Koontz and O'Donnell   Management: A Book of Readings
Koontz and O'Donnell   Principles of Management: An Analysis of Managerial Functions
Levin, McLaughlin, Lamone, and Kottas   Production/Operations Management: Contemporary Policy for Managing Operating Systems
Luthans   Contemporary Readings in Organizational Behavior
Luthans   Organizational Behavior
McNichols   Policy Making and Executive Action
Maier   Problem-solving Discussions and Conferences: Leadership Methods and Skills
Margulies and Raia   Organizational Development: Values, Process, and Technology
Mayer   Production and Operations Management
Miles   Theories of Management: Implications for Organization Behavior and Development
Mundel   A Conceptual Framework for the Management Sciences
Newstrom, Reif, and Monczka   A Contingency Approach to Management: Readings
Petit   The Moral Crisis in Management
Petrof, Carusone, and McDavid   Small Business Management: Concepts and Techniques for Improving Decisions
Pigors and Pigors   Case Method in Human Relations
Porter, Lawler, and Hackman   Behavior in Organizations
Prasow and Peters   Arbitration and Collective Bargaining: Conflict Resolution in Labor Relations
Ready   The Administrator's Job
Reddin   Managerial Effectiveness
Richman and Copen   International Management and Economic Development
Sartain and Baker   The Supervisor and His Job
Schrieber, Johnson, Meier, Fischer, and Newell   Cases in Manufacturing Management
Shore   Operations Management
Shull, Delbecq, and Cummings   Organizational Decision Making
Steers and Porter   Motivation and Work Behavior
Steiner   Managerial Long-Range Planning
Sutermeister   People and Productivity
Tannenbaum, Weschler, and Massarik   Leadership and Organization
Vance   Industrial Administration

THIRD EDITION

PRODUCTION AND OPERATIONS MANAGEMENT

RAYMOND R. MAYER

Professor of Management
Loyola University of Chicago

McGRAW-HILL BOOK COMPANY

New York   St. Louis   San Francisco   Auckland
Düsseldorf   Johannesburg   Kuala Lumpur   London
Mexico   Montreal   New Delhi   Panama   Paris
São Paulo   Singapore   Sydney   Tokyo   Toronto

Library of Congress Cataloging in Publication Data

Mayer, Raymond R
    Production and operations management.

    (McGraw-Hill series in management)
    First–2d ed. published under title: Production
management.
    Bibliography: p.
    1. Production management. I. Title.
TS155.M3428 1975   658.5 74–9961
ISBN 0–07–041023–2

PRODUCTION AND OPERATIONS MANAGEMENT

  34567890 DODO 79876

This book was set in English by University Graphics, Inc. The editors were Thomas H. Kothman and Claudia A. Hepburn; the cover was designed by Rafael Hernandez; the production supervisor was Sam Ratkewitch. New drawings were done by J & R Services, Inc.
The printer was Segerdahl Corporation; the binder, R.R. Donnelley & Sons Company.

TO HELEN
AND MARK, JOHN, MARY, JANE

CONTENTS

PREFACE

Much of what is usually included in the preface of a book has, in this case, been placed in the introductory chapter of the text. Among these items of information are such things as a statement of the way in which the subject matter is being defined, a description of the specific topics to be considered, the reasons for the selection of these topics and the exclusion of others, and an explanation of the manner in which the material will be presented. Such comments are designed to place everything that follows in the desired perspective. Because of the importance of this function, it was decided to make these observations in the first chapter, which is likely to be studied by more readers than is the preface.

At this point, however, we might note that this book is intended to serve as an introduction to the subject of production and operations management. In the preparation of any book of an introductory nature, one must constantly overcome the inclination to consider every aspect of the discipline involved. Failure to overcome this inclination can have a number of undesirable consequences. At one extreme, the presentation may be thorough, but the by-product is a work of such length and complexity that it cannot be assimilated by the reader within a reasonable time period. Any attempt to circumvent this undesirable outcome can lead to the other extreme. This would be a superficial presentation of each of an exhaustive set of topics, that is, a presentation in which description replaces exposition, with the result that the reader comprehends only a limited amount of the material and retains even less. In either case, justice is not being done to either the discipline or the reader.

For these reasons, the treatment of production and operations management in this book is one in which the emphasis is placed only on fundamentals. As a result, each of these can be covered in a thorough and, yet, fairly concise manner. This has been done with the belief that the reader will thereby find the subject to be more comprehensible, will retain significantly more of the material than he otherwise would, and will acquire the foundation necessary for more advanced work in the field.

All this suggests, and correctly so, that the book is designed primarily for use in the first course taken in this field by business and engineering students at either the undergraduate or graduate level. This, however, does not preclude its being employed under a different set of circumstances. For example, in combination with case-study materials, a book of readings, or a text of a more advanced nature, it could be used in a series of two or more courses in production and operations management. And of course, there is no reason why it cannot be used by anyone engaged in independent study of the subject.

In spite of the fact that selectivity has been exercised in the choice of topics, the book does contain a significant amount of material. An attempt has been made to present this material in a way which will enable the student to acquire an understanding of much of it through independent study. Furthermore, it may be found that some of the material has already been or will be covered in other courses. Nevertheless, some teachers will find that, for any number of reasons, an insufficient amount of classroom time is available to permit an exposition of the remaining topics. What should be done under such circumstances is, of course, a matter of judgment. One possibility is to concentrate on only the first 14 chapters which are a relatively self-contained unit dealing with the areas of production planning and control. An alternative is to consider every part of the book but to treat only the methods of analysis that are representative of those contained in each part; what these representative methods are will be, to some degree, a matter of opinion, and, therefore, no specific recommendations are being made.

It will be noted that questions and problems appear at the end of each chapter. The questions are designed to aid the student when he is reviewing the material and to serve as a basis for classroom discussions. The problems are intended to provide the student with an opportunity to apply the methods of analysis discussed and, very often, to suggest applications other than those explicitly considered in the respective chapters. A teachers' manual is available for use in conjunction with the problems.

Because a significant portion of the book is devoted to quantitative approaches, the question arises concerning how much prior knowledge of mathematics and statistics is required of the reader. In general, this question can be answered by stating that the quantitative courses currently required of all students in secondary schools are such that it is unlikely that anyone will be unable to cope with the material in this book.

RAYMOND R. MAYER

PRODUCTION AND OPERATIONS MANAGEMENT

PART ONE
INTRODUCTION

ONE

THE PRODUCTION AND OPERATIONS FUNCTION

In a lecture delivered in 1883, Professor William Graham Sumner of Yale University made the following statement: "Wealth comes only from production." Those who agree with this position do so after first having defined wealth and production in a certain way. To begin with, wealth would be considered to be the aggregate amount of goods and services that had been generated during some given time period. Goods would include such things as automobiles, clothing, houses, food, furniture, roads, ships, books, radios, television sets, airplanes, schools, dams, paintings, sculptures, pencils, and medicines. Services would be represented by the end result of activities engaged in by such individuals as physicians, salespeople, lawyers, teachers, barbers, clergymen, entertainers, repairmen, computer programmers, reporters, economists, waitresses, accountants, administrators, pilots, truck drivers, cooks, and policemen.

The meaning of production follows from the foregoing definition of wealth. With reference to goods, we should say that production is the fabrication of a physical object through the use of men, materials, and equipment; whereas, with reference to services, we should say that production is the discharge of a function which has some utility. Admittedly, this interpretation of the production activity is a very broad one and, as such, does not coincide with the fairly common one in which production is equated with manufacturing. Instead, the position being maintained is that there is no difference in principle between an action which provides someone with a tangible material item and an action which provides someone with information, advice, help, aid, or assistance. In either case, something is being produced which did not exist earlier.

Unfortunately, many individuals and organizations continue to apply the term "production" solely to the manufacturing activity. Therefore, the task of instilling an understanding and an acceptance of the more comprehensive meaning of the term remains to be completed. The efforts that have been expended in an attempt to accomplish this have manifested themselves in many forms. A fairly recent one is to substitute the word "operations" for "production," with the result that references to operations management rather than production management are appearing with increasing frequency. We shall take cognizance of this by occasionally substituting the one phrase for the other, but, at all times, the two will be used synonymously.

A SYSTEMS APPROACH

Given our definition of the operations function, it follows that every organization is engaged in the production of either a physical good or a service. The organization may be a manufacturing firm, hospital, educational institution, governmental agency, department store, warehouse, consulting firm, automobile distributor, or the like. As this suggests, production is essential to any organization's continued existence and, of course, to society's well-being. But other activities are equally important.

One of these other activities is marketing. Specifically, most organizations must engage in market research to determine the nature of the market for their products or services and, then, must promote, sell, and distribute these products or services.

However, production and marketing require the expenditure of money which, it is hoped, will be recovered through the revenues these activities will bring about. But in the meantime, the production and marketing functions must be financed, and methods for doing so must be developed and exercised.

Finally, successful results in the areas of production, marketing, and finance can be attained only through the efforts of qualified people. Hence, it becomes necessary that an organization concern itself with personnel recruitment, selection, training, motivation, and management.

In brief, the typical manufacturing or service organization can be looked upon as representing a system whose elements are production, marketing, finance, and personnel relations. It is a system in the sense that these functions are interrelated and, therefore, must be coordinated because what is done in any one of these areas will have an effect on the others. This can be illustrated with reference to the production activity. The character of the firm's marketing program will affect the demand for its products, and this will determine what is to be produced and the quantities to be produced. Similarly, the firm's financial position will affect the amount of money available for capital expenditures, and this may affect the type of facilities which can be made available for production purposes. In the same manner, the firm's personnel policies will have an influence on the caliber and morale of the work force, and the consequences will manifest themselves in the production area. As all this suggests, operations management is not independent of marketing, financial, and personnel management.

Conversely, the consequences of decisions in the operations area will be felt in the organization's other functional areas. As examples, we might note that a firm's production capacity will affect what and how much can be sold, that the nature of the production processes will influence the level of required expenditures for equipment and buildings, and that the kind of operations performed will determine the type of personnel needed.

THE PRODUCTION SYSTEM Having recognized that any organization can and must be treated as a system, we might also take cognizance of the fact that the operations activity itself is a subsystem, that is, a system within a system. Let us consider why this is so.

To say that production is a system is to say that the operations activity consists of a number of interrelated elements. Some of these are performed in sequence, while others are carried out concurrently. The important thing, however, is that the manner in which one element of the operations activity is conducted will most likely have an effect on one or more of the other elements. This becomes evident when we consider what is involved in the management of a firm's operations.

The operations personnel in any organization can be said to have four basic responsibilities. These are to produce the firm's products or services in a way such that (1) quantity requirements will be satisfied, (2) established delivery or completion dates will be met, (3) quality requirements will be fulfilled, and (4) the most economical methods for accomplishing the foregoing will have been selected and applied.

Quantity requirements and established completion dates will, of course, reflect the demands of the consumers of the firm's products or services. To satisfy these demands, operating personnel, as a rule, will be compelled to plan the production activity prior to the point at which the demands actually occur. This is true for a number of reasons. First, unless the required factors of production are on hand at the time an order for a given quantity is received, it is unlikely that the delivery date desired by the customer can be met, because the time required to procure manpower, materials, equipment, and buildings usually far exceeds what is generally accepted as being a reasonable delivery time. And second, even if this were not the case, the firm that would procure and utilize factors of production only at the time at which they are required to satisfy customer orders would, more often than not, find that it would be producing and purchasing in uneconomic lot sizes and experiencing wide fluctuations in the output capacity required at any single moment; this would serve to generate excessive costs.

For these reasons, every concern engages in *production planning*. This involves forecasting the demand for the firm's products and services and translating this forecast into its equivalent demand for various factors of production. These resultant factor-of-production demand schedules might be adjusted to eliminate wide fluctuations or to permit producing and purchasing in economic lot sizes. In their final form, however, they provide the operations manager with information on the kind and amount of materials, manpower, and production facilities which will be required at various future points in time. Arrangements can then be made to procure these factors of production prior to the times at which they will actually be needed. Doing so facilitates the production department's being able to meet delivery dates on orders it subsequently receives.

However, even if the needed factors of production are on hand at the time actual orders are received, quantity requirements and stipulated delivery dates can be satisfied only if steps are taken to utilize these factors in an efficient manner. This calls for scheduling the required work, providing operating departments with necessary instructions, checking on production progress, and inaugurating corrective action when such action is needed. All this is called "production control."

But as has been mentioned, in addition to being responsible for satisfying quantity requirements and meeting stipulated delivery dates, the operations manager is also responsible for the quality of the organization's output. The quality of goods and services can be maintained only if measures are employed which will increase the likelihood that the firm's output will meet specifications. Such measures are available, and they are referred to as the techniques of "quality control."

And finally, we have noted that operating personnel are expected to produce the organization's products and services not only in the required quantities, at the required times, and with the required quality, but also in the most economical manner. As a consequence, *methods analyses* must be made of the alternative ways in which the firm's goods and services can be produced with a view toward determining the most efficient of these alternative work methods. Also, a need is created for *materials handling analyses* and for *plant and office layout analyses* whose purpose is to develop a handling system and an arrangement of departments and work stations which will serve to minimize the cost to be associated with the movement of personnel and materials from one location to another. To continue, *inventory control* becomes a necessity, because inventory levels of supplies, raw materials, component parts, and finished goods will affect, among other things, the cost of carrying inventories and the risk of shortages and the corresponding stockout costs. Furthermore, *work measurement* techniques must be applied to ascertain the amount of time that should be required to perform a task so that the labor costs generated by the production activity can be controlled. And in many cases, the cost of operations can be reduced still further through the use of *wage incentives* which motivate operating personnel to maximize their efficiency by relating their earnings to the quantity and the quality of their output.

To summarize all this, operations managers must concern themselves with a number of interrelated areas. In the order in which we have considered them, they are production planning, production control, quality control, methods analysis, materials handling, plant layout, inventory control, work measurement, and wage incentives. This is not to suggest, however, that operations managers will not become involved in other areas of decision making. They will, and some of the specific ones are plant location, building design, and product development. Also, because the decisions made in the functional fields of marketing, finance, and personnel will affect the production activity and vice versa, production managers will be expected to contribute to the solution of marketing, financial, and personnel problems. But these other areas and problems are not their primary responsibility, and we shall concentrate only on those that are so as to keep the scope of this presentation within manageable proportions.

THE ASSUMED MODEL

As has just been noted, the topics we shall consider in our treatment of the subject of production management will be those related to the areas which are the primary responsibility of the operations manager. In this treatment, it shall be necessary, for purposes of illustration, to relate the material to specific production activities. This requires making a decision regarding the type of activities to be selected for purposes of illustration. The choice should be such that it enables us to demonstrate the various applications of the principles of operations management, reveals the need for a systems approach to operations management, and permits us to keep the presentation to a reasonable length.

To demonstrate that the principles of operations management are applicable in any organization engaged in the production of a physical good or service, consideration might be given to the possibility of relating these principles to every type of enterprise. If this were done, means of, say, work scheduling would be explained with reference to a manufacturing organization, and then to a merchandising organization, and finally to a service organization. The same could be done with inventory control, methods analysis, and so on. Unfortunately, the result of such an approach would prove to be a work of formidable length, and, hence, this alternative is not a feasible one.

There is still another way in which the general applicability of the principles of operations management could be demonstrated. This would be to illustrate some of these principles with reference to a manufacturing organization, others with reference to a merchandising organization, and still others with reference to a service organization. For example, work scheduling could be explained in terms of its application by a textile manufacturer, inventory control in terms of its application by a department store, and methods analysis in terms of its application by a hospital. However, this alternative also has a serious limitation. This is that it would tend to obscure the fact that production is a system. This is to say that the interrelationships among the various elements of the operations function cannot be readily seen when these elements are explained in terms of examples drawn from radically different types of enterprises. And while it is important that the extensive applicability of the concepts we shall discuss be recognized, it is equally important that we demonstrate that the management of operations is the management of a system.

The remaining alternative, and it is the one we shall select, is to begin by explaining each of the areas of operations management with reference to a single type of enterprise; doing so will enable us to recognize the impact of decisions in one area on what occurs in other areas. This approach, however, will be coupled with pauses at appropriate points to comment on the applicability of what is being considered to enterprises of a type other than the one assumed for purposes of illustration; in this manner, we shall be able to indicate in a fairly concise manner other possible applications of the material being discussed. Also, the problems that appear at the end of each chapter will be selected with a view toward demonstrating these other applications.

Of course, a need now arises for selecting the type of organization to be used for purposes of illustration. The model we shall select is a manufacturing firm. The reason for this choice is that the most comprehensive type of production problem is the one that exists in a manufacturing enterprise. More specifically, the management of production in manufacturing concerns necessitates becoming involved in every aspect of operations management. This is not the case with other types of concerns, as suggested by the fact that an educational institution does not have to determine what inventories of its product should be maintained, a public relations firm does not have to design a materials handling system, a retail establishment does not have to prepare a production schedule, a hospital does not have to make decisions regarding product design, a construction firm does not have to develop a layout of its production facilities, a library does not have to develop a method for controlling the quality of its output, and a public utility does not have to decide what items it should produce. We could go on this way, but these examples suffice to bring out the fact that, although nonmanufacturing organizations must manage their operations, they can do so without necessarily becoming involved in each of the areas of operations management. But a manufacturing organization must, and, consequently, it is a more suitable model for our purposes. Its use will create no difficulties at the points at which we shall relate the subject matter to the management of operations in other kinds of organizations.

When illustrating certain points with examples drawn from a manufacturing firm, we shall find it necessary to refer to specific manufacturing processes. More often than not, we shall consider metalworking processes. This will be done for a number of reasons. First, these processes have the advantage of consisting of only six basic operations which can be easily described, illustrated, and understood. Second, they are processes with which most people are already acquainted; for those individuals who are not, a brief description is presented in Appendix A. Third, although the processes are simple, they generate more complex problems in the field of production management than do many other processes. And last, they happen to be the processes engaged in by a very large proportion of manufacturing concerns.

METHOD OF PRESENTATION

Before we begin our discussion of the methods of operations management, let us consider the manner in which the material will be presented.

If all the elements of the production system were sequential, the task of describing and analyzing the system would be greatly simplified. There would be no question about the order in which the elements should be presented and studied, because this should obviously be the order in which they occur. Furthermore, the only interrelationships that would have to be analyzed would be those that exist between succeeding elements. And finally, the fact that the written word is a medium of description by means of which only one aspect of a subject can be treated at a time would present no difficulty, because only one element of the system would be occurring at any one time. But as we know, although some of the elements of the production system are performed sequentially, others are performed simultaneously. Consequently, the task of describing and analyzing the system proves to be a relatively complex one.

Nevertheless, there is no doubt but that the framework of this presentation must consist of the sequential elements of the system. These are the ones that have already been referred to as the production planning and control activities, which begin with a forecast of the future orders the firm might receive for its products and which end with the shipment of the products called for by the orders the firm did receive. With the use of this framework as a core, we shall build the rest of the production structure by adding on the system's concurrent elements. These elements were also referred to earlier; they consist of quality control, methods analysis, materials handling, plant layout, inventory control, work measurement, and wage incentives. Some of these will be introduced as the framework of production planning and control is being constructed, and the remainder after the framework has been completed.

In each of the foregoing areas, we shall find that the operations manager must choose from alternative courses of action. Another way of stating this is that he must make decisions. The nature of these decisions can be determined only after one has become familiar with the production management area under consideration. For this reason, we shall begin the discussion of each of these areas with a description of the activities it encompasses. This will be followed by an account of the problems that will be encountered in any attempt to manage these activities. An understanding of the problems will enable us to determine the factors that are relevant to their solution. Having become acquainted with these factors, we shall finally be in a position to analyze how they enter into and are used in the decision-making process. In brief, description must precede analysis. Consequently, each of our presentations will consist of two phases, the first of which will be descriptive.

The second phase will be analytical. In this phase, we shall concern ourselves with decision-making procedures. When doing so, we shall discover that some problems and the factors relevant to their solution are such that the decision-making process will, of necessity, have to be qualitative, that is, based on judgment. In other cases, it will be found that a quantitative approach can be employed because a mathematical or statistical model can be developed and employed as a means for describing the relevant factors and their interrelationships. In still other cases, and these are the prevalent ones, we shall find that some combination of a qualitative and quantitative approach must be used, because certain aspects of the problem lend themselves to numerical analysis while the remaining ones do not.

In most of the approaches to be considered, it will be necessary to process data. When presenting the method of analysis involved, we shall begin with the assumption that the data are to be processed manually, that is, without the use of automatic data processing equipment. This will necessitate our considering and explaining every step in the computational procedure, and there is reason to believe that the result will be a greater understanding of the underlying principles than would otherwise be acquired. However, a growing number of organizations are finding that the procedures can be implemented more efficiently with the use of punched card equipment and computers. Therefore, although manual methods will be assumed for expository purposes, we shall comment, at appropriate points, on the applicability of automatic data processing equipment in the area under consideration. For those individuals who are unacquainted with automatic data processing systems, the fundamentals are presented in Appendix B.

Finally, it will become evident in the analytical phase of our presentation that every method of analysis has its advantages and disadvantages, Care will be taken to stress what these are, because they must be taken into consideration when choosing among alternative analytical techniques. However, we shall find that, regardless of the approach selected, some risk of error always remains. While this proves to be troublesome, it also serves to add interest to the decision-making process.

This brings us to the end of our preliminary observations. We shall now go on to consider what can most accurately be described as the art and science of production and operations management.

QUESTIONS

1-1 How is production and operations management defined?

1-2 Is operations management independent of marketing, financial, and personnel management? Explain.

1-3 Why is it said that the production activity is a system?

1-4 What are the basic responsibilities of an organization's operations personnel?

1-5 Define the following:
   a Production planning
   b Production control
   c Quality control
   d Methods analysis
   e Plant layout
   f Materials handling
   g Inventory control
   h Work measurement
   i Wage incentives

1-6 What is the difference between a qualitative approach and a quantitative approach to decision making in the area of production and operations management?

PART TWO
FACILITIES PLANNING

TWO
FORECASTING FUTURE DEMAND

Most firms are not in a position to wait until orders are actually received before they begin to determine what production facilities are required and in what amounts. The reason for this is that their customers usually demand delivery in a reasonable period of time. What a reasonable time period is cannot be defined precisely, but it would be the rare customer who would be willing to wait five years until the supplier builds a plant, or one year until he procures equipment, or often even one month until he obtains the necessary machine accessories, manpower, and material. This means that the manufacturer must anticipate the future demand for his product and, on this basis, provide the production capacity which will be required. This is referred to as production planning. The activity calls for forecasting the future sales of a given product, translating this forecast into the demand it generates for various production facilities, and arranging for the procurement of these facilities.

Preparation of the sales forecast is not ordinarily the responsibility of the production manager. However, some knowledge of sales forecasting techniques contributes to a better understanding of the other aspects of production planning. For this reason, we shall consider the fundamentals of the more important sales forecasting methods.

SOME GENERAL OBSERVATIONS ON SALES FORECASTING

In the most comprehensive case, a firm will be producing both standard and special products. Standard products are those which the company produces for stock. It is able to do so because there is a continual demand for these products, and their specifications are somewhat predictable. Examples of this type of item would be automobiles, washers, bricks, soft drinks, furnaces, and wire.

As opposed to this, the company may also be producing nonstandard products, which are often referred to as specialty, or custom-made, items. They are not manufactured for stock but directly to customer order. This means that the item is produced only after an order for it has been received, and, as a rule, it is built in accordance with the customer's specifications. The reason such products are nonstock items is that there is no continual demand for them and their exact character is unpredictable. Examples of such products would be production equipment of special design, custom-made furniture, and tailor-made clothing.

The difference between standard and nonstandard items has been pointed out because the same approach cannot be employed when forecasting the demand for each of these types of products. Having noted this, we shall first discuss methods of forecasting the sales of standard products and then consider the case of special products.

With regard to standard products, it should also be mentioned that the company will usually attempt to forecast its future sales for each individual standard product it manufactures. In some cases, however, it is not possible to do so. The reason for this is that the company may be producing such a multitude of products that any attempt to forecast by individual items would prove to be too costly and time-consuming. For example, a company may be producing 18,000 different valves and fittings. Intuitively, one would balk at the suggestion that an effort be made to make 18,000 individual forecasts. In a situation such as this, it is common to think in terms of product groups and to prepare forecasts accordingly. This is to say that the company will classify its products by type and then forecast sales for each of these classifications. In general, items of similar design which require a similar sequence of operations on similar equipment would be considered to be members of a single product group. For example, an oil refinery would be inclined to include all the different grades of gasoline it produces in a single product group; a manufacturer of farm equipment would be inclined to include all the different tractors he produces in a single product group; and a producer of plumbing supplies would be inclined to include all the different faucets he manufactures in a single product group.

COLLECTIVE OPINION

The first sales forecasting method we shall consider is called "collective opinion." Although this approach can take various forms, a representative one is as follows: The procedure may begin with the firm's salesmen being asked to submit estimates of future sales in their respective territories. In their estimates, they would be influenced by such things as customer reaction to the product and the trend their sales have been following. Branch sales managers would review these figures and make adjustments to reflect their knowledge of the individual salesmen. Some of the latter may have demonstrated in the past that they are consistently optimistic, and their estimates may be revised downward; others may be known to be somewhat pessimistic, and their estimates may be revised upward; the remainder may have proved themselves to be realistic, and their estimates may remain unaltered. These adjusted figures are then made available to a committee responsible for making the final forecast. The members of this committee might include the firm's sales manager, treasurer, production manager, chief engineer, marketing manager, and economist. They would review the estimates in light of certain factors with which the salesmen and branch sales managers would not be acquainted. These might include such things as expected changes in product design, a plan for increased advertising, a proposed increase or decrease in selling prices, new production methods which will improve the product's quality, changes in competition, and changes in such economic forces as purchasing power, income distribution, credits, population, and employment. Consideration of these factors would result in still another revision of the salesmen's original estimates. This final revision would represent the sales forecast.

At this point, the sales forecast may be expressed in terms of either dollars or physical units. If it is in dollars, it must be converted to equivalent physical units for production planning purposes. This is because it is customary to describe material, manpower, and equipment requirements in terms of quantities needed per unit of output. Hence, product demand can be translated into a corresponding demand for factors of production only when the product demand is expressed in physical units.

If a dollar forecast has been made for each individual product, the conversion to physical units presents no problem. Estimated dollar sales for each product are simply divided by its expected selling price per unit.

The problem becomes more complex when the forecast is made in terms of total dollar sales for a product group. In this case, it is necessary that the total be first broken down into expected dollar sales for each item in the group. The simplest way to do this is to analyze past dollar sales of the product group and determine what percentage of this total was attributable to each of the items in the group. This percentage will probably vary from period to period for any single item. For example, a product group may be composed of four items, one of which we shall call "product A." Annual sales for the past three years for the entire group and for product A may be as follows:

Year	Total sales for product group	Total sales for product A	Percent of sales attributable to product A
1	$ 40,000	$ 8,000	20
2	60,000	13,200	22
3	50,000	12,000	24
Total	$150,000	$33,200	22

One alternative is to calculate the average percentage for each product and apply this percentage to the expected sales for the entire product group. In our illustration, the average percent for product A is 22. If the sales forecast for the product group for the fourth year is $70,000, the forecast for product A can be obtained by taking 22 percent of $70,000, which will yield $15,400.

Another alternative is to analyze past percentages for each item to determine whether a trend exists. In our example, the percent of sales attributable to product A is increasing at a rate of 2 percent per year. Therefore, for the fourth year, the firm may want to assume that product A will account for 26 percent of the product group sales. As a result, if the forecast for the group is $70,000, the forecast for product A will be obtained by multiplying the $70,000 by 26 percent, which will yield $18,200.

In any event, once these respective percentages have been determined, they can be used to obtain the expected sales for each item in the group. These dollar sales can then be converted to physical units by dividing each one of them by the expected selling price of the corresponding product.

A similar procedure must be followed when the sales forecast for a product group is made in terms of physical units. In this case, the number of units to be associated with each item in the group can be determined by analyzing past sales and calculating the percentage of total unit sales accounted for by each of the products. If this percentage varies from period to period, either the average or a trend value can be used. In this case, however, the past percentages used are percentages of past total *unit* sales, whereas in the case of a forecast of total dollar sales, the past percentages used are percentages of past total *dollar* sales.

The need to convert expected dollar sales to unit sales can be eliminated only by making the initial forecast in terms of physical units. On occasion, this is possible but not done because the individuals making the estimates are accustomed to thinking in terms of dollars and find it more convenient to continue doing so. On other occasions, an initial forecast in physical units is not even possible because the items included in a product group may be such that they cannot be described in terms of a common physical unit. To illustrate, one of the product groups in a company may consist of building materials such as gravel, lumber, bricks, cement, and sand. While some of these are measured in units of weight, others are measured in units of length or number. As a result, it may be necessary to use dollars as the least common denominator.

AN EVALUATION   The collective opinion approach is relatively simple and straightforward. One of its advantages is that it makes use of the people in the organization who are directly involved in the activities which will influence the level of sales, who are in a position to become acquainted with the forces and factors which will affect sales, and who probably have had the opportunity to acquire the experience and judgment which will enable them to evaluate the effects of these forces and factors. An added advantage of the method is that, unlike some other techniques, it requires no special technical skill. Finally, the method lends itself to use in the forecasting of sales of new products. The latter application would, of course, call for some variation in the approach as we have described it. The firm may begin with the results of a market survey rather than with sales-men's estimates. Also, if a new product group is under consideration, judg-ment will play a more important role in the ascertainment of the proportion of total forecast sales to be attributed to each product in the group.

However, the method does have disadvantages. The most important is that it is almost completely subjective. This is of no consequence if the firm is fortunate enough to have personnel in its sales and managerial ranks who have the ability to make this type of subjective analysis, but not all organizations are endowed with personnel of this type.

Also, there is reason to believe that the method, at best, can yield a reasonably good forecast for a period of about one year. The seriousness of this limitation varies with the application of the sales forecast. In pro-duction planning, it will be used to determine future building requirements, and three to five years may be required to design, erect, and prepare a building for use. If this is the case, a one-year forecast will be inadequate. Next, the forecast will be used to ascertain future equipment requirements. Standard equipment can, as a rule, be procured within one year, while equipment of special design may involve a procurement time of approxi-mately two years. Consequently, a one-year forecast will probably be ade-quate from the standpoint of its ability to provide information in time to order and install standard equipment but inadequate for the same purpose insofar as special equipment is concerned. Further, the sales forecast will be translated into a demand for machine accessories, materials, and man-power. Required procurement times for these factors will vary, but they will probably be less than one year. Therefore, a one-year forecast would suffice. In brief, a long-term forecast is required for determining the probable demand for buildings and special equipment, and such forecasts based on collective opinion are likely to contain a high risk of error.

A final criticism is that the individuals making the forecast are often capable of making fairly accurate estimates of future sales in terms of sales for the entire year or even by quarters for the coming year, but their accuracy diminishes rapidly when they are required to forecast sales by the month or by the week. This is serious because sales may fluctuate widely from week to week or from month to month, and if this is the case, it should be known. While this limitation is a real one, steps can be taken to alleviate the resultant difficulties. If the collective opinion approach yields only an annual forecast, the problem may be one of distributing this total over a 12-month period. This can be done by means similar to those employed in breaking down estimated sales for a product group. Past annual sales can be analyzed to determine what percentage of these sales was made during each month of the year. If these percentages vary from year to year, the company can compute the average percentage for each month or it can select a percentage suggested by an existing trend. These percentages can then be applied to the forecasted annual sales to arrive at corresponding monthly sales. The same approach can be employed to obtain weekly sales if it is necessary to do so. Naturally, if a new product is being considered, no past records exist, and the company will have to rely solely on judgment or, if possible, on its experience with similar products.

ECONOMIC INDICATORS

A second approach to sales forecasting is based on the use of economic indicators. These indicators describe economic conditions prevailing during a given time period. In many cases, companies find that there is a direct relationship, or correlation, between the sales of some or all of their products and these conditions. Where this is true, the availability of appropriate indicators provides the firm with a means for estimating what its sales will be. Some commonly used indicators are as follows:

Construction contracts awarded	Consumer installment debt
Personal income	New durable goods orders
Automobile production	Wholesale commodity prices
Farm income	Bank deposits
Employment	Steel production
Gross national product	Industrial production
Consumer prices	Automobile registrations

Data of this type are compiled and published by such departments of the federal government as Labor, Commerce, and Agriculture, by the Federal Reserve Board, and by various private organizations such as trade associations.

DESCRIPTION OF THE TECHNIQUE   To illustrate the principles underlying this method, suppose that a manufacturer of fishing tackle finds that the number of rods of a certain type he has sold per year during the past 10 years and the corresponding values of a specific economic indicator, expressed as an index, are as follows:

Year	Sales (10,000 units)	Economic index
1	2.1	104
2	1.9	101
3	2.3	106
4	1.5	99
5	1.2	95
6	2.7	109
7	3.6	120
8	1.4	98
9	0.9	90
10	2.0	103

If he were to plot the values of the index against his annual sales, the indicated relationship would be as shown in Figure 2-1.

The positions of the points on this graph reveal that a very strong linear relationship or correlation exists between sales and the economic indica-

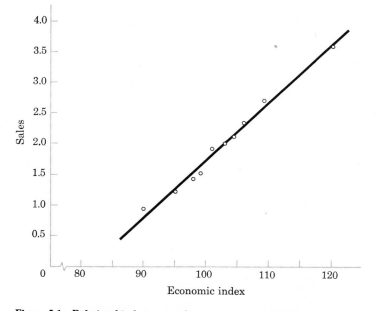

Figure 2-1 Relationship between sales and an economic index

tor. The exact nature of this relationship can be described by means of a line of best fit which we shall assume for the time being will be located on the basis of judgment. If this is done as shown in Figure 2-1, the firm can make use of the resultant line to forecast the value of sales for some future time period for which the value of the indicator is available. To illustrate, if the value of the index for the twelfth year is expected to be 112, the line of best fit reveals that an index value of 112 yields a sales value of 28,600 units.

It should be mentioned that if the predicted value of the index takes us beyond the values of the index on the basis of which the line of best fit was determined, it becomes necessary to extrapolate the line. This is an unsound practice, because we do not know what the relationship between the variables will be beyond the points generated by the available data. However, chances are that the increase in the value of the indicator for any one period will not be appreciable, and, hence, the risks to be associated with the extrapolation will not be too great.

In any event, if the forecast is expressed in terms of physical units for a single product, the information is in the form required for production planning purposes. But if the resultant forecast is in terms of dollar sales for a single product or product group, it must be converted to physical units per product. This is done just as it was in the collective opinion method.

Mention should be made of the fact that it is unfortunate that, in the case under consideration, sales of fishing rods do not lag behind the index. Instead, the relationship between the index and these sales is such that an increase or decrease in the value of the index for a particular year results in an increase or a decrease in the amount of sales for that same year. This is unfortunate because the actual index for a given year will be known only after the year has ended, and this is too late to permit its use to predict the sales for that year.

The ideal index is one which leads sales, that is, one behind which sales lag. For example, the number of construction contracts awarded in one period may determine the amount of building material which will be sold in the following period. Therefore, a producer of building materials will have some indication at the end of a given period of what his sales will be during the following period. Or farm income in one year may determine the amount of farm equipment which will be sold in the following year. Therefore, a published index of farm income at the end of a certain year can be used by a manufacturer of farm equipment to forecast his sales for the following year.

It follows that a company should try to find an economic indicator which is correlated with its sales and behind which its sales lag. This, however, is not always possible. In a case such as this, the firm may still find it possible to use a nonleading indicator if some organization or government agency forecasts the magnitude of the economic indicator for some future period. Although a forecast is not as desirable as an accomplished fact, it is sometimes the best alternative available to the firm. If nothing else, the company has the assurance that the agencies or groups making these forecasts usually have better-qualified personnel engaged in this activity than are to be found in the company itself.

In summary, the company should try to find an indicator which leads its sales, or, if this is not possible, an indicator which coincides with its sales but whose magnitude is forecast by organizations best able to do so. Once such an indicator is found, the firm will determine the relationship between its sales and the indicator and make use of this relationship to forecast sales for some future time period. This determination of the relationship involved is sometimes referred to as "regression analysis."

METHOD OF LEAST SQUARES In our example, a linear relationship was found to exist between the firm's sales and the selected economic indicator. In other cases, it may be that the two variables are not related linearly but are related curvilinearly. However, for purposes of simplicity, we considered and shall continue to consider only linear relationships.

But even in the relatively simple case of an existing linear relationship, the use of judgment to locate the line of best fit may present some difficulty. For this reason, it is a fairly common practice to determine the line of best fit by a less subjective approach called the "method of least squares."

The method of least squares yields an equation which describes and locates the line of best fit. This line can be described in terms of two things. One is the point at which it intersects the Y axis; this point is called the "Y-intercept." The other is the "slope" of the line; the slope is the amount by which the Y variable increases for an increase of one unit in the value of the X variable. All this is shown in Figure 2-2.

If we know the Y-intercept and the slope, the equation of the line can be determined from the general expression for the equation of any line, which is as follows:

$$Y' = a + bX \tag{2-1}$$

where Y' = calculated value of the dependent variable, which is the variable whose value is to be predicted

a = Y-intercept of the line of best fit

b = slope of the line of best fit

X = given value of the independent variable, which is the variable in terms of which the value of the dependent variable is to be predicted

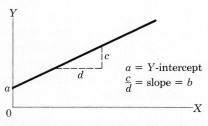

Figure 2-2 Slope and Y-intercept of a line

To relate this to our sales forecasting application, Y' would represent the value of sales because this is the variable whose value is to be predicted, and X would represent the value of the economic indicator because this is the variable whose value will be supplied.

With the least-squares method, we determine the values of the Y-intercept and of the slope of the line by working with the given data. This can be done by making the appropriate substitutions in the following expressions:

$$\sum Y = na + b\sum X \qquad\qquad (2\text{-}2)$$
$$\sum XY = a\sum X + b\sum X^2 \qquad\qquad (2\text{-}3)$$

where $\sum$ = summation sign

X = given values of the independent variable, which in our problem would be the economic indicator

Y = given values of the dependent variable, which in our problem would be sales

n = number of given paired observations

It should be noted that a distinction is being made between a given value of sales, Y, and a calculated value, Y'. In any case, if Eqs. (2-2) and (2-3) are solved for a and b, the following expressions are obtained:

$$b = \frac{n\sum XY - (\sum X)(\sum Y)}{n\sum X^2 - (\sum X)^2} \qquad\qquad (2\text{-}4)$$

$$a = \frac{\sum Y - b\sum X}{n} \qquad\qquad (2\text{-}5)$$

APPLICATION OF THE LEAST-SQUARES METHOD Let us now apply this approach. In the following table, we have the past values of the economic indicator and of sales with which our manufacturer of fishing tackle was working; in addition, other values required for substitutions we shall be making are shown.

Index (X)	Sales (Y)	XY	X^2	Y^2
104	2.1	218.4	10,816	4.41
101	1.9	191.9	10,201	3.61
106	2.3	243.8	11,236	5.29
99	1.5	148.5	9,801	2.25
95	1.2	114.0	9,025	1.44
109	2.7	294.3	11,881	7.29
120	3.6	432.0	14,400	12.96
98	1.4	137.2	9,604	1.96
90	0.9	81.0	8,100	0.81
103	2.0	206.0	10,609	4.00
1,025	19.6	2,067.1	105,673	44.02

If we substitute an n of 10 and the relevant totals from this table in Eqs. (2-4) and (2-5), we obtain the following:

$$b = \frac{10\,(2,067.1) - 1,025\,(19.6)}{10\,(105,673) - (1,025)^2} = 0.0952$$

$$a = \frac{19.6 - 0.0952\,(1,025)}{10} = -7.80$$

Therefore, the equation of the least-squares line becomes

$$Y' = -7.80 + 0.0952X \tag{2-6}$$

To locate the line on a graph as was done in Figure 2-1, it is necessary only to locate two points through which the line passes and then to draw the line through these points. The points can be found by substituting any two values of X in Eq. (2-6) and solving for the corresponding Y' values. Once the line has been located in this manner, it can be used to obtain the value of sales which corresponds to some given value of the economic indicator in the same way that a line located on the basis of judgment can be used. However, a more efficient method for obtaining such a sales value is simply to make the necessary substitution in the equation of the line. For example, the firm in our illustration expected the value of the index to be 112 for some future year. When we substitute this value in Eq. (2-6), we obtain

$$Y' = -7.80 + 0.0952\,(112) = 2.86$$

This means that sales of 28,600 fishing rods are indicated which coincides with the value obtained earlier from Figure 2-1.

PROPERTIES OF THE LEAST-SQUARES LINE   Let us now consider the characteristics of the least-squares line. If all the points do not fall on the line, as is the case in Figure 2-1, substitution of the given values of X in the equation of the least-squares line will not yield calculated values of the Y variable equal to the actual, that is, given, values. For example, substitution of a value of 90 for the economic index in Eq. (2-6) yields a calculated value, Y', of sales of 7,680 fishing rods. But an examination of the manufacturer's sales data for the past 10 years reveals that when the value of the indicator was 90, as it was in the ninth year, the actual value, Y, of sales was 9,000 units. Therefore, the deviation between the actual and calculated values is equal to

$$Y - Y' = 9,000 - 7,680 = 1,320 \text{ units}$$

Similar deviations would be found to exist between actual and calculated sales for the other nine given years. However, one of the characteristics of the least-squares line is that the sum of these deviations, that is $\Sigma(Y - Y')$, will always be equal to zero. This is to say that the sum of the vertical distances between the line and the points that fall above it will always be equal to the sum of the vertical distances between the line and the points that fall below it.

Once these respective deviations have been calculated, it is possible to go on to compute the squares of these deviations, that is, $(Y - Y')^2$. The sum of these deviations squared, $\Sigma(Y - Y')^2$, will be some positive number. A second characteristic of the least-squares line is that it will yield a minimum value for this sum. This means that if a line had been drawn in any other position, the sum of the squares of the resultant deviations would be greater than the sum obtained with the least-squares line.

COEFFICIENT OF CORRELATION   Small deviations between past actual sales and their corresponding calculated values suggest that only small differences will occur between predicted and actual sales. But as these deviations increase, a weaker linear relationship or correlation between the two variables is indicated and larger errors in forecasted values would be expected. In some cases, the deviations prove to be so large that the firm would conclude that the existing linear relationship is not sufficiently strong to serve as a basis for a sales forecast.

On occasion, a decision regarding the strength of the linear relationship between an economic indicator and sales can be made by means of a visual examination of a constructed graph such as the one shown in Figure 2-1. In that figure, the points are so close to the least-squares line that there is little doubt but that an extremely strong linear relationship exists between the two variables. However, there may be cases in which it would be helpful to have a quantitative measure of the strength of the linear relationship. Such a measure exists, and it is called the "coefficient of correlation." The expression from which this coefficient r can be calculated is as follows:

$$r = \sqrt{1 - \frac{\Sigma(Y - Y')^2}{\Sigma(Y - \bar{Y})^2}} \tag{2-7}$$

where $\bar{Y}$ = average of the given values of the dependent variable, which in our problem would be sales

What this expression involves can best be understood by analyzing Figure 2-3. This figure shows four given points, the line obtained by the method of least squares, the line which represents the average value of the dependent variable, and $(Y - Y')$ and $(Y - \bar{Y})$ for one of the points. As can be seen, the numerator of the fraction which we subtract from 1 in Eq. (2-7) reaches a minimum value of zero when every point falls on the line, that is, when the actual values equal the calculated values. But when this numerator is zero, the coefficient of correlation reaches its maximum value of the square root of 1, or 1. However, since this occurs only when we have a perfect fit, we say that the coefficient of correlation is 1 whenever the two variables are correlated perfectly. The weaker the relationship between the two variables, the greater will be the squared vertical deviations of the actual points from the line of best fit. This will increase the size of the fraction in Eq. (2-7) and reduce the value of the coefficient of correlation. The minimum value this coefficient can assume is zero, which would indicate a complete absence of any relationship between the variables. Finally, whether we assign a positive or negative sign to the value of the coefficient depends on the slope of the least-squares line; if the slope is positive, the coefficient is said to be positive, but if the slope is negative, the coefficient is said to be negative.

Exactly where the division is between a high and a low degree of correlation is difficult to define, but the following represents a generally accepted rule of thumb:

Absolute value of correlation coefficient	Interpretation
.90–1.00	Very high correlation
.70– .90	High correlation
.40– .70	Moderate correlation
.20– .40	Low correlation
0– .20	Slight correlation

We have seen that the form of Eq. (2-7) enables us to observe what happens to the value of the coefficient of correlation as the deviations

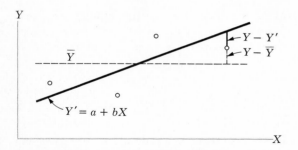

Figure 2-3   Quantities considered when computing the coefficient of correlation

between actual and calculated values of the dependent variable increase. However, the formula presents computational difficulties because it requires that we begin by ascertaining the calculated values, Y', of the dependent variable. This also means that the coefficient can be computed only after the equation of the least-squares line has been determined. But it may be that the computed value of the coefficient reveals that a sufficiently strong linear relationship between the variables does not exist. Consequently, time and effort were expended in obtaining a least-squares line which cannot be used for forecasting purposes. As this suggests, it would be better if we could begin by calculating the coefficient of correlation from the given data. Then, if the coefficient proves to be sufficiently high, the firm could go on to determine the equation of the least-squares line.

It so happens that given data can be used to obtain the value of the coefficient. If Eq. (2-7) is subjected to a few algebraic operations, it will assume the following form:

$$r = \frac{n\sum XY - (\sum X)(\sum Y)}{\sqrt{n\sum X^2 - (\sum X)^2}\sqrt{n\sum Y^2 - (\sum Y)^2}} \tag{2-8}$$

Let us now apply this formula to the example with which we have been working. All the values required for substitution in the formula can be obtained from the table on page 23. Their substitution yields the following:

$$r = \frac{10(2,067.1) - 1,025(19.6)}{\sqrt{10(105,673) - (1,025)^2}\sqrt{10(44.02) - (19.6)^2}} = 0.99$$

Because the coefficient of correlation is close to 1, a very strong relationship exists between the economic indicator and sales of fishing rods. This coincides with the conclusion suggested by a visual examination of Figure 2-1. Therefore, the indicator involved does lend itself for use in forecasting future sales of the product under consideration.

PROBLEMS AND LIMITATIONS   The use of economic indicators to forecast sales poses various difficulties.   One is the need for finding an appropriate indicator. In some cases, a given economic indicator will obviously be the correct one. But in other cases, no one indicator will be obviously applicable, and a trial-and-error approach must be employed. This can be a very tedious and time-consuming procedure because, first, many different indicators are available and, second, the appropriate indicator may vary with the product or product group under consideration. Often only a detailed study will reveal the appropriate indicator and whether it is correlated with the firm's unit sales, current dollar sales, or constant dollar sales for a given product or product group. Further, it may be that sales will be a function of more than one indicator, and this fact will complicate the analysis to an even greater degree.

Also, after investigating all the possible alternatives, the company may find that no single or combination of indicators is suitable. In such a case, this method of forecasting cannot be used. However, the firm may find that although its sales are not correlated with any economic indicator, the industry's sales are. This would be the case when the company's share of the market is fluctuating widely. In such situations, the firm may want to forecast the industry's sales and then go on to estimate its share of the market by some other method such as collective opinion.

Another difficulty stems from the fact that the relevant indicator may be, say, an annual index, whereas the company may want to forecast its sales on a month-by-month basis. If so, the company would have to forecast annual sales and then break this total down by month. This would be done just as it was in the collective opinion method.

A further limitation of the method is that it does not lend itself to a forecast of sales for a new product because no past data exist on which a correlation analysis can be based. At best, if the product has been produced in the past by other firms, the company can prepare an industry forecast through the use of economic indicators and estimate its share of these sales on the basis of some form of collective opinion.

Next, there is reason to believe that, at best, this technique can be expected to yield fairly accurate sales forecasts for a period of approximately one to two years. If an economic indicator is found which leads sales, it would be very unusual for sales to lag behind any such indicator by more than one year; however, a sales forecast for the second year could be made if a forecasted value of the indicator is available. And if no lag exists and the company must rely on a predicted value of the indicator it is using, it is unlikely that reliable predictions for more than a year in advance would be available. Therefore, the company will very often have difficulty planning its requirements for such things as special equipment and buildings, which may involve a procurement time of from two to five years.

But one of the most important limitations of the approach is the following: Even if there is overwhelming evidence that an extremely strong relationship exists between a company's past sales and some economic indicator, this simply proves that a *past* relationship existed, and it is not necessarily true that this relationship will continue in the future. There is always the possibility that certain changes have taken place or will take place which will alter the nature of this relationship. For example, at one time there was some relationship between the number of private dwellings constructed and the sale of tile for roofing. This relationship no longer exists because of the change which has taken place from tile to asphalt roofs. In brief, the product has become obsolete. Other changes may occur in price, design, advertising, quality, marketing methods, and competition, which would alter the nature of the relationship.

This suggests that it would be the rare firm that would take a reading from a graph or the answer from a formula and accept the result as representing its sales forecast. Instead, this estimate would be used as a starting point in its analysis. The firm would then take into consideration that the correlation was not perfect, that the value of the indicator it is working with may itself be a forecast, and that the conditions which will exist in the future will not necessarily duplicate those of the past. The preliminary forecast would then be modified in light of these other considerations. The nature and extent of this modification will be determined on the basis of the judgment, intuition, and experience of concerned individuals.

This means that, even if economic indicators are used as a basis for forecasting, the method will contain elements of the collective opinion approach. Similarly, the collective opinion approach will contain elements of the method based on economic indicators. This was suggested in the earlier discussion of the collective opinion approach when reference was made to the fact that, among other things, the forecasting committee would consider economic factors. The basic difference between the two methods is that a forecast based on collective opinion begins with estimates submitted by, say, sales personnel, whereas a forecast based on economic indicators begins with estimates obtained by a regression analysis. The latter may provide management with a better starting point for making its final forecast.

TIME SERIES ANALYSIS

A third method of sales forecasting is called "time series analysis." In this approach, a company analyzes its past sales to determine if there is a trend. This trend is then projected into the future, and the resultant indicated sales are used as the basis for a forecast. The mechanics of this technique can be best explained by means of an illustration.

Suppose that a manufacturer of paint-roller frames decides to forecast the next-year sales of his product by this method. He begins by collecting data on his sales for the past four years. From experience, he knows that his sales in any one year fluctuate because of seasonal variations in demand. In fact, he has found that his sales are at a minimum during the first quarter of the year because fewer people paint during this season. Improved weather during the second quarter usually results in an increase in sales. For the same reason, a still greater increase takes place during the third quarter. However, with the onset of less favorable weather in the fourth quarter, sales decrease. As a result of these quarterly variations, he prefers to develop a forecast by quarter for production planning purposes. To do this, he must, for purposes of analysis, break down his sales for the past four years by quarters. When he does, he obtains the following results:

Quarter	Sales (1,000 units)	Quarter	Sales (1,000 units)
1	1	9	2
2	3	10	4
3	4	11	6
4	2	12	3
5	1	13	2
6	3	14	5
7	5	15	7
8	3	16	4

It will be noted that the quarters are numbered consecutively, beginning with number 1, which represents the first quarter of the first year, and ending with number 16, which represents the fourth quarter of the fourth year. If the sales are plotted against the quarter in which they took place, a graph representing the time series is obtained. The graph for our data is shown in Figure 2-4.

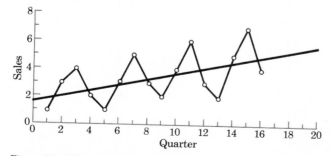

Figure 2-4 Sales by quarter and the resultant trend line

An examination of this graph reveals that the sales are following an upward trend. The next step is to develop some measure of the nature and the magnitude of this trend. This is done by fitting a trend line to the points depicting the firm's sales. A number of ways for doing this exist, but a fairly common one is to construct a straight line by the method of least squares. In doing so, one assumes the trend to be linear, whereas it may actually be curvilinear. If the latter is true, more complex methods of constructing the trend line must be employed. However, we shall limit ourselves in this presentation to linear trends for purposes of simplicity.

The equation of the least-squares line is determined as it was earlier. Since sales are to be forecast, they are considered to be the dependent variable Y. Also, since sales will be assumed to vary with time, the quarters will be the independent variable X. The Y-intercept and the slope of the line are found with the use of Eqs. (2-4) and (2-5). Working with the given data, we obtain the following:

Quarter (X)	Sales (Y)	XY	X²
1	1	1	1
2	3	6	4
3	4	12	9
4	2	8	16
5	1	5	25
6	3	18	36
7	5	35	49
8	3	24	64
9	2	18	81
10	4	40	100
11	6	66	121
12	3	36	144
13	2	26	169
14	5	70	196
15	7	105	225
16	4	64	256
136	55	534	1,496

When we make the necessary substitutions in the equations, we obtain the following:

$$b = \frac{16(534) - 136(55)}{16(1,496) - (136)^2} = 0.1956$$

$$a = \frac{55 - 0.1956(136)}{16} = 1.775$$

Therefore the equation of the line of best fit is equal to

$Y' = 1.775 + 0.1956X$

where X = quarter number, given that the value of 1 has been assigned to
the first quarter of the first year

Y' = sales in thousands of units

The trend line represented by this equation is also shown in Figure 2-4.
An examination of this line reveals that most of the points representing
actual sales do not fall on it. For this reason, one would be reluctant to
forecast sales by projecting the line and reading off the value of sales for
some future quarter. Instead, consideration would be given to the fact
that, in the past, actual sales varied from the sales as calculated from the
equation of the line. Since these variations existed in the past, there is
reason to believe that they will exist in the future, and it would be natural
to modify the value of future sales obtained from the trend line to reflect
the expected variation.

The total variation of sales around a trend line is assumed to be composed of three different types of variations. The first is seasonal variation,
whose nature has already been suggested in the example under consideration. The second is called "cyclical variation," and it is caused by fluctuations in the business cycle, that is, in economic conditions. The third is
called "residual variation" and represents all other causes. These may
include such things as wars, strikes, and unusual weather, all of which may
have an influence on the company's sales during a specific period.

It follows, therefore, that if the trend line value of future sales is to be
used as a basis for a forecast, it must be adjusted to take into account expected seasonal, cyclical, and residual variations.

Unfortunately, no reliable quantitative methods for handling cyclical
and residual variations exist. However, somewhat satisfactory methods
for adjusting the trend value of future sales for seasonal variations have
been developed. We shall consider one of these, which, although relatively simple, is often used. It is called the "ratio-to-trend method," and
it can be best described by means of an illustration. For this reason, we
shall continue to work with our example.

THE RATIO-TO-TREND METHOD   In this method, it is assumed that the
trend line based on past sales data has been determined. For the case under
consideration, the equation of this line was found to be as follows:

$$Y' = 1.775 + 0.1956X \qquad (2\text{-}9)$$

Next, actual sales values are compared with trend sales values, and the total
variations are computed. This requires a knowledge of the trend values,

and these can be obtained for the data in our problem by substitution in Eq. (2-9). For example, the trend value for the first quarter of the first year would be equal to

$$Y' = 1.775 + 0.1956\,(1) = 1.97$$

Similarly, the trend value for the second quarter of the fourth year would be equal to

$$Y' = 1.775 + 0.1956\,(14) = 4.51$$

Different measures of total variation around the trend line can be used, but the simplest and most straightforward one would be computed as follows: It will be noted that, for the first quarter, the actual sales are 1 and the calculated sales, that is, the trend value, are, as was just shown, 1.97. We shall describe this variation by expressing the actual sales Y as a percentage of the calculated sales Y'. In this case, we obtain

$$\frac{Y}{Y'} = \frac{1.00}{1.97} = 51\%$$

In other words, the actual sales in the first quarter were 51 percent of the calculated sales. As another example, let us turn to the second quarter of the fourth year, which is the fourteenth quarter in our series. We have just shown that the trend line yields a value of 4.51 for sales for this quarter. The actual sales were 5. Therefore, we find that

$$\frac{Y}{Y'} = \frac{5.00}{4.51} = 111\%$$

This tells us that in the fourteenth quarter actual sales were 111 percent of the calculated sales.

If we go through the same steps for each of our 16 quarters, we obtain the following results:

Quarter (X)	Actual sales (Y)	Calculated sales (Y')	Y/Y', %
1	1	1.97	51
2	3	2.17	138
3	4	2.36	170
4	2	2.56	78
5	1	2.75	36
6	3	2.95	102
7	5	3.14	159
8	3	3.34	90
9	2	3.54	56
10	4	3.73	107
11	6	3.93	152
12	3	4.12	73

Quarter (X)	Actual sales (Y)	Calculated sales (Y')	Y/Y', %
13	2	4.32	46
14	5	4.51	111
15	7	4.71	149
16	4	4.90	82

It will be recalled that we want to forecast future sales by quarters, because this is the seasonal pattern of this firm's sales. The first step in making this forecast is to obtain the trend value for the future quarter under consideration. For example, if we want to forecast sales for the first quarter of the fifth year, which is the seventeenth quarter, the trend value will be

$$Y' = 1.775 + 0.1956\,(17) = 5.10$$

However, we want to adjust this value to provide for expected seasonal variations. We determine the magnitude of this seasonal adjustment factor by finding the average of the past variations during the first quarter of each year. In the preceding table, we find that the quarters numbered 1, 5, 9, and 13 represent first quarters. In quarter 1, actual sales were 51 percent of calculated sales; in quarter 5, actual sales were 36 percent of calculated sales; in quarter 9, actual sales were 56 percent of calculated sales; in quarter 13, actual sales were 46 percent of calculated sales. The average percentage for the first quarter is equal to

$$\frac{51 + 36 + 56 + 46}{4} = 47\%$$

This means that, on the average, first-quarter sales for each year are 47 percent of the sales as calculated from the trend equation. So, for the first quarter of the coming year, we obtain the sales forecast, adjusted for seasonal variations, by multiplying the trend value, which we found to be 5.10, by 0.47. This yields 2.40, or a forecast of 2,400 paint-roller frames to be sold.

It might be claimed that the adjustment factor we obtain by this averaging process reflects not only seasonal variations but also cyclical and residual variations, because we are calculating the average of the total variations around the trend line. It would be well if this were true, but unfortunately it is not. This becomes evident if we keep the following in mind: In every year, the seasonal causes of variation will always act in the same direction during a particular quarter; that is, they will always result in the sales for, say, the summer quarter being higher than the trend value and the sales for, say, the winter quarter being lower than the trend value. As opposed to this, cyclical and residual causes of variation for a particular quarter may act in either a positive or negative direction. For example, during the winter quarter of one year, economic conditions may be extremely favorable, while during the winter quarter of some other year, economic conditions may be very unfavorable. In the long run, therefore, we say that the cyclical-residual variations for a particular quarter, such as the winter quarter, will cancel out; that is, there will be as many acting in the positive direction as in the negative direction. Consequently, if our time series covers a sufficiently long period, averaging the total variations for a particular quarter will yield an average which is free of cyclical and residual variations. What remains is the average seasonal variation.

Let us now return to our problem and resume our calculation of the seasonal adjustment factors for the other quarters. Working with values from the preceding table, we are able to summarize our calculation of the seasonal adjustment factor for each of the four quarters in the following manner:

	Actual sales as a percent of calculated sales				
Quarter	Year 1	Year 2	Year 3	Year 4	Average, %
1	51	36	56	46	47
2	138	102	107	111	115
3	170	159	152	149	157
4	78	90	73	82	81

If we were asked to forecast the sales for the fifth year by quarters, this would now be done as was illustrated earlier. For each of the four quarters, the steps would be as follows:

Quarter (X)	Trend value of sales ($Y' = 1.775 + 0.1956X$)	Seasonal adjustment factor	Forecast ($Y' \times$ adjustment factor)
17	$1.775 + 0.1956(17) = 5.10$	0.47	2.4
18	$1.775 + 0.1956(18) = 5.30$	1.15	6.1
19	$1.775 + 0.1956(19) = 5.49$	1.57	8.6
20	$1.775 + 0.1956(20) = 5.69$	0.81	4.6
Total			21.7

The last column represents the forecast in thousands of units for each quarter of the coming year, adjusted for seasonal variations. When we obtain these values, we have completed the final computational step in the time series approach to sales forecasting. It might be mentioned that a seasonal adjustment of the trend value would not be necessary if we were working with a time series based on annual data; in that case, there would be no seasonal variation to consider. In any event, the forecast which results from the time series analysis must now be modified by the firm to reflect anticipated cyclical and residual variations. This means that the effect of changes in economic conditions, prices, product acceptance, advertising, and the like must be evaluated on the basis of judgment and incorporated in the final forecast.

At this point, unless it is already in those terms, the forecast must be converted to physical units per product by means described earlier. We might recall, however, that in our earlier discussion of the procedure for doing this, it was mentioned that the percentage of sales attributable to a single product may vary from period to period. One alternative was to use an average percentage; a second was to use a percentage which would reflect the presence of a trend. Although the latter could be done on the basis of judgment, many firms make a time series analysis of the varying percentages to obtain a trend value.

ADVANTAGES AND DISADVANTAGES The time series analysis approach to sales forecasting exists because there are certain advantages to be associated with it. However, other methods also exist because many firms believe that these advantages are more than offset by the disadvantages.

Supporters of the time series analysis method point out that it is less subjective than collective opinion. Also, as opposed to the use of economic indicators, its use is not dependent on the company's ability to find an appropriate economic indicator; all the required information is available in the company's records. Finally, if the company wants to forecast by months, it can very easily do so by analyzing its past monthly sales; if it wants to forecast by quarters, it can do so by analyzing its past quarterly sales; and if it wants to forecast by year, it can do so by analyzing its past annual sales. This is simpler than taking an annual sales forecast, which may be obtained by the collective opinion or economic indicator method, and then breaking it down by quarter or month.

With regard to the last point, let us digress for a moment to elaborate upon something that was mentioned earlier. It was stated that, with the collective opinion or economic indicator method, the initial result might be an annual forecast. However, the company could distribute this total over, say, the months of the year by analyzing its past annual sales and determining what percentage of these sales was made during each month. If the percentage for a given month varied from year to year, the average percentage could be used, or a percentage which would reflect the presence of a trend could be selected. This latter percentage for a particular month could be determined by making a time series analysis of the past percentages for that month.

To return to the evaluation of the time series method for sales forecasting, the method has a number of limitations. First, the approach cannot be used to forecast the sales of a new or relatively new product because no past data or insufficient past data exist. At best, if the product has been produced by other firms in the past and the company has access to past sales data for these firms, it can use a time series approach to forecast industry sales and then estimate its share of the market by some form of collective opinion.

Also, the trend value is obtained by extrapolating the trend line. This is contrary to the belief that a line should not be extrapolated beyond the values of the variables which were used to determine the nature and location of the line. The reason for this is that there is no way of knowing what the relationship between the variables will be beyond these points. Past data may suggest that an upward trend is taking place. This may be attributable to changes in the general level of population, consumer acceptance of the product, competition, people's habits and tastes, and so on. However, an assumption that these changes will follow the same pattern in the future as they have in the past may not be correct. And the farther we project the line into the future, the greater is the probability of the assumption being incorrect. It is for this reason that the time series approach is rarely recommended for use as a means to forecast sales for more than a year or two into the future.

Next, an adjustment is made for seasonal variations which are caused by forces whose exact future nature and magnitude are unknown. The usual way of making this adjustment is to assume that past variations are representative of what will take place in the future. Whether or not this is true is questionable. Therefore, a seasonal adjustment factor, which may be incorrect, is applied to a trend value obtained on the basis of what may be an erroneous assumption about the future trend. The combined effect of this might be that the forecast will be in error by an appreciable percentage.

Finally, there is no way in which the effects of changes in selling prices, product quality, marketing methods, promotional efforts, and economic conditions can be incorporated into the method itself. This can be done only on the basis of judgment, experience, and intuition, which suggests that no firm can limit its sales forecasting to the use of a time series analysis alone. Instead, the results of the method will simply provide a starting point for making the forecast. From that point on, elements of the collective opinion and economic indicator methods will enter into the procedure.

SOME FINAL OBSERVATIONS

We have considered three methods of sales forecasting. All were introduced as approaches which could be employed to forecast the sales of standard products.

Of the methods discussed, the one adhered to by most companies is collective opinion. There are a number of reasons for this. To begin with, some companies are unacquainted with the approaches based on economic indicators and time series analyses. Others have learned of them but have been obtaining fairly good results with the collective opinion method and are reluctant to make the change. Still others believe that the use of these other methods cannot be justified because of their limitations. At the other extreme, there are companies that employ all three methods for a given product or product group. One initial forecast may be based on collective opinion, a second on economic indicators, and a third on a time series analysis. As a rule, the results will differ from each other, and the task becomes one of reconciling these differences.

Also, a firm might use one method for some of its products, a second method for others, and a third for still others. For example, the collective opinion approach may be applied to new products. Products which have been produced in the past may be subjected to a regression analysis if appropriate economic indicators are available. If not, a time series analysis may be made.

Finally, there are companies which employ a hybrid method of some type. One such approach has already been suggested. Sales for a product group might be forecast on the basis of collective opinion, but the sales for each item in the group might be determined by making a trend analysis of past sales to determine what percentage of the total should be assigned to each item in the group.

Regardless of the method adhered to, the results provide management with nothing more than a starting point for making the final forecast. At all times, the results must be modified to account for factors that were not considered explicitly in the initial analysis. This requires judgment, intuition, and experience. Hence, whatever approach is employed, a risk of error is to be associated with the final result. It is for this reason that no firm will make, say, an annual forecast and then adhere to it for the entire year. Instead, it is customary to review the forecast periodically, which may be at the end of each month, and make revisions in light of new developments. As a result, the company might begin with a forecast on January 1 for the coming 12 months, broken down by month. One month later, it might review and revise, if necessary, the forecast for the remaining 11 months and also extend it for one more month. A month later, this procedure would be repeated and would continue to be repeated at the end of each month. In effect, a forecast would be made for the coming 12 months at the end of each month on the basis of the latest information available.

LONG-RANGE AND SPECIAL-PRODUCT FORECASTS With regard
to sales forecasting, two points remain to be discussed. One of these is long-
range forecasting. It was mentioned earlier that the methods we have presented can, at best, be expected to yield fairly reliable forecasts for a
period of one to two years. This, however, is usually inadequate for determining building and special-equipment requirements far enough in
advance.

Unfortunately, no really satisfactory means exist for making forecasts
of the length required for this purpose. And yet, the firm must engage in
this type of planning. It does so, ordinarily, by means which are based
primarily on judgment. Since judgment is involved, little can be said about
it except to state that this judgment will be based on such things as population studies, market surveys, predicted economic conditions, and, of
course, experience. This does not mean that no formal approach will be
used. What is basically the collective opinion method may be employed,
with the difference that opinions are obtained with regard to sales for the
next five years rather than for just one year. Or a regression analysis may
be employed on the basis of five-year forecasts of the values of an economic indicator. Or a time series analysis may be adhered to by extrapolating the trend line five years into the future. However, the uncertainty to
be associated with such forecasts is many times that to be associated with a
one-year forecast made by these methods. Consequently, judgment
will play a more important role in the evaluation and modification of the
results obtained by these means.

The second point that remains to be considered is forecasting the demand for nonstandard products. However, for reasons that will become
apparent later, we shall postpone the consideration of the approach that
can be employed to make this forecast until we have first considered how
the sales forecast for standard products can be translated into the demand
it creates for various factors of production.

QUESTIONS

2-1   What constitutes production planning?

2-2   How do standard products differ from nonstandard products?

2-3   Under what conditions would the firm prepare a sales forecast for product
      groups rather than for individual products?

2-4   Describe and evaluate the collective opinion approach to sales forecasting.

2-5   How can economic indicators be used to forecast sales? Evaluate this
      approach.

2-6   What are some of the more commonly used economic indicators, and what
      are their sources?

2-7   Describe and evaluate the method of sales forecasting based on a time series
      analysis.

2-8 Why is it necessary that the sales forecast be expressed in terms of physical units for production planning purposes?

2-9 When a dollar sales forecast has been made for an individual product, how can the equivalent physical units be obtained?

2-10 How can the expected dollar sales for a product group be converted to expected unit sales for the individual products involved?

2-11 By what means can the expected unit sales for a product group be converted to expected unit sales for the individual products involved?

2-12 Under what conditions would the firm make an initial sales forecast in terms of dollars rather than physical units?

2-13 What is the length of the future time period for which a sales forecast must be prepared for production planning purposes?

2-14 If future sales are estimated for, say, the entire coming year, how can the result be broken down into, say, expected quarterly sales?

PROBLEMS

2-1 On the basis of collective opinion, it has been estimated that, during a future time period, the sales of an item stocked by a retail food market will total $43,500. If the unit selling price will be $1.25, how many units of the item are expected to be sold?

2-2 Soon after the forecast mentioned in the preceding problem has been made, it is decided to raise the unit selling price by 10 percent. However, this is expected to increase total dollar sales of the item by only 5 percent. What would be the revised unit sales forecast? (Ans. 33,218)

2-3 A wholesale distributor of automobile supplies finds that the number of batteries of a given type he has sold per year during the past seven years and the corresponding values of a certain economic index are as follows:

Year	Sales (1,000 units)	Economic index
1	13.1	87
2	17.4	122
3	15.3	119
4	22.8	130
5	11.6	93
6	19.2	124
7	14.7	118

a Determine the equation of the least-squares line that describes the relationship between sales and the economic indicator. $(Y' = -5.67 + 0.194X)$

b Construct a graph in which the seven given points and the least-squares line are shown.

    c Determine the strength of the relationship between the two variables by computing the value of the coefficient of correlation. (Ans. 0.83)

    d If the value of the index for year 9 is predicted to be 127, what sales can be expected during that period? (Ans. 18,970)

2-4 A manufacturer compares the annual sales of one of his products with the values of three different economic indexes for the same years. The values of the sales and these indexes are as follows:

Year	Sales ($10,000)	Index 1	Index 2	Index 3
1	8	101	98	110
2	18	103	107	116
3	22	103	112	104
4	14	112	103	101
5	12	116	101	107

    a Which of the indexes is most suitable for sales forecasting purposes? Explain.

    b Construct a graph which depicts the relationship between sales and the selected index; locate the line of best fit on the basis of judgment. With the use of the graph, forecast sales for the sixth year.

    c Determine the equation of the line of best fit by the least-squares method. With the use of this equation, calculate the value of sales for the sixth year.

    d Compute the value of the coefficient of correlation between sales and the selected index.

2-5 A department store decides to forecast the demand for an item it sells by means of a time series analysis. Quarterly sales for the past three years were as follows:

Year	Quarter	Sales ($1,000)
1	1	20
	2	30
	3	50
	4	70
2	1	30
	2	40
	3	60
	4	80
3	1	40
	2	60
	3	80
	4	90

In spite of the limited amount of data available, determine the equation of the trend line. With this equation, calculate the trend value of quarterly sales for the coming year, that is, year 4. Then adjust these values to provide for expected seasonal variations. (Ans. $Y' = 24.40 + 4.58X$; $83,940, $88,520, $93,100, $97,680; $53,720, $74,360, $107,060, $132,840)

2-6 A manufacturer's semiannual sales of one of his products during the past four years have been as follows:

Year	Semiannual period	Sales (100,000 units)
1	1	4.5
	2	3.2
2	1	4.1
	2	2.9
3	1	3.8
	2	2.5
4	1	3.4
	2	2.2

Perform a time series analysis of these data to obtain a seasonally adjusted forecast for semiannual sales during the sixth and seventh years.

2-7 With the collective opinion approach, a consulting firm has forecast its revenues for the first quarter of the coming year. These are expected to be $140,-000. However, for operations planning purposes, the firm must break down this forecast by months.

An analysis of past revenues for the first quarter of each year reveals the following:

Month	Percent of dollar sales for quarter		
	Year 1	Year 2	Year 3
January	58	56	54
February	30	31	32
March	12	13	14
Total	100	100	100

Translate the $140,000 quarterly forecast into a monthly forecast by working with:

a The average percentage for each month as calculated from past data. (Ans. $78,400, $43,400, $18,200)

b A percentage for each month which reflects the presence of a trend as determined by a visual examination of past percentages. (Ans. $72,800, $46,200, $21,000)

2-8 An organization that services, among other things, television sets has estimated that it will sell about 750 replacement picture tubes during the coming year. Insofar as a specific type of tube is concerned, a study of the organization's records for the last six years reveals that this tube's unit sales accounted for the following percentages of the total unit sales of replacement tubes:

Year:	1	2	3	4	5	6
Percent:	9	13	15	19	24	29

How many units of this type of tube would the organization expect to sell during the coming year (year 7), if it chooses to work with:

a The average percentage of past total unit sales attributable to the tube under consideration?

b A trend percentage value obtained by making a least-squares trend analysis of the past annual percentages?

2-9 On the basis of a forecast, sales for a group of three products are expected to be $2,500,000 during the coming year. An analysis of past annual sales reveals that, on the average, the first product accounts for 20 percent of the annual dollar sales of this group, the second for 50 percent, and the third for 30 percent. Using these percentages, convert the sales forecast for the product group to a forecast for each product in the group.

If the unit selling price of the first product is $2, of the second $4, and of the third $3, what is the sales forecast in physical units for each product?

THREE

DETERMINATION OF FACTOR-OF-PRODUCTION REQUIREMENTS

Insofar as the firm's production department is concerned, the sales forecast is important for one reason, namely, that it permits the determination of the factors of production which must be on hand if the shipping schedule suggested by the sales forecast is to be met. Therefore, once the sales forecast in terms of physical units for various products has been prepared, the next task is to translate this forecast into the demand it generates for various factors of production. Let us now consider how this is done.

THE GENERAL PROCEDURE

We shall begin with an extremely simple illustration. Suppose that a company is manufacturing, among other things, a tapered metal pin and that the forecast for some month in the future stipulates that 5,700 pins are expected to be sold. The next step in the production planning procedure calls for determining what factors of production are needed to manufacture this item and the quantities required to produce 1 unit of the item. This is accomplished in the following manner:

Prior to a part's being produced for the first time, whoever is responsible for the design of the part will summarize the results of his work in the form of a blueprint. The blueprint will permit concerned individuals to visualize the shape of the part and will state the material from which the part is to be produced, the dimensions that must be adhered to, the tolerances or allowable variations in the dimensions that are permitted, and the finishes that are required.

Following this, a process engineer will study the blueprint and decide how the part is to be manufactured. He will determine what operations are required, the amount of time required to perform each of these operations per unit of output, the sequence in which these operations should be performed, the machine accessories such as jigs, fixtures, gauges, and cutting tools required for each operation, and how the equipment is to be operated with regard to speed, feed, and depth of cut. All this information is presented on what is called an "operation sheet," or a "routing sheet," such as the one shown in Figure 3-1.

PART NAME	Rear Electrode						PART OR CODE NO.	P-75497		
NEXT ASY NO. P-75554		SHEET 1 OF 1 DATE					DRWG NO. P-75497 ISSUE NO. 1			
APPARATUS K-500 Telephone		ISSUE NO. 6 PROC. ENG.								
		STD ENG.					PRODUCTION CONTROL			
	DISTRIBUTION	KIND Naval Brass Alloy A					S.O. NO.			
ONE (1) SEPIA COPY TO PRODUCTION CONTROL FOR GENERAL DISTRIBUTION INTO EACH DEPT. PERFORMING OPERATION. ONE (1) HARD COST ESTIMATING SHEET.		SIZE 3/4 dia. x 12' SHAPE Round TEMPER Hard FINISH SPEC. GM 338 FT. OR LBS PER/M 44# CODE NO.					DATE ISSUED _____ SIGN. _____ QUANTITY DATE REQ'D STOCK _____ TO STOCK _____			
DEPT.	L.G. NO.	OPER. NO.	OPERATION DESCRIPTION		TOOLS, GAGES AND GUARDS	MACH. TYPE	PCS PER HR.		HRS PER/M
							D.W.	INC.	
21	5	20	Set up (set of -3- #2 B & S Cams)		V-19392	#2 B&S	.33		
21	8	30	Feed stock to stop, rough center 78°L front form		Gage Nos.			174	5.8
			rear form, drill finish center 78°L ream and cut off.		N-11850				
			NOTE: Use Texaco "Cleartex-140" or approved		N-11853				
			equal cutting oil. DO NOT use sulphurized		N-11855				
			cutting oil.		N-11857				
					N-11858				
					N-11866				
					N-11947				
07	8	40	Set up		V-19007	Dr. Pr.	4		
07	12	50	Ream center hole (.166 dia.) to remove burr		N-12024			960	.9
19	10	60	Roto finish (5000 pcs. per load; tumble for 2 hours)		#12 alum. oxide	Small	4000		.25
					W/#600 comp.	barrel			
19	9	70	Gold plate #107 per GM #264, wash, oven dry			Barrel &	300		3.3
			inspect & pack in glass container.			Oven			
11	11	80	Inspect for proper finish.			Bench	400		2.5

FORM 1964 B

Figure 3-1   Operation, or routing, sheet

As all this suggests, the operation sheet contains most of the information required to determine factor-of-production requirements. Therefore, returning to our illustration, we should begin by turning to the operation sheet for the tapered metal pin. Let us assume that the operation sheet reveals that the required equipment, accessories, material, and direct labor are as follows:

Factor of production	Requirements per unit of output
Equipment:	
Saw	2 min
Lathe	10 min
Grinder	3 min

Factor of production	Requirements per unit of output
Machine accessories:	
Saw accessories	2 min
Lathe accessories	10 min
Grinder accessories	3 min
Material:	
SAE bar stock, ½ in.	4 in.
Direct labor:	
Saw operator	2 min
Lathe operator	10 min
Grinder operator	3 min

It will be noted that these data contain no information about indirect labor, supplies, building, and materials handling equipment requirements per unit of output. However, it is customary at this point in the production planning procedure not to translate the sales forecast into the demand it generates for these items. With regard to indirect labor, it is impossible to ascertain how much labor time per unit of a given product is required for such things as maintenance, materials handling, and machine repair. For that reason, the usual procedure is to apply some percentage, based on past experience, to the direct labor-hours or machine-hours to obtain the hours of indirect labor of different types that will be needed. Judgment based on experience would be employed in the determination of needed supplies, such as coolants and lubricants. Insofar as buildings and materials handling equipment are concerned, again, there is no way of ascertaining how much floor space or what fraction of a forklift truck is required per unit of output. Instead, these factors are treated as a whole in the development of an appropriate plant layout and in the design of a materials handling system, which we shall discuss in the chapters that follow.

Therefore, to return to our illustration, the firm will concern itself at this time only with the factors of production described directly or indirectly in the operation sheet. The demand generated for these factors by the metal pin in the month under consideration would be found by multiplying the respective unit requirements by the number of units expected to be sold. However, the expected sales would be adjusted to reflect the amount of defective work which may be produced. Similarly, unless the time requirements contained in the operation sheet already do so, they would have to be adjusted to reflect expected unavoidable delays and labor efficiency.

In our example, if we assume that 6,000 units will have to be scheduled for production because of anticipated scrap and that the given time requirements allow for unavoidable delays and expected labor efficiency, we should obtain the equivalent demand for the required factors of production by multiplying each of the unit requirements shown in the preceding table by 6,000. Doing so, we should obtain the results shown in the following table:

Factor of production	Requirements for 6,000 units of output
Equipment:	
Saw	200 hr
Lathe	1,000 hr
Grinder	300 hr
Machine accessories:	
Saw accessories	200 hr
Lathe accessories	1,000 hr
Grinder accessories	300 hr
Material:	
Bar stock	2,000 ft
Direct labor:	
Saw operator	200 hr
Lathe operator	1,000 hr
Grinder operator	300 hr

For production planning purposes, we have expressed the sales forecast in meaningful terms. The production department now knows that, in the month under consideration, it must enable the firm to ship, in effect, 200 hours of saw time, 1,000 hours of lathe time, 2,000 feet of bar stock, 300 hours of grinder operator time, and so on. And these things can be shipped only if they have been made available. However, if the forecast is prepared far enough in advance, steps can be taken to procure these factors of production in the required quantities for shipment during that month. The only thing that remains to be determined is the time at which these factors must be on hand. If we assume that the 5,700 tapered metal pins can all be manufactured in the month in which they are to be shipped, it will not be necessary to have the required factors of production on hand any earlier than the beginning of the month under consideration.

THE CASE OF A MORE COMPLEX PRODUCT   The preceding illustration was an extremely simple one for two reasons. First, the product consisted of only one part. Second, it was assumed that all the operations could be completed in the month in which the units were to be shipped. Unfortunately, these conditions will not always prevail. If they do not, translating the sales forecast becomes somewhat more difficult.

Suppose that the product is an assembly. In a case such as this, the first step in the production planning procedure calls for determining the component parts which must be manufactured or purchased to produce one assembly. If the product has been produced in the past, this information will already be on hand in the form of a bill of materials. If a new product is being considered, a bill of materials must be prepared. A bill of materials is a listing of all the component parts of an assembly, the quantity of each required for 1 unit of the assembly, and the source of each part, that is, whether it is to be purchased or manufactured. An example of a bill of materials is shown in Figure 3-2.

On the basis of this information, the total quantity of each component part which must be procured or produced if the number of finished assemblies stipulated in the sales forecast is to be shipped can be calculated. After having translated the product forecast into a component-part forecast, the firm must ascertain the nature and amount of the various factors of production which will be required to process the calculated quantities of each of the manufactured component parts. This will be done just as it was in the illustration of the tapered metal pin.

At this point, then, we have the sales forecast for an assembled product

ORDER NO.		DESCRIPTION		WT. PER UNIT	PART NO.		
		Motor Drive			Unit 1214-75		
QUANT. ORD	DATE ISSUE	MODEL			SHEET		REVISION DATE
					OF 1 SHEETS 1		———→
	DATE START						
MACH. LOAD	DATE FINISH						

QUANTITY		✓	PART NUMBER	LOCATION	DELIVER TO DEPT.	SYMBOL	DESCRIPTION OF MATERIAL	REMARKS
TOTAL	PER UNIT							
1	1		1214-3000		ST		Adjusting Bracket	
2	2		1214-3001		ST		Eye Bolt	
1	1		1214-111		ST		Motor Bracket Support	
1	1		1214-112		ST		Motor Bracket Shaft	
1	1		1214-123		ST		Motor Bracket	
1	1		514-3036		ST		Belt Guard - Motor	
1	1		514-3037		ST		Back Plate	
1	1		Purchased		OP		QD Sheave 12.0 PD 4 Gr. E Hub	
4	4		Purchased		OP		C75 Goodyear HYT Green Seal Vee Belt	
4	4		4259		AF		5/8 - 11 Full Nuts	
1	1		Purchased		EL.		40 HP T.E.F.C. 1800 RPM Motor Frame	
1	1		Purchased		OP		Worthington QD Sheave 9.0 PD 4 Gr.	

Figure 3-2 Bill of materials

translated into an equivalent demand for specific factors of production which will now include purchased parts. The one thing that remains to be considered is the times at which these factors must be made available if the shipping schedule is to be met. And it is here that we may encounter a complication.

As in the tapered-metal-pin illustration, it is possible that, if certain factors of production are to be shipped in a certain month, the nature and the length of the production process may be such that these factors of production can be shipped during the month if they are made available during that month. In some cases, however, this is not possible. Instead, it may be that so many component parts are involved and that some of the operations are so time-consuming that the first operation must be started one or two months prior to the month in which the final product is to be shipped. This means that we cannot always assume that the required factors of production must simply be on hand during the month in which the product is to be shipped. On the contrary, some of them might have to be available months before. To illustrate this, we shall consider a relatively simple case.

Suppose that a certain number of units of a finished product are expected to be sold in December. The product is an assembly which consists of three complex component parts, each of which requires a number of time-consuming operations. Given the required processing times, we may find the required operation schedule to be as shown in Figure 3-3.

From Figure 3-3 it is evident that, although the product is to be shipped in December, some of the factors of production must be on hand in November. This, however, becomes apparent only after an operation schedule has been prepared. Therefore, a need is created for an additional step

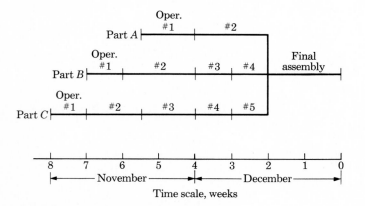

Figure 3-3 A possible operation schedule

in the production planning activity. This calls for developing a probable operation schedule at the time the firm is translating its sales forecast into an equivalent demand for factors of production.

Unfortunately, this need sometimes presents a difficult problem for the following reason: The goal of production planning is the determination of the production facilities required at various points in time. As has been shown, this may call for the development of an operation schedule. And yet, the exact nature of the operation schedule can be determined only if it is known what production facilities will be available. To illustrate, if two machines of a certain type are available, it may be possible to perform certain required operations in one week. If only one machine is available, two weeks may be necessary. The production planning personnel, however, want to know how many machines will be required and when. This cannot be done unless they make some assumption about the number of machines which will be on hand. Hence, they find themselves in a vicious circle.

It should be noted, however, that this problem arises only in long-range planning. There is no comparable difficulty in the case of short-range planning because, in the short run, equipment capacity is fixed at the level available at the present time due to the fact that additional equipment cannot, as a rule, be procured immediately. But in long-range planning, consideration must be given to what the equipment capacity will be in the distant future, and this capacity is a variable at the present time. About all that can be said is that the planning personnel must assume various levels of available capacity until they find one which, in their judgment, yields a reasonable operation schedule. A similar assumption would be made with regard to manpower and machine accessories.

Another problem of comparable difficulty stems from the fact that a variety of arrangements for performing the required operations is possible. For example, Figure 3-3 suggests that operation 1 will be completed on all the units of part A before operation 2 is begun. As a result, the factors of production associated with operation 1 are needed in November, and the factors of production associated with operation 2 are needed in December. However, another arrangement would be to perform the first operation on half the lot and then to send these items to the second work station for the next operation. Meanwhile, the first operation would continue to be performed on the remaining half of the lot. This would serve to move up the date at which the factors of production associated with operation 2 would be needed. This is only one possibility; there are many others. Again, there is no fixed way in which a single alternative can be decided upon. All that can be said is that this will probably be left to the discretion of the planning department.

THE FACTOR-OF-PRODUCTION DEMAND SCHEDULE

The next step in the production planning activity is to find the total demand for specific factors of production at various points in time. This is done by the simple process of addition. For a given factor and time period, the respective demands generated by various products are totaled. To illustrate, it may be that, during some coming month, five products will be manufactured which require a certain number of milling machine-hours. The hours for each of these products may be as follows:

Product	Required milling machine-hours
1	44
2	70
3	22
4	17
5	31
Total	184

This tells the firm that 184 hours of milling machine time must be made available during that month if the required operations on these five products are to be completed on schedule.

Or it may be that final assembly operations are to be started during that month on three products, each of which requires the same kind of purchased gear. The number of gears required for each product may be as follows:

Product	Required purchased gears
1	212
2	107
3	541
Total	860

This tells the firm that 860 gears of this type must be purchased and made available for that month if the required number of units of each of these products is to be assembled in the month under consideration.

The end result of this phase of the planning activity will be that, for each of the future time periods being considered, the company will have a list of the different kinds and amounts of factors of production that must be on hand. However, these totals will have the serious limitation of being based on the sales forecast, and the sales forecast accounts for only standard products. As a result, if the firm makes the indicated requirements available, it will not have provided for the manufacture of nonstandard products. This brings us to the point at which we are compelled to face the problem of forecasting the sales of special products.

THE NONSTANDARD PRODUCT FORECAST Because the specifications of nonstandard products are not known prior to their being ordered, a sales forecast for these items in terms of physical units is not possible. At best, the firm can do the following: An analysis can be made of the respective factors of production required to satisfy the demand for special products in the past. If these requirements are broken down by time period, the firm will have what amounts to a time series for each of these factors of production. For example, it may be that the demand for assembly-hours accounted for by special products during the last 12 quarters is as shown in Figure 3-4.

The future demand for such assembly-hours can be estimated by making a time series analysis of these past data for this factor of production. The future trend value can be obtained and, if warranted, a seasonal adjustment factor can be computed and applied. The result would then be modified, on the basis of judgment, to reflect special conditions which are expected to prevail in the future.

This type of analysis would have to be made for each of the factors of production which had been involved in the processing of nonstandard items in the past. The adjusted projected values would then be added to the demand for corresponding factors of production which had been estimated as being required for the production of standard products. The result would be a total factor-of-production demand schedule which would reflect anticipated future sales of both standard and nonstandard items.

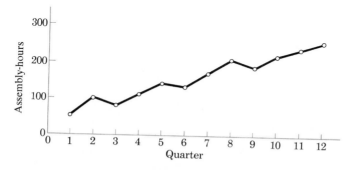

Figure 3-4   A demand schedule for assembly-hours

Although the time series approach has been suggested here, many firms have found it simpler to adhere to some rule of thumb developed on the basis of judgment and past experience. For example, after having determined the demand for various factors of production created by anticipated sales of standard products, they will increase this indicated demand by some factor, such as 10 percent, to provide for probable sales of special products.

ADJUSTMENTS IN FACTOR-OF-PRODUCTION DETERMINATION

It was mentioned that, in the determination of required factors of production, expected sales must be adjusted to reflect the amount of expected defective work. Also, unit time requirements should reflect expected labor efficiency and the fact that unavoidable delays will be experienced. In brief, the purpose of the analysis is to determine the factors of production required under actual rather than ideal conditions. And under actual conditions, some output is scrapped, operators work at efficiencies other than 100 percent, and unavoidable delays take place. We shall now consider how these occurrences are treated in the analysis.

ADJUSTMENT FOR SCRAP Suppose that the forecast for a particular month states that 1,900 *good* units of a given part are required. Further, the operation sheet for that part reveals that a drilling machine must be used to perform one of the operations. Finally, it is estimated that 5 percent of the output from the machine will be defective in the sense that it must be scrapped. Under these conditions, the number of units scheduled for production must be

$$\text{Scheduled units} = \frac{1,900 \text{ units}}{1.00 - 0.05} = 2,000 \text{ units}$$

Because 95 percent of the output will be satisfactory, we find that, if the 2,000 scheduled units are multiplied by this percentage, a result of 1,900 good units is obtained.

ADJUSTMENTS FOR UNAVOIDABLE DELAYS AND EFFICIENCY The operation sheet for the part being considered will also state the required time per unit of output. This time, when multiplied by the 2,000 units scheduled for production, will yield the required drilling machine-hours, man-hours, and machine accessory-hours. However, the indicated unit time requirement might be the *actual* time or the *standard* time or the *normal* time.

Actual time is the true time required per unit of output as determined by taking into consideration labor efficiency and unavoidable delays such as machine breakdowns, material shortages, and rest periods. Standard time is the time determined by taking into consideration the occurrence of unavoidable delays but assuming that labor efficiency will be 100 percent. Normal time is the time that would be required if labor efficiency were 100 percent and there were no unavoidable delays.

Consequently, for production planning purposes, if the operation sheet contains normal times, these times must be adjusted to reflect expected unavoidable delays and labor efficiency. If it contains standard times, these times must be adjusted to reflect expected labor efficiency. If it contains actual times, no adjustment is required.

To illustrate how necessary adjustments are made, let us begin by assuming that we are given the normal time for the drilling operation in our example and that this is 0.126 hour per unit.[1] If unavoidable delays are expected to account for 25 percent of the total time, the standard time for the operation would be found in the following manner:

$$\text{Standard time} = \frac{0.126 \text{ hr/unit}}{1.00 - 0.25} = 0.168 \text{ hr/unit}$$

Next, if it is estimated that the labor efficiency will be 120 percent, this standard time would be adjusted in the following manner to obtain the actual time:

$$\text{Actual time} = \frac{0.168 \text{ hr/unit}}{1.20} = 0.140 \text{ hr/unit}$$

Because the firm is interested in ascertaining the actual requirements for the various factors of production, these requirements would be determined by multiplying the actual time per unit by the number of units that must be scheduled for production. In our example, doing so would yield

$$\text{Required hours} = 2,000 \text{ units} \times 0.140 \text{ hr/unit} = 280 \text{ hr}$$

This means that, for the month under consideration, the demand for 1,900 good units of this part is equivalent to a demand of 280 hours for drilling machine-hours, drilling man-hours, and drilling machine accessory-hours. These hours can be converted to the number of machines, men, and accessories they represent by dividing them by the monthly capacity of 1 unit of these factors of production. For example, if the plant will operate on a 40-hour-a-week schedule, any one drill is theoretically capable of operating 173 hours a month. Consequently, 280 machine-hours are equivalent to the following number of machines:

---

[1] Methods for determining the normal time are described in Chapters 20 and 21.

$$\text{Required machines} = \frac{280 \text{ hr}/\text{month}}{173 \text{ hr}/\text{machine}/\text{month}} = 1.62 \text{ machines}$$

LEVELING THE PRODUCTION FACTOR DEMAND SCHEDULE

A total factor-of-production demand schedule will exist for each of the different factors of production. Graphically, the schedule for one of these, which we shall assume to be drill press-hours, might appear as shown in Figure 3-5.

It would be convenient, from the production planning standpoint, if the firm could simply adopt the production schedule implied in the demand schedule for each factor of production and formulate its procurement policy accordingly. This, however, is rarely possible. Invariably, as shown in Figure 3-5, the demand for a given factor of production is a fluctuating one. If these fluctuations were accepted and no attempt made to modify them, problems would arise for reasons we shall now consider.

DEMAND FOR EQUIPMENT AND ACCESSORIES Let us begin with the factor of equipment, in which we shall include machine accessories because of the close relationship between the two. It may be that the demand schedule for a certain type of equipment is as shown in Figure 3-6.

Figure 3-6 also contains a line which represents the firm's present capacity insofar as this equipment is concerned. In determining what the present capacity is, the company will have to decide what the plant hours of operation will be. An eight-hour-day schedule five days a week will permit the machine to run a maximum of 173 hours a month. On the other hand, a two-shift operation increases a single machine's capacity to 346

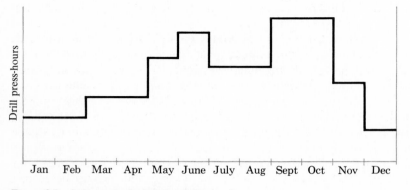

Figure 3-5   A demand schedule for drill press-hours

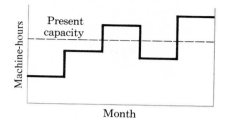

Figure 3-6 A demand schedule for equipment

hours per month. Therefore, the available capacity of equipment of a certain type will be expressed in terms of so many hours per time period and will be equal to the number of machines of that type on hand times the number of hours each machine can be operated during the period.

Showing the present capacity in Figure 3-6 reveals that, if the firm accepts the demand schedule involved, the present capacity will be inadequate during certain periods. It might be proposed that additional equipment be procured. But if this is done, the capital investment in equipment is increased with the result that a corresponding increase takes place in depreciation. Also, there is a cost to be associated with financing the investment. Finally, more floor space may have to be acquired to house the additional equipment.

Another proposal might be to schedule overtime work or add an additional shift. But this alternative generates the cost of overtime or shift premiums. Furthermore, it is not unusual for labor efficiency to be lower during overtime periods and on night shifts, with the result that an additional increase occurs in unit production costs.

Consequently, a better proposal might be that the company attempt to level out the demand for this factor of production. While, as we shall see, there are costs to be associated with this alternative, they are very often lower than those generated by the other possible courses of action. This proposal would be in order even if present capacity were sufficient for indicated peak periods, because leveling out the demand might permit a reduction in the investment in equipment at some saving to the firm.

DEMAND FOR LABOR Insofar as the factor of labor is concerned, it may be that the demand schedule for a certain type of labor is as shown in Figure 3-7.

Again, if the company were to adhere to this schedule, it would be compelled to select one of a number of alternatives. One would be to hire additional personnel during one period and lay off personnel during an-

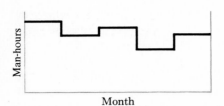

Figure 3-7   A demand schedule for labor

other. A second would be to hire the maximum number of personnel required at any one time and keep the excess on the roll during periods of reduced activity. A third would be to have existing personnel work overtime during periods of greater activity.

Any one of these alternatives may be undesirable. Alternately hiring and laying off people tends to increase unit labor costs because of the costs to be associated with the procurement and training of personnel, with the laying off of personnel, and with the firm's getting a reputation as being an undesireable place to work because of the little security it offers. The disadvantage of the second alternative is obvious; the firm cannot operate economically if it adheres to a policy of keeping surplus personnel on the roll. The third alternative calls for the payment of overtime premiums, and lower labor efficiency during overtime periods may also contribute to higher unit costs.

Therefore, as in the case of equipment and machine accessories, we conclude that the solution to the problem of a fluctuating demand for labor may lie in leveling out this demand.

DEMAND FOR MATERIALS   Let us now consider the factor of materials, which will include purchased parts. Suppose that the demand schedule for a given material is as shown in Figure 3-8.

The case of materials differs from that of the other factors of production, because fluctuations in material demand might be of no consequence

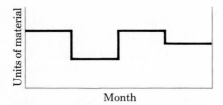

Figure 3-8   A demand schedule for materials

whatsoever. It may be that the company can place its order for whatever quantity is required for a particular time period without incurring any additional cost due to the variation in the size of these orders.

On the other hand, it may be that the quantity required for a particular time period is so small that this quantity can be procured only at a higher unit purchase cost, or the quantity may be so large that storage becomes a problem. In such cases, savings may be possible by leveling out the demand for raw materials and purchased parts.

In summary, there may or may not be something to be gained by leveling out the demand schedule for materials. Therefore, most firms will emphasize the need for leveling out the demand for equipment, machine accessories, and labor. This will not always be the case, but, for purposes of simplicity, we shall concentrate on this prevalent condition.

In brief, after the sales forecast has been translated into a demand schedule for various factors of production, the firm will not necessarily adopt and adhere to these schedules. Instead, if wide fluctuations in demand are evident, an effort will be made to minimize these fluctuations. We shall now consider methods for doing so.

METHODS OF LEVELING PRODUCTION SCHEDULES   One method of leveling production schedules is to produce to stock during slack periods. This has the effect of cutting off one or more of the peaks in the demand schedule and allocating the output corresponding to these peaks to earlier time periods during which the demand is somewhat lower. For example, an original production schedule may be altered in the following manner:

Month	Original production schedule, units	Revised production schedule, units
1	120	170
2	130	170
3	260	170
Total	510	510

It should be noted that the firm will be carrying higher inventories than it otherwise would, and there are certain costs to be associated with this. And it may be that the higher inventory costs will more than offset the savings· to be associated with the leveling out of the demand for various factors of production; this can be determined by means of a cost analysis. Furthermore, eliminating fluctuations in the production schedule for a given product may not have a salutary effect on all the factor-of-production demand schedules. It may be, for example, that two machines are used in the production of that product; suppose these are a punch press and a drill. The original production schedule, based on the sales forecast, may yield a total demand schedule for drilling time which has an undesirable peak. However, the same may not be true for punch-press time because the production schedules for the firm's other products, which also require punch presses, are such that the composite demand for this factor of production is fairly uniform. Consequently, it is possible that altering the production schedule of the item under consideration so as to level out the demand for drilling time will create peaks in the demand for punch-press time which did not exist with the original schedule. Therefore, the required analysis may become somewhat complex.

A second method for minimizing fluctuations in the factor-of-production demand schedules calls for making an effort to alter the sales pattern of certain products. We know that the firm has some control over what this pattern will be. For example, the amount of a given product that will be sold will be a function of the selling price and the amount of sales effort expended. Therefore, a given sales forecast is based on an assumed selling price and on an assumed level of sales effort. If this forecast generates non-uniform demand schedules for various factors of production, it is possible to take steps which will alter the forecast and, therefore, the factor-of-production demand schedules. One of these steps may be to reduce selling prices during periods of reduced demand. Another may be to increase the amount of sales effort during these periods. Again, these alternatives involve a price. The required reduction in selling price and the cost of the additional sales effort may be such that they more than offset the advantages of leveled-out demand schedules. Whether or not this is the case can be determined by means of a cost comparison. Also, as mentioned earlier, while an altered sales pattern may have a desirable effect on the demand schedule for one factor of production, it may have an undesirable effect on the demand schedule for some other factor. All this must be taken into consideration.

If one of the two preceding methods for leveling out demand schedules is not feasible, the company has a third alternative, namely, to promise later delivery dates during peak periods. The effect of this is to postpone the production of a certain number of units of some of its products until a later date when the required capacity will be available. The consequences of this will vary. In some cases, it may be that the customer is perfectly willing to accept a later delivery date. In other cases, it may be that the order will be lost. Where this is true, the firm will have to decide whether the cost of lost orders is more than offset by the savings to be realized from the resultant leveling out of production-factor demand schedules.

The fourth and final method for minimizing fluctuations calls for the introduction of new products into the firm's product line. These items would have to have one important characteristic, which is that the sales pattern they would follow and the factors of production they would require would be such that they could be produced on what would otherwise be idle production facilities. If this is possible, the sum of the production-factor demand schedules for the existing and new products would yield a combined demand schedule which would be fairly uniform.

Although we have discussed each of these methods individually, more than one of them may be adopted by a single firm. Also, it is possible that none of these methods will be practical for a given firm, and as a result, the company may be compelled to adopt the production schedule which generates fairly wide fluctuations in the demand for various factors of production. Where this is true, the firm must adapt itself to these fluctuating demands. This might necessitate procuring additional equipment by buying or leasing, hiring additional personnel during peak periods and laying them off during slack periods, scheduling overtime work or a two-shift operation during peak periods, subcontracting some of the excess work, and so on.

It should also be mentioned that the alteration of the demand schedules may not be limited to leveling out these schedules but may also involve adjusting them to provide for producing economic lot sizes and for building up or decreasing inventories. But we shall consider this aspect of the problem in the chapters on inventory control. In any event, after having either accepted or altered the original demand schedules for the different factors of production, the company has completed the last step in the production planning procedure as it is related to the determination of equipment, machine-accessory, direct-labor, and material requirements. All that is necessary now is that provision be made for obtaining these factors in the required quantities by the dates indicated in the final schedules. As this suggests, the procurement time for the various factors of production will determine the length of the future time period for which a schedule of demand will be prepared.

There is also the question concerning whether these schedules should show the demand by day, week, month, or quarter. If the demand is expected to vary radically from day to day, a daily schedule would be in order. On the other hand, if the demand is expected to be fairly stable from day to day in any given week but is expected to vary considerably from week to week, a weekly schedule would be in order. The same reasoning may suggest a schedule broken down by month or quarter. However, since the demand for one factor may vary from week to week while for another factor only from month to month, it may be that the weekly demand will be determined for one factor and a monthly demand for some other.

USE OF DATA PROCESSING EQUIPMENT

It is evident that production planning can be a tremendous task. However, certain things can be done to simplify the procedure. To begin with, translating the sales forecast into an equivalent demand for various factors of production need not be done for each individual product. Often a number of products differ only in minor respects, with the result that they require the same factors of production in about the same quantities and in the same sequence. In such cases, they can all be handled as if they were a single product.

Next, for a single product, the equipment capacity of a certain type that will be required will usually be equal to the capacity required of a corresponding type of labor and machine accessory. One computation, therefore, may serve to determine the required capacity for three factors of production.

Even with these simplifications, the production planning procedure is a difficult and complex one. The simple mechanics of processing data for the sales forecast, of translating the forecast into a factor-of-production demand schedule, and of altering these schedules are tedious and time-consuming. The only relief from these elements of the procedure lies in the use of automatic data processing equipment.

If the economic indicator approach is employed in sales forecasting, such equipment can be used to compute the degree of correlation between past sales and various indicators; in this manner, an appropriate indicator, if one exists, can be found. Then the equation of a line which describes the relationship between sales and the indicator can be determined. Finally, the equipment can be used to compute, with the use of the resultant equation of the least-squares line, the volume of sales that corresponds to some given value of the indicator.

In the event that a time series analysis is performed, data processing equipment can be utilized to ascertain the equation of the trend line, to compute the values of the seasonal adjustment factors, and, with the use of these factors and the equation of the trend line, to calculate the expected values of future sales.

If the resultant forecast is for a product group, past sales can be analyzed to determine the percentages of these sales attributable to the individual items contained in the group. For a given item, the average or trend value of these percentages for various time periods can be calculated and applied to the group forecast to obtain the expected sales for the item.

Data processing equipment can also be used to convert dollar forecasts for individual products to unit forecasts by dividing the dollar values by unit selling prices.

Finally, in the case of special products, the equipment can be applied in the determination of the kinds and amounts of factors of production required in the past to manufacture these products. These data can then be processed to obtain an average or trend value for each factor; this value would then be used as an estimate of future requirements.

Data processing equipment can also be used to convert the sales forecast into the demands it generates for raw materials, purchased parts, manpower, equipment, and machine accessories. Bills of materials and operation sheets required for this purpose can be prepared and maintained in the form of punched cards or tapes. The bills of materials and quantity requirements for assembled products permit the determination of the purchased and manufactured parts needed for the assemblies involved. The operation sheets and quantity requirements for manufactured parts permit the determination of the materials, manpower, equipment, and accessories needed for the parts involved. In the course of these determinations, the data processing equipment can also make the necessary adjustments for expected scrap, labor efficiency, and machine downtime due to unavoidable delays.

When all this has been done, the equipment can be used to obtain total requirements by time period for the various factors of production. If the resultant demand schedules contain undesirable fluctuations, data processing equipment can be utilized to develop more uniform schedules and to evaluate these alternative schedules on the basis of a cost comparison.

SOME REMAINING OBSERVATIONS

The relative complexity of production planning should not obscure the fact that the results are likely to contain errors. This is because the entire procedure is intended to yield information about the future, and there is no accurate method for predicting the course of future events. However, the usual errors are not calamitous. Their adverse effects are reduced by the firm's ability to maintain safety stocks of raw materials and finished parts, to increase or decrease the hours of work, and to alter the demand for its products by changing its prices and sales effort. While the need for these corrective actions may prove to be costly, it will probably not prove to be disastrous.

It should also be noted that some managements engage in no formal production planning. If one were to mention forecasting sales or preparing demand schedules for production factors to them, they would simply say that these things cannot be done in their firms because of the nature of their operations. This does not mean, however, that they do not engage in production planning. If they did not, they would never maintain inventories of any kind, hire a person, buy a piece of equipment, move into a larger plant, and so on. These managements do these things, and they do them because they believe there will be a need for the factors involved. This is production planning. The difference between the respective approaches is that theirs is based solely on judgment and intuition.

Let us also take cognizance of the fact that production planning is required in every type of enterprise. For reasons stated in the introductory chapter, we are using the manufacturing activity as the model in terms of which the principles of operations management will be considered. However, operations must be managed in such other enterprises as retail and wholesale establishments, law firms, hospitals, accounting firms, educational institutions, governmental agencies, automobile repair shops, brokerage firms, and so on. In each of these cases, the managements of these enterprises must anticipate the future demand for the products and services their organizations provide and take steps to procure the manpower, equipment, materials, supplies, and space that must be on hand if these demands are to be satisfied. Their specific production or operations planning procedures will differ in various respects from those employed in a manufacturing organization. Nevertheless, the concepts underlying them will be the same as those we have considered and described.

But to return to our manufacturing model, we should recall that the procedures we have considered do not provide the firm with information regarding future requirements for buildings and materials handling equipment. As noted earlier, these can be ascertained only in the course of developing an appropriate plant layout and designing a materials handling system. So let us go on to consider this aspect of the production planning activity.

QUESTIONS

3-1   Describe an operation, or routing, sheet in terms of the information it contains.

3-2   Describe a bill of materials in terms of the information it contains.

3-3   How is the sales forecast for a manufactured part translated into the demand it generates for various factors of production?

3-4   How is the sales forecast for an assembly translated into the demand it generates for various factors of production?

3-5   What is an operation schedule? How does it enter into the production planning process?

3-6   What methods can be employed to forecast the demand for factors of production generated by the sale of nonstandard products?

3-7   Define actual time. Normal time. Standard time.

3-8   What disadvantages are to be associated with wide fluctuations in the demand schedule for equipment? For manpower? For materials?

3-9   Describe the methods by means of which it may be economically feasible for the firm to minimize fluctuations in the demand schedules for factors of production.

3-10 What specific functions can be performed with the use of automatic data processing equipment in the area of sales forecasting? In the determination of demand schedules for factors of production?

3-11 Give some examples of activities, other than manufacturing, which require the planning of future operations.

PROBLEMS

3-1 A sales forecast for an assembly indicates that 800 units can be expected to be sold in a particular month. The bill of materials for this product indicates that it consists of two component parts, A and B. Further, part A is manufactured, and part B is purchased. Finally, 2 units of part A and 1 unit of part B are required for each assembly.

The operation sheet for part A indicates that the following factors of production are among those required to produce 1 unit of part A:

Factor of production	Requirements per unit of output
Material:	
Casting #1783	1
Equipment and accessories:	
Drill	0.079 hr
Planer	0.168 hr
Direct labor:	
Drill operator	0.079 hr
Planer operator	0.168 hr

Translate the sales forecast into an equivalent demand for these factors of production.

3-2 An estimate has been made of the number of manufactured assemblies of a certain type that will be demanded during a given week. From the bill of materials for this product, the firm determines the number of good component parts that must be manufactured to satisfy this demand. Further, on the basis of past experience, an estimate is made of the percentage of the output of each of these parts that will probably be scrapped. The results can be summarized as follows:

Part number	Number of good units required	Expected scrap, %
1697	70	3
2581	140	5
2902	70	1
4714	210	2

What quantity of each component part would have to be scheduled for production? (Ans. 73, 148, 71, 215)

3-3 Two thousand good copies of a report are needed. The printing process requires three successive operations. The output at the end of each processing stage is inspected and any unsatisfactory work discarded. It is expected that 4 percent of the output will be scrapped after the first operation, 2 percent of the remainder will be scrapped after the second operation, and 5 percent of the balance will be scrapped after the third operation. In the determination of the factors of production required for the first operation, consideration will have to be given to the number of copies of the report that will undergo that operation. What should that number be? (Ans. 2,238)

3-4 The normal time for processing orders in a warehouse is given as 35.120 hours per 100 orders. It is estimated that unavoidable delays will account for 20 percent of the total time and that labor efficiency will be 90 percent. What will be the standard time per order? The actual time? (Ans. 0.439, 0.488)

3-5 The average actual time for keypunching cards used in a data processing installation is 1.05 minutes per card. Average labor efficiency on this job has been 115 percent, and 25 percent of the total time has been spent on unavoidable delays. What is the standard time for the activity? The normal time?

3-6 An analyst finds that, in a particular month, a special fixture will be required to process 1,390 units of a part and that the actual time per unit of output will probably be 30 minutes. If the plant were to operate on a single shift, each fixture of this type would be available for 173 hours per month. However, plans are to work two shifts during the period under consideration. Under these circumstances, how many fixtures of this type would be required? (Ans. 2.0)

3-7 A proposed production schedule stipulates that 420 good units of a specific part are to be manufactured in a certain week. The routing sheet for the part indicates that one of the operations calls for a power hacksaw and that the normal time for the operation is 0.072 hour per unit.

Calculate the number of machines of this type that will be required to process this part in the week under consideration if:

a No scrap is expected, labor efficiency will be 100 percent, each saw will be scheduled to operate 40 hours per week, and no unavoidable delays will be experienced.

b Five percent of the output will be scrapped, labor efficiency will be 100 percent, each saw will be scheduled to operate 40 hours per week, and no unavoidable delays will be experienced.

c Three percent of the output will be scrapped, labor efficiency will be 105 percent, each saw will be scheduled to operate 40 hours per week, and no unavoidable delays will be experienced.

d Four percent of the output will be scrapped, labor efficiency will be 70 percent, each saw will be scheduled to operate 50 hours per week, and no unavoidable delays will be experienced.

e One percent of the output will be scrapped, labor efficiency will be 120 percent, each saw will be scheduled to operate 44 hours per week, and unavoidable delays will account for 22 percent of the total time. (Ans. 0.74)

3-8 A bank provides its customers with a number of special services which involve activities of a nonstandard nature. A study of the bank's records reveals that, in the past, the number of man-hours expended on these activities were as follows:

Year	Required man-hours
1	2,100
2	2,700
3	3,100
4	3,600
5	4,000
6	4,500

For operations planning purposes, the bank will estimate the man-hours required for special services by making a time series analysis of the data compiled. If this is done by the least-squares method, what will be the calculated requirements for the seventh and eighth years? (Ans. 4,973; 5,442)

3-9 A monthly production schedule, suggested by the expected demand for a product, is as follows:

Month	Units to be produced
January	2,200
February	3,400
March	2,400
April	2,200
May	3,200
June	1,800
July	2,000
August	2,800
September	2,000
October	2,000
November	1,800
December	2,200

The firm decides to reduce the fluctuations in this schedule by producing to stock during the relatively slack periods and, thereby, carrying higher inventories of the involved item. Prepare a revised production schedule that reflects this decision.

PART THREE

FACILITIES LAYOUT AND MATERIALS HANDLING

FOUR
THE DEPARTMENTAL ARRANGEMENT

It has been stated that future building requirements can be determined only by giving consideration to the required layout of the production facilities in the plant. This is so because it is in this manner that the firm can ascertain how much and what kind of space will be needed. But this does not mean that the firm engages in the plant layout activity only when a need arises for determining future building requirements. Every manufacturing concern is confronted by plant layout problems on other occasions. To begin with, when an analysis is made of the work methods at a work station, consideration must be given to the possibility of improving these methods by rearranging the facilities with which the operator is working. In other cases, a change in product design or production processes may result in a revised sequence of operations, a new set of operations, the replacement of old equipment by new equipment, and the like. As a consequence, a need for more or less space may be generated, existing work stations may become unnecessary and new work stations necessary, or the flow of work from one department to another may now leave something to be desired. Then there are situations in which new items are added to the company's product line, existing items are discarded, or a change takes place in the required levels of output. The consequences of this might be that new equipment will be installed, old equipment will be removed, or space requirements will change, with the result that a layout problem is created. Finally, a company may find that its overall plant layout is such that the utilization of the most efficient available materials handling equipment is not possible, that work in process is unduly high because of an inefficient flow of work, or that a space shortage exists because the available floor space is not being used effectively.

All this suggests that the scope and magnitude of the plant layout problem vary widely. At one extreme, and this is the most common case, the nature of certain events will be such that relatively minor adjustments in the existing layout will be called for. One department or work station may be relocated or rearranged, a new production line may be installed in an available area, and so on.

At the other extreme, the company may find it necessary to re-layout its entire plant. This may be done in the building it already occupies and in which it has been operating, in a different building to which it has decided to move and which already exists, or in a new building which has yet to be designed and constructed.

THE PROBLEM TO BE CONSIDERED

The details of the plant layout procedure vary with the nature of the problem. Consequently, a need arises for defining the type of plant layout problem we shall discuss. This will be the one in which the company finds it necessary to review, and possibly revise, the entire layout of an existing plant. Further, we shall assume that the purpose of the analysis is to determine what specific layout is required if the firm is to be able to satisfy the future demand for its products. In the process, the firm will also determine its future building requirements.

This type of problem is the most comprehensive one, because the method for analyzing the existing layout with a view toward making a complete revision calls for giving consideration to more factors than does the method for analyzing any other layout problem. Consequently, if we become acquainted with all these factors, there should be no difficulty in adapting the approach to the solution of a less complex problem.

In the process of developing this approach, we shall find that consideration must be given to three things. One is the arrangement of the production and service departments in the plant. The second is the arrangement of work stations in these departments. And the third is the arrangement of the facilities with which an operator must work at a particular work station. In each of these cases, the goal is the development of an arrangement which will permit the most efficient flow of work. However, it will not be enough for the analyst to concern himself with only the location of departments, work stations, and work facilities. While it is true that the end result of doing so will be a layout which may permit the most efficient flow of work, it is also true that such a layout will not in itself bring about the desired efficiency. This is so because the cost to be associated with a given flow pattern will be affected by the choice of materials handling equipment. Hence, consideration must be given to alternative methods of handling materials. And furthermore, space for this equipment must be provided in the layout. In brief, plant layout and materials handling are interrelated, and this interrelationship must be taken into account. We shall do so by concentrating on plant layout and relating it to materials handling as the need to do so arises.

THE DETERMINATION OF EQUIPMENT REQUIREMENTS

The initial step in any plant layout analysis is the determination of what is to be laid out. For this reason, the firm will begin by ascertaining the kind and amount of equipment that will be required to manufacture its products. The procedure for accomplishing this has already been discussed. But it should be mentioned that, for plant layout purposes, the demand schedules for equipment must be prepared for a fairly long future time period. In fact, it is not unusual for the company to think in terms of 5 to 10 years in the future when evaluating its existing plant layout. One reason for this is that, if it is found that existing space is inadequate for future needs, sufficient time must be allowed for the procurement of additional space. Another is that if the result is an extensive revision of the existing layout, the expense of such a project calls for making every effort to develop a layout which will be satisfactory for more than just a year or two. Of course, any attempt to forecast sales for a 5- to 10-year period is likely to yield results which are anything but accurate, but this risk of making an error must be assumed.

In any event, after the respective demand schedules have been leveled out or have been adjusted to permit production in economic lot sizes, the analyst can calculate equipment requirements in the manner described in the last chapter. To illustrate, for a given future month, the expected production schedule may generate demands for a specific kind of equipment such as the demands summarized in Figure 4-1.

If the indicated 514 hours of grinder time have been obtained by taking into consideration expected scrap, unavoidable delays, and labor efficiency, these hours can be converted to the equivalent number of machines by dividing them by the monthly capacity of one grinder, which may be 173 hours. Consequently, 514 machine-hours would be equivalent to the following number of machines:

$$\text{Required machines} = \frac{514 \text{ hr}/\text{month}}{173 \text{ hr}/\text{machine}/\text{month}} = 2.95, \text{ or 3 machines}$$

Although the calculated number of machines was rounded off to the next higher whole number, there is no general rule which states that this should always be done. With a calculated figure of something like 2.95, there can be little doubt that three machines will be required. But if the calculated figure were, for example, 3.11, the firm might decide to provide only three machines on the assumption that the demand might not be as great as expected, that the operating efficiency might be greater than expected, that the amount of defective work might be less than expected,

MACHINE DESCRIPTION:	
Heald #74 grinder	
MONTH UNDER CONSIDERATION:	
March 19___	
PART NUMBER	REQUIRED MACHINE HOURS
2337	206
2681	23
2972	190
3102	54
Special	41
Total	514

Figure 4-1   A summary of machine
requirements

or that the monthly machine capacity could be increased by scheduling overtime work.

It might also be noted that, if equipment requirements fluctuate from one period to another and these fluctuations cannot be eliminated, space will have to be provided in the layout for the maximum number of units that will be needed during any single period. In any case, after all such determinations have been made, the analyst is in a position to go on to the next step in the plant layout activity, which is the determination of departmental space requirements.

DETERMINATION OF SPACE REQUIREMENTS FOR PRODUCTION DEPARTMENTS

The task of laying out an entire plant calls for, first, locating the departments in the existing building and, then, locating the work stations in the various departments. Therefore, before work stations can be planned, it is necessary that the analyst decide where the individual departments are to be located. This cannot be done, however, until he has made an estimate of the space each department will require. It is this problem with which we shall now concern ourselves. For the moment, we shall concentrate on the determination of space requirements for production departments. The need for making similar estimates for service departments will then be considered.

INTERMITTENT VERSUS CONTINUOUS MANUFACTURING The determination of space requirements for production departments begins with the departmentalization of the firm's manufacturing activities. How this is done depends on whether the firm engages in intermittent or continuous manufacturing.

Intermittent manufacturing is characterized by the fact that a given product is manufactured intermittently and not continuously. This means that the item will appear in the production schedule for a limited period of time and then drop out. At some later date, it will again appear in the schedule. An example of this would be a nonstandard product which is produced directly to customer order. Another would be a standard product for which the demand is so small that it need not be manufactured continuously; instead it may be that the requirements for an entire month can be economically produced in, say, one day. Consequently, the item would enter the production schedule for one day during each month.

As opposed to this, a firm may be producing an item for which the demand is such that continuous production is warranted. Once this product enters the company's production schedule, it stays there continuously. Of course, continuously does not mean forever. Products become obsolete, demand patterns change, strikes occur, and equipment breaks down, but, in general, a fairly long period of time is involved. In all such cases, the item would be a standard product.

This one difference between intermittent and continuous manufacturing suggests another. If an item is produced continuously, the quantities involved are such that the firm can usually justify investing in equipment which is specially designed to process this product and which will be limited to the processing of this product. As opposed to this, equipment used to process an item which is produced intermittently must be flexible enough so that it can be adapted to the processing of other products. Otherwise, a given piece of equipment would be utilized for an extremely limited period of time, and this would be uneconomical. Therefore, a firm which engages in intermittent manufacturing will tend to use general-purpose equipment, whereas a firm which engages in continuous manufacturing will tend to use equipment of special design.

Another difference is that, given two companies of comparable size, the one engaged in intermittent manufacturing will be producing more different products than will the firm engaged in continuous manufacturing. This follows from the fact that, in intermittent manufacturing, relatively small quantities of each product will be produced while in continuous manufacturing, relatively large quantities of each product will be produced. If the respective overall plant operations are of equal scope, the smaller quantities will be coupled with many products and the larger quantities with few products.

Finally, a firm which is engaged in intermittent manufacturing will adhere to a system of departmentalization which differs from that adhered to by a firm which is engaged in continuous manufacturing. In continuous manufacturing, the firm will adopt a product layout, whereas in intermittent manufacturing, it will adopt a process layout. The difference between the two layouts is as follows: In a product layout, all the machines employed in the manufacture of a single product or part are grouped together, and every such grouping is considered to be a department. In a process layout, all machines of the same type are grouped together, and every such grouping is considered to be a department. Let us now elaborate upon this.

THE PRODUCT LAYOUT   Suppose that a company is producing a part which requires five different operations. These operations are performed on the following equipment:

Operation number	Required equipment
1	Lathe
2	Drill
3	Milling machine
4	Drill
5	Grinder

It may be that the quantities being produced are large enough so that two lathes are needed continuously to perform the first operation, one drill to perform the second operation, two milling machines to perform the third operation, one drill to perform the fourth operation, and one grinder to perform the fifth operation. Because of this, it would be natural to group this equipment together to bring about an efficient flow of work. In other words, the establishment of a production line for the processing of this part would be justified. The resultant line may appear as shown in Figure 4-2.

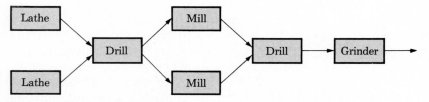

Figure 4-2   A production-line layout

Further, if the company had a number of other parts whose quantity requirements also justified the establishment of individual production lines, the final plant layout would consist of a collection of such lines, each devoted to the manufacture of a single part. Also, every line would be looked upon as representing a single department. In brief, the company would have a product layout, that is, a layout in which machines are grouped in accordance with the part, or product, they process.

If the product is an assembly, the arrangement of equipment may be more complex. To illustrate, the company may be manufacturing, on a continuous basis, a product which consists of three component parts. If so, the production line may consist of a combination of three series of machines, each series devoted to the manufacture of one of the component parts, and a series of assembly stations. This arrangement is indicated in Figure 4-3. In a case such as this, all the work stations required to process and assemble the three component parts might be looked upon as constituting a single department.

Up to this point, it has been assumed that a given production line will be devoted to the processing of only one product. On occasion, however, more than one part will be processed on the line. This will occur when a number of parts differ only slightly from one another, in the sense that they can be produced on the same line if minor changes are made in the manner in which the equipment is set up and operated. For example, a printing firm can print pages of different sizes on the same equipment if the equipment is adjusted accordingly.

BALANCING PRODUCTION LINES Before going on to the process layout, let us consider the need for balanced production lines in the product layout. To illustrate the meaning of a balanced line, suppose that we have a line which consists of a series of four machines, each performing a single operation. The unit operating times may be as follows:

Operation number	Required time per unit of output, min	Output per hour, units
1	10	6
2	20	3
3	10	6
4	20	3

From an examination of these operating times, it is clear that if one machine is assigned to each operation, the line will not be balanced. The reason is that the first and third machines produce twice as many units

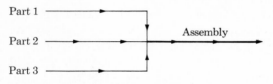

Figure 4-3 A production line for the manufacture of an assembly

per hour as do the second and fourth machines. As a consequence, materials would start piling up at the second station and, in time, the third station would be operating at 50 percent capacity.

To correct this situation, one of a number of things can be done. First, it would be possible to assign two machines to each of the bottleneck operations. This would double the output at these stations, and the line would now be balanced. If this is done, the output capacity of the line would be 6 units per hour.

However, it may be that a capacity of 6 units per hour is not required. For example, suppose that the line can be operated a maximum of 150 hours per month. With an output capacity of 6 units per hour, the monthly capacity becomes 900 units. But if the production schedule calls for only 450 units, the line will be idle 50 percent of the time, and this is not economical. Therefore, a more desirable alternative may be to assign only one machine to each operation but to have the machines performing the second and fourth operations operate twice as many hours as do the other two machines. The excess output could be stored temporarily at the second and fourth stations. Although the first and third machines would be idle 50 percent of the time, the other two would be operating at full capacity, and, as a result, the line would be utilized more completely than it would have been with the first alternative.

Yet, the fact that some idle capacity continues to exist suggests that still another alternative may be more attractive. This one calls for taking steps to change the time requirements for the various operations. For example, it may be possible to procure machines whose individual output capacities are such that a better balance will be obtained. Or if some of the elements of the operations are manual, it may be possible to redistribute the work or to vary the number of operators so that the lack of balance is eliminated, or at least minimized.

Finally, there are always those cases in which the only way a satisfactory degree of balance can be attained is to establish a single work station as an integral part of more than one production line. For example, a firm may be planning to produce two parts on two different production lines. Each of these parts undergoes one operation which is common to both. However, suppose it has been found that if a separate machine were to

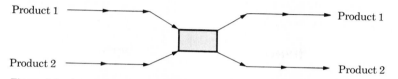

Figure 4-4 An arrangement in which one machine is a part of more than one line

be installed in each of the lines for the performance of this operation, this equipment would be used only 50 percent of the time. Under these circumstances, it may be possible to have one unit of the equipment service both lines, as shown in Figure 4-4.

These, then, are the more important ways in which production lines can be balanced to yield the desired output capacity. Regardless of which one or combination of these alternatives is selected, chances are that a perfect balance will never be attained.

THE PROCESS LAYOUT We shall now consider the conditions under which a process layout would be in order. Suppose that a part is to be manufactured in such quantities that it appears in the production schedule approximately once every two weeks. Furthermore, these quantities are such that the first operation on every lot can be performed on a lathe in six hours, the second on a drill in three hours, the third on a milling machine in five hours, the fourth on a drill in three hours, and the fifth on a grinder in three hours. Intuitively, one would reject the suggestion that a production line be established to process the part. If such a line were established, it would permit an efficient flow of work so far as this part is concerned. Unfortunately, this flow would take place for only a few hours every month. During the remaining time, the company could either allow the line to stand idle or schedule other work on the equipment. Since no firm will find it economical to allow its equipment to be idle the majority of the time, other work would be scheduled on the equipment. But chances are that the very line which permits the most efficient flow of work for one part will yield an inefficient flow of work for some other parts. To begin with, even if the other parts are to be processed on the same equipment which is contained in the line, the equipment might be required in a different sequence, with the result that there would be an appreciable amount of backtracking of materials. Even worse, some of the other parts may require equipment all of which is not present in any one line. As a result, the work would have to be routed from one line to another in the shop, and excessive production control and materials handling costs would be experienced.

All this suggests that, when parts are produced intermittently, the pro-

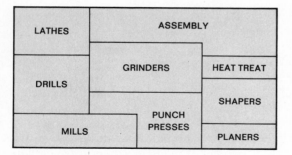

Figure 4-5   A process layout

duction-line or product layout usually proves to be unsatisfactory. Instead, it has been found that, under these conditions, a process layout in which similar machines are grouped together yields a more satisfactory flow of work. With this type of layout, all the lathes are placed in one department, all the drills in a second, all the milling machines in a third, all the planers in a fourth, and so on. The result may be as shown in Figure 4-5.

THE PRODUCT AND PROCESS LAYOUT CASE   In any one firm, some departments may consist of groups of dissimilar machines used to process a single part or product, and other departments may consist of groups of similar machines used to process a variety of parts or products. This is because some of the items in a company's product line might be manufactured continuously and others intermittently.

The responsibility for determining how a specific part or product is to be produced is the responsibility of the company's manufacturing engineers. At the time they are preparing operation sheets, they must decide whether the quantity requirements, as related to a specific item, are such that a production line is warranted. If it is, the operation sheets will be prepared accordingly, and the manufacturing engineers will call for the establishment of what amounts to a single-purpose special machine for the manufacture of the item involved. Otherwise, the item will be produced on general-purpose equipment which will also be used to process other products.

Therefore, at the time the plant layout analyst is determining the firm's equipment requirements, he will be able to ascertain which machines will be engaged in continuous manufacturing and which will be engaged in intermittent manufacturing. This enables him to group the equipment accordingly for purposes of departmentalization. Having done this, he is now confronted by the task of determining space requirements for these departments.

CALCULATING SPACE REQUIREMENTS The space-requirement cal- culations for production departments are not complicated. But this is not because the computations are inherently simple. It is because the analyst has very little information at his disposal at this point and, hence, has no choice but to make a simple and crude calculation.

Specifically, the analyst knows only two things. One is the equipment to be located in each department. The other is the square feet of floor space each piece of equipment will occupy. The latter information can be obtained from the manufacturer's specifications or the firm's equipment records. Therefore, the analyst can calculate the total amount of floor space that will be occupied by the equipment to be located in each depart- ment.

This total, however, represents only a fraction of the space that must be allotted to any one department. A production department will contain not only production equipment but also aisles, workbenches, storage space, personnel, and materials handling equipment. But the analyst will know nothing about the space required by such things until he locates the work stations, prepares their layouts, and selects a materials handling system. However, none of these can be done prior to the departmentaliza- tion of the plant. Hence, the analyst finds himself in a position in which he must calculate departmental space requirements without knowing how much space will be needed for things other than production equipment.

He can find his way out of this quandary by studying the existing layout to determine what average percentage of the total departmental area is occupied by production equipment. It is likely that the percentage for departments laid out on a product basis will be higher than the percentage for departments laid out on a process basis. One reason for this is that more storage space must be allowed in intermittent manufacturing because materials will probably not be processed as soon as they are delivered to the work station, nor will the work be removed as soon as it is com- pleted. Also, as will be seen when we discuss materials handling and work- station layouts, more space will usually be required in intermittent manu- facturing for the movement of materials handling equipment and for such things as workbenches and storage cabinets for the machine operator.

In any event, the analyst can obtain one percentage which will represent the average amount of floor space occupied by the production equipment in departments engaged in continuous manufacturing, and a second per- centage which will represent the average amount of floor space occupied by the production equipment in departments engaged in intermittent man- ufacturing. These percentages would then be used in the following man- ner: If the percentage for departments laid out on a process basis is 20, the analyst will multiply the space which he has calculated as being required by machines in each such department by a factor of 5, which is obtained by taking the reciprocal of 20 percent; this will provide him with an estimate of the total space requirement for each such department. Similarly, if the percentage for departments laid out on a product basis is 30, the analyst will multiply the space which he has calculated as being required by the machines in each such department by a factor of 3.33; this will give him an estimate of the total space requirement for each such department.

Of course, if the analyst has reason to believe that the existing layout is characterized by congested departments, he may increase the value of the computed adjustment factor by some amount based on judgment. If the existing layout is characterized by wasted space, the value of the computed factor will be decreased by some estimated amount. But regardless of the factor employed, the resultant departmental requirements are only approximations and are tentative in the sense that they may be revised after the analysis has progressed. At this time, they should be looked upon as providing the analyst only with a point from which he is able to continue his study.

DETERMINATION OF SPACE REQUIREMENTS FOR SERVICE DEPARTMENTS

Every plant will contain service departments as well as production departments. The more important of these are the following:

Shipping and receiving

Inspection

Maintenance

Toolrooms, tool cribs, and stockrooms

Shop offices

Washrooms and locker facilities

Cafeterias

Shop hospital

We shall now consider the factors which the analyst must take into consideration when estimating the amount of space to be allotted to each of these departments.

SHIPPING AND RECEIVING DEPARTMENTS Every firm receives raw materials, supplies, and parts which are to be used in the manufacture of its products, and provision must be made for the receipt of these items.

Because the receiving department must have the capacity required during periods of peak activity, a precise determination of the space requirements for this department would call for knowing, first, the times at which the receipt of shipments will be at a maximum. These times might be represented by specific days or hours during specific days. Second, the analyst would have to know the number of carriers, which may be trucks or freight cars, that will arrive during these periods. Third, information would have to be obtained with regard to the amount of floor space which will be occupied by the materials delivered by each of these carriers. This can be calculated if the analyst knows what specific materials will be contained in each order, the size and shape of these materials, the number of units in each order, and the manner in which these items will be packaged and stacked. Finally, the length of time during which any one order will remain in the receiving department would have to be known.

Unfortunately, there is no way of predicting all this. At best, the analyst can check the existing receiving department to determine whether the present floor space is adequate. If it is, he may provide the same space in the future layout or he may increase or decrease it to reflect an anticipated increase or decrease in the volume of materials to be handled. If it is inadequate, he will revise the presently available space to reflect both this and any anticipated changes in the volume of materials to be handled. The amount by which the existing space should be altered will be determined primarily on the basis of the judgment of the analyst and the personnel responsible for the receiving activity.

In addition to receiving goods, every manufacturing firm ships materials to subcontractors and finished products to its customers. The problems encountered in estimating space requirements for the shipping department are the same as those just described with regard to the receiving department. For that reason, the same general approach would be used.

INSPECTION The inspection activity in any one firm may be decentralized, centralized, or some combination of the two. In decentralized inspection, the inspection activity is performed at stations in the production departments. In centralized inspection, the inspection activity is separated from manufacturing by establishing inspection departments to which materials, parts, and products are delivered to be inspected.

As a rule, receiving and final inspection are centralized. Insofar as receiving inspection is concerned, it is usually more economical to inspect incoming lots at some central location while the items are still in a single lot. Furthermore, unsatisfactory lots can be identified before the items they contain have been issued to the production departments.

Final inspection is often centralized because it takes place at the end of the production process, and the firm may find that many of its finished products find themselves in a central location after they have undergone the last operation. Also, a number of the product's characteristics must usually be checked, and this may be a time-consuming procedure. As a result, it may be impossible to incorporate it into a balanced assembly or production line.

No generalization is possible about the inspection of work in process. In any one company, some of the work-in-process inspection may be centralized and the remainder decentralized. For example, if certain products are being manufactured continuously, the firm would be inclined to incorporate the inspection activity right into the line so as not to disrupt the flow of work. Similarly, in intermittent manufacturing, the firm would be inclined to have the required inspection performed in the production departments so as to eliminate the need for additional moves to and from an inspection department. However, it may be that the inspection calls for the use of certain delicate instruments which must be kept free from dirt and vibration if they are to function properly, and this may necessitate transporting work in process to a separate inspection department, in which the proper conditions can be maintained. In another case, the cost of an inspection device used to inspect a number of different products may be extremely high, and it may be that if one of these devices were assigned to each of the production departments involved, the degree of utilization would be extremely low. To reduce the required investment in this instrument, the company might find it necessary to centralize the inspection activity even if a less efficient flow of work results.

The importance of all this lies in the fact that, if all inspection is decentralized, the analyst will not have to provide space for an inspection department. Otherwise, an inspection department will have to be established.

The decision concerning how and where inspection is to take place will be made by quality control personnel, and the plant layout analyst will be notified accordingly. If an inspection department is to be established, the analyst will be told what facilities will be used to perform various inspections and what unit inspection times will be. Therefore, knowing what items are to be inspected centrally, what inspection equipment will be required for each of these items, and the unit inspection times, the analyst can determine what equipment is to be located in the inspection department. He will do this by working with the tentative production schedules established for the sales forecast period and going through the same steps he did when determining production equipment requirements.

The analyst should encounter no difficulty in ascertaining the amount of space required by the various types of inspection facilities and, therefore, the amount of space that must be allowed for the housing of these facilities in the inspection department. However, additional space must be allowed for storage, aisles, personnel, materials handling equipment, and so forth. But the amount of this space that will be needed cannot be determined until the inspection department is being laid out in detail and until the materials handling system has been designed. Consequently, at this point, the analyst has no alternative but to multiply the space required by the inspection facilities by some factor to obtain an estimate of the total space requirement. As was mentioned in regard to a similar problem related to production departments, this factor can be calculated by analyzing the existing inspection department or can be based on recommendations of quality control personnel.

It should also be noted that the centralized inspection department will not necessarily be a single department. In order to minimize the distances to be traveled, a receiving inspection department may be located close to the receiving department or raw-material stockroom, a final inspection department close to the shipping department or finished-goods storeroom, and work-in-process inspection departments in the production areas.

MAINTENANCE Another service department for which the analyst must provide space is the maintenance department. This department will contain the supplies, spare parts, and equipment which maintenance personnel use in their work. It is extremely difficult to forecast for any appreciable period of time the exact nature of these items or the quantities in which they will be stored. For this reason, the analyst has no alternative but to consult with representatives of the maintenance department in an effort to obtain some estimate of the amount of space that will be needed. By examining the existing arrangement and considering the expected future increase or decrease in required maintenance work, they can usually make some realistic estimate.

As a rule, an attempt will be made to centralize the maintenance department. Doing so usually results in more effective supervision of the activity and fuller utilization of maintenance personnel. However, if the plant is extremely large, it may be that these advantages will be more than offset by the long distances that maintenance personnel must travel to obtain supplies and equipment and to receive assignments and instructions. Where this is true, the decentralization of the maintenance department into smaller units located throughout the plant may be in order.

TOOLROOMS, TOOL CRIBS, AND STOCKROOMS Most firms that engage in machining processes will have a toolroom in which tools, jigs, and fixtures are manufactured or repaired, or both. This department will contain equipment with which this work is done; storage facilities for incoming work, completed work, and required materials; space for materials handling equipment and aisles; and workbenches and cabinets. In brief, the arrangement will have the appearance of a miniature shop engaged in intermittent manufacturing. However, it is characterized by the fact that it is engaged primarily in the production of special products to customer order. The customers in this case would be the plant's production departments. We say that the products are special because the exact nature of the tools, jigs, and fixtures that will be produced in the future is unknown. Therefore, there is no way in which an accurate long-range forecast can be made of the items that will be produced, of the quantities in which they will be produced, and of the points at which they will be produced. Even more uncertainty is to be associated with the future demand for repair work.

For this reason, the analyst is compelled to adhere to one of two approaches in his determination of this department's future equipment requirements. One is to rely on the collective opinion of those individuals responsible for the toolroom activity. A second is to make a trend analysis of the different kinds of machine-hours which had been required in the past and then to convert the results to equivalent machines of each type. After this has been done, the space required by this equipment can be calculated and multiplied by some factor to obtain the total space requirement for the department. The magnitude of this factor can be estimated by making an analysis of the existing toolroom to determine the proportion of the total space currently being occupied by machines.

With regard to the question of centralization versus decentralization, the most common arrangement is to have a centralized toolroom. Ordinarily, the greater ease of supervision and the more effective utilization of facilities more than offset the added cost of materials handling.

In addition to toolrooms, the firm will also have tool cribs, in which tools, jigs, and fixtures will be stored and from which the machine operators will draw these items as they are needed. If the plant is relatively small, one central tool crib will be established, because the time required by employees to obtain and return machine accessories will not be appreciable. On the other hand, if the plant is large, individual tool cribs will be located throughout the plant. Each of these will service a specific production department or group of production departments. While the cost of supervision and the investment in machine accessories will ordinarily be higher with this arrangement, these added costs will tend to be offset by the saving in travel time on the part of the employees.

The determination of tentative space requirements for tool cribs must also be based primarily on judgment. These requirements will be affected by the size of the individual machine accessories, the quantities to be stored, and the method of storage. However, the nature of these factors for an extended future time period is somewhat unpredictable. About all the analyst can do is to rely on the opinion of tool-crib personnel, who will take into consideration the adequacy or inadequacy of the presently available space and the expected change in the level of plant activity. Another alternative is to calculate the amount of floor space currently being occupied by the tool cribs in terms of square feet per unit of production equipment in operation in the plant. This factor can then be multiplied by the total number of machines expected to be in operation in the future to obtain an estimate of future space requirements.

It is necessary also to determine space requirements for raw-material and finished-goods stockrooms. Theoretically, the analyst would have to know the different raw materials, parts, and products which will be stored, the unit sizes of these items, the maximum number of units which will be in stock at any one time, and the method of storage. The items to be stored can be ascertained from the translated sales forecast. The unit size of these items can also be determined. But the analyst will encounter serious difficulties in any attempt to estimate the maximum number of units which will be in stock at any one time. The method of storage also is not easily determined for each of the items involved. Some may be stored in bins, others on shelves, and still others by stacking to various heights. However, there is no way of predicting these methods with any degree of confidence.

All these difficulties preclude the analyst's calculating the cubic feet of required storage space for, say, the next five years. As a result, the required space can be estimated only on the basis of the pooled judgments of the plant layout analyst, stockroom personnel, and inventory control personnel.

Insofar as centralization or decentralization of stockrooms is concerned, no generalization is possible. The smaller the plant, the greater is the inclination to centralize in order to simplify record keeping and exert closer control over inventories. But even here, if the receiving department is at one end of the plant and the shipping department at the other, the decision may be to store purchased materials and parts near the receiving department and finished goods near the shipping department. As the plant increases in size, there will be a tendency to decentralize raw-material stockrooms so as to reduce the distances over which materials must be transported as they are delivered to the various work stations.

SHOP OFFICES In addition to their general administrative offices, most firms will have offices located in the shop. These offices will be used by shop supervisors, timekeepers, engineers, time study men, dispatchers, methods analysts, and the like. They may be centralized or decentralized, depending on the size of the plant and the nature of the activity.

Usually, the determination of space requirements for these offices is begun by having the appropriate supervisors submit estimates of the number of personnel they expect to have stationed in shop offices. Then, some rule of thumb is employed to convert the number of employees to the amount of floor space they will require. For example, a fairly common rule is that 50 to 75 square feet of working space must be allowed per employee. This figure takes into account the area occupied by desks, chairs, filing cabinets, storage cabinets, and the like.

EMPLOYEE FACILITIES A large group of plant services can be classified as employee facilities. These include such things as washrooms, cafeterias, and first-aid stations. In determining the space requirements for these facilities, the analyst will be governed by the number of shop employees who will make use of these services. This number can be determined by translating the sales forecast into the demand it generates for manpower.

Once this estimate has been made, the determination of space requirements is fairly simple. The reason is that suppliers of lunchroom equipment, plumbing fixtures, lockers, medical equipment, and the like are able to advise the firm on what facilities will be required and in what quantities for a given number of employees. Further, they will provide estimates of total space requirements for such things as lunch counters, dining areas, wash basins, and toilets. These recommendations provide the analyst with a means for making a tentative estimate, which may be revised later when the detailed layout of these areas is being made.

The only other thing that might be mentioned with regard to employee facilities is that they tend to be centralized in small plants and decentralized in large plants, for the same reasons we mentioned when discussing the centralization or decentralization of other service departments.

Having considered employee facilities, we have reached the last of the important services for which space must be provided in the plant layout. Other types of service departments exist, but those we have considered are the major ones and are the ones that are to be found in most plants. About the only generalization that can be made about the approach to the determination of space requirements for most of these departments is that judgment is probably its predominant element.

At this point in the study, then, the analyst has a list of the various production and service departments for which space must be allowed and an estimate of the amount of space each of these departments will require.

The next step is the tentative allocation of areas to these departments. It is this task with which we shall now concern ourselves.

DATA ON EXISTING BUILDINGS AND LAYOUT

The analyst begins this phase of the analysis by obtaining plot plans of the existing buildings and grounds. The plot plans will show the location of the buildings on the grounds which the company occupies and the location of such things as rail lines and sidings, highways and roadways, canals or rivers, and platforms and docks. The importance of these data lies in the fact that they indicate the route which materials must follow as they are being delivered to the plant and the route which finished goods must follow as they are being taken away from the plant. Consequently, they will play an important role in the determination of the location of the receiving and shipping departments.

The next item of information which the analyst must obtain consists of floor plans of the buildings in which the production and service departments are to be housed. These floor plans should show the location and size of such things as columns, walls, doors, windows, sprinkler systems, stairwells, elevator shafts, and plant utilities. Plant utilities will include sewers, drains, ventilating equipment, water mains, electric power lines, gas lines, air lines, and steam lines. The information contained in the floor plans will also play a role in the determination of the location of the various departments. For example, if the activities in a certain department call for the maximum amount of natural light, the analyst would want to know the positions and sizes of windows so that the department can be located accordingly.

The analyst should also obtain cross-sectional drawings of existing buildings. The most important information contained in these drawings will be ceiling heights and the load capacities of floors in various parts of the buildings. These data will also influence the location of departments. For example, if a particular department is to contain some equipment which is 15 feet high, the analyst will want to place the department in a section of the building in which ceiling heights are adequate.

Finally, the analyst will require drawings in which the present layout of departments and work stations is shown. This information will be used to evaluate a proposed area allocation plan. When a layout exists, any decision to make major changes in the location of departments must be appraised in light of the costs of making these changes. Therefore, the analyst will be influenced in his determination of departmental locations by the present location of these departments.

THE PREPARATION OF OPERATION PROCESS CHARTS

The analyst now has a description of the physical environment in which the production and service departments are to be located. But before he can go on to the allocation of the available area to the various departments, it is necessary that operation process charts for each of the company's products be prepared. The necessary information for doing so is to be found in the bills of materials and the operation sheets for the products involved.

The operation process chart for a given product shows, first, the materials which enter into the production process and, second, what happens to each of these materials in terms of operations and inspections. An operation is said to occur when an object is changed in any of its physical or chemical characteristics or when an object is assembled with another object. An inspection is said to occur when an item is verified for quality.

The operation chart is a graphic presentation, and symbols are used to depict operations and inspections. These symbols are a circle for an operation and a square for an inspection. All this is illustrated in the example of an operation process chart shown in Figure 4-6.

Operation process charts are of value at this stage of the analysis because they suggest the relative positions which the production and inspection departments should occupy. We shall illustrate this, first, by considering those products which are to be manufactured intermittently. As we know, the equipment used to manufacture these items is grouped on a process basis. However, these departments are not located in the plant haphazardly. Instead, the analyst attempts to arrange the departments so that an efficient interdepartmental flow of work will result. He does this by analyzing each part and product with a view toward determining what the most common sequence of operations is. For example, let us take a simple case in which the firm is producing three parts intermittently. Each of these parts requires four different kinds of equipment used in the following sequence:

Operation number	*Equipment required*		
	Part 1	*Part 2*	*Part 3*
1	Lathe	Drill	Lathe
2	Drill	Lathe	Drill
3	Shaper	Grinder	Shaper
4	Grinder	Shaper	Grinder

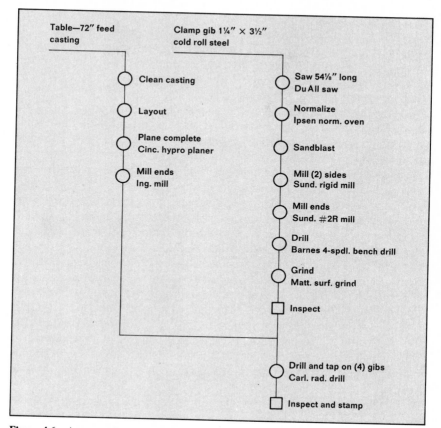

Figure 4-6   An operation process chart

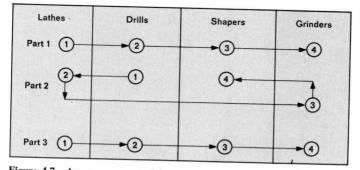

Figure 4-7   An arrangement of four departments in which three parts are produced

From a study of these data, one would be inclined to arrange the four different departments in a manner similar to that shown in Figure 4-7. As can be seen, this arrangement yields the most efficient flow of work for two of the three products. If the departments were arranged in the best straight-line sequence for part 2, the other two parts would be characterized by a less efficient flow pattern.

Of course, this example is somewhat unrealistic, because only three parts are involved; in an actual case, the analyst may be confronted by hundreds of parts which must be studied in order to determine the most common sequence of operations. Also, it was assumed that the best arrangement will be the one which will yield the most efficient flow of work for the greatest number of parts. This may not necessarily be true. For example, in our illustration, it may be that part 2 accounts for 95 percent of the total volume or weight to be associated with the three parts being produced. If this is true, part 2 is the item with which the major portion of the materials handling activity is to be associated. Therefore, we can conclude that the departments should be arranged in a manner which will provide for the efficient flow of the greatest amount of material rather than of the greatest number of parts. This fact sometimes tends to simplify the analyst's task in one respect. When hundreds of different parts or products are involved, the analyst will often find that relatively few of these items account for most of the volume or weight of materials to be handled. The sequence of operations and inspections which these relatively few items undergo can then be reviewed to determine the relative positions which the various departments should occupy.

The information contained in operation process charts is also of value when the analyst is considering products which are manufactured continuously. It was stated that a department laid out on a product basis will contain all the facilities required to produce a given product. In a specific case, however, it may be that the product consists of a number of component parts and subassemblies, each of which calls for a rather extensive series of operations and inspections. Where this is true, the analyst might consider each of the component production lines, each of the subassembly lines, and the final assembly line to be a separate department. Similarly, in another case, it may be that one production line is employed to produce a part which is a component of four or five different products. Such a line might be looked upon as being a single department.

In both these instances, the analyst will have to concern himself with the position of one production line, or department, relative to another. And just as the operation process chart for a product being manufactured intermittently suggested the relative locations of the departments involved, so does the operation process chart for assemblies being manufactured continuously suggest the relative locations of the production lines involved.

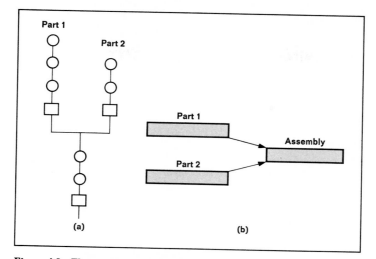

Figure 4-8   Flow pattern suggested by an operation process chart for an assembly being manufactured continuously

For example, an operation process chart such as shown in Figure 4-8*a* suggests a production-line layout such as shown in Figure 4-8*b*.

There is still another set of conditions under which operation process charts are of value when the analyst is making a product layout. It was pointed out that, even in continuous manufacturing, inspections may be performed in a separate department if conditions on the production line are such that inspection devices cannot function properly or if the utilization of expensive inspection instruments will be extremely low. For similar reasons, other activities may be removed from various production lines and grouped in separate departments. For example, painting operations may be segregated in one department, where the necessary equipment can be installed more economically and utilized more completely. Or grinding operations which require expensive exhaust and dust-collecting equipment may be performed in a separate department, where the equipment can be installed at a lower cost and also utilized more completely. Or cleaning activities which require steam and drainage facilities that cannot be economically installed at various locations in the plant may be grouped in a single department. Or noisy equipment and equipment causing vibrations, such as forge hammers, whose operation would affect other activities or employees adversely might be segregated.

In brief, even so-called continuous production lines may be discontinuous in the sense that the work which passes through these lines may be routed to other departments for operations or inspections which have not been incorporated in the line for one reason or another. If this is the case, the fact that these activities are to be performed in another department can be noted on the operation process chart. With this information at his disposal, the analyst can then try to locate these other departments, relative to the production lines they service, so that the necessary materials handling is kept to a minimum.

THE APPROACH TO AREA ALLOCATION

The analyst is now able to begin the location of departments on a copy of the floor plan. Unfortunately, there is no fixed set of rules which will enable him to determine exactly what the most efficient allocation of the existing area will be. As a result, no two analysts working separately are likely to recommend the same departmental arrangement. This is not surprising, given that an infinite number of different arrangements are possible. To begin with, any one department can assume any number of different shapes. And in addition to this, any one of these different-shaped departments can be placed in any number of locations in the plant.

Admittedly, the majority of these possible combinations will obviously be unsatisfactory and can be immediately rejected. For example, the analyst will not consider placing the receiving department in the center of the shop. But even if he ignores such obviously unsatisfactory alternatives, a large number remain to be evaluated.

However, the situation is not hopeless because the analyst can adhere to certain established guides which will serve to limit the number of arrangements to which he should give serious consideration.

SOME GENERAL CONSIDERATIONS   As a rule, the analyst will begin by locating the receiving and shipping departments. When doing so, he will be influenced by the location of the rail lines and sidings, highways and roadways, and existing docks and platforms which will be shown on the plot plan. It can be argued that, on occasion, it is a mistake to be governed by the existing location of these facilities because they can be constructed in new locations, and it may be wiser to do so if this permits a more efficient positioning of the receiving and shipping departments. While this is true, it is also true that such projects prove to be quite costly, and, hence, most firms make the assumption that the location of these facilities is fixed.

After having decided upon the general location of these departments, the analyst will go on to determine their shape. In doing so, he must consider the number of square feet of space which had been estimated as being required, the dimensions of the existing departments, and the shape of the section of the building in which these departments are to be housed. Beyond this, he is compelled to rely on his judgment. But it is important to note that any decision he makes is not a final one, and revisions can be made at a subsequent point in the analysis.

Having tentatively located the receiving and shipping departments, the analyst has located the points at which the flow of materials begins and ends in the plant. The remaining departments must now be located so that the flow of materials between these starting and ending points can be accomplished at the lowest possible cost.

The analyst begins this task by working with the results of his analysis of the operation process charts for the products which are to be manufactured. Insofar as those items which are to be produced intermittently are concerned, an attempt will be made to arrange the process departments in an order which will correspond to the most common sequence of operations. This can be done by means of various flow patterns. To illustrate, suppose that six different process departments are involved and that these departments have been numbered 1 to 6 to designate the order in which they will be used to process most of the materials. If the departments are arranged as shown in Figure 4-9a, the result will be a straight-line flow pattern. This pattern would be given serious consideration if the receiving department were at one end of the plant and the shipping department at the other. But even in this case, an alternative flow pattern is possible. This is the serpentine pattern, which a departmental arrangement such as the one shown in Figure 4-9b would yield.

However, if the receiving and shipping departments were combined and located at one end of the plant, either of these two arrangements would call for transporting finished goods across the whole plant to get them back to the shipping department. To eliminate the need for doing so, it might be better to arrange the six departments so that a U-shaped flow pattern would be generated. This could be done as shown in Figure 4-9c. An alternative would be to locate the departments so as to obtain a circular flow pattern. This could be done by means of an arrangement such as the one shown in Figure 4-9d.

In each of these cases, of course, the departments would adjoin each other although they have been separated in Figure 4-9 so that the resultant flow of work can be seen more easily. In any event, these examples of flow patterns bring out the fact that the determination of the most common sequence of operations will not serve to indicate the exact relative position of one process department to another. Other factors, which we shall consider shortly, must be taken into account.

Similarly, a review of the operation process charts for products to be manufactured continuously will give the analyst only a general idea of what the relative position should be of one production line to another or of one

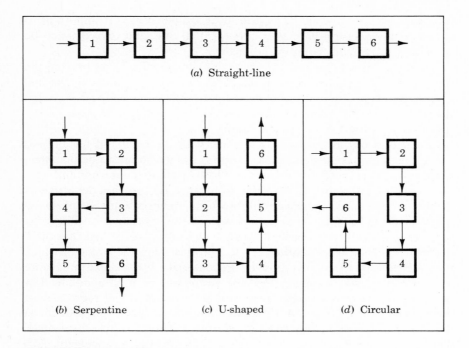

Figure 4-9   Alternative flow patterns

production line relative to some centralized activity such as inspection. For example, the operation process chart for a particular product may reveal that the manufacture of this product calls for the operation of three production lines. However, these three lines could conceivably be located

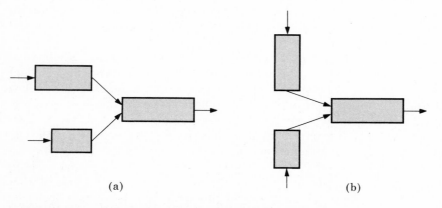

Figure 4-10   Two different arrangements of three related production lines

in either of the two positions shown in Figure 4-10. Still other arrangements are possible. Furthermore, any one of the three lines can assume a straight-line, serpentine, circular, or U-shaped pattern. But as in the case of process departments, the most desirable flow pattern can be ascertained by the analyst only after he has considered other factors. Let us now consider what these are.

GUIDES TO DEPARTMENTAL LOCATION The location of production departments will also be affected by factors whose nature is suggested by a number of guides to which the analyst will adhere. These guides are as follows:

1 Departments requiring the use of heavy equipment should be placed in areas in which the floor load capacity is adequate.
2 Departments requiring the use of high equipment should be placed in areas where ceiling heights are adequate.
3 Departments requiring the use of special plant utilities should be placed where these utilities can be made available at a reasonable cost.
4 Departments in which dangerous operations are performed should be placed where the adverse effects of a mishap can be kept to a minimum.
5 Departments which are characterized by noise, heat, vibration, and dirt should be located so that they interfere as little as possible with the satisfactory performance of other operations and the comfort of shop personnel.
6 Departments which can use natural light to advantage should be located accordingly.
7 Departments in which the temperature and humidity must be controlled should be placed where the necessary control equipment can be installed and operated at a reasonable cost.

These guides apply primarily to production departments, although some of them may be applicable to certain service departments, such as storage and inspection. However, the analyst also has guides which are directly related to service departments. They are as follows:

1 The raw-material storeroom should be located close to the receiving department. If it is decentralized, the individual storerooms should be located close to the points at which the raw materials they contain are to be used.
2 The finished-goods stockroom should be located close to the shipping department.
3 The receiving inspection department should be located close to the receiving department.
4 The final inspection department should be located close to the finished-goods stockroom or shipping department.
5 Work-in-process inspection departments should be located in areas free from vibration and dirt and close to the production departments which they service.

6   Locker areas and washrooms should be located close to the points at which employees enter and leave the plant. This minimizes the distances employees must walk after they enter the plant to prepare for work and after they have washed and changed clothes prior to going home.

7   Toilets should be located at points which make them easily accessible to the employees.

8   Lunchrooms should be located so as to minimize the travel time for employees who will be using them.

9   Tool cribs, shop offices, and the maintenance department should be located near the departments which they service.

Finally, the analyst must keep in mind, regardless of whether he is considering the location of a production department or of a service department, that if he decides to place a particular department in a location different from the one it currently occupies, the cost of moving the equipment involved may be quite high. On occasion, the magnitude of this cost may be such that it more than offsets the benefits to be associated with relocating the department.

These, then, are the other factors which will influence the analyst in his approach to area allocation. It might be noted that the guides reveal why, at an earlier point, the analyst obtained information with regard to floor load capacities, ceiling heights, the existing layout, and the location of utilities, windows, and plant entrances and exits. Admittedly, no set of guides will serve to divulge the one best location for any single department. But they do eliminate certain possible locations and, therefore, reduce the amount of judgment the analyst must exercise. But some judgment is still involved both in the selection of the exact location for a particular department and in the determination of the shape which the area to be allocated to a particular department should assume. With regard to the latter, about all that can be said is that this will be affected by the shape of the building, location and size of stairwells and elevator shafts, the shape of adjoining departments, the size of the facilities to be housed in the department, the shape of existing departments, and so on.

Also, it should be noted that the process of locating departments is not one in which the analyst draws in the first department on a blank floor plan and then proceeds to do the same with the remaining departments until he reaches the last department, which happens to fit into the last remaining space. Instead, a number of trials may be made before everything works out satisfactorily. And there will be occasions when the available floor space just does not appear to be adequate. When this occurs, the analyst may review the estimated departmental space requirements to determine whether any can be reduced. If it appears that they cannot, chances are that no decision to expand the plant will be made at this time. Instead, somewhat arbitrary reductions in the allotted space will probably be made in the hope that, when the actual work stations are laid out, the reduced space will prove to be adequate.

Similarly, if all the available floor space does not appear to be needed, estimated space requirements for some or all of the departments might be increased to increase the probability of sufficient space being available for the work stations involved.

FLOW DIAGRAMS After having developed what is still a tentative departmental arrangement, the analyst will prepare a flow diagram. This is done by drawing in the flow pattern for each product or product group on the completed departmental arrangement. To illustrate this, suppose that only six departments had to be located. Further, the operation process chart reveals that the materials used in producing a particular product pass through the first, third, fourth, and sixth of these departments. If the six departments had been located as shown in Figure 4-11, the flow diagram for this product would consist of Figure 4-11 in its entirety.

A flow pattern such as this would be drawn for each product or product group on the same copy of the departmental arrangement. To distinguish between different products or groups of products, lines can be drawn in different colors.

The reason the analyst will, as a rule, prepare a flow diagram is that a careful examination of the diagram will give him some idea of the adequacy of his proposed arrangement. Such things as relatively straight-line flows, zigzag flows, and backtracking will be readily apparent. If an examination of the diagram reveals that the bulk of the materials will not follow an efficient path of travel, the analyst prepares a new departmental arrangement.

Eventually, an arrangement will be prepared which appears to be satisfactory, and the analyst will be able to go on to the next phase of the analy-

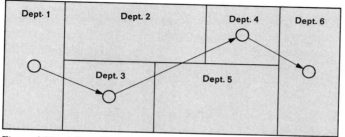

Figure 4-11 A flow diagram

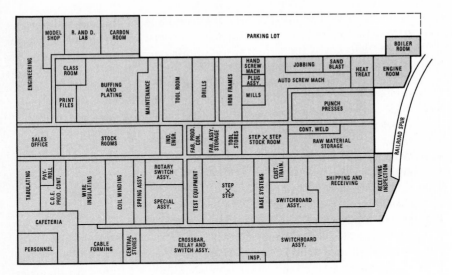

Figure 4-12 A departmental arrangement

sis. The results of his efforts up to this point will resemble the example of a departmental arrangement shown in Figure 4-12.

QUESTIONS

4-1   What is the purpose of the plant layout activity?

4-2   How are the plant layout activity and the selection of materials handling equipment interrelated?

4-3   What are some of the occasions on which it becomes necessary to engage in the plant layout activity?

4-4   How does the firm ascertain the kind and amount of equipment for which space must be provided in the plant?

4-5   What are the differences between intermittent and continuous manufacturing?

4-6   What is the difference between a product layout and a process layout? Under what conditions would each be adopted? Why?

4-7   How is a determination made of the kinds and number of production departments to be established in the plant?

4-8   How is an estimate made of total space requirements for the respective production departments?

4-9   What is the difference between centralized and decentralized inspection? Under what conditions would the one arrangement be preferred over the other?

4-10 What are the advantages and disadvantages to be associated with decentralized as compared with centralized maintenance, storage, and employee facilities?

4-11 How are space requirements estimated for the following service departments: (a) shipping and receiving, (b) inspection, (c) maintenance, (d) toolroom, (e) tool crib, (f) stockrooms, (g) shop offices, and (h) employee facilities?

4-12 What information is contained in data on existing buildings and layout? Of what significance is this in the development of a departmental arrangement?

4-13 What information is contained in an operation process chart? How is it used in the development of a departmental arrangement?

4-14 What are some of the specific guides to which the analyst will adhere when locating production and service departments?

4-15 Describe the following flow patterns: (a) straight-line, (b) serpentine, (c) U-shaped, and (d) circular. Under what conditions would each be adopted?

4-16 What is a flow diagram? How is it used in the development of a departmental arrangement?

PROBLEMS

4-1 A company has taken its sales forecasts and translated them into production schedules with a view toward manufacturing in economic lot sizes and minimizing fluctuations in demand schedules for factors of production. The result is that the theoretical number of machines of a certain kind that will be required during a typical 12-month period has been calculated to be as follows!

Month	Machines required	Month	Machines required
1	38.6	7	35.0
2	38.2	8	34.6
3	38.1	9	35.3
4	32.7	10	47.9
5	32.5	11	46.5
6	32.8	12	48.1

In the computations, it had been assumed that the plant would operate five days per week, one shift per day, with no overtime work scheduled. Scrap, efficiency, and unavoidable delay percentages were estimated on the basis of what they had been in the past.

At this time, the plant layout analyst must ascertain the amount of space to be allotted to the department which will contain this equipment. Consequently, he must decide on the number of machines for which space must be provided. What would your recommendation be? Explain.

4-2 The production schedule for a certain part calls for manufacturing approximately 220 units per week. While there is some fluctuation in this requirement, it is extremely small. The operation sheet reveals that production of the part calls for five operations to be performed on five different machines. The time requirements for these operations, adjusted for delays, labor efficiency, and expected scrap, are as follows:

Operation number	Required time per unit, hr
1	0.190
2	0.400
3	0.394
4	0.196
5	0.200

a Calculate the number of machines required to perform each operation if the plant is scheduled to work 44 hours per week. (Ans. 1, 2, 2, 1, 1)

b What kind of layout (process or product) would you recommend for the processing of this part?

c Prepare a sketch of one possible arrangement of these machines.

4-3 Four operations must be performed in the course of processing a part. The actual time requirements for these activities are as follows:

Operation number	Required time per unit, min
1	6
2	15
3	14
4	16

Approximately 30 units of the item are to be produced per day for an extended period of time. If the plant will operate eight hours per day, under what arrangement would you suggest that the part be manufactured? Explain.

4-4 All the typists in a governmental agency are to be located in a single area. The equipment to be contained in the area will require 850 square feet of floor space. An analysis of the existing layout in areas in which similar activities are conducted reveals that these areas occupy a total of 20,000 square feet, of which 6,000 are utilized by equipment. In general, these areas do not appear to be congested, nor do they seem to contain wasted space. What might be a good estimate of the total space requirement for the area under consideration? (Ans. 2,833)

4-5 In an existing arrangement, the facilities located in a restaurant occupy 30 percent of the total floor space. However, the restaurant appears to be overcrowded, and it is decided that it would be better if the total floor space were increased by 20 percent. If this could be accomplished, what percentage of the total floor space would then be occupied by the restaurant's facilities?

4-6 Select a manufacturing activity which you are able to observe and then describe it by means of an operation process chart.

4-7 Select a nonmanufacturing activity which you are able to observe and then describe it by means of an operation process chart.

4-8 Eight parts are to be produced intermittently on equipment which can be identified by the number of the department in which it is located. The parts and the order in which the equipment is used to process them are as follows:

	Part							
	A	B	C	D	E	F	G	H
Dept.	#1	#3	#1	#4	#2	#1	#4	#4
	3	1	3	2	1	3	2	2
	2	4	2	3	4	2	3	3
	4	6	4	5	6	4	5	5
	6	5	6	6	...	6	6	6
	5	...	5	...	...	5	...	...

Develop a possible departmental arrangement which will yield an efficient flow pattern. When doing so, assume that each of the eight parts calls for handling the same amount of materials. State any other assumptions you made in the course of locating the departments. Finally, prepare a flow diagram to show the resultant path of travel of materials.

4-9 Ten departments are to be located in a plant which is to be laid out on a process basis. It has been estimated that the floor-space requirements for each of these departments are as follows:

Department number	Space requirements, sq ft	Department number	Space requirements, sq ft
1	40,000	6	35,000
2	20,000	7	60,000
3	30,000	8	12,000
4	24,000	9	18,000
5	25,000	10	36,000

Given that the size of the plant is 500 by 600 feet, arrange these departments so that the resultant flow pattern is: (a) straight-line, (b) serpentine, (c) U-shaped, (d) circular.

When making these different arrangements, assume that (1) the bulk of the materials will flow through the departments in the order in which the latter are numbered and (2) any department can be located anywhere in the plant from the standpoint of ceiling heights, floor load capacities, plant utilities, lighting, and so forth.

FIVE
THE DETAILED LAYOUT AND MATERIALS HANDLING

Having completed the departmentalization of the plant, the analyst is able to begin his determination of the precise locations for all the production and service facilities. We shall consider the approach he must adhere to in this determination by, first, concentrating on the problem of making the detailed layout of the production departments and, then, turning to the service departments.

The final phase of the plant layout analysis, as related to production departments, calls for the analyst's making two decisions simultaneously. First, he must decide where the physical facilities are to be located. At the same time, he must decide what kind of materials handling equipment is to be used so that space can be provided for this equipment. Neither of these things can be done without regard for the other for the following reason: The method of handling materials can be decided upon only after two things are known. One is the kinds and amounts of materials to be transported. The second is the locations from and to which materials are to be transported. These locations, however, will be determined by the locations of the respective work stations. But the analyst cannot locate the work stations without taking into consideration the space which must be provided for the loading, unloading, and movement of materials handling equipment. Consequently, the locations of work stations will influence the choice of materials handling equipment, and the choice of materials handling equipment will influence the locations of work stations.

In spite of this, we shall consider the location of work stations and the selection of materials handling equipment separately. We shall do this by assuming that the analyst knows the nature of the handling equipment which will be employed and by then going on to consider the problem of work-station location. After we have completed this, we shall consider the factors which will affect the design of a materials handling system. The reason for choosing this method of presentation is that the approach to work-station location and the approach to materials handling equipment selection are sufficiently complicated to necessitate describing them individually. Further, even though we shall consider these interrelated activities separately, it will be evident how they would be combined in practice.

THE LAYOUT OF WORK STATIONS

A work station is the area occupied by the operator and by the equipment with which he works. The equipment might include such things as the machine; benches; tool cabinets or racks; materials handling equipment; and skids, pallets, and containers used to store both materials delivered to the work station and work which has been completed at the station.

While this definition is, in general, a correct one, a work station does not always consist of one operator and one machine plus other miscellaneous items. To begin with, it is possible that the work station will not contain a machine because the operation involved is manual in nature. Or it may be that the nature of the machine being used to perform an operation is such that it requires the attention of two or more men; in this case, the work station would include the one machine and whatever number of men are assigned to it. On the other hand, it may be that one man is assigned to operate two machines, two men to operate three machines, and so on; in such cases, the work station would include the one man and two machines, the two men and three machines, and so on.

In any event, every production department consists of a collection of work stations. Therefore, the detailed layout of a production department will be the final arrangement of the work stations contained in that department. However, in the process of arranging work stations in some order, it is necessary that the analyst also lay out the individual work stations, that is, decide where the physical objects which the work station contains are to be located. We shall now consider the procedure for developing this detailed layout.

TEMPLATES AND MODELS   The analyst begins by preparing a plant layout board. The plant layout board consists of a piece of wood, metal, fiberboard, or plastic which is covered by a floor plan of the building in which the layout is to be made. This floor plan is marked off in squares, drawn to some scale, and shows the departmental locations which have been decided upon. Further, it shows the locations of columns, windows, doors, stairwells, elevators, walls, and utilities, because these items will have some effect on the final layout. Although the entire floor plan will often be represented on a single board, there are cases in which the floor space involved is so large that a number of boards will be prepared and a section of the building depicted on each.

Next, the analyst will prepare or obtain templates or models, constructed to the same scale as was the floor plan, of the physical facilities to be laid out in each department. A template is a flat piece of material cut to the shape which the facility it represents would assume if it were projected on the floor. Examples of templates are shown in Figure 5-1. As opposed to templates, models are three-dimensional representations of the physical objects they depict. A few examples are shown in Figure 5-2.

Templates are usually constructed from cardboard, wood, sheet metal, or plastic. In the process of making the detailed layout, the analyst will position them at various locations on the layout board until the most satisfactory locations are decided upon. When the templates are in any one location, they will be fastened to the board by means of tacks, double-sided adhesive, or magnets if both the templates and board are made of metal. Similarly, models are constructed from wood, metal, or plastic. As a rule, they are not fastened to the board, because their weight is sufficient to keep them in position.

The sources from which templates and models are obtained vary. The

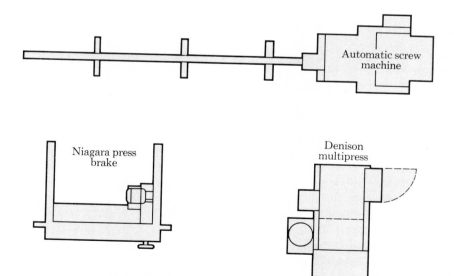

Figure 5-1   Two-dimensional templates

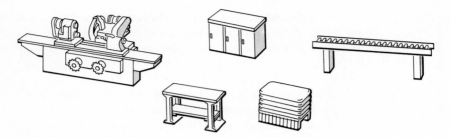

Figure 5-2   Three-dimensional models (Courtesy of VISUAL Plant Layouts, Inc.)

firm making the layout often constructs them itself. In other cases, they may be purchased from firms which specialize in their production. Finally, the company is sometimes able to obtain them from equipment manufacturers. As might be expected, models are more expensive to construct or purchase than are templates, but the resultant three-dimensional layouts are more easily visualized. This is true especially in those cases in which the plant is characterized by many overhead installations.

LAYING OUT WORK STATIONS   There is no completely objective approach to the laying out and locating of work stations. At best, we can describe only the factors that should be taken into account.

As a rule, the analyst will lay out one department at a time while keeping in mind the direction of the flow of work into and out of the department as indicated on the flow diagram he prepared after completing his departmental arrangement. In the most common situation, each work station will include one machine and one operator. For the moment, let us consider this to be the case and assume that the analyst will be working with templates. Since he knows what machines are to be located in a particular department, he also knows the number and general nature of the work stations which the department will contain. Therefore, he will begin by selecting the template for one machine, placing it on the plant layout board, and constructing the work station represented by this machine. The construction of this work station is basically a problem in methods analysis.

To begin with, the analyst must decide what other equipment should be included in the work station to permit the operator to work efficiently. If the operator has to have a place to study blueprints, load and unload jigs, or inspect his work, a bench should be provided for this purpose. If machine accessories are to be stored temporarily or permanently at the work station, a tool rack or cabinet must be provided. If raw material and finished work are to be stored temporarily at the work station, storage facilities must be made available; these may consist of skids, pallets, or containers. If the size and weight of materials to be processed at the station are such that the machine cannot be loaded or unloaded manually, appropriate handling equipment must be provided for the operator's use. The exact nature of any one of these physical facilities will vary from case to case. The nature of the required bench will be affected by the use to which it will be put; the nature of the required storage facilities will be affected by the kinds and quantities of items to be stored at any one time; the nature of the handling equipment will be affected by the materials to be handled.

If the work station happens to be an integral part of a continuous production line, all these things are somewhat predictable. But if the work station is engaged in intermittent manufacturing, the analyst will depend, to an appreciable degree, on his judgment and experience. It is necessary for him to do so because there is no method by which he can forecast exactly what work will be performed at the work station and the frequency with which new orders will be delivered and completed orders removed. At best, he can only review the nature of the parts which might possibly be processed on that particular machine and obtain some information about what the most likely lot sizes will be.

After the physical facilities to be contained in the work station have been decided upon, the analyst must determine how they are to be arranged. In doing so, he will take cognizance of the fact that the operator must have space in which to move around. Also, space must be allowed for loading and unloading the machine and for the projection of materials which have been loaded in the machine; this space requirement can be estimated by reviewing the parts and products which, according to the operation sheets, will possibly be processed on that particular machine. In addition, space must be allowed to enable the operator or maintenance personnel to perform whatever maintenance work may be required on the machine. Finally, space must be allowed for the materials handling equipment which will be used to deliver materials to and remove work from the station.

Keeping these space requirements in mind, the analyst will lay out the work station in such a way as to permit the operator to adhere to an efficient work pattern. The result may be similar to the typical work-station layouts shown in Figure 5-3.

If the analyst decided, or was told, for example, that one operator was to operate two machines, he would employ exactly the same approach. The only difference would be that this particular work station would contain two machines, and these machines and other production facilities would have to be arranged so as to permit the operator to follow an effi-

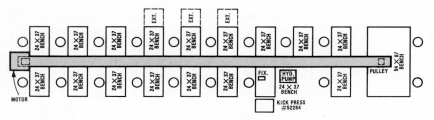

Figure 5-3 Layout of work stations in a production line

cient work pattern. The same would hold true for all other types of work stations, including those at which no machine would be present.

Although there is no way to determine whether the most efficient work-station layout has been developed, the analyst is often able to evaluate his final decision by constructing a flow diagram which will show the operator's path of travel in the proposed work station. This flow diagram will be similar to the one constructed for the evaluation of the departmental arrangement. But instead of showing the path of travel of material from one department to another, it will show the path of travel which the operator will follow as he moves from one location to another at the work station in the course of performing his duties. An examination of the indicated flow pattern would enable the analyst to determine whether it is an efficient one.

LOCATING WORK STATIONS The task of making work-station layouts is further complicated by the fact that the analyst must select the location of the work station at the same time that he is laying it out. The reason for this is that the location of the work station will often have some effect on the arrangement of the production facilities contained in the work station. For example, if the work station is located in an area in which no supporting column is present, no space has to be allowed for the column. However, if a column is present, not only must space be allowed for the column, but the relative positions of the production facilities included in the work station may be different from what they otherwise would be. To illustrate, the skid which is used to store finished work may now have to be moved to a new position because the column, even though it occupies only 1 square foot of floor space, blocks the path materials handling equipment could follow if no column were present.

When locating work stations, the analyst will concern himself with a number of factors. We have already mentioned columns. If columns in some part of the area occupied by a particular work station will prohibit the development of the most efficient work-station layout, an attempt will be made to locate the work station elsewhere, but, if this is not possible, the analyst will do the best he can with the area in which a column is present. Also, care will be taken in locating work stations so as not to block elevators, doors, and stairwells. Further, work stations which require the use of special utilities will be located either where these utilities are already available in the department or where they can be economically installed. In addition, the analyst will concern himself with the location of walls so as not to locate a work station in a position which would prevent maintenance personnel from gaining access to certain sections of the machine for necessary repair work. Next, work stations that require the presence of natural light not only will be located near windows but also will be arranged so that the operator will be working in a position which enables him to take full advantage of this light. Also, work stations containing heavy and vibrating equipment will be located in those sections of the department in which floor load capacities are adequate. Further, work stations that are noisy and dirty will be located where they will be as isolated as possible within the department. Finally, every attempt will be made to locate work stations so that the most efficient flow of work will be obtained in the department itself. This last point is particularly relevant in the case of departments which consist of work stations which represent a continuous production line. In these cases, the analyst will refer to the operation process chart and arrange the work stations within the department so that there will be a smooth flow of work with no backtracking. Whether this has been accomplished can be checked by constructing a flow diagram in which the path of travel which the material will follow, as it moves from one work station to another in the line, can be shown. This flow may be straight, circular, serpentine, or U-shaped, depending on the shape of the department, the length of the line, and so on. And, of course, the analyst will note at all times the present locations of work stations so as not to recommend a layout whose advantages are more than offset by the cost of moving existing work stations to new locations.

Just as the analyst has to locate work stations at the time he is laying them out, so must he make provision for aisle space at the time he is locating work stations. With regard to aisles, suffice it to say that they must be provided for the movement of personnel, materials, and production facilities from one location to another in the plant. Aisle widths will be affected by the number of personnel which will be using them, the size of materials handling equipment which will travel over these aisles, the size of the materials which this equipment will handle, and the size of the production facilities which on occasion will have to be moved through the plant. The location of aisles must be such that all these factors of production can reach the various work stations and departments at which they may be required.

To summarize, in the process of making the detailed layout of production departments, the analyst must concern himself with work-station layouts, work-station locations, and aisle widths and locations. Given the nature of the procedures involved, he will probably have laid out each work station in a number of different ways, located each work station at a number of different points, and positioned aisles in a number of different locations on the plant layout board before reaching a final decision.

It was stated that after having considered production departments, we should turn to service departments. Generally speaking, the same approach would be followed in laying out service departments as was employed in laying out production departments. Consequently, we shall limit our remarks to the statement that, insofar as service departments are concerned, the analyst will consider the physical facilities to be laid out in these areas and try to arrange them so as to obtain an efficient flow of men and materials. In doing so, he will be governed by the same factors he had to take cognizance of in his analysis of production departments.

It should also be pointed out that the detailed layout of production and service departments may result in changes in the space allotted to the various departments and in the shape of the respective departments as shown on the departmental arrangement prepared earlier. At the time we discussed departmental arrangements, it was mentioned that the results were tentative primarily because the required space requirements were only estimates. More likely than not, when making his detailed layout, the analyst will find that the allotted space for a particular department is either more or less than adequate and that the shape of the department may have to be altered to accommodate the facilities involved. If the revisions in one department are offset by revisions in another department, there is no cause for concern. But if the net result is that the overall available space appears to be inadequate, the analyst will review the detailed layout to see whether the facilities can be rearranged to eliminate the difficulty. Only after it had definitely been proved that this could not be done would plans be formulated for an addition to the existing floor space. On the other hand, if all the floor space has not been utilized, work-station layouts might be reviewed to determine whether they could be improved upon in light of the availability of additional space, or the remaining space might be reserved for future expansion.

In conclusion, it should be mentioned that in the course of preparing the detailed layout, it is not unusual for the analyst to develop alternative plans, which would then be evaluated with a view toward selecting the best one. Any single completed plan would have the general appearance of the section of a detailed layout shown in Figure 5-4.

Thus far, we have assumed that the nature of the materials handling system was known. As a result, we were able to say simply that space must be provided in work stations for materials handling equipment and that aisles must be provided for the movement of this equipment. But for reasons mentioned earlier, the analyst will select the method of handling materials while he is making the detailed layout. We shall now consider the factors that will affect this selection.

MATERIALS HANDLING EQUIPMENT

A prerequisite to the design of a materials handling system is a knowledge of the different kinds and types of materials handling equipment that are available. Although there are hundreds of different kinds and types of handling equipment, all can be placed in three major categories. Let us begin with a general description of each of these categories. At the end of each of these descriptions, sketches of some of the more important types of equipment which are to be found in the category under consideration will be presented.

CONVEYORS   The first major class of materials handling equipment consists of conveyors. A conveyor is any device which moves materials, in either a vertical or horizontal direction, between two *fixed* points, and this movement can take place either continuously or intermittently.

One of the distinguishing characteristics of conveyors is that they create a relatively fixed route. Consequently, they are employed primarily in continuous manufacturing in which materials leaving one work station invariably go to some other specific work station in the production line; therefore it is possible to connect two such work stations by materials handling equipment which is capable of moving materials only between two fixed points. In intermittent manufacturing, however, materials leaving one work station may go to any number of other work stations. Obviously, it would not be feasible to set up a network of conveyors which would provide all the possible routes which materials may have to follow.

A second characteristic of conveyors is that, unless they are of the portable type, they occupy space continuously. As a result, they must be installed in locations in which they will not interfere with the flow of other traffic. For example, if two work stations are located on opposite sides of an aisle which is used as a path of travel by men and trucks, a floor-mounted conveyor could not be used to link these two work stations. Therefore, unless cross traffic can be bypassed, no serious consideration would be given to the use of conveyors.

Insofar as a listing of the different types of conveyors is concerned, the ones most frequently encountered are the following:

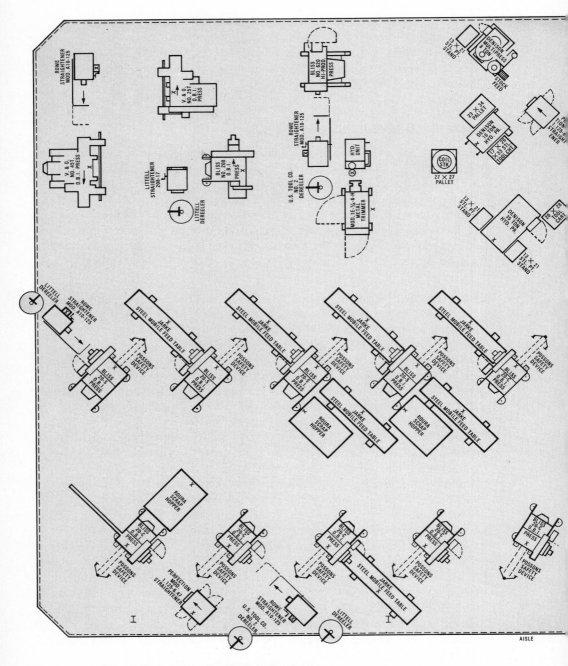

Figure 5-4 A section of a detailed plant layout

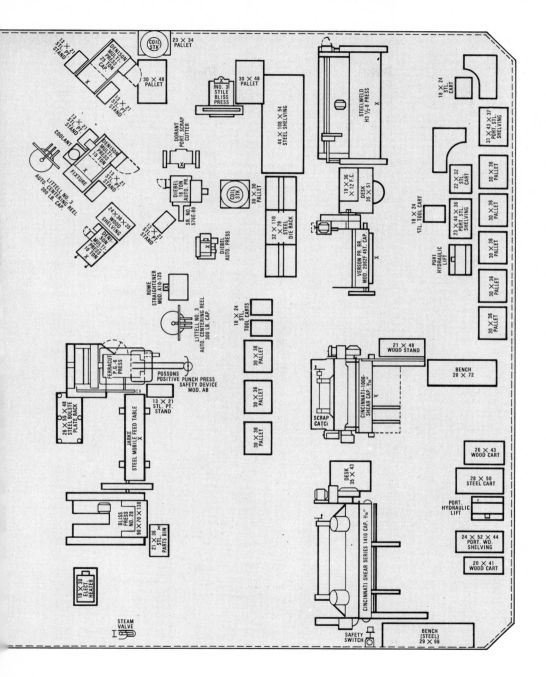

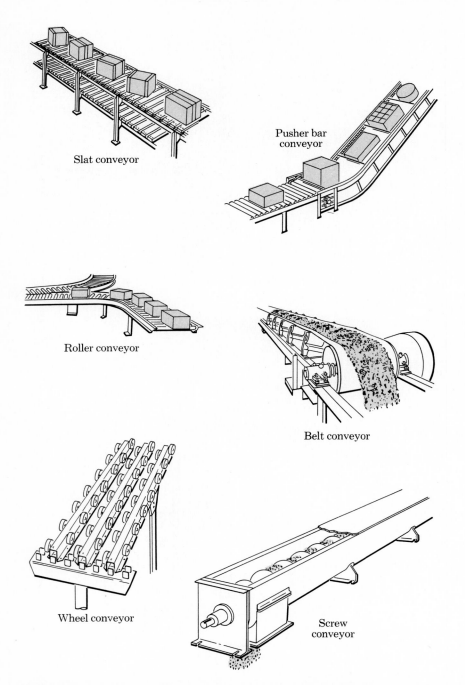

Figure 5-5   Types of conveyors (Courtesy of Conveyor Equipment Manufacturers Association)

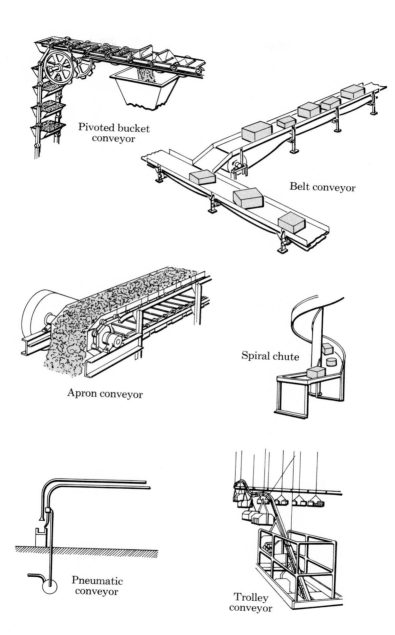

Pivoted bucket conveyor

Belt conveyor

Apron conveyor

Spiral chute

Pneumatic conveyor

Trolley conveyor

Roller	Screw
Belt	Pneumatic
Wheel	Bucket
Apron	Chute
Pusher bar	Trolley
Slat	

All these are depicted in sketches which have been prepared by the Conveyor Equipment Manufacturers Association and which are shown in Figure 5-5. An examination of these sketches will reveal the more important characteristics of each of these conveyors.

INDUSTRIAL TRUCKS   Industrial trucks, which represent the second category of materials handling equipment, are vehicles, powered by hand, by gasoline, or by electricity, which are capable of transporting materials horizontally between any two points. As opposed to a conveyor, a truck is able to move from one location to any other location so long as suitable traveling surfaces are available and its path of travel is not obstructed. For this reason, the prevalent method of handling materials in a firm engaged in intermittent manufacturing is by means of trucks. The variable path of travel they are able to follow permits them to transport materials from one work station to any of a number of other work stations at which a subsequent operation is scheduled to be performed.

A second desirable feature of trucks is that they occupy a given amount of space intermittently. This means that a certain amount of space in a given location is required to house a truck for only as long as the truck is in that location. As soon as the vehicle is moved, the space is free for other uses. Therefore, this equipment can be used wherever cross traffic exists or does not exist. For example, if an operator is assigned two machines, he must be provided with a path which he can follow to move back and forth between these machines. There is no reason why a truck cannot use this same path or cross this path, because in doing so it will, at worst, interfere with the movement of the operator for only occasional short periods of time.

As in the case of conveyors, there are many types of trucks, and each of these can be equipped with a variety of attachments. But the most important ones are as follows:

Hand-operated vehicles	Forklift trucks
Tractors	Straddle carriers
Platform trucks	

Sketches which have been prepared by the Industrial Truck Association and which serve to describe these various types of mobile equipment are shown in Figure 5-6.

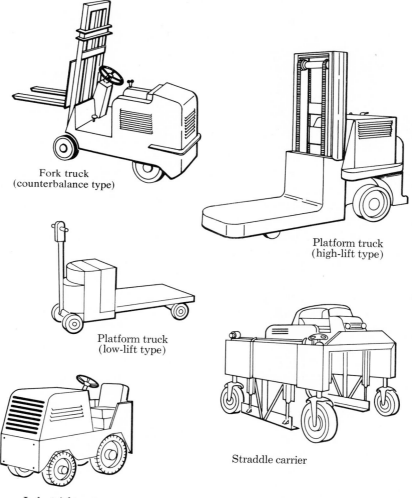

Fork truck
(counterbalance type)

Platform truck
(high-lift type)

Platform truck
(low-lift type)

Straddle carrier

Industrial tractor

Figure 5-6   Types of mobile equipment (Courtesy of Industrial Truck Association)

CRANES AND HOISTS   The third classification of materials handling equipment consists of cranes and hoists. This equipment is able to move materials vertically and laterally in any area of limited length, width, and height. It is used primarily when materials must be lifted prior to being moved from one point to another. These points may represent different work stations or different locations at a single work station. For example, if a part is large or heavy, the operator may find it necessary to use a hoist to aid him in loading and unloading the machine. Subsequently, a crane may be used to move the part to another work station.

One of the advantages of cranes and hoists is that they are able to transport objects through the overhead space in the plant. Consequently, space is utilized which would otherwise be unused, and floor space is freed for other uses. To illustrate, it might be possible to move a large heavy casting by means of a truck from one work station to another. However, this would create a need for wide aisles at appropriate locations in the plant. If floor space is at a premium, a more desirable alternative would be to transport the item through the air by means of a crane which would either eliminate the need for certain aisles or, at least, permit the use of narrower aisles which may be required for the movement of smaller objects. But there are cases in which cranes and hoists are used, not because they free floor space, but because they are the best available means of positioning material in a particular location. One such case was suggested when we spoke of the need for some mechanical means for loading a heavy or large part in a machine.

However, when considering cranes and hoists, it is important to keep in mind that any one unit of this equipment is capable of serving only a limited area. The size and shape of this area will vary with the kind of crane or hoist being used. Nevertheless, the equipment is somewhat more flexible in this respect than are conveyors, but not as flexible as are industrial trucks. Also, it will be found that cranes and hoists are as likely to be used in intermittent as in continuous production.

Again, there are many types of equipment which are placed in the crane and hoist category. However, the most common ones are the following:

Overhead traveling bridge cranes	Chain hoists
Gantry cranes	Air hoists
Jib cranes	Electric hoists
Elevators	

Sketches which suggest the manner in which these pieces of equipment function are shown in Figure 5-7.

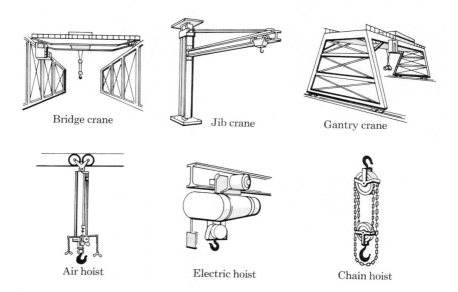

Figure 5-7   Typical cranes and hoists (Source: *Material Handling Engineering Directory and Handbook.* **The Industrial Publishing Corp., Cleveland, 1958)**

FACTORS IN THE SELECTION OF MATERIALS HANDLING EQUIPMENT

Because of the many kinds and types of materials handling equipment available, the task of selecting the specific equipment which should be used to handle a particular material is not a simple one. However, the analyst is able to reduce the number of alternatives appreciably by taking into consideration certain factors.

Before we consider these factors, it should be mentioned that the points at which materials handling is necessary will become apparent to the analyst at the time he is making his detailed layout. When laying out the receiving department, he will realize that provision must be made for unloading the carriers by which materials, parts, and supplies will be delivered to the plant. When laying out the raw-material stockroom, he will realize that provision must be made for the delivery of materials from the receiving department to the stockroom and from the stockroom to the work stations. When laying out the work stations, he will realize that provision must be made for the delivery of materials to the work station and the removal of completed work from the work station. Similarly, when laying out certain service departments, he will realize that provision must be made for the delivery of materials to these departments and the removal of materials from these departments.

Further, given a point at which materials must be picked up, no special problems will be experienced in the determination of the area to which they must be delivered. All the information necessary for this purpose can be obtained from the operation process charts prepared earlier for each product and from the flow diagrams the analyst prepared in the course of developing his departmental arrangement. This does not mean that the exact point to which a given material must be delivered can always be ascertained. For example, if a certain product is manufactured intermittently, the involved production departments will be laid out on a process basis, and the analyst will know only the departments to which the work in process must be transported. On the other hand, if a certain product is manufactured continuously, the analyst will usually know the exact work station to which the work in process must be transported. But in either case, the available information will be adequate for purposes of selecting appropriate materials handling equipment.

Let us now go on to a discussion of the factors which will influence the analyst's choice of equipment.

REQUIRED PATH OF TRAVEL The first factor to be considered is the path of travel which will be followed by materials leaving a particular location. If all the materials leaving a work station always go to some other specific work station, the analyst will give serious consideration to the use of equipment which is characterized by a lack of variability in its path of travel. Examples of this type of equipment are chutes, belt conveyors, elevators, and pipes. Since it is in continuous manufacturing that materials usually follow a fixed path of travel, fixed-path equipment has its widest application in this type of manufacturing.

On occasion, the analyst will find that while the materials leaving a given location do not all go to some other single location, they may go to one of only two or three different locations. To illustrate, a work station may be an integral part of two different production lines. This means that the work processed at this station will go to one of two different points. Where this is true, the analyst might select equipment which has limited variability in its path of travel. Conveyors with switching systems are an example of this type of equipment. After moving down a length of the conveyor, the material can be switched to one of two other sections of the conveyor, each of which travels in a different direction. Under other circumstances, a bridge crane, which is capable of operating within a limited area of the plant and hence is limited in its path of travel, will be capable of handling materials which are to be delivered to or removed from locations contained in that area.

Finally, the analyst may encounter cases in which materials at a particular point will have to be moved to any one of a large number of different and widely scattered locations. This is usually the situation in intermittent manufacturing. In cases such as this, equipment which has unlimited variability in its path of travel would be required, and, hence, the analyst will consider hand trucks, forklift trucks, tractor-trailer trains, and the like.

It is clear that if the required path of travel varies, variable-path equipment must be employed. However, it may not be clear that if the required path of travel does not vary, fixed-path equipment should be employed. In the latter case, variable-path equipment would also be capable of performing the required service. Nevertheless, where variability is not required, there is a tendency to use fixed-path equipment for a number of reasons. To begin with, the first cost of fixed-path equipment is usually lower; a roller conveyor, for example, does not cost as much as a forklift truck. Second, operating costs of fixed-path equipment are usually lower; a truck always requires an operator, whereas a pipe or a conveyor does not. Third, fixed-path equipment requires no supervision because it ordinarily involves no manpower. Finally, variable-path equipment requires more space in which to maneuver about. All these things are not true in every case, and even when they are, they are offset to some degree by certain characteristics of fixed-path equipment. For example, conveyors utilize space continuously, whereas trucks do not. But more often than not, it has been found that, where variability is not required, fixed-path equipment is more economical.

NATURE OF MATERIALS   A second factor which will affect the choice of materials handling equipment is the nature of the materials to be transported. There are various ways of classifying materials, and one of these calls for differentiating between bulk and packaged materials. Bulk materials would be such things as sand, flour, grain, water, and oil. Packaged materials would include all items packed in containers such as boxes, bags, and barrels. If the analyst is confronted by the need for handling bulk materials in the form of liquids, he will consider pipes rather than roller conveyors. Similarly, bulk materials in the form of a powder would suggest the use of belt conveyors, screw conveyors, or bucket conveyors rather than cranes, hoists, or forklift trucks. Packaged materials, on the other hand, would lend themselves to handling by such things as roller conveyors, tractor-trailer trains, and forklift trucks when the materials are properly stacked on skids.

Materials can also be classified according to their size, shape, and weight. Considering these characteristics, the analyst would probably decide that items of small and irregular shape can be transported more effectively on belt conveyors than on roller conveyors. But if the items are fairly large and flat, a roller conveyor of appropriate size would be given serious consideration. Further, if the material is quite large and heavy, the use of an overhead crane may be in order.

Finally, the durability of the materials to be handled would have some effect on the method of handling. At one extreme, fragile objects made of glass may be moved from one location to another by hand. But if the material is sheet metal or an iron casting, there would be little danger of breakage, and, hence, any number of mechanical handling methods could be given consideration.

PHYSICAL CHARACTERISTICS OF THE BUILDING The analyst will also consider the factor of building characteristics. The floor load capacity will have some effect on the weight of the materials handling equipment which can be used in certain areas. Ceiling heights and truss strength may permit or prohibit the installation of an overhead traveling bridge crane. Column spacing and door sizes will often limit the size of the equipment which can be used. The location of columns will affect the path conveyors can follow. The degree to which certain areas can be ventilated may determine whether fume-producing gasoline-powered trucks can be used or whether trucks powered by electric batteries must be employed. If the building is multistoried and the various levels are connected by ramps, trucks can possibly be used; otherwise, elevators and chutes may have to be relied upon. These few illustrations demonstrate the role building characteristics will play in the selection of handling equipment.

SPACE REQUIREMENTS OF HANDLING EQUIPMENT It has been mentioned that some equipment requires floor space, whereas other equipment requires overhead space. Also, some equipment uses a certain space continuously, whereas other equipment uses it intermittently. Therefore, floor-operated equipment can utilize floor space continuously or intermittently, and overhead equipment can utilize overhead space continuously or intermittently. For example, a roller conveyor uses a given area of floor space continuously, while a truck uses it intermittently; a trolley conveyor uses a given area of overhead space continuously, while a traveling crane uses it intermittently.

It follows that the kind and amount of space available in the plant will have to be taken into consideration by the analyst when he is selecting materials handling equipment. If it appears that floor space is at a premium and overhead space is available, an attempt would be made to recommend equipment which would not require the use of floor space. On the other hand, if a low ceiling or high equipment precludes the use of overhead space in certain areas, overhead materials handling equipment would not be a real alternative.

Even after the choice has been tentatively made between floor space and overhead space, the analyst would go on to evaluate equipment alternatives in terms of the amount of this space they will require and in terms of whether they require the space continuously or intermittently. For example, if a limited amount of space is available either on the floor or overhead, the analyst would favor smaller trucks, conveyors, and cranes. Also, if cross traffic exists either on the floor or overhead, the analyst would choose equipment which uses space intermittently rather than continuously.

REQUIRED HANDLING CAPACITY   After the analyst decides what kind of equipment should be used to transport materials between two points, he will take into account what the total handling capacity of this equipment must be. By doing this, he will be able to determine how many units of equipment of some specific type will be required. As this suggests, it is not enough to conclude on the basis of other factors that, for example, a forklift truck will be used. Instead, it is necessary to describe the required forklift truck in terms of the output capacity it must possess and to calculate the number of such trucks that will be required.

The output capacity per unit of any type of materials handling equipment is a function of two things. One is the load capacity of the equipment, that is, the weight or number of items it can carry at any one time; the other is the speed at which the equipment can transport materials.

Therefore, the analyst must specify the load capacity the equipment must possess and the speed at which it must be capable of operating. This, coupled with information about the amount of material that must be handled and the distances it must be transported, will enable him to determine the number of units of equipment of this type that will be required.

To illustrate all this, suppose that materials are to be moved continuously from one location in the plant to another. The two locations are separated by a distance of 0.1 mile. The materials are stacked on skids, and one loaded skid weighs 500 pounds. A total of 500,000 pounds of materials is to be moved from the one point to the other during an eight-hour day. Although it has been decided to employ forklift trucks for this purpose, no determination has been made of the number of trucks, of some specific load and speed capacity, that will be required.

The analyst would begin this determination by taking cognizance of the fact that the minimum possible load is 500 pounds, because this is the weight of one loaded skid. This means that one alternative is a truck whose load capacity is 500 pounds. It may be that a truck of this type is available which is capable of an average speed of 5 miles per hour; this was arrived at by taking into account the speed under load, the speed without load on the return trip, downtime for repairs and maintenance, and so on.

Knowing these operating characteristics of the equipment, the analyst can compute the amount of material one truck is able to transport between the two points per day. At an average speed of 5 miles per hour, in an eight-hour day, one truck can travel 5 times 8, or 40, miles. Given that a round trip between the two points is 0.2 mile, one truck can make 40 divided by 0.2, or 200, trips per day. Because the load per trip will be 500 pounds, one truck can handle 200 times 500, or 100,000, pounds of material per day. To transport the stipulated 500,000 pounds of material per day, 500,000 divided by 100,000, or five, trucks of this type would be required.

Undoubtedly, other alternatives will be available. For example, consideration might be given to a truck with a load capacity of 1,000 pounds and, say, an average speed of 4 miles per hour. In that case, some number of trucks other than five would be needed. As this suggests, various combinations of load capacity, speed, and number of trucks will generate the required total handling capacity.

COST CONSIDERATIONS   One major factor remains to be considered, and this is the cost to be associated with a specific type of equipment.

Regardless of how thoroughly the analyst studies a materials handling problem in light of the factors we have already discussed, he will usually find that more than one alternative is available. To begin with, the analyst will very often have to decide whether the company should continue to use the equipment which is currently in operation or whether this equipment should be replaced by new equipment of more efficient design. Or it may be that a roller conveyor is just as capable, in the physical sense, of performing a given service as is a belt conveyor, and a choice must be made between the two. Or it may be that a belt conveyor is called for, but basically the same conveyor can be obtained from either of two different manufacturers, and the firm must decide which manufacturer should receive the order. Or it may be that the required handling capacity can be provided in various ways, and a specific combination of load capacity, speed, and number of units of equipment must be selected.

In all such cases, the only way that a decision can be made is by means of a cost comparison. When computing the cost of any one of the alternatives, the analyst will consider the investment it requires and the interest cost to be associated with this investment, the equipment's probable service life, its future salvage value, and its operating costs. Operating costs will include such things as labor, maintenance, taxes, insurance, power, and supervision. A number of methods for making the necessary cost comparisons are available, and one will be considered in the part beginning with the next chapter.

CHECKING THE FINAL LAYOUT

The procedures involved in laying out a plant and designing a materials handling system are such that it is likely that a number of different layouts and materials handling systems will evolve in the course of the analysis. When this occurs, a decision about which of these alternatives is the best must be reached on the basis of a cost comparison.

But regardless of the number of alternatives to be evaluated, the analyst will review each proposal to determine whether anything has been overlooked. In the process of doing so, he will probably make use of one of many available check sheets. One of the most comprehensive of these lists is that developed by Apple.[1] It is shown in Figure 5-8, and it should be examined carefully because it covers a number of minor points which we have not considered.

It should also be noted that, although reference has been made to a single analyst, many individuals with various backgrounds will participate in the described activities. This is true for a number of reasons. First, the task of laying out an entire plant and designing a complete materials handling system is of such a magnitude that, if it is to be completed in a reasonable period of time, it becomes necessary that a number of analysts work on the project. Second, the project calls for taking into consideration so many different factors that it would be difficult to find any one individual who possessed all the required knowledge and experience. Consequently, some of the analysts may concentrate on materials handling problems, others on the layout of stockrooms, others on the layout of shop offices, others on the layout of machining departments, still others on the layout of assembly departments, and so on. Third, regardless of how skilled the respective analysts are, there will be certain things they are not familiar with or may have overlooked, and, for that reason, it is customary for them to consult with representatives of other departments. The plant engineering department may be asked to estimate the cost of installing utilities in a certain location or the cost of moving equipment; the methods department may be asked to review certain methods of operation; the quality control department may be asked to evaluate the proposed layout of an inspection department; the maintenance department may be asked

[1] J. M. Apple, *Plant Layout and Materials Handling,* The Ronald Press Company, New York, 1950, pp. 242–243.

A. MATERIALS HANDLING

1. Are materials received and shipped in unit loads utilizing pallets, gondolas, skids, or racks?
2. Do incoming materials go directly to the work areas whenever possible?
3. Are materials handled in one trip, or do they have to be handled and rehandled?
4. Have the processes involving heavy materials been located as near the receiving department as possible?
5. Do conveyors and materials handling systems run from the receiving department to work areas, to assembly areas, and then to shipping areas?
6. Does the materials handling system operate for straight-line production with a minimum of back-tracking?
7. Has gravity been used in materials handling wherever possible?
8. Can mechanical handling equipment be used within the manufacturing process?
9. Have all the avoidable manual handling operations been eliminated, and has the total number of handling operations been minimized?
10. Do subassemblies flow into the assembly line directly?
11. Is materials handling equipment designed to carry materials in a position so as to conserve space?
12. Are aisles likely to get "cluttered up" with unused materials and equipment?
13. Have the conveyors and machines been guarded for the safety of the employees?
14. Are widely separated work areas connected by suitable conveyor systems?
15. What provision has been made for auxiliary flow lines in the event of machine or conveyor breakdown?
16. When finished work is disposed of by one operator, can it be readily picked up by the next operator?
17. What are the sources of possible delays or "bottlenecks"?
18. Is the flow planned so that inventory checking and inspection can be carried out right in the immediate work area?
19. Are inspection points located at vital and convenient points along the materials handling system?
20. Has proper storage been allowed for materials in process between operations?
21. Are the containers used to transport materials in process designed to speed up and assist the process?
22. Are the lift trucks and motorized equipment kept busy all the time?
23. Does each materials handling installation fit in as an integral part of the over-all plant system?
24. Do any of the conveyors "box" anyone in?
25. Do the materials handling devices bring materials right up to the operator so as to reduce walking?

B. PRODUCTION AND PRODUCTION CONTROL

1. Are conditions such that quality of work can be maintained?
2. Is floor area fully utilized?
3. Are machines so arranged that their full capacity can be utilized?
4. Are machines readily accessible for supplying them with materials and for repair and maintenance work?
5. Can individual operators tend more than one machine?
6. Are aisles and doorways free of obstacles and clearly marked off for traffic purposes?
7. Has an approved color scheme been adopted for painting machines and work areas?
8. Do the machines "block in" anyone; i.e., is enough work space left around the machines for proper operation?
9. Are machines and equipment located to give maximum motion efficiency during processes?
10. Are tool cribs located where they will save steps in tool issuing?
11. Does machine overtravel extend into the aisles or interfere with operator's work space?
12. Is there room for departmental expansion?
13. Is the maximum use being made of each piece of equipment?
14. Are machine cycles balanced?
15. Can supervisors and foremen easily oversee their entire departments?

Figure 5-8 Plant layout and materials handling check sheet

16. Does the arrangement of machines give maximum flexibility?
17. Has space been allowed for foremen's desks or small booths for production control records, etc.?
18. Have standard machines and equipment been used wherever possible instead of highly specialized machines?
19. Can men smoke on the job? If not, has a smoking area been designated?
20. Can repair and maintenance be performed so as not to interfere with production?
21. Are service controls readily accessible?
22. Can quick exits be made around, over, or under conveyors?
23. What has been done to eliminate noise?
24. Are hazardous operations located in isolated areas?

C. THE BUILDING AND ITS SURROUNDINGS
1. Are floors overloaded?
2. Has space been left for pillars, walls, and supports?
3. Are electrical outlets convenient to the machines so that power lines can be easily connected or disconnected?
4. Are exits, fire doors, and fire escapes adequate and properly located for maximum safety?
5. Have drinking fountains been provided?
6. Is artificial illumination adequate?
7. Has natural light been used to full advantage?
8. Is ventilation adequate in all areas?
9. What provisions are necessary for heating or air conditioning?
10. Are floors level?
11. Have the sources of power been studied as to availability, cost of power, advisability of buying primary or secondary power?
12. Is there danger of smoke or other contamination from nearby plants or industries?
13. Have the plant and process plans been checked by the insurance companies and by the proper local officials?
14. Are the layout and the building itself such as to facilitate good housekeeping and neatness?
15. Are aisles and doors wide enough to accommodate trucks carrying loaded pallets or skids?
16. Whenever possible do doors open and close automatically?
17. Are ramps kept at the lowest possible grade?
18. Can building repairs be made with ease?
19. Are loading and unloading docks covered against weather?
20. Has parking space been provided for the employees?
21. What are the possibilities of natural catastrophe such as earthquake, flood, or tornado?
22. Can fire protection equipment be easily transported to various parts of the plant?

D. PRODUCT DESIGN AND ENGINEERING
1. Have the considerations of product versus process layout been thoroughly weighed?
2. Has the nature of the product been taken into account; i.e., are there any peculiarities of the product that have been overlooked?
3. What will happen to the layout in case of product changes, improvements, and redesigns, etc.?
4. Has criticism been invited from all groups having anything to do with the product?
5. Can new or additional equipment be installed without disrupting the present production?
6. Are specialized machines necessary for turning out the product, or will standard machines and equipment serve the purpose with equal economy?
7. Can existing machines be readily retooled to fit new requirements?

E. SERVICE AREAS AND EMPLOYEE COMFORT
1. Are service areas easily accessible from all parts of the plant?
2. Are there sufficient washrooms, lockers, drinking fountains, etc., for the convenience of all?
3. Has proper heating, ventilating, and lighting been provided?
4. Are all danger areas clearly marked and guarded?
5. Are there first-aid stations located throughout the plant?
6. Is there proper storage space for inflammable materials?
7. What are the employee recreational facilities?

to review a proposed detailed layout to determine whether the location of the equipment permits it to be repaired with no difficulty; the personnel department may be asked to comment on the location and layout of employee facilities; the production planning department may be asked to pass judgment on the amount of space allowed for future expansion. Some of these consultations will take place while the work is in progress, and others after a tentative layout has been completed and submitted for approval.

RELATIONSHIP TO PRODUCTION PLANNING

In conclusion, it should be recalled that we have considered a problem which is the exception rather than the rule. Most layout and materials handling problems do not involve laying out an entire plant or designing a complete materials handling system. In most cases, the task is one arising from the need to add a new department, expand an existing department, rearrange an existing work station, enlarge the existing materials handling capacity, replace existing materials handling equipment, and the like. In brief, the more common problem is fairly narrow in scope. But, as was mentioned, one advantage of considering the most comprehensive problem is that the resultant approach can be adapted for use in the analysis of problems of a simpler nature.

The other advantage stems from the fact that it is this most comprehensive problem by which the firm is confronted in that phase of the production planning activity devoted to the determination of future requirements for buildings and materials handling equipment. The kind and amount of space that will be needed can be ascertained only after the entire plant layout has been prepared. Similarly, the kind and amount of materials handling equipment that will be needed can be determined only by giving consideration to the design of the entire materials handling system.

Fortunately, a problem of the scope that has been considered can be simplified to some degree with the use of automatic data processing equipment. Such equipment can be used to carry out the calculations involved in the determination of production and materials handling equipment requirements, in the balancing of production lines to yield the needed output capacity, in the determination of the sequence of operations to which the bulk of materials are subjected, in the computation of departmental space requirements, and in the comparison of costs to be associated with alternative layouts and handling methods.

It might also be noted that, when layout and materials handling analyses become necessary in operations other than manufacturing, these analyses must be based on the principles and concepts involved in our production model. The specifics of the appropriate approach will vary, of course, depending on whether the operations under consideration are taking place in a store, office, hospital, repair shop, warehouse, restaurant, or theater. But in each such case, the approach must begin with a determination of what facilities are to be contained in the layout, continue with the grouping of these facilities, and end with an arrangement of these facilities which will yield an efficient flow of materials, employees, customers, or clients.

QUESTIONS

5-1 What are the more common things for which space must be provided in a work station?

5-2 What are the advantages and disadvantages of using templates when preparing the detailed layout? Of using models?

5-3 How does the analyst go about laying out work stations in a given department? How can a flow diagram be used in this activity?

5-4 What factors are taken into consideration when locating work stations in a department? How can operation process charts and flow diagrams be used in this activity?

5-5 At what point in the plant layout analysis might the firm conclude definitely that the existing building capacity will be inadequate to satisfy future requirements?

5-6 What are some of the more common types of (a) conveyors, (b) industrial trucks, and (c) cranes and hoists?

5-7 How do the following factors affect the firm's choice of materials handling equipment: (a) required path of travel, (b) nature of materials, (c) building characteristics, (d) equipment space requirements, (e) required handling capacity, and (f) cost considerations?

5-8 It has been stated that the development of a satisfactory plant layout and materials handling system calls for the cooperative efforts of representatives of the plant engineering, maintenance, personnel, production planning, and other departments. Explain.

5-9 How can automatic data processing equipment be used in plant layout and materials handling analyses?

5-10 What are some examples of activities, other than manufacturing, in which consideration must be given to the layout of facilities and the handling of materials?

PROBLEMS

5-1 We know that work stations in a production line can be arranged so as to yield straight-line, serpentine, U-shaped, or circular flow patterns. Assume that a given production line consists of 12 work stations. By means of sketches on which the path of travel of materials is indicated, show how these work stations might be arranged so that each of the aforementioned flow patterns would be obtained. Under what conditions would these respective arrangements be favored?

5-2 Select a manufacturing operation which is to be performed at a single work station. Describe the elements of the operation and state your assumptions with regard to equipment requirements, storage requirements, materials handling methods, and the like. After having done this, lay out the work station and present your recommendations in the form of a scale drawing. Finally, construct a flow diagram on this drawing, showing the path of travel of either the man or the material, depending on which you believe to be the more relevant.

5-3 Select a nonmanufacturing activity which is to be carried out at a single work station. Then do everything called for in problem 5-2.

5-4 A construction contractor must move earth from one location to another. The amount to be transported is such that dump trucks will be assigned solely to this task for an extended period of time.

The two locations are separated by a distance of 3.75 miles. The type of truck that will be used for this activity has a load capacity of 15 tons. Its average speed will be about 6 miles per hour; this takes into account the speed under load, the speed without load on the return trip, loading and unloading time, delays, downtime for repairs and maintenance, and so on.

If 350 tons of soil are to be moved from the one location to the other during every 10-hour day, how many trucks of this type will be required? (Ans. 2.9)

5-5 Castings loaded on skids are to be moved continuously from one department to another by means of a platform truck. The departments are separated by a distance of 660 feet. Each casting weighs 10 pounds, and 20 such castings can be loaded on one skid.

The trucks used for this activity can carry one skid per trip at an average speed of 2 miles per hour. If 12,000 castings, weighing a total of 60 tons, are to be moved from the one location to the other during a 40-hour week, how many trucks will be required for this activity?

5-6 Visit a manufacturing concern and obtain, for one or more of its departments, information with regard to the existing layout and materials handling system. Review this layout and system, and develop what you believe to be a more appropriate combination.

In your report, describe the original layout and handling methods, the factors taken into consideration in the analysis, and your recommendations. In the event that no improvements appear to be possible, state your reasons for reaching this conclusion.

5-7 Visit an organization which engages in activities other than manufacturing. Then do everything called for in problem 5-6.

PART FOUR

PART FOUR

CAPITAL EXPENDITURE ANALYSIS

SIX
RELEVANT COSTS AND FACTORS

The final step in many analyses in the field of operations management is a cost comparison of the available alternatives. We have already seen that this is true in the production planning activity when, for example, it becomes necessary to select the most economical method for leveling demand schedules for factors of production. Similarly, in the plant layout activity and in the design of a materials handling system, a point is reached at which an evaluation must be made of alternative layouts and handling systems. As we go on to a consideration of other areas of production management, we shall find that, again, more than one way of performing a task evolves and that there is a need for determining the best course of action.

A number of techniques have been developed for use in the determination of the most economical, that is, the most profitable alternative. One of the most basic of these is the *uniform annual cost* method. It is with this method that we shall now concern ourselves.

CAPITAL AND OPERATING COSTS

The most comprehensive alternative is one which requires that the company incur two types of costs. The first of these is capital costs; the second is operating costs. *Capital costs* are those expenditures which, when made, provide the company with a service for a period of time greater than one year. An example of an expenditure of this type is the first cost of a piece of production equipment which has an estimated life of, say, 10 years. Another example is the expenditure made to overhaul or rehabilitate a production facility which results in its life being extended by a period greater than one year.

Operating costs, on the other hand, are those expenditures which provide the company with a service for a period of time equal to or less than one year. An example of an expenditure of this type is the cost of labor. If the employees are paid every two weeks, the payment of these wages is the payment for a service which was provided for a period of less than one year. The cost of materials is another example. As a rule, the size of a lot of purchased materials is such that they will be utilized within a period of less than one year. Other expenditures which would fall into this category are routine maintenance, heat, light, power, supervision, repairs, taxes, insurance, and the like.

The reason for giving consideration to these basic costs is that a comparison of alternatives necessitates taking cognizance of the costs to be associated with each alternative. This is not to say, however, that the most economical alternative is always the one with which the lowest cost is to be associated. To say so would be to suggest that the goal of any firm is cost minimization rather than profit maximization. If this were true, every firm could develop a program for the attainment of this goal with little difficulty. This program would simply be to terminate its activities. The result would be that no costs would be experienced. But a proposal of this type would, as a rule, be rejected, because the zero costs it would bring about would be accompanied by zero revenues and, consequently, by zero profit.

THE IMPORTANCE OF REVENUES

The foregoing suggests that the revenues to be associated with a particular course of action cannot be ignored. It may be that a given alternative will generate capital and operating costs which will be higher than the comparable costs for any other alternative. And yet, the nature of this more costly alternative may be such that it will bring about an increase in revenues which will more than offset the extra cost. In other words, the profit to be realized with this alternative will be greater than that to be realized with any other alternative. If this is the case, it follows that this would be the most economical alternative, in spite of the fact that it does not minimize costs.

To illustrate, let us assume that two different machines are available for the production of a specific product. An analysis reveals that the average annual costs with machine A will be $25,000, while with machine B they will be only $23,000. On the basis of these figures, machine B appears to be the more economical alternative.

However, it may be that machine A is capable of producing a product whose quality is higher than the quality of the output from machine B. The result may be that the firm can increase its unit selling price without experiencing a decrease in unit sales if machine A is procured. Consequently, revenues from machine A will be greater than they would be from machine B. Suppose that the estimated annual revenues from machine A are $30,000 as compared with $27,000 from machine B. Let us now see whether this alters the situation. If we were to compute the annual profit to be associated with each alternative, we should obtain the following results:

Item	Machine A	Machine B
Annual revenues	$30,000	$27,000
Annual costs	25,000	23,000
Annual profit	$ 5,000	$ 4,000

A comparison of these respective profits reveals machine A to be the more economical alternative, whereas a comparison of the respective costs erroneously suggested that machine B was the more desirable investment. It follows, therefore, that the most economical alternative is to be selected on the basis of a profit comparison rather than on the basis of a cost comparison.

Of course, if revenues are not affected by the choice of alternative, the more economical alternative can be identified by means of either a cost or profit comparison. To illustrate this, suppose that machines A and B were both expected to generate annual revenues of $27,000. In that case, a profit comparison would yield the following:

Item	Machine A	Machine B
Annual revenues	$27,000	$27,000
Annual costs	25,000	23,000
Annual profit	$ 2,000	$ 4,000

An examination of these data reveals that, because revenues are constant, the machine that minimizes costs also maximizes profits. This means that, if the firm has reason to believe that the alternatives in a given case will all yield the same revenues, it can select the most economical one on the basis of a cost comparison.

The fact remains, however, that a profit comparison will always reveal the most economical course of action, whereas a cost comparison will not. Consequently, if we are to choose one of these two approaches, it is clear that the choice must be the profit comparison approach. Yet a decision to do this poses a problem. The term "cost comparison" is so widely and habitually used that there is little hope for the adoption of the term "profit comparison." Because of this, we shall accept the term "cost comparison" and use it in this presentation. We can do so without error if we define revenues as if they were *negative* costs. Doing so permits one to arrive at the correct decision in all cases by making a cost comparison. For example, in our first illustration, the annual revenues to be associated with machines A and B were given as $30,000 and $27,000, respectively. Treating these as negative costs would yield the following comparison of total annual costs:

Item	Machine A	Machine B
Annual revenues	−$30,000	−$27,000
Annual costs	+ 25,000	+ 23,000
Total annual cost	−$ 5,000	−$ 4,000

Since −$5,000 is less than −$4,000, the *cost* comparison indicates that machine A is the more economical alternative. This coincides with what we found in our earlier *profit* comparison.

Let us now state explicitly what we shall do from this point on. The most economical alternative will be found by making a cost comparison of alternatives. The alternative with the lowest cost will be the more economical one. In this comparison, consideration will be given to capital costs, operating costs, and revenues. Capital and operating costs will be treated as positive costs. Revenues will be treated as negative costs.

DEPRECIATION AS AN ELEMENT OF CAPITAL COST

We now know that three factors must be taken into consideration in any cost comparison. These are capital costs, operating costs, and revenues. The nature of the factors of operating costs and revenues is such that they require no further elaboration. The same cannot be said of capital costs.

Capital costs consist of two elements. The first of these is depreciation. The term "depreciation" has many definitions, but, in our application, it will be used to represent the amount by which an asset actually decreases in market value during a given time period. For example, if a production facility is purchased at a cost of $50,000 and has a value of $40,000 a year later, the depreciation for that year is $50,000 minus $40,000, or $10,000. If it has a value of $32,000 at the end of the second year of its life, the cost of depreciation for the second year is the difference between the value of the facility at the beginning of the second year, which is $40,000, and the value of the facility at the end of the second year, which is $32,000. This yields a depreciation charge for the second year of $8,000. To find the depreciation charge for the entire two-year period, we compute the difference between the first cost of the facility, which is $50,000, and the value of the facility at the end of the second year of its life, which is $32,000. The result is a depreciation cost of $18,000. The *average* annual cost of depreciation would be this $18,000 divided by the two-year period, or $9,000.

It is evident that a decrease in the value of an investment in an asset is a real cost to be associated with the procurement of that asset. If a piece of equipment is purchased and it decreases in value by $18,000 in two years, this $18,000 is as much a cost of owning that equipment as are the wages paid to the operator of the equipment. Hence, the expense of depreciation must be taken into consideration in any cost comparison. The reason we designate depreciation as a capital cost, even when it is computed on an annual basis, is that it stems from an expenditure which provides a service for a period of more than one year.

DATA REQUIRED TO CALCULATE DEPRECIATION From the preceding explanation of the method for calculating the depreciation charge, it is clear that it is necessary to have certain data at one's disposal. To begin with, it is imperative that one identify the time period under consideration. A depreciation of $18,000 in 2 years is one thing, and a depreciation of $18,000 in 10 years is another. Next, it is necessary to know the investment represented by the facility at the beginning of the time period under consideration and the investment represented by the facility at the end of this time period. Let us now consider what these factors of time period, initial value, and future value would be represented by in a cost comparison.

Suppose that a firm is considering the replacement of an existing machine by a new piece of equipment. However, before it can be certain that the new machine will be an improvement, it must make a cost comparison of the two alternatives. One of these is to retain the old machine; the second is to procure the new machine. The question with which we shall concern ourselves is: What must we know about the old and new machines in order to be able to compute their respective depreciation costs?

We shall begin with the new machine. Insofar as the time period for which the depreciation charge is to be determined is concerned, it is evident that the period we should be interested in is the one which represents the service life of the new facility. This means that an evaluation of this alternative would require an estimate of the number of years the equipment will be used by the company if it is procured.

Next, we must determine the investment in the facility at the beginning of its service life. In general, this investment will be equal to the first cost of the equipment. However, care must be taken in defining the first cost. On occasion, the supplier of the equipment will quote a certain price, but this price will not include delivery charges and installation costs. If delivery charges and installation costs will be incurred, these should be added to the quoted price to arrive at the total first cost. Also, there are instances in which there is a loss of production while the new equipment is being installed. If sales are lost because of this, the cost of these lost sales should be included as a part of the required investment.

Finally, the value of the asset at the end of its service life must be determined. This amount is the future salvage value of the equipment. Because this is something which will take place in the future, the disposal value of the facility at the end of its service life must be forecast.

To summarize, the depreciation cost to be associated with new equipment can be determined only if its first cost, salvage value, and service life are known or can be estimated. For example, if we are told that the first cost is $35,000, the estimated salvage value is $1,000, and the estimated service life is 10 years, we can say that the facility is expected to decrease in value by $34,000 in 10 years.

Let us now turn to the second alternative, the old machine. With regard to the factors of time period and future value, we arrive at the same conclusions as we did with the new machine. The time period for which we should want to know the depreciation cost is equal to the expected future service life of the old equipment. If it is believed that the remaining life of the equipment is four years, four years is the period for which we should want to determine the depreciation charge. Similarly, the future value of the facility is its salvage value at the end of its expected service life. For example, if it is estimated that the remaining service life is four years and that the equipment will have a disposal value of $500 at that time, $500 would be the future value with which we should work in computing the depreciation expense.

This leaves only the present value of the equipment to be considered. It is the determination of this value that sometimes presents a problem, because we are considering a facility which is already on hand and, consequently, no cash outlay is required. But as a rule, it will be found that the investment in an existing facility is its present market value. For example, a survey of the used equipment market may reveal that, if the company disposes of equipment it owns, it will receive $2,000. Therefore, a decision to retain the old equipment is a decision not to convert it into $2,000. Now, if a piece of equipment calls for a cash outlay of, say, $2,000, it is apparent that this is the investment required by the equipment. But in principle, this is no different from a decision not to convert a physical asset into $2,000 in cash. The actual cash outlay for a new asset results in the firm's having $2,000 less than it would otherwise have. Likewise, retention of an existing asset which has a cash value of $2,000 results in the firm's having $2,000 less than it would otherwise have. We say, therefore, that the required investment, that is, the present value of an existing facility, is its market value.

There is, however, one exception to the preceding statement. It may be that when a company decides to sell its old machine, all it can get is $2,000. But it may also be that, if it wanted to procure a facility just like it, the company would find that it would have to spend $2,300. In brief, the replacement cost is higher than the market value. When this occurs, the question arises of whether the replacement cost or the market value is the relevant figure. There is no single answer to this question.

Let us continue to assume that the replacement cost is $2,300 and the market value $2,000. The usual situation is one in which the company will dispose of the old equipment if it does procure the new facility. When it does, $2,000 is what it will receive. In brief, the old machine has proved to be the equivalent of $2,000, and, consequently, this market value is the actual value of the equipment.

On occasion, however, a somewhat unusual situation will exist. The company may require a replica of the old machine in one of its other departments. If the old machine is replaced by a new one, it will not be sold. Instead, it will be moved to the other department. But—and this is important—if the old machine is not replaced, it will be necessary for the firm to buy one just like it for the other department at a cost of $2,300, which is the replacement cost and not the market value. Therefore, a decision to replace the old facility is a decision which will eliminate the need for spending $2,300 for its replica. In this special case, the replacement cost, and not the market value, represents the present value of the old machine. But in the remainder of this presentation, to simplify the discussion, we shall assume either that the special condition does not exist or that the market value is equal to the replacement cost, and, hence, we shall refer to the market value as being the relevant figure.

BOOK VALUES   There is another value which incorrectly is sometimes said to represent the investment in an existing facility. This is the book value. The book value of an asset is determined in the following manner: When a company procures a fixed asset, it will not show the entire cost of the asset as one of the costs of operating the business during the first year of the asset's life. To do so would be to overstate the expense and understate the profit for that year because the asset will have a life of more than one year. Instead, the company will depreciate the asset over its estimated life. For example, the asset may have a first cost of $30,000, an estimated life of five years, and an expected salvage value of $10,000.

This means that it is assumed that the asset will decrease in value by $20,000 during the five-year period. The average annual depreciation charge would therefore be $4,000.

A fairly common method of depreciation for accounting purposes is to assume that the asset will decrease in value at this uniform rate of $4,000 per year and to consider this $4,000 to be one of the annual expenses of operating the business during each year of the five-year period. This means that, during the first year, the asset will be assumed to have decreased in value by $4,000, or that its value at the end of the first year is only $30,000 minus $4,000, or $26,000. This value of $26,000 is called the book value at the end of the first year. Similarly, it will be assumed that the asset has decreased in value by another $4,000 during the second year. This yields a book value of $26,000 minus $4,000, or $22,000, at the end of the second year. If we went on this way, we should find the respective end-of-year book values to be as follows:

Year	Depreciation charge	End-of-year book value
0	$ 0	$30,000
1	4,000	26,000
2	4,000	22,000
3	4,000	18,000
4	4,000	14,000
5	4,000	10,000
Total	$20,000	

But it is important to keep a number of things in mind. First, just because it was estimated that the service life would be five years, it does not mean that it will be five years. Also, just because it was expected that the salvage value would be $10,000 at the end of five years, it does not mean that it will be $10,000. Finally, just because it was assumed that the total depreciation of $20,000 would take place at a uniform rate of $4,000 per year, it does not mean that this will definitely occur. In brief, the book values were derived from the use of a method which is based on estimates and assumptions. As a result, the book value may or may not coincide with the market value at any point in the asset's life. For example, at the end of the fifth year, the market value may actually be $12,000 or $8,000 instead of the $10,000 it was expected to be.

If at a particular point in the asset's life the book value is less than the market value, it means that the amount by which the asset was shown to have depreciated in the company's books is too great and that this particular expense was overstated. As a result, the company's profit has been understated. Conversely, if at a particular point in the asset's life the book value is greater than the market value, it means that the amount by which the asset was shown to have depreciated in the company's books is too small and that this particular expense was understated. As a result, the company's profit has been overstated.

Of course, the fact that a discrepancy often exists between the book value and market value is not surprising, because the method and rate of depreciation are decided upon at the beginning of an asset's life on the basis of what is expected to happen in the future. And what is expected to occur and what actually occurs may not coincide. In spite of this, there are some individuals who maintain that it is the book value, rather than the market value, which represents the firm's investment in an asset. This position is usually maintained when the book value exceeds the market value. When the market value exceeds the book value, a different conclusion is ordinarily reached. For example, suppose that, in the case of the asset we have been discussing, consideration is being given to replacing it at the end of the fourth year of its life. At that time, it has a book value of $14,000. However, the analyst finds that the facility has a market value of $20,000. It would be the rare company which would not insist that the facility has an actual value of $20,000 at this point.

But if, for example, the book value is $14,000 and the market value is only $8,000, the firm may insist that the actual value is $14,000 and that this amount represents the investment in the facility. Actually, the fact that the book value exceeds the market value by $6,000 simply means that the cost of depreciation for the preceding four years has been understated by $6,000. Anything that is done with the asset at this point will not change this fact. And yet, many firms will maintain that if the asset is disposed of at this time, the company will suffer a "loss" of $6,000. They, in effect, ignore the fact that the $6,000 has already been lost and that selling the asset now will simply compel the firm to state this explicitly by making the necessary adjustments in its accounts. It is true, however, that, if the company disposes of the asset, the discrepancy between the book and market values may result in a capital gain or loss which will be relevant for tax purposes. But we shall not be getting into tax accounting in this presentation, and for that reason we shall ignore tax considerations.

Let us now summarize our conclusions regarding the alternative which involves retaining the old equipment: The amount which represents the value of the equipment at the beginning of the time period under consideration is the market value of the equipment. Under certain conditions, it will be the replacement cost. Further, the time period in which we shall be interested is the remaining service life of the facility. Finally, the value of the asset at the end of this time period will be its salvage value at that time. If we have all this information, we can compute the depreciation cost of this alternative. For example, if an old machine has a market value and a replacement cost of $2,000, an estimated remaining life of four years, and an expected terminal salvage value of $800, we say that one of the costs to be associated with this alternative is a $1,200 depreciation, which will take place during a four-year period.

COST OF MONEY AS AN ELEMENT OF CAPITAL COST

The second element of capital cost is the cost of money, which we shall refer to as the "interest charge." Interest is the amount an individual must pay for the use of borrowed money. For example, a person may borrow $100 with the understanding that he will return $110 at the end of one year. The $100 is called the "principal," and the additional $10 is called the "interest charge." Interest can also be expressed in terms of a rate. The rate is the interest charge expressed as a percentage of the principal. In our illustration, in which $10 interest was paid on a principal of $100, the interest rate is simply $10 divided by $100, or 10 percent.

However, just as in the case of the depreciation charge, the interest charge, or rate, tells us little unless we know the length of the time period involved. In our example, we were told that the $10 in interest would have to be paid at the end of one year. Therefore, we should state that the interest charge is $10 per year, or 10 percent per year. If the $110 had to be returned at the end of two years, the interest charge would still be $10, and the interest rate 10 percent, but now it would be $10 per two years, or 10 percent per two years.

Although we have chosen to describe interest as an amount paid for the use of borrowed money, it is also possible to describe interest as an amount received by the lender for the use of his money. In every loan, there is a borrower and a lender. Consequently, for every person who pays interest, there is a person who receives interest. Thus, the lender would look upon interest as money received. For example, in our illustration, the individual who loaned the $100 for one year would say he is receiving an interest payment of $10 per year, or an interest rate of 10 percent per year. He would probably refer to the 10 percent as his rate of return.

Having described what interest is, we can now go on to a consideration of why interest is an element of capital cost.

THE RELEVANCY OF INTEREST Let us assume that a firm is considering an investment alternative which calls for an initial outlay of $10,000 for a piece of materials handling equipment. It so happens that this amount of money is not available internally, and, consequently, if this alternative is selected, the firm will have to borrow the $10,000. In other words, the investment will be financed with external rather than internal funds. It may be that external funds are available at an interest rate of 6 percent per year. This means that a decision to buy the equipment is a decision to spend $10,000. But a decision to spend $10,000 is a decision which will necessitate borrowing $10,000. And borrowing $10,000 means paying an annual interest charge of 6 percent times $10,000, or $600, for as long as the principal is retained. In brief, a decision to buy the equipment is a decision which entails incurring an interest charge. If the investment were not made, no money would be borrowed, and there would be no interest expense. It follows, therefore, that in a situation such as this, the interest charge must be one of the expenses to be associated with the alternative. The reason we call this expense a capital cost is that it stems from an expenditure for an asset which will, as a rule, provide a service for a period of time greater than one year.

But let us now suppose that there is no need for the company to borrow money if it procures the equipment. It may be that it has the required funds on hand or some of its other assets can be converted into cash. Or it may be that the equipment being considered is already owned, that the $10,000 is its market value, and that the question is whether the equipment should be retained.

Even in a case such as this, the firm would be incurring an interest expense. The difference is that it is not an out-of-pocket cost but an opportunity cost. It is an opportunity cost in the following sense: If the investment were not made in this alternative, the company would have $10,000 more cash than it would have if the investment were made. This additional $10,000 could be invested elsewhere at a certain rate of return. Elsewhere could be in stocks, bonds, a new product, inventories, accounts receivable, and the like. Each of these investments would yield a rate of return in one form or another. Stocks would provide dividends; bonds, an outright interest payment; a new product, increased profits; inventories, certain benefits to be associated with larger inventories; and accounts receivable, an ability to finance more customers and thereby increase sales and profits. But if the company chooses to invest the $10,000 in the materials handling equipment, it will forgo the opportunity to invest this money in sources from which a rate of return can be realized. And in principle, there is no difference between a decision which results in an out-of-pocket expense of, say, $600 a year and a decision which results in the company's not receiving $600 which it otherwise would. Both represent a real expense of $600. Therefore, if the company is using internal funds which could be invested elsewhere at a rate of return of 6 percent, this opportunity cost is as much a cost as is the 6 percent interest charge the company would incur if it found it necessary to borrow the money from external sources. And this cost must be charged against the alternative under consideration.

Up to this point we have shown only that interest exists as a business fact and why it must be taken into consideration when evaluating an investment alternative. All this was relatively straightforward. However, the need for taking interest into consideration serves to complicate the technique for making cost comparisons. For that reason, it is necessary to spend some time on a presentation of how interest is handled in certain typical problems.

COMPOUND INTEREST

The type of interest that prevails in the business world is compound interest. To illustrate how it is computed, suppose that someone borrows $100 at a compound interest rate of 10 percent per year. The repayment plan calls for his returning the principal plus all the accumulated interest at the end of two years. We should calculate the amount to be paid at the end of two years in the following manner: The interest charge for the first year would be equal to the *principal* owed at the beginning of that year times the interest rate per year. This yields $100 times 10 percent, or $10. As a result, the borrower owes $110 at the end of the first year, which coincides with the beginning of the second year. The interest charge for the second year would be equal to the *principal plus accrued interest* owed at the beginning of the second year times the interest rate per year. This yields $110 times 10 percent, or $11. Therefore, at the end of the second year, the borrower must return what he owed at the beginning of the second year plus the interest charge for the second year. This is equal to $110 plus $11, or $121.

It should be noted that repayment plans other than the one just described are possible under a compound interest arrangement. For example, the borrower in the preceding example may choose or be required to pay, at the end of the first year, the earned interest of $10. As a result, there would be no accrued interest at the beginning of the second year, and, therefore, he would owe only the $100 principal at that point. Consequently, the interest charge for the second year would be 10 percent of this $100, or $10. The borrower would then be required to pay this $10 interest charge and to repay the $100 principal.

Although the borrower would repay a total of $120 instead of the $121 repaid under the first plan, the lender receives $10 of this $120 at the end of the first year. Therefore, he is able to lend it to someone else at a rate of 10 percent and receive $1 in interest on this loan at the end of the second year. This $1 plus the $10 interest he will receive from the original borrower at the end of the second year will yield a total interest receipt of $11 for that year, which coincides with the $11 he earned under the first repayment plan. And, of course, if compound interest is being received, compound interest is being paid. In brief, with the second repayment plan, the earned interest is lent to another borrower, whereas in the first repayment plan it was lent to the original borrower for another year.

To summarize, a variety of repayment plans is possible involving compound interest. All are characterized by the fact that at no time does the borrower retain accrued interest without paying interest on the amount accrued.

SINGLE-PAYMENT COMPOUND AMOUNT FACTOR

Compound interest computations can become somewhat complex. However, general expressions have been derived which enable us to solve the various types of compound interest problems with a minimum of difficulty. One such type of problem is suggested by the following.

Suppose that a firm decides to level out the demand schedules for factors of production by manufacturing some items in advance during what would otherwise be periods of relatively low activity. Doing so, however, will increase inventories of the products involved. To finance the investment in these inventories, the firm borrows $10,000 at an annual interest rate of 6 percent. The terms of the loan call for the repayment of the principal and the earned interest in a single sum at the end of the four years. The firm would like to determine what the total amount owed at that point will be.

Before we begin this determination, let us describe the problem by means of a time line. When we do, we obtain the following:

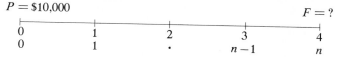

As can be seen, the time line contains various items of information. First, it shows the number of years being considered, which in our problem is 4. Second, it shows that $10,000 is borrowed at point 0, which marks the beginning of the first year. Third, it shows that we want to know how much will be owed at point 4, which marks the end of the fourth year. In terms of the symbols shown on the time line, the $10,000 is equal to P, the elapsed time of four years is equal to n, and the future amount that will be owed is equal to F. Finally, although this is not shown on the time line, the annual interest rate of 6 percent is equal to i.

THE COMPUTATION With the use of the method described earlier, we can compute the amount to be repaid by the company in the following manner:

Year (a)	Amount owed at beginning of year (b)	Interest earned during year ($c = b \times 0.06$)	Amount owed at end of year ($d = b + c$)
1	\$10,000	\$10,000(0.06) = \$600	\$10,000 + \$600 = \$10,600
2	\$10,600	\$10,600(0.06) = \$636	\$10,600 + \$636 = \$11,236
3	\$11,236	\$11,236(0.06) = \$674	\$11,236 + \$674 = \$11,910
4	\$11,910	\$11,910(0.06) = \$715	\$11,910 + \$715 = \$12,625

It is apparent that the steps in the computation are tedious and time-consuming even in a problem such as this in which a short time period is involved. But fortunately, an algebraic expression has been developed which enables us to obtain the answer directly. This expression is as follows:

$$F = P(1 + i)^n \tag{6-1}$$

If we substitute the data in our problem in Eq. (6-1), we obtain

$$F = \$10,000(1 + 0.06)^4 = \$10,000(1.2625) = \$12,625$$

which coincides with what we found earlier.

Eq. (6-1) tells us that we can find F by multiplying P by $(1 + i)^n$. The expression $(1 + i)^n$ is called the "single-payment compound amount factor," for which we shall use the abbreviation F/P. Therefore, we shall say that

$$F = P(F/P)$$

The value of a specific single-payment compound amount factor can be found by substituting the appropriate values of n and i in the algebraic expression for this factor. However, if the exponent n is fairly large, logarithms must be used to obtain the numerical value of the factor, and this is inconvenient. For this reason, values of the single-payment compound amount factor for various interest rates and numbers of years have been calculated and made available in table form. Table C-1 (see Appendix) is representative of the many versions that are available.

To illustrate the use of Table C-1, let us return to our example. The specific single-payment compound amount factor we want to find is for an i equal to 6 percent and an n equal to four years. Therefore we can say that in our problem

$$F = \$10,000(F/P)_{n=4}^{i=6}$$

Turning to Table C-1, we go to the first column, number of years, and read down until we reach 4. Then we go to the right until we reach the 6 percent interest column. This yields a value of 1.262 which means that

$$(1 + 0.06)^4 = 1.262$$

Consequently, we are able to say that the company must make a payment of

$$F = \$10,000\,(1.262) = \$12,620$$

which differs slightly from the amount calculated earlier because of the rounded value of the factor which appears in the table.

In any case, we can say that $10,000 today is equivalent to $12,620 in four years from today at an annual interest rate of 6 percent. On the basis of this statement, we can define the symbols we have been using in more general terms. These definitions are as follows:

$P =$ present sum of money

$n =$ number of years during which interest is earned

$i \ =$ interest rate per year

$F =$ future sum of money n years from the present time which is equivalent to P at an interest rate i

SINGLE-PAYMENT PRESENT WORTH FACTOR

Let us now suppose that we are confronted by the following problem: A company estimates that it will need $60,000 in 15 years from now to finance an addition to its plant. It wants to provide for this future expenditure by investing a sum of money in a source which will yield a rate of return of 8 percent per year. What management wants to know is: How much must be invested at this time so that the investment will yield $60,000 in 15 years from now? All this can be described on a time line as follows:

$P = ?$ $F = \$60,000$

```
|--+--+--+--+--+--+--+--+--+--+--+--+--+--+--|
 0  1  2  3  4  5  6  7  8  9 10 11 12 13 14 15
```

In the absence of a general expression from which the unknown quantity can be found, it would be necessary to use a trial-and-error approach to the solution of the problem. Different values of P would have to be assumed until one was finally found which would be equivalent to $60,000 in 15 years from now at an annual interest rate of 8 percent. Fortunately, there is an easier way than this. Earlier, we found that

$$F = P(1 + i)^n$$

If we divide both sides of this expression by $(1 + i)^n$, we obtain

$$P = F\left[\frac{1}{(1 + i)^n}\right] \tag{6-2}$$

In our problem, we know the values of F, i, and n. When we substitute these values in Eq. (6-2), we find that the present sum of money P which must be invested is equal to

$$P = \$60,000\left[\frac{1}{(1 + 0.08)^{15}}\right] = \$18,912$$

This permits us to say that $18,912 today is equivalent to $60,000 in 15 years from today at an interest rate of 8 percent per year. A common way of stating this is to say that the present worth of the $60,000 is $18,912.

As indicated in Eq. (6-2), P is found by multiplying F by $1/(1 + i)^n$. This expression is the reciprocal of the single-payment compound amount factor and is called the "single-payment present worth factor" for which we shall use the abbreviation P/F. Therefore, Eq. (6-2) can be expressed in the following form:

$$P = F(P/F)$$

As in the case of the single-payment compound amount factor, the value of the single-payment present worth factor can be found by substitution of the specific values of n and i with which we are concerned. But again, this presents computational difficulties, and, for this reason, a table of single-payment present worth factor values has been developed for various interest rates and time periods. These values for selected interest rates and time periods are shown in Table C-2.

With the use of this table, we should begin the solution to our problem by stating that

$$P = \$60,000 \, (P/F)_{n=15}^{i=8}$$

The value of the single-payment present worth factor as found in Table C-2 is equal to 0.3152. With the use of this value, we find that

$$P = \$60,000 \, (0.3152) = \$18,912$$

which agrees with what we found earlier.

CAPITAL RECOVERY FACTOR

The two compound interest factors we have considered are called single-payment factors for a special reason. They are applied in those cases in which we want to find the single sum of money at some point in time which is equivalent to a single sum of money at some other point. One of these was a case in which a company borrowed a single sum of money P and it became necessary to determine the future single amount F that would have to be returned in payment of the principal and accumulated interest.

But let us assume that a different type of repayment plan is involved. Specifically, suppose that a firm borrows $1,000 at an interest rate of 6 percent per year. However, the loan is to be repaid by means of a series of three uniform annual payments. The first of these payments will be made at the end of the first year, and the last at the end of the third year. The question is: What must be the size of these annual payments, for which we shall use the symbol A, so that when the last one is made, the debt is paid in full?

Our problem can be depicted on a time line as follows:

$P = \$1,000$ $A = ?$ $A = ?$ $A = ?$

```
├────────┼────────┼────────┤
0        1        2        3
```

As an examination of the time line reveals, the series of payments has three characteristics: (1) Every payment in the series will be made at the *end* of the year; (2) a payment will be made at the end of *every* year in the time period under consideration; (3) the payment will be uniform, that is, each of the payments will be of the same magnitude.

In the absence of a known relationship between P and A, this problem can be solved only by a trial-and-error method. However, an expression has been derived for the relationship between these two quantities, from which we can find A directly. This expression is as follows:

$$A = P \left[\frac{i(1 + i)^n}{(1 + i)^n - 1} \right] \tag{6-3}$$

where A = annual uniform end-of-year payment continuing for n years which is equivalent to P at an interest rate of i

The terms P, i, and n continue to be defined as before. But we said earlier that P was a present sum of money which was equivalent to some future sum F. Now we can also say that

P = present sum of money which is equivalent to a series of uniform end-of-year payments continuing for n years at an interest rate i

THE COMPUTATION To return to our problem, we know the values of P, i, and n. Substitution of these values in Eq. (6-3) yields the following result:

$$A = \$1,000 \left[\frac{0.06(1 + 0.06)^3}{(1 + 0.06)^3 - 1} \right] = \$374$$

Therefore, if the firm pays $374 at the end of each year for a period of three years, it will have paid off its debt after having made the last payment.

Or if we want to place ourselves in the position of the lender, we can say that if the lender receives $374 at the end of each year for a period of three years, he will have recovered his investment and his earned interest. In general, $374 at the end of each year for three years is equivalent to $1,000 at the beginning of the first year at an interest rate of 6 percent per year.

The factor $[i(1 + i)^n]/[(1 + i)^n - 1]$, by which we multiply P to find A, is called the "capital recovery factor." Our abbreviation for this factor will be A/P. Therefore we can say that

$$A = P(A/P)$$

Before we go on with the discussion of the capital recovery factor, let us pause for a moment to show exactly what is happening to the firm's debt as it makes its annual payments of $374. As we know, $1,000 was borrowed at an interest rate of 6 percent per year. Consequently, at the end of the first year, the company owes the $1,000 of principal plus the interest on this $1,000. This interest charge will be 6 percent times $1,000, or $60. The total debt is therefore $1,060. However, it will pay $374 at the end of the first year. This leaves a balance of $1,060 minus $374, or $686, at the beginning of the second year. At the end of the second year, the company will owe this $686 plus the interest charge for the second year. Since it owed $686 at the beginning of the year, its interest charge, if we work to the closest dollar as we have heretofore, will be 6 percent times $686, or $41. The total debt at the end of the second year is therefore $686 plus $41, or $727. But at this point the company will make a second payment of $374. As a result, the balance will be $727 minus $374, or $353, at the end of the second year, which is also the beginning of the third year. At the end of the third year the company will owe this $353 plus the interest charge for the third year. This interest charge will be equal to 6 percent of the amount owed at the beginning of the year, or 6 percent times $353, or $21. Therefore, the total debt at the end of the year will be $353 plus $21, or $374. Obviously, when the company makes its third payment of $374 at this point, the balance will be zero. As this demonstrates, the capital recovery factor does yield the correct answer.

Let us now return to our discussion of the capital recovery factor as such. It will be recalled that the algebraic expression for the capital recovery factor is somewhat complex. However, we do have tables of numerical values for this factor for various interest rates and time periods. The particular table we shall work with is shown as Table C-3. We shall demonstrate the use of this table with a different problem.

ANOTHER APPLICATION   Suppose a person deposits $10,000 in a savings account on which he will be earning an interest rate of 5 percent. His withdrawal plan is as follows: At the end of each year, for a period of

10 years, he will withdraw a certain amount of money. These withdrawals will be uniform and of such a magnitude that when he makes his last one, the fund will be exhausted. We are asked to determine the size of these uniform withdrawals.

If the problem is described on a time line, we have the following:

$P = \$10,000$

$$A = ? \quad A = ? \quad A = ? \quad A = ? \quad A = ? \quad A = ? \quad A = ? \quad A = ? \quad A = ? \quad A = ?$$

$$\begin{array}{cccccccccccc} | & | & | & | & | & | & | & | & | & | \\ 0 & 1 & 2 & 3 & 4 & 5 & 6 & 7 & 8 & 9 & 10 \end{array}$$

The expression with which we must work is as follows:

$$A = P(A/P)$$

The appropriate capital recovery factor is one for an i of 0.05 and an n of 10. Therefore, in our problem, the specific equation becomes

$$A = \$10,000 \, (A/P)_{n=10}^{i=5}$$

We find the value of the capital recovery factor in Table C-3 to be 0.12950. Substituting this value in our equation, we find that

$$A = \$10,000 \, (0.12950) = \$1,295$$

Therefore, if the depositor invests \$10,000, he will exhaust his fund in 10 years by making a series of uniform end-of-year withdrawals of \$1,295 each. Or \$10,000 at the beginning of the first year is equivalent to \$1,295 at the end of each year for 10 years at an interest rate of 5 percent per year.

THE EQUIVALENT UNIFORM ANNUAL CAPITAL COST Before we go on to the next compound interest factor, we shall elaborate on the capital recovery factor, because it is a factor which will play an important role in our cost comparison technique. Let us return for a moment to the problem we have just solved. When our depositor makes his annual withdrawals of \$1,295, he is recovering two things: (1) his capital investment and (2) his earned interest. It is important to note that the \$10,000 he invests in the savings account is, in effect, the first cost of this investment alternative. Also, the fact that the account will exist for 10 years means that, in effect, this investment alternative will have a service life of 10 years. Finally, because the account will contain no money at the end of 10 years, the salvage value of this investment alternative is zero; in other words, the account has depreciated by \$10,000 in 10 years, or at an average rate of \$1,000 per year. The latter suggests that \$1,000 of the total annual withdrawal of \$1,295 is the average annual rate at which the initial investment is recovered and the balance of \$295 is the average annual earned interest.

Now, let us assume that our depositor has a second investment alternative at the beginning of this 10-year period. This second alternative is a piece of production equipment which also has a first cost of $10,000, a life of 10 years, and a salvage value of zero at the end of this life. If he chooses this alternative, instead of the one that calls for opening a savings account, he is forsaking an investment which would yield $1,295 a year for 10 years. Therefore, he could reason that, if he buys the equipment for $10,000, he will not be able to invest the $10,000 in a savings account from which he could withdraw $1,295 a year for the 10 years which coincide with the equipment's service life. Consequently, the equipment will, in effect, be costing him $1,295 a year for 10 years. Of this total, $1,000 will be the average annual depreciation expense, and the balance of $295 will be the average annual interest expense.

The situation would be no different if he had to borrow the $10,000 at an annual interest rate of 5 percent to buy the equipment. In a case such as this, if he wanted to pay off his debt by making 10 uniform end-of-year payments, each payment would have to be $1,295. Then he could reason that, if he buys the equipment for $10,000, he will be compelled to borrow the money which will necessitate his making annual payments of $1,295 a year for the 10 years which coincide with the equipment's service life. Consequently, the equipment will, in effect, be costing him $1,295 a year for 10 years. Again, $1,000 of this total will be the average annual depreciation expense, and $295 the average annual interest expense.

From this, we can see that the capital recovery factor will be useful in calculating the equivalent annual capital cost of an investment alternative. This uniform annual equivalent is a capital cost because it will stem from an expenditure for an asset which will ordinarily provide a service for more than one year. Also, it will be composed of two elements: depreciation and interest. The depreciation element will reflect the fact that the investment is decreasing in value; the interest element will reflect the fact that there is either an opportunity cost or an out-of-pocket interest charge, depending on whether internal or external funds are used.

SERIES PRESENT WORTH FACTOR

One more compound interest factor remains to be considered. The conditions under which it will be employed are similar to those which prevail. when the use of the single-payment present worth factor is indicated. It will be recalled that there may be a case in which a company would like to provide for the availability of a specified single sum of money in the future by investing a single sum at the present time. The required present sum of money can be found by multiplying the specified future sum by the single-payment present worth factor.

But suppose that the firm wants to provide not for a single payment in the future, but for a series of payments. For example, let us assume that a company has just procured a fleet of trucks which have an estimated service life of five years. These trucks will require servicing at the end of each year which will cost $500. There is an outside firm which does this type of work. This firm proposes the following plan: If the owners of the trucks make a single payment at the present time, the firm will service all the trucks at the end of each year for five years. The company that owns the trucks is interested in knowing what the correct single payment should be if the cost of money is 10 percent per year.

The problem can be depicted on a time line as follows:

$$P = ? \qquad A = \$500 \qquad A = \$500 \qquad A = \$500 \qquad A = \$500 \qquad A = \$500$$
$$0 \qquad\qquad 1 \qquad\qquad 2 \qquad\qquad 3 \qquad\qquad 4 \qquad\qquad 5$$

The total present value of this series of $500 payments could be found with the use of single-payment present worth factors if we consider each of the payments as a single sum of money. Doing so, we should obtain the following:

$$P = \$500\,(P/F)_{n=1}^{i=10} + \$500\,(P/F)_{n=2}^{i=10} + \cdots + \$500\,(P/F)_{n=5}^{i=10}$$

But if a series is of any appreciable length, this approach is somewhat unsatisfactory. For this reason, it is desirable that a single factor be found which will enable us to find the unknown present value in a more efficient manner.

In the section on the capital recovery factor, we found that the following was true:

$$A = P\left[\frac{i(1+i)^n}{(1+i)^n - 1}\right]$$

But in our problem, P is the unknown, while A is known. However, if we solve the preceding equation for P, we obtain

$$P = A\left[\frac{(1+i)^n - 1}{i(1+i)^n}\right] \tag{6-4}$$

When we substitute the values given in our problem for A, i, and n in Eq. (6-4), we find that

$$P = \$500\left[\frac{(1+0.10)^5 - 1}{0.10(1+0.10)^5}\right] = \$1,895$$

This permits us to say that a payment of $1,895 at the present time is equivalent to five end-of-year payments of $500 each at an interest rate of 10 percent per year. This is so, because if the firm were to invest $1,895 today at an annual interest rate of 10 percent, it could withdraw $500 at the end of each year for five years if the first withdrawal is made one year from today.

The quantity $[(1 + i)^n - 1]/[i(1 + i)^n]$ in Eq. (6-4) is called the "series present worth factor," and it is the reciprocal of the capital recovery factor. For this factor we shall use the abbreviation P/A. As a result, Eq. (6-4) can be expressed in the following form:

$$P = A(P/A)$$

As with the other factors, tables are available in which the numerical values of the series present worth factor are given for various interest rates and time periods. A typical one is shown as Table C-4. To illustrate the use of this table, let us consider how it would be employed in our problem.

The appropriate series present worth factor in this case is the one for an i equal to 0.10 and an n equal to 5. Therefore, we can say that

$$P = \$500 \, (P/A)_{n=5}^{i=10}$$

The value of this particular factor is found from Table C-4 to be 3.791. Substituting this value in our equation, we find that

$$P = \$500 \, (3.791) = \$1,895$$

which is to say that the present worth of the series of $500 services is $1,895.

A SUMMING UP

In total, we have considered four different compound interest factors. With these factors, we were able to develop four different expressions, which can be summarized as follows:

Given P, to find F:

$$F = P(F/P)$$

Given F, to find P:

$$P = F(P/F)$$

Given P, to find A:

$$A = P(A/P)$$

Given A, to find P:

$$P = A(P/A)$$

A knowledge of these relationships permits us to go on to a discussion of the technique for making cost comparisons of investment alternatives.

QUESTIONS

6-1 Define capital costs and operating costs. Give examples of each.

6-2 Why is it necessary to evaluate an investment alternative in terms of whether it maximizes profits rather than whether it minimizes costs?

6-3 Why must revenues be considered in any comparison of investment alternatives?

6-4 Under what conditions would the investment alternative that minimizes costs also maximize profits?

6-5 What are the two elements of capital cost? Define each.

6-6 What must be known about an investment alternative before its annual depreciation cost can be computed?

6-7 What would represent the required investment in an asset whose procurement the firm is considering?

6-8 What would represent the present investment in an asset the firm already owns? Explain.

6-9 Why must interest be considered as a cost to be associated with an investment alternative?

6-10 What is compound interest?

6-11 Under what conditions is each of the following employed: (*a*) single-payment compound amount factor, (*b*) single-payment present worth factor, (*c*) capital recovery factor, and (*d*) series present worth factor?

PROBLEMS

6-1 The demand for an accounting firm's services is a highly fluctuating one. If the firm operates in accordance with this demand pattern, it will experience average annual costs of approximately $870,000, while revenues will be about $960,000. The costs can be reduced to $750,000 a year if the company reduces the variation in the demand for factors of production by failing to satisfy the entire demand for its services. However, average annual revenues will then probably decrease by $130,000. What course of action should the firm follow?

6-2 An item of a particular design is expected to generate average annual revenues of $150,000 and average annual costs of $120,000. A simpler design would have an adverse effect on sales, in the sense that annual revenues would be 10 percent less. What percentage decrease in annual costs would have to occur to make the simpler design as economical as the more complex one? (Ans. 12.5)

6-3 A building was purchased by a railroad for $750,000. Ten years later, it was sold for $525,000. What was the total depreciation cost? The average annual depreciation cost? The average weekly depreciation cost?

At the time of its purchase, the building was expected to have a 40-year life and a $75,000 terminal salvage value. If the straight-line method of depreciation was adhered to, what was the asset's book value at the time of its sale?

6-4 A company is considering replacing an old piece of production equipment with a new machine. The price of the new equipment is $80,000, but there will be a $300 delivery charge and a $700 installation expense.

The old machine was purchased with borrowed funds at a cost of $50,000, of which $12,000 remains to be repaid. Its replacement cost is $9,500; its book value is $10,000; and its resale value is $9,000.

What investment is called for by the new equipment? What amount represents the present value of the old equipment if its replacement will be followed by its disposal? If retention of the old equipment necessitates the firm's buying another unit just like it for some other use, how much will the company have decided to invest in the old equipment by retaining it?

6-5 The owner of an automobile service station borrows $25,000 with the understanding that he is to repay the lending institution $28,750 at the end of one year. What is the interest charge? The interest rate?

6-6 The proprietor of a medical laboratory borrows $10,000 at an annual compound interest rate of 7 percent. The terms of the loan call for his returning the principal and earned interest in a single sum at the end of the fourth year. What is the interest charge for the *fourth* year?

6-7 A warehousing firm borrows $50,000 to finance an investment in materials handling equipment. This amount and all accumulated interest is to be repaid at the end of a three-year period. If interest is 10 percent compounded annually, how much is owed at the time payment is due? Determine this, first, without the use of a compound interest factor and, then, with the use of an appropriate factor. (Ans. $66,550)

6-8 It is estimated that $75,000 will be required in five years to revise an advertising firm's office layouts. Management wants to provide for this expenditure by investing a single sum of money at the present time. If 8 percent compounded annually can be earned on such an investment, how much must be invested so that the required sum will be available when needed? (Ans. $51,045)

6-9 How much must a land development company invest now, at an annual interest rate of 6 percent, to provide for promotional expenses of $400,000 in two years, of an additional $200,000 in four years, and of a final $100,000 in six years? (Ans. $584,920)

6-10 Suppose that municipal bonds have been available which yield a rate of return of 5 percent compounded annually. During a 10-year period, an individual has made the following purchases of these securities: $20,000 at the beginning of the first year, $15,000 at the end of the third year, $30,000 at the beginning of the sixth year, and $25,000 at the end of the tenth year. If interest was accumulated rather than paid at the end of each year, what is the total investment at the end of the tenth year in terms of principal plus earned interest? (Ans. $116,965)

6-11 A university wants to establish a fund which will enable it to rehabilitate some of its laboratories in five years. If a deposit of $60,000 is made now, a second deposit of $70,000 one year from now, a third deposit of $80,000 two years from now, and a fourth deposit of $90,000 three years from now, how much will the university have in a fund at the end of five years if it earns 8 percent per year on its deposits?

6-12 A program for the replacement of production equipment has been developed which calls for an expenditure of $200,000 five years from now, $150,000 eight years from now, and $375,000 eleven years from now. What single sum would have to be invested now, at an interest rate of 12 percent compounded annually, to provide for these expenditures?

6-13 A publishing firm is going to invest $90,000 now, at 10 percent per year, to provide for bonuses for its editors at the end of each year for the next three years. What maximum uniform amount can be withdrawn for this purpose at the end of each year? After having determined this, calculate the respective balances in the account after each withdrawal has been made. (Ans. $36,190)

6-14 What is the maximum justifiable investment in a methods improvement which will save a public utility $16,000 in labor costs at the end of each year for five years? The company's rate-of-return requirement is 15 percent per year. (Ans. $53,632)

6-15 In a given company, subcontracting costs are expected to total $44,000 a year for the next four years. If these are treated as if they will occur at the end of each year and the appropriate interest rate is 6 percent compounded annually, what single payment at the present time is equivalent to this series of costs?

6-16 To level out expected demand schedules for factors of production, a company is giving consideration to the production of a new item whose nature is such that it will probably be in demand for only seven years. The cost of introducing the product at this time is expected to be about $300,000. On investments of comparable risk and tax status, the firm can earn a rate of return of approximately 15 percent. What is the equivalent of this initial expenditure in terms of a uniform series of end-of-year costs?

6-17 In the preceding problem, suppose that management wants to find a uniform series of *beginning*-of-year payments that is equivalent to the required initial expenditure. What would this be? (Ans. $62,705)

6-18 A farm equipment dealer is considering renting storage space for a period of 10 years. The terms of the lease call for a payment of $20,000 at the *beginning* of each year for the first four years and $30,000 at the *beginning* of each year for the last six years. At an interest rate of 10 percent compounded annually, what expenditure at the beginning of the first year would be equivalent to these rental charges? What would be the uniform end-of-year equivalent of the annual rental charges? (Ans. $167,900; $27,326)

SEVEN
THE UNIFORM ANNUAL COST METHOD

It has been mentioned that the method for evaluating investment alternatives we shall consider is the uniform annual cost method. In this approach, each alternative is described in terms of the investment it requires, its service life and salvage value, and the revenues and operating costs it is expected to generate. These data are then used to calculate the average or uniform annual cost to be associated with each alternative. The alternative with the lowest annual cost is considered, in the absence of any irreducible factors, to be the most economical one. We shall describe this method of analysis with the aid of an illustration.

THE ASSUMED PROBLEM

Suppose that a company is *considering* the production of a new product. It has been found that the item can be manufactured in one of two different ways. The first involves the procurement and use of one type of equipment, which we shall call alternative K. The second involves the procurement and use of some other type of equipment, which we shall call alternative L.

Alternative K is expected to have a first cost of $80,000, a service life of four years, and no salvage value. Furthermore, it is expected to yield annual revenues of $55,000 and annual operating costs of $32,000. These operating costs include such things as labor, material, floor space, utilities, insurance, and administrative expense.

Alternative L is expected to have a first cost of $100,000, a service life of six years, and a salvage value of $10,000. Its annual revenues are also estimated to be $55,000. However, the operating costs are estimated to be $30,000 a year for the first three years of its life and $35,000 a year for the last three years.

In addition, the company's management has decided that the cost of money, that is, the interest rate, is 10 percent per year. Finally, the more economical alternative is to be selected on the basis of a uniform annual cost comparison.

THE COMPUTATION

We shall begin the uniform annual cost computation by considering alternative K. This alternative can be described on a time line in the following manner:

```
        $(55,000)    $(55,000)    $(55,000)    $(55,000)
$80,000    32,000       32,000       32,000       32,000
  ├──────────┼────────────┼────────────┼────────────┤
  0          1            2            3            4
```

Before we go on, let us examine this time line. The first cost of $80,000 is shown as having been incurred at the beginning of the first year of the four-year service life, which is as it should be. Next, we have a series of $55,000 figures, which represent the annual revenues. There are two things to note with regard to these figures. First, they are shown in parentheses. The reason for this is as follows: It will be recalled that revenues will be treated as negative costs. Therefore, it is important to signify on the time line that the figures which represent revenues are of opposite sign from actual costs. This could be done by showing a negative sign where necessary; however, parentheses will be somewhat more conspicuous. Hence, on the time line only, we shall use parentheses to denote revenues, or negative costs. The absence of parentheses denotes a positive cost.

The second thing to note is that annual revenues are shown as taking place at the *end* of each year. Actually, revenues may be realized every week, day, or even hour. However, it is difficult enough to estimate revenues on an annual basis without trying to forecast them by week, day, or hour. For this reason, annual estimates are considered to be sufficiently precise. But given annual revenues, a need arises for deciding at what point in the year they will be shown as having occurred. A very common practice is to show them as having occurred at the end of the year, and this is what we shall do. It is for this reason that an end-of-year series was assumed in the development of the series compound interest factors.

The same can be said for the series of annual operating costs of $32,000. Although these costs may be incurred every day, hour, or even minute, the best that can be hoped for is a fairly good annual estimate. Also, these annual costs are shown as having taken place at the end of each year for the same reason that annual revenues are. Finally, they are shown on the time line as positive costs, which means that they are not shown in parentheses.

But to continue, what we want to do is find the total uniform annual equivalent of the costs and revenues associated with this alternative. This total is to be expressed in terms of an end-of-year series. As can be seen, the operating costs and revenues are already expressed in the desired form, so nothing has to be done with these factors. The same, however, cannot be said of the first cost. Here, we have a single payment of $80,000 at the beginning of the first year, which must be expressed in terms of its uniform annual equivalent. This is easily done. We know that

$$A = P(A/P)_n^i$$

In our problem, the interest rate is given as 10 percent and the number of years as 4. Therefore, we can say that the equivalent uniform annual capital cost is equal to

$$A = \$80,000\,(A/P)_{n=4}^{i=10} = \$80,000\,(0.31547) = \$25,238$$

If we substitute this equivalent series for the first cost on the time line, we obtain:

$$
\begin{array}{ccccc}
\$25,238 & \$25,238 & \$25,238 & \$25,238 \\
(55,000) & (55,000) & (55,000) & (55,000) \\
32,000 & 32,000 & 32,000 & 32,000 \\
\end{array}
$$

```
|--------+--------+--------+--------|
0        1        2        3        4
```

To find the total uniform annual cost of alternative K, we add the annual capital cost, the annual operating costs, and the annual revenues. When we do so, we obtain

$$
\begin{array}{lr}
\text{Annual capital cost} \quad = & \$25{,}238 \\
\text{Annual operating costs} = & 32{,}000 \\
\text{Annual revenues} \quad = (-)\ & 55{,}000 \\
\hline
\text{\textit{Total}} = & \$\ 2{,}238 \\
\end{array}
$$

Let us now consider alternative L. This alternative can be described on a time line as follows:

$$
\begin{array}{ccccccc}
 & & & & & & \$(10,000) \\
 & \$(55,000) & \$(55,000) & \$(55,000) & \$(55,000) & \$(55,000) & (55,000) \\
\$100,000 & 30,000 & 30,000 & 30,000 & 35,000 & 35,000 & 35,000 \\
\end{array}
$$

```
|------+------+------+------+------+------|
0      1      2      3      4      5      6
```

As compared with K, alternative L has a salvage value of $10,000 which is shown as a revenue to be received at the end of the sixth year. Furthermore, annual operating costs are not expected to be uniform throughout the six-year life. Consequently, there is a need for calculating the uniform annual equivalent not only of the first cost, but of the salvage value and operating costs as well.

Insofar as the first cost is concerned, we find its uniform annual equivalent by multiplying it by the capital recovery factor for an interest rate of 10 percent and a time period equal to the service life, which in this case is six years. Doing so yields

$$A = \$100,000 \, (A/P)_{n=6}^{i=10} = \$100,000 \, (0.22961) = \$22,961$$

Turning to the salvage value, we find that it is necessary to ascertain the uniform annual equivalent A of a future sum of money F. However, in the preceding chapter, we considered only the uniform annual equivalent of a present sum of money P which we found to be

$$A = P(A/P) \tag{7-1}$$

But we also found that

$$P = F(P/F)$$

If we substitute $F(P/F)$ for P in Eq. (7-1), we obtain

$$A = F(P/F)(A/P)$$

In brief, we can find the uniform annual equivalent of a future sum of money by, first, calculating the present worth of this sum and, then, determining the uniform annual equivalent of the resultant present value. Keeping in mind that the salvage value is a negative cost, we should find the uniform annual equivalent of the $10,000 salvage value in our problem in the following manner:

$$A = (-)\$10,000 \, (P/F)_{n=6}^{i=10} \, (A/P)_{n=6}^{i=10}$$
$$= (-)\$10,000 \, (0.5645)(0.22961) = (-)\$1,296$$

This approach also serves to suggest how the uniform annual equivalent of nonuniform operating costs can be found. The procedure is to find the total present worth of the individual future operating costs and then to calculate the uniform annual equivalent of this total present worth. In the case of alternative L, this would be done as follows:

$$A = [\$30,000 \, (P/A)_{n=3}^{i=10} + \$35,000(P/F)_{n=4}^{i=10} + \$35,000 \, (P/F)_{n=5}^{i=10}$$
$$+ \$35,000 \, (P/F)_{n=6}^{i=10}] \, (A/P)_{n=6}^{i=10}$$
$$= [\$30,000 \, (2.487) + \$35,000 \, (0.6830) + \$35,000 \, (0.6209)$$
$$+ \$35,000 \, (0.5645)] \, (0.22961)$$
$$= \$32,145$$

It might be noted that, because the $30,000 annual operating costs for the first three years represent a uniform series, we were able to employ the series present worth factor to obtain the present worth of these costs at the beginning of the first period of the series.

When we turn to the annual revenues, we find that they are uniform and, hence, in the desired form. However, if they were nonuniform, their uniform annual equivalent would be found by the same method as the one employed when calculating the uniform annual equivalent of nonuniform operating costs.

We can now substitute our calculated equivalents for the data contained in the original time line which served to describe alternative L. When we do, we obtain the following:

$22,961	$22,961	$22,961	$22,961	$22,961	$22,961
(1,296)	(1,296)	(1,296)	(1,296)	(1,296)	(1,296)
32,145	32,145	32,145	32,145	32,145	32,145
(55,000)	(55,000)	(55,000)	(55,000)	(55,000)	(55,000)
0	1	2	3	4	5	6

To find the total uniform annual cost of alternative L, we add these four annual equivalents. This yields

```
Uniform annual equivalent of first cost      =      $22,961
Uniform annual equivalent of salvage value   = (−)   1,296
Uniform annual equivalent of operating costs =      32,145
Uniform annual equivalent of revenues        = (−) 55,000
                                     Total  = (−)$ 1,190
```

In summary, the respective total uniform annual costs for the two alternatives are equal to

	Alternative K	*Alternative L*
Total annual cost	(+)$2,238	(−)$1,190

THE COMPARISON

If the two alternatives had equal service lives, the calculated annual costs could be compared and, because alternative L has the lower cost, a conclusion reached that it is the more economical alternative. Unfortunately, our problem involves unequal service lives, and, hence, a comparison of these two annual costs does not, theoretically, permit us to make a decision. The reason for this is that they represent two different things. The +$2,238 is really +$2,238 per year for four years, while the −$1,190 is really −$1,190 per year for six years. Let us elaborate upon this.

As we know, the company was willing to assume a six-year life for the equipment represented by alternative L. This suggests that the service provided by this equipment will be required for at least six years. We say "at least" because it is possible that the equipment will be replaced at the end of six years by another facility which will continue to provide the same service. But we are sure that at least six years of service will be required. Consequently, if alternative K were selected, the equipment it involves would have to be replaced at the end of its four-year life because of the continuing need for the service it provided.

Now we saw that a direct comparison of our computed annual costs suggests that alternative L should be selected at this time because its annual costs are −$1,190 as compared with +$2,238 for alternative K. However, it may be, although not necessarily, that in four more years an extremely efficient type of new equipment will be available. In fact, it may be so efficient that it will be worth the company's while to choose alternative K now and experience higher annual costs for four years in order to be able to take advantage of the opportunity to purchase the more efficient equipment which will be available at that time.

Of course, the only way this can be determined is to forecast what will take place in the future. To return to our alternatives, the company may go on to estimate that if the equipment represented by alternative K is selected, it will be replaced in four years by equipment which will have a first cost of $20,000, a life of two years, a salvage value of zero, annual operating costs of $25,000, and annual revenues of $55,000. This means that a decision to select alternative K is a decision which will generate the following costs during the coming six years:

				$20,000		
	$(55,000)	$(55,000)	$(55,000)	(55,000)	$(55,000)	$(55,000)
$80,000	32,000	32,000	32,000	32,000	25,000	25,000
0	1	2	3	4	5	6

In brief, these are the costs to be associated with the equipment represented by alternative K and its replacement. To find their uniform annual equivalent, we can begin by calculating their total present worth. This would be done in the following manner:

$$P = \$80,000 + \$32,000\,(P/A)_{n=4}^{i=10} + \$25,000\,(P/F)_{n=5}^{i=10}$$
$$\quad + \$25,000\,(P/F)_{n=6}^{i=10} - \$55,000\,(P/A)_{n=6}^{i=10}$$
$$\quad + \$20,000\,(P/F)_{n=4}^{i=10}$$
$$= (-)\,\$14,812$$

We can now find the uniform annual equivalent of this present sum of money. This would be done as follows:

$$A = (-)\,\$14,812\,(A/P)_{n=6}^{i=10} = (-)\,\$3,401$$

This means that a decision to select alternative K is a decision which will result in the company's experiencing average annual costs of −$3,401 for the next six years. On the other hand, as we found earlier, a decision to choose alternative L is a decision which will result in the company's experiencing average annual costs of −$1,190 for the next six years. These two figures can now be compared directly, because six years from the present time the company will have the same choice of alternatives regardless of what it chooses to do at the present time. Consequently, the time period beginning six years from now can be ignored. Therefore, if our forecasts for the next six years are correct, alternative K should be selected in spite of the fact that it will yield higher annual costs for the first four years. This is true, of course, only because of the nature of its replacement. With another type of replacement, a different conclusion might be reached.

In theory, then, this is how the problem of unequal service lives is handled. We simply keep forecasting the costs and revenues which will be generated by each of the presently available alternatives until we end up with equal time periods. One alternative then becomes a series of investments headed by one of the presently available alternatives; the other becomes another series of investments headed by the other presently available alternative. The next step is to find the uniform annual equivalents of these respective series. Finally, we compare these uniform annual costs and select the series with the lower cost.

A SIMPLIFYING ASSUMPTION   Actually, this theory is difficult to apply in practice. The difficulty stems from the fact that it is almost impossible to predict the nature of future investment alternatives, especially when it becomes necessary to describe a fairly long series of replacements. To illustrate, suppose it were believed that alternative K in our example would be replaced by a facility with a service life of five years. This would take us to a total of nine years in the future. But alternative L will last only six years. So now we have nine years as compared with six. This necessitates forecasting what alternative L will be replaced by. If the replacement will have a life of eight years, we shall then have a total of fourteen years as compared with nine. We could go on this way, but this suffices to bring out the size of the estimation problem involved.

For this reason, just about every method proposed for making cost comparisons of alternatives with unequal service lives involves a simplifying assumption about the nature of future investment alternatives. These assumptions vary, but every one has the effect of permitting the firm to ignore the nature of future investment alternatives. A fairly common one, *and it is the one we shall adopt,* is that, regardless of which of the presently available alternatives is selected, it will be replaced at the end of its service life by a series of alternatives just like it.

To return to our problem, this means that, if we select alternative K, we assume it will be replaced by an alternative which will also require an investment of $80,000 and will have a service life of four years, a salvage value of zero, annual operating costs of $32,000, and annual revenues of $55,000. Similarly, this first replacement will be followed by the same kind of alternative, and so on.

Insofar as alternative L is concerned, the assumption is to be interpreted as stating that L will be replaced at the end of six years by an alternative just like it. Furthermore, this first replacement will be succeeded by the same kind of alternative, and so on.

This assumed series of replacements in each case would continue until a point is reached at which the time period covered by the one alternative is equal to the period covered by the other. In our problem in which alternative K has a four-year life and alternative L a six-year life, this time period would have to be 12 years. Specifically, the series headed by alternative K, if we omit the thousands, would appear on a time line as follows:

```
                            $80                      $80
          $(55) $(55) $(55) (55)  $(55) $(55) $(55) (55)  $(55) $(55) $(55) $(55)
    $80     32    32    32   32     32    32    32   32     32    32    32    32
    ├─────┼─────┼─────┼─────┼─────┼─────┼─────┼─────┼─────┼─────┼─────┼─────┤
    0     1     2     3     4     5     6     7     8     9    10    11    12
```

and the series headed by alternative L would appear as follows:

```
                                       $100                                    $(10)
                                       (10)                                    (55)
          $(55) $(55) $(55) $(55) $(55) (55)  $(55) $(55) $(55) $(55) $(55)
    $100    30    30    30    35    35   35     30    30    30    35    35    35
    ├─────┼─────┼─────┼─────┼─────┼─────┼─────┼─────┼─────┼─────┼─────┼─────┤
    0     1     2     3     4     5     6     7     8     9    10    11    12
```

Let us now consider the effects of the assumption on our computations. We have shown that the cost of alternative K would be +$2,238 a year for four years. However, no additional calculations are required to determine the annual cost of its replacements. If its replacements are just like it, our computations would show that the annual cost of the replacements is also +$2,238 a year. Therefore, we can say that the series headed by alternative K will cost +$2,238 a year for 12 years.

We also found that the cost of alternative L would be −$1,190 a year for six years. But again, no additional computations are required to determine the annual cost of its replacements. If these replacements are just like it, our computations would show that their annual cost would be −$1,190. Therefore, we can say that the series headed by alternative L will cost −$1,190 a year for 12 years.

As this suggests, the assumption in effect is that the annual cost of the one alternative will continue, because of the nature of its assumed replacements, for a time period which will be equal to the least common denominator of the service lives of the two alternatives being compared. Likewise, the annual cost of the other alternative will continue, because of the nature of its assumed replacements, for the same time period. Consequently, no additional computations are required. We can simply calculate the annual cost for the one alternative on the basis of its service life and compare this directly with the annual cost calculated for the other alternative on the basis of its service life. To illustrate, we found the cost of alternative K to be +$2,238 a year for four years and of alternative L to be −$1,190 a year for six years. We can compare these two annual costs directly and select the more economical alternative. The assumption that these costs will continue until equal time periods are reached is implicit in this direct comparison. And, to repeat, we shall make this assumption in each of our comparisons unless stated otherwise. Therefore, in our problem, we conclude that L is the more economical alternative. But it is possible that, if we knew the characteristics of the *actual* replacements, we should reach a different conclusion.

INTERPRETATION OF THE RESULTS

In the preceding problem, it was stated that the cost of money to the company is 10 percent per year. As a result, an interest rate of 10 percent entered into the computations. More often than not, a company will refer to this 10 percent as its rate-of-return requirement.

Let us now examine the results of the preceding analysis with a view toward determining whether these results suggest that the firm's 10 percent rate-of-return requirement is being satisfied. Insofar as alternative K is concerned, the annual costs were found to be as follows:

Annual capital cost	=	$25,238
Annual operating costs	=	32,000
Subtotal	=	$57,238
Annual revenues	= (−)	55,000
Total	=	$ 2,238

The capital cost of $25,238 consists of two elements. One of these is an average annual depreciation expense of $20,000 which, in the absence of a salvage value, is obtained by taking the $80,000 first cost and dividing it by the four-year service life. The second element is the remaining $5,238, which is the average annual interest expense generated by the 10 percent interest rate. This interest of $5,238 is a *cost,* and a cost can never represent a rate of return on an investment. Only revenues are capable of doing so. Therefore, if a return is to be realized, it can be realized only through the revenues the investment makes possible and not through the costs it generates.

Keeping this in mind, let us examine the figures shown in the foregoing table. We have positive costs, which total $57,238 a year, and these include depreciation, interest, and operating costs. The company hopes to recover these costs through the revenues the alternative will make possible. Now, if the revenues were exactly $57,238 a year, the company would just recover its annual costs of $57,238. But this means that it would just recover its operating costs, its depreciation cost, and its interest charge of 10 percent per year. In other words, among other things, the firm would be just reimbursed for an interest charge of 10 percent, which is synonymous with saying that it would be realizing a rate of return equal to exactly 10 percent. On the other hand, if revenues were less than $57,238, they would be insufficient to reimburse the company for the interest charge of 10 percent, which is synonymous with saying that the firm would be realizing a rate of return equal to less than 10 percent. Finally, if revenues were greater than $57,238, they would be more than sufficient to reimburse the company for the interest charge of 10 percent, which is synonymous with saying that the firm would be realizing a rate of return equal to more than 10 percent.

In our problem, annual revenues from alternative K happen to be $55,000, which is less than the annual costs of $57,238. Therefore, we can say that this alternative would yield a rate of return of less than 10 percent.

An indication of whether or not the interest charge is being recovered is the sign of the total annual cost. If the total annual cost is negative, as it would be if annual revenues with alternative K were, say, $58,000, it means that the rate of return is greater than the interest rate used in the computations. If the total annual cost is positive, as it is for alternative K, it means that costs exceed revenues, and, therefore, the rate of return is less than the interest rate used in the computations. Finally, if the total annual cost is zero, it means that costs equal revenues, and, therefore, the rate of return is equal to the interest rate used in the computations.

In summary, we can say that alternative K, which yields an annual cost of +$2,238, will provide a rate of return of less than 10 percent on the total investment of $80,000.

Let us now turn to alternative L and make the same analysis. Alternative L can be described as follows:

Annual capital cost   = $21,665
Annual operating costs =   32,145
           Subtotal = $53,810
Annual revenues   = (−) 55,000
            Total = (−)$ 1,190

The annual capital cost of $21,665 is the difference between the $22,961 uniform annual equivalent of the first cost and the $1,296 uniform annual equivalent of the salvage value. In any event, the fact that the total cost is negative means that the rate of return on the total investment of $100,000 in alternative L is greater than 10 percent. Or more precisely, alternative L yields a rate of return of 10 percent *plus* an additional amount of $1,190 a year.

It would be wrong, however, to conclude from all this that the sole reason for rejecting alternative K is that it does not satisfy the rate-of-return requirement. The alternative could satisfy this requirement and still be rejected. For example, if the revenues generated by alternative K had been estimated to be $58,000 a year, the total annual cost would then have been as follows:

Annual capital cost   = $25,238
Annual operating costs =   32,000
           Subtotal = $57,238
Annual revenues   = (−) 58,000
            Total = (−)$ 762

Nevertheless, L would continue to be the more economical alternative, because its annual cost of −$1,190 is less than −$762. In brief, in this case, both alternatives would yield revenues which are able to cover all the costs they generate, including the 10 percent interest expense. However, after having done so, alternative L provides an additional amount of $1,190 a year, which exceeds the additional amount of $762 a year provided by alternative K.

All this suggests that, when evaluating investment alternatives, the firm must consider whether its rate-of-return requirement will be satisfied. To return to our original problem, it was mentioned that the company was *considering* the production of a new product and that there were two alternative methods of producing this product. We then went on to select the more economical of these two alternatives. However, it is extremely important that we take cognizance of the following fact: Because one of these two alternatives is more economical than the other, it does not mean that this alternative will be selected. The reason is that there is a third alternative which exists but which has not been described explicitly. This third alternative is not to produce the product at all. For example, suppose that the estimated revenues for each alternative were only $50,000 a year. If all the other data remained the same, we should obtain the following total annual costs:

	Alternative K	*Alternative L*
Annual capital cost	$25,238	$21,665
Annual operating costs	32,000	32,145
Subtotal	$57,238	$53,810
Annual revenues	(—) 50,000	(—) 50,000
Total	$ 7,238	$ 3,810

A comparison of these totals reveals that alternative L is still the more economical of the two. However, because both totals are positive, both investments are yielding a rate of return of less than 10 percent. And if the company has to borrow the required capital at 10 percent or could invest available capital in other sources of comparable risk at 10 percent, it would clearly be unwise to select L, even if it is more economical than K, because L does not yield a satisfactory rate of return on the total investment it requires. In brief, the company would be better off not producing the product at all. If it selects this third alternative of doing nothing, its revenues will be zero but so will its costs. Therefore, the total annual cost of this alternative would be zero, which is less than the $3,810 annual cost of alternative L.

In general, then, the first question that must be answered in an evaluation of investment alternatives is whether any capital investment should be made. This can be answered by computing the total annual costs of the alternatives which call for making a capital investment. Those alternatives which yielded positive total annual costs, that is, those alternatives which did not yield a satisfactory rate of return on total investment, would be dropped from further consideration. Of the remaining alternatives, that is, those alternatives which yielded a zero or negative total annual cost, the one with the lowest cost would be selected. If no alternatives fell into this latter category, no investment would be made.

COST RELEVANCY

In spite of the need for ascertaining whether the most "economical" alternative satisfies the rate-of-return requirement on total investment, in many studies, no attempt is made to satisfy this need. There are reasons why this is so.

Before it is possible to determine whether the rate-of-return requirement is being met, it is necessary that all the revenues and costs generated by a particular investment alternative be known or estimated. Very often, this is not possible. For example, suppose that a proposal for a methods improvement calls for replacing one unit of equipment in a production line that may contain 25 units of equipment and that may be used to process 15 similar but different products. It would be the rare company that would attempt to estimate what portion of the revenues from these products is attributable to this particular machine. Similarly, it might be impossible to estimate what fraction of the total cost of administration, marketing, supervision, indirect labor, indirect materials, and the like is attributable to this machine. The problem is even more obvious when we consider something like a unit of materials handling equipment. How does one determine what revenues are made possible by the presence of a conveyor or forklift truck?

In brief, there are many investment alternatives whose natures are such that it is impossible to describe them in terms of the *total* revenues and costs they generate. At best, the company can, in certain cases, estimate some of the costs and, in other cases, only the expected increases or decreases in costs or revenues. Where this condition prevails, determination of the rate of return on total investment is not feasible.

And yet, alternatives of this type are evaluated all the time. An evaluation is possible because of an assumption made by management. This assumption, which is a decision based on judgment, is that the alternatives available for the solution of a given problem do satisfy the rate-of-return requirement. Given this assumption, the analyst has only to select the most economical of the available alternatives, from which the alternative of making no investment is excluded.

In the presence of an assumption such as this, the problem of estimation is greatly simplified, because the need for estimating all the revenues and all the costs is eliminated. Instead, the analyst has to consider only those revenues and costs whose magnitudes will be affected by the choice of alternative.

Let us illustrate this by returning to the problem with which we have been working. Suppose that the company assumes that the rate of return on the total investment in either of the two alternatives will be satisfactory. This means that the firm has already decided to produce the new product, and it is to be produced in one of these two ways. If this is the case, the analyst will be interested only in determining which of these two alternatives has the lower annual cost, and he can do this even if he ignores those costs and revenues that are common to both alternatives. For example, we found the equivalent uniform annual costs and revenues to be as follows:

	Alternative K	Alternative L
Annual capital cost	$25,238	$21,665
Annual operating costs	32,000	32,145
Annual revenues	(—) 55,000	(—) 55,000
Total	$ 2,238	(—)$ 1,190

A comparison of these totals revealed that alternative L is more economical than K by $3,428 a year and, further, that it satisfies the firm's rate-of-return requirement. Now, if revenues had been ignored because they were expected to be the same for each alternative, the "total" cost would have been found to be as follows:

	Alternative K	Alternative L
Annual capital cost	$25,238	$21,665
Annual operating costs	32,000	32,145
Total	$57,238	$53,810

Again, although the values for the total costs have changed, alternative L continues to be the more economical alternative by $3,428 a year. However, the fact that these total costs are now positive is of no significance, because they are not totals in the strict sense of the term. But if the firm assumes that the rate-of-return requirement is being satisfied, this is of no consequence.

Similarly, if certain operating costs were the same for each alternative, ignoring them would have changed the totals but would not have changed the difference between the totals. The same would hold true if only the differences between revenues or certain operating costs had been considered. In brief, when the rate of return on total investment is assumed to be satisfactory, anything is permissible that does not alter the difference between the resultant total annual cost figures, because it is this difference which will serve to identify the more economical alternative.

To summarize, there are cases in which no explicit steps will be taken to determine whether available investment alternatives satisfy the rate-of-return requirement. Instead, it will simply be assumed that they do. Where this condition prevails, the most economical alternative can be selected by considering only those costs and revenues whose magnitudes will be affected by the choice of alternative.

PROBLEMS OF ESTIMATION

The uniform annual cost method has been described with the aid of a problem which is above average in complexity. The alternatives were characterized by the presence of salvage values, nonuniform annual operating costs, and unequal service lives. In many cases, one or more of these complicating factors are not present, and the computations are somewhat simpler.

However, the problem was also characterized by the fact that only two alternatives had to be evaluated. But there are situations in which three or more alternatives have to be considered. Where this is true, the basic approach remains unchanged. It becomes necessary only to calculate the uniform annual cost of each of these alternatives and select the one with the lowest cost.

It should also be noted that in the presentation of the uniform annual cost method, the emphasis has been placed on the factors that must be taken into consideration and on how these factors enter the analysis once they have been expressed in quantitative terms. However, the difficulties one encounters in any attempt to express these factors in quantitative terms have not been mentioned. The fact that these difficulties do exist cannot be ignored, because given a correct method of analysis, the results are only as accurate as the estimates on which the analysis is based.

The nature of this problem of estimation is quite evident when we consider the need to forecast the magnitudes of such things as future service lives, salvage values, operating costs, and revenues. But the firm also finds it necessary to select an interest rate for use in the analysis, and the determination of an appropriate rate is no simple task. Let us consider why this is true.

DETERMINATION OF THE INTEREST RATE In theory, the rate-of-return requirement should be that interest rate which will permit the firm to allocate its available capital in the most efficient manner. Selection of this rate requires that management determine its supply and demand schedules for capital. At various interest rates, different amounts of capital will be both made available to and required by the company for investment. In general, as management is willing to pay higher interest rates for the use of money, it will have more opportunities to obtain money, and its supply of capital will increase. On the other hand, as management demands higher rates of return from its investments, it will have fewer opportunities to invest money, and its demand for capital will decrease. At some interest rate, the capital supply and demand will be equal. If all available investment opportunities are of comparable risk and tax status, it is this interest rate which should be used as the rate-of-return requirement.

The reason it is necessary to speak in terms of comparable risk and tax status is easily demonstrated. With regard to the risk factor, an individual may estimate the potential rate of return from a high-risk venture, such as introducing a new product, to be about 20 percent. At the same time, he may have an opportunity to invest the money in stock which involves less risk but will yield a return of only 10 percent. Because of the difference in the degree of risk, the 10 percent may actually be more attractive than the 20 percent. The same holds true when we consider the factor of tax status. Two bonds may be available which involve the same degree of risk. One pays an interest rate of 7 percent, but the interest payment is considered to be taxable income. The other pays an interest rate of only 4 percent, but the interest payment is tax free. Given this difference in tax status, the 4 percent bond may be more attractive to a particular investor than the 7 percent bond.

Unfortunately, the determination of the interest rate is much more difficult in practice than it is in theory. To begin with, it is almost impossible for a given firm to ascertain what amounts of money are available at various rates of interest. In fact, difficulties are many times encountered in determining what the cost of money actually is, as in the case of financing by the sale of shares in the business. Therefore, the supply schedule of capital exists but cannot be accurately described. The same is true for the demand schedule. Its determination necessitates investigating all internal and external opportunities for investing funds and making accurate estimates in order to compute probable rates of return. For all practical purposes, this is impossible to do. But even if all these obstacles to the determination of capital supply and demand schedules were overcome, the resultant interest rate would have a number of deficiencies. First, it would represent a state of equilibrium only at a given moment in time; this means that it would reflect neither future changes in investment opportunities nor future changes in capital availability. Next, the resultant interest rate would have to be modified to provide for both the different levels of risk inherent in various investment opportunities and for the possible differences in the tax status of these investment opportunities; no completely satisfactory methods for doing so exist at this time.

For these reasons, judgment plays an important role in the selection of a rate-of-return requirement. The only thing the firm can ascertain with some degree of certainty is the minimum value this rate should assume. This value would be the rate which can be obtained from other investments of comparable risk and tax status. But as has been suggested, the amount by which this value should be increased to permit the most efficient allocation of available capital does not lend itself to determination by a quantitative approach.

Given the difficulty of selecting an appropriate interest rate and the problem of estimating the values of the other factors that enter the analysis, the question that now arises is whether this problem of estimation destroys the usefulness of such techniques as the uniform annual cost method. Actually, there can be little doubt that the techniques of investment analysis are a valuable analytical tool. In many cases of decision making, management will find that a limited number of alternatives are available. Also, the nature of these alternatives is such that, although a quantitative description is difficult, it is not impossible. Where this is true, and it often is, uniform annual cost calculations can usually provide a better basis for selecting the most economical alternative than can judgment or the variety of rules of thumb to which many companies adhere.

This is not to say that one should not appreciate the reluctance of some companies to adopt these more refined methods. They do pose problems of estimation, and this fact cannot be ignored. Because of this, the real need at the present time is for practical guides to aid companies in their attempt to express the factors incorporated in these methods in quantitative terms. Automatic data processing equipment can be of some help in this respect. The availability of such equipment permits the firm to maintain more complete records of the past service lives, salvage values, and operating costs it has experienced with fixed assets of various types. These historical data may provide a starting point in the estimation procedure. The equipment can also be used to carry out the computations involved in the application of the uniform annual cost method, and to determine how sensitive the decision regarding the most economical alternative is to changes in the estimated values of the relevant factors. Incidentally, data processing equipment can also be used to generate tables of values of compound interest factors for various combinations of interest rates and service lives.

IRREDUCIBLE FACTORS Because estimates are involved, decisions cannot be made solely on the basis of the numerical results of a uniform annual cost computation. These results must be interpreted in light of so-called irreducibles. Irreducibles are those factors which cannot be expressed in quantitative terms. They assume a major role in the decision-making process when a comparison reveals that the annual costs generated by the alternatives are not significantly different. In such cases, the final decision is very often based on the irreducible factors. It is not possible either to develop an exhaustive list of such factors or to consider the role each would play under every possible set of conditions. At best, only examples can be given. Some of these are as follows:

If the firm has reason to believe that more attractive alternatives will be available in the future, it will be inclined to select the shortest-lived of the presently available alternatives.

In another case, if indications are that the prices of materials and labor might increase in the near future, the firm will give preference to that alternative which would reduce the required amounts of these factors of production.

Or if management suspects that the future cost of money will be lower than it is at the present time, it will be disposed toward the alternative that requires the lowest initial investment.

As a final example, the firm will favor that alternative which will (1) improve the quality of its products, (2) result in greater safety for the users of its products or for its employees, (3) provide the firm with greater output capacity which might possibly be required in the future, (4) bring about better public relations, (5) improve employee morale, or (6) enable the firm to make faster deliveries to its customers.

Of course, if a dollar value can be assigned to any of these or similar factors, they cease to be irreducibles. But the facts are that some irreducibles will always remain and that the estimates of other factors are subject to error. Nevertheless, there is reason to believe that, at least, the use of the uniform annual cost method will reduce the areas in which judgment and intuition must play a role and will compel management to take all the relevant factors into consideration. If it does nothing more than this, it will have made an important contribution. And, of course, it can make this contribution in areas other than manufacturing. An organization that services television sets, radios, and phonographs must choose from among various available types of diagnostic equipment; a university must select the most economical kind of laboratory equipment; an operator of a restaurant has a choice of automatic dishwashers; a management consulting firm must decide what kind of office equipment it will procure; and a railroad must attempt to identify the most efficient type of locomotive. In each of these and similar cases, the required analysis can be made with the aid of a technique such as the uniform annual cost method.

QUESTIONS

7-1 Describe in general terms the uniform annual cost method for the evaluation of investment alternatives.

7-2 How is the uniform annual equivalent of the following found: (a) initial investment in an alternative, (b) future salvage value of an asset, and (c) nonuniform annual revenues or disbursements?

7-3 Why is it necessary to consider equal time periods when comparing investment alternatives?

7-4 When all the revenues and costs generated by an alternative have been taken into consideration, what is the significance of a calculated total annual cost of zero? Of a positive total annual cost? Of a negative total annual cost? Explain.

7-5 It has been mentioned that, on occasion, revenues and certain costs can be ignored when comparing investment alternatives. When is this possible, and under what conditions would it be permissible to do so? What are the advantages of being able to do so?

7-6 What factors should the firm take into consideration when determining its rate-of-return requirement?

7-7 Define irreducible factors. How do they enter into the decision-making process? Under what conditions do they assume a major role? Give some examples of these factors and explain how each would affect the firm's choice of alternative.

7-8 Evaluate the uniform annual cost approach to the determination of the most economical investment alternative.

PROBLEMS

7-1 An analysis has been made of the layout of a large department store, and three alternate layouts have been developed. Adoption of any one of them will entail an expense, because departments and facilities within departments will have to be relocated and rearranged. However, each is expected to generate some benefit, because the flow of stock, employees, and customers will be more efficient than it is with the present arrangement. The expense and corresponding benefit for each plan are a follows:

	Plan 1	Plan 2	Plan 3
Installation cost	$48,000	$36,000	$65,000
Annual benefit	11,000	8,000	14,000

If management's rate-of-return requirement is 7 percent, which of these plans should it select if there is reason to believe that a new layout would be satisfactory for five years? Make your decision on the basis of a uniform annual cost comparison. (Ans. $707, $780, $1,853)

7-2 A stockbroker may decide to install an automatic data processing system. The equipment involved can be either leased or purchased.

The leasing arrangement would call for an annual rental charge of $84,000, which includes the cost of maintenance. If purchased, the same equipment would have a first cost of $420,000, a probable service life of six years, an estimated salvage value of $70,000, and average annual maintenance costs of $6,000.

Whether the equipment is rented or purchased, the cost of such things as site preparation, programming, operating personnel, power, and supplies would be the same.

After ascertaining which of these two alternatives is the more attractive, the firm will go on to evaluate this alternative in light of the costs to be associated with its present data processing system. If the cost of money is 10 percent per year, would it be more economical to lease or to purchase the equipment?

7-3 A methods analysis has been made of a certain activity at a cost of $750. It is proposed that changes be made in the existing method which will yield an annual saving in material costs of $2,400. Furthermore, the man-hours required for the activity could be reduced by 320 per year which would represent an annual saving of $2,240; however, it is noted that the nature of the work is such that the involved employee could not be assigned to some other task during these hours and, consequently, would simply have more idle time. The cost of installing the method, which would have a probable life of three years, would be $6,000. If the company's rate-of-return requirement is 6 percent per year, is the proposed method more attractive than the present one?

7-4 A proposal has been submitted which calls for the replacement of a packaging line by new facilities. If the new equipment is procured, the old facilities will be sold for $20,000. The new equipment involves a purchase price of $97,000 and an installation cost of $3,000. Other relevant data are as follows:

	Existing line	Proposed line
Annual operating costs	$90,000	$82,000
Expected life	5 years	10 years
Salvage value	0	$10,000
Interest rate	12%	12%

Does a uniform annual cost comparison suggest that the extra investment required by the new equipment can be justified? (Ans. $95,548, $99,128)

7-5 In the preceding problem, suppose that the analyst chooses not to make the assumption that the nature of future replacements is such that the respective calculated uniform annual costs will continue until the same point in time is reached with each alternative. Instead, he estimates that, if the old packaging line is retained, it will be replaced at the end of its five-year life by equipment with a required initial investment of $45,000, a life of five years, a $5,000 salvage value, and annual operating costs which continue at $90,000. What effect will these new data have on the calculated uniform annual cost of the alternative which calls for keeping the old packaging line? Does this alter the decision reached in the preceding problem? (Ans. $97,774)

7-6 A cleaning establishment is going to install one of two types of air-conditioning systems. These alternatives can be described as follows:

	Type 1	Type 2
First cost	$6,000	$8,000
Service life	8 years	12 years
Salvage value	$ 500	$ 500
Annual disbursements	$1,400	$ 900

At an annual interest rate of 15 percent, which of these systems is the more economical?

7-7 Two different tractors are being considered for purchase by a landscaping firm. Both have an estimated life of four years. However, tractor A will have a first cost of $10,000, whereas the cost of tractor B is $8,000. Annual disbursements for such things as labor, maintenance, repairs, and power will also differ. With tractor A, they are expected to be $8,500 during the first year and will increase at a rate of $100 per year thereafter. With tractor B, they are expected to be $9,000 during the first year and will increase at a rate of $150 per year thereafter. Finally, tractors A and B will probably have salvage values of $1,885 and $1,600, respectively. Having been told that the firm has a 10 percent rate-of-return requirement, you are asked to select the more economical alternative after computing the uniform annual cost of each tractor. What is your recommendation? Explain. (Ans. $11,386, $11,386)

7-8 A firm is planning to manufacture a new product. If it does, it will do so by one of two alternative methods. These can be described in part as follows:

	Alternative X	Alternative Y
First cost	$200,000	$500,000
Life	10 years	20 years
Salvage value	$ 20,000	$ 50,000
Annual revenues	$110,000	$116,000

Total annual disbursements for alternative X will be $70,000 a year for the first four years and $80,000 a year for the last six years of its life. Total annual disbursements for alternative Y will be a uniform $60,000 throughout its life.

The company's rate-of-return requirement is 8 percent. What is the total annual cost to be associated with each alternative?

Management wants to know whether or not it should manufacture the new product and, if so, by which of the two alternative methods. What is your recommendation and why? Would the fact that there is a high probability that annual revenues have been overestimated by $10,000 in each case have any effect on your decision? Explain.

7-9 Suppose that the original estimates given in the preceding problem are accurate. However, there is reason to believe that, if alternative X is selected, it will be succeeded at the end of its 10-year life by a method which will have a first cost of $300,000, a life of 10 years, a zero salvage value, uniform annual revenues of $110,000, and uniform annual disbursements of $60,000. Would this alter the original decision reached in the preceding problem? (Ans. −$6,125, −$6,168)

PART FIVE

PART FIVE

INVENTORY CONTROL

EIGHT

RELEVANT FACTORS IN INVENTORY CONTROL

In our discussion of production planning, mention had been made of the fact that a company may not adopt the production schedule suggested by the demand for the firm's products. Instead, this schedule might be adjusted to permit the firm to level out the demand for various factors of production and to produce or procure items in economic lot sizes. However, alternative production and procurement schedules must be evaluated on the basis of the costs to be associated with each, and one of these costs is the cost of carrying the inventories generated by the schedules under consideration. As this indicates, the subject of inventory control is an integral part of production planning, and we shall now examine this aspect of the planning procedure.

The area of inventory control is one in which the firm must decide what levels of inventory can be economically maintained. These inventories consist of raw materials and component parts which the company procures from external sources and component parts and finished assemblies which the company manufactures itself. The reason that a decision must be made concerning what quantities of purchased and manufactured items will be kept in stock is that there are certain cost advantages and disadvantages to be associated with every unit of inventory the firm maintains. However, for a given item, there will be some level of inventory which will yield a total cost which will be lower than the total cost generated by any other level. What the firm must do is determine what this most economical level is for each purchased and manufactured item and then maintain the inventory at this level.

THE FUNCTION OF INVENTORIES

Every firm must concern itself with the control of inventories because inventories perform certain important functions. To begin with, they serve to offset errors contained in the forecast of the demand for the company's products. If we ignored all other reasons for maintaining inventories, an ability to forecast the exact demand for various products would eliminate the need for maintaining any inventories. In a case such as this, raw materials and purchased parts could be scheduled to be delivered at the specific times at which they were required for production purposes. Similarly, finished goods could be scheduled to be completed at the specific times at which they were required to meet customer demand. However, this is rarely possible. Since the demand may be greater than anticipated, the firm may want to stock some additional raw materials, purchased parts, manufactured parts, and finished assemblies as a safety measure.

Next, inventories often permit more economical utilization of equipment, buildings, and manpower when the nature of the business is such that fluctuations in demand exist. As was pointed out earlier, a translation of the sales forecast into its equivalent demand for factors of production may yield a factor-of-production demand schedule which is characterized by fairly wide fluctuations. This is undesirable and suggests a need for leveling out these demand schedules. One way of doing so is to produce to stock during slack periods.

Another reason for maintaining inventories is that a willingness to do so permits the company to purchase or manufacture in economic lot sizes. To illustrate, a lot size equal to a one-day supply of an item may yield a negligible inventory of that item and, therefore, a negligible cost of carrying that inventory. However, this may be accompanied by an excessive annual ordering cost because of the large number of orders that will have to be placed per year. A larger lot size of, say, a one-month supply would, of course, increase the inventory level and, therefore, the annual inventory carrying cost. But this increased cost may be more than offset by the resultant decrease in the annual ordering cost. As we shall see, there is some order quantity that will minimize the sum of the inventory carrying cost and the ordering cost. This quantity is called the economic lot size, and it will usually be some quantity that exceeds the quantity required to satisfy the immediate demand for the item.

Inventories also contribute to the degree to which the various activities in the operations area are independent of each other. Raw-materials inventories eliminate the need for having the material delivered right at the moment its processing is scheduled to begin. Work-in-process inventories eliminate the need for having one operation completed right at the moment the next operation is scheduled to begin. And finished-goods inventories eliminate the need for having the last operation completed right at the moment the product is to be shipped to a customer. As this suggests, if the firm is willing to incur the costs of carrying inventories, it can realize reductions in the cost of coordinating the various phases of the production activity.

INVENTORY CLASSIFICATION

The inventory control problem is a difficult one if for no other reason but that the typical firm may find it necessary to carry inventories of thousands of different raw materials, supplies, parts, subassemblies, and assemblies. An attempt to maintain close control over the stock of each of these items may prove to be uneconomical from the standpoint of the demand such rigid control would generate for time and personnel. For this reason, it is usually advisable that management establish classifications which will enable it to decide upon the degree to which the individual items that are stocked should be controlled.

Various criteria exist on the basis of which a classification system can be developed. The most common of these is the annual dollar rate of use of the items. This would be obtained by multiplying each item's unit purchase or production cost by the number of units purchased or produced per year. Such an analysis may reveal that, during the past year, $500,000 worth of a given raw material was used. As opposed to this, the cost of another raw material during the same period may have been only $200. Obviously, the inventories of the first item should be controlled to a greater degree than those of the second.

This type of classification proves to be helpful because, as a rule, the firm will find that a relatively small percent of the items account for a large percent of the total rate of use. To illustrate, as shown in Figure 8-1, it may be that 10 percent of the items stocked account for 60 percent of the total annual usage, 25 percent of the items for 80 percent of the total annual usage, and the remaining 75 percent of the items for only 20 percent of the total annual usage. As also indicated in Figure 8-1, the resultant three categories of items are labeled A, B, and C, respectively. For this reason, this approach to inventory classification is called the "ABC system." But the important thing is that the results of such an analysis suggest that tight control be exercised over class A items, moderate control over class B items, and loose control over class C items. Of course, there is no reason why a firm cannot establish more than three such classifications.

Another basis for classifying inventories is the dollar investment in the respective items. For example, at the time an analysis is being made, it may be found that the inventory of one product represents a capital investment of $120,000 and that the inventory of some other product represents an investment of only $1,300. It is likely that a higher degree of control is

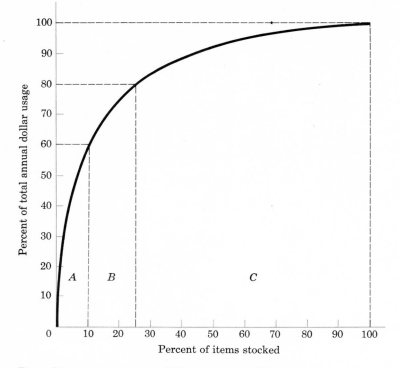

Figure 8-1   An example of an ABC inventory classification system

called for in the case of the first item than in the case of the second. In any event, this method of classification will also reveal that, very often, tight control need be exercised over a small percent of the total items being stocked. To illustrate, the results of the analysis depicted in Figure 8-2 show that 5 percent of the items account for about 50 percent of the dollar inventory investment at a given point in time, 25 percent of the items for about 90 percent of the investment, and the remaining 75 percent of the items for only 10 percent of the investment. Such findings can serve as the basis of an ABC or some similar classification.

Criteria of a nonquantitative nature may also be established for use in conjunction with those we have just considered. Tight control would probably be applied to those items whose supply is endangered by a threatened strike, to those items whose prices are characterized by wide and frequent price fluctuations, to those items which are subject to sudden obsolescence, to those items that are critical in the sense that a shortage would bring production activities to a standstill, and so on. But regardless of the

ABC CLASSIFICATION

ITEM NUMBER	PERCENT ITEMS	ON HAND INVESTMENT	CUM. ON HAND INVESTMENT	CUM. PERCENT INVESTMENT
9,034	5	467,170.00	467,170.00	51.81
9,282	10	187,170.00	654,340.00	72.57
*9,846	15	98,770.00	735,110.00	83.53
5,322	20	41,328.00	794,438.00	88.11
9,102	25	26,877.50	821,315.50	91.09
2,026	30	22,089.36	843,404.86	93.54
1,981	35	17,945.00	861,349.86	95.53
6,621	40	12,802.00	874,151.86	96.95
6,267	45	7,080.00	881,231.86	97.74
9,339	50	6,008.75	887,240.61	98.40
8,565	55	3,760.00	891,000.61	98.82
9,655	60	3,559.97	894,560.58	99.21
6,832	65	1,856.00	896,416.58	99.42
3,320	70	1,850.00	898,266.58	99.63
7,061	75	1,327.50	899,594.08	99.77
2,018	80	767.50	900,361.58	99.86
7,036	85	525.00	900,886.58	99.92
9,986	90	352.50	901,239.08	99.96
2,620	95	228.00	901,467.08	99.98
5,415	100	108.10	901,595.18	100.00

*NOTE: 15% of the item accounts for 83.53%
of the capital investment in inventory

Figure 8-2   An analysis of the total investment in inventories (Courtesy of The NCR Corporation)

criteria selected, they serve only to simplify the inventory control problem and not to eliminate it.

RELEVANT FACTORS

In the presentation of the major reasons for maintaining inventories, it was stated that there are specific costs which will be reduced if inventories are carried and that there are other costs that will be increased. In brief, certain factors encourage the maintenance of higher inventories, while others encourage the maintenance of lower inventories. Let us continue by considering the specific costs that fall into each of these categories. For purposes of illustration, we shall speak in terms of their average magnitude per year.

QUANTITY DISCOUNTS   In the case of purchased materials, the firm is often able to obtain a reduction in the unit purchase price if it purchases these items in larger lots. Since the same average number of units will be purchased per year regardless of the lot size, a lower unit purchase price will reduce the average annual purchase cost.

However, a decision to increase lot sizes in order to take advantage of available quantity discounts is a decision to increase the average inventory of these materials. Therefore, the factor of quantity discounts encourages the purchase of larger lots and, hence, the maintenance of larger inventories of purchased materials and parts.

SETUP COSTS   Setup costs are incurred every time a firm inaugurates production of a given item. These costs are fixed per setup because the same expense is incurred in setting up equipment which will then be used to manufacture 1 unit as is incurred in setting up equipment which will then be used to manufacture 1,000 units. The only exception to this statement would be the case in which a decision to manufacture larger lot sizes would result in the use of different manufacturing methods and, hence, a different setup. But for a given method of production, setup costs will remain constant. Consequently, since the same average number of units will be produced per year regardless of the lot size, larger lot sizes mean fewer setups per year and, therefore, lower setup costs per year. However, as the lot size increases, the average inventory of the item being produced will increase, and, hence, this cost element encourages the maintenance of larger inventories of manufactured parts and products.

DIRECT MATERIAL COSTS   Ordinarily, direct material costs are constant per unit of output. However, there are cases in which a relatively fixed number of units of scrap are produced before the correct adjustments can be made in equipment being set up for production purposes. When this occurs, it follows that the larger the lot size, the lower will be the average amount of material required per good unit of output. Consequently, the annual cost of materials will decrease, because the same number of good units will be produced per year, regardless of the lot size. This, of course, encourages the production of larger lot sizes and, therefore, the maintenance of higher average inventories.

DIRECT LABOR COSTS   As the size of the manufactured lots increases, the direct labor cost per unit of output may decrease for one or both of two reasons. The first of these coincides with the reason for unit direct material costs' decreasing under the same conditions. When a relatively fixed number of units of output are scrapped in the process of setting up and trying out the equipment, the scrap represents not only a material cost but also a labor cost. Consequently, just as the direct material cost per unit of output and per year goes on to decrease as the lot size increases, so will the direct labor cost.

Unit and annual direct labor costs will probably decrease as lot sizes increase for still another reason. It has been found that, when an operator begins to work on a new job, he passes through a warm-up period. During this period, his efficiency is likely to be lower than it will be in the subsequent period. Since the length of the warm-up period is relatively fixed for a specific task, the operator's average efficiency will increase as the length of the subsequent period increases. And the length of the subsequent period will increase as the lot size increases. In brief, larger lot sizes will probably be accompanied by a higher average labor efficiency. This will reduce the direct labor time and, in the absence of certain types of wage incentive plans, the direct labor cost per unit of output. With the average annual output remaining the same, the result is a lower average annual direct labor cost. Therefore, the factor of direct labor cost encourages the scheduling of larger lot sizes, which will serve to increase the average level of inventories.

PRODUCTION CONTROL AND PROCUREMENT COSTS Every time a product is to be manufactured, the production control department must schedule the work, prepare various forms and instructions for the shop, and determine the progress of production. The nature of these activities is such that the cost of performing them may be independent of the size of the order or may increase somewhat as the order size increases, but at a relatively lower rate. As a result, as lot sizes increase, fewer orders will be processed, and average annual production control costs will decrease. This will encourage the production of larger lots and, therefore, the maintenance of higher average inventories of the items involved.

Similarly, when materials or parts are to be purchased, purchase requisitions must be prepared, purchase orders must be placed, and paper work must be performed when the materials are received. As in the case of production control activities, the cost of these procurement activities may be independent of the size of the order or may increase by a smaller percentage than the percentage increase in the size of the order. Consequently, the firm would have an incentive to reduce the number of purchase orders by increasing the size of purchased lots and, therefore, the average level of its inventories. Doing so would reduce average annual procurement costs for purchased materials and parts.

OVERTIME AND SHIFT PREMIUM COSTS The factors considered thus far are characterized by the fact that they all will have some influence on the lot sizes in which a firm should produce or purchase. Let us now turn to a cost element which suggests a need for leveling out factor-of-production demand schedules by building up inventories. If the company adheres to demand schedules generated by the sales forecast, it may find that there will be periods in which plant capacity is inadequate. To provide the necessary capacity during these peak periods, the firm could schedule overtime work or add a second shift. If this is done, the company will usually have to pay an overtime premium or a shift premium to those employees assigned to the second or third shift. Obviously, this will raise labor costs for a given level of annual output. In addition, employees who work overtime or are assigned to the second or third shift often operate at a lower efficiency than do other employees. This tends to increase annual labor costs further. A possible alternative is to have the shop produce in advance during periods of lower demand. This will result in an increase in inventories of finished parts and products but will eliminate or minimize the additional costs to be associated with overtime or extra-shift operations. Therefore, we say that the existence of this cost element encourages the maintenance of higher average inventories of finished parts and products.

HIRING, TRAINING, AND LAYOFF COSTS   If the company chooses not to schedule overtime and extra-shift work during periods of peak demand, it has the alternative of hiring additional personnel during these periods and laying them off during periods of reduced demand. However, there are costs to be associated with this alternative. When new personnel are to be hired, they must be recruited and interviewed, their applications must be processed, appropriate records must be established, and very often they must be trained. Similarly, laying off personnel involves some paper work, interviews, and very often severance pay. Further, if the firm obtains a reputation of being unable to offer stable employment, it may encounter difficulties in its attempt to recruit qualified personnel. Those that are recruited may be relatively inefficient, with the result that labor costs for a given level of annual output will increase. Again, all these costs suggest a need for leveling out the demand for manpower, and this can be done by building up inventories during periods in which a reduced demand exists for the company's products. These cost factors, therefore, encourage the maintenance of higher inventories of finished parts and products.

It might also be mentioned that, if the company attempts to eliminate hiring, training, and layoff costs by retaining excess personnel on the roll during slack periods, average annual labor costs will be higher than they need be. Because of this, the incentive to level out the real demand for manpower will remain.

DEPRECIATION COSTS A policy of varying the number of employees on the roll also tends to increase the depreciation expense which the company incurs. If the company's goal is to avoid overtime and extra-shift work, it must provide its employees with the maximum building and equipment capacity they will require. For example, if a maximum of 50 lathe operators will be required at a particular point in time, 50 lathes must be made available for their use. If in a subsequent time period only 20 lathe operators will be employed, 30 lathes will simply be idle. However, the cost of depreciation is primarily a function of time rather than a function of the degree to which the asset is utilized. Therefore, during slack periods, the idle production facilities will continue to decrease in value.

The most effective method the firm has at its disposal for minimizing these depreciation costs is to minimize its capital investment. It can do this by leveling out the demand for its production facilities, and this can be accomplished by building up inventories during periods of reduced demand. By doing so, the firm will be utilizing each of its fixed assets more completely and, hence, can manage to meet the demand for its products through the use of fewer assets than would otherwise be necessary. Therefore, the factor of depreciation encourages the maintenance of higher average inventories of finished parts and products in the sense that it suggests that steps be taken to level out production schedules.

LOST CUSTOMER ORDERS Another factor which encourages the firm to carry higher inventories is the fact that, as the level of inventory decreases, the risk of not being able to meet the delivery date desired by a customer increases. The result may be that potential orders will be lost. The cost of this is the profit the firm would have realized on these orders.

This risk can be minimized if the firm stocks larger amounts of raw materials, purchased parts, and finished goods. The finished-goods inventory will, in some cases, enable the company to promise immediate delivery of the items called for on an order. In other cases, the raw-material and component-part inventories will enable the firm to begin processing the products called for on an order in time to establish what the customer will consider to be a satisfactory delivery date.

It may be argued, however, that if the receipt of an order is endangered because the promised delivery date may prove to be unsatisfactory, special arrangements can be made to "rush" the order to completion. This usually involves taking steps to expedite the procurement of purchased materials, rearranging shop schedules to permit the earlier completion of the order under consideration, working overtime, and so on. While it is true that this course of action may be effective, it is also true that it can be followed only at some cost to the company. A rush order is an order that calls for special attention, and this kind of attention costs money.

DETERIORATION Up to this point, we have considered cost factors which encourage the firm to carry relatively large inventories. But there are forces which act in the opposite direction. The first of these is the factor of deterioration. Deterioration is an expense to the company because the items involved may have to be scrapped, reworked, or sold at a lower price. And, of course, if something is subject to deterioration, the more of it the firm has on hand, the greater will be the amount of total deterioration. Therefore, this factor encourages the maintenance of lower inventories.

OBSOLESCENCE Another factor which encourages the firm to carry smaller inventories is obsolescence. Raw materials, component parts, or finished products become obsolete when the demand for them decreases to a point at which they must either be scrapped or sold at a reduced price. A new automobile dealer who has a stock of the current year's model will find that his stock is somewhat obsolete as soon as next year's model is available. A retailer of women's dresses may find that some of his stock has become obsolete because new styles are now being promoted. In all such cases, the occurrence of obsolescence creates some loss to the firm that is carrying inventories of the affected items. These items might be not only the finished products but also the materials and component parts used to manufacture them. Again, it is obvious that the average annual cost of obsolescence will vary in proportion to the size of the inventories being maintained. Consequently, the presence of this potential cost encourages the maintenance of lower inventories.

TAXES For tax purposes, the value of the inventories a company has on hand is very often included in the assessed valuation of the property it owns. As a result, the greater the investment in inventories, the higher will be the firm's taxes. It follows, therefore, that when inventories are subject to a property tax, the company will be inclined to carry lower inventories than it otherwise would.

INTEREST Inventories are just like any other asset in that they call for a capital investment. Some firms find it necessary to borrow money to be able to make the required investment in inventories; if so, they obligate themselves not only to return the borrowed funds but also to pay an interest charge. Other companies are able to finance inventories through the use of internal funds; if so, they give up the opportunity to invest these funds in other sources from which they could realize a rate of return. Therefore, whether it uses external or internal funds, the company experiences an interest expense when it invests in inventories. It is clear that the larger the investment, the greater will be this interest cost. As a result, insofar as this factor is concerned, it is to the company's advantage to keep the size of its inventories as small as possible.

STORAGE COSTS As a rule, an increase in the level of inventories carried by the company is accompanied by an increase in storage costs. Storage costs include such things as the cost of floor space, the cost of heat, light, and maintenance for the area in which inventories are stocked, and the cost of insurance. When these costs increase as inventories increase, this factor encourages the maintenance of lower inventories.

HANDLING COSTS Two more factors will be considered. They are unique in the sense that they can either discourage or encourage the maintenance of higher levels of inventory. The first of these is the cost of handling. Materials and parts must be transported from the receiving department to the storeroom, from the storeroom to the point of use, from one work station to another, and from the final work station to the stockroom. On occasion, the cost per move will be almost constant for a certain range of quantities handled. For example, it may cost about as much to have a materials handler transport a single skid containing 50 parts as it does to have him transport a single skid containing 100 parts. In all such cases, handling costs per unit produced or purchased will decrease as the quantities handled are increased, and these quantities will increase as the manufactured and purchased lot sizes increase. Lower unit handling costs will yield lower annual handling costs because the amount of material handled per year will be unaffected by the amount of material handled at any one time. Therefore, the factor of handling costs encourages the procurement and production of larger lot sizes, which is synonymous with maintaining higher inventories.

In other cases, however, it may be that increased inventories will result in the overcrowding of storage areas. When this is true, the handling of materials may become more difficult and, therefore, more time-consuming. Consequently, annual handling costs will tend to increase. When this occurs, it proves to be a force which encourages the firm to carry smaller inventories.

PRICE CHANGES The second factor which may tend to encourage or discourage the maintenance of larger inventories is that of anticipated price changes. At a given point in time, purchased items will be available at a certain price. If the firm has reason to believe that these prices will increase in the near future, it will be inclined to buy additional stocks at the present time when it can take advantage of the more favorable price. Conversely, if the firm has reason to believe that these prices will decrease in the near future, it will be inclined to keep its purchases at a minimum at the present time and replenish its stocks after the prices have dropped. As a result, anticipated price increases encourage the building up of inventories of purchased materials and parts, and anticipated price decreases encourage the reduction of these inventories.

This brings us to the close of our presentation of the relevant inventory costs. However, we have not considered an exhaustive list of relevant factors, but only those most frequently encountered. One could add such things as the threat of a strike in a supplier's plant, plans to shut down certain production facilities for rehabilitation, and so on.

In any single problem, of course, not all the factors discussed will have to be considered. This is so because, in any one case, the magnitudes of some of these costs will not be affected by the choice of inventory level. When this occurs, the costs involved can be ignored.

INVENTORY LEVELS AND PRODUCTION SCHEDULES

At this point, it might be noted that one type of problem in the area of inventory control can be analyzed with a technique we have already discussed, namely, the uniform annual cost method. The problem is that of determining the most economical production schedule when significant fluctuations exist in the demand for a firm's product. Such a schedule will generate the most economical combination of manufacturing costs and inventory carrying costs.

In general, the determination will begin with a description of alternative production schedules. At one extreme, the firm can adopt the fluctuating schedule suggested by the expected demand for the product. If it does so, the resultant inventories will be at a minimum. At the other extreme, the firm can adopt a uniform production schedule. Doing so will reduce manufacturing costs but will generate a need for carrying inventories of finished goods. Between these extremes, there will be a number of alternatives with the following characteristics: (1) Each will reduce but not eliminate the fluctuations in the production schedule suggested by the demand for the firm's product, and (2) each will increase the inventories being carried by a smaller amount than would the uniform production schedule.

After the firm has determined all such alternative production schedules, it can go on to the second step in the analysis. In this step, cognizance is taken of the fact that any one production schedule can be met in a number of different ways. Each of these ways can be said to represent an operating plan. Let us consider what some of these operating plans might be with reference to a fluctuating production schedule.

One way in which such a schedule can be met is to procure the buildings, equipment, and manpower needed, during the period of peak production, with a one-shift operation and no overtime work; furthermore, during periods of reduced output, the firm could keep the excess employees on the roll to reduce hiring, training, and layoff costs. A second operating plan would be like the one just described with the exception that employees would be hired, trained, and laid off as required so as not to have idle manpower capacity at any time. Still another operating plan would be to procure buildings, equipment, and manpower needed during the period of minimum output but to schedule overtime work when a greater level of output is required.

We could develop other plans, but these suffice to bring out the fact that a given production schedule can be met in more than one manner and that the resultant manufacturing cost will be affected by the operating plan selected. In any event, all such alternative plans must be described for each schedule and the plan which will minimize the manufacturing cost for a given schedule determined. This determination can be made by calculating the uniform annual capital and operating costs generated by each plan and selecting the plan which yields the minimum total annual cost. The end result of all this would be that the most economical operating plan for meeting each of the production schedules being considered would now be known. Further, in the process of determining this plan for the respective schedules, the firm will have determined the minimum possible average annual manufacturing cost to be associated with each of these production schedules.

The firm must now go on to compute the cost of carrying the inventories generated by the respective production schedules. If manufacturing costs have been expressed in terms of a uniform annual equivalent, it becomes necessary that the inventory carrying cost also be described in terms of an average annual cost. This calls for estimating the cost of carrying 1 unit of inventory in stock for one year. Next, the average inventory to be associated with each production schedule must be ascertained. A knowledge of the average inventory and the unit annual carrying cost permits the firm to compute the average annual inventory carrying cost. This cost, when added to the annual manufacturing cost, yields the total annual cost of the production schedule being considered. The determination of these totals for the alternative schedules and their corresponding inventory levels enables the firm to select the most economical alternative, which is that combination of production schedule and inventory level which will minimize the total annual cost.

The difficulties of application one would encounter with the use of this quantitative method of analysis are easily recognized. The determination of alternative production schedules and operating plans is no simple matter. Furthermore, there is the task of making the estimates that are necessary for the determination of the annual cost of each alternative, and these estimates are likely to contain errors. However, these difficulties must be accepted because of the unavailability of a better approach. Nevertheless, the presence of these difficulties requires that management exercise judgment when reviewing the results of the analysis and selecting the course of action to be followed.

Let us now go on to consider the approaches that can be employed in the analysis of other types of inventory control problems.

QUESTIONS

8-1   What is meant by inventory control?

8-2   Why does the typical company carry inventories of raw materials, component parts, and finished goods?

8-3   What cost factors encourage the firm to adopt production and procurement policies which bring about an increase in average inventory levels? Explain why each does so.

8-4   What factors encourage the firm to adopt production and procurement policies which bring about a decrease in average inventory levels? Explain why each does so.

8-5   What are some examples of factors that might either encourage or discourage the maintenance of higher inventories? Explain.

8-6   How are *relevant* inventory costs defined?

8-7   In what respect are production scheduling and inventory control interrelated?

8-8   Describe the approach that can be employed to determine the production schedule which will minimize the sum of the resultant manufacturing and inventory carrying costs.

8-9   What is the purpose of an inventory classification system such as the ABC method?

PROBLEMS

8-1   It is estimated that 15,000 units of a given product will be manufactured during the coming year. Setup and production control costs are fixed at $36 per order. What will be the annual setup and production control costs if the item is produced in lot sizes of 500 units? Of 5,000 units?

8-2   Approximately 60,000 units of an item are purchased per year by a mail-order firm. When 10,000 units are procured at a time, ordering and receiving costs are $72 per order. However, these costs increase by only 25 percent when the lot size is doubled. What will be the annual ordering and receiving costs when lot sizes are 10,000 and 20,000 units, respectively?

8-3   If a company produces in accordance with the expected demand for one of its products, the resultant inventories will be negligible. An alternative is to adopt a production schedule which will level out the demand for factors of production but will also generate an average inventory of 450 units. Each of the units represents an investment of $120 by the company.

Carrying costs consist of deterioration, storage, and interest. The monthly deterioration expense is estimated to be 1 percent of the total investment in inventory, the storage expense to be 0.8 percent, and the interest expense to be 1.25 percent. What total annual carrying cost is to be associated with the 450-unit average inventory level? (Ans. $19,764)

8-4   A hospital's annual rate of use of a pain reliever of a certain type is 60,000 tablets. The price of the item is $0.10 per unit when purchased in quantities of 1,000 units, $0.09 in quantities of 5,000, and $0.08 in quantities of 10,000. What annual purchase cost would each of these order quantities generate?

8-5   The procurement time for an item sold by a men's clothing store is one month. At the beginning of a particular week, 28 units of the item are in stock. A replenishment order is expected in three weeks. For every unit demanded but not in stock, the store incurs a loss of $12. The actual demand during the week proves to be 41 units. What will be the cost of lost customer orders because of the resultant shortage? What would the stockout cost have been had the beginning-of-week inventory been 35 units?

8-6   The required quantity of a given product can be manufactured in the week during which it is demanded. The sales forecast for the item for a future 10-week period is as follows:

Week	Demand, units	Week	Demand, units
1	650	6	820
2	1,040	7	250
3	1,310	8	1,660
4	520	9	950
5	1,480	10	1,720

a If the firm is interested only in minimizing inventories of the item, to what production schedule should it adhere? What will be the resultant end-of-week inventories?

b If the firm is interested only in leveling the demand for factors of production, to what production schedule should it adhere? What will be the resultant end-of-week inventories?

c Give an example of a production schedule which will reduce the fluctuations in demand for factors of production but will not maximize the amount of inventory carried. What will be the resultant end-of-week inventories?

8-7   On the basis of a five-year sales forecast, a company has developed a number of alternative production schedules. For each of these, possible operating plans have been prepared. To illustrate, three such plans have been developed for one of the production schedules. The first calls for the procurement of an amount of equipment such that no overtime work would be required and for hiring and laying off employees as the demand for manpower varies. This plan would require a $200,000 investment in facilities which would have a salvage value of $20,000 at the end of the five-year period. Annual operating costs would be $64,000.

A second plan would necessitate the procurement of the minimum required amount of equipment. Specifically, only $150,000 would have to be invested in facilities which are expected to have a $15,000 salvage value at the end of five years. Furthermore, the plan calls for fewer employees but significantly more overtime work with the result that annual operating costs would be $75,000.

Finally, the third plan would call for an amount of equipment which exceeds that involved in the second plan but is less than that involved in the first. Some overtime work would be scheduled, and excess employees would be kept on the roll during slack periods. The result of all this is that $175,000 would be invested in equipment whose salvage value would be $17,500 in five years and that annual operating costs would be $69,000.

Which of these operating plans would yield the minimum uniform annual cost at an interest rate of 12 percent per year? (Ans. Plan 2, $114,251)

8-8   A company is considering two alternative schedules for the production of a part which is a component of a number of different assemblies. The most economical operating plan for each of these schedules can be described as follows:

	Schedule 1	Schedule 2
Required investment	$275,000	$340,000
Life	8 years	10 years
Salvage value	$ 25,000	$ 20,000
Annual disbursements	$110,000	$ 95,000
Additional annual revenues	$ 0	$ 2,000

Schedule 1 is expected to generate an average inventory of 2,100 units, and schedule 2 of 1,300 units. Annual inventory carrying costs are estimated to be $6 per unit. The cost of money to the firm is 15 percent per year. Which schedule is the more attractive on the basis of a uniform annual cost comparison?

NINE

INVENTORY CONTROL UNDER CERTAINTY

The basic technique for making cost comparisons is the uniform annual cost method. But in addition to this technique, other quantitative methods of analysis have been developed for use in the area of inventory control. It is these approaches that we shall now consider, beginning with the method for ascertaining the lot sizes in which it is most economical to produce or purchase items when the demands for these items are known with certainty.

THE MAXIMUM-MINIMUM SYSTEM

The economic lot size approach to the maintenance of satisfactory inventory levels is best exemplified by the maximum-minimum system of inventory control. The mechanics of this system are as follows: The company will specify, for a given material, part, or product, three things: (1) the minimum inventory it wants to have on hand, (2) the reorder point, that is, the point at which additional units are to be ordered, and (3) the reorder quantity, or lot size. If the rate of use of the item is constant and if the entire lot is delivered at one time, this system can be described schematically as shown in Figure 9-1.

To illustrate how this system works, let us suppose, first, that the company decides that it wants to have a minimum of 100 units of an item on hand at any one time. Second, whenever it orders the item for stock-replenishment purposes, it will order 500 units. The question that arises is: At what point should the company place its order for these 500 units? To answer, we must know two things. One of these is the lead time or procurement time, that is, the length of time required to obtain an order after it is placed. The other is the rate at which the item is being used. Let us assume that, in our example, one month is required for procurement of the 500 units and that the item is used at a rate of 200 units per month. Therefore, after the order is placed, one month will elapse before it is

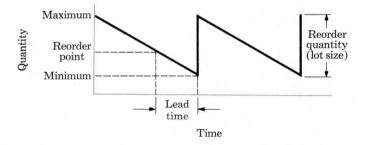

Figure 9-1   A schematic presentation of the maximum-minimum system of inventory control

delivered. However, the rate of use is 200 units per month. As a result, 200 units will be used during the procurement period. Since the company does not want the inventory to drop below 100 units, an order must be placed when the inventory level reaches 300 units. This is equal to the minimum inventory of 100 units plus the 200 units which will be used while the order is being processed. In equation form, we can say that

Reorder point = minimum inventory
        + (procurement time × consumption rate)

When using this equation, one must take care to express the consumption rate and the procurement time in the correct units. If the consumption rate is given as a rate per day, the procurement time must be stated in days. If the consumption rate is given as a rate per week, the procurement time must be stated in weeks. In our example, the consumption rate was given as being 200 units per month and the procurement time as one month. Substituting these values and the minimum inventory of 100 units in our equation, we obtain

Reorder point = 100 units + (1 month) (200 units/month)
       = 300 units

To continue with our example, we can say that the minimum inventory will be 100 units, the reorder point will be 300 units, and the reorder quantity will be 500 units. Since these 500 units are expected to be delivered when the inventory reaches 100 units, the maximum inventory on hand at any one time will be the sum of these two figures, or 600 units.

BASIC ASSUMPTIONS   Before we go on, let us note the assumptions which underlie the described system. First, it is assumed that the rate of use of the item involved is constant. Second, it is assumed that the entire lot will be delivered at one time. Third, since the reorder point is a function of the procurement time and the rate of use, it is assumed that these can be estimated with a fair degree of accuracy and that the procurement time, like the rate of use, will be constant. If any one of these assumptions is incorrect, the system cannot be used. However, if a different set of conditions prevails, a similar system can sometimes be developed which will reflect these conditions. At a later point in this presentation, we shall consider one such variation.

AVERAGE INVENTORY   While the application of the system is extremely simple, it can be applied only after the company has selected a minimum inventory and the reorder quantity. We are ignoring the need for knowing the rate of use of the item involved and the procurement time because the values of these factors are determined on the basis of estimates. As opposed to this, the determination of the values of the minimum inventory and reorder quantity calls for an analytical approach on the part of the company. The reason for this is that the average inventory being carried will be a function of both the minimum inventory and the reorder quantity. To illustrate, let us return to our example in which the minimum inventory was 100 units and the reorder quantity 500 units. If everything takes place as planned, the 500 units will be delivered when the inventory on hand reaches 100 units. As a result, the maximum inventory will be 600 units. If the rate of use is uniform, the average inventory will simply be the average of the maximum and minimum inventories, or 350 units. This can be found from the following expression:

$$\text{Average inventory} = \frac{\text{minimum inventory} + \text{maximum inventory}}{2}$$

$$= \frac{100 + 600}{2} = 350 \text{ units}$$

Now, if the reorder quantity is kept at 500 units and the minimum inventory is reduced to 0, the maximum inventory drops to 500 units. The average inventory will then be as follows:

$$\text{Average inventory} = \frac{0 + 500}{2} = 250 \text{ units}$$

Similarly, if the minimum inventory is kept at 100 units and the reorder quantity is increased to 700 units, the maximum inventory is raised to 800 units. The average inventory will then be as follows:

$$\text{Average inventory} = \frac{100 + 800}{2} = 450 \text{ units}$$

All this brings out the fact that variations in either the minimum inventory or the reorder quantity cause variations in the average inventory.

But since the cost of maintaining inventories will vary with the size of
the average inventory, the firm must determine the average level at which
this cost will be a minimum. Before we begin this determination, let us
first investigate the reason for maintaining a minimum inventory in excess
of 0 units.

MINIMUM INVENTORIES

The reason for maintaining minimum inventories is suggested by the name
many firms assign to these inventories. They are referred to as "safety
stocks." If it were true that the item being stored would be used at a uniform predictable rate and that the procurement time for a replenishment
order would be some fixed predictable time period, the firm would be
able to adhere to a minimum inventory of zero. Under these conditions,
replenishment stock would be received just at the point at which the existing inventory was exhausted. This arrangement would be desirable because, with a given reorder quantity, it would serve to minimize the average inventory being carried.

However, a realistic approach to the problem compels the company
to accept the fact that rates of use and procurement times will, on occasion, be greater than those estimated. In either case, the result is that the
demand during the procurement period will be greater than anticipated.
For example, the firm may estimate that the rate of use will be 200 units
per month and the procurement time, one month. If this were always true
the firm could place an order when the stock on hand reached a level of
200 units, and the additional stock would be received just when the balance
on hand reached zero. But it may be that a particular lot is not received
in a month; instead, 1½ months elapse. If this were the case and the rate
of use remained at 200 units per month, the storeroom would run out of
stock one-half month before the replenishment order was received. During
this period, it would receive requests for 100 units of the item which it
would be unable to satisfy. In another case, it may be that the replenishment order will be received in the estimated time of one month but that
the rate of use will increase to 300 units per month during this time. Again,
with a reorder point of 200 units, the storeroom would find that it could
not fill all the requests for the item.

Because there are costs to be associated with an out-of-stock condition, the firm will ordinarily maintain some positive minimum inventory.
In doing so, it provides a safety stock from which the storeroom can draw
in the event that the demand during the procurement period is greater
than expected.

As all this suggests, the function of the minimum inventory is not to enable the firm to produce or purchase in economic lot sizes, but to provide for unexpected increases in demand. Because our primary interest at this point is in the determination of the economic lot size, we shall drop the topic of safety stocks for the moment and go on to consider the size of reorder quantities. This means that we shall assume, first, that the company is able to predict exactly what the rate of use and procurement time for a given item will be and, second, that no variations will take place in this rate of use and procurement time. Consequently, the company will have no need for maintaining safety stocks, and the minimum inventory will be zero.

ECONOMIC LOT SIZE DETERMINATION

With a given minimum inventory, as the reorder quantity increases, so does the average inventory. As a result, we expect an increase in the lot size to be accompanied by a rise in such costs as storage, interest, obsolescence, deterioration, and taxes per time period. On the other hand, as the reorder quantity increases, fewer lots must be ordered per time period. As a result, we expect an increase in the lot size to be accompanied by a drop in such costs per unit and per time period as setup, material, labor, purchase price, materials handling, production control, and ordering. The result is that we have two opposing forces at play. One encourages and the other discourages the production and purchase of larger lot sizes.

Usually, as the lot size of a given item begins to increase, those costs per time period that tend to decrease as the lot size increases will decrease at a *faster* rate than the rate at which the other costs will increase. Consequently, the total cost per time period will continue to decrease as the lot size is increased. At some point, however, this cost will reach a minimum. Beyond this point, those costs that tend to decrease as the lot size increases will decrease at a *slower* rate than the rate at which the other costs will increase. Therefore, the total cost per time period will begin to increase as the lot size is increased beyond the point at which the minimum cost is reached. This can be depicted graphically, as is done in Figure 9-2.

In Figure 9-2, the lot size which yields the lowest cost per time period is noted by the letter Q on the X axis. This lot size is called the economic lot size and represents the reorder quantity to which the company should adhere for a given raw material, component part, or finished product if it wants to minimize its costs.

One possible approach to the determination of this lot size is obvious. The company can assume different values for the reorder quantity, estimate the relevant costs to be associated with each of these assumed values,

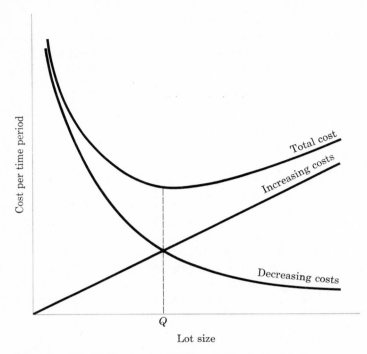

Figure 9-2   Cost patterns generated by variations in the lot size

calculate the total cost of each, and then select that lot size which yields the lowest total cost. Let us illustrate this approach by means of an example.

AN ILLUSTRATION   Suppose that a manufacturer of small electric motors purchases the housings for one type of these motors. The housings are used in the assembly of the motor at a uniform rate of 300 units per day. Since the plant operates an average of 250 days per year, this is equivalent to a demand of 75,000 housings per year.

The manufacturer has decided to maintain a minimum inventory of zero units. Therefore, he has only to calculate the order quantity which represents the economic lot size. He begins this calculation by estimating the values of what he considers to be the relevant costs. First, he notes that the purchase price is $0.50 per housing regardless of the quantity he buys at any one time and, therefore, can be ignored in the cost comparison. Next, he estimates the ordering cost to be fixed at $20 per order; this consists of the cost of placing the order, receiving it, and transporting it to the stockroom. Furthermore, the cost of carrying the average inventory generated by the lot size is expected to be $0.077 per unit per year;

the elements of this cost in this case are storage, deterioration, obsolescence, and interest. Finally, although he considers other factors, the manufacturer concludes that they will be unaffected by the order quantity.

In summary, the data given to us and the symbols we shall assign to these data are as follows:

C = consumption rate = 75,000 units per year

P = purchase price = $0.50 per unit

B = ordering cost = $20 per order

E = carrying cost = $0.077 per unit per year

M = minimum inventory = 0 units

Our problem is to calculate the economic lot size. We shall do this by assuming different lot sizes until we find that lot size which will yield the lowest cost per year. The reason we shall work with annual costs is that much of our cost data is already expressed in terms of costs per year. However, we could have worked with, say, average daily costs just as well.

Let us begin by arbitrarily selecting a lot size of 1,000 housings. Now, regardless of what the order quantity is, the firm will purchase an average of 75,000 housings per year. Therefore, with a lot size of 1,000, the annual purchase cost of the housings will be equal to the 75,000 units times the $0.50 purchase price per unit, or $37,500. But because this cost is not affected by the lot size, it can and will be ignored in our analysis.

Next, we are told that the ordering cost is $20 per order. If lots of size 1,000 are purchased and 75,000 units are to be procured, the number of orders that must be placed per year is equal to 75,000 divided by 1,000, or 75. Since the cost of procurement is $20 per order, the annual ordering cost will be equal to the 75 orders per year times the $20 per order, or $1,500. Using the symbol X to represent the lot size and the other given symbols to represent the other factors, we can say that

$$\text{Annual ordering cost} = \frac{C}{X}(B) = \frac{75,000}{1,000}(\$20) = \$1,500$$

What remains to be considered is the annual inventory carrying cost. But before we can calculate this cost, we must determine the average inventory that will be carried. We saw earlier that, when the rate of use is constant, the average inventory is equal to the average of the minimum and maximum inventories. If the minimum inventory is 0 units, as it is in this case, a reorder quantity of 1,000 units yields a maximum inventory of 1,000 units. Therefore,

$$\text{Average inventory} = \frac{0 + 1,000}{2} = 500 \text{ units}$$

To put this more simply, we can say that, when the minimum inventory is 0 units, the average inventory will be equal to one-half the lot size.

Since an average of 500 units will be carried and the carrying cost is $0.077 per unit per year, the annual carrying cost will be equal to 500 units times the $0.077 per unit per year, or $38.50. In terms of symbols

$$\text{Annual carrying cost} = \frac{X}{2}(E) = \frac{1,000}{2}(\$0.077) = \$38.50$$

This takes care of all the relevant factors. To obtain the total annual cost of a policy of adhering to a lot size of 1,000 units, we need only find the sum of the annual ordering cost and the annual carrying cost. When we do so, we obtain the following:

Total annual cost = $1,500 + $38.50 = $1,538.50

This total cost can be expressed in the following form:

$$\text{Total annual cost} = \frac{CB}{X} + \frac{XE}{2} \tag{9-1}$$

An examination of Eq. (9-1) reveals that the only variable it contains is the lot size X. All the other symbols represent data which are fixed in a given problem.

Once we have a general expression of this type for the total annual cost, the computation of the annual costs to be associated with other lot sizes becomes a matter of arithmetic. We need only substitute other values for the lot size X in Eq. (9-1) and solve for the annual cost. If our assumed values of the lot size increase in steps of 1,000, beginning with 1,000 and ending with 10,000, Eq. (9-1) will yield the following annual costs:

Lot size (X)	Ordering cost	Carrying cost	Total cost (Y)
1,000	$1,500	$ 38.50	$1,538.50
2,000	750	77.00	827.00
3,000	500	115.50	615.50
4,000	375	154.00	529.00
5,000	300	192.50	492.50
6,000	250	231.00	481.00
7,000	214	269.50	483.50
8,000	187	308.00	495.00
9,000	167	346.50	513.50
10,000	150	385.00	535.00

An examination of this table reveals that the minimum total cost is reached when the lot size is about 6,000 units. We say about 6,000 units because we only know that a lot size of 5,000 or 7,000 generates a higher cost. But it may be that a lot size of, say, 5,900 or 6,200 will yield a lower cost. To be certain, we should have to assume lot sizes slightly below and slightly above 6,000. In any case, we can say that the manufacturer should purchase the housings in lots of approximately 6,000 units.

A SIMPLER APPROACH

The approach we have considered is not difficult. However, it can be tedious and time-consuming. For this reason, a simpler method has been developed which will yield the same result. This method calls for deriving, from the total annual cost equation, a formula for the lot size that will yield the minimum total annual cost. The use of this expression eliminates the need for a trial-and-error approach. We shall consider two means for obtaining the formula.

THE ECONOMIC LOT SIZE FORMULA   In our example, we found the equation for the total annual cost Y to be

$$Y = \frac{CB}{X} + \frac{XE}{2}$$

The first term in this expression represents the annual ordering cost; and the second, the annual carrying cost. It has been found that the nature of this total cost function is such that the total cost will be a minimum for that value of the lot size X at which the annual ordering cost is equal to the annual carrying cost. Therefore, we can say that the total annual cost will be a minimum when

$$\frac{CB}{X} = \frac{XE}{2}$$

Solving this expression for the unknown lot size X, we obtain

$$X = \sqrt{\frac{2CB}{E}} \tag{9-2}$$

By substituting the data given to us in this formula, we can solve for the economic lot size directly.

THE USE OF CALCULUS   A knowledge of calculus permits one to find the minimum cost point in still another way. Again, we should begin with the total cost function which we know to be

$$Y = \frac{CB}{X} + \frac{XE}{2}$$

Next, to obtain the value of X at which the total annual cost Y will reach a minimum, we find the first derivative D_x of the function and equate this derivative to 0. Doing so yields

$$D_x = -\frac{CB}{X^2} + \frac{E}{2} = 0$$

Then we solve for the lot size X and find that the total annual cost Y reaches a minimum when

$$X = \sqrt{\frac{2CB}{E}} \tag{9-3}$$

It should be noted that Eq. (9-3) is the same as Eq. (9-2) and, hence, that we obtain the same result by each of the two methods.

THE FORMULA APPLIED To return to our example, if we substitute our given numerical values in Eq. (9-3), we find that the economic lot size is equal to

$$X = \sqrt{\frac{2\,(75,000)\,(\$20)}{\$0.077}} = 6,250 \text{ units}$$

The explanation for the difference between this result and the result obtained by our trial-and-error method has already been suggested. When assuming different values for the lot size, we increased these assumed values in steps of 1,000. Therefore, our earlier result of 6,000 units was as close as we were able to get to the correct answer. As opposed to this, given a certain set of data, Eq. (9-3) yields the exact answer and has the added advantage of being based on an approach which, from the standpoint of time and effort, is more satisfactory than the original one.

It might also be mentioned that Eq. (9-3) is called an economic lot size formula. Because the value of the lot size it yields is the economic lot size, whereas the symbol X represents a variable lot size, it is customary to substitute a different symbol for this particular value of the lot size. The symbol most commonly used is Q. Therefore, we shall say that

$$Q = \sqrt{\frac{2CB}{E}} \tag{9-4}$$

where $C =$ consumption rate per period

$B =$ cost of placing and receiving an order

$E =$ cost of carrying 1 unit of inventory for 1 period

The only restrictions on the use of this general formula are that the rate of use of the item be uniform, that the entire lot be received at one time, and that the unit cost of the item be constant. However, when applying this formula, care must be taken to express the factors it contains in the correct units. The cost of placing and receiving an order will always be some amount per order. But if the consumption rate is the rate *per year,* then the carrying cost must be the cost per unit *per year.* If the consumption rate is a rate *per day,* then the carrying cost must be the cost per unit *per day,* and so on. In brief, these two factors must be expressed in terms of the same time period.

In conclusion, it should be stated that although this economic lot size formula has been developed on the basis of an illustration involving a purchased item, it can be applied as well to cases in which the item is manufactured. The only difference will be that when the item is manufactured, the specific factors which represent the cost of placing and receiving an order will be different. These fixed costs per order would then take the form of production control costs, handling costs, setup costs, and the like.

ANOTHER ECONOMIC LOT SIZE FORMULA

If the assumptions that underlie the economic lot size formula we have just developed are not valid, the formula cannot be used. However, other formulas have been derived for other sets of conditions. We shall now consider one of those other sets of conditions and develop a formula that would be appropriate for use under those conditions.

In some cases, the entire lot is not delivered at one time but at a uniform rate over a period of time. For example, it may be that a firm's stockroom will submit a manufacturing requisition for 500 units of a given item. The shop may go into production on this item a week later. When it does, it may produce the item at a rate of 100 units a day for five days. However, rather than temporarily store the completed units until the entire order is completed, the shop may arrange to have 100 units delivered to the stockroom each day. As a result, the delivery would take place over a five-day period. During this period, there would, of course, be some demand for the item. If the rate of use is, say, 20 units per day, the inventory will be built up at a rate of 100 minus 20, or 80, units per day for five days.

We shall now describe this condition by means of a graph. But before

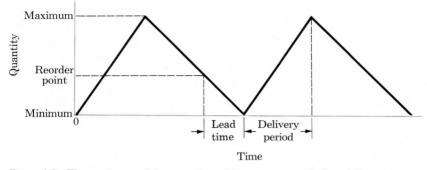

Figure 9-3   **The maximum-minimum system of inventory control when delivery occurs over a period of time**

we do, let us note all the assumptions underlying this system. First, we shall assume, as before, that the minimum inventory is to be zero. Second, the rate of use is assumed to be constant. Third, it is assumed that the item will be received at a uniform rate over some period of time. Finally, an implied assumption is that the procurement time is constant and that the rate of use and the rate of delivery can be predicted with a fair degree of accuracy. Given all these assumptions, the system can be described in general terms as shown in Figure 9-3.

On the basis of these assumed conditions, let us determine how the economic lot size can be ascertained. The approach to be employed can best be explained by means of an illustration.

AN ILLUSTRATION   Suppose that a company manufactures a gear which is a component part of a number of its finished products. At the present time, the gear is produced in lot sizes of 3,000 units. The rate of production is 1,000 units per day, and this is the rate at which completed gears are delivered to the stockroom. The demand for the part is a uniform 600 units per day.

The company, however, wants to determine whether the 3,000 lot size to which it is adhering is the economic lot size. The firm begins its analysis by estimating the values of what it considers to be the relevant costs. First, it finds that the total cost of the production control, setup, and handling activities is relatively fixed at $10 per lot. Direct production costs amount to $2 per gear. Also, there are certain carrying costs to be associated with each unit of inventory. These include interest, taxes, deterioration, and obsolescence. The total of these carrying costs is estimated to be $0.001 per unit per day. This total has been estimated on a per day basis, because the inventory will be increasing at some rate per day. Consequently, other relevant factors will have to be expressed in terms of the same time period.

With these data at its disposal, the firm is in a position to determine the economic lot size. Before we see how this is done, it should be mentioned that the fact that the company is currently adhering to a lot size of 3,000 units is of no significance. This information was included because we shall use this lot size in the development of the general expression for the total cost to be associated with a given lot size. In any case, let us begin by summarizing the data given to us and listing the symbols which will be used to represent each of these items of information. This summary and these symbols are as follows:

R = delivery rate = 1,000 units per day

C = consumption rate = 600 units per day

V = direct production costs = $2 per unit

B = ordering cost = $10 per order

E = carrying cost = $0.001 per unit per day

The first step in the analysis calls for developing the general expression for the total cost generated by the lot size. In this case, we shall consider the total average *daily* cost, because the data involving a time element are given on a per day basis. This total cost will consist of the ordering cost and the carrying cost. As this suggests, the average daily production cost will be ignored, because it is unaffected by the lot size.

Insofar as the ordering cost is concerned, the average number of orders placed per day will be equal to the consumption rate per day of 600 units divided by the lot size X of 3,000 units, or $\frac{1}{5}$. In other words, one order will be placed every five days, because, with a rate of use of 600 units per day, an order for 3,000 units is an order for a five-day supply. To calculate the average daily ordering cost, we multiply this $\frac{1}{5}$ of an order per day by the $10 ordering cost and obtain $2. Therefore, in terms of our symbols, we can say that

$$\text{Average daily ordering cost} = \frac{600}{3,000}(\$10) = \$2 = \frac{C}{X} \ (B)$$

Having developed the general expression for the ordering cost, we can now turn to the inventory carrying cost. This cost will be affected by the average inventory, which is a function of the minimum and maximum inventories. The minimum inventory presents no problem because we have been told it is to be zero. The maximum inventory, however, is not so easily ascertained.

To calculate the maximum inventory, we must first take into consideration the rate of inventory growth. This growth will take place during the delivery period, and its rate will be equal to the difference between the delivery rate of 1,000 units per day and the consumption rate of 600 units per day, or 400 units per day. Therefore, we can say that

Rate of inventory growth $= 1{,}000 - 600 = 400$ units/day
$$= R - C$$

Because this growth continues for the length of the delivery period, the inventory will reach its maximum level at the end of this period. In our example, with a lot size of 3,000 units and a delivery rate of 1,000 units per day, the order will be delivered over a three-day period. During this period, the inventory increases at a rate of 400 units per day. Therefore, the maximum inventory will be the 3 days times the 400-unit increase per day, or 1,200 units. In summary, we can say that

$$\text{Maximum inventory} = \frac{3{,}000}{1{,}000}(1{,}000 - 600) = 1{,}200 \text{ units}$$

$$= \frac{X}{R}(R - C) = X(1 - C/R)$$

When this maximum is reached, the quantity on hand begins to drop, because the demand for the item continues but deliveries have stopped. In our example, the inventory will then begin to decrease at a rate of 600 units per day, because this is the consumption rate. Consequently, the units on hand will decrease from a maximum of 1,200 to a minimum of 0 within two days after the maximum has been reached, and the cycle will repeat itself. All this is shown in Figure 9-4.

Knowing the minimum and maximum inventories, we can now determine the average inventory by simply computing the average value of these minimum and maximum inventories. An examination of Figure 9-4 will clarify why this is so. During the three-day delivery period, the inventory rises from its minimum value of 0 units to its maximum value of 1,200 units. Since this is a straight-line increase, the average inventory during this period will be the midpoint between these two values, or 600 units. During

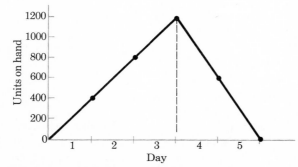

Figure 9-4   A specific inventory pattern.

the following two-day period, the inventory decreases from its maximum value of 1,200 units to its minimum value of 0 units. Again, since this is a straight-line decrease, the average inventory during this period will be the midpoint between these two values, or 600 units. With an average inventory of 600 units during each of these two periods, the average inventory for the entire period must also be 600 units. But this value is equal to the average of the minimum and maximum inventories, or, since the minimum inventory is zero, to one-half of the maximum inventory. Therefore, the expression for the average inventory will be equal to

$$\text{Average inventory} = \tfrac{1}{2}(1,200) = 600 \text{ units} = \frac{X}{2}\left(1 - \frac{C}{R}\right)$$

The average daily carrying cost will be equal to this average number of units being carried times the carrying cost per unit per day. In our problem, the unit carrying cost has been given to us as $0.001 per unit per day. Therefore, the average daily cost of carrying 600 units would be the 600 units times $0.001, or $0.60, per unit per day. In terms of an equation, we can say that

$$\text{Average daily carrying cost} = 600\,(\$0.001) = \$0.60$$
$$= \frac{X}{2}\left(1 - \frac{C}{R}\right)(E)$$

Having accounted for all the factors which enter into the analysis, we can now develop the general expression for the total daily cost to be associated with various lot sizes. This expression for the total daily cost, which is the sum of the daily ordering cost and the daily carrying cost, will take the following form:

$$\text{Total average daily cost} = \frac{C}{X}(B) + \frac{X}{2}\left(1 - \frac{C}{R}\right)(E) \tag{9-5}$$

For the lot size of 3,000 units with which we have been working, substitution in this expression will yield the following total daily cost:

$$\begin{aligned}
\text{Total average daily cost} &= (600/3{,}000)(\$10) \\
&\quad + (3{,}000/2)(1 - 600/1{,}000)(\$0.001) \\
&= \$2 + \$0.60 = \$2.60
\end{aligned}$$

We could now find the economic lot size by assuming different values for the lot size, making the appropriate substitutions in Eq. (9-5), and solving for the total daily cost. Eventually, we should find that lot size which would generate the minimum total daily cost. However, it will be easier to derive a formula which will enable us to find this lot size directly.

THE FORMULA   The first term in Eq. (9-5) represents the average daily ordering cost; the second term represents the average daily carrying cost. As in the earlier case we had considered, it has been found that the nature of this total cost function is such that the total average daily cost Y will be a minimum for that value of the lot size X at which the average daily ordering cost is equal to the average daily carrying cost. This permits us to say that the total cost will be a minimum when

$$\frac{CB}{X} = \frac{X}{2}\left(1 - \frac{C}{R}\right) \quad (E)$$

When we solve this expression for the unknown lot size X, we obtain

$$X = \sqrt{\frac{2CB}{E(1 - C/R)}}$$

With the use of this formula, we can substitute the data given to us in our problem and solve for the economic lot size directly.

THE USE OF CALCULUS   Another way of obtaining the formula for the economic lot size is with the use of calculus. We begin with the total cost function which was given to us in Eq. (9-5) as

$$Y = \frac{C}{X}(B) + \frac{X}{2}\left(1 - \frac{C}{R}\right) \quad (E)$$

Next, we find the derivative D_x of this function and equate it to 0. When we do this, we obtain

$$D_x = -\frac{CB}{X^2} + \frac{E}{2}\left(1 - \frac{C}{R}\right) = 0$$

Finally, we solve this expression for the lot size X and find that the total average daily cost reaches a minimum when

$$X = \sqrt{\frac{2CB}{E(1 - C/R)}}$$

which coincides with what we obtained with the use of the first approach.

THE FORMULA APPLIED   The preceding enables us to say that the formula for the economic lot size Q in the case under consideration is equal to

$$Q = \sqrt{\frac{2CB}{E(1 - C/R)}} \quad (9\text{-}6)$$

where $C =$ consumption rate per day

$B =$ ordering cost per lot

$E =$ carrying cost per unit per day

$R =$ delivery rate per day

If we substitute the data from our illustration in Eq. (9-6), we obtain the following value for the economic lot size:

$$Q = \sqrt{\frac{2(600)\,(\$10)}{\$0.001\,(1 - 600/1,000)}} = 5,480 \text{ units}$$

As in the case of the first economic lot size formula we derived, care must be taken to express the factors contained in Eq. (9-6) in the correct units. The ordering cost will always be the cost per lot. But if the level of inventory increases at some rate *per day,* then the consumption rate, carrying cost, and delivery rate must be described on a *per day* basis. If we tried to work with annual costs and rates when the inventory increases at some rate per day, we should find it impossible to do so. An attempt to substitute in Eq. (9-6) would reveal that the average annual consumption rate and the average annual delivery rate are equal. Therefore, the denominator of the equation would become zero, and the expression could not be solved. In brief, the units in which the rate of inventory increase must be expressed will dictate the units in which the consumption rate, carrying cost, and delivery rate must be expressed.

It should also be recognized that Eq. (9-6) can be applied to purchased items as well as to manufactured items. In those cases, the ordering cost will be the cost to be associated with placing and receiving an order, and the delivery rate will be the rate at which the supplier delivers the item.

This economic lot size formula is the last one we shall develop. The two we have considered suffice to demonstrate that a unique formula must be derived for every combination of circumstances. Furthermore, the circumstances must be such that they permit the construction of a total cost function, from which one can derive the appropriate economic lot size formula.

QUANTITY DISCOUNTS

One of the restrictions on the use of the foregoing economic lot size formulas is that, in the case of a purchased item, the unit purchase price be constant or that, in the case of a manufactured item, the direct unit manufacturing cost be constant. When this condition is not satisfied, it becomes necessary to modify the way in which the formulas are used to obtain the economic order quantity. To consider how this is done, we shall return to the example employed in the derivation of the first economic lot size formula, in which it was assumed that the entire lot is delivered at one time.

It will be recalled that, in that example, a firm was purchasing housings for electric motors. The part was used at a rate C of 75,000 units per year; the ordering cost B was \$20; and the annual unit carrying cost E was \$0.077. Substitution of these data in Eq. (9-3) yielded an economic lot size of 6,250 units. Furthermore, the unit purchase price P was \$0.50, but because it was constant, it was ignored in the analysis. Nevertheless, had we wanted to obtain the total annual cost, including the purchase cost, generated by the economic lot size, we could have done so in the following manner:

$$Y = \frac{75,000\,(\$20)}{6,250} + \frac{6,250\,(\$0.077)}{2} + 75,000\,(\$0.50) = \$37,981$$

Now, suppose that the supplier notifies the firm that, if it purchases the housings in lot sizes of 10,000 or more, the price of every unit purchased will be reduced to \$0.45. In other words, the firm is being offered a quantity discount. Obviously, this will serve to reduce the annual purchase cost, because 75,000 units will continue to be purchased per year even if the order size is increased to 10,000 units or more. However, it may be that the larger lot size will cause an increase in the sum of the annual ordering and carrying costs which will more than offset the decrease in the annual purchase cost. The only way to determine whether this will be the case is to calculate the total annual cost that will be experienced with the quantity discount and the larger lot size it necessitates. But before this can be done, the firm must determine the value of the economic lot size at the \$0.45 unit price. This is done as follows:

As a rule, the unit carrying cost will be affected by the unit value of the item being carried in inventory. But the value of the item will be affected by its unit purchase or manufacturing cost. Consequently, the firm in our example may have originally estimated the annual unit carrying cost to be 15.4 percent of the unit purchase price of \$0.50, or \$0.077. It follows that, if the price drops to \$0.45, the unit carrying cost will decrease to 15.4 percent of \$0.45, or to \$0.0693 per year. This suggests that we begin the determination of the economic lot size at the \$0.45 unit price by substituting the 75,000-unit annual rate of use, the \$20 ordering cost, and the new annual unit carrying cost of \$0.0693 in Eq. (9-3). When this is done, we find that

$$Q = \sqrt{\frac{2\,(75,000)\,(\$20)}{\$0.0693}} = 6,580 \text{ units}$$

However, since the quantity discount is available only with lot sizes of 10,000 units or more, the manufacturer cannot adhere to the calculated theoretical value of the economic lot size of 6,580 units and obtain the discount. He must buy at least 10,000 units. But if the theoretical minimum total cost at the $0.45 price occurs with a lot size of 6,580 units, the total cost will increase as the lot size increases beyond this point. Therefore, with a lot size of 10,000 units, the total cost will be greater than it would be with a lot size of 6,580 units. Similarly, with lot sizes in excess of 10,000 units, the total cost will be still greater. In brief, the total cost pattern generated by the data in our example is as shown in Figure 9-5. Consequently, if the manufacturer decides to take advantage of the quantity discount, he should do so by just satisfying the supplier's requirement, that is, by buying in quantities of 10,000 units.

To determine whether it is advisable for him to do so, we must calculate the total annual cost caused by the lot size of 10,000 units. When we do, we find this cost to be as follows:

$$Y = \frac{75,000\,(\$20)}{10,000} + \frac{10,000\,(\$0.0693)}{2} + 75,000\,(\$0.45) = \$34,246$$

Whether this is a more economical alternative than the one involving a lot size of 6,250 units and a unit purchase price of $0.50 can be ascertained by comparing their respective total annual costs, which must include the annual purchase cost because this cost is affected by the choice of alternative. As was shown earlier, a lot size of 6,250 units yields a total annual cost of $37,981. But the lot size of 10,000 units yields a total annual cost of $34,246. Therefore, the latter alternative is more economical, and the manufacturer should adhere to a lot size of 10,000 units.

In our example, the economic lot size at the lower price proved to be equal to the minimum quantity of 10,000 units the company had to buy to

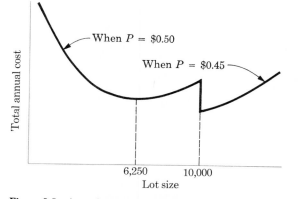

Figure 9-5   **A total cost curve generated by two unit prices** *P*

realize this price. But this will not always be the case. To illustrate, if the lower purchase price had caused a radical reduction in the annual unit carrying cost to, say, $0.0248, the calculated theoretical value of the economic lot size would then be

$$Q = \sqrt{\frac{2(75,000)(\$20)}{\$0.0248}} = 11,000 \text{ units}$$

Because the company can adhere to this lot size and take advantage of the quantity discount, the economic lot size at the lower price is now 11,000 rather than 10,000 units. This is to say that the minimum total cost at the $0.45 price and the corresponding $0.0248 carrying cost will occur when the lot size is 11,000 units. As a result, the total cost pattern generated by the two alternatives is as shown in Figure 9-6. Therefore, the firm should go on to compute the total annual cost with this lot size of 11,000 units and compare it with the $37,981 total annual cost to be associated with a lot size of 6,250 units. If the computed cost is lower than $37,981, the item should be purchased at the reduced price in lots of 11,000 units.

In brief, when quantity discounts are available, the analysis begins with a determination of the economic lot size for each price level. For a given price level, this lot size is ascertained by first substituting the corresponding carrying cost in the economic lot size formula. If the calculated lot size is less than or equal to the minimum quantity that must be purchased to obtain that price, this minimum quantity is the economic lot size at that price. But if the calculated lot size exceeds this minimum quantity, the calculated lot size is the economic lot size at that price. Once the economic lot size for each price level has been determined, the firm can go on to

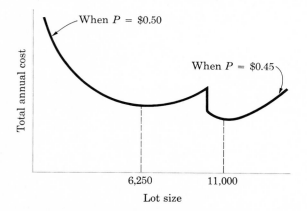

Figure 9-6   Another total cost curve generated by two
unit prices P

compute the total cost generated by each of the alternatives and identify the one that yields the minimum cost.

Although this procedure has been explained with an example involving a purchased item, the same approach would be employed when the unit cost of a manufactured item decreases when the lot size reaches a certain value. This is not too common, but it can occur when a larger lot size calls for a change in the method of production with the result that unit direct manufacturing costs decrease to some new level.

The same general method of analysis can also be applied when the lot is delivered at some uniform rate over a period of time rather than all at one time. However, the economic lot size and the total cost at each price or manufacturing cost level would have to be computed with the economic lot size formula and total cost equation that correspond to this delivery pattern.

EVALUATION OF ECONOMIC LOT SIZE FORMULAS

In any attempt to apply the economic lot size approach to inventory control, the firm will experience certain difficulties. One of these stems from the need to estimate such things as rates of use, ordering costs, carrying costs, and lead times. These estimates are not easily made, and a risk of error always exists. But if an appropriate economic lot size formula can be derived, the company must use either the formula or judgment. However, when a company stores thousands of different items, as many do, one would be reluctant to recommend that order quantities for what may be the majority of these items be selected on the basis of judgment. Hence, it becomes almost mandatory that the inventories of some of these items be controlled by a semiautomatic routine such as the economic lot size approach. While it is true that some of the estimates may prove to be relatively poor, it is possible that they will yield approximate results which, for all practical purposes, will be satisfactory.

It should also be recognized that the application of economic lot size formulas may serve to introduce undesirable fluctuations in the production schedule. For example, the demand for a manufactured part might be fairly uniform. This suggests the use of an economic lot size formula that will yield an order quantity which, if adhered to, will create peaks in the production schedule for this item. And as we know, there are costs to be associated with the resultant fluctuations. Unfortunately, there is no way of incorporating these costs in the economic lot size calculation itself. Of course, it is possible that, when the fluctuating production schedules for many such parts are combined, the result will be a fairly level composite schedule. But if not, the company might find that the most economical production schedule is not the one based on the results of economic lot size computations.

Finally, there are many cases in which the economic lot size approach to inventory control must be abandoned for the simple reason that an appropriate formula cannot be derived. Such formulas are possible only if the forces at play, such as demand, unit prices, procurement time, carrying costs, and ordering costs, are of a nature which permits the development of a mathematical expression which serves to describe the total cost function. Yet, in the real world, the nature of the factors relevant to the inventory problem is such that their combined effect cannot always be described by means of a mathematical model. Consequently, an appropriate formula cannot be derived. When this is true, many companies adopt rules of thumb to arrive at order quantities for certain raw materials, component parts, and finished products. This is to say that they conclude that the proper lot size for one class of items is a one-month supply, for another a three-month supply, for still another a six-month supply, and so on. Very often, the only way to arrive at such ordering rules is on the basis of judgment and intuition. But on other occasions, there is an alternative. In brief, it requires that more than one rule of thumb be considered and that the most economical of these be identified by means of a cost comparison. Let us now consider this approach.

RULE-OF-THUMB SELECTION[1]

When it is decided on some basis that the order quantity for some item should be, for example, a one-month supply, this suggests that the company is able to prepare a fairly accurate forecast of the monthly demands for the item. Otherwise, there would be no way of translating the proposed rule of thumb into specific order quantities. Let us suppose, for purposes of illustration, that the estimated future monthly demands during a one-year period for a given item are as shown in the first two columns of Table 9-1.

With a "one-month supply" ordering rule, one order would be placed some time before the beginning of each month so as to obtain delivery at the beginning of the month. The quantity ordered would be equal to the demand expected during the month under consideration. Therefore, as also is shown in Table 9-1, the beginning inventory for any one month would be equal to the expected demand, and the ending inventory would be equal to zero.

---

[1] The material in this section is based on an article by the author entitled "Selection of Rules-of-Thumb in Inventory Control," which appeared in the May 1972 issue of the *Journal of Purchasing*.

Table 9-1 The Inventory Pattern Generated by a "One-Month Supply" Ordering Rule

Month	Units demanded	Beginning inventory	Ending inventory	Average inventory
1	450	450	0	225
2	120	120	0	60
3	570	570	0	285
4	710	710	0	355
5	340	340	0	170
6	230	230	0	115
7	890	890	0	445
8	160	160	0	80
9	110	110	0	55
10	650	650	0	325
11	370	370	0	185
12	200	200	0	100

At this point, the firm can continue the analysis by estimating the total cost associated with this rule. This total cost will consist of two elements, one of which will be the inventory carrying cost and the other the ordering cost.

Insofar as the carrying cost is concerned, its calculation must begin with a determination of the average inventory for each month. If the demand is fairly uniform during any one month, a good approximation can be obtained by simply computing the average of the beginning and ending monthly inventories. When this is done, the values shown in the last column of Table 9-1 are obtained. The overall average now can be computed by taking the total of these monthly averages, which is 2,400 units, and dividing this total by the number of months involved, which is 12. Doing so yields an overall average of 200 units. The cost of carrying this quantity will be a function of the unit carrying cost. If this is estimated to be $2 per unit per year, the annual carrying cost will be

Carrying cost = 200 units ($2/unit/year) = $400/year

If the firm has reason to believe that wide fluctuations in the item's rate of use will occur, say, from week to week, a better approximation of the average inventory would be obtained by forecasting the weekly rather than the monthly demands and then computing the average inventory for each week and finally determining the overall average of these weekly averages.

In any event, the firm now must go on to ascertain the ordering cost. With the ordering rule being considered, 12 orders will be placed per year.

If the fixed cost associated with each order is estimated to be $75, the annual ordering cost will be

Ordering cost = 12 orders/year ($75/order) = $900/year

The total cost will be the sum of the carrying cost and the ordering cost, and this is equal to

Total cost = $400/year + $900/year = $1,300/year

This total cost could be assumed to be a minimum if it were generated by an order quantity determined by means of an economic lot size formula. But no such assumption can be made when the order quantity is determined by means of a rule of thumb based on judgment. Therefore, there is nothing about the calculated total cost of $1,300 which enables the firm to conclude whether or not the rule is satisfactory. It can determine this only by going on to consider alternate ordering rules.

ALTERNATIVE ORDERING RULES   Judgment must be exercised in the selection of the next ordering rule to be evaluated. Nevertheless, there probably would be general agreement that, at this point, consideration should be given to a rule calling for the procurement of a two-month supply of the item.

As can be seen in Table 9-2, the total demand for the first two-month period is expected to be 570 units. Therefore, an order would be placed for this amount in time to obtain delivery at the beginning of the first month. A beginning inventory of 570 units and an expected demand of 450 units yield an ending inventory of 120 units for the first month and an average inventory of 345 units. With a beginning inventory of 120 units for the second month and an expected demand of 120 units, we should have an ending inventory of zero for that month and an average inventory of 60 units. The remaining data in Table 9-2 can be developed in the same general manner.

The overall average of the monthly average inventories would be found to be 372.5 units. Consequently, the annual carrying cost to be associated with this ordering rule will be

Carrying cost = 372.5 units ($2/unit/year) = $745/year

As was to be expected, this exceeds the cost of carrying the inventories that resulted from the "one-month" rule. However, this should be offset to some degree by a reduction in the annual ordering cost. Because only six orders now will be placed per year, the annual ordering cost will decrease to

Ordering cost = 6 orders/year ($75/order) = $450/year

Table 9-2   The Inventory Pattern Generated by a "Two-Month Supply" Ordering Rule

Month	Units demanded	Beginning inventory	Ending inventory	Average inventory
1	450	570	120	345
2	120	120	0	60
3	570	1,280	710	995
4	710	710	0	355
5	340	570	230	400
6	230	230	0	115
7	890	1,050	160	605
8	160	160	0	80
9	110	760	650	705
10	650	650	0	325
11	370	570	200	385
12	200	200	0	100

The sum of the carrying cost and the ordering cost for this rule will, therefore, be equal to

Total cost = $745/year + $450/year = $1,195/year

A comparison of this total with the total cost of $1,300 per year for the "one-month" rule reveals that it is more economical to purchase a two-month supply of the item whenever an order is placed.

But because the total cost decreased when the order quantity was increased, it might be worthwhile to consider still another rule of thumb involving even larger order quantities. A logical one would be a rule calling for an order quantity equal to a three-month supply of the item. The manner in which this rule would affect inventories can be determined in the same general way as for the "two-month" rule. The results that would be obtained are shown in Table 9-3.

The overall average inventory with this alternative would be found to be 467.5 units, and this would yield the following carrying cost:

Carrying cost = 467.5 units ($2/unit/year) = $935/year

Also, one order every three months will result in four orders per year, so the ordering cost would be

Ordering cost = 4 orders/year ($75/order) = $300/year

Therefore, the total of these two cost elements would be as follows:

Total cost = $935/year + $300/year = $1,235/year

Table 9-3 The Inventory Pattern Generated by a "Three-Month Supply" Order-ing Rule

Month	Units demanded	Beginning inventory	Ending inventory	Average inventory
1	450	1,140	690	915
2	120	690	570	630
3	570	570	0	285
4	710	1,280	570	925
5	340	570	230	400
6	230	230	0	115
7	890	1,160	270	715
8	160	270	110	190
9	110	110	0	55
10	650	1,220	570	895
11	370	570	200	385
12	200	200	0	100

This total exceeds the total of $1,195 calculated for the "two-month" rule; hence, the rule that a two-month supply be ordered remains the most economical. Moreover, because the larger order quantities that evolved from the "three-month" rule brought about a higher total annual cost, there is no point in going on to evaluate rules calling for still larger order quantities.

INTERPRETING THE RESULTS Three proposed rules of thumb were considered in the illustration, and their respective annual costs were found to be as follows:

Ordering quantity	Total annual cost
One-month supply	$1,300
Two-month supply	1,195
Three-month supply	1,235

As has been noted, the most economical of these rules is the one that specifies an order quantity equal to a two-month supply. However, it would be incorrect to assume that this is the optimum rule. It may be that some rule which has not been considered thus far will yield a still lower cost. Let us consider why this is true.

The three rules evaluated were selected from an unlimited number of rules to which the firm could adhere. For example, consideration also could have been given to ordering a one-day supply, a one-week supply, or a one-year supply. Fortunately, the relative magnitudes of the calculated total costs are such that most of these alternatives can be discarded immediately. Specifically, the pattern created by these total costs indicates that the minimum cost will be realized with an order quantity that exceeds a one-month supply but is less than a three-month supply. But this does not mean that the minimum cost will be attained with the "two-month" rule. It may very well be that, say, a six-week or a ten-week supply will yield the true minimum. However, the expense of a more-detailed analysis is usually such that an evaluation of these other alternatives is not warranted. Furthermore, estimates of demand and costs are involved with the result that, at best, only a good approximate solution can be obtained. Therefore, it probably would be advisable that the firm in this illustration simply conclude that the "two-month supply" rule is the most economical. Although this rule may not represent an optimum solution, there is reason to believe that it will prove to be more economical than a rule of thumb selected solely on the basis of judgment and intuition.

This brings us to the close of our discussion of analytical techniques that can be employed to control inventories under what can be referred to as the "condition of certainty." This condition is said to prevail when each of the relevant factors is expected to have a single value and it is assumed that this value is known with certainty. Consequently, in each of the problems considered, we dealt with a single value of the demand during a specific time period and with a single value for the procurement time. When this condition of certainty does not prevail, other methods of analysis must be utilized.

QUESTIONS

9-1 Describe, in general terms, the maximum-minimum system of inventory control.

9-2 How are the reorder point and maximum inventory determined in this system? Why is a minimum inventory, or safety stock, maintained?

9-3 What is the procedure for the determination of the economic lot size in the absence of an appropriate formula?

9-4 Describe the steps in the development of an economic lot size formula.

9-5 How is the economic lot size determined when a quantity discount is available?

9-6 What are the difficulties a firm can encounter in its attempt to derive and apply economic lot size formulas? How serious are these problems?

9-7 What are some examples of rules of thumb a company might apply to control inventories? Under what conditions would it be inclined to adopt such ordering rules?

9-8 Describe the method for evaluating alternative rules of thumb. Why is it said

that this method may not yield the optimum rule? What are the advantages
and disadvantages of this method?

9-9 How is the condition of certainty defined in the area of inventory control?

PROBLEMS

9-1 The inventory level of a product stocked by a distributor of pharmaceuticals
is controlled by means of the maximum-minimum system. For control purposes, the firm divides each year into 13 four-week periods.

The product under consideration is received from a supplier in lot sizes
of 1,600 units, all of which are delivered at one time. The item is used at a
uniform rate during each of the four-week periods, and the demand is 800
units per period. The lead time is two weeks, and no minimum inventory is
maintained.

   a Calculate the values of (1) the maximum inventory, (2) the average inventory, and (3) the reorder point.

   b If at a subsequent date it is decided to carry a safety stock of 100 units,
   what effect will this decision have on (4) the maximum inventory, (5) the
   average inventory, and (6) the reorder point? (Ans. 1,700; 900; 500)

9-2 An oil refinery operates every day of the year. The entire lot of an item it
produces intermittently is delivered to a warehouse at one time, from which
it is shipped to the firm's dealers at a uniform rate. The warehouse's reorder
point is 1,000 cases, which was arrived at by taking into consideration, among
other things, a 10-day procurement time. The order quantity is such that the
average inventory is 1,450 cases.

   a If the foregoing data reflect a decision to carry no safety stock, what is
   (1) the maximum inventory, (2) the lot size, and (3) the rate of use per week?

   b But if the foregoing data reflect a decision to maintain a safety stock of
   200 cases, what is (4) the maximum inventory, (5) the lot size, and (6) the
   rate of use per week? (Ans. 2,700; 2,500; 560)

9-3 A savings and loan association uses a certain form at a uniform rate of 60
pads per week during each of the 52 weeks per year it is in operation. Every
replenishment order it places is delivered at one time. No minimum inventory
is to be carried. Ordering costs are estimated to be $10 per order. The pur-
chase cost is $2 per pad. Carrying costs will consist of storage and interest
on investment; in terms of the amount per pad per year, these costs are
estimated to be 26 percent of the unit purchase price of $2. The procurement
time is one week.

   a Determine the approximate value of the economic lot size by assuming
   different values for the lot size and calculating the total cost to be associated with each. Begin with a lot size of 300 units and increase this in
   steps of 20. (Ans. 340)

b Determine the value of the economic lot size by means of an appropriate formula. (Ans. 346)

c With the use of the given data and the calculated value of the economic lot size, determine the following:

1 Reorder point
2 Maximum inventory
3 Average inventory
4 Orders per week
5 Ordering cost per week
6 Carrying cost per week
7 Total cost per week
8 Total cost per year

(Ans. 60; 346; 173; 0.173; $1.73; $1.73; $3.46; $179.92)

9-4 A manufacturer wants to calculate the economic lot size for one of his products. The entire manufactured lot is delivered to the stockroom at one time. Furthermore, the product is shipped to the firm's customers at a uniform rate of 100 units per day in each of the 250 days per year during which the plant operates.

The fixed costs per order are estimated to be $24 for production control, $14 for handling, and $12 for setup. Carrying costs per unit per year are expected to be $3 for interest, $0.80 for storage, and $0.20 for insurance and taxes.

Although the economic lot size will be computed as if the condition of certainty prevails, the manufacturer decides, on the basis of judgment, to maintain a minimum inventory equal to a three-day supply of the item. Finally, the lead time is estimated to be five operating days.

a What is the economic order quantity?

b With the selected safety stock, calculated lot size, and other given data, what will be the following?

1 Reorder point
2 Orders per year
3 Maximum inventory
4 Average inventory
5 Ordering cost per year
6 Carrying cost per year
7 Total cost per year

c Why is the annual ordering cost not equal to the annual carrying cost as it was in the preceding problem?

9-5 A bakery which supplies a large number of retail outlets uses an ingredient every day of the year at a rate of 2,000 pounds per day. When an order for the material is placed, the source delivers the item at a rate of 8,000 pounds per day over a time period whose length depends on the quantity ordered.

No safety stock is carried. The procurement time is one week. The cost of placing, receiving, and handling an order is $75.

Carrying costs are estimated in terms of some amount per pound per year but converted to a per day basis by dividing the annual cost by the number of days per year. This yields a cost of $0.001 per pound per day.

a Compute the value of the economic lot size. (Ans. $20,000)

b Determine the resultant (1) maximum inventory, (2) average inventory, (3) average number of orders per day, (4) average daily carrying cost, (5) average daily ordering cost, (6) average total daily cost, and (7) reorder point. (Ans. 15,000; 7,500; 0.1; $7.50; $7.50; $15; 14,000)

9-6 A company manufactures a component part for one of its assemblies. The part is processed at a rate of 500 units per day, and this quantity is delivered to the stockroom each day during the entire production run. The company's assembly department uses the part at a rate of 250 units per day, and the item is withdrawn from the stockroom accordingly.

Production control, setup, and handling costs are relatively fixed at $20 per order. Carrying costs include interest, storage, insurance, taxes, and deterioration and are expected to amount to $1.168 per unit per year based on a 365-day year.

a In what lot size should the part be manufactured?

b Calculate the total annual cost that will be generated by this lot size.

c Assume that the lead time is two days and that the company will carry a minimum inventory of 750 units and will adhere to the calculated lot size. Construct a graph which describes the resultant inventory pattern. On this graph, show the minimum inventory, maximum inventory, average inventory, reorder point, lead time, length of delivery period, and time between orders.

9-7 Compute the uniform annual cost that will be experienced if, to realize a quantity discount, the firm adheres to the 11,000-unit lot size in the situation depicted in Figure 9-6.

9-8 A company purchases a part which is a component of one of the assemblies it manufactures. This component is used at a uniform rate throughout the year, and the supplier delivers the entire lot at one time. The manufacturer finds it necessary to take the following factors into consideration when ascertaining the economic lot size:

C = consumption rate per year = 25,000 units

B = cost of placing and receiving an order = $14

E = cost of carrying 1 unit of inventory for 1 year
   = 20 percent of unit purchase price

P = unit purchase price
   = $1 for lot sizes of 1 to 1,999 units

$P = \$0.50$ for lot sizes of 2,000 to 4,999 units
$= \$0.30$ for lot sizes of 5,000 or more units

What is the economic lot size at each of these prices? What annual cost will each of these lot sizes yield? (Ans. 1,871; 2,646; 5,000; $25,374; $12,764; $7,720)

9-9   A company manufactures an item intermittently. When it does, the output is 200 units per day, and this quantity is delivered to the stockroom each day. The stockroom ships 40 units of the item every day.

Ordering costs are $90 per order. Direct manufacturing costs are $60 per unit for lot sizes of less than 325 units. But production economies are possible when lot sizes of 325 units or more are processed, and, as a result, direct unit manufacturing costs decrease to $55 with these larger lots.

a If carrying costs are unaffected by manufacturing costs and are equal to $0.10 per unit per day, what is the economic lot size?

b In what quantities should the product be produced if the carrying cost is $0.10 per unit per day when lot sizes are less than 325 units but decreases to $0.07 per unit per day with larger lot sizes because of the lower investment in each unit made possible by reduced manufacturing costs?

9-10   A distributor of small electrical appliances has his own repair department which services items returned by customers. A certain replacement part is common to many of the appliances. The demand for the part during a future six-week period is expected to be as follows:

Week	Demand, units	Week	Demand, units
1	21	4	108
2	84	5	36
3	43	6	72

A weekly forecast has been prepared, because the part is used at a fairly uniform rate during any one week, but, as indicated, the demand varies significantly from week to week.

Ordering costs are about $25 per order, and carrying costs are estimated to be $0.14 per unit per week.

On the basis of judgment, the distributor has selected two possible ordering rules. The first calls for ordering a three-week supply of the item so that one order would be received by the beginning of the first week and another by the beginning of the fourth week. A second calls for ordering a six-week supply which means that a single order would be received by the beginning of the first week. Which of these two ordering rules would you recommend?

9-11 The expected demand for a raw material during a future 12-month period is as follows:

Month	Demand, units	Month	Demand, units
1	180	7	130
2	220	8	360
3	190	9	110
4	140	10	280
5	270	11	250
6	210	12	160

The item is used at a uniform rate during any one month. Ordering costs are $40 per order. The unit purchase price is $5 for lot sizes of less than 500, and $4.90 for lot sizes of 500 or more units. Annual carrying costs per unit of inventory are approximately 30 percent of the unit purchase price. The procurement time is one week.

Three ordering rules have been proposed. These are that the order quantity should be equal to (a) a one-month supply, (b) a two-month supply, and (c) a three-month supply. Which of these proposals is the most economical on the basis of an annual cost comparison? (Ans. $13,136; $13,068; $12,862)

TEN

INVENTORY CONTROL UNDER RISK AND UNCERTAINTY

During a given period, the actual demand for some raw material, part, or product will assume a single value. For example, at the end of a specific month, the firm may find that, in that month, the demand for one of its products was equal to 7,400 units. However, for production planning purposes, it is necessary that the firm forecast the demand for that month some time in advance. If the condition of *certainty* prevails, we say that, when it is preparing the forecast, the firm will know that the value of this future demand is 7,400 units.

But the more common situation is one in which the condition of certainty does not exist. Instead, the individuals making the forecast might conclude that the demand for the item will assume one of a number of different possible values. To return to our example, they may estimate that the future demand will be either 7,200 units or 7,400 units or 7,600 units. If they can go on to estimate the probabilities of occurrence that correspond to each of these possible demand values, the condition of *risk* is said to exist.

In any case, the question to be answered is: Should the firm in our example arrange to have 7,200 units or 7,400 units or 7,600 units in stock to satisfy the demand during the period under consideration? The answers to such questions can be arrived at by means of a method of analysis we shall now consider.

A RISK PROBLEM[1]

Suppose that the distributor of an item wants to determine how many

[1] The material in this section is based on an article by the author entitled "Determination of Order Sizes under Risk," which appeared in the August 1968 issue of *The Purchasor*.

units should be purchased to satisfy the demand for the article during a specific month. On the basis of past experience and judgment, he concludes that, for the period involved, the possible demands and their corresponding probabilities of occurrence are as follows:

Demand, units	Probability of occurrence
500	0.20
600	0.30
700	0.50
Total	1.00

The distributor purchases the item at a cost of $10 per unit. He sells it at a price of $15 per unit, but, for each unit sold, a selling expense of $1 is incurred. However, the article is subject to deterioration and obsolescence with the result that all units that remain in stock at the end of the month have a salvage value of only $4 per unit.

Finally, the procurement time for the item is six weeks. This means that there will be no opportunity to replenish the stock during the month under consideration if it becomes apparent that the demand will exceed the supply. Consequently, the distributor must decide whether a purchase order should be placed for 500, 600, or 700 units.

EXPECTED PROFITS   One approach to the determination of the economic order quantity calls for ascertaining the *expected profit* to be associated with each of the alternative order quantities and selecting that quantity which will yield the maximum expected profit. This procedure begins with the calculation of the profit that will be realized with each possible combination of order quantity X and demand D. These respective profits can be computed by finding the difference between the revenues and the costs generated by each combination of order quantity and demand. In our example, these differences can be found with the expressions developed in the following table:

	When $X > D$	When $X \leq D$
Sales	(+) $15D$	(+) $15X$
Salvage	(+) $4(X - D)$	(+) 0
Purchase cost	(−) $10X$	(−) $10X$
Selling expense	(−) $1D$	(−) $1X$
Total (Profit)	$10D - $6X$	$ 4X$

To illustrate the application of the resultant expressions for profit, let us assume that 600 units are purchased but that the actual demand proves to be only 500 units. From the preceding table, we learn that, when the order quantity X exceeds the demand D,

$$\text{Profit} = \$10D - \$6X = \$10(500) - \$6(600) = \$1,400$$

But suppose that, when the 600 units are purchased, the actual demand proves to be either 600 or 700 units. The preceding table reveals that, because the order quantity is now less than or equal to the demand, the resultant profit will be

$$\text{Profit} = \$4X = \$4(600) = \$2,400$$

Continuing in this manner, we can determine the profit for the remaining combinations of order quantity and demand and then summarize our results in the form of the following *profit matrix:*

Order quan-tity (X)	Demand (D)		
	500	600	700
500	$2,000	$2,000	$2,000
600	1,400	2,400	2,400
700	800	1,800	2,800

With the use of the profit matrix and the demand schedule for the item, we can now go on to ascertain the expected profit for each alternative.

Among other things, the profit matrix reveals that if 700 units are ordered, the profit will be $800 when 500 units are demanded, $1,800 when 600 units are demanded, and $2,800 when 700 units are demanded. The demand schedule states that the probability of the demand's being 500 units is 0.20, of its being 600 units is 0.30, and of its being 700 units is 0.50. This means that, in the long run, a policy of consistently adhering to an order quantity of 700 units will generate an $800 profit 20 percent of the time, a $1,800 profit 30 percent of the time, and a $2,800 profit 50 percent of the time. The *expected* profit per order to be associated with this order quantity of 700 units is defined as the weighted average of the three possible profits and is equal to

$$\text{Expected profit} = 0.20(\$800) + 0.30(\$1,800) + 0.50(\$2,800) = \$2,100$$

In the same manner, we should find the expected profit for an order quantity of 600 units to be

$$\text{Expected profit} = 0.20(\$1,400) + 0.30(\$2,400) + 0.50(\$2,400) = \$2,200$$

And finally, for an order quantity of 500 units, the expected profit would be

$$\text{Expected profit} = 0.20(\$2,000) + 0.30(\$2,000) + 0.50(\$2,000) = \$2,000$$

Our findings can now be summarized as follows:

Order quantity	Expected profit
500	$2,000
600	2,200
700	2,100

An examination of these results reveals that the maximum value of the expected profit is $2,200 and that this value is generated by an order quantity of 600 units. Therefore, this is the order size to which the distributor should adhere.

EXPECTED COSTS   A second approach to the determination of the economic order quantity calls for ascertaining the *expected cost* of each alternative and selecting that quantity which will generate the minimum expected cost. Because the cost approach yields the same result as does the profit approach, the specific procedure to be followed is very often a matter of personal preference. In some cases, however, the data available for the analysis may permit the determination of costs but not of profits; when this is true, the expected cost approach must be employed.

To illustrate the determination of expected costs, let us return to the problem with which we have been working. The procedure begins with the calculation of the total cost to be associated with each possible combination of order quantity and demand. This cost consists of two elements. The first of these is the stockout cost; in some cases, this will be represented by the cost of lost customer orders, and in others, by the cost of disrupted production schedules. The second cost element is the inventory carrying cost.

In our problem, the stockout cost is the cost of lost customer orders, that is, the profit that is lost when the demand exceeds the supply; specifically, for each unit demanded but not on hand, the distributor loses the $15 selling price minus the $10 purchase cost minus the $1 selling expense, or $4. The carrying cost is the cost of deterioration and obsolescence experienced when the supply exceeds the demand; specifically, for each unit that remains unsold at the end of the month, the distributor loses the $10 purchase cost minus the $4 salvage value, or $6. Knowing this, we can develop the general expressions with the use of which we can compute the cost to be associated with a given combination of order quantity X and demand D in our problem. This would be done as follows:

	$X > D$	$X < D$	$X = D$
Carrying cost	$6(X - D)$	$ 0	$0
Stockout cost	0	$4(D - X)$	0
Total cost	$6(X - D)$	$4(D - X)$	$0

By making the appropriate substitutions in these expressions, we can construct the following *cost matrix:*

Order quan-tity (X)	Demand (D)		
	500	*600*	*700*
500	$ 0	$400	$800
600	600	0	400
700	1,200	600	0

These costs and their corresponding probabilities of occurrence, as determined from the demand schedule, are then used to find the expected cost for each alternative. The procedure for doing so is the same as the one for computing expected profits. When applied in our example, it will yield the following results:

Order quantity	Expected cost
500	$520
600	320
700	420

Because the order quantity of 600 units generates the minimum expected cost of $320, it would be considered to be the most economical order size. This coincides with what we concluded on the basis of a comparison of expected profits. It is also worth noting that the differences between the respective expected costs correspond to the differences between the respective expected profits computed earlier.

As all this suggests, the given data in the problem under consideration are such that either the expected profit or the expected cost approach proves to be suitable as a method of analysis. However, if we had simply been given unit stockout and carrying costs, we should have had no choice but to adopt the expected cost approach.

AN EVALUATION   The analytical technique for the determination of order sizes under risk has been presented with the use of an example in which only three demand values appeared. Ordinarily, a firm will conclude that the demand for an item can assume many more values. This does not mean, however, that every single possible value must be considered. Instead, it may suffice to estimate demands to the closest hundred or thousand units. Also, extreme values may have such a small chance of occurring that there is no harm in ignoring them, which is to say that the probabilities involved would be assigned a value of zero. But regardless of the number of values that serve to make up the demand schedule, the method of analysis is as we have described it to be.

Our simple illustration also suffices to suggest some of the difficulties that will be experienced in the application of the approach. To begin with, there is the need to estimate such things as revenues, carrying and stock-out costs, and the possible demands and their probabilities of occurrence. Because errors in these estimates are possible, the firm cannot be certain that the decision reached will be correct. Also, even if all the estimates happen to be accurate, the calculated maximum expected profit or minimum expected cost per order will be realized only in the long run, that is, only after an extremely large number of orders of a given size have been placed for the item. For any one order or short series of orders, the average profit or cost might be greater or smaller than the expected value.

However, the alternative to an analytical approach is judgment and intuition. Admittedly, this alternative may prove to be the more effective under a special set of circumstances. But more commonly, the advantage lies with an approach that compels the firm to take all the relevant factors into consideration, requires that these factors be expressed in quantitative terms, and insures that these factors are then processed correctly.

THE SAFETY STOCK PROBLEM[2]

The foregoing method of analysis, with some modification, can also be employed in the determination of the minimum inventory that should be maintained when the company adheres to the economic lot size approach to inventory control. It will be recalled that the function of the minimum inventory is to provide a safety stock in the event that unexpected increases occur in the demand or procurement time.

---

[2] The material in this section is based on an article by the author entitled "The Interrelationship between Lot Sizes and Safety Stocks," which appeared in the July–August 1965 issue of *The Journal of Industrial Engineering.*

When determining the safety stock to be carried, the company takes cognizance of the fact that, as the safety stock is increased, certain costs decrease but others increase. The decreasing costs are those to be associated with lost customer orders or disrupted production schedules, that is, the stockout costs. The increasing costs are those of carrying the safety stock. But for some safety stock level, the total of these decreasing and increasing costs will be at a minimum. Therefore, the firm must assume different possible values for the safety stock level, determine the costs to be associated with each, and select that level which yields the minimum total cost. We shall now consider the details of this general approach.

NEED FOR SAFETY STOCKS One of the assumptions which underlay each of the economic lot size formulas we developed was that an item was used by the firm at a constant rate. If this is not the case, the formulas cannot, strictly speaking, be employed to find the economic lot size. However, in the real world, absolute uniformity in the rate of use is rarely found. Therefore, for practical purposes, it becomes necessary to define a constant rate of use as a rate in which fluctuations are not too great or in which fluctuations are the exception rather than the rule. For example, it may be that a firm estimates the actual demand schedule for an item to be as follows:

Monthly demand, units	Probability of occurrence	Cumulative probability of occurrence
2,000	0.02	0.02
2,500	0.03	0.05
3,000	0.90	0.95
3,500	0.03	0.98
4,000	0.02	1.00

These possible demands and their corresponding probabilities of occurrence would yield the following average or expected demand:

$$\text{Expected demand} = 0.02(2{,}000) + 0.03(2{,}500) + 0.90(3{,}000)$$
$$+ 0.03(3{,}500) + 0.02(4{,}000) = 3{,}000 \text{ units/month}$$

Because the probability is relatively small that the demand will be other than the expected value of 3,000 units per month, the firm would most likely assume that no serious error would be introduced in the economic lot size computation if it were to treat the demand as being a constant 3,000 units per month. But this is not to say that it will completely ignore the fact that the demand might, in a particular month, be greater than 3,000 units. Instead, the firm will consider the possibility of maintaining a safety stock to meet this increased demand when it does occur.

In its determination of what amount of safety stock should be carried, the firm must begin with the realization that the inventory control system under consideration is able to make an automatic partial adjustment for unexpected increases in demand. Specifically, if the actual consumption rate proves to be greater than the expected rate, the reorder point will be reached sooner and a new order will be placed sooner than it otherwise would. However, once the reorder point is reached and the order for replenishment stock placed, the firm can do nothing but wait until the new lot is received. If an unexpectedly high demand occurs during this period, the firm will either have to draw on its safety stock or, if none exists, fail to satisfy the additional demand. This can be seen in Figure 10-1, in which it is assumed that the entire lot is delivered at one time.

The importance of this lies in the fact that it enables us to see that the risk of an out-of-stock condition arises only at the time the reorder point is reached. Now, it might be argued that this is not always true. For example, the reorder point may be 3,000 units and a request for 4,000 units may come in when the balance on hand is 3,500 units, If there is no safety stock, the entire 4,000 units cannot be delivered in spite of the request's having been received prior to the reorder point's having been reached. However, it should be noted that when the request for 4,000 units is received, the reorder point will be reached when 500 of these units are drawn from stock. Theoretically, a replenishment order would be placed at that

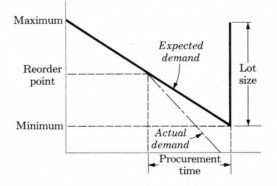

Figure 10-1   Inventory pattern when actual demand exceeds expected demand

moment. The request for the entire remaining 3,500 units cannot be satisfied because it was expected that the demand during the procurement period would be only 3,000 units. The actual demand has turned out to be at least 3,500 units, and possibly more, if additional requests for the item are received during the procurement period. Hence, the out-of-stock condition resulted from a demand which took place after the reorder point was reached.

But to continue, because an increase in the lot size results in a decrease in the number of orders per year and, therefore, in the number of times the reorder point is reached per year, it becomes apparent that the frequency with which a firm assumes the risk of an out-of-stock condition is affected by the lot size. This suggests that the problem of safety stock determination cannot be considered independently of the lot size.

Having concluded this, we can now go on to the method for calculating the required amount of safety stock. Before doing so, however, we should note that an out-of-stock condition can arise, while the firm is waiting for delivery of a new lot, for another reason: For a given order, the actual procurement time may be greater than the expected procurement time employed in the determination of the reorder point. However, we shall begin by assuming that the only variable is the rate of use and that the procurement time is constant.

THE STOCKOUT COST The first step in the analysis calls for determining the alternative safety stock levels. To explain how this is done, let us suppose that the actual demand for an item can be described in terms of the preceding demand schedule; this schedule yielded an expected value of the demand equal to 3,000 units per month. Furthermore, if the procurement time for a replenishment order is estimated to be a constant one month, the expected demand during the procurement period is 3,000 units.

One alternative, of course, is to maintain a minimum inventory of 0 units. With a one-month lead time and an expected demand of 3,000 units per month, this alternative yields a reorder point of 3,000 units. As a result, any demand of 3,000 units or less during the one-month procurement period can be satisfied.

But the demand schedule reveals that the actual demand during this period might also be 3,500 units. If it is, a minimum inventory of 0 units and the 3,000-unit reorder point it generates will result in a shortage of 500 units. To prevent this, the firm can carry a minimum inventory of 500 units, and this becomes the second alternative.

Finally, the demand schedule states that the actual demand during the one-month procurement period might be 4,000 units. If this proves to be the case, a minimum inventory of 0 units and its corresponding reorder point of 3,000 units will bring about a shortage of 1,000 units. A minimum inventory of 1,000 units will prevent this occurrence, and, therefore, this quantity represents the third alternative.

In summary, the firm in our illustration must evaluate three possible safety stock levels. These are 0 units, 500 units, and 1,000 units. It can begin this evaluation by determining the total stockout cost to be associated with each of these alternatives. To do so, it must first estimate the unit cost of not having required stock on hand. Suppose this is expected to be $1 for each unit demanded but not available. Next, the possible shortages with each minimum inventory level must be determined. For a given safety stock alternative, the shortages will depend on the demand during the procurement period. We have already seen that, with a minimum inventory of 0 units, the shortages will be 0 units with a demand of 3,000 units or less, 500 units with a demand of 3,500 units, and 1,000 units with a demand of 4,000 units. If the minimum inventory is increased to 500 units, the shortages will be 0 units with a demand of 3,500 units or less, and 500 units with a demand of 4,000 units. Finally, when a minimum inventory of 1,000 units is maintained, the shortage will be 0 units with a demand of 4,000 units or less. At a cost of $1 per unit, these shortages will generate the total stockout costs shown in the following cost matrix:

Minimum inventory (M)	Demand during procurement period (D)		
	3,000	3,500	4,000
0	$0	$500	$1,000
500	0	0	500
1,000	0	0	0

These results are to be interpreted as follows: If, for example, the firm maintains a minimum inventory of 0 units, it will experience a stockout cost of $0 during 95 percent of the procurement periods, because the demand schedule tells us that the probability is 0.95 that the demand during a one-month procurement period will be 3,000 units or less. Similarly, the stockout cost will be $500 during 3 percent of the procurement periods, and $1,000 during the remaining 2 percent. Therefore, the expected value of the stockout cost with the alternative of maintaining a 0-unit minimum inventory will be

Expected stockout cost $= 0.95(\$0) + 0.03(\$500) + 0.02(\$1,000)$
$$= \$35/\text{procurement period}$$

The expected stockout costs for the other alternatives are obtained in the same way, and the results can be summarized as follows:

Safety stock, units	Expected stockout cost per procurement period
0	$35
500	10
1,000	0

At this point, it is worth noting that these stockout costs can also be treated as an expected fixed cost per order. Let us explain this for a minimum inventory of 500 units. With this safety stock, the expected stockout cost is $10 per procurement period. However, a procurement period begins with the placing of an order. Therefore, every time an order is placed, a period follows during which a stockout cost occurs that has an average value of $10. In principle, there is no difference between this stockout cost and the fixed ordering cost which is incurred every time an order is placed.

MINIMUM COST DETERMINATION Having determined the expected stockout costs per order, the firm must now go on to determine the economic lot size that corresponds to each minimum inventory level. This is necessary, because the economic lot size is a function of the fixed cost per order and this fixed cost is affected by the minimum inventory being carried. We begin by recalling that

$C =$ expected consumption rate $= 3,000$ units per month
$$= 36,000 \text{ units per year}$$
$M =$ minimum inventory $= 0$ or 500 or $1,000$ units
$S =$ expected stockout cost $= \$35$ or $\$10$ or $\$0$ per order

Now, suppose the firm estimates that

$B =$ ordering cost $= \$110$ per order
$E =$ carrying cost $= \$0.40$ per unit per year

If the entire lot is delivered at one time, we know that the general expression for the economic lot size is

$$Q = \sqrt{\frac{2CB}{E}}$$

But this must now be modified to reflect the fixed stockout cost S per order. When this is done, we obtain

$$Q = \sqrt{\frac{2C(B + S)}{E}} \tag{10-1}$$

Therefore, with a minimum inventory of 0 units and its stockout cost of \$35 per order, the economic lot size becomes

$$Q = \sqrt{\frac{2(36,000)(\$110 + \$35)}{\$0.40}} = 5,109 \text{ units}$$

To determine the total annual cost generated by this combination of minimum inventory and economic lot size, we can substitute in the following expression:

$$Y = \frac{C}{X}(B) + \frac{C}{X}(S) + \frac{X}{2}(E) + ME \tag{10-2}$$

in which the first term represents the annual ordering cost, the second term the annual stockout cost, the third term the annual cost of carrying the average inventory generated by the lot size, and the fourth term the annual cost of carrying the minimum inventory. When we compute this cost for a minimum inventory of 0 units and the corresponding lot size of 5,109 units, we obtain

$$Y = \frac{36,000(\$110)}{5,109} + \frac{36,000(\$35)}{5,109} + \frac{5,109(\$0.40)}{2} + 0(\$0.40)$$
$$= \$2,044/\text{year}$$

Insofar as the alternative of carrying a minimum inventory of 500 units is concerned, this safety stock yielded a stockout cost per order of \$10. Consequently, the economic lot size with this alternative becomes

$$Q = \sqrt{\frac{2(36,000)(\$110 + \$10)}{\$0.40}} = 4,648 \text{ units}$$

and the resultant total annual cost is found to be

$$Y = \frac{36,000(\$110)}{4,648} + \frac{36,000(\$10)}{4,648} + \frac{4,648(\$0.40)}{2} + 500(\$0.40)$$
$$= \$2,059/\text{year}$$

Finally, the last alternative of carrying a minimum inventory of 1,000 units was characterized by a stockout cost of \$0 per order. As a result, it yields an economic lot size of

$$Q = \sqrt{\frac{2(36,000)(\$110 + \$0)}{\$0.40}} = 4,450 \text{ units}$$

and the total annual cost with this combination of minimum inventory and lot size will be

$$Y = \frac{36,000\,(\$110)}{4,450} + \frac{36,000\,(\$0)}{4,450} + \frac{4,450\,(\$0.40)}{2} + 1,000\,(\$0.40)$$

$$= \$2,180/\text{year}$$

In summary, the results of the analysis are as follows:

Safety stock, units	Corresponding economic lot size, units	Total annual cost
0	5,109	$2,044
500	4,648	2,059
1,000	4,450	2,180

From this, it is apparent that, in the absence of irreducible factors, the firm should procure the item involved in a lot size of 5,109 units and maintain a safety stock of 0 units, because this yields the minimum total annual cost of $2,044.

VARIABLE PROCUREMENT TIMES   In this illustration, we assumed that the procurement time was constant. But as was mentioned earlier, there is usually some probability that the procurement time will vary, and, therefore, safety stocks must be maintained to provide for unexpected increases in this time. Also, combinations of variations in the rate of use and procurement time are possible which will result in potential shortages. However, as can be shown, the exact cause of a potential shortage will have no effect on the method of analysis.

When there is reason to believe that the rate of use will be constant but that the procurement time might be longer than expected, the firm must begin by estimating the various values these procurement times can assume and their corresponding probabilities of occurrence. For example, in our problem, the firm might estimate these to be as follows:

Procurement time, months	Probability of occurrence
0.75	0.04
1.00	0.92
1.25	0.04

If the rate of use is estimated to be a constant 3,000 units per month, the demand for the item during each of the possible procurement periods will be

Procurement time, months	Demand during procurement period, units	Probability of occurrence
0.75	2,250	0.04
1.00	3,000	0.92
1.25	3,750	0.04

By converting the variable procurement times into the equivalent demands during these periods, we have succeeded in translating the problem into a variable demand problem. From this point on, the analysis would proceed in the manner described in the preceding example.

Insofar as possible combinations of unexpected rates of use and unexpected procurement times are concerned, the firm must translate these various combinations into the number of units that will be consumed while the firm is awaiting delivery of a new lot in each of these cases. The analysis would then proceed as before.

We can conclude, therefore, that if variations occur in the rate of use or procurement time, or both, the approach the firm would employ to identify the most economical alternative remains the same, although the problem of estimation grows as the number of variables increases.

A FIXED-INTERVAL SYSTEM   This brings us to the end of our description of this particular method of analysis. As is to be expected, it has its limitations. There is, to begin with, the problem of estimating the values of the demands for the item, procurement times, ordering costs, stockout costs, and probabilities of occurrence. With regard to probabilities, it should be stressed that, even if these estimates are correct, they are correct only in the long run. For example, in our illustration, it may be that the probability to be associated with a demand of 4,000 units per month is actually 0.02 as was estimated. This means that, in the long run, the demand will be 4,000 units in 2 out of 100 months. But this does not preclude the demand's being 4,000 units during, say, 3 months of a single 6-month period. Consequently, the calculated economic safety stock may not prove to be best for that short-run period, and the firm may experience significant losses as a result. For this reason, we speak of *expected* values, which may coincide with the actual values in the long run but not necessarily in the short run.

Because of these limitations, the firm will have to evaluate the results of its quantitative analysis on the basis of judgment. Having done so, it may decide to adhere to a different combination of safety stock and lot size than the one called for by the analysis. To illustrate, we found that a safety stock of 0 units and a lot size of 5,109 units yielded the minimum total cost of $2,044 per year. However, because of the risk of error, the firm may decide to adopt the combination of a safety stock of 1,000 units and a lot size of 4,450 units, which yielded an annual cost of only $136 more, that is, of $2,180. In fact, even this lot size might be rounded to the more convenient figure of 4,500 units.

At this point, we are able to take cognizance of another disadvantage of the maximum-minimum system of inventory control which has not yet been mentioned. This is the cost of keeping inventory records required to operate the system. Let us explain this with reference to our example in which the expected demand was 3,000 units per month. Suppose that, as has just been suggested, the firm does decide to maintain a safety stock of 1,000 units and adhere to a lot size of 4,500 units. The result is a *fixed-order* system, in the sense that the order size is fixed at 4,500 units. If the demand were a constant 3,000 units per month, the reorder point would be reached every 1.5 months, because a 4,500-unit lot size represents a 1.5-month supply. But the demand schedule reveals that the monthly demand is expected to vary from 2,000 to 4,000 units. Therefore, any one reorder point may be reached sooner or later than the date suggested by the expected value of the demand. As a consequence, it becomes necessary that the firm maintain a record-keeping system which reveals the quantity on hand at any moment in time, so that it will know when the reorder point is reached. Such systems can prove to be expensive. Also, because the intervals between orders will not be fixed, it may be that occasionally the firm will be placing separate orders with the same supplier for five or six different items within an extremely short time period. A significant reduction in ordering cost might have been realized had the firm been able to place a single order for all these items at one time.

These disadvantages of a fixed-order system have resulted in some firms' adopting a *fixed-interval* system in which the time between orders is fixed but the order quantity varies. The length of the interval is some-times determined on the basis of judgment, but it can also be based on the results of an economic lot size calculation. We shall now consider the latter approach.

In our example, the expected value of the variable demand was 3,000 units per month, and the procurement time was estimated to be a constant 1 month. The most economical combination of minimum inventory and lot size was found to be 0 and 5,109 units, respectively. But we shall assume that, because of irreducible factors, the firm decides to modify this result by adopting a minimum inventory of 1,000 units and a lot size of 4,500 units. However, the firm prefers to keep the interval between orders fixed and, if necessary, to vary the order quantity.

The first step in the analysis calls for determining the length of the interval between orders. This is done by simply dividing the expected monthly demand of 3,000 units into the 4,500-unit lot size that would have been adhered to with a fixed-order system. The result is a 1.5-month interval, which is to say an order will be placed every 1.5 months.

Next, the size of the order to be placed at a given point in time must be computed. This computation begins with the realization that the service period covered by any one order is equal to the procurement or lead time plus the interval between orders. To illustrate, suppose that the firm in our example is going to place an order on March 1. Given a 1-month lead time, that order will be received on April 1. But because the order interval is 1.5 months, the next order will not be received until May 15. Therefore, the quantity on hand on March 1 and the size of the order placed on that date must be sufficient to satisfy the demand between March 1 and May 15. With an expected demand of 3,000 units per month, the expected demand during this 2.5-month service period will be 3,000 times 2.5, or 7,500 units. Furthermore, the firm will need an additional 1,000 units to satisfy its minimum inventory requirement of 1,000 units. When we add this 1,000-unit safety stock requirement to the 7,500-unit expected demand, we obtain a total requirement of 8,500 units. However, it may be that 3,700 units are on hand at the time the order is being placed on March 1. If so, the order size need be only the 8,500-unit total requirement minus the 3,700 units on hand, or 4,800 units.

To develop an expression which can be used to calculate the order quantity in a more straightforward manner, let us assign the following symbols to our factors:

T_P = procurement or lead time = 1.0 month

T_I = interval between orders = 1.5 months

T_S = service period = $T_P + T_I$ = 2.5 months

C = expected demand = 3,000 units per month

M = minimum inventory = 1,000 units

A = amount on hand at reorder time = 3,700 units

X = order quantity

In terms of these symbols, we can say that

$$X = (T_P + T_I)(C) + M - A \tag{10-3}$$

and, therefore, the quantity to be ordered is

$$X = (1.0 + 1.5)(3,000) + 1,000 - 3,700 = 4,800 \text{ units}$$

If the quantity on hand at the time an order is being placed is 4,000 units, the order quantity, as found from Eq. (10-3), decreases to 4,500 units.

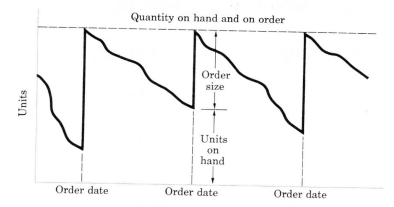

Figure 10-2 Inventory pattern generated by a fixed-interval system

In brief, for a given item, the quantity to be ordered will be affected by, among other things, the quantity on hand at the time an order is to be placed. Therefore, the inventory record-keeping system need provide the company only with information regarding the units on hand at those times. Furthermore, it may be possible to establish the same reorder date for a number of items being obtained from the same source, with the result that only a single order has to be placed for all these items. In these respects, a fixed-interval system, which can be described graphically as shown in Figure 10-2, is superior to a fixed-order system.

MONTE CARLO SIMULATION

Mention has been made of the fact that, quite often, a mathematical model cannot be developed which will serve to yield an optimum ordering policy. Or if developed, the model proves to be of limited value because of the difficulties experienced when estimating the values to be assigned to the relevant cost factors. For one or both of these reasons, a company may adopt rules of thumb as a means for controlling its inventories. The evaluation of such rules under the condition of certainty has already been considered. We shall now see how this can be done under the condition of risk with the use of simulation.

A SIMULATION EXAMPLE   Suppose that a company wants to determine the lot sizes in which one of its manufactured parts should be produced. A study of the past demand for the part by the firm's assembly department results in the following estimate of the future demand schedule:

Demand, units per week	Probability of occurrence
15	0.50
20	0.40
25	0.10

It has been proposed that the order quantity be a one-week supply of the part. However, there seems to be no basis for arriving at an accurate estimate of the future demand during any specific week. For this reason, the firm decides to define a one-week supply to be the *expected* value of the weekly demand. From the data contained in the demand schedule, this value is found to be

Expected demand $= 0.50(15) + 0.40(20) + 0.10(25) = 18$ units/week

Specifically, the proposal is that the part be produced in lot sizes of 18 units. Taking into consideration the required lead time, the production control department would schedule production so as to have these units delivered to the stockroom at the beginning of each week.

If this ordering rule is adopted on the basis of judgment, the firm will in time learn what the consequences of the rule are in terms of stockout, ordering, and carrying costs. Unfortunately, this may prove to be an expensive method for ascertaining that the rule is unsatisfactory. In brief, it would be better to have a method for determining in advance what the probable results of a proposed decision rule will be. Simulation is such a method. In the simulation process, one pretends that something is happening. Therefore, in the application of simulation to inventory control, the firm pretends that the proposed decision rule is in effect and proceeds to determine on paper what is being experienced.

SIMULATING THE DEMAND In the problem under consideration, the consequences of the proposed ordering policy can be ascertained only by comparing the resultant inventories with the demands for the item. However, we do not know what the individual weekly demands will be with certainty; so, working with the demand schedule, we must generate a demand series. This can be done most easily with the use of a table of random numbers or a computer, but, for purposes of simplicity, we shall employ the following approach:

We know that, on the average, the demand will be 15 units in 50 out of 100 weeks, 20 units in 40 out of 100 weeks, and 25 units in 10 out of 100 weeks. Therefore, we can take 100 slips of paper and write the term "15 units" on 50 of them, the term "20 units" on 40 of them, and the term "25 units" on 10 of them. These slips can then be placed in a container. If the weekly demands are assumed to be independent of each other, one slip can now be selected at random, the number written on it recorded, and the slip returned to the container. A second slip would then be selected, the number written on it recorded, and the slip returned to the container. This would be repeated a large number of times and the resultant series of numbers looked upon as the series of future demands for the part. If the series is long enough, the derived distribution of demands will approach the assumed distribution.

This process of random selection by means of which a demand pattern is generated is referred to as a "Monte Carlo process," and, for this reason, when it is employed in the simulation procedure, we say that Monte Carlo simulation is involved.

But to continue, the firm can now go on to evaluate its decision rule in light of the demands which have been generated. If a computer is available, a fairly long demand series can be treated with little difficulty; otherwise, manual methods are necessary, and these can be tedious and time-consuming. Because we shall make use of the latter approach, we shall work with a short series of generated demands. Specifically, let us assume that one series of ten draws of slips of paper in our illustration is representative of a much longer series and that it yielded the following results:

15 – 20 – 15 – 25 – 15 – 20 – 15 – 20 – 20 – 15

We assume that these numbers represent the weekly demands for this representative 10-week period and that these demands will occur in the order in which the slips were drawn. At an earlier point, we learned that, with a "one-week supply" ordering rule, 18 units of the part would be delivered to the stockroom at the beginning of each week. With this delivery pattern and the simulated demand pattern, we can now determine the resultant inventory pattern, which would be as follows:

Week	Units received	Beginning inventory	Simulated demand	Ending inventory
1	18	18	15	3
2	18	21	20	1
3	18	19	15	4
4	18	22	25	−3
5	18	15	15	0
6	18	18	20	−2
7	18	16	15	1
8	18	19	20	−1
9	18	17	20	−3
10	18	15	15	0

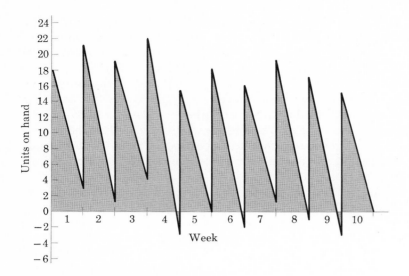

Figure 10-3   Results obtained from a Monte Carlo simulation

It might be noted that a stockout condition occurs in 4 of the 10 weeks. In each of those cases, although the physical ending inventory would be zero, a negative value is shown, and this negative quantity is added to the quantity received to arrive at the beginning inventory for the following week. This is because items not on hand when demanded are back-ordered and must be supplied when replenishment stock is received. Given that the component part involved is used by the firm's assembly department, this is likely to be the case. But in the absence of back-ordering, the beginning inventory in such instances would be equal to the units received. In any event, the resultant inventory pattern, in graphical form, for the typical 10-week period would be as shown in Figure 10-3.

Admittedly, a series of this length is not sufficient to indicate what the long-run effects of the decision rule will be, but it serves to demonstrate the mechanics of Monte Carlo simulation and suggests the nature of the possible results.

The next step in the analysis is the evaluation of the results obtained with the ordering rule being tested. This could be done by calculating the ordering, carrying, and stockout costs that would be experienced during the 10-week period and then converting these to an average total cost per week. Because this procedure has already been demonstrated a number of times, it will not be repeated here. Suffice it to say that the calculated average weekly cost will not serve to prove whether or not the proposed rule of thumb is satisfactory. To determine this, the company must go on to simulate the consequences of other proposed rules of thumb. For example, consideration might now be given to a "two-week supply" rule which would result in 36 units of the part being received at the beginning of every two-week period. Given the simulated weekly demands, the consequences of this rule could be ascertained in the manner outlined and the resultant costs calculated. For reasons mentioned when we evaluated rules of thumb under the condition of certainty, an ordering rule selected with this approach may not necessarily be an optimum solution to the problem, but it is likely to be more economical than one arrived at solely on the basis of judgment and intuition.

OTHER DECISION CRITERIA   It has been mentioned that, on occasion, it may not be possible to estimate the values of the factors needed to calculate the costs generated by a proposed ordering rule. When this is true, the firm may establish criteria, other than costs, in terms of which the rule is judged. One of these may be the number of orders that would have to be placed per time period; in our example, this would be one per week. A second may be the percent of time periods during which a stockout occurs; in our example, shortages occurred in 4 out of 10, or 40 percent, of the time periods. A third may be the average number of items back-ordered in each time period; in our example, a total shortage of 9 items was experienced in the 10-week period, or an average of 0.9 unit per week. A fourth may be the service level, that is, the percent of the total demand that can be satisfied without delay; in our example, the total simulated demand was 180 units of which 171, or 95 percent, could be met immediately.

Some combination of such criteria would simply serve to aid the decision maker when he is asked to pass judgment on an ordering rule whose costs cannot be forecast. If these criteria place the proposed policy in an unfavorable light, the consequences of another policy can be simulated and then evaluated in terms of the same criteria. This would continue until a final decision, based on informed judgment, is reached.

AN EVALUATION   Having concluded our consideration of simulation, we can appreciate why this approach is sometimes described as a trial-and-error method which is applied in a systematic manner. Although the application of this technique has been explained with reference to inventory control, it can be employed to test proposed decision rules in other areas of operations management. Nevertheless, it is important to recognize that simulation does involve predictions of future events, and the firm has no assurance that these predictions will prove to be accurate in either the short or long run. Or they may prove to be correct in the long run but not in the short run. Furthermore, the method for generating a series of future demands is based on the assumption that the respective demands are independent of each other; if this is not true, the approach should not be employed. Finally, the nature of most problems which might be analyzed by this method is such that a manual analysis will prove to be a formidable task; consequently, electronic data processing equipment is usually necessary for use in the analysis.

CONDITION OF UNCERTAINTY[3]

Each of the problems we have considered thus far in this chapter had two characteristics. One was that the future demand for the item could assume one of a number of values. And the other was that a probability of occurrence could be assigned to each of these values. If such probabilities cannot be assigned because they are completely unknown, the condition of *uncertainty* is said to exist. We shall now consider some approaches to order size determination that have been proposed for use under this condition.

MAXIMIN AND MAXIMAX CRITERIA   The first method to be considered is one developed by Abraham Wald. To illustrate its application, let us suppose that a firm has reason to believe that the demand for a purchased item will assume one of the following values for the period under consideration:

Demand

12,000
13,000
14,000
15,000

Furthermore, the purchase price is $6 per unit; the selling price is $10 per unit; the selling expense is $1 for every unit sold; and the net salvage value of every unit that remains unsold at the end of the period is $2. Finally, the firm has no idea of what the probability is of the demand's assuming each of the aforementioned values. Nevertheless, a decision on the quantity to be ordered must be made.

The firm can begin its analysis by constructing a profit matrix. This would be done by calculating, for each possible order quantity X, the

[3] The material in this section is based on an article by the author entitled "Order Size Determination under Uncertainty," which appeared in the August 1968 issue of the *Journal of Purchasing*.

profit that would be generated by each of the possible demands D. The general expressions with which these respective profits can be calculated are as follows:

	When $X > D$	When $X \leq D$
Sales	(+) $10D	(+) $10X
Salvage	(+) 2(X − D)	(+) 0
Purchase cost	(−) 6X	(−) 6X
Selling expense	(−) 1D	(−) 1X
Total (Profit)	$ 7D − $4X	$ 3X

Appropriate substitutions in these expressions would yield the following profit matrix, in which all units are in thousands:

Order quan-	Demand (D)			
tity (X)	12	13	14	15
12	$36	$36	$36	$36
13	32	39	39	39
14	28	35	42	42
15	24	31	38	45

The analysis would continue with an examination of the profit matrix to determine the minimum profit that would be realized with each of the alternative order quantities. In our illustration, these values are as follows:

Order quantity	Minimum profit
12,000	$36,000
13,000	32,000
14,000	28,000
15,000	24,000

Finally, the firm would identify and select that order quantity which will yield the maximum minimum profit, that is, the *maximin*. In our example, this quantity is 12,000 units.

It is apparent that the maximin criterion is one which would appeal to a decision maker who is inclined to believe that the most likely demand to be associated with a specific order quantity is the one which will provide the minimum gain. As opposed to this type of person, an optimist would tend to place emphasis on the maximum gain to be associated with each course of action. More specifically, such an individual would examine the profit matrix and determine the maximum profit that might be experienced with each order quantity. When he did so, he would obtain the following:

Order quantity	Maximum profit
12,000	$36,000
13,000	39,000
14,000	42,000
15,000	45,000

He then would be inclined to select that alternative which yields the maximum maximum profit, that is, the *maximax*. In our illustration, this alternative would be an order quantity of 15,000 units.

As all this indicates, a pessimist would react favorably to the maximin criterion. But an optimist would reject it in favor of the maximax criterion.

THE MINIMAX CRITERION   The second method to be considered is one developed by Leonard J. Savage. Whereas Wald concentrates on the profit to be realized by a firm, Savage places the emphasis on the regret, or opportunity cost, the firm might experience. The opportunity cost to be associated with a specific order quantity is defined as the difference between the actual profit the firm will realize with a given combination of order quantity and demand and the profit that could have been realized had the order quantity been equal to the demand.

To illustrate this, let us return to the preceding profit matrix and note that, when the order quantity is 12,000 units and the demand is 13,000 units, the profit is $36,000. But if the company had ordered 13,000 instead of 12,000 units, the profit would have been the $3 unit profit times 13,000 units, or $39,000. Consequently, the firm experiences an opportunity cost or regret of $39,000 minus $36,000, or $3,000. As another example, when the order quantity is 15,000 units and the demand is 12,000 units, the profit is $24,000. But if the firm had ordered 12,000 instead of 15,000 units, the profit would have been the $3 unit profit times 12,000 units, or $36,000. The result is an opportunity cost of $36,000 minus $24,000, or $12,000. Proceeding in this manner, we develop the following opportunity cost or regret matrix, in which all units are in thousands:

Order quan-tity (X)	Demand (D)			
	12	13	14	15
12	$ 0	$ 3	$ 6	$ 9
13	4	0	3	6
14	8	4	0	3
15	12	8	4	0

An examination of this matrix reveals that the maximum regret to be associated with each of the alternative order quantities is as follows:

Order quantity	Maximum regret
12,000	$ 9,000
13,000	6,000
14,000	8,000
15,000	12,000

With this method, the firm selects that order quantity which will minimize the maximum regret, that is, the *minimax*. In our case, this quantity is 13,000 units. It will be recalled that the maximin criterion yielded an order quantity of 12,000 units.

Although the two approaches produced different results in this illustration, the minimax criterion, like the maximin, represents a conservative method of analysis. This is so because it is based on the implied belief that, for a specific order quantity, the most likely regret is that represented by the maximum value of the opportunity cost. However, the pessimist who prefers to concentrate on the profit that could have been realized, instead of the profit that will be realized, would find the Savage approach to be more attractive than the Wald approach.

AN EVALUATION   Three different criteria were employed in the problem we have been considering for illustrative purposes in this presentation. These criteria, and the order quantities they yielded, are as follows:

Criterion	Order quantity
Maximin	12,000
Maximax	15,000
Minimax	13,000

As can be seen, the three criteria generated three different results. This, of course, suggests that, if one of the results is correct, then the others must be incorrect. Consequently, the need remains for determining which, if any, of the recommended order quantities is the correct one. In brief, we seem to have returned to the question with which we began the analysis.

However, a somewhat more judicious reaction to our findings may be in order. An exact solution to a problem is possible only if all the relevant data are known and processed correctly. In the determination of an order quantity under uncertainty, all the relevant data are not known; specifically, the firm is ignorant of the demand schedule for the item involved. Hence, no analytical approach can be developed which will yield the correct answer with certainty. At best, it may be possible to develop a method which, although deficient in some respects, is preferable to judgment or intuition.

It so happens that more than one such method has been developed for use when uncertainty prevails and that each of these methods may yield a different result. Admittedly, this has its disadvantages. However, it also has an important advantage. In the absence of certainty, the decision reached in a specific case cannot help but be affected by the attitude of the decision maker toward risk or uncertainty. Under a given set of circumstances, it is not surprising to find that a pessimist reacts one way and an optimist a second way; furthermore, some individuals are governed by what is to be gained and others by what is to be lost. When the condition of uncertainty exists, there is no way of knowing which of these attitudes is correct in a specific case. Therefore, one can conclude that it is fortunate that more than one rational approach to the determination of order sizes under uncertainty is available, because an individual is then free to select that approach which reflects the value system to which he adheres.

SOME REMAINING OBSERVATIONS

We have considered a number of basic quantitative approaches to the determination of economic inventory levels. Other techniques of a more advanced nature have been developed for use, but those described typify the methods by means of which the firm can reduce its dependence on judgment and intuition. Nevertheless, in spite of the availability of these and other quantitative techniques, there are many items for which inventory levels cannot be established in this manner. Reasons for this have already been suggested—the construction of an appropriate mathematical model may not be feasible, meaningful estimates of the relevant factors may not be possible, short-term considerations may outweigh those of the long term, the cost of a quantitative analysis may be excessive, and so on. In such cases, ordering policies must, of necessity, be based on the judgment of qualified individuals.

It should also be noted that, as suggested by some of our examples, the need to control inventories exists in various types of organizations. Manufacturers must control inventories of raw materials, component parts, and finished products. Wholesalers and retailers must control inventories of the items they sell. Hospitals must control inventories of medicinal supplies, food, linens, and maintenance supplies. Repair firms must control inventories of spare parts. Offices must control inventories of forms and stationery. The important thing to recognize, however, is that the principles of inventory control are unaffected by the organization in which the need for such control exists.

Finally, we might note that the use of automatic data processing equipment enables many organizations to control inventories with greater ease than would otherwise be possible. In this area of activity, there is a need for extensive record keeping and report preparation. Data processing equipment can be employed to maintain such records as quantities received, used, and on hand; to prepare reports in which items for which reorder points have been reached are listed and their corresponding reorder quantities shown; and to analyze past records to obtain a starting point for estimating future demands, lead times, and their relative frequencies of occurrence.

The equipment can also be used to carry out the computations involved in the determination of economic lot sizes, the evaluation of available quantity discounts, the comparison of alternative combinations of manufacturing schedules and inventory levels, the selection of safety stocks, and the choosing of order quantities under conditions of risk and uncertainty. And as has already been mentioned, the application of Monte Carlo simulation almost necessitates the use of a computer to generate a sufficiently long demand series and to ascertain the consequences of alternative decision rules in light of this generated demand pattern.

Of course, data processing equipment can perform these useful and important functions only after it has been instructed how to do so, and these instructions can be prepared only by someone who is acquainted with the elements of the methods of analysis we have considered.

QUESTIONS

10-1 How is the condition of risk defined?

10-2 What is meant by the *expected* value of such things as demand, revenues, costs, and profits? How is this value determined?

10-3 Describe and evaluate the procedure for determining the quantity of an item that should be in stock at the beginning of a given period if the demand during the period can assume different specific values for which the respective probabilities of occurrence are known.

10-4 What is the advantage of carrying safety stocks? The disadvantage?

10-5 Why is it said that the problem of safety stock determination cannot be considered independently of the lot size involved?

10-6 Describe and evaluate the method for determining the combination of lot size and safety stock which will minimize the total inventory cost when the demand for the item under consideration is not constant. When the procurement or lead time is not constant.

10-7 What is the difference between a fixed-order system and a fixed-interval system? What advantages does the latter have as compared with the former?

10-8 How are order intervals and quantities determined in a fixed-interval system?

10-9   What is Monte Carlo simulation? How is it applied in inventory control?

10-10   What are the criteria, other than costs, in terms of which a company might evaluate the consequences, as determined by the simulation process, of an inventory decision rule?

10-11   Evaluate Monte Carlo simulation as a decision-making tool in the area of inventory control.

10-12   How is the condition of uncertainty defined?

10-13   Ordering rules under the condition of uncertainty can be selected on the basis of a maximin, maximax, or minimax criterion. Describe the methods for obtaining the values of each of these criteria and evaluate these respective approaches to the determination of order quantities.

10-14   Under what conditions would a firm be unable to employ quantitative methods of analysis in the area of inventory control?

10-15   What are some examples of operations, other than manufacturing, in which the need for controlling inventories exists?

10-16   How can automatic data processing equipment be used in the area of inventory control?

PROBLEMS

10-1   The profit matrix shown on page 231 contains nine profit values. The text contains the expressions for determining two of these values. Show how the other seven were obtained.

10-2   The cost matrix on page 233 contains values which yielded the expected costs listed in the table that follows the matrix. Show how the nine matrix values and the three expected costs were obtained.

10-3   A company has decided to purchase a group of automatic machines of special design which have an estimated service life of five years. Spare parts can be obtained at this time and kept in stock, or they can be ordered at the time they will actually be needed. The estimated demand schedule for spares during the five-year period is as follows:

Sets of spares required	Probability of occurrence
0	0.90
1	0.05
2	0.03
3	0.02

For every set of spares purchased now, the carrying cost for the involved time period is expected to be $5,000; this consists of depreciation, storage, and interest. For every set of spares required but not on hand, the cost is estimated to be $90,000; this represents the increased cost of any spares ordered at a later date and the expense of the resultant serious production delays.

What are the expected costs of the alternatives? How many sets of spare parts should be procured at this time? (Ans. $15,300; $11,300; $11,800; $15,000)

10-4 The unit purchase cost of a monthly magazine distributed by a vendor is $0.20, and the selling price is $0.50. At the end of a given month, the vendor receives no refund on any unsold magazines and simply discards them. The magazines are kept in stock for such a short time that the cost of storage and interest is considered to be negligible. Selling expenses are estimated to be $0.07 for each magazine sold. The monthly demand schedule for the magazine is as follows:

Number demanded	Probability of occurrence
500	0.60
550	0.30
600	0.10

If only one order can be placed for a given issue of the magazine, what should the order size for each issue be? Determine this, first, by computing the expected profit for each alternative and, then, by computing the expected cost of each alternative. (Ans. $115.00, $113.60, $105.75; $5.75, $7.15, $15.00)

10-5 In the situation described in the preceding problem, suppose that the supplier of the magazine changes his policy regarding unsold copies. Specifically, it is revised to allow the vendor to return all unsold magazines at the end of a given month and receive a refund of $0.12 per copy. What effect will this have on the expected profit for each alternative? On the expected cost?

10-6 A research institute receives a certain chemical at a rate of 80 gallons per day during the delivery period. Ordering costs are fixed at $32 per order. The procurement time is a constant five days. Carrying costs are $0.065 per gallon per day. Stockout costs, attributable to disrupted work schedules, are about $16 for every gallon needed but not on hand. The estimated demand schedule for the chemical is as follows:

Demand per procurement period, gal	Probability of occurrence
90	0.02
100	0.96
110	0.02

Because the probability is so small of the demand's being other than 100 units during the five-day lead time, it is decided to determine the economic order quantity as if the demand were a constant 20 units per day. Nevertheless, consideration will be given to maintaining a safety stock to provide for a greater demand. What combination of lot size and safety stock will yield the minimum average daily cost? (Ans. 170; 0; $8.28)

10-7   The entire lot of a packaging material is delivered at one time and used at a uniform rate. Ordering costs are approximately $45 per order, and carrying costs for the resultant inventories are about $0.08 per unit per week. Stockout costs stemming from lost customer orders are estimated to be $6 for each unit demanded but not available. The lead time is a constant one week. The demand schedule for the item is as follows:

Demand per week, units	Probability of occurrence
800	0.04
900	0.06
1,000	0.80
1,100	0.06
1,200	0.04

Management considers the variation in demand to be negligible in the sense that the economic lot size will be computed on the assumption that the demand is uniform and equal to the expected value of the possible demands. However, a safety stock might be maintained to provide for the occurrence of greater demands. What should the lot size and minimum inventory be?

10-8   The determination of economic minimum inventory levels when procurement times are expected to vary was discussed in the section beginning on page 241. It was pointed out that the first step in the procedure calls for converting variable procurement times into the equivalent demands during these periods. This was illustrated with an example in which the demand was given as a constant 3,000 units per month. This demand, when coupled with the variable procurement-time schedule, yielded the following:

Procurement time, months	Demand during procurement time, units	Probability of occurrence
0.75	2,250	0.04
1.00	3,000	0.92
1.25	3,750	0.04

The other relevant items were that the entire lot was received at one time, ordering costs were $110 per lot, carrying costs were $0.40 per unit per year, and stockout costs were $1 per unit. What combination of lot size and minimum inventory should the firm adopt? What will be the resultant annual cost? (Ans. 5,020; 0; $2,008)

10-9   A firm manufactures a component part which is used by its assembly department at a uniform rate of 75 units per day. The manufacturing process is such that, when a lot is being manufactured, the items are delivered to the stockroom at a uniform rate of 100 units per day during the entire production run. Ordering costs are $80 per lot, and the inventory carrying costs are $0.012 per unit per day.

The average procurement time for a replenishment order is three days. However, past experience suggests that the actual distribution of these times is likely to be as follows:

Procurement time, days	Probability of occurrence
2	0.08
3	0.84
4	0.08

Given that the out-of-stock cost is estimated to be $3 per unit, what lot size and minimum inventory would you recommend that the firm adhere to for this item?

10-10 In a fixed-interval system of inventory control, what will the order quantity be under the following conditions?

a The time between orders is 4 weeks, the specified safety stock is 500 units, the lead time is 1 week, the expected demand is 1,400 units per week, and the quantity on hand is 1,650 units.

b The quantity in stock is 495 units, the expected demand is 32 units per working day, the procurement time is 15 working days, the interval between orders is 45 working days, and the established minimum inventory is 0 units.

10-11 A department of the federal government uses stationery at a fairly uniform rate throughout the year. The annual demand is 720 packages, and the lead time is one-half month.

It was determined that the most economic combination of order quantity and minimum inventory is 116 and 10 packages, respectively. However, the lot size was rounded off to 120 packages, with the result that, on the average, an order would be placed every two months. The actual time between orders would, of course, vary because there are fluctuations in the rate of use during any one year.

Because of the disadvantages to be associated with a fixed-order system, the department decides to place orders for the stationery at fixed intervals. The length of the selected interval is obtained by taking into consideration the annual demand and the rounded value of 120 packages for the economic lot size. The decision to carry a safety stock of 10 packages remains unchanged.

At the time an order for replenishment stock is to be placed, what should the order quantity be under each of the following circumstances?

a The quantity on hand is 40 packages. (Ans. 120)

b The quantity on hand is 25 packages.

c The quantity on hand is 57 packages.

10-12 The results of a specific application of Monte Carlo simulation are contained in the table shown on page 247. Suppose that the involved firm goes on to ascertain the consequences of a "two-week supply" ordering rule. What would be the resultant inventory pattern for the 10-week period considered in the text example in which a "one-week supply" rule was evaluated? After developing this pattern, determine the following for the "two-week supply" rule:

a Number of orders placed per week. (Ans. 0.5)

b Percent of weeks during which a stockout occurred. (Ans. 30)

c Average number of units back-ordered per week. (Ans. 0.6)

d Percent of total demand that can be satisfied without delay. (Ans. 96.7)

10-13 On the basis of judgment and past experience, a firm derives the following demand schedule for one of its products:

Demand per month, units	Probability of occurrence
2,200	0.09
2,300	0.38
2,400	0.31
2,500	0.22

The product is shipped at a uniform rate during any one month. Further, the demand in a given month is not affected by demands during other months. Also, stockouts do not result in back orders but in lost sales. Finally, the lead time is one week.

Inventory control personnel are considering, among others, an ordering rule which provides for the receipt of an order in the stockroom at the beginning of each month. The size of this order would be constant and equal to the *expected* value of the demand per month. To obtain some idea of the effects of this policy, the firm tests the rule by means of Monte Carlo simulation. In the process, it generates a long series of monthly demands, but the values for a 12-month portion of this series are fairly representative of the entire series. These values are as follows:

Month	Simulated demand, units	Month	Simulated demand, units
1	2,300	7	2,400
2	2,200	8	2,400
3	2,500	9	2,500
4	2,500	10	2,400
5	2,300	11	2,300
6	2,300	12	2,300

With these simulated demands and the proposed ordering rule, what will the following be:

a Number of orders placed per year?

b Number of months per year in which a stockout will occur? Percent of months?

c Average shortage in terms of units per month?

d Percent of total demand that cannot be satisfied? That can be satisfied?

10-14 Show how the 16 values contained in the profit matrix on page 251 were obtained.

10-15 Sample calculations were given for 2 of the 16 values contained in the opportunity cost or regret matrix which appears on page 252. Show how the other 14 values were obtained.

10-16 A florist can place only one order for a certain type of cut flower to satisfy the demand that will occur during a given weekend. He estimates that the demand, to the closest ten dozen, will assume one of the following values in the period under consideration:

Demand, dozens

    100
    110
    120
    130
    140

All flowers that remain unsold by the close of the weekend are donated to a local hospital. The flowers cost the florist $3 per dozen, and other expenses average $2 for every dozen sold. The selling price is $9 per dozen. If there is no basis for arriving at the probabilities to be associated with the various demand values, what order size is suggested by each of the following criteria: (*a*) maximin, (*b*) maximax, and (*c*) minimax? (Ans. 100, 140, 120)

10-17 A combination of long lead time and high ordering cost permits a distributor of Christmas tree ornaments to place only one order to obtain a supply of a certain type of ornament for the season. The cost of the item is $10 per case; the selling price is $30 per case; and the selling expense is $5 per case sold. To eliminate the need for storage until the following year, all remaining cases are disposed of at the close of the season by reducing the selling price to $8 a case; a selling expense of $5 per case is also experienced with these sales.

The distributor expects the demand before the close of the season to be 600 or 700 or 800 cases, as estimated to the closest hundred cases. But he is unable to arrive at the probabilities to be associated with these respective demands.

Determine the order quantity that would be obtained by a (*a*) maximax analysis, (*b*) maximin analysis, and (*c*) minimax analysis.

PART SIX

PRODUCTION CONTROL

ELEVEN

PRODUCTION CONTROL IN INTERMITTENT MANUFACTURING

The end result of decisions in the areas of facilities planning, plant layout, materials handling, and inventory control is that, at a given moment in time, the firm will have a certain output capacity. This is to say that specific types and amounts of production equipment, machine accessories, manpower, floor space, materials handling equipment, raw materials, and purchased parts will be available for use in the production activity.

After this capacity has been established, actual orders for given quantities of various products will be coming in. These orders might be for standard or nonstandard products. Insofar as standard products are concerned, these will have been produced for stock on the basis of a sales forecast. However, as the inventories of these items are depleted in the course of satisfying customer demands, the stockroom, in effect, will be placing replenishment orders with the production department for quantities determined by methods discussed in the chapters on inventory control. Insofar as nonstandard products are concerned, these will not have been produced in advance, and, hence, the production department will, in effect, be receiving orders for these items directly from the firm's customers rather than from the stockroom.

All orders received by the production department will stipulate the expected delivery dates, in addition to the required quantities of the products involved. Therefore, the manufacturing department will be expected to produce the firm's products, not only in the required quantities but also in time to meet preestablished delivery dates. As a rule, this can be accomplished only if some control is exercised over the plant's activities. This control, which we call "production control," involves the development and implementation of a plan which is capable of yielding the desired results.

Every such plan calls for the preparation of an operation schedule. For a given order, the operation scheduling activity will involve determining what operations are required, the type and amount of production facilities that must be employed, and the points at which each of these operations must be started and completed if the established delivery date is to be met. After the operation schedule has been established, necessary instructions must be issued to the manufacturing departments. Then, procedures must be established for determining the progress of production, for evaluating this progress in light of the existing schedule, and for making adjustments for departures from this schedule.

But a production control system cannot accomplish miracles. If the stipulated order quantities and delivery dates are unrealistic in the sense that they impose impossible demands on the firm's output capacity, there is little, if anything, the production control department can do to rectify the situation. In brief, production control is incapable of eliminating the adverse effects of poor production planning; at best, if can only hope to minimize them. This does not mean, however, that sound production planning eliminates the need for production control. Even though the required plant capacity has been provided, action must be taken to utilize this capacity effectively. Unless this is done, orders may not be processed in time even in the presence of excess capacity.

BASIC PRODUCTION CONTROL SYSTEMS

In this presentation, we shall discuss two basic production control systems. One of them is called "order control"; the other is called "flow control." Order control is adhered to by those firms which engage in intermittent manufacturing, while flow control is adhered to by those firms which engage in continuous manufacturing.

The existence of these two different methods of production control is attributable to the fact that intermittent manufacturing differs from continuous manufacturing in certain important respects which we have already discussed. The influence of these characteristics on the corresponding production control systems will become apparent when the respective systems are described. But even at this point, one can see intuitively that intermittent manufacturing will call for the more complex procedure. If for no other reason, this is true because of the greater number of products whose production must be controlled. In addition to this, a great deal of preparatory work is involved every time production is to begin on a given product, and in intermittent manufacturing, production of a single product will be inaugurated many times a year as compared with maybe once for a product which is manufactured continuously. Finally, the fact that a given piece of equipment may be used to process scores of different products in intermittent manufacturing also presents special difficulties. Provisions must be made for a variety of setups at a single work station, for informing the supervisor and operator of what is to be done next, for making the proper materials and machine accessories available when needed, and so on. In continuous manufacturing, on the other hand, a single set of instructions will suffice to keep a work station active for an appreciable length of time.

Before we go on to a description of order control and flow control, it should be mentioned that, in any one company, both these systems may exist at the same time. This is because some of the firm's products may be manufactured intermittently and some of them continuously. But even more important, many firms will have a system which contains elements of both order control and flow control. The reason for this is that there are cases in which manufacturing is basically, although not completely, continuous. As an example, there is the case of an automobile assembly plant. In general, the plant is producing a single product continuously. The assembly line has been designed specifically for the performance of the required operations, and all the component parts flowing through the line undergo the same processes. Yet, not every automobile coming off this line is the same. Some have two doors, others have four; some are green, others are black; some have white-walled tires, others do not. In brief, there are variations in the final product, and some provision must be made for handling these variations. Suffice it to say that the production control system which will be designed to cope with this situation will be a cross between order control and flow control. Exactly which elements of each will be present should be evident after we have considered the respective systems.

NATURE OF PRESENTATION We shall begin our presentation with a discussion of order control. Because this is the more complex of the two systems, if it is considered first, the details of flow control can be understood with less difficulty. In this presentation of order control and the subsequent presentation of flow control, we shall describe each of the steps in somewhat general terms. As this suggests, no attempt will be made to describe the specific approach employed by a given company. The reason for this is that no two systems of either order control or flow control are exactly alike. Instead, each is designed to reflect the unique operating characteristics and needs of the firm in which it will be used. Consequently, the procedures and forms we shall consider are only suggestive of those that may be applied in a specific case. However, the basic functions of production control are as we shall describe them to be, even though the means for performing them may vary from firm to firm.

Furthermore, we shall refer to the production control department as being responsible for all the steps in the procedure. In a particular firm, however, many of these responsibilities may be assigned to individuals who are members of some other group. In fact, there are companies which do not have a department specifically called "production control." But as long as the function is one of production control, we shall speak of it as being performed by the production control department.

AUTHORIZATIONS TO PRODUCE

In intermittent manufacturing, the entire production control activity is inaugurated by the production control department's being told what is to be produced, the quantities to be produced, and the date by which the stipulated quantity of a given product is to be produced. We shall refer to the form in which all this information is presented as an authorization to produce. Actually, producing authorizations can take one of three forms. The first of these is a sales order; the second, a manufacturing requisition; and the third, a master schedule. We shall discuss them in this order.

SALES ORDERS   We know that products manufactured intermittently may be nonstandard items produced directly to customer order. When a sales order is received for a nonstandard product, a copy of this order can be sent to the production control department. Insofar as this department is concerned, the relevant information contained in the order would be the description of what is to be produced, the required quantities, and the delivery date. In most cases, the sales department will arrive at the delivery date by first consulting with the production control department. At the time an inquiry is received from the customer, the production control department will be asked to make a somewhat general study of the available factors of production and, on the basis of its findings, to furnish the sales department with a possible delivery date. If this proves to be unsatisfactory to the customer, the date will be reviewed to see if any improvement is possible. There are cases, however, in which the sales department will promise a delivery date independently of the production control department. This would be possible when the sales department is somewhat acquainted with the production potential of the plant and, on the basis of past experience with orders of a similar nature, is able to arrive at a fairly realistic date. Then, of course, there are cases in which sales personnel will promise any date they have to, to make the sale, and then let production control worry about it. This may create special problems, which we shall consider later.

In any event, when the production control department does receive a copy of a sales order of this type, it has authorization to schedule the production of the items and quantities involved. A form which is typical of an order such as this is shown in Figure 11-1.

MANUFACTURING REQUISITIONS The sales order would not be applicable to those products manufactured for stock. As we know from our discussion of inventory control, some of these standard items will be produced in uniform lot sizes, which should be the economic lot size, while others will not. In the case of those products that are manufactured in uniform lot sizes, the authorization to produce will take the form of a manufacturing requisition.

For the items that fall into this category, an inventory record of the type shown in Figure 11-2 will be maintained. When the indicated reorder point for a given part or product is reached, stockroom or inventory control personnel will prepare a manufacturing requisition and send a copy to the production control department. This requisition will identify the

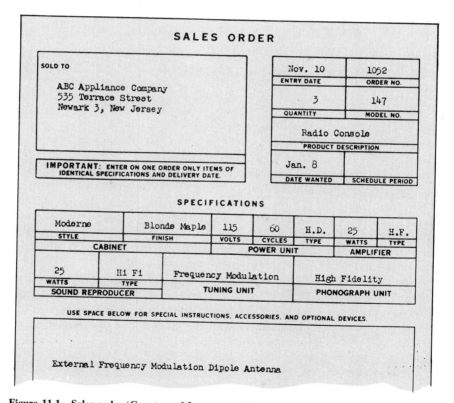

Figure 11-1 Sales order (Courtesy of International Business Machines Corporation)

INVENTORY RECORD

PART NUMBER	DESCRIPTION	P A / A S / R S / T Y	UNIT COST	UNIT OF MEAS	LEAD TIME	ORDERING RULES				VENDOR NO.	ON HAND
						DISCRETE			A		
						REORDER POINT		EOQ	B		
						MIN		MAX	C		
42309683	SHAFT	[X] [ ]	7.50	01	3	10		100	B	19630	40

	CURRENT	1	2	3	4	5	6	7	8	OVER 8
ON ORDER *Released Orders	100*	100*		100*		100	100			
REQUIREMENTS	110	90	20	80	30	80	90	20		
NET AVAILABLE	30	40	20	40	10	30	40	20	20	

RELEASED SHOP OR PURCHASE ORDERS

STOCK DATE	QTY	ORDER NO.	STOCK DATE	QTY	ORDER NO.	STOCK DATE	QTY	ORDER NO.	STOCK DATE	QTY	ORDER NO.
125	100	13842	130	100	14910	140	100	15895			
STOCK DATE	QTY	ORDER NO.	STOCK DATE	QTY	ORDER NO.	STOCK DATE	QTY	ORDER NO.	STOCK DATE	QTY	ORDER NO.

Figure 11-2   Inventory record (Courtesy of International Business Machines Corporation)

item and stipulate the quantity needed for stock replenishment purposes. The quantity, of course, will be equal to the predetermined economic lot size, which is also shown in the inventory record.

Insofar as the expected delivery date is concerned, it will be recalled that the reorder point is affected by the length of the procurement period. Therefore, an estimate of the length of this period would have been obtained from the production control department prior to the establishment of the reorder point. This expected delivery time may be shown on the manufacturing requisition, or if not, it will be assumed that the production control department knows when delivery is expected.

Therefore, when the production control department receives a manufacturing requisition, it receives authorization to schedule production of the items called for in this requisition, and it is expected to arrange for the delivery of the stipulated quantities within a certain period of time. A typical manufacturing requisition is shown in Figure 11-3.

MASTER SCHEDULES   As we learned in our discussion of inventory decision rules, not all standard products will be manufactured in uniform

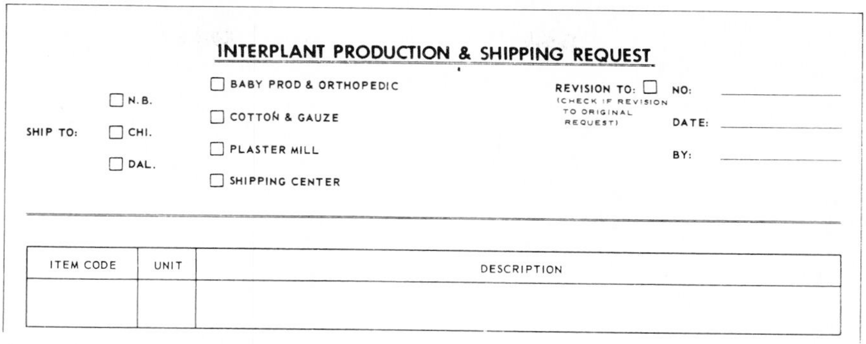

INTERPLANT PRODUCTION & SHIPPING REQUEST

☐ BABY PROD & ORTHOPEDIC   REVISION TO: ☐ NO: _____

☐ N.B.   (CHECK IF REVISION
                                                   TO ORIGINAL
☐ COTTON & GAUZE   REQUEST)   DATE: _____

SHIP TO: ☐ CHI.

☐ PLASTER MILL   BY: _____

☐ DAL.

☐ SHIPPING CENTER

ITEM CODE	UNIT	DESCRIPTION

Figure 11-3   A manufacturing requisition

lot sizes. Instead, the lot size may vary from order to order. Where this is true, no single value for the reorder point and reorder quantity can be shown in the inventory record for the item involved, and, hence, some form other than the manufacturing requisition must be employed to authorize the production of these products. The authorization that is used is called a "master schedule," and it is prepared as follows:

After having determined the pattern of production that will be adhered to in the manufacture of these standard items, the inventory control personnel will notify the production control department accordingly. Specifically, they will identify the products which are to be produced, the quantities of each to be produced, and the points in the period under consideration at which they are to be produced. These points represent the dates by which the last required operation on the various products is to be completed. These instructions, which we call the master schedule, usually assume a tabular form. However, for our purposes, the information contained in the master schedule can more clearly be depicted graphically, and this is done in Figure 11-4.

The schedule shown in Figure 11-4 is to be interpreted as follows: Taking the first week for purposes of illustration, we note that 100 units of product 1 are required in that week. This means that 100 units of this product are to be ready for delivery during that week; this may necessitate inaugurating operations on these units a week or two before. During the same week, 200 units of product 2 are to be ready for shipment, and so on.

In brief, then, the master schedule, manufacturing requisition, and sales order are the means by which the production control department can be notified concerning what is to be produced, in what quantities it is to be produced, and when it is to be produced. In any one company, one or more of these three types of production authorization will be in use.

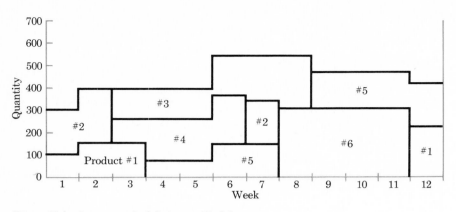

Figure 11-4   A master schedule in graphical form

PROCESSING INSTRUCTIONS

After the production control department has been told what is to be manufactured and when, it must arrange for the production of these items. Before it can do this, however, it must know how the product is to be manufactured, and, therefore, it must receive processing instructions. These processing instructions can take various forms.

In the most comprehensive case, instructions will be required for an assembly which is to be produced for the first time. Where this is true, the first step in the preparation of these instructions will call for the drawing of blueprints. On the basis of these prints, someone must prepare a bill of materials, such as the one shown earlier as Figure 3-2, and make it available to the production control department. Given the number of assemblies called for in the authorization to produce, the bill of materials enables the production control department to enumerate the different parts required and the total quantities of each needed to produce the stipulated number of assemblies. This enumeration can be referred to as the "exploded assembly requirements" and may assume the form shown in Figure 11-5.

Next, an operation or routing sheet, such as the one shown earlier as Figure 3-1, must be prepared for each of the manufactured parts. These sheets, in combination with the bill of materials, provide the processing instructions for the product under consideration.

It was mentioned that an assembly to be produced for the first time represents the most comprehensive case. The reason for this is that if the product to be manufactured is not an assembly, no product explosion, and, hence, no bill of materials, is required. Further, if the product has

ASSEMBLY ORDER

ASSEMBLY NUMBER   20136818
ASSEMBLY DESCRIPTION   PUMP ASSY
ORDER QUANTITY   50

ORDER NUMBER   337813

PART NUMBER	DESCRIPTION	U/M	QUANTITY PER ASSY	EXTENDED QUANTITY
531674	SCREW	01	6	300
531690	WASHER	01	5	250
728419	SCREW	01	5	250
1431478	SEAL	01	2	100
3519794	MOTOR	01	1	50
3572133	SPRING	01	2	100
20136130	PUMP SHAFT ASSY	01	1	50
20136301	SET COLLAR	01	1	50
20136315	CLAMP MOUNTING	01	1	50
20136338	SHIFTER COLLAR	01	1	50
20136345	SCREW	01	4	200

Figure 11-5 An example of an exploded assembly requirement (Courtesy of International Business Machines Corporation)

been produced in the past, a bill of materials and operation sheets will already exist, and there will be no need for preparing them at this particular time.

AVAILABILITY OF FACTORS OF PRODUCTION

At this point, the production department knows what is to be produced, how much is to be produced, when it is to be produced, and how it is to be produced. It would appear that the next step is the actual scheduling of operations. However, one more thing remains to be done; namely, the department must check on the availability of factors of production. This involves a series of activities. In discussing these activities, we shall assume that the product involved is an assembly; the case of a single part is, of course, much simpler.

We know that, with the use of the bill of materials, the production control department has developed a list of all the part and quantity requirements for an order which may have emanated from a customer or the stockroom. Some of these parts are purchased, and some are manufactured. However, not all of them will necessarily have to be purchased or manufactured at this time for this specific order. The reason for this is that some of these parts may have already been purchased or produced on the basis of decisions made during the production planning activity and are currently in stock. Therefore, the production control department will begin by checking its list of required parts against what is in stock. Insofar as purchased parts are concerned, the required quantities of those on hand will be reserved for this order, and purchase orders will be placed for no less than the remainder and possibly more if the ordering rule calls for a larger reorder quantity. At the time these orders are placed, the production control department will obtain the probable delivery dates. Insofar as the manufactured parts are concerned, the required quantities of those on hand will also be reserved, and no less than the remainder will be scheduled for production and possibly more if the ordering rule calls for a larger reorder quantity.

Now that the production control department has a list of all the parts and quantities that must be manufactured for this order, it can begin the work which is preliminary to the actual scheduling of operations. To begin with, these part requirements must be expressed in terms of their equivalent factors of production. First, the kinds and amounts of materials required must be determined. The information necessary to do this can be obtained from the respective operation sheets. By taking the material requirements per unit of output for each part and multiplying them by the units to be produced, the production control department can ascertain the total material requirements for each part. It should be mentioned, however, that the units to be produced will be increased by some percentage, determined on the basis of past experience or estimates, to allow for the occurrence of scrap. After material requirements have been computed, the production control department will check with the stockroom to determine which of these raw materials are on hand. Those that are will be reserved. The remainder or possibly some larger quantity will be ordered, and information with regard to probable delivery dates will be obtained.

Second, equipment requirements will be determined. Again the information required to do this will be contained in the operation sheets. For each part to be produced, the operation sheet will list the equipment to be used and the amount of time required per unit of output to perform the operations in which this equipment is involved. Knowing the total units to be produced, and this total will include an allowance for scrap, the production control department can compute the total machine-hours of different types that will be required. Now, if the time requirements shown in the operation sheet are based on the assumption that machine operators will work at 100 percent efficiency and that the machine will be operated at 100 percent capacity, the calculated totals of required machine-hours must be adjusted to reflect actual labor efficiency and the fact that there will be a certain amount of downtime to be associated with each machine. After all this has been done, the production control department must check on the availability of the required equipment. It does this by reviewing its machine load cards. A machine load card will exist either for each piece of equipment in the plant or for each group of machines of the same kind. In addition to an identification of the machine involved, the card will contain a list of the work already scheduled to be performed on the machine and the hours each of these jobs is expected to take. Therefore, if 72 hours of work are scheduled on a machine which is operated eight hours a day, the production control department knows that this machine will be available for additional work in nine days. A typical machine load card is shown in Figure 11-6.

Next, the production control department must determine machine-accessory requirements, such as tools, jigs, fixtures, and gauges. The procedure for doing this is like the one employed in the determination of equipment requirements. From the operation sheets, needed accessories can be ascertained. The amount of each required in terms of hours can be determined by working with unit operating times and total units to be produced. As before, an adjustment would be made for scrap, labor efficiency, and machine downtime and other delays. The availability of these accessories would be determined by checking with the tool crib, where records of all the accessories on hand would be maintained. If some of these accessories had never been procured, they must be ordered and probable delivery dates obtained.

Finally, manpower requirements must be computed. A major portion of this work will already have been done when equipment requirements were determined. The reason for this is that the hours of machine operator time will coincide with the hours of machine time, or with some multiple or fraction of this time if more than one or less than one operator is assigned to a machine. However, there may be operations which do not require the use of equipment, such as packaging or assembly, and the manpower requirements for these activities must also be determined. As before, the operation sheets will show what these operations are and

WORK CENTER MANUFACTURING ORDER LIST											
WORK CENTER		NUMBER OF SHIFTS	NO. OF MEN OR MACH.	TOTAL WKLY. CAPAC-ITY	ADJ. WKLY. CAPAC-ITY	PART NO.	ORDER NO.	ORDER QTY.	OP. NO.	DATE COMP.	LOAD HOURS SCHED.
NO.	NAME										
115	MON. 12*36 LATHE	1	1	40.0	38.5	1334216	24972	70	25	1110	3.1
						1249174	25237	140	35	1110	2.1
						1101319	24881	90	20	1110	4.0
						1272818	25201	75	40	1111	3.5
						1331016	24842	40	60	1111	4.0

Figure 11-6 A machine load card (Courtesy of Royal McBee Corporation)

their time requirements per unit of output. Working with total production requirements for each part, adjusted for scrap, the production control department can calculate the total man-hours of various types that will be required in addition to those required to operate equipment. These man-hours must also be adjusted to reflect expected labor efficiency and unavoidable delays. With this information at its disposal, the production control department can now go on to check the availability of manpower. A portion of this task will also have already been accomplished. With regard to manpower required to operate equipment, it will be assumed that, when the equipment is available, the operator will be available. If this were not true, the corresponding machine load card would not have been in the active file. Insofar as the remaining labor requirements are concerned, the production control department must determine the total amount of this manpower, by type, that is in the company's work force. Then, by comparing these totals with the work these individuals are already scheduled to perform, it can determine when each of these various labor classifications will be available for work on the order under consideration. Existing work loads for the various types of labor can be found from load records similar to those maintained for equipment.

It will be noticed that nothing has been said about indirect labor. The reason for this is, as was suggested when we were considering production planning, that the production control department would find it impossible, for all practical purposes, to determine exactly how much indirect labor is required for a specific order. Therefore, the common assumption is that a sufficient amount of this type of labor will be available when needed.

Let us now summarize what the production control department has at this point. First, it has complete information on the amount of each factor of production that will be required to process the order, and this information includes processing times for each operation. Second, it has information on purchased and manufactured parts in stock and promised delivery dates on purchased parts ordered. Third, it has information on materials in stock and promised delivery dates on materials ordered. Fourth, it has information on when various types of equipment will be available. Fifth, it has information on what machine accessories are in stock and promised delivery dates on machine accessories ordered. Sixth, it has information on when various types of direct labor will be available. And, of course, it has instructions about how all these factors of production are to be used to perform the required operations. With all this information at its disposal, the production control department is now ready to schedule the performance of these operations, that is, to prepare the required operation schedule.

THE OPERATION SCHEDULE

Preparing the operation schedule is one of the most difficult tasks in production control. The operation sheets tell the production control department what sequence the operations should follow, what unit processing times are for each operation, and what factors of production are required to perform each operation. The preparatory work it has done up to this point tells the production control department the times at which the required factors of production will be available. The task at hand is analogous to the fitting together of the pieces of a jigsaw puzzle, with one important difference. While the pieces of a jigsaw puzzle go together in only one way, a variety of operation schedules is possible, and there is no way of knowing for certain which is the best. To illustrate this, let us consider a simple case in which three operations are required on a single part. It may be that the availability of the required factors of production is such that the three alternatives shown in Figure 11-7 are possible.

These three alternatives are only representative of the many which can possibly be adopted. However, one may say that each of these three alternatives will yield a different completion date, and some of them may be unsatisfactory in light of the required delivery date. This is true. On the other hand, it may be that, given the plant's available capacity, the preestablished delivery date is relatively far away, and, consequently, it can be met with any of these three alternatives. If the production control department schedules the work so that it is completed in the shortest period of time, this will serve to increase the firm's inventories and the costs to

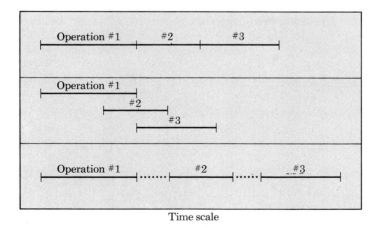

Time scale

Figure 11-7   Three alternative operation schedules

be associated with these inventories. On the other hand, if the production control department schedules the work so that it is completed just in time for delivery, the company will have idle capacity at the present time, and it may be that, at the later date when the order is being processed, a number of other orders will have been received and existing capacity will be inadequate. In either case, a gamble is involved, and there is no way of knowing for certain what should be done.

About all that can be said is that, in general, there are two basic approaches that can be employed in operation scheduling. One is to start with the desired delivery date and the last required operation and then work backward by scheduling each preceding operation on the basis of the availability of the factors of production and required processing times until the starting date for the first operation on the first part is reached. The result may be as shown in Figure 11-8.

The second alternative is to schedule the first operation on the first part as soon as the required factors of production are available and then work forward by scheduling each succeeding operation on the basis of the availability of the factors of production and required processing times until the completion date for the last operation on the last part is reached. The result of this procedure may be as shown in Figure 11-9. Of course, with this basic approach, the variations suggested in Figure 11-7 are possible, and judgment must be used.

It should also be mentioned that, when scheduling the required operations, the production control department will allow some time for the transporting of work in process from one work station to another and for the time an order may have to remain at a work station before processing begins. These times are difficult to estimate with any accuracy, and, consequently, a rule of thumb, such as four hours per operation, may be developed on the basis of past experience.

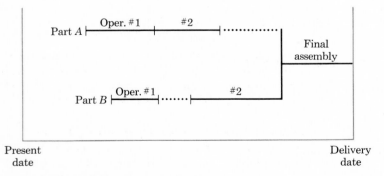

Figure 11-8   A possible operation schedule

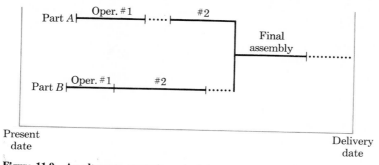

Figure 11-9 An alternate operation schedule

If the production planners have done their job well in the sense that the forecasts of required factors of production prove to be sound, a satisfactory operation schedule can be developed without too much difficulty. However, since all the predictions will not be perfect, it may be that the availability of the factors of production is such that the operation schedule developed by the production control department will not enable the firm to deliver the product on what is considered to be a satisfactory date. In such cases, the firm will do whatever it can to correct the condition. This corrective action may consist of one or more of the following: (1) schedule overtime work; (2) inaugurate a second shift; (3) subcontract some of the work; (4) expedite the delivery of ordered materials, purchased parts, and machine accessories; (5) hire more people; (6) perform some operations on equipment normally used for other purposes; and (7) make required factors of production available earlier by rescheduling less critical orders.

It is obvious that the selection of the proper form of corrective action will often be a matter of judgment, intuition, and experience. And there will always be those cases in which corrective action is impossible in either the physical or economic sense. In such cases, the delivery date simply will not be met.

PREPARATION OF REQUIRED SHOP FORMS

After the operation schedule has been developed, the production control department must prepare various forms which will be sent to the shop. These forms perform two functions. One is to provide instructions to the shop concerning what is to be done, how it is to be done, and when it is to be done. The second is to provide the shop with authorizations which will enable it to obtain some of the necessary factors of production which are ordinarily kept in storerooms.

Forms of an instructional nature are manufacturing orders and move orders. The nature of the manufacturing order will vary from company to company, but in its most comprehensive form it will show: (1) order number, (2) part number and description, (3) quantity to be produced, (4) operations to be performed, (5) required equipment and accessories, (6) materials to be used, (7) operating times per unit for each operation, and (8) the scheduled completion date. If the product involved is an assembly, one such order would be prepared for each of the component parts to be manufactured.

The manufacturing order can take one of two forms. One of these is called a shop order. If a shop order is used, all the relevant information is presented on one form similar to the one shown in Figure 11-10. In some cases, however, job tickets are used. The only difference between a shop order and a job ticket is that one shop order is prepared for all the operations to be performed in the production of a given part, while one job ticket is prepared for each of the operations to be performed in the production of a given part and would contain information relevant only to that operation. An example of a job ticket is shown in Figure 11-11.

It was mentioned that the information contained in a manufacturing order includes the scheduled completion date. In some cases, the scheduled completion date will be shown for each operation; in others, only for each part; and in still others, only for the final product. But since the production control department does prepare an operation schedule, one may wonder why the scheduled completion date for each operation is not always shown. It is sometimes omitted to provide the shop supervisors with some flexibility in the scheduling of work in their departments. On occasion, the supervisor may find it advantageous to schedule the work a little later or sooner than called for by the production control department's operation schedule to take advantage of an existing setup on a machine or to take advantage of the availability of a particular operator who is best qualified to perform the work. If it is found that these slight variations in operation scheduling offset each other in the sense that the final completion date is still met, the production control department will not bother to specify the completion date for each operation or, sometimes, even for each part. In brief, it relies on the supervisors to use their judgment and will simply furnish them with the final completion date. Actually, this does not involve too much of a risk. The production control department has satisfied itself that the availability of factors of production is such that the scheduled delivery date can be met. If skilled and experienced supervisors are available, they can usually be relied upon to use these factors in the most advantageous manner. Of course, if this assumption proves to be false, the production control department will lose little time

Figure 11-10   Shop order (Courtesy of Royal McBee Corporation)

MANUFACTURING ORDER ROUTE SHEET

| MANUFACTURING ORDER NO. 24347 | PART NO. 3143211 | MODEL NO. 8461 | SHEET 1 | OF 1 |

| ORDER QUANTITY 656 | PART DESCRIPTION ACTUATOR SCREW | | BY LB |

| DATE START 1016 | DATE COMPLETE 1124 | DATE ISSUE 1002 | RAW MATERIAL NO. 60431 | RAW MATERIAL DESCRIPTION 241 SP. 1/2" RD. |

| TOTAL QUANTITY RAW MATERIAL 81.25 FT. | RAW MATERIAL PER UNIT .125 FT. | DELIVER TO DEPT. 14 |

SCHEDULE DATE COMPLETE	WORK CENTER	OPER. NO.	OPERATION DESCRIPTION	TOOLS AND FIXTURES	SPEED	FEED	JOB CODE	SET-UP HOURS	STANDARD HOURS PER HUNDRED	PIECES PER HOUR
1018	142	10	TURN .475 DIA., TURN .350 DIA. TURN FOR 1/4 – 16 THREAD, GROOVE, DEBURR, CUT OFF				197	1.50	3.300	30
1022	282	20	DRILL (1) .135/.140 DIA. HOLE REAM (1) .135/.140 DIA. HOLE							
1025	543	30	MILL TEETH							
1030	549	40	STRADDLE MILL .312 DIAM.							
1102	549	50	RADIUS CORNERS PER END VIEW							
1105	920	60	DEBURR AND RADIUS							
1107	950	70	CLEAN FOR HEAT TREAT							
1109	901	80	HEAT TREAT							
1126	314	85	GRIND 1/4 – 16 THREADS							
1128	951	90	DEGREASE							

WORK CENTER OPERATION TICKET

| MANUFACTURING ORDER NO. 24347 | PART NO. 3143211 | MODEL NO. 8461 |

| ORDER QUANTITY 656 | PART DESCRIPTION ACTUATOR SCREW |

| DATE START 1016 | DATE COMPLETE 1124 | DATE ISSUE 1002 | RAW MATERIAL NO. 60431 | RAW MATERIAL DESCRIPTION 241 SP. 1/2" RD. |

| TOTAL QUANTITY RAW MATERIAL 81.25 FT. | RAW MATERIAL PER UNIT .125 FT. |

SCHEDULE DATE COMPLETE	WORK CENTER	OPER. NO.	OPERATION DESCRIPTION	JOB CODE	SET-UP HOURS	STANDARD HOURS PER HUNDRED	PIECES PER HOUR
1018	142	10	TURN .475 DIA., TURN .350 DIA. TURN FOR 1/4 – 16 THREAD, GROOVE, DEBURR, CUT OFF	197	1.50	3.300	30

DATE

BAL. PC'S.

Figure 11-11   Job ticket (Courtesy of Royal McBee Corporation)

in changing to a more rigid control procedure in which completion dates for each operation will be specified and enforced.

It was also stated that instructions in the form of move orders would be sent to the shop. A move order of the type shown in Figure 11-12 would be prepared for every occasion on which the work in process has to be transported from one work station to another. These are necessary in intermittent manufacturing because every order being processed at a single work station will not necessarily go to the same work station for the next operation. Therefore, materials handling personnel must be instructed about where a given order should be taken. They obtain these instructions from the move orders which accompany the work and which stipulate the location in the plant to which the work in process should be transported.

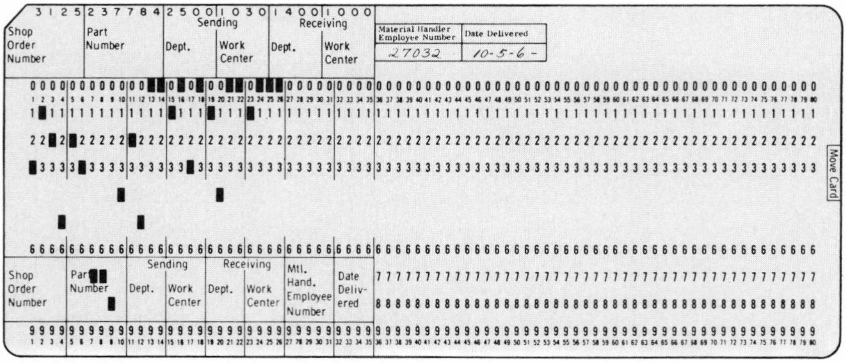

Figure 11-12   Move order (Courtesy of International Business Machines Corporation)

The second category of forms would be those which authorize the shop to obtain necessary factors of production. These factors would be those which are stored and, therefore, would not include equipment and manpower. This leaves raw materials, manufactured or purchased finished parts, and machine accessories which are not kept at the work stations. The authorization to obtain raw materials is called a "raw-material requisition," and it will contain a description of the material and the amount of this material which should be issued to the shop for a particular order. An example of a material requisition form is shown in Figure 11-13.

Similarly, finished-part and machine-accessory requisitions would be prepared in which a description of the items involved and the amounts to be issued for a particular order would be shown. A typical finished-part requisition is shown in Figure 11-14, and a typical machine-accessory requisition in Figure 11-15.

After having been prepared, all the forms related to a specific order, together with any blueprints the shop may require, are sent to the plant. If the product involved is an assembly, the forms will be grouped according to the component part to which they are related. This means that everything required for one of the component parts will be prepared as a single package, everything required for another of the component parts as a second package, and so on. These packages would then be sent to the respective locations at which the first operation on each of these parts is to be performed.

DISPATCHING THE WORK

The manner in which the aforementioned forms are handled in the shop depends on how much direct control the production control department exercises over shop operations. Where production control is a highly cen-

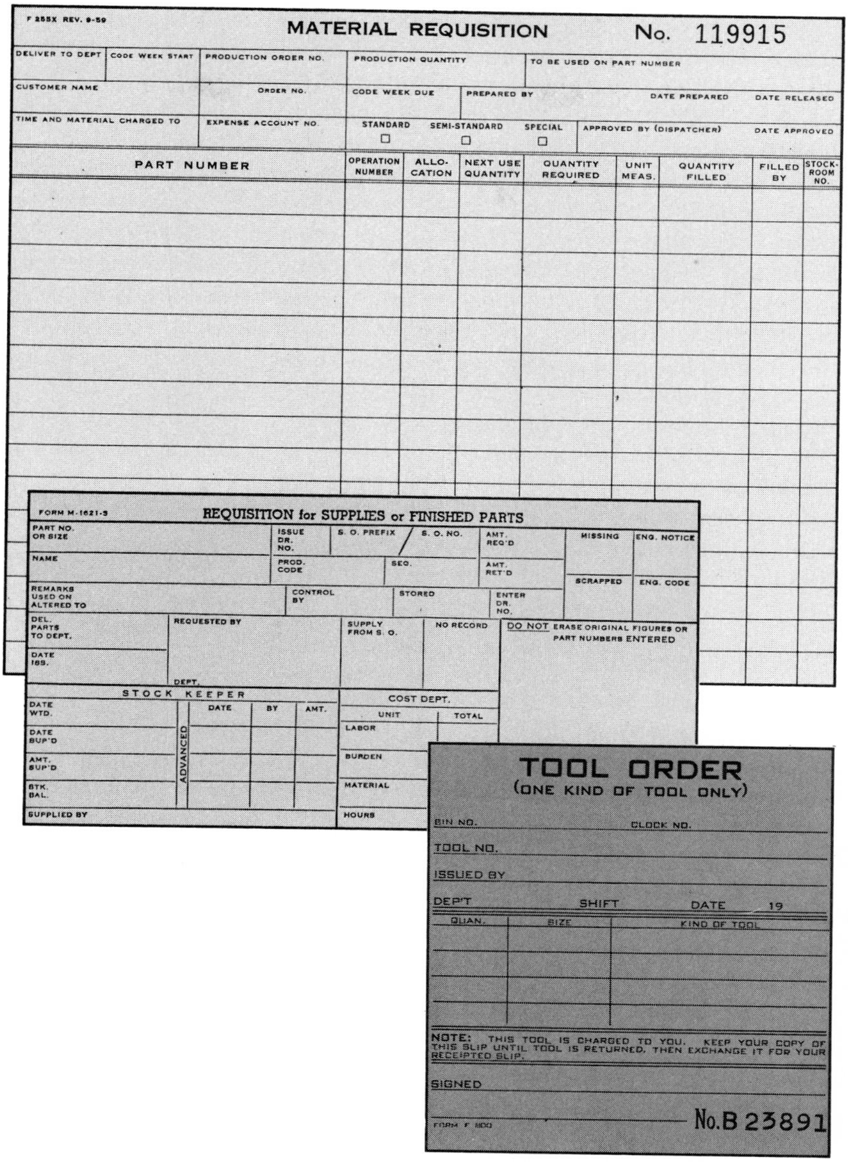

| F 255X REV. 9-59 | | MATERIAL REQUISITION | | | | No. 119915 | | | | | |

MATERIAL REQUISITION — Form F 255X REV. 9-59 — No. 119915

| DELIVER TO DEPT | CODE WEEK START | PRODUCTION ORDER NO. | PRODUCTION QUANTITY | | TO BE USED ON PART NUMBER | | |

CUSTOMER NAME — ORDER NO. — CODE WEEK DUE — PREPARED BY — DATE PREPARED — DATE RELEASED

TIME AND MATERIAL CHARGED TO — EXPENSE ACCOUNT NO. — STANDARD ☐ SEMI-STANDARD ☐ SPECIAL ☐ — APPROVED BY (DISPATCHER) — DATE APPROVED

PART NUMBER	OPERATION NUMBER	ALLO-CATION	NEXT USE QUANTITY	QUANTITY REQUIRED	UNIT MEAS.	QUANTITY FILLED	FILLED BY	STOCK-ROOM NO.

REQUISITION for SUPPLIES or FINISHED PARTS — FORM M-1621-9

PART NO. OR SIZE — ISSUE DR. NO. — S. O. PREFIX / S. O. NO. — AMT. REQ'D — MISSING — ENG. NOTICE

NAME — PROD. CODE — SEQ. — AMT. RET'D — SCRAPPED — ENG. CODE

REMARKS USED ON ALTERED TO — CONTROL BY — STORED — ENTER DR. NO.

DEL. PARTS TO DEPT. — REQUESTED BY — SUPPLY FROM S. O. — NO RECORD — DO NOT ERASE ORIGINAL FIGURES OR PART NUMBERS ENTERED

DATE ISS. — DEPT.

STOCK KEEPER | COST DEPT.

DATE WTD. — DATE — BY — AMT. — UNIT — TOTAL

DATE SUP'D — LABOR

AMT. SUP'D — ADVANCED — BURDEN

STK. BAL. — MATERIAL

SUPPLIED BY — HOURS

TOOL ORDER
(ONE KIND OF TOOL ONLY)

BIN NO. — CLOCK NO.

TOOL NO.

ISSUED BY

DEP'T — SHIFT — DATE ___ 19

QUAN.	SIZE	KIND OF TOOL

NOTE: THIS TOOL IS CHARGED TO YOU. KEEP YOUR COPY OF THIS SLIP UNTIL TOOL IS RETURNED, THEN EXCHANGE IT FOR YOUR RECEIPTED SLIP.

SIGNED

FORM F 800 — No. B 23891

Figure 11-13   Material requisition
Figure 11-14   Finished-part requisition
Figure 11-15   Machine-accessory requisition

tralized activity, the forms may be sent to a member of the production control department who is located in the shop and is known as a dispatcher. One such dispatcher may be stationed in each department. When a given piece of equipment and an operator are free to begin work on a new order, the dispatcher will decide what order should be assigned to the equipment and will issue blueprints and job instructions to the operator. He will do this on the basis of scheduled completion dates for the respective operations, parts, or products. He will also issue material and finished-part requisitions to the stockrooms and machine-accessory requisitions to the tool crib with instructions about when and where the stipulated items should be sent. Further, he will issue move orders to materials handling personnel when an order is ready to be moved to another work station.

Where production control is decentralized to some degree, the forms are sent directly to the foremen. The foremen will then perform all the functions of the dispatcher and, in some cases, may even assign some of them to the machine operator. For example, the operator may be given the requisitions and told to obtain the items himself or arrange for their delivery to his work station.

PREPARATION OF PROGRESS REPORTS

Once the order is in the shop, the production control department will employ some means for determining whether the established schedule is being met. To do this, it must develop procedures for ascertaining what the actual progress on a specific order is. There are a number of ways in which this information can be obtained from the shop.

The first of these requires that the foreman or dispatcher in each department prepare a report at, say, the end of each day, in which he would list the orders which had been received in the department, the orders which had been processed in the department, and the orders which had left the department during that day. With this information at its disposal, the production control department can determine the present status of any order.

A second method is possible when job tickets are employed. Arrangements could be made to have a copy of the job tickets for all completed operations sent to the production control department. Since there would be a job ticket for every operation, the job tickets received would serve to identify those operations which had been completed. The one deficiency of this method is that there would be no way of knowing whether the next scheduled move had been made.

Another alternative would be to have a copy of the move orders which had been carried out sent to the production control department. A reported move by the materials handling department would indicate that all the operations scheduled to be performed prior to the move had been completed. However, a drawback of this procedure would be that a certain operation might have been completed but the order had not, as yet, been moved to the next work station. As a result, the production control department would have no way of knowing that the operation had already been performed.

Finally, the firm can make use of inspection reports. For example, after completing an inspection, the inspector can be required to fill out a form similar to that shown in Figure 11-16. Such reports will show the order number, the last operation completed, and the results of the inspection. If the production control department arranges to receive a copy of this report, it will know that the inspection and all the preceding operations had been completed. However, until the report is received, the department

SCRAP REPORT

PART NO.			REG. NO.	
PART NAME			AMOUNT	
S.O. PREFIX	SHOP ORDER NO.		DR. NO.	
FOR DEPT. OR VENDOR		TIME SPENT ON SPECIALS		
AMT. GOOD	AMT. SCRAP	QTY. IN LOT	LAST OPER. DONE	
SCRAPPED ON OPER.	STD./PIECE	OPERATOR PREFIX	OPERATOR NO.	
CODE	CHARGE DEPT.	☐ CHARGE CURRENT ☐ CHARGE RETROACTIVE	☐ NO CHARGE	
AMT.	REASON FOR REJECTION			
A.				
B.				
C.				
D.				
MATERIAL				
REMARKS				
ORIGINATOR AND/OR FOREMAN			DATE	
% SCRAP	COST	HOURS		

Figure 11-16   Inspection report

would not know whether the individual preceding operations had been performed.

In practice, unless detailed reports were being submitted by the foremen or dispatchers, the production control department would probably receive copies of job tickets if they are used, of move orders, and of inspection reports. In combination, these would provide a relatively complete picture of the status of every order in the shop. Inspection reports would also serve to indicate whether the amount of defective work was greater than anticipated. If it was, additional parts would possibly have to be scheduled for production.

PROGRESS REPORT FORMS   After these reports have been received, the production control department will compare actual progress with scheduled progress. These comparisons can assume innumerable forms. One of these involves the use of what is referred to as a Gantt chart. To illustrate its use, we shall assume, for purposes of simplicity, that the orders being processed involve single parts. If this is the case, the Gantt chart will appear as shown in Figure 11-17. As can be seen from an examination of this figure, the order numbers are listed in the left-hand column. Then, for each order, a line representing the operation schedule will be shown. Below this line, a second line will be drawn to represent the actual progress being made on the order.

In addition to Gantt charts of the order control type, some companies will maintain Gantt charts for machines which represent bottleneck operations. In charts of this type, the machine number is listed in the left-hand column, and a line is drawn on which are shown the orders scheduled to pass through this machine. A second line, depicting progress

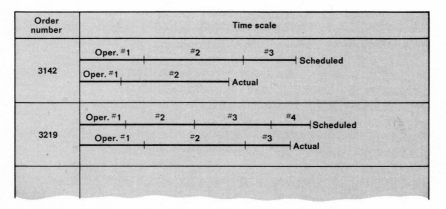

Figure 11-17   A Gantt order control chart

against this schedule, is then drawn in. An example of this type of chart is shown in Figure 11-18. When machine load charts of this type are maintained, they can also be used by the production control department for operation scheduling purposes. In such cases, they serve as substitutes for machine load cards.

Some companies also make use of man load Gantt charts, which are just like the machine load chart, with the exception that employee numbers rather than machine numbers are listed. These would be used when certain skills, which are associated with specific employees, represent potential bottlenecks. These charts can also be used for operation scheduling purposes.

Although a great deal has been written about Gantt charts and charts of a similar nature, they are not employed very extensively. Most firms have found that the cost of maintaining them can be fairly high. Also, the time required to make the necessary postings can be so long that the charts fail to depict the current status of an order. Finally, the charts may "fall behind" while changes are being made in them to reflect revisions in schedules which unexpected events have made necessary.

If charts of the Gantt type are not maintained, the production control department will set up tabular forms of its own design which will provide for a comparison of actual progress with scheduled progress. The specific form will vary from company to company, but the one shown in Figure 11-19 serves as an example. A more comprehensive report might contain a listing of all the operations required to complete an order, a listing of the scheduled completion dates for each of these operations, and a listing of the actual completion dates for each of these operations.

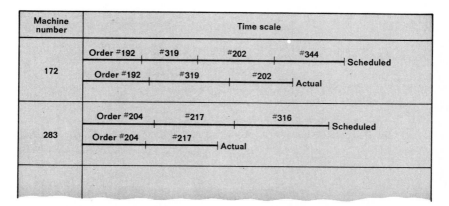

Figure 11-18   A Gantt machine load chart

	WORK-IN-PROCESS STATUS												

SHOP DATE 615

RAMAC ADDR.	SHOP ORDER		STOCK DATE	QUANTITY ORDERED	TOTAL STD. HRS.	TOT. ACT. HRS. TO DATE	STD. HRS. TO COMPL.	NO. OPS.	LAST OP.		DAYS		REASON CODE
	PART NO.	LOT NO.							DAY	NO.	EARLY	LATE	
20400	358006	020–0	632	68	1597	269	1414	13	612	50		3	1
20800	358006	030–0	649	69	1615	80	1582	13	613	20	2		
21800	358117	040–0	617	100	975	815	161	16	614	180		1	4

Figure 11-19 **A progress report (Courtesy of International Business Machines Corporation)**

INAUGURATING CORRECTIVE ACTION

When comparing actual progress with scheduled progress, the production control department will be interested in both ahead-of-schedule and behind-schedule conditions. If the shop is ahead of schedule on some orders, certain production facilities, such as equipment, machine accessories, and manpower, will be available for other orders sooner than was expected. Therefore, this will be taken into consideration when scheduling future orders. Also, existing schedules for orders which are still awaiting processing may be revised in light of the earlier availability of these factors of production.

If the shop is behind schedule on some orders, one of two general courses of action will be followed. In the simplest case, the condition may be of little, if any, concern to the production control department, and no attempt will be made to correct it. This would be true when the plant is operating well below capacity and delays are of no consequence because all the orders will be completed in advance of their scheduled shipping dates anyway. But even in these instances, the production control department will take cognizance of the fact that certain production facilities will not be available as soon as they were expected to be. As a result, existing schedules for orders which are still awaiting processing on these facilities may be revised, and future orders will be scheduled on the basis of this altered availability of certain factors of production.

More commonly, however, a behind-schedule condition will affect established shipping dates for one or more orders adversely. In those cases, the production control department must make a concerted effort to find the cause of the delay. This cause may be poor dispatching in the shop, employee absenteeism, unexpected machine breakdowns, unsatisfactory materials handling, late deliveries of materials or purchased parts or machine accessories, poor supervision, and the like. To prevent the situation from becoming worse, steps would have to be taken to eliminate the cause of the delay, and the nature of the cause would dictate the appropriate course of.action. To eliminate or improve the behind-schedule condition, it might be necessary for the firm to hire additional labor, subcontract some of the work, work overtime, start a second shift, and so on. If none of these alternatives provides a solution, the condition will just have to be accepted, and schedules for existing orders will have to be revised and schedules for future orders established on the basis of the altered availability of the affected factors of production.

Having considered the action that might be taken on the basis of a comparison of actual progress and scheduled progress on an order, we have reached the close of our description of order control. We shall now go on to consider flow control.

QUESTIONS

11-1   In general terms, what constitutes production control?

11-2   What are the two basic production control systems? Under what conditions is each adhered to?

11-3   What general information is contained in authorizations to produce?

11-4   What forms can authorizations to produce assume? Answer this and all subsequent questions in this section with reference to order control.

11-5   How do production control personnel ascertain how an assembly is to be processed?

11-6   In what way is a determination made of the kinds and amounts of component parts that must be manufactured at this time for a specific order when the product involved is an assembly?

11-7   How are factor-of-production requirements and the availability of these factors determined?

11-8   What are the two basic procedures for the preparation of an operation schedule?

11-9   What shop forms must be prepared in order control, and what information do they contain?

11-10   Describe the dispatching activity.

11-11   How can the work that has been completed on an order be determined by the production control department?

11-12   Describe a Gantt order control chart. A Gantt machine load chart. A Gantt man load chart.

11-13   Why might the production control department be interested in learning of an ahead-of-schedule condition?

11-14 What can be done to prevent a behind-schedule condition from becoming any worse?

11-15 If the shop is significantly behind schedule on an order, what steps might be taken to eliminate or improve the condition?

PROBLEMS

11-1 A product consists of four different manufactured parts. Parts 1 and 2 each undergo six operations and an inspection and are then brought together to make up a subassembly. Parts 3 and 4 each undergo five operations and an inspection and are then brought together to make up another subassembly. The two subassemblies are then assembled with a purchased part to make up the final product, which is subjected to a final inspection.

Prepare a hypothetical operation schedule for these activities in the form suggested by Figure 11-8. Go on to assume actual starting and completion times for the operations and inspections involved. Finally, construct an appropriate Gantt chart on which scheduled and actual progress are depicted.

11-2 Select a firm which manufactures certain products intermittently and is willing to discuss the production control system to which it adheres in the processing of these items. Describe this system in detail in the terms we have considered. Finally, compare the details of this system with those of the one we have studied and explain the differences.

11-3 Select an organization that engages in nonmanufacturing activities on an intermittent basis. Then determine the system by means of which these operations are controlled. Describe this system in terms of the same elements considered in the description of production control in intermittent manufacturing.

TWELVE

PRODUCTION CONTROL IN CONTINUOUS MANUFACTURING

The production control system used in continuous manufacturing is called "flow control," because its primary purpose is to control the rate at which a product *flows* through the plant, that is, the rate at which the product is manufactured. In order control, on the other hand, the production control department is concerned with getting a particular *order* for a given product through the plant.

Although flow control is much simpler than order control, there is no major difference between the elements of the two systems. In flow control, as in order control, the entire production control activity begins with a receipt of an authorization to produce and ends with action being taken as a result of discrepancies between scheduled progress and actual progress. To bring this out clearly, we shall consider flow control in terms of the same elements as those used to describe order control.

AUTHORIZATION TO PRODUCE

In continuous manufacturing, the production control department must be told what is to be produced, in what quantities, and by what date. But before we discuss the form which this authorization to produce will take, let us reconsider certain relevant characteristics of continuous manufacturing.

All products which are manufactured continuously are standard products. As a result, they are always produced for stock and not to customer order. This does not mean that the quantities produced will necessarily remain in stock for weeks or months, as they may in the case of intermittent manufacturing. Actually, much of the output may never reach the company's stockroom. Instead, shortly after having been produced, it may be shipped directly to the firm's distributors, but we think of the stocking function as being performed by the distributors.

The items produced are also produced continuously. However, it is important to realize that a product which is manufactured continuously is not necessarily a product which will be manufactured at a uniform rate. The more common situation is one in which variations occur in this rate. It is primarily because of these variations that a need exists for controlling production in continuous manufacturing.

For a given period of time, the rate at which a specific product is to be produced will be determined by the company on the basis of a sales forecast. The production schedule suggested by the sales forecast might then be adjusted to bring about desired changes in inventory levels and to level out the demand for various factors of production. It is this adjusted production schedule which serves as the production control department's authorization to produce.

The exact form which the authorization takes is called a "production program release." It is very similar to the master schedule used in intermittent manufacturing in the sense that it states, for some future time period, the specific quantities of various products that should be completed and ready for shipment, either to the stockroom or to a distributor, at stipulated points during this time period. A production program release may cover a two- to four-week period, depending on the accuracy with which sales forecasts can be made. This does not mean that sales forecasts will not be made for longer time periods for production planning purposes. However, for production control purposes, there is no real need for authorizing production for any longer period of time, and the shorter the period, the more accurate the forecast is likely to be.

The actual form of the production program release may appear, in part, as shown in Figure 12-1. However, graphically, the information it contains can be presented as shown in Figure 12-2.

The schedule depicted in Figure 12-2 states, for example, that on the first day of the time period under consideration, 200 units of product 1, 400 units of product 2, and 300 units of product 3 are to be completed. Naturally, the nature of these products and the length of the production cycle may be such that initial operations on these items must be started some time in advance. This would be likely in those cases in which the products happened to be complicated assemblies.

PROCESSING INSTRUCTIONS

As in intermittent manufacturing, the production control department can schedule the required operations only if it knows how the product is to be

PART NUMBER	PART DESCRIPTION	SCE	REQUIRED FOR PRODUCT	PERIOD REQUIREMENTS						TOTAL QTY. REQ'D
				1	2	3	4	5	6	
27002	CHASSIS	1	147	30	35	42	56	64	82	
27002	CHASSIS	1	148	26	32	39	51	62	78	
27002	CHASSIS	1	149	29	33	41	60	86	95	
27002	CHASSIS	1	150	40	45	52	45	46	66	
				125	145	174	212	258	321	1235
27058	CONDENSER	2	147	32	36	40	53	61	75	
27058	CONDENSER	2	148	25	30	38	48	65	81	
27058	CONDENSER	2	149	27	29	35	57	73	90	
27058	CONDENSER	2	150	38	42	49	41	+3	62	
				122	137	162	199	242	308	1170

CONSOLIDATED REQUIREMENTS

BY PRODUCT AND PERIOD

DATE

Figure 12-1 Production program release (Courtesy of International Business Machines Corporation)

processed. In discussing these processing instructions, let us consider the most complicated case, which will be the one in which the product is an assembly. In this case, the production control department must know what the components of the assembly are and which of these are to be manufactured and which are to be purchased. This information can be obtained from a bill of materials.

Next, the production control department must be told how each of the manufactured parts is to be produced. This information, however, assumes a much simpler form in continuous manufacturing than it does in intermittent. Although the production department must know what raw materials are required for each part and the quantities of these materials required for 1 unit of each part, there is no need for a detailed description of the operations that must be performed, of the equipment and machine

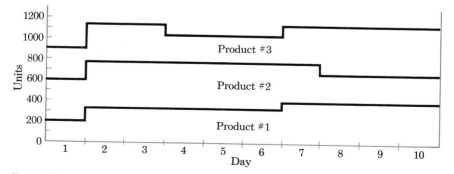

Figure 12-2 A production program release in graphical form

accessories required for each operation, and of unit operating times. This is true for the following reason: The volume of output for a single product manufactured continuously is such that the firm can justify the procurement of equipment especially designed for the production of the item under consideration. Further, a given piece of equipment will be used to process only a single product or, at most, a number of products which differ in some minor respect. Consequently, in continuous manufacturing, it is common to speak in terms of a production line or lines for a particular product.

At the time plans are being made to manufacture a new product, it is necessary that the appropriate lines be designed, constructed, and placed in operation. This, however, is primarily an engineering function. On the basis of long-term sales forecasts, the firm's engineers will be told what the production schedule for a given product is expected to be. They will then explode this forecast into its component-part requirements and begin the design of a production line for each of the manufactured parts. In this design, they will be governed, first, by the required output capacity of the line. Next, they will have to provide for the performance of all operations required to process a given part. The task then becomes one of ascertaining what equipment and machine accessories are needed to perform these operations on the raw materials involved in such a way that a well-balanced production line will result. After the design has been completed, the line will be constructed and installed. At this point, the company has what amounts to a single special-purpose machine which is capable of producing a single part at a given rate per hour.

Because of this, when the production control department receives an authorization to produce a certain product, it is not necessary that it be told what individual operations must be performed on each part or what equipment and machine accessories are needed to perform each of these operations. These specific instructions are said to be built into the production line for that part. If the raw materials are delivered to the beginning of the line, the line itself will perform the required operations, in the correct sequence and with the appropriate equipment and accessories.

Therefore, insofar as the production control department is concerned, there is no need for its working with operation sheets for each part. It is sufficient that it have, for each manufactured part, a summary card of some type which will show the kind of raw material from which the part is produced, the amount of raw material required per unit of output, the identification of the line on which the part is to be produced, and the output capacity of the line in units per hour. This, together with the bill of materials, is the only processing instruction required.

AVAILABILITY OF FACTORS OF PRODUCTION

The next step requires that the production control department determine what factors of production are needed to produce the number of units of the finished product called for by the production program release. If the product is an assembly, this is done by first translating the finished-product requirements into component-part requirements by means of the bill of materials. This translation will yield a list of the different purchased and manufactured parts needed and the required quantities of each. As a result, at this point, the production control department will know one of the factors of production required, namely, the purchased parts.

Manufactured parts, however, must now be expressed in terms of materials, equipment, machine accessories, and manpower. This is easily done. With regard to materials, the production control department knows the kind and amount of materials needed per unit for each part. These unit requirements are multiplied by the number of units of each part scheduled to be manufactured to obtain the total material requirements by type. The number of parts scheduled would, of course, contain some allowance for expected scrap.

Equipment, machine accessories, and manpower pose an even less difficult task. These three factors of production are the elements of any production line. Therefore, since the production control department knows the output capacity in units per hour for the production line through which a given part is to be processed, it has only to divide the total unit requirements for this part by the output capacity of the line in order to arrive at the number of line-hours needed to produce the calculated quantities of this part. This procedure would be followed for each of the required manufactured parts. If the output capacity of the line contains an allowance for breakdowns and delays of some other type, nothing more need be done. If not, the calculated line-hours would be increased by some factor, determined on the basis of past experience or a study of some type, to provide for these unavoidable delays.

As in intermittent manufacturing, no effort is made to calculate indirect labor requirements. For reasons discussed earlier, it is simply assumed that an adequate amount of indirect labor will be available.

After the required factors of production have been determined, consideration must be given to the availability of these factors. This was a fairly difficult task in intermittent manufacturing. In continuous manufacturing, it is not. Insofar as the production line for a given part is concerned, this line will always be available for this part because no other part is processed through the line. This, therefore, takes care of the availability of equipment, machine accessories, and manpower and leaves only raw materials and purchased parts.

It is extremely important that materials and purchased parts be available when required. Because of the continuous production-line arrangement which is present in this type of manufacturing, the lack of even one item may sometimes bring a number of lines to a standstill at a tremendous cost to the company. For this reason, the production program release will be prepared and issued far enough in advance so that, after material and purchased-part requirements are determined and the operating schedule developed, ample time remains in which to procure the necessary items in the required quantities and at the required times. This means that, as soon as the production control department makes its calculations, it will notify the stockroom personnel of what is required and when. If the quantities currently on hand or on order are inadequate, steps will be taken by the company's purchasing department to place the necessary orders and arrange for the delivery of the required items by the dates on which they will be needed. The dates on which the materials and purchased parts will be needed will be known, of course, only after the operating schedule has been developed. Therefore, after ascertaining the raw-material and purchased-part requirements, the production control department will inmmediately establish an operating schedule so as to provide the firm's purchasing department with as much time as possible to procure these items in the event that stocked or ordered quantities are not adequate.

We speak in terms of an "operating" rather than an "operation" schedule, because, in continuous manufacturing, the individual operations are an integral part of the production line. Consequently, it is necessary to schedule only operating times for the production lines involved. Let us now consider how this operating schedule is prepared.

THE OPERATING SCHEDULE

As a rule, an attempt is made in continuous manufacturing to produce the finished product no sooner than the day stipulated in the production program release. The reason for this is that, because of the relatively large quantities being produced, the firm will strive to maintain some balance between the rate at which its products are being manufactured and the rate at which they are being shipped from the plant. Unless this balance exists, inventories may build up very rapidly, resulting not only in excessive carrying costs but also in excess output that the firm may be physically unable to store. For the same reasons, a similar balance will be maintained between the rate at which raw materials and purchased parts are delivered to the plant and the rate at which they are being used in production. The only times high raw-material, purchased-part, or finished-goods inventories would be maintained would be in those cases in which there were indications that a shortage of these items was imminent because of a strike, national emergency, or the like.

In intermittent manufacturing, on the other hand, most firms have little reluctance to process an order completely before its scheduled shipping date. The smaller quantities involved do not present as great a storage problem, and if it is a customer order, the customer will usually accept earlier shipment. Also, there is more uncertainty about what the future demand for factors of production will be, and, hence, the firm usually prefers to have as much capacity available in the future as possible in the event that an unexpected increase in demand occurs.

This difference between continuous and intermittent manufacturing serves to simplify the scheduling of work in continuous manufacturing in the sense that it practically dictates that the production control department establish the operating schedule by starting with the completion date called for in the production program release and working backward. In the case of an assembled product, this would be done as follows: If the production program release, adjusted for expected scrap, calls, for example, for 240 units of a given product to be produced on, say, May 15, and the production capacity of the final assembly line, adjusted for delays, is 60 units per hour, the production control department would schedule four hours of work on the final assembly line for that day. In a similar manner, given the manufactured component-part requirements and the output capacity of the respective component-part production lines, the production control department would calculate the number of hours each of these lines would have to be operated. Working backward, it would then determine when each of these lines would have to be started in order to keep the final assembly line supplied with the necessary parts in the required quantities. In this manner, the complete operating schedule would be developed for the stipulated quantity of the product under consideration. If the assembly is fairly complex, in the sense that its components call for time-consuming operations, it may be that some or all of the component-part lines may have to begin work on the necessary parts in advance of the day on which the quantities called for in the production program release are to be assembled. Otherwise, it may be that both the component parts and the finished assemblies can be produced in the same day.

THE NEED FOR ALTERING LINE CAPACITY As can be seen, this scheduling is simple as compared with what was required in intermittent manufacturing. The only complication that may arise stems from the fact that the output capacity of a line may have to be changed in order to arrive at a satisfactory schedule. This can often be done, because this capacity is not necessarily fixed. Ordinarily, when the firm states that the output capacity of one of its lines is, say, 60 units per hour, it means that this is the expected hourly output when the line is operated under normal conditions. Normal conditions, however, are defined in terms of the number of operators that are usually assigned to the line, the number of units of equipment that are usually in operation, the speeds at which this equipment is usually operated, and so forth. But it is very often possible to alter the hourly output capacity of a line by altering the manner in which the line is operated. For example, if a line is composed primarily of manual operations, the output capacity can be increased or decreased by increasing or decreasing the number of workers assigned to the line. If mechanical equipment is involved, it may be possible to vary the output capacity by changing the speed at which the equipment is operated and making any necessary corresponding change in the number of workers assigned to the line. Or if a line consists of, say, four work stations, the output capacity can be reduced by operating only the first two stations, building up a bank of parts, terminating operations at the first two work stations, and beginning operations at the last two work stations. These illustrations are only typical of the number of ways in which output capacity per hour can be altered.

Having suggested that the normal output capacity may have to be altered on occasion to arrive at a satisfactory operating schedule in continuous manufacturing, we shall now illustrate this. Ordinarily, the production control department will begin its development of the operating schedule on the basis of the normal output capacity of the respective production lines. The results, however, may be unsatisfactory, for one of a number of reasons. First, it may be that the normal output capacity of one of the lines is inadequate to meet the established completion date for the finished product. For example, the production program release may call for 500 units to be assembled on a certain day, but the final assembly line may have a normal output capacity of only 50 units per hour. This calls for 10 hours of operation. If the plant is operating only eight hours a day, the production control department has a problem. At this point, it must decide whether to request authorization for two hours of overtime work or to make an attempt to increase the line's output capacity. If the second alternative is selected, means for increasing the capacity must be found. In some cases, these means are obvious; in others, their determination calls for some ingenuity on the part of the personnel involved. Further, if this capacity is altered, it may be necessary to alter the output capacity of the lines feeding into the final assembly line in order to maintain the required balance. Hence, the task grows in magnitude.

A problem may also arise when the production control department finds that the operating schedule, as determined on the basis of normal output capacity, calls for some of the lines to be operated for only a portion of the day. The problem may stem from the fact that no other work can be found for the rest of the day for all the operators assigned to the lines, and, furthermore, the firm cannot or does not want to send them home without paying them for the remaining hours. In a case such as this, the obvious alternative is to reduce the output capacity by reducing the amount of manpower assigned to these lines. If this can be done, it may be that the reduced number of excess employees can be utilized effectively elsewhere in the plant, or if the condition appears to be somewhat permanent, the excess personnel can be laid off. But as in the preceding case, the individuals concerned may have to tax their imaginations to determine how this desired reduction in output capacity can be brought about. Also, the change may necessitate a corresponding change in related production lines.

In brief, then, the need to alter the output capacity of one or more lines to arrive at a satisfactory schedule is unique to continuous manufacturing and can often pose a fairly difficult problem. And, of course, there will always be those cases in which it is impossible to develop a satisfactory schedule simply by varying the output capacity. When this is true, if output capacity is excessive, the lines will simply have to be operated for limited periods of time, and if no other work can be found for the excess personnel, they will have to be sent home, or, if this is not possible, they will simply be idle or assigned to "make-work" activities. If output capacity is insufficient, overtime work will have to be scheduled or a second shift started; if this does not solve the problem, then the production program release is unrealistic and must be revised.

PREPARATION OF REQUIRED SHOP FORMS AND DISPATCHING

After the operating schedule has been completed, the production control department will immediately notify the individuals concerned of what raw materials and purchased parts are required and the dates by which they must be on hand.

Following this, instructions will be prepared for the shop. These instructions assume a very simple form. In intermittent manufacturing, manufacturing orders had to be prepared which served to tell the shop what was to be manufactured, the quantities to be manufactured, the date by which something was to be manufactured, the operations to be performed, and the equipment and accessories to be used. In continuous manufacturing, much of this information is unneccesary. While something similar to a manufacturing order is prepared, no special form is employed.

Instead, a simple notice will be prepared for each production line stating the time at which a certain run should begin, the expected length of the run, the number of units to be produced during the run, and, if the line is not to be operated in the usual manner, the specific manner in which it should be operated. No need exists for describing the operations to be performed or the equipment and machine accessories that should be used, because all this information is built into the line. These notices are then sent either to dispatchers located in the shop, who will pass the information on to the appropriate line supervisors, or directly to the supervisors.

Insofar as raw-material, finished-part, and machine-accessory requisitions are concerned, these are unnecessary. Machine accessories are an integral part of the line. Raw materials and finished parts are not withdrawn from the stockroom for a specific order because specific orders, as such, do not exist. In fact, in many instances, the various raw materials and finished parts are stored close to the point at which they are required, and no authorization is needed to withdraw them. The line personnel simply use these items as they are required. In other cases, the production control department will prepare notices for storeroom personnel, such as the one shown in Figure 12-3, in which it will stipulate what materials and parts are to be delivered to specific points, the quantities in which they are to be delivered, and the times at which they are to be delivered. The exact nature of all this information would be dictated by the operating schedule. These notices would be sent either to the dispatchers or directly to the storeroom personnel.

Finally, nothing like a move order is necessary. In a given production

MATERIAL-PARTS REQUISITION

	☒ STANDARD COST ☐ CHARGE ACCOUNT NO.		DATE FILLED 9-10-7- FILLED BY			
SIGNED *RJB*						

DATE	SHORTAGE NO.	QUANTITY	PART NUMBER	PART DESCRIPTION	ORDER REF.	PAGE
9-10-7-	5200029	1000	5A15654	ARM ASSEMBLY	432761	1

PART NUMBER	PART DESCRIPTION	STOCK LOCATION	DELIVER TO	QUANTITY	USE U/M	DATE NEEDED
5A15656	ARM	FF	49-020	1000	EA	9-19-7-
5A12458	STUD	FA	49-020	1000	EA	9-19-7-
5A12455	ARM	FG	49-020	1000	EA	9-19-7-
5A12457	STUD	FB	49-020	1000	EA	9-19-7-
5A12456	HUB	FC	49-020	1000	EA	9-19-7-

Figure 12-3   A statement of required parts (Courtesy of NCR Corporation)

line, the material may be moved automatically from one work station to another. But even if this is not the case, materials from one work station will always be transported to the same next work station. This also holds true for items moved from one production line to another; from one line, the work will always be transported to some other specific line. Therefore, after the production lines have been set up, materials handling personnel will be told what the paths of travel of the various items are, and no need exists for repeating these instructions.

In summary, then, after the operating schedules have been prepared, the production control department need only notify concerned individuals when materials and purchased parts must be available, notify dispatchers or supervisors when and how specific production lines should be operated, and notify dispatchers or stores personnel where and when materials and purchased parts should be delivered.

PREPARATION OF PROGRESS REPORTS

From this point on, all the production control department can do is observe the progress of production in the shop, compare it with the established schedule, and take whatever action is necessary to eliminate any discrepancy between the two. The only information required for the preparation of progress reports is a count of the output from each line. These counts can be obtained by asking the supervisor of each line to submit a verbal or written report periodically throughout the day. The supervisor may determine the actual output from his line by providing for a physical count to be taken or, in some cases, by taking a reading from a counting device which may be installed right in the line. If an inspector is stationed at the end of each line, another alternative is to have him submit a periodic inspection report, in which the cumulative number of good and defective items inspected would be recorded. These reports would also serve to reveal whether additional units must be scheduled for production to offset an excessive amount of scrap.

At the times these reports are received, the production control department will compare actual output with the scheduled output for each production line. These comparisons can be tabular or graphical. Graphically, for a given line, the information would take the form shown in Figure 12-4.

INAUGURATING CORRECTIVE ACTION

Some difference between actual output and scheduled output for a particular production line will probably always exist. If these differences are minor, it is unlikely that anything will be done about them. However, if

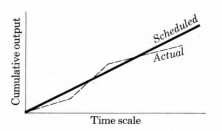

**Figure 12-4   A comparison of actual
and scheduled output**

they begin to assume major proportions, corrective action must be taken.

If the actual output exceeds the scheduled output, the production control department has only two alternatives. The first is to reduce, if possible, the output capacity of the line operating ahead of schedule by means described earlier. The second alternative is to allow the line to operate until the total scheduled number of parts has been produced and then to shut the line down. However, this may create problems. To begin with, it may be that the line involved is supposed to be balanced with some subsequent line. If the second line cannot keep up with the first, the output from the first line must be banked. But it may be that the amount of storage space is inadequate. If this is the case, the first line may not be allowed to complete its run. Instead, after a small bank of parts has been built up, the line may be stopped until the bank is used up and then started again. Another possibility would be to increase the output capacity of the second line.

If the line is running behind schedule, the first thing the production control department must do is determine the cause. This may be a material shortage, an unskilled worker assigned to the line, frequent machine breakdowns, defective materials, the line's being operated improperly, and the like. To prevent the behind-schedule condition from becoming worse, the cause of the trouble must be eliminated if at all possible. To make up the discrepancy between actual and scheduled outputs, the production control department will have to increase the hours the line is scheduled to operate or increase the output capacity of the line or both. Again, if the behind-schedule condition on one line affects other lines adversely, the production control department may be compelled to alter the operating schedules or output capacities of these other lines.

However, there will always be behind-schedule conditions which cannot be corrected. In those cases, production schedules for subsequent time periods will probably have to be revised to make up the difference between realized output and expected output.

This, then, is production control in continuous manufacturing. Special problems arise, of course, which we have not considered. As an example, it may be that the required quantities of one of the manufactured component parts are such that a single production line cannot be economically established to produce just this item. Instead, it and similar parts will be produced intermittently on general-purpose machines and their production controlled by a system which will have many of the characteristics of order control. Or it may be that a single line is used to manufacture a number of similar parts which differ in certain minor respects. Yet, the nature of the differences may necessitate making changes in the setups of the equipment in the line. This calls for issuing special instructions to the shop. But in spite of the fact that these special problems do arise, flow control is, in general, simpler than order control.

DATA PROCESSING IN PRODUCTION CONTROL

As mentioned earlier, it is important to bear in mind that each of the two described systems of production control represents an extreme case, and the system actually adhered to by any one company contains, more often than not, elements of both. Further, the specific procedures adhered to for implementing a given system will vary. To illustrate, one approach will be employed by a firm which has an automatic data processing installation and another by a company which does not. Let us consider how such an installation might affect control procedures.

The production control activity begins with the release of authorizations to produce. In order control, data processing equipment can be used to prepare periodically a list of the standard products to be produced, the required quantities, and the scheduled delivery dates; such a report would replace individual manufacturing requisitions and the master schedule. Similarly, in flow control, the equipment can be used to prepare the equivalent of a production program release.

As in production planning, the equipment could then be employed to ascertain component-part requirements for assembled products. These requirements can be automatically compared with the inventories of the parts involved to determine which of the items must be purchased or manufactured at this time. Insofar as manufactured parts are concerned, automatic data processing would continue with a determination of the raw-material requirements for parts produced continuously and with a determination of raw-material, direct labor, equipment, and machine-accessory requirements for parts produced intermittently. In flow control, a report would then be prepared which would serve to notify the stockroom of what raw materials must be on hand by a specified date. In order control, the data processing equipment would be used to check manpower, equipment, and accessory requirements against load cards to find out when these factors would be available for the order under consideration; with regard to raw materials, the requirements would be compared with records of the amounts in stock to determine whether additional quantities must be ordered.

Scheduling of the required work could also be done with the use of data processing equipment if some specific procedure for developing such schedules has been established. One such procedure might call for beginning with the stipulated completion date and working backward while taking into consideration processing times and the availability of factors of production. Of course, if the resultant schedule proves to be unsatisfactory in some respect, modifications might have to be made by manual methods.

Data processing equipment can also be applied in the preparation of required shop forms. In order control, these would be shop orders, job tickets, move orders, and the various requisitions. In flow control, they would be printed notices informing shop supervisors of the quantities to be manufactured on the production lines involved and instructing stockroom personnel with regard to raw-material and purchased-part requirements at stipulated locations in the plant.

Finally, the equipment can be employed in the determination and evaluation of progress being made in the shop. Employees can be instructed to record the completion of their tasks on job tickets and move orders, or the foreman can be asked to provide reports of completed work. These data can then be recorded on tape or punched cards and the data processing equipment used to compare actual with scheduled progress and to prepare appropriate reports.

In conclusion, it might be mentioned that many of the figures in this and the preceding chapter on production control contained forms and reports that were prepared and used in connection with an automatic data processing installation.

OTHER CONTROL APPROACHES

Regardless of how elaborate a control system is developed, things will not work out perfectly at all times. Operation schedules developed by the most scientific methods will be disrupted because an employee decides to take the day off or because a supplier addresses a shipment incorrectly or because someone inadvertently drops his lunch pail into the working parts of a machine. Further, a number of the elements of any production control system involve the use of judgment or are based on predictions of the future course of events, and errors in judgment and in forecasting are commonplace. Fortunately, however, perfection is not required. Production is not an activity which calls for split-second timing, and so long as the firm's mistakes are no more serious than those of its competitors, there is little cause for major concern.

It might also be repeated that, in our presentation, we assumed that the firm would have a production control department, which would develop and implement procedures of a somewhat formal nature. This will not necessarily be the case. Just as a firm may not adhere to formal production planning methods, a firm may also be without a centralized production control department. Instead, the production control functions will be performed by manufacturing personnel on the basis of judgment, experience, and rules of thumb. And this type of arrangement may, on occasion, prove to be satisfactory. This is not to say that an informal approach to production control is just as desirable as the systematic approaches we have considered. It is simply that there are firms that adhere to an informal approach with success, firms that adhere to a formal approach with success, and firms that adhere to some combination of the two with success. But regardless of the nature of the approach followed, the factors we have discussed must be considered and the activities we have described must be performed, and there is no single method for doing so which will be best for every firm.

With regard to somewhat informal approaches, these are likely to prevail in organizations that engage in activities other than manufacturing. For a number of reasons, operations in medical centers, restaurants, educational institutions, service organizations, department stores, government agencies, and the like do not lend themselves to control by means of the specific approach we considered with reference to a manufacturing model. Some of these reasons are that the work methods involved very often cannot be standardized, time requirements may be difficult to determine in advance, employees may be working on a number of tasks simultaneously, activities may be primarily mental rather than physical, and so on. But even under such circumstances, some system of control must be developed and adhered to. As suggested, it may be relatively loose and informal. Nevertheless, it should contain provisions for determining what is to be done, how it is to be done, and when it is to be done. Concerned individuals must then be notified and instructed accordingly and some means provided for determining and evaluating progress. Admittedly, many aspects of the resultant system will involve a great deal of judgment and a dependence upon a significant amount of oral communication. But given the circumstances, this simply has to be accepted.

QUESTIONS

12-1 What is the function of a production program release? Answer this and all subsequent questions in this section with reference to flow control, unless directed otherwise.

12-2 Why is it said that a production line is equivalent to a single special-purpose machine and that certain processing instructions are built into the line?

12-3 What form do the processing instructions for an assembly assume?

12-4 How are the required factors of production determined and arrangements made to have them on hand when they will be needed?

12-5 How is the operating schedule prepared?

12-6 What is meant by the *normal* output capacity of a production line? How can this capacity be altered?

12-7 After an operating schedule has been prepared, what kinds of instructions are sent to shop supervisors, dispatchers, and store personnel?

12-8 How is production progress ascertained and evaluated in flow control?

12-9 What action, if any, might be taken when actual output is found to be exceeding scheduled output? When actual output is significantly less than scheduled output?

12-10 How can automatic data processing equipment be used to control production in intermittent and continuous manufacturing?

12-11 What will be the similarities and the differences between the system used to control production in a nonmanufacturing operation and the system used in a manufacturing operation? Why do the differences exist?

PROBLEMS

12-1 Select a firm which manufactures certain products continuously and is willing to discuss the production control system to which it adheres in the processing of these items. Describe this system in detail in the terms we have considered. Finally, compare the details of this system with those of the one we have studied and explain the differences.

12-2 Select an organization that engages in nonmanufacturing activities on a continuous basis. Then determine the system by means of which these operations are controlled. Describe this system in terms of the same elements considered in the description of production control in continuous manufacturing.

THIRTEEN
LINEAR PROGRAMMING

In the course of discussing production control procedures, we noted that, on occasion, the firm may find that the factors of production on hand, at a given moment in time, may be such that all the demands for these factors cannot be satisfied. When such situations arise, management is said to be confronted by an allocation problem in which a determination must be made of the most efficient way of allocating scarce resources among the demands that exist for them.

One example of a problem of this type is that of capacity allocation. Although it is true that, in the long run, available output capacity is variable, it is relatively fixed in the short run. This is to say that, because of the time required to procure various factors of production, significant changes cannot usually be made in the firm's output capacity for some specific time period in the near future. If the demand for the company's products during this period is greater than that which can be satisfied, a decision must be made concerning what quantities of specific products should be produced.

Another example of this kind of problem is that of routing or loading. It may be that a number of jobs must be performed but that their nature is such that the operations involved can be performed on different types of equipment. However, for a given job, not all this equipment may be equally efficient. If equipment capacity is limited, an analysis must be made to ascertain the most efficient allocation of the different types of available machine time to the various jobs that must be performed.

In all problems of this kind, a basic analytical technique, such as the uniform annual cost method, can be used to identify the alternative which will maximize profits. However, when an extremely large number of alternatives must be evaluated, such methods prove to be relatively inefficient, and a need exists for an approach which will serve to identify the best alternative in a more direct manner. We found this to be the case in the economic lot size problem. However, we also found in the economic lot size problem that, under certain conditions, a more direct approach can be developed and applied. Similarly, in allocation problems, a more direct method of analysis is available for use under certain conditions. This method is called "linear programming."

The conditions under which linear programming can be employed are those of linearity and certainty. By *linearity,* we mean that all the relationships among the variables in a given problem can be described in terms of linear equations; for example, if two of the variables are output and manufacturing costs, a linear relationship would have to exist between these variables. By *certainty,* we mean either that no variations will occur in the expected numerical values of the relevant factors or that the size of any such variations will be insignificant.

In this chapter, we shall consider the fundamentals of the linear programming method. These fundamentals will be presented with the aid of two problems of a relatively simple nature so that the emphasis can be placed on the principles underlying the approach rather than on its mechanics.

A PRODUCT-MIX PROBLEM

Suppose that, among other things, a company manufactures two assemblies, XX and YY. Each unit of these respective products requires a certain amount of machining time and a certain amount of assembly time. Specifically, these requirements are as follows:

	Required hours per unit	
Product	*Machining*	*Assembly*
XX	4	2
YY	6	1

The individuals responsible for the preparation of the production schedule for the coming month find that the maximum available machining capacity is 2,400 hours and that the maximum available assembly capacity is 700 hours. Furthermore, because of time limitations, nothing can be done to increase these capacities for the period under consideration.

The demand for each of these items is expected to exceed the maximum number of units of each product that can possibly be manufactured with the available factors of production. In other words, a demand exists for any feasible combination of units of products XX and YY.

The problem confronting the scheduling personnel is one calling for the determination of the quantities of the respective products that should be manufactured during the time period being considered. Because the product mix that should be adhered to is the one that will maximize profits, it is necessary that something be known about the respective products' contributions to the firm's profits. Let us assume that it is estimated that the difference between the unit selling price and the variable manufacturing cost of product XX is $20 per unit; although this represents the item's contribution to profits and the covering of fixed costs, for purposes of simplicity we shall refer to this amount as the "profit." Insofar as product YY is concerned, it is estimated that it will generate a $25-per-unit contribution to profits and the covering of fixed costs.

THE CONSTRAINTS   The linear programming method for arriving at a solution to an allocation problem begins with a statement of the existing constraints. These are the restrictions that are imposed upon the decision maker and which serve to reduce the number of possible solutions to the problem.

In our example, if we let X represent the number of units of product XX to be manufactured, we can begin by stating that this quantity cannot be less than 0, that is,

$X \geq 0$

To continue, if we let Y represent the number of units of product YY to be manufactured, we can say that this quantity cannot be less than 0, that is,

$Y \geq 0$

However, only 2,400 machining hours are available, and, therefore, the total output of these two products is restricted by this available capacity. Given that unit machining times for products XX and YY are 4 and 6 hours, respectively, the following constraint can be said to exist:

$4X + 6Y \leq 2,400$

which can also be stated as

$6Y \leq 2,400 - 4X$

or

$Y \leq 400 - (2/3)\, X$

A similar limitation exists because of available assembly capacity. A maximum of 700 assembly-hours is available, and unit assembly times for products XX and YY are 2 hours and 1 hour, respectively. Hence, another constraint is as follows:

$2X + 1Y \leq 700$

or

$Y \leq 700 - 2X$

In summary, we have the following four constraints:

$X \geq 0$

$Y \geq 0$

$Y \leq 400 - (2/3) X$

$Y \leq 700 - 2X$

The third and fourth of these have been expressed in a form similar to the general equation of a line

$Y = a + bX$

because this form will prove to be a more convenient one at a subsequent point in the analysis.

THE OBJECTIVE FUNCTION   The next step in the linear programming method calls for the development of the objective function. In our problem, the objective is to maximize the total profit P. Given that each unit of product XX contributes $20 to profit and that each unit of product YY contributes $25, the profit function, that is, the objective function, becomes

$P = 20X + 25Y$

The task now is to determine those values of X and Y which will maximize the value of P without violating the existing constraints. This can be accomplished either algebraically or graphically. We shall adhere to the latter approach, because it serves to demonstrate more clearly the concepts underlying the linear programming method.

THE SOLUTION   The first step in the graphical method calls for constructing a graph on whose X axis are shown possible manufacturing quantities for the one product and on whose Y axis are shown possible manufacturing quantities for the other product. The graph with which we shall be working is shown in Figure 13-1.

Next, the constraints are shown on the graph. Beginning with the restriction, $X \geq 0$, we first locate the line, $X = 0$, as indicated in Figure 13-1. Then, arrows pointing to the right are shown to reflect the fact that X can also be greater than 0.

After we locate the second constraint, $Y \geq 0$, in the same general manner, we turn to the machining constraint, which was found to be

$Y \leq 400 - (2/3) X$

This expression tells us that the maximum value Y can assume is

$Y = 400 - (2/3) X$

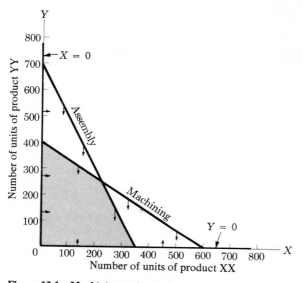

Figure 13-1   Machining and assembly constraints

To locate this line, we require only two points through which the line passes. Two such points can be found by selecting two arbitrary X values, substituting these values in the equation of the line, and calculating the corresponding Y values. For example, the following X values will yield the indicated Y values:

X	Y
0	400
600	0

When we plot these points on the graph and connect them, we obtain the "machining line" shown in Figure 13-1. Consequently, we can say any combination of X and Y values that represents a point on this line satisfies the machining-capacity limitation. However, the constraint states that Y can also be less than the value calculated with some given X value, that is, that the maximum capacity does not have to be utilized. Therefore, any point below the line also satisfies the constraint.

The fourth and last constraint is the one which reflects the available assembly time and which was found to be

$$Y \leq 700 - 2X$$

As a result, the maximum allowable value for Y in this case is

$$Y = 700 - 2X$$

The following two X values and the indicated Y values they generate enable us to determine two points through which this line passes and, therefore, to locate the line in Figure 13-1:

X	Y
0	700
350	0

Again, because the maximum assembly capacity does not have to be utilized, any point on or below this line yields a combination of X and Y output values that satisfies the assembly constraint.

However, it should be noted that all four constraints must be satisfied, and, consequently, only the points contained in the shaded area of Figure 13-1 represent feasible solutions to the problem. This area is referred to as the "solutions area." In any case, the task that now remains is one of determining which of the many points in the solutions area will maximize the profit function.

We shall begin this determination by expressing the profit function in a somewhat different form. We know that

$$P = 20X + 25Y \tag{13-1}$$

Solving for Y, we obtain

$$Y = (1/25) P - (4/5) X \tag{13-2}$$

Equation (13-2) can be referred to as the equation of the "profit line." An examination of this equation reveals that it has a negative slope equal to 4/5. But its Y-intercept is equal to $P/25$, which is to say that the value of the Y-intercept depends on the value of the profit. To illustrate this, let

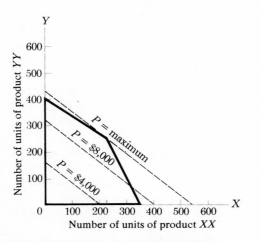

Figure 13-2 Solutions area and profit lines

us suppose that we want to obtain the equation of the profit line for a profit of \$4,000. When we substitute this value for P in Eq. (13-2), we obtain

$$Y = (1/25) (4,000) - (4/5) X$$
$$= 160 - (4/5) X$$

To locate this line on the graph, we can select two arbitrary values for X and solve for the corresponding Y values. For example, we can do this in the following manner:

X	Y
0	160
200	0

If we plot these points on the graph and draw a line through them, we obtain the \$4,000-profit line shown in Figure 13-2, which also depicts the solutions area for our problem. The significance of this line is that it contains all the points, each of which represents some combination of outputs for products XX and YY, that will yield a profit of \$4,000. To demonstrate this, let us take the point at which X is 200 and Y is 0. When we substitute these values in Eq. (13-1), we obtain

$$P = \$20 (200) + \$25 (0) = \$4,000$$

The same result would be obtained with any other point selected from this line. Incidentally, it might be noted that all the points on the line fall within the solutions area.

But let us now suppose that the firm would like to increase its profit to, say, \$8,000. When we substitute this value for P in Eq. (13-2), we obtain

$$Y = 320 - (4/5) X$$

This \$8,000-profit line can be located, as it has been, in Figure 13-2 with the same approach employed when locating the \$4,000-profit line. From the resultant line, we can obtain all the combinations of X and Y that will yield a profit of \$8,000. However, it should be noted that, in this case, all these combinations do not fall within the solutions area. For example, one of these points yields an X of 400 units and a Y of 0 units. With these outputs, the profit would be

$$P = \$20 (400) + \$25 (0) = \$8,000$$

However, an examination of Figure 13-2 reveals that this point does not fall within the solutions area, which is to say that it does not satisfy all the constraints. Therefore, if the firm wants to realize a profit of \$8,000, it must do so by selecting a point from that segment of the \$8,000-profit line which passes through the solutions area.

The two arbitrarily selected profits of \$4,000 and \$8,000 served to demonstrate a number of things. First, the Y-intercept of the profit line is a function of the profit. Second, all the profit lines in this problem have the same slope and, as a result, will be parallel. And third, the profit increases as the profit line is moved away from the origin. As this last observation suggests, the maximum-profit line will be the one that is as far from the origin as possible and, yet, yields a product mix which falls within the solutions area.

To obtain the maximum-profit line, we return to Figure 13-2. From this figure, we determine, either graphically or visually, that we can keep moving the profit line away from the origin until we reach the point at which the machining and assembly constraint lines intersect and still obtain a feasible solution. This point yields a value of 225 units for product XX and 250 units for product YY.

After it has been found that the solution lies at the intersection of two constraint lines, it is sometimes difficult to get an accurate reading of the values involved from the graph. If so, the equations of the two intersecting lines can be solved simultaneously to obtain the coordinates of the point of intersection. In our problem, these two equations are

$$Y = 400 - (2/3)\ X$$

$$Y = 700 - 2X$$

Solving these two simultaneous equations, we obtain an X of 225 units and a Y of 250 units, as we did with the use of the graph.

When these quantities are produced, the resultant total contribution to profit and the covering of fixed costs will be

$$P = \$20\ (225) + \$25\ (250) = \$10,750$$

Any other product mix would yield a smaller total profit.

It might be mentioned that, if our profit function had a slope other than the one it has, a different solution to the problem might have been obtained. For example, the profit function could possibly have a slope which is equal to the slope of the line representing the assembly constraint. Such a profit line is shown in Figure 13-3. In that case, more than one product mix would maximize profits, and any of the points that fall on the involved section of the assembly constraint line would represent a solution to the problem.

On the other hand, the profit function could have a slope such that the optimum product mix is represented by the point at which either the machining or the assembly constraint line intersects one of the axes. A profit line of this type is also shown in Figure 13-3.

It becomes apparent, therefore, that the specific point or points that

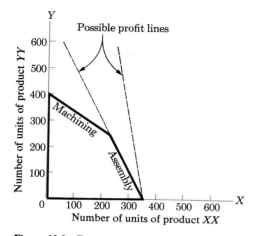

Figure 13-3   Examples of other profit functions

represent the optimum product mix can be ascertained by the described method only after the profit line in a given problem has been located relative to the constraint lines and the direction in which this line must be moved to increase profits is determined.

However, the examples of profit functions with different slopes that we have considered suffice to permit us to make the following generalization: The solution to the problem will always lie at one of the corners of the solutions area, and the specific corner will depend on the slope of the profit function. This statement is correct even when the solution consists of all the points that fall on a segment of one of the constraint lines, because each of the end points of the segment will lie at a corner of the solutions area.

Once this fact has been recognized, an alternate approach to the solution of the problem presents itself. This is to locate the constraint lines on the graph, determine the values of X and Y at each corner of the resultant solutions area, compute the profit for each of these combinations of X and Y values, and select the one that maximizes profits. If two of these points yield the same maximum-profit value, the maximum-profit line apparently coincides with the constraint line that passes through these points, and, therefore, any point on the relevant segment of that constraint line will also maximize the profit function. Of course, the coordinates of the corners of the solutions area can also be determined algebraically by solving simultaneously the equations of each pair of lines which intersect to form a corner.

A LOADING PROBLEM

We shall now consider another example of the application of linear programming. This problem is characterized by the fact that revenues are not affected by the choice of alternative, and, as a result, the firm's objective is to minimize costs.

The firm under consideration has two plants, I and II. Three of its products, which we shall identify as D, E, and F, are manufactured at each of these plants. The products are similar to the degree that all require the same kind and amount of material per unit of output. However, the type of equipment and its condition varies from the one plant to the other, with the result that unit manufacturing costs for the respective products depend on the plant in which they are produced. Specifically, these costs are as follows:

	Unit manufacturing costs		
Plant	Product D	Product E	Product F
I	$30	$25	$15
II	$20	$35	$10

The production control department is notified that, for the coming week, it is to arrange for the production of 110 units of product D, 80 of E, and 60 of F. A check with the stockrooms of the two plants reveals that plant I has a sufficient amount of raw materials on hand to manufacture a total of 150 units of some combination of products D, E, and F and that plant II has a sufficient amount to manufacture a total of 100 units. Further, it is concluded that it would not be economical to ship raw materials from the one plant to the other and that there is an insufficient amount of time for either of the plants to obtain additional materials from a supplier.

Given these circumstances, the production control department must determine the quantities of each of the products that should be scheduled for production at the respective plants. This schedule, of course, should be the one that will minimize total production costs and yet will satisfy the demand for the items.

THE SOLUTION   We shall begin the solution to this problem by letting X represent the number of units of product D to be manufactured at plant I and Y the number of units of product E to be manufactured at the same plant. Keeping in mind the total quantity of each product to be manufactured and the total output possible at each plant, we can describe the production schedule to be established in the following manner:

Plant	Product D	Product E	Product F	Total
		Production schedule in units		
I	X	Y	$150 - X - Y$	150
II	$110 - X$	$80 - Y$	$60 - (150 - X - Y)$	100
Total	110	80	60	250

An examination of this table reveals that, if the two unknown quantities, X and Y, are determined, the data given to us will permit the determination of the values of the other four quantities. To ascertain the values of these quantities, we begin, as in the preceding problem, with a statement of the constraints.

It so happens that some of these constraints have already been considered and satisfied in the process of constructing the preceding table. For example, one constraint is that 110 units of product D are to be manufactured; consequently, because X of these units are to be manufactured in plant I, the number of units to be produced in plant II was shown to be 110 minus X. Given that this and other constraints related to total output have been satisfied, the only ones remaining are that each of the six unknown production quantities must be greater than or equal to zero. Specifically, these constraints are as follows:

$$X \geq 0$$
$$Y \geq 0$$
$$150 - X - Y \geq 0 \text{ or } Y \leq 150 - X$$
$$110 - X \geq 0 \text{ or } X \leq 110$$
$$80 - Y \geq 0 \text{ or } Y \leq 80$$
$$60 - (150 - X - Y) \geq 0 \text{ or } Y \geq 90 - X$$

Next, we must develop the expression for the cost function which is to be minimized. The total cost C will simply be the sum of the terms obtained by multiplying each of the six quantities by their corresponding unit production costs. When we do this, we obtain the following:

$$C = 30X + 25Y + 15(150 - X - Y) + 20(110 - X)$$
$$+ 35(80 - Y) + 10[60 - (150 - X - Y)]$$
$$= 5X - 15Y + 6,350$$

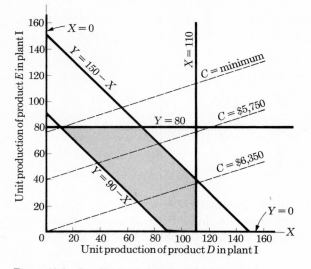

Figure 13-4   Graphical solution to scheduling problem

Having formulated the constraints and the objective function, we can go on to locate the constraint lines on a graph and determine the region which contains all the feasible solutions to the problem. These lines and this region, which is represented by the shaded area, are shown in Figure 13-4.

To locate the point that will yield the optimum production schedule, we return to the cost function which we know to be

$$C = 5X - 15Y + 6,350$$

which is equal to

$$15Y = (6,350 - C) + 5X$$

or

$$Y = \frac{6,350 - C}{15} + \frac{1}{3}X \qquad (13\text{-}3)$$

If we substitute a cost of, say, $6,350 in this expression, we obtain the cost line shown in Figure 13-4. This suffices to reveal the slope of the line but does not tell us the direction in which the line must be moved to reduce the cost. However, if we substitute a cost of, say, $5,750 in Eq. (13-3), we find, as also indicated in Figure 13-4, that the line moves upward. But it should be noted that this will not always be the case in a minimization problem. In any event, if we continue to move the line upward while maintaining its slope, we determine that the minimum cost point occurs at the intersection of the following lines:

$Y = 80$

$Y = 90 - X$

From either the graph or these two equations, X is found to be 10 units and Y to be 80 units. With the use of these two values and the earlier table in which the production schedule was described in terms of six unknown values, we find the optimum quantities of each product to be manufactured in the individual plants to be as follows:

	Production schedule in units			
Plant	*Product D*	*Product E*	*Product F*	*Total*
I	10	80	60	150
II	100	0	0	100
Total	110	80	60	250

The total cost that will be experienced with this schedule is as follows:

$C = \$5X - \$15Y + \$6{,}350$

$\quad = \$5(10) - \$15(80) + \$6{,}350$

$\quad = \$5{,}200$

It is apparent, therefore, that the same general approach is employed in a cost minimization as in a profit maximization problem. In brief, the line which represents the objective function must be located and moved in the proper direction on the graph which depicts the constraints and the feasible solutions area. With this approach, the solution will always be found to occur at a corner of the solutions area. For this reason, cost minimization problems, as well as profit maximization problems, can also be solved by first determining, either graphically or algebraically, the coordinates of each corner of the solutions area. Each set of these values can then be substituted in the objective function and the set selected which enables the firm to attain its objective.

OTHER PROBLEMS AND PROCEDURES

The method of linear programming we have described is the graphical method. This approach is an efficient one when the problem under consideration contains only two variables, as happened to be the case in each of our illustrations. However, the graphical method becomes somewhat awkward when three variables, that is, three unknowns, are involved. An example of such a problem would be one in which the same factors of production are used to process three different products; if inadequate amounts of these factors are available, three unknowns exist in the sense that there is a need to ascertain what quantities of three products are to be produced if the firm's objective is to be realized. A problem of this type can be handled geometrically by adding a third axis to the graph. When this is done, the constraints become planes rather than lines, and the feasible solutions are contained in a space enclosed by intersecting planes rather than in an area. But it is fairly obvious that a graphical approach calling for the construction and analysis of a three-dimensional figure is appreciably more difficult than an approach involving a two-dimensional figure.

What is of even greater significance is that a geometric solution becomes impossible when the problem contains four or more variables. And problems of this type are the rule rather than the exception. When they do occur, they must be solved with the use of special computational techniques called "algorithms." The most common of these is the simplex method; others are the transportation method and the assignment method.

The *simplex method,* which can be employed to solve any linear programming problem, consists of a series of repetitive operations which are performed after the constraints and objective function have been determined and by means of which an optimum solution is ultimately reached. We shall not consider this iterative procedure, because the graphical method suffices to demonstrate the fundamentals of linear programming. However, it might be noted that, if carried out manually, the simplex technique proves to be rather tedious and time-consuming. This is particularly true when a large number of variables and constraints must be manipulated. An extreme example of such a problem is one in which a company had to consider approximately 2,500 variables and 800 constraints. But even in problems of much more limited scope, it is very often found that the manual application of the simplex method proves to be physically or economically impracticable; the same can be said with reference to other available special techniques, such as the transportation method. In these cases, the algorithm must be applied in conjunction with an electronic computer which has been programmed to carry out the necessary operations. As a matter of fact, it is only a slight exaggeration to say that the solution of most realistic linear programming problems requires the use of electronic data processing equipment. Fortunately, special computer programs have been prepared for this purpose and are readily available.

In brief, the graphical approach we have discussed may not be the one that is actually employed to obtain the solution to a given problem, but it does serve to acquaint one with the fundamentals of linear programming. Similarly, the problems considered do not represent an exhaustive set of applications of linear programming. For example, the method can also be used to solve blending problems in which the least costly mix of product ingredients must be found, to decide how a limited amount of suitable land is to be allocated among several crops to obtain optimum results, to determine how available funds should be distributed among various advertising media to attain some given objective, to determine the most economical distribution pattern when products manufactured at different locations must be transported to various distribution centers, and to ascertain how capital should be allocated among alternative investment projects to maximize the rate of return. Other examples could be given, but these suffice to suggest that linear programming can be utilized to solve a variety of problems in both manufacturing and nonmanufacturing areas.

However, it is important not to lose sight of the fact that, in all cases, the condition of linearity and certainty must, for all practical purposes, be satisfied before linear programming can be applied. Furthermore, the results are meaningful only if the firm has been able to make fairly good estimates of the numerical values that must be assigned to the relevant factors. And finally, there must be some indication that the benefits will more than offset the cost of a linear programming analysis.

QUESTIONS

13-1 What is meant by an allocation problem? Give some examples of such problems, in both manufacturing and nonmanufacturing areas.

13-2 Under what conditions can linear programming be utilized in the solution of allocation problems?

13-3 Define the following: (a) constraint line, (b) objective function, and (c) solutions area.

13-4 Describe, in general terms, the graphical method for the solution of a linear programming problem. Under what conditions can this approach be employed?

13-5 When is a firm likely to make use of a computer in the solution of a linear programming problem?

13-6 What benefits and limitations are to be associated with the linear programming technique?

PROBLEMS

13-1 A company manufactures three products, each of which has the same selling price. Furthermore, each of the products is processed in the same two departments. The man-hours required per unit of output in each of these departments are as follows:

Product	Required man-hours per unit	
	Dept. F	Dept. G
1	0.4	0.5
2	0.8	0.6
3	0.9	1.0

The cost of labor is $6.20 per hour in department F and $5.10 in department G. A maximum of 3,500 man-hours is available in a given month in department F and 3,700 in department G.

The only other relevant cost is that of direct materials. Specifically, material cost is $8.30 per unit of product 1 and $4.55 per unit of product 2 and $2.40 per unit of product 3.

The firm would like to produce a combined total of 5,000 units of the three products during the month; however, because of shipping commitments, at least 1,000 units of each product must be produced.

On the basis of what constraints and objective function would the firm determine what quantity of each product should be manufactured? Can this problem be solved by a graphical method? Why or why not?

13-2 A tobacconist sells four blends of pipe tobacco. Each of these blends contains three types of tobacco in the following proportions:

Blend	Type of tobacco		
	K	L	M
A	20%	50%	30%
B	35	40	25
C	50	30	20
D	60	25	15

At the present time, the quantities of tobacco on hand are 220 pounds of type K, 240 pounds of type L, and 110 pounds of type M. No additional amounts can be obtained during the coming week.

The tobacconist realizes a profit of $1.95 on each pound of blend A he sells, $1.90 on blend B, $1.70 on blend C, and $1.45 on blend D. The demand for these blends during the coming week is expected to be such that the entire supply of whatever product mix is prepared can be sold.

What are the constraints and the objective function which should be taken into consideration when determining how many pounds of each blend should be prepared? Can this problem be solved by a graphical method? Why or why not?

13-3 A bakery, which has to decide what quantities of two different kinds of cookies are to be produced, determines the constraints to be as follows:

$$0 \leq X \leq 12$$
$$0 \leq Y \leq 9$$
$$3X + 6Y \leq 66$$

The objective function to be maximized is as follows:

$$P = 2X + 4Y$$

What are the optimum values of X and Y? What will be the resultant value of P? (Ans. $P = 44$)

13-4 In a machine-assignment problem, the constraints are found to be as follows:

$$X \geq 0$$
$$Y \geq 0$$
$$2X + 8Y \geq 80$$
$$5X + 2Y \geq 50$$
$$3X + 3Y \leq 66$$

The objective function, which is to be minimized, is as follows:

$$C = 30X + 10Y$$

Find the required values of X and Y and the resultant value of C. (Ans. 2; 20; 260)

13-5 Two of a firm's products are manufactured with the use of the same kind of manpower. The maximum number of man-hours of this type that will be available during the coming month is 16,000.

The first product yields a profit of $6 per unit, and its processing requires 2.4 man-hours per unit. It is estimated that the demand for this product will be 4,200 units in the month under consideration.

The second product yields a profit of $9 per unit, and its processing requires 3.2 man-hours per unit. It is estimated that a maximum of 2,500 units of this product can be sold in the same period.

What number of units of each product should the firm schedule for production? What will be the resultant profit?

13-6 A distributor of garden supplies produces a plant food by mixing two ingredients, A and B. The final product must weight exactly 10 pounds. Different amounts of A and B can be combined to accomplish this. However, established specifications are such that every unit of the item must contain a minimum of 4 and a maximum of 7 pounds of ingredient A, and a minimum of 3 and a maximum of 6 pounds of ingredient B. Ingredients A and B each costs $0.35 a pound.

What should the composition of the final product be, as determined by the linear programming method? What will be the total cost of material in each 10-pound mix?

13-7 A company manufactures one of its products in two different plants. The quantities produced per week at each location are as follows:

Plant	Output, units
1	800
2	500

From these two plants, the product is shipped to three different warehouses. Weekly requirements at these locations are as follows:

Warehouse	Requirement, units
R	600
S	400
T	300

Unit shipping costs to a given warehouse depend on the plant at which the product was manufactured, that is, from which it is being shipped. Specifically, these costs are as follows:

Warehouse	Unit transportation cost	
	Plant 1	Plant 2
R	$0.70	$0.55
S	0.45	0.40
T	0.60	0.75

How should the output from the two plants be distributed among the three warehouses? What weekly transportation cost will this schedule generate?

13-8 A new animal food, which a company has just developed, consists of two elements. Each pound of element H costs $1 and contains 8 units of carbohydrates, 4 units of protein, and 2 units of fat. Each pound of element I costs $0.80 and contains 3 units of carbohydrates, 5 units of protein, and 6 units of fat.

There is no weight specification, but each bag of the food must contain at least 24 units of carbohydrates, 20 units of protein, and 12 units of fat.

For each element, determine the number of pounds per bag that will yield the most economical mix. What will be the cost of these amounts per bag? (Ans. 2.14, 2.29, $3.97)

FOURTEEN
CRITICAL PATH
SCHEDULING

In the discussion of production control systems and procedures, consideration was given to the manner in which work is scheduled. But the activities
considered for purposes of illustration were of a routine and somewhat
repetitive nature. On occasion, however, the firm will find itself confronted
by large and complex projects in which many tasks are involved and in
which the interrelationships among these tasks must be taken into account. Examples of such projects are the design and manufacture of special-purpose equipment, the development and introduction of a new
product, and the construction of a building.

Special methods for the planning and scheduling of projects of this
type are available for use. Although their specific characteristics vary,
all are similar in the sense that they are employed to determine the minimum time in which a project can be completed and to ascertain the tasks
that are likely to delay this completion. They do this by identifying the
most time-consuming series of tasks. This series of tasks is said to represent a *critical path,* and, for this reason, these special methods are said
to involve critical path scheduling.

We shall consider two such methods of scheduling. The first is the Critical Path Method (CPM), and the second is the Program Evaluation and
Review Technique (PERT). Each of these approaches will be described
with the aid of a simple illustration.

THE CRITICAL PATH METHOD

The Critical Path Method begins with a determination of each job that
makes up a project; these individual jobs are identified by means of a
number or letter. Furthermore, the jobs that must be completed before
a specific job can be started are determined; these jobs are referred to
as "predecessor jobs," and the last job in a series of predecessor jobs is
called the "immediate predecessor." Conversely, jobs that follow a specific

job are referred to as "successor jobs," and the first job in a series of successor jobs is called the "immediate successor." Finally, the time required to complete each job is estimated; the nature of the projects which would be controlled by a Critical Path Method and the manner in which they would be broken down into jobs are usually such that estimated time requirements are expressed in terms of calendar days or weeks.

Let us illustrate this phase of the method by considering a relatively simple project which will be described in fairly general terms so that we can concentrate on the fundamentals of the approach. Suppose that a firm has received an order for a nonstandard product which is an assembly consisting of two manufactured component parts. To plan and schedule the production of the required quantities by the Critical Path Method, concerned personnel describe the jobs that must be performed, identify the immediate predecessor for each job, and estimate time requirements. The results are as follows:

Job	Description	Immediate predecessors	Required time, days
G	Start		0
H	Procure materials for part 1	G	4
I	Procure materials for part 2	G	3
J	Machine part 1	H	6
K	Machine part 2	I	5
L	Assemble parts 1 and 2	J, K	2
M	Inspect and test assemblies	L	1
N	Finish	M	0

It will be noted that jobs with no real predecessors are said to be preceded by "Start." Similarly, jobs with no real successors are said to be followed by "Finish." Neither of these requires any time.

In any case, completion of this phase of the analysis may be followed by the preparation of a project graph. The graph is a useful rather than an essential part of the method, because computer programs can be written by means of which the necessary subsequent computations can be made without reference to a graph. However, the project graph contributes to an understanding of these computations, and, therefore, we shall assume that it is to be constructed for the project under consideration.

In general, the graph is a pictorial representation of the jobs that make up a project and of their interrelationships. Its construction calls for the use of a circle, ellipse, or rectangle to depict each job; if, say, a circle is

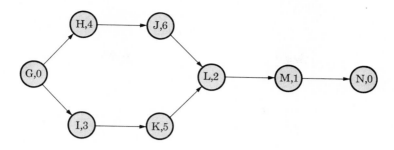

Figure 14-1 A project graph

used, the circle for a given job will contain the letter or number identification of the job and the time estimated for its completion. From any one circle, arrows are drawn to all the immediate successor jobs. The graph for the project in our illustration would appear as shown in Figure 14-1.

With the use of the project graph, the firm can ascertain the minimum time required to complete the project. One way to begin this determination is to enumerate the different routes or paths that can be followed from the start to the finish of the project. As an examination of Figure 14-1 reveals, there are only two such paths in our example. The first of these is represented by the job sequence G–H–J–L–M–N, and the second by the job sequence G–I–K–L–M–N. We now go on to determine the total time requirement for each of these paths. The individual required times for the jobs in the first path are 0, 4, 6, 2, 1, and 0 days; the sum of these times is 13 days. As opposed to this, the jobs in the second path have required times of 0, 3, 5, 2, 1, and 0 days; these yield a total required time of 11 days. The minimum amount of time required to complete the project will be determined by the most time-consuming sequence of jobs, which in this case is the 13-day one of G–H–J–L–M–N.

The path represented by this most time-consuming sequence is called the "critical path." Every job in this path is considered critical in the sense that any delay in the completion of these jobs will increase the total time required to complete the project. This is not true of the jobs in the non-critical path. In our example, the noncritical jobs are I and K, whose estimated time requirements are 3 and 5 days, respectively, which yield a total requirement of 8 days. This total could be increased by 2 days, and the project would still be finished in 13 days. The reason for this is that assembly cannot begin until both parts have been machined. However, the procurement of materials for the first part and the subsequent machining are estimated to require 10 days. It follows that, if the procurement of materials for the second part and the machining of that part also take 10 days instead of the estimated 8, no delay will be experienced in the start of the assembly job and, therefore, in the completion of the project. These additional 2 days that are available for the completion of the non-critical jobs are called the "total slack time."

EARLY START AND FINISH TIMES   Unfortunately, the foregoing method for determining the critical path usually proves to be an inefficient one in practice. The typical project, for which the expense of a critical path analysis can be justified, very often contains scores and sometimes hundreds of paths. Their enumeration would be very time-consuming, and there would also be a high risk of overlooking certain paths. As a result, it is customary to ascertain the critical path in a different manner. In the description of this alternate approach, we shall make use of the following terms:

$S =$ earliest possible starting time for the *project*

$ES =$ earliest possible starting time for a given *job*

$t =$ time required to complete a given *job*

$EF = ES + t =$ earliest possible finish time for a given *job*

$F =$ earliest possible finish time for the *project*

The analysis begins with a determination of the earliest points in time at which each job can be started and finished. The procedure for doing so in our illustration can probably be best explained with the aid of Figure 14-2. Beginning with the first job G, we show the date which represents the earliest possible starting time S for the project. Let us assume this is

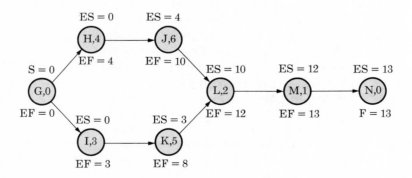

Figure 14-2   Determination of early start and finish times

to be May 1. However, for the sake of convenience, we shall assign a value of 0 to this point in time and number subsequent dates accordingly. To continue, because the time t for job G is 0 days, its early finish time EF will be the starting time of 0 plus the required completion time of 0 days; this yields 0, which, of course, means 0 days from the project starting date.

Following the first path, we go on to job H. This job can be started no sooner than when its immediate predecessor G is finished; therefore, its early start time ES will be equal to its immediate predecessor's early finish time, which was found to be 0. To obtain the early finish time for job H, we take its early start time of 0 and add the 4 days required to perform the job to arrive at an early finish time of 4.

The early finish time of 4 for job H is the early start time for its immediate successor J. The early finish time for job J is found by taking this early start time of 4 and adding to it the required time of 6 days for the job. In this manner, an early finish time of 10 is obtained.

Had we followed the second possible path, we should have calculated the early start and finish times shown in Figure 14-2 for jobs I and K in the same way. When we reach job L, however, we find that it has two immediate predecessors, J and K. Furthermore, J has an early finish time of 10, and K of 8. But we know that job L cannot be started until *both* predecessor jobs are finished. Therefore, the early start time for job L will be governed by the early finish time for J, because it is later than the early finish time for K. As a result, an early start time of 10 is recorded for job L. From that point on, we proceed as before until we reach a finish time F for the project of 13 days from its start. This means that, if the starting time were established as May 1, the earliest possible completion date would be May 14.

LATE START AND FINISH TIMES The analysis continues with a determination of the latest points in time at which each job must be started and finished if a target completion date is to be met. This target completion date may be equal to the earliest possible finish time that has been calculated for a project, or it might be some other date established on the basis of other considerations. For purposes of illustration, we shall assume that a target completion date of May 14, or point 13, has been established for our project; this means that the target completion date is equal to the early finish time we found earlier.

In general, the procedure employed to obtain the desired late times is the reverse of the one followed to obtain early start and finish times. We begin with the target completion time for the last job and work backward until we reach the late start time for the first job. How this is done will be

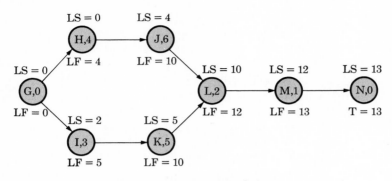

Figure 14-3   Determination of late start and finish times

explained with the aid of Figure 14-3 and with the use of the following notation:

T = target completion time for the *project* or the latest possible finish time for the project

LF = latest possible finish time for a given *job* if the target completion time *T* is to be met

t = time required to complete a given *job*

LS = *LF* − *t* = latest possible starting time for a given *job* if the target completion time *T* is to be met

We begin by noting a target completion date *T* of 13 for job N. Given this late finish time of 13 and a required time of 0 days to perform job N, we find the late start time for this job to be the difference between these two times, which is 13.

For the preceding job M, the late finish time must be equal to the late start time of 13 for its immediate successor N. Therefore, with a required time of 1 day for the job, the late start time for M must be this time of 1 day subtracted from its late finish time of 13, or 12.

We continue to work toward the first job G in this same manner. When we reach G, we find that its immediate successors, H and I, have late start times of 0 and 2, respectively. However, the late finish time for job G will be governed by the immediate successor which has the earlier, that is, the more demanding, late start time. This is job H, and, consequently, the late finish time for G becomes 0.

DETERMINATION OF SLACK   The results of our analysis can be sum-marized as shown in the following table:

	Possible start times		Possible finish times		Slack time
Job	Earliest (ES)	Latest (LS)	Earliest (EF)	Latest (LF)	(LS−ES) or (LF−EF)
G	0	0	0	0	0
H	0	0	4	4	0
I	0	2	3	5	2
J	4	4	10	10	0
K	3	5	8	10	2
L	10	10	12	12	0
M	12	12	13	13	0
N	13	13	13	13	0

The last column contains the slack time, in days, for each job. Although the concept of slack time was introduced earlier, we can now see how it can be obtained in a systematic manner. For any job, the slack time is the difference between the late start and the early start times for that job or between the late finish and the early finish times for that job. This will be explained with reference to job K. The preceding table tells us that we are able to start this job at point 3; however, it also tells us that the target completion date can be met even if the job is started as late as point 5. The difference of 2 days between these late and early start times represents the total slack time. Similarly, the table reveals that we are able to finish this job at point 8 but that it does not have to be finished until point 10. Again, the difference of 2 days between these late and early finish times represents the total slack time. It should be emphasized that this slack time of 2 days is the total allowable delay in the completion of all the jobs in the noncritical path. These are jobs I and K. Therefore, if job I requires, say, 1 more day than originally estimated, only 1 more day than originally estimated can be allowed for job K if the target completion date is to be met.

When the target completion time for a project is equal to its earliest possible finish time, the slack times for all critical jobs will be zero. All noncritical jobs will have a larger slack. As this suggests, an examination of job slack times permits the determination of the critical path. In our example, it would be the path represented by all the jobs with zero slack, and these are G–H–J–L–M–N. This coincides with what we found by the earlier method of totaling individual job times for the various paths.

It should also be noted that when the target completion time for the project is later than its earliest possible completion time, the slack for critical jobs will be greater than 0 by an amount equal to the difference between these two times. However, a corresponding increase will take place in the slack times for the noncritical jobs. For example, if the early start time for the first job is May 1, the early finish time for the project will occur 13 days later, or on May 14. If the target date is also May 14, critical jobs will have 0 slack, and a noncritical job, such as I, will have a slack of 2 days. But in the event that the target completion date is, say, May 18, which is 4 days later than the early finish date of May 14, the slack time for the critical jobs will increase from 0 to 4 days and for a noncritical job, such as I, from 2 to 6 days.

In general, we can say that the critical path consists of those jobs with the minimum value of slack. The jobs involved are critical in the sense that any delay in the completion of these jobs will increase the total time required to complete the project. Whether this increase will preclude the firm's meeting an established target completion date depends on the minimum slack value and on the length of the delay. If, for example, the minimum slack value is 4 days, the target completion date will be met if the delay is 3 days but not if it is 5.

The preceding observations are based on the assumption that the minimum calculated slack time is not less than 0. In the event that negative slack values are obtained, the firm must conclude that the target completion date is not feasible with the planned work methods. This would be the case, if, say, a target completion date of May 12 had been established for the project for which we had computed an early finish time of May 14. When this occurs, steps must be taken to reduce critical job time requirements, or the target completion date must be revised.

BENEFITS OF CRITICAL PATH ANALYSIS We have seen how the project graph is constructed, how the critical path is determined, and how slack times for the various jobs are calculated. Let us now consider what benefits a firm is able to realize from the application of the Critical Path Method.

From our earlier discussion of operation scheduling in order control, we know that scheduling is of value to the firm if for no other reason than that it enables management to determine what the probable completion dates will be with alternative plans; these dates can then be evaluated in light of the costs involved and the required completion date. Furthermore, a schedule permits the firm to evaluate the progress which is being made toward the completion of a project. But these are advantages to be associated with almost any approach to scheduling and are not unique to critical path scheduling.

The Critical Path Method has the additional advantage of being able to identify that sequence of jobs that determines the earliest possible completion date for the project. Consequently, if this date extends beyond the target date, management knows which job times must be reduced if the target date is to be met. Of course, if steps are taken to reduce required times for these critical jobs, some other path may then become the critical one, and any further reductions in total project time could be realized only by reducing the times for these new critical jobs. The methods for bringing about these reductions in critical job times involve technical and economic considerations, but the important thing is that a knowledge of the critical jobs serves to eliminate the fairly common and costly practice of rushing all jobs to reduce the total project time.

A critical path analysis also provides management with information on slack time to be associated with each job in the project, and this knowledge is of value in the development of work schedules. Because the starting times for activities with positive slack are flexible to the degree suggested by the calculated early and late start times, the specific starting time for a given job can be selected with a view toward minimizing fluctuations in work schedules.

In brief, critical path scheduling has advantages which traditional approaches do not. However, as was mentioned earlier, there is more than one method of this kind, and we shall now consider one of these others. This is the Program Evaluation and Review Technique.

PROGRAM EVALUATION AND REVIEW TECHNIQUE

The PERT method is a refinement of the Critical Path Method. In this approach to critical path determination, the analysis begins with a description of the project in terms of activities and events. An activity represents the actual performance of a task and, therefore, is comparable to a job in CPM. An event represents the start or completion of a task, and, unlike an activity, requires no time or resources.

After the activities and events have been determined, a preliminary PERT network can be prepared. The PERT network is similar to the project graph used in CPM, but there are important differences. In the network, activities are depicted by arrows, and events by circles, ellipses, or rectangles. Each circle, for example, contains a description of the event it represents and an identifying number or letter. Therefore, the preliminary network for the project with which we have been working may appear as shown in Figure 14-4.

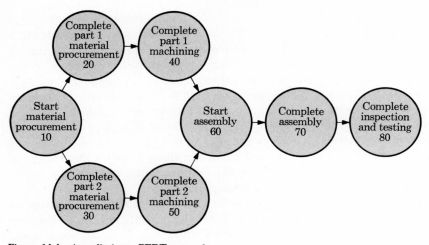

Figure 14-4   A preliminary PERT network

As a rule, start events are not shown in the network unless absolutely necessary, because it is taken for granted that the completion of an activity coincides with the start of its immediate successor. Of course, one point at which a start event must be indicated is at the beginning of the network, that is, at the point at which the first activity begins; in Figure 14-4, this point is represented by event number 10.

In addition, it may be necessary to show start events on occasion to maintain the logic of the network. An example of such an occasion is event 60 in Figure 14-4. If this event were not included, the affected section of the network would appear as indicated in Figure 14-5. This presentation

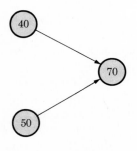

Figure 14-5   The result
of excluding event 60
from Figure 14-4

would prove to be somewhat confusing, because it misleadingly suggests that activities 40–70 and 50–70 both represent the assembling of parts 1 and 2. A clearer picture is obtained when event 60, start assembly, is inserted. But to return to Figure 14-4, it should be noted that the inclusion of event 60 creates activities 40–60 and 50–60, neither of which represents the performance of an actual task. In PERT, all such activities are called "dummy activities," and they require no time or resources.

Development of the preliminary network is followed by an estimate of the required times, in calendar days or weeks, for the activities involved. Three different time estimates are made for each activity. These are as follows:

Optimistic time = the minimum time in which an activity is likely to be completed

Most likely time = the time which has the highest probability of occurrence associated with it

Pessimistic time = the maximum time which an activity might require

Let us illustrate this by returning to our example. One of the activities in the project called for the procurement of materials for part 1. In the Critical Path Method, the required time was estimated to be 4 days. But with PERT, it might be estimated that the optimistic time is 3 days, the most likely time 4 days, and the pessimistic time 6 days. These three times would be inserted above the arrow, which represents the activity in the network, in the following manner:

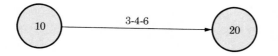

After these three times have been estimated for every activity, the average time t_e for each activity is computed. For reasons we shall consider later, the average time is calculated with the use of the following expression:

$$t_e = \frac{a + 4m + b}{6} \tag{14-1}$$

where a = optimistic time
m = most likely time
b = pessimistic time

As an examination of Eq. (14-1) reveals, the average is obtained by a weighting process in which the most likely time is assigned a weight of 4 and the other two times a weight of 1. Therefore, the average time for the activity of procuring materials for part 1 would be

$$t_e = \frac{3 + 4(4) + 6}{6} = 4.2$$

This time is inserted in the network below the arrow that represents the activity being considered. As a result, the complete description of the 10–20 activity in the network would appear as follows:

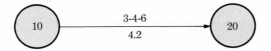

To summarize, after the preliminary network has been developed, three time estimates would be made and their weighted average computed for each activity. These data would then be inserted in the chart to arrive at the completed PERT network. For the project on which our illustration is based, the estimated times may be such that the network shown in Figure 14-6 is obtained.

THE ANALYSIS After the network has been completed, the analysis proceeds with a determination of the slack times and the critical path. In general, an approach similar to the one employed in CPM is followed. More specifically, the calculated average times are used as the required times for the various activities, and the early finish and late finish times are ascertained for each activity. However, the notation for these finish

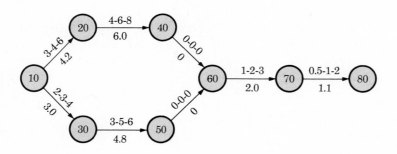

Figure 14-6   A completed PERT network

times differs from that adhered to in CPM. Instead, the following symbols are used:

T_E = earliest possible time that an *event* can be reached or an *activity* completed

T_S = target completion time for the *project*

T_L = latest possible time that an *event* can be reached or an *activity* completed if the project target completion time is to be met

To determine the early time T_E for each event, we begin with the first event shown in Figure 14-7 and work in the direction of the last event. If we assign an early time value of 0 to the first event, number 10, we add the average required time of 4.2 days for activity 10–20 to this value to obtain an early time of 4.2 for the successor event, number 20. Similarly, the addition of the average required time of 6.0 days for activity 20–40 to this result yields an early time of 10.2 for event 40. The only thing that might be noted is that, for reasons given in our explanation of CPM, the early time for an event, such as number 60, is obtained by working with the later of the early times for its two immediate predecessors.

Upon the completion of all such calculations, we obtain the results shown in Figure 14-7 and find that the earliest possible completion time for the project is 13.3 days. Because the required activity times differ

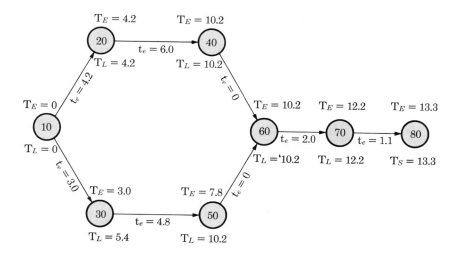

Figure 14-7 **Determination of early and late completion times**

somewhat from those used in the CPM illustration, this result does not coincide with the 13 days we obtained in that earlier analysis. In any case, we know that the length of the critical path is 13.3 days. The specific path involved can be found by ascertaining the slack time for each event.

To determine the slack times, we continue by calculating the latest possible time T_L that each event can be reached if the project target completion date is to be met. This is done by beginning with the target completion time for the last event and working backward until the first event is reached. If we assume, as we did in the CPM example, that the target time T_S is equal to the early time T_E for the last event, the late time for event 80, as indicated in Figure 14-7, becomes 13.3. From this value, we subtract the average required time of 1.1 days for activity 70–80 to obtain the late time of 12.2 for event 70.

Continuing in this manner, we obtain the results shown in Figure 14-7. It might be noted that the late times for events 20 and 30 are 4.2 and 5.4, respectively. The activity which precedes event 20 yields a late time of 0 for the predecessor event number 10, while the activity which precedes event 30 would yield a late time of 2.4 for the same event. But for the reason given when we considered the Critical Path Method, the late time for event 10 is shown as the more demanding, that is, the earlier of these two times, which is 0.

The slack times for the events can now be obtained by taking the difference between the late and early times for each event. Working with the results of our analysis, we find these slack times to be as follows:

| Event | Possible completion times | | Slack time $(T_L - T_E)$ |
	Early (T_E)	Late (T_L)	
10	0	0	0
20	4.2	4.2	0
30	3.0	5.4	2.4
40	10.2	10.2	0
50	7.8	10.2	2.4
60	10.2	10.2	0
70	12.2	12.2	0
80	13.3	13.3	0

From the preceding table, we learn, for example, that event 40 must be reached at point 10.2 if the project is to be completed in 13.3 days and that this is also the earliest point at which it can be reached; therefore, there is no slack time. As another example, we learn that event 50 must be reached at point 10.2 if the project is to be completed in 13.3 days but it can be reached as early as point 7.8; therefore, a delay of 2.4 days can be experienced in reaching this event without increasing the total time required to complete the project. On the basis of such observations, we conclude that the critical path is represented by events 10–20–40–60–70–80, because they have the least amount of slack time, which in this case is 0.

Of course, if the target completion date were later than the earliest possible completion date, the critical events would have a slack time greater than 0, but this slack would continue to be less than the slack for noncritical events. Also, if the target completion date preceded the earliest possible completion date, the minimum slack time would still be associated with the critical events, but this slack time would now have a negative value. As a result, the target completion date would not be met unless actual activity times proved to be sufficiently lower than the expected activity times.

It might also be noted that, as with CPM, there is an alternate method for determining the critical path. This is the one in which all the paths from start to finish are enumerated and the total time for each path is determined by finding the sum of the average times for the activities involved. The critical path would be the one with the maximum total time requirement. To illustrate, working with the average activity times shown in Figure 14-6, we obtain a total of 10.9 days for path 10–30–50–60–70–80 and 13.3 days for path 10–20–40–60–70–80. The latter, therefore, is the critical path, because a total delay of 2.4 days can be experienced in completing activities 10–30 and 30–50 without increasing the total time of 13.3 days required to complete the project. But, as mentioned earlier, this approach proves to be unwieldy when more complex projects are being analyzed.

UNDERLYING STATISTICAL CONCEPTS It is evident that the PERT and CPM approaches to scheduling are basically alike. Hence, PERT has the same advantages over conventional scheduling methods as does CPM. However, PERT is said to have an additional advantage stemming from the fact that it takes into account possible variations in required activity times. Let us elaborate upon this by considering the statistical concepts which underlie the PERT method.

When an activity that is an integral part of a project is performed once, the elapsed time will assume some single value. For example, when part 2 in our illustration is actually machined, the required time may prove to be exactly 4 days. But if this same part were to be machined again, some

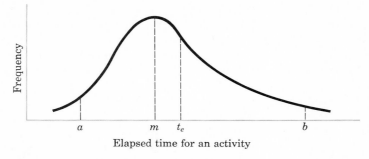

Elapsed time for an activity

Figure 14-8 A distribution of activity times

other required time might be experienced. In brief, the amount of time required for a given activity will not ordinarily be constant; instead, it will vary from one occasion to another. As a result, we say that, if a task is performed repeatedly, a distribution of elapsed times will be obtained. In the PERT method, it is assumed that this distribution can be described by means of a theoretical distribution known as the "beta distribution." The beta distribution does not have a single shape, but it may assume the form shown in Figure 14-8.

As indicated in Figure 14-8, when concerned individuals are asked to estimate the most likely time m for an activity, they are asked to estimate the time that would occur more frequently than any other if the activity were performed an infinite number of times. A common definition of the optimistic time a, which is also indicated in Figure 14-8, is that it is a value which would be exceeded 99 percent of the time if the task were performed repeatedly. And finally, the pessimistic time b is commonly defined as that value which would be exceeded 1 percent of the time in the long run. However, there is no general agreement on these definitions of the optimistic and pessimistic times; for example, some individuals maintain that 5 percent of the area under the curve should lie to the left of a and 5 percent to the right of b. In any case, the average or expected time t_e for the activity is defined as the average of this assumed distribution of elapsed times.

It so happens that the determination of the average of a beta distribution is relatively difficult. Consequently, an attempt is made to obtain only a good approximation of this value, and Eq. (14-1) was developed to yield this approximation. When we calculate the average time with this equation, we obtain a value which is an average in the sense that, in the long run, the actual time for the activity will be greater than this average value 50 percent of the time and less than this average value the remaining 50 percent. But because the total time required to complete the project is computed with the use of these average activity times, it follows that the resultant total time is also an average value. This means that the calculated total time of 13.3 days in our example is to be interpreted as follows: If the project were to be carried out a large number of times, the actual time requirement would exceed 13.3 days half the time and be less than 13.3 days the other half. This permits us to make certain observations regarding the probability of meeting a target completion date. Specifically, in our example, if the target completion date is 13.3 days from the project starting date, the probability of completing the project on or before the target date is 0.50. Also, if the target completion date is more than 13.3 days from the project starting date, the probability of completing the project on or before the target date is greater than 0.50. And finally, if the target completion date is less than 13.3 days from the project starting date, the probability of completing the project on or before the target date is less than 0.50.

There is provision in the PERT method for calculating the exact value of such a probability for some given target completion date. It calls for taking into consideration the dispersion of the distribution of required times for each activity and the resultant dispersion of the distribution of total required times for the project. However, we shall not consider this refinement of the method. Its use is somewhat limited, because serious questions can and have been raised regarding the validity of the underlying assumptions. Among these assumptions is that the beta distribution provides an accurate description of the actual distribution of required times for an activity and that the formulas for calculating the average and dispersion of this theoretical distribution yield good approximations.

APPLICATION OF THE METHODS

Although there are benefits to be realized from the application of critical path scheduling, it is also true that the methods involved do have their limitations. To begin with, there is the danger that certain activities and interrelationships may be overlooked when the preliminary project graph or network is being prepared. The risk of this is not great when the project is a relatively simple one. But as the project becomes more complex, the risk increases. And in practice, complexity is to be expected; for example, one firm reports that one of its projects contained 2,000 tasks.

This is not to say that there is only one correct way in which a specific project can be broken down into the activities it entails. In fact, it is un-likely that two groups, working independently of each other, will construct identical graphs or networks for the same project. This is true if for no other reason than that one group's description will contain fewer but more comprehensive steps than will the other's. But if any description does not contain a required task or take cognizance of an existing interrelationship between two or more tasks, the calculated critical path and slack times may prove to be erroneous.

Additional difficulties stem from the need for estimating time require-ments for the various activities. If these estimates are not accurate, the results of the analysis will prove to be incorrect. It should also be noted that when making these estimates, the individuals concerned must take into consideration the kinds and amounts of resources that will be em-ployed in the performance of the tasks involved. Because these resources can be controlled by the firm to some degree, alternative methods of operation are available, and the required time will depend on the method adopted. Therefore, it becomes necessary that the alternatives be deter-mined, that the schedule generated by each be ascertained, and that the optimum schedule be identified. This identification, of course, can only be made on the basis of a cost comparison of the alternatives.

As all this suggests, the preparation of the project graph or network can be a demanding task from the standpoint of time and cost. The same can be said for the subsequent determination of the critical path and slack times. In a complex project, the number of required computations may be such that the use of a computer becomes almost a necessity. If so, data processing equipment can be used with CPM to ascertain early start, early finish, late start, late finish, and slack times and to determine the critical path. Similarly, with PERT, the equipment can be applied in the calcula-tion of average times once optimistic, most likely, and pessimistic times have been estimated, in the computation of early and late completion times, and in the determination of slack times and the critical path.

After the project is inaugurated, there is the need for comparing actual progress with scheduled progress. If these do not coincide, it may be necessary to revise the schedule accordingly, determine whether the critical path has changed, and recalculate slack times.

In brief, the application of PERT and CPM can prove to be costly and time-consuming. For this reason, the use of these and similar methods can be justified only when the nature of the project is such that there is reason to believe that the benefits of a critical path analysis will more than offset its cost. This is usually the case when the project is fairly large and complex.

It has been stated that the results may be in error because of incorrect time estimates and inaccuracies in the project graph or network. However, there is no other scheduling approach which is free of this limitation. Consequently, an increasing number of firms are concluding that, for projects of the type we have described, problems of estimation do not destroy the benefits to be realized from critical path scheduling. As a result, this analytical technique is being adopted with greater frequency for use in scheduling such things as cost reduction programs, construction projects, computer system installations, rehabilitation projects, and research and development programs. These representative applications suggest that critical path scheduling can be and is being employed in nonmanufacturing as well as in manufacturing areas.

With this, we conclude our discussion of selected special techniques that are available for use at various points in the production planning and control activity. We shall now go on to a consideration of other areas of production management.

QUESTIONS

14-1 Under what conditions is critical path scheduling usually employed?

14-2 What information does this scheduling approach yield?

14-3 What is meant by the critical path?

14-4 In the Critical Path Method, how is each of the following defined: (a) predecessor jobs, (b) successor jobs, (c) project graph, (d) early start times, (e) early finish times, (f) late start times, (g) late finish times, and (h) slack time?

14-5 In the Program Evaluation and Review Technique, how is each of the following defined: (a) activities, (b) events, (c) PERT network, (d) dummy activities, (e) optimistic, most likely, pessimistic, and average times, (f) early completion times, and (g) late completion times?

14-6 Describe the statistical concepts that underlie the PERT method.

14-7 How can computers be used in the application of critical path scheduling?

14-8 What are some representative applications of critical path scheduling in manufacturing and nonmanufacturing areas?

14-9 What benefits are to be associated with the use of critical path scheduling methods? What are the limitations of these methods?

PROBLEMS

14-1 A bank has decided to install automatic data processing equipment. The project will begin with the determination of the alternatives and end with the transfer of processing operations to the equipment that has been selected and installed. In any case, the bank's management wants to plan and schedule the project by the Critical Path Method.

The personnel involved determine the jobs that must be performed in the course of carrying out the project, ascertain their interrelationships, and estimate their time requirements. The results are as follows:

Job	Immediate predecessors	Required time, weeks
A	—	0
B	A	6
C	B	3
D	B	2
E	B	9
F	B	5
G	C, D	10
H	E, F	16
I	G, H	7
J	I	12
K	J	0

a Construct a project graph. Then suppose that the earliest point at which the project can be started is designated as point zero. Determine the early start and early finish times for each job and show these on the project graph.

b Continue by assuming that the established target completion date is 54 weeks from point zero. Determine the late start and late finish times for each job and show these on a second copy of the project graph.

c Find the slack times for the respective jobs by working with, first, the calculated start times and, next, the calculated finish times. Then analyze these results to determine the critical path. (Ans. A–B–E–H–I–J–K)

d Repeat the foregoing with an established target completion date of 50 weeks from point zero. With an established target completion date of 48 weeks from point zero. Can the latter be met? Explain.

e Determine the critical path by enumerating the available paths from the start of the project to its finish, obtaining the total time for the respective paths, and comparing these total times.

14-2 A construction firm has received a contract to build a shopping center. The project is to be planned and scheduled with the use of the Program Evaluation and Review Technique. With this in mind, the firm has described the necessary activities in fairly broad terms and developed the following three time estimates for each of these activities:

Activity	Estimated times, months
10–20	1.5–2.0–4.1
20–30	2.0–3.0–4.5
20–40	0.8–1.0–1.2
20–50	2.3–4.0–5.3
30–70	4.0–6.0–7.0
40–60	0.0–0.0–0.0
50–60	0.0–0.0–0.0
60–70	1.1–2.0–2.4
70–80	0.7–1.0–1.2
70–90	2.6–3.0–4.1
80–100	0.0–0.0–0.0
90–100	1.6–2.0–2.9
100–110	6.4–7.0–9.0

a Construct a PERT network in which you show the events, the estimated activity times, and the average time for each activity as calculated to one decimal place.

b If the earliest the project can be started is two months from now, what are the early times for each event? Show these in the network.

c If the target completion date for the project is 26 months from now, what will be the late times for each event? Show these in the network.

d Determine the slack times for the respective events, and the resultant critical path. (Ans. 10–20–30–70–90–100–110)

e Suppose it is proposed that the target completion date be changed to 24 months from now. What effect will this have on the events' early times, late times, and slack times? On the critical path? What is your reaction to this proposal?

f Ascertain the critical path by enumerating the six paths from the start of the project to its finish, obtaining the total time for the respective paths, and comparing these total times.

14-3 A firm is making an attempt to obtain an order for a complex assembly consisting of many component parts, each of which will require a large number of operations. Although the assembly is a nonstandard item, it has been produced in the past.

In the course of its negotiations with the customer, the company finds it necessary to determine the earliest possible delivery date. As a part of this determination, the production control department is asked to prepare a schedule for its activities, beginning with its receiving the authorization to produce the assembly and ending with its preparing and issuing the necessary shop forms.

The department concludes that the tasks it must perform and their estimated time requirements are as follows:

Job	Description	Immediate predecessors	Time, days
A	Receive production authorization		0
B	Determine part requirements	A	2
C	Determine production factors	B	4
D	Determine material availability	C	6
E	Determine manpower availability	C	3
F	Determine equipment availability	C	5
G	Prepare operation schedule	D, E, F	8
H	Prepare and issue shop forms	G	7

Following this, it is decided to make a CPM analysis in which the earliest point at which the last job can be completed will be accepted as the target completion date for the production control activity. What will be the critical path? Determine this by working with, first, early and late start times and, then, early and late finish times.

14-4 Suppose that, in the preceding problem, the production control personnel had decided to make a PERT analysis. As a consequence, they described their responsibilities in the project under consideration in the following manner:

Activity	Description	Times, days
10–20	Receive production authorization	0.0–0.0–0.0
20–30	Determine part requirements	1.6–2.0–3.0
30–40	Determine required production factors	3.2–4.0–6.0
40–50	Determine material availability	4.8–6.0–9.0
40–60	Determine manpower availability	2.4–3.0–4.5
40–70	Determine equipment availability	4.0–5.0–7.5
50–80	Dummy activity	0.0–0.0–0.0
60–80	Dummy activity	0.0–0.0– 0.0
70–80	Dummy activity	0.0–0.0– 0.0
80–90	Prepare operation schedule	6.4–8.0–12.0
90–100	Prepare and issue shop forms	5.6–7.0–10.5

Furthermore, they are told that shop forms should be issued no later than 30 days after the production authorization has been received. Under these circumstances, what will be the early and late times for each event, and the critical path as determined from these times?

PART SEVEN
QUALITY CONTROL

FIFTEEN
CONTROL CHARTS FOR VARIABLES

Thus far, we have concentrated on the need to produce the items demanded by the firm's customers in the required quantities and in time to meet established delivery dates. But every organization is also concerned with the quality of its output, which means that the quality of this output must be controlled.

Quality control, however, is not to be confused with inspection. In the inspection activity, the emphasis is placed on the quality of past output. This is to say that steps are taken to determine whether what has been produced meets established specifications. As opposed to this, the emphasis in the quality control activity is on the quality of future output. There are various ways of controlling this quality. For example, care may be taken to procure the proper factors of production and then to provide operating personnel with correct instructions prior to the production of an item. However, some of the more important methods are based on techniques of a statistical nature. It is with methods of this type that we shall concern ourselves in this presentation.

SOME BASIC STATISTICAL CONCEPTS

Each of the techniques we shall consider is based on certain statistical concepts. Therefore, we shall begin with a presentation of some of these concepts and introduce others as the need to do so arises.

THE MEANING OF A DISTRIBUTION   Let us start with a review of what is meant by a *distribution.* Suppose that an operator at a given work station is responsible for producing shafts. The raw material comes to him in the form of bar stock cut to the correct length, and his job is to perform an operation so as to get the diameter of the stock down to 2.500 ± 0.005 inches. In this case, the diameter is the *variable,* that is, the characteristic of the part with which the operator will be concerned.

After a large number of shafts have been produced, it will be found that

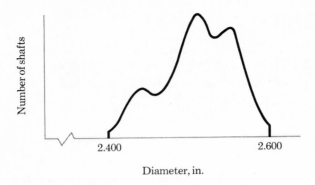

Figure 15-1   A distribution of shaft diameters

there is some variation in their respective diameters due to chance causes. These resultant shaft diameters are referred to as a "population" which can be described in a number of ways. The most complete description would be obtained by measuring and recording the diameter of every shaft that has been manufactured. These data could be summarized by listing, in one column, the different shaft-diameter values that had been obtained and, in a second column, the frequency with which each of these values occurred. Graphically, the results may appear as shown in Figure 15-1.

But whether the findings are presented in the form of a table or a graph, the result is called a "distribution," because it describes the way in which the various diameters are distributed among the shafts in the population.

A MEASURE OF CENTRAL TENDENCY   On occasion, it may be convenient to describe a distribution in a more concise manner. Various measures for doing so are available. One of them is the arithmetic mean or average.

The arithmetic mean is found by taking the sum of the values of the items contained in the population and dividing this total by the number of such items. In terms of a formula, this can be expressed as follows:

$$\mu = \frac{\Sigma X_i}{N} \tag{15-1}$$

where $\mu(m\bar{u})$ = the population mean
X_i = the value of an individual item
N = the number of items in the population

To illustrate the use of this formula, let us assume that 10,000 shafts had been manufactured and that the sum of their individual diameters was found to be 25,020 inches. The mean of this population of shaft diameters would be

$$\mu = \frac{25{,}020}{10{,}000} = 2.502 \text{ in.}$$

MEASURES OF DISPERSION Although the arithmetic mean provides us with some knowledge of the nature of a distribution, the resultant description is inadequate, because two distributions can have the same average and still be quite different from each other. For example, a population of 10,000 shafts might be produced, each of which has a diameter of 2.502 inches; the average of the resultant distribution would be 2.502 inches. On the other hand, a population of 10,000 shafts might be produced of which one half has a diameter of 2.402 inches and the other half of 2.602 inches; this distribution would also have an average of 2.502 inches. However, although the respective means are alike, there is a greater variation in the values of the individual items in the second population than in the first; another term for this variation is "dispersion." Therefore, to describe a distribution more completely, it becomes necessary that we have some measure of its dispersion.

The simplest available measure is the range R. The range is equal to the difference between the maximum and minimum values of the variable in the distribution being considered. This is to say that

$$R = X_{max} - X_{min} \tag{15-2}$$

To demonstrate how the range is computed, let us consider a small population of only five shaft diameters which have the following values:

Item	Value
X_1	2.499
X_2	2.499
X_3	2.503
X_4	2.504
X_5	2.505

The largest diameter is represented by X_5 and the smallest by either X_1 or X_2, and, therefore, the range is equal to

$$R = 2.505 \text{ in.} - 2.499 \text{ in.} = 0.006 \text{ in.}$$

A second measure of dispersion is the standard deviation. The standard deviation, σ' (sigma prime), of a population is found with the use of the following expression:

$$\sigma' = \sqrt{\frac{\Sigma(X_i - \mu)^2}{N}} \qquad\qquad (15\text{-}3)$$

To illustrate the application of this formula, let us compute the standard deviation of the population of five shaft diameters whose range we just calculated. We shall begin with the determination of the value of the arithmetic mean, which is equal to

$$\mu = \tfrac{1}{5}\,(2.499 + 2.499 + 2.503 + 2.504 + 2.505) = 2.502 \text{ in.}$$

The value of the numerator in Eq. (15-3) can now be obtained as follows:

X_i	$X_i - \mu$	$(X_i - \mu)^2$
2.499	$2.499 - 2.502 = -0.003$	0.000009
2.499	$2.499 - 2.502 = -0.003$	0.000009
2.503	$2.503 - 2.502 = +0.001$	0.000001
2.504	$2.504 - 2.502 = +0.002$	0.000004
2.505	$2.505 - 2.502 = +0.003$	0.000009
	$Total =$	0.000032

Substituting this total in the numerator of the formula and the population size of 5 in the denominator, we find the standard deviation to be

$$\sigma' = \sqrt{\frac{0.000032}{5}} = 0.0025 \text{ in.}$$

As is apparent from these calculations, the value of every item in the population is taken into account in the determination of the standard deviation. Further, as an examination of the numerator of Eq. (15-3) reveals, the smaller the differences between these individual values and the center of the distribution, as represented by the mean, the smaller will be the calculated standard deviation. This is as it should be, because a smaller spread of individual values should be reflected in a smaller calculated value of the measure of dispersion.

THE NORMAL DISTRIBUTION   The characteristics of actual distributions vary. However, many actual distributions have, for all practical purposes, the characteristics of a theoretical distribution known as the "normal distribution."

The normal distribution, when depicted graphically, is bell-shaped and

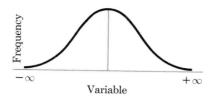

Figure 15-2   The normal distribution

symmetrical. Also, it is continuous in the sense that the variable can assume all the values on a continuous scale. Furthermore, it represents a population of infinite size. In addition, if its mean is shown as zero, the values of the variable involved range from minus to plus infinity. All these characteristics are shown in Figure 15-2.

Another important characteristic of this distribution is that it can be described completely in terms of its mean and standard deviation. This is done in Table C-5 (see Appendix). From this table, we learn, for example, that, as shown in Figure 15-3, approximately 68.3 percent of the area under the curve falls within 1 standard deviation of the mean, 95.5 percent within 2 standard deviations, and 99.7 percent within 3 standard deviations.

To illustrate this, we shall return to our population of shaft diameters. Let us assume that a normal population is produced which has a mean of 2.502 inches and a standard deviation of 0.004 inch. If this is the case, 95.5 percent of the shafts would have diameters between $2.502 \pm 2(0.004)$, or a diameter of no less than 2.494 inches and no greater than 2.510 inches. Consequently, if one shaft were selected in a random manner from this population, the probability is 0.955 that its diameter would be between 2.494 and 2.510 inches.

With the use of Table C-5, it is possible to determine the percentage of items in this population that would have a diameter between two stipulated values. For example, we may want to know what percentage of the shafts

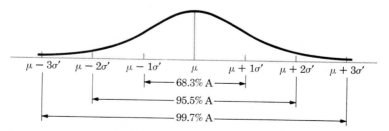

Figure 15-3   Areas under the normal curve

will have a diameter between 2.492 and 2.508 inches. The first step in this determination calls for expressing each of these values in terms of the population mean and standard deviation. Insofar as the 2.508 value is concerned, this dimension is 0.006 inch greater than the mean. With a standard deviation of 0.004 inch, this is equivalent to 1.5 standard deviations. Therefore, we can say that 2.508 inches is equal to $\mu + 1.5\sigma'$. In a similar manner, we find that 2.492 inches is equivalent to $\mu - 2.5\sigma'$.

In general, we can find the number of standard deviations Z that a given value of the variable X is away from the population mean μ with the use of the following expression:

$$Z = \frac{X - \mu}{\sigma'} \tag{15-4}$$

Substituting the values in our example in this equation, we obtain

$$Z_1 = \frac{2.508 - 2.502}{0.004} = +1.5$$

$$Z_2 = \frac{2.492 - 2.502}{0.004} = -2.5$$

From Table C-5, we find that 43.32 percent of the area is contained between μ and $\mu + 1.5\sigma'$ and 49.38 percent between μ and $\mu - 2.5\sigma'$. The sum of these two percentages is 92.7. Therefore, 92.7 percent of the shafts will have a diameter between 2.492 and 2.508 inches.

The foregoing computation was based on the assumption that the distribution of shaft diameters is normal. But this cannot be the case in our example. First, it is certain that the population does not contain an infinite number of shafts. Second, the diameter is being measured to the closest thousandth of an inch, and as a result, the variable is not continuous but increases in steps of one-thousandth. And third, even if we subtracted the value of the mean from each shaft diameter to obtain a distribution with an average of zero, the resultant values of the individual diameters would not range from minus to plus infinity. Consequently, the most we can assume is that the actual distribution is, *for all practical purposes,* normal. This would be true if it represented a large population and had a shape which is fairly close to that of a normal distribution. Under such circumstances, no serious error is introduced if we treat it, for purposes of analysis, as if it were normal. And, as mentioned earlier, many actual distributions are approximately normal.

DISTRIBUTION OF SAMPLE AVERAGES   Many times, the distribution of individual items in a population is far from being normal. For example, it may be rectangular, as shown in Figure 15-4. However, it has been determined that if we (1) have almost any shaped distribution involving a large number of items, (2) take an infinite number of samples of a given size from the underlying population, (3) calculate the average of each sample, and (4) plot the different sample averages obtained against the frequencies with which they occur, the resultant distribution of sample averages will be practically normal. Unless the underlying population is extremely large, this sampling should be with replacement; that is, after an item is selected and measured, it should be returned to the population before another item is selected. Also a sample of sufficient size is required to transform a nonnormal to a normal distribution. What this size is will be affected by the nature of the underlying population, but for populations usually generated by manufacturing processes, a sample size of 4 or greater is probably adequate.

The distribution of sample averages will have a mean and a dispersion just as any distribution does. With regard to the mean, it has been found that, when the number of samples approaches infinity, the mean of the sample averages will be equal to the mean of the individual items contained in the population from which the samples have been taken.

Insofar as the dispersion is concerned, it can be described in terms of the standard deviation of the sample averages. This standard deviation is called the "standard error of the mean," for which the symbol $\sigma_{\bar{x}}$ is used. Again, it has been found that, when the number of samples approaches infinity, there is a relationship between the standard error of the mean $\sigma_{\bar{x}}$ and the standard deviation σ' of the items in the population from which the samples have been taken. This relationship is as follows:

$$\sigma_{\bar{X}} = \frac{\sigma'}{\sqrt{n}} \tag{15-5}$$

where n = the sample size

An examination of Eq. (15-5) reveals that if samples of size 1 are taken, the standard error of the mean is equal to the standard deviation of the underlying population; this was to be expected, because samples of size

Figure 15-4 A rectangular distribution

1 serve to reproduce the original population. But as the sample size is increased, the dispersion of the sample averages decreases; this is attributable to the fact that the larger the sample size, the more likely it is that the sample average will approach the population average and, hence, the smaller will be the resultant dispersion of sample averages.

To illustrate all this, let us return to our population of shaft diameters which had a mean of 2.502 inches and a standard deviation of 0.004 inch. If repeated samples of, say, size 4 were taken from this population, the resultant distribution of sample averages would have a mean of 2.502 inches and a standard error of the mean of

$$\sigma_{\bar{x}} = \frac{0.004}{\sqrt{4}} = 0.002 \text{ in.}$$

Further, because the sample averages are normally distributed, we can say, for example, that 99.7 percent of them will fall between $\mu \pm 3\sigma_{\bar{x}}$. This means that if four items are selected and their average shaft diameter is calculated, chances are 99.7 out of 100 that this average will fall between $2.502 \pm 3(0.002)$ inches. With the use of Table C-5, we could also ascertain the percentage of sample averages that would fall between any two specified values.

In summary, by working with sample averages, we can transform almost any distribution into a normal distribution for purposes of analysis. Also, by varying the sample size, we can control the degree of dispersion of the resultant distribution of sample averages. We shall now go on to consider how all this can be applied in the control of product quality.

CONTROL CHARTS FOR AVERAGES

The quality of an item can be determined by, first, measuring its relevant characteristic and, then, comparing the result with the specification for this characteristic. If the result falls within the specification limits, the part is considered to be good; otherwise it is classified as a defective. For example, a manufacturing order may call for drilling a hole with a diameter of 1.200 ± 0.003 inches. A good part would be one with a hole whose diameter is no greater than the upper specification limit of 1.203 inches and no less than the lower specification limit of 1.117 inches. Consequently, the firm would make an attempt to establish a combination of factors of production such that parts of this nature would be manufactured.

However, it can also be said that an attempt will be made to establish a combination of factors of production which will generate an acceptable *population* of parts. Such a population would be one with a satisfactory mean and dispersion. What the values of this mean and dispersion are would be determined by the specification for the variable under consideration. To return to our example of hole diameters, if the average hole diameter of all the manufactured parts is equal to the specified 1.200 inches, the probability of the individual parts' being good is greater than it would be if the average diameter were 1.205 inches. Nevertheless, it could be that the average of 1.200 inches is being obtained by drilling holes of which half have a diameter of 1.300 inches and the other half of 1.100 inches. Given the specification limits of 1.203 and 1.117 inches, all the parts in this population would be defective in spite of the fact that their average is satisfactory. This is so because their dispersion is greater than that allowed by the 0.003 tolerance stipulated in the specification.

In summary, a satisfactory population is one with a satisfactory mean and dispersion. We shall now describe how the firm will attempt to establish and maintain a combination of factors of production which will yield such a population. In this description, we shall begin with a discussion of the method for determining whether a satisfactory average is being maintained and then go on to a consideration of the population dispersion.

THE POPULATION AVERAGE Let us return, for purposes of illustration, to our example of shaft diameters. Suppose that the firm establishes a combination of factors of production that will yield a population of individual diameters which will have a mean of 2.502 inches and a standard deviation of 0.004 inch; how these numerical values are ascertained will be discussed at a later point. Furthermore, the specification for the variable is such that this mean and standard deviation are considered to be satisfactory; therefore, the firm would like conditions at the work station to remain such that no change will take place in the mean and dispersion of the population of shaft diameters being produced. But since we are interested, for the time being, only in the mean, we shall simply say that the company wants the nature of the equipment, materials, and operator to remain such that a population of shafts with an average diameter of 2.502 inches will continue to be produced. This means that, if there is any indication that a shift has taken place in the population average, that is, if there is reason to believe that the average diameter being generated has increased or decreased, corrective action will be inaugurated. The problem then becomes one of devising some means of determining whether a shift has taken place.

One way of ascertaining this would be to record the diameters of all the shafts being produced and then to calculate the average when the entire population has been manufactured. Unfortunately, in addition to the cost involved, the procedure has the disadvantage of providing management with information after it is too late to do anything about any undesirable change which may have taken place. This defeats the entire purpose of quality control, which is to govern the quality of future output. Another limitation of this approach is that, even if the overall average were found to be exactly 2.502 inches, this would not prove that no changes had occurred. It is possible that significant shifts did take place but their nature was such that they canceled each other out. At the time of any single change, however, quality might have been affected adversely.

In brief, it is necessary that any shift in the population average be recognized at the time that it takes place, or soon after. The way in which this can be accomplished is to take samples of the output during the course of production, inspect the items in each sample, and pass judgment on the process on the basis of the quality of the items in each sample. To show how this is done, we shall continue to consider the work station at which we had a combination of production factors that will generate a population of shafts with an average of 2.502 inches and a standard deviation of 0.004 inch. Our task is to keep conditions such that the average remains at 2.502 inches.

The first thing that must be done is to ensure that we shall be working with a normal distribution so as to have a distribution which lends itself to precise description. This can be done by dealing with samples of size 4 or greater. If the quality control analyst decides on a sample size of 4, he knows that the resultant distribution of sample averages will have, as shown earlier, an average of 2.502 inches and a standard error of the mean of 0.002 inch. Therefore, the distribution can be partially described as shown in Figure 15-5.

From this point on, the procedure is as follows: Some time after production has started, the analyst will go to the work station, take a random sample of four shafts, measure the diameter of each, and calculate the average. If the sample average is equal to the desired population average, it will be assumed that the population average is being maintained. The same assumption will be made if the sample average does not differ signifi-

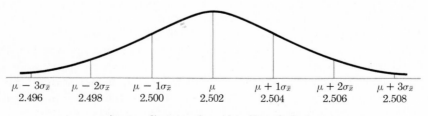

$\mu - 3\sigma_{\bar{x}}$	$\mu - 2\sigma_{\bar{x}}$	$\mu - 1\sigma_{\bar{x}}$	μ	$\mu + 1\sigma_{\bar{x}}$	$\mu + 2\sigma_{\bar{x}}$	$\mu + 3\sigma_{\bar{x}}$
2.496	2.498	2.500	2.502	2.504	2.506	2.508

Average diameter of samples of four shafts, in.

Figure 15-5   Distribution of sample averages

cantly from the desired population average. But if a significant differ-ence exists between the sample average and the desired population average, it will be assumed that the latter is no longer being maintained.

Of course, the need remains for defining a significant difference. Suf-fice it to say that, for reasons to be considered, the following practice has evolved: So long as the sample is with 3 standard errors of the mean of the population average, it is assumed that any variation between the sample average and the desired population average is due to chance, that is, to unassignable causes. However, as soon as the sample average varies from the desired population average by more than 3 standard errors of the mean, it is assumed that the variation is not due to chance but to assign-able causes and that a shift has taken place in the population average.

Applying this rule to our example, we should conclude from an examina-tion of Figure 15-5 that, if a sample average between 2.496 and 2.508 inches is obtained, it will be assumed that the sample has come from a population with a mean of 2.502 inches. But if the sample average is found to be less than 2.496 inches, it will be assumed that the population mean has decreased to some value less than 2.502 inches. And finally, a sample average of more than 2.508 inches will suggest that the population mean has increased to some value greater than 2.502 inches.

When the analyst decides that a change has taken place, the next step is to find the assignable cause. This calls for investigating the equipment, materials, and the operator's work methods. For example, it may be found that the machine is not being operated correctly or that the machine has deteriorated to a point which precludes maintaining the required dimen-sions. Whatever the cause, it must be found and eliminated, so that future output is not affected adversely.

CHANCES OF MAKING AN ERROR It might be asked why a change is ordinarily assumed to have taken place when the sample average exceeds the 3-sigma limits rather than, say, something like 2- or 4-sigma limits. This question can be answered only by giving consideration to the conse-quences of establishing any given set of limits. Whenever the analyst decides that a change has taken place in the population average, an in-vestigation is made to determine the cause. This investigation is often time-consuming and costly, and therefore, ideally, it would be conducted only when an actual shift occurs. With 3-sigma limits, since 99.7 percent of the sample averages from a given population will fall within these limits, the remaining 0.3 percent will fall outside the limits. This means that in the long run, 3 sample averages out of every 1,000 will fall outside the 3-sigma limits even if no change takes place in the population average. As a result, on these occasions, the analyst will be looking for an assignable cause of

variation when none exists. This is referred to as a "type 1 error." Specifically, a change is assumed when none has taken place, and, consequently,
time and money are spent on a needless investigation. However, if the firm
were to work, for example, with 2-sigma limits, the probability of making
this error would be even greater than 0.3 percent. This is because, in the
long run, 4.5 percent of the sample averages will fall outside the 2-sigma
limits even if the population average remains constant.

It becomes apparent that, to minimize the cost of needless investigations,
the firm should not establish limits which are too close to the assumed
population average. This suggests that, in the absence of any other consideration, the wider the limits, the better. Unfortunately, there is another
consideration. It so happens that, with a given sample size, as the probability of making a type 1 error decreases, the probability of making
another error increases. This other error is to assume that no change has
taken place in the population average when actually a change has taken
place. This error is referred to as a "type 2 error." To demonstrate
how it may occur, suppose that the firm in our illustration decides to work
with 5-sigma limits. The result would be that a shift in population average
would be assumed to have occurred only when a sample average beyond
$2.502 \pm 5(0.002)$ inches is encountered. Consequently, if a sample average
of 2.497 inches were obtained, no action would be taken because the situation would be as shown by the solid-line distribution in Figure 15-6.

It may be, however, that the population has shifted to the left, as indicated by the broken-line distribution also shown in Figure 15-6, and that
the sample average of 2.497 inches comes from the right side of the new
distribution and thus happens to fall within the established 5-sigma limits.
As a result, the analyst would erroneously assume that everything is in
order when actually it is not. During the interval between this and the
subsequent sample, shafts would be produced which might fail to meet
specifications. But this error would not have been made if, for example,
2-sigma limits had been established. The lower 2-sigma limit would have

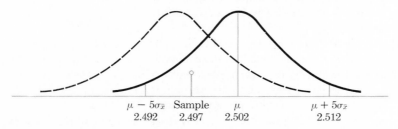

$\mu - 5\sigma_{\bar{x}}$ Sample μ $\mu + 5\sigma_{\bar{x}}$
  2.492   2.497   2.502   2.512

Figure 15-6   Occurrence of a type 2 error

been 2.502 minus 2(0.002), or 2.498, inches. The sample average of 2.497 inches would have fallen below this limit, and the population shift would have been detected. In brief, the narrower the limits, the lower the probability of making a type 2 error.

There is a way, however, of decreasing the probability of making one type of error without increasing the probability of making the other. This is by working with a larger sample size. For example, to return to the case described in Figure 15-6, with 5-sigma limits, there is some fixed probability of making a type 1 error. But the numerical values of these limits will be affected by the sample size. To illustrate, if samples of size 25 rather than 4 were taken, the limits would now be as follows:

$$\text{Upper limit} = \mu + 5\frac{\sigma'}{\sqrt{n}} = 2.502 + 5\frac{0.004}{\sqrt{25}} = 2.506$$

$$\text{Lower limit} = \mu - 5\frac{\sigma'}{\sqrt{n}} = 2.502 - 5\frac{0.004}{\sqrt{25}} = 2.498$$

Therefore, the sample average of 2.497 inches would have fallen below the lower limit, and the population shift would have been detected. Consequently, no type 2 error would have been committed. However, the larger sample size would serve to increase the cost of taking and inspecting the sample.

In any event, the fact remains that, for a given sample size, there is a need for finding a balance between the two types of errors. Each involves a cost, and the problem is to find that combination which will minimize the total cost. Because of the difficulty of estimating these costs in a specific situation, a rule of thumb has evolved which calls for the use of 3-sigma limits. This practice is not universal, and, therefore, other limits are sometimes employed. But, in general, industry adheres to 3-sigma limits.

This, then, is the theory which underlies the technique for maintaining a given population average at a specified point. The mechanics of applying this theory in practice will now be presented.

METHODS OF APPLICATION   As stated, once management selects the limits to be adhered to, the analyst must take periodic samples, find the average of each sample, and then determine whether the average falls within the established limits. This last step is usually carried out with the aid of a chart designed for this purpose. As can be seen in Figure 15-7, the normal distribution and the generally used 3-sigma limits can be shown in a slightly different position. Further, for purposes of quality

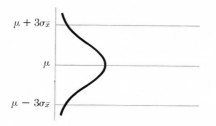

Figure 15-7 Alternate presentation of the distribution of sample averages

control, no need exists for showing the shape of the distribution. It suffices to depict only the desired population average and the 3-sigma limits. The resultant chart is shown in Figure 15-8.

As indicated in Figure 15-8, the line representing the location of the population average is called the "central line"; the line representing the location of $\mu + 3\sigma_{\bar{x}}$, the "upper control limit"; and the line representing the location of $\mu - 3\sigma_{\bar{x}}$, the "lower control limit." The chart itself is referred to, in general, as a "control chart for averages," or specifically, the "$\bar{X}$ chart." The reason for this is that the chart is used to plot values of sample averages, for which the symbol $\bar{X}$ is used.

After having constructed this chart, the analyst will make periodic visits to the work station, take a random sample, calculate its average, and plot the value on the control chart. The values of the sample averages are plotted in the order in which the samples are taken, with the central line serving as the time axis. Therefore, after five samples, the $\bar{X}$ chart may appear as shown in Figure 15-9, in which, for purposes of clarification in this discussion, numbers are shown by the respective points to designate the sample represented by a particular point.

In general, and this will be qualified later, so long as the sample averages stay within the control limits, the production process is allowed to con-

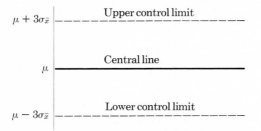

Figure 15-8 General form of the control chart for averages

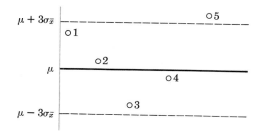

Figure 15-9 Sampling results as shown on the
$\overline{X}$ **chart**

tinue without interference. The process is said to be "in control"; that is, the variations in sample averages are said to be chance variations and not attributable to an assignable cause. But as soon as a point falls outside one of the control limits, as in the case of point 5 in Figure 15-9, the process is said to be "out of control"; that is, the variation is said to be no longer a chance variation but attributable to an assignable cause. A point above the upper control limit would indicate an increase in the population average, and a point below the lower control limit would indicate a decrease. An immediate investigation would be made of the factors of production to find and eliminate the cause of the assumed change.

CONTROL CHARTS FOR RANGES

Thus far, we have concerned ourselves with the method for maintaining the population average at some desired level. But we know that it is also important that the dispersion of the population be controlled. Unless this is done, a satisfactory dispersion, such as the one depicted by the solid-line distribution in Figure 15-10, may become the unsatisfactory dispersion depicted by the broken-line distribution in the same figure. Therefore, some means must be devised for determining whether a desired population dispersion is being maintained.

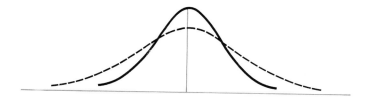

Figure 15-10 Change in the population dispersion

THE RANGE AS A MEASURE OF VARIABILITY A population with a satisfactory dispersion is defined as a population with a satisfactory standard deviation. Therefore, to return to our shaft illustration in which we had a population of shaft diameters with a standard deviation of 0.004 inch, if this is satisfactory, the firm will want to keep the standard deviation at 0.004 inch.

One way of determining whether the standard deviation has remained at 0.004 inch would be to wait until the entire population had been produced and then to calculate its standard deviation. But this is unsatisfactory for the same reasons that this alternative was rejected when we were considering the population average. The alternative is to reach a decision regarding the standard deviation of the population by analyzing the standard deviations of samples drawn from this population.

While a sample standard deviation can be used as a means of checking the value of the population standard deviation, most firms work with the sample range, which is more readily calculated and understood than is the standard deviation. To demonstrate that a population's dispersion is reflected in the ranges of the samples drawn from that population, let us consider an extreme case in which all the items in a population are alike. This means that the population standard deviation is 0. If we were to take a sample of, say, size 4 from this population, we should expect the four items in the sample to be alike, that is, the range of the sample to be 0. Likewise, if we were to take a sample from a population with a standard deviation greater than 0, we should expect the range of our sample to be greater than 0. In fact, the larger the standard deviation of our population, which means that we have a greater spread of values, the larger would be our expected sample range. This suggests that sample ranges can be used to estimate the population standard deviation. Let us see how this is done.

THE DISTRIBUTION OF SAMPLE RANGES If a series of samples is taken from a population with a standard deviation greater than 0, the values of the sample ranges will vary because of chance causes, For example, in the shaft illustration in which we had a population standard deviation of 0.004 inch, it may be that, in one sample, the difference between the largest and smallest shaft diameters is 0.002 inch; in another, 0.010 inch; in another, 0.000 inch, and so on. As a result, after taking a large number of random samples, we should obtain a distribution of sample ranges. It has been found that the general shape of this distribution is as shown in Figure 15-11.

The distribution of sample ranges, like any distribution, has a mean and dispersion. Its mean $\bar{R}$ is simply the average of the sample ranges. Its

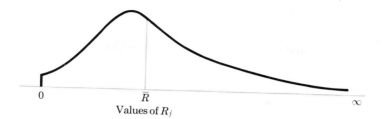

Figure 15-11   **Distribution of sample ranges**

dispersion is described in terms of the standard deviation of the sample ranges σ_R, which is called the "standard error of the range."

Statistical theory tells us that a relationship exists between the average range $\bar{R}$ and the standard deviation σ' of the population from which the samples are taken. It also tells us that a relationship exists between this standard deviation σ' and the standard error of the range σ_R. The nature of these two relationships is shown in the following equations:

$$\bar{R} = d_2\sigma'$$
(15-6)

$$\sigma_R = d_3\sigma'$$
(15-7)

It will have to suffice to say that it has been found that the factors d_2 and d_3 are a function of the sample size. Values of these factors for various sample sizes have been determined, and these are shown in Table C-6.

With this information at our disposal, we can compute the average range and standard error of the range for the population of shaft diameters which had a standard deviation of 0.004 inch. Eq. (15-6) and Table C-6 tell us that, with a sample size of 4, the average of the distribution of sample ranges will be

$$\bar{R} = 2.059\,(0.004) = 0.00824 \text{ in.}$$

Eq. (15-7) and Table C-6 tell us that, with a sample size of 4, the standard error of the range will be

$$\sigma_R = 0.880(0.004) = 0.00352 \text{ in.}$$

In brief, a population of shaft diameters, whose standard deviation is 0.004 inch, will generate a variety of sample ranges if a large number of samples of size 4 are taken from this population. These values of the sample range will have a distribution whose average is 0.00824 inch and whose standard error of the range is 0.00352 inch. This distribution can be described, in part, as shown in Figure 15-12.

To summarize, with a population of shaft diameters whose standard deviation is 0.004 inch, if we take a large number of samples of size 4,

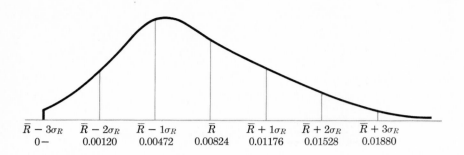

$\bar{R} - 3\sigma_R$	$\bar{R} - 2\sigma_R$	$\bar{R} - 1\sigma_R$	$\bar{R}$	$\bar{R} + 1\sigma_R$	$\bar{R} + 2\sigma_R$	$\bar{R} + 3\sigma_R$
0—	0.00120	0.00472	0.00824	0.01176	0.01528	0.01880

Figure 15-12   A specific distribution of sample ranges

we shall obtain a distribution of sample ranges whose average is 0.00824 inch. With some other population standard deviation, we should have some other average sample range. In any case, to say that we want to maintain the standard deviation of the population at 0.004 inch is the same as saying that we want to maintain the average of the distribution of sample ranges at 0.00824 inch.

METHOD FOR CONTROLLING VARIABILITY Whether the desired average sample range is being maintained can be determined by taking a sample of, in this case, 4, calculating the sample range, and deciding whether the value of this range suggests that the sample range was drawn from a population of sample ranges whose average is 0.00824 inch. If the difference between the sample range and the desired average range is insignificant, it will be assumed that no change has taken place in the mean of the population of sample ranges and, therefore, in the dispersion of the population of individual shaft diameters. But if the difference is significant, it will be assumed that a shift has occurred and that corrective action must be inaugurated.

In the determination of whether a significant difference exists between the sample range and the desired average range, it is assumed that, although the distribution of sample ranges is not normal, no serious error results from treating it as if it were. Next, so long as the sample range is not more than 3 standard errors of the range away from the desired average range, it is assumed that no change has taken place in the mean of the sample ranges. However, if a sample range falls outside the 3-sigma limits, a shift is assumed to have occurred. In the selection of this criterion, industry was governed by the same considerations as prevailed in the selection of a criterion for passing judgment on the population average. With a given sample size, narrow limits would increase the probability of making a type 1 error, while wide limits would increase the probability of making a type 2 error. As before, it was decided that 3-sigma limits provide the most economical combination.

Once the desired limits have been determined, the analyst constructs a control chart for ranges which is referred to as the R chart. The R chart will show the average sample range which is to be maintained and the limits within which the sample ranges are expected to fall if no change has occurred in the population dispersion. Given 3-sigma limits, the chart will appear as shown in Figure 15-13.

Following the construction of the R chart, the analyst will make periodic visits to the work station, take a random sample, calculate its range, and plot the value on the control chart. Since the firm will probably also be maintaining an $\overline{X}$ chart, there is no reason why the sample cannot be used to obtain both the sample average and sample range so that a single sample will yield a point for each of the control charts. In any event, if the calculated sample range falls within the control limits, the assumption will be made that no change has taken place in the population dispersion, and the production process will be allowed to continue without interference. However, as soon as a sample range falls beyond the control limits, the process will be said to be out of control, and the variation will be attributed not to chance but to an assignable cause. An investigation would be made of the equipment, materials, and operator, with a view to determining the cause. This would be done even when a sample range falls below the lower control limit, which suggests a decrease in the population dispersion. The desirable change in the dispersion may prove to be temporary unless the cause is found and incorporated as a permanent characteristic of the manufacturing process. On the other hand, it may be found that the improvement is being brought about by a change in method which will prove to be uneconomical and, hence, should be eliminated. Finally, there is always the chance that the unusually small sample range is attributable to an inspection error, and if this proves to be the case, a check should be

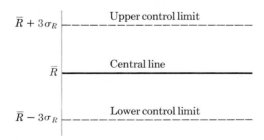

Figure 15-13   General form of the control chart for ranges

made of the qualifications of the individual making the measurements. Of course, if indications are that a permanent reduction has taken place in the population standard deviation σ', the $\overline{X}$ and R charts would have to be revised accordingly since both are affected by the value of the standard deviation.

PROBLEMS OF ESTIMATION

At this point, we have a method for controlling two characteristics of the population of parts being produced. These are the average and dispersion. The population average is controlled by means of an $\overline{X}$ chart. The basic expressions for the central line and limits for this control chart are as follows:

$$\text{Upper control limit} = \mu + 3\sigma_{\overline{X}} = \mu + 3\frac{\sigma'}{\sqrt{n}} \tag{15-8}$$

$$\text{Central line} = \mu \tag{15-9}$$

$$\text{Lower control limit} = \mu - 3\sigma_{\overline{X}} = \mu - 3\frac{\sigma'}{\sqrt{n}} \tag{15-10}$$

The population dispersion is controlled by means of the R chart, for which the basic expressions are as follows:

$$\text{Upper control limit} = \overline{R} + 3\sigma_R = d_2\sigma' + 3d_3\sigma' \tag{15-11}$$

$$\text{Central line} = \overline{R} \tag{15-12}$$

$$\text{Lower control limit} = \overline{R} - 3\sigma_R = d_2\sigma' - 3d_3\sigma' \tag{15-13}$$

An examination of Eqs. (15-8) to (15-13) reveals that, to construct the control charts, the analyst must know, among other things, the value of the sample size n and the values of d_2 and d_3. The sample size, of course, will be known, and available tables will yield the corresponding values of d_2 and d_3. However, the mean μ and the standard deviation σ' of the population of parts being produced are also required. Unfortunately, with a given combination of equipment, materials, and manpower, there is no way of knowing what these values are for the population that is being or will be produced. And yet, the equations require that these values be determined. We shall consider two different approaches the analyst can employ in this determination.

AIMED-AT VALUES   The simplest method for obtaining the necessary values of the population average and dispersion calls for the establishment of desired values of μ and σ'. What these should be will depend on the specifications for the job characteristic involved. We shall explain this by continuing to work with shaft diameters, but so as not to create any confusion, we shall introduce values dissimilar from those used earlier.

Suppose that the blueprint for some shaft, other than the one we have been considering, shows that the required dimension for the diameter is 3.557 ± 0.013 inches. As this specification suggests, the desired value is 3.557. It follows that this 3.557 inches is the logical value to select for the desired mean μ of the population of shaft diameters to be produced, because it falls at the midpoint of the established specification limits.

Insofar as the desired population dispersion is concerned, its value will be affected by the allowed variation in shaft diameters. The blueprint states that this tolerance is ± 0.013 inch. To convert this to a desired value of the population standard deviation, the firm must begin by defining satisfactory quality. This definition might be as follows: A population of individual shaft diameters is to be generated such that 98 percent of the shafts will satisfy the established specifications. In other words, 98 percent of the shaft diameters should fall within ± 0.013 inch of the population mean of 3.557 inches.

Before the analyst can proceed, he must make an assumption about the distribution of *individual* shaft diameters which may or may not be correct. If he is willing to assume that this distribution is normal, he can go on to ascertain from the table of areas under the normal curve that 98 percent of the shaft diameters will fall within 2.33 standard deviations of the mean. As shown in Figure 15-14, 98 percent of the output will be within specification limits if these two points, $\mu \pm 2.33\ \sigma'$, coincide with the specification limits, 3.557 ± 0.013. This is to say that the following requirement must be satisfied:

$$2.33\sigma' = 0.013$$

from which we obtain a desired value of 0.0056 inch for σ'.

The desired values of 3.557 for μ and 0.0056 for σ' can now be substituted in Eqs. (15-8) to (15-13), and the control charts established.

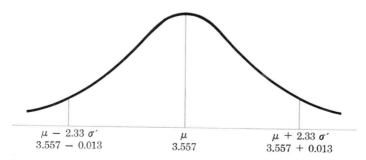

Figure 15-14   An example of a desired distribution of a variable

Prior to applying the resultant charts, production personnel will attempt to establish a combination of factors of production which will yield these desired values of the population mean and standard deviation. Once this has been done, periodic samples will be taken and the respective sample averages and ranges plotted on the control charts to determine whether these "aimed-at" values of μ and σ' are being realized. If they are not, corrective action will be inaugurated.

The advantage of this approach is that it provides a simple way of obtaining the values necessary for the determination of the central lines and control limits for the $\bar{X}$ and R charts. However, it is based on the assumption that the individual shaft diameters are normally distributed, and this may not be true. In the event that it is not, more or less than 2 percent of the output might be defective, even though the aimed-at values of μ and σ' are being attained. The exact percent will depend on the nature of the actual distribution, but this is unknown.

Another disadvantage of the approach is that it assumes that the aimed-at values are the only acceptable values of the population average and standard deviation. Consequently, if indications are that these values are not being realized, time and money will be spent to alter the population being generated. However, it may be that the average and dispersion of this population are such that, although they differ from the desired values, in combination they will yield a distribution of individual parts which will prove to be satisfactory. For example, it may be· that, in our illustration in which the desired mean is 3.557 inches, a population with a mean of 3.560 inches is being produced. Furthermore, this same population may have a standard deviation of only 0.0043 inch, instead of the aimed-at value of 0.0056. As a result, if the shafts are normally distributed, 98 percent of them will have diameters between $3.560 \pm 2.33(0.0043)$, or 3.570 and 3.550 inches, respectively. These values happen to be within the specification limits, and, hence, the firm's definition of satisfactory quality is being satisfied in spite of the fact that neither the desired mean nor the desired standard deviation is being attained. It is primarily because of this disadvantage of the described approach that another method is usually employed to arrive at values of μ and σ' to be used in the construction of the control charts.

ESTIMATED VALUES   The alternate method calls for setting up the operation to be performed in such a way that there is reason to believe that the specification limits will be met by practically all the parts. Then, while the population of parts is being produced, the mean and standard deviation of this population are estimated. Finally, a decision is reached regarding the suitability of this mean and standard deviation. We shall describe this method by assuming that the production process has already begun and by starting at the point at which estimates are to be made of the mean and standard deviation of the population being generated.

Different rules of thumb for making the necessary estimates have been developed, but we shall consider only one, which is in fairly common use. The method requires that the analyst take about 25 random samples of the output from the work station for which the control charts are to be constructed. The average and range of each sample are then determined. Next, the mean of the sample averages is calculated, and this is assumed to be equal to the population average μ. Then the mean of the sample ranges is found, and this is assumed to be equal to the average of the distribution of sample ranges $\bar{R}$, which can then be translated into a corresponding σ' value. Let us illustrate this procedure with reference to the shaft-diameter example we have just considered, in which the specification was 3.557 ± 0.013 inches.

The analyst begins by taking 25 random samples from the shafts being produced at the work station under consideration. Let us suppose that he chooses to work with a sample size of 5. After taking his samples, the analyst will inspect the items contained in each and record the magnitudes of the variable with which he is concerned; in our illustration, this is the shaft diameter. He then calculates the average and range of the diameters contained in each sample and finds them to be as shown in Table 15-1.

As an estimate of the population average, the analyst will use the mean of the sample averages. Its value will be found by substitution in the following expression:

$$\mu \doteq \frac{\sum\limits_{j=1}^{k} \bar{X}_j}{k} \tag{15-14}$$

where k = the total number of samples

Therefore, the estimated population average in our example, in which the sum of the sample averages is 88.7738 inches, will be

$$\mu \doteq 88.7738/25 = 3.5510 \text{ in.}$$

As his estimate of the average of the population of sample ranges, the analyst will use the mean of the ranges of the samples he has taken. The expression for this average $\bar{R}$ will be as follows:

$$\bar{R} \doteq \frac{\sum\limits_{j=1}^{k} R_j}{k} \tag{15-15}$$

In our illustration, in which the sum of the ranges of the 25 samples is 0.222 inch, the estimated average of the population of sample ranges will be

Table 15-1   Data for Estimating the Population Mean and the Average Sample Range

Sample number (j)	Sample average, in. ($\bar{X}_i$)	Sample range, in. (R_i)
1	3.5492	0.005
2	3.5546	0.004
3	3.5488	0.009
4	3.5464	0.008
5	3.5516	0.015
6	3.5496	0.006
7	3.5548	0.007
8	3.5544	0.010
9	3.5506	0.003
10	3.5470	0.005
11	3.5534	0.008
12	3.5526	0.012
13	3.5468	0.020
14	3.5480	0.004
15	3.5488	0.008
16	3.5506	0.007
17	3.5534	0.009
18	3.5470	0.010
19	3.5608	0.011
20	3.5540	0.023
21	3.5506	0.005
22	3.5498	0.011
23	3.5476	0.006
24	3.5520	0.010
25	3.5514	0.006
Total	88.7738	0.222

$$\bar{R} \doteq 0.222/25 = 0.00888 \text{ in.}$$

Finally, we know that

$$\bar{R} = d_2\sigma'$$

from which we obtain

$$\sigma' = \frac{\bar{R}}{d_2}$$

For a sample size of 5, Table C-6 shows that the value of d_2 is 2.326. Therefore, in our example, the estimated standard deviation will be

$$\sigma' = 0.00888/2.326 = 0.00382 \text{ in.}$$

TRIAL CONTROL LIMITS   Having made these estimates, the analyst is now able to determine, with the use of Eqs. (15-8) to (15-13), the location of the central lines and control limits for the $\overline{X}$ and R charts. For the $\overline{X}$ chart, these will be as follows:

$$\text{Upper control limit} = 3.5510 + 3\frac{0.00382}{\sqrt{5}} = 3.5561 \text{ in.}$$

$$\text{Central line} = 3.5510 \text{ in.}$$

$$\text{Lower control limit} = 3.5510 - 3\frac{0.00382}{\sqrt{5}} = 3.5459 \text{ in.}$$

Likewise, for the R chart, we should obtain

$$\text{Upper control limit} = 0.00888 + 3(0.864)(0.00382) = 0.019 \text{ in.}$$

$$\text{Central line} = 0.009 \text{ in.}$$

$$\text{Lower control limit} = 0.00888 - 3(0.864)(0.00382) = 0 \text{ in.}$$

With regard to the computations for the R chart, two things should be noted: (1) The value of d_3 is obtained from Table C-6; and (2) if the actual computation for the lower control limit were carried out, a negative figure would be obtained; but since a negative range is not possible, zero is used as the lower limit.

The analyst can now construct his control charts. The $\overline{X}$ chart will appear as shown in Figure 15-15 and the R chart as shown in Figure 15-16.

The limits shown in these figures are referred to as "trial" control limits because they are subject to revision. The reason for this is that the analyst has no assurance that his 25 samples came from a stable population. It may have been that changes were taking place in the population average and dispersion during the period in which the samples were being drawn. But unless a process is in control during the estimating period, that is, unless a stable population is being produced, no sound estimate can be made of the average and dispersion. Therefore, the analyst examines his data for any evidence of instability. This is usually done by plotting the averages and ranges of his 25 samples on the constructed $\overline{X}$ and R charts. If all these points fall within the trial control limits, it is assumed that the samples

Figure 15-15   Trial control limits for the $\overline{X}$ chart

Figure 15-16   Trial control limits for the R chart

were drawn from a stable population, and the control limits are no longer considered to be trial control limits but actual control limits. However, if some of the points fall outside the control limits on either of the two charts, the analyst assumes that a change took place in the population during the estimating period. This suggests that the estimates could not have been accurate and that revised estimates are necessary. Before we consider the procedure for revising estimates, let us put our data on the 25 samples through the required check.

Comparing the sample averages in Table 15-1 with the trial control limits for the $\overline{X}$ chart shown in Figure 15-15, we find that the average of sample 19 exceeds the upper limit. The analyst would assume that this sample was drawn from a population with an average which differed from the average of the population from which the other 24 samples were drawn.

In the same manner, the values of the sample ranges would be compared with the control limits for the R chart shown in Figure 15-16. Doing so reveals that the ranges of samples 13 and 20 exceed the upper control limit. The analyst would assume that these samples were drawn from a population of sample ranges with an average which differed from the average of the population of sample ranges from which the other 23 samples were drawn.

Estimates are revised by basing the new estimates on the sample values which appear to represent a stable population. In our case, the one out-of-control sample average would be discarded and a new estimate of μ made on the basis of the remaining 24 sample averages. Also, the two out-of-control sample ranges would be discarded and a new estimate of σ' made on the basis of the remaining 23 sample ranges.

The new mean of the sample averages would be found by first finding the total of the remaining 24 sample averages, which is 85.2130 inches, and then dividing this total by the number of samples it represents, which is 24. This yields 3.5505 inches. The new mean of the sample ranges would be found by first finding the total of the remaining 23 sample ranges, which is 0.179 inch, and then dividing this total by the number of samples it represents, which is 23. This yields 0.0078 inch. The revised estimate of $\overline{R}$ provides a revised estimate of σ'. Dividing $\overline{R}$ by d_2, we obtain 0.0078 divided by 2.326, or 0.00335, inch. The analyst now uses these revised estimates to compute a new set of central lines and control limits for his $\overline{X}$ and R charts. For the $\overline{X}$ chart, the results would be as follows:

$$\text{Upper control limit} = 3.5505 + 3\frac{0.00335}{\sqrt{5}} = 3.5550 \text{ in.}$$

$$\text{Central line} = 3.5505 \text{ in.}$$

$$\text{Lower control limit} = 3.5505 - 3\frac{0.00335}{\sqrt{5}} = 3.5460 \text{ in.}$$

For the R chart, the analyst would obtain the following:

$$\text{Upper control limit} = 0.0078 + 3\,(0.864)\,(0.00335) = 0.016 \text{ in.}$$

$$\text{Central line} = 0.008 \text{ in.}$$

$$\text{Lower control limit} = 0.0078 - 3\,(0.864)\,(0.00335) = 0 \text{ in.}$$

These revised limits are still referred to as trial control limits for the time being. Again, the reason for this is that the analyst has no assurance that the remaining samples, on which these limits are based, were drawn from a stable population. The only check he has is to plot the remaining sample averages and ranges on the revised $\overline{X}$ and R charts and see whether all the points fall within the trial control limits. If they do, the designation "trial" is dropped.

When we compare the remaining sample values in our illustration with the revised control limits, we find that no out-of-control points appear. The analyst would, therefore, assume that these samples were drawn from a stable population and that his estimates are sufficiently accurate to permit using the revised limits as actual control limits. However, if out-of-control points had appeared, the estimates would have to be revised again, and a new set of trial control limits determined. This would be done by following the same procedure employed in the first revision. The new out-of-control points would be discarded and new estimates made, as before, on the basis of the remaining data. New trial control limits would then be computed, and the remaining sample averages and ranges checked against these limits. If none of these is out of control, the limits are adhered to. Otherwise, the entire procedure is repeated. Sometimes, the analyst will find that so many of the samples must be discarded before all the remaining points fall within the control limits that little of the original data remains. In that event, he is compelled to assume that the degree of instability which prevailed precludes the making of sound estimates because no single population is being generated. His only alternative is to study the

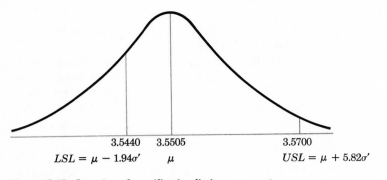

$$LSL = \mu - 1.94\sigma' \qquad \mu \qquad \qquad USL = \mu + 5.82\sigma'$$

Figure 15-17   Location of specification limits

production process and eliminate the assignable causes of variation. Having done so, he will take 25 new samples and begin again.

EVALUATION OF THE LEVEL OF CONTROL

When the control charts are based on aimed-at values of the population mean and standard deviation, subsequent application of the charts may indicate that these values are being realized; if so, the firm knows that the population of parts being produced will satisfy its definition of satisfactory quality. Similarly, when the charts are based on estimates of what population mean and standard deviation are actually being generated, subsequent application of the charts may indicate that these values are being maintained; but in this case, the firm has no assurance that these values are satisfactory, that is, that the process is being kept in control at a satisfactory level. As this suggests, prior to applying control charts constructed on the basis of estimated values of μ and σ', the analyst must determine whether these values reflect a satisfactory population of parts. Let us see how this would be done by continuing to work with our example.

In our illustration, the mean was estimated to be 3.5505 inches and the standard deviation to be 0.00335 inch. Therefore, if we assume that the items in this population are normally distributed, we can locate the mean μ, the upper specification limit USL, and the lower specification limit LSL, as shown in Figure 15-17.

This figure also contains a description of the specification limits in terms of the population mean and standard deviation. The description was obtained, with the use of Eq. (15-4), in the following manner:

$$Z_1 = \frac{3.5700 - 3.5505}{0.00335} = +5.82$$

$$Z_2 = \frac{3.5440 - 3.5505}{0.00335} = -1.94$$

From Table C-5, we learn that the area to the right of the upper specification limit is practically zero and to the left of the lower specification limit is 0.0262. This means that 2.62 percent of the shaft diameters will be defective in the sense that they will be undersized. Consequently, they cannot be reworked, as they could if they were oversized, but must be scrapped.

It should be stressed that, at best, this calculated percentage is only an approximation, because the individual items may not be normally distributed. But without the assumption of normality, no such determination could be made, because the exact nature of the underlying population is unknown. In any event, the firm must now decide, on the basis of cost considerations, whether the estimated percentage of defective work is acceptable. If it is decided that it is not, steps would have to be taken to reduce this percentage. What these steps are will vary. In our problem, an examination of Figure 15-17 reveals that the amount of defective output would be reduced if the population mean were increased; therefore, an attempt should be made to alter the factors of production to bring this about. In other situations, it may be appropriate to alter factors of production with a view to changing the population dispersion or the population's mean and its dispersion.

But whatever the case, after changes in the process are made, a new set of control charts must be constructed to depict the altered population. The analyst will, again, take about 25 samples, make his estimates, compute trial control limits, and so forth. This is continued until a combination of production factors is established which will generate a satisfactory population.

Of course, it is sometimes found that nothing can be done to bring about a desired change in the average or dispersion of the population of parts produced by a given manufacturing process. This may be true for economic or technological reasons. In such instances, the analyst has two alternatives. The first is to request the engineering department to revise the specification limits in a way which will serve to reduce the amount of defective output. But if the specifications cannot be changed, the firm must accept the fact that a certain proportion of the output will not meet quality requirements. This is, in effect, the second alternative: maintaining the process in control at a level which may be somewhat unsatisfactory and accepting the consequences. But where this alternative must be chosen, management should realize that the plant supervisor or operator cannot be held responsible for this normal amount of defective output. If it does accept this, time and effort will not be spent in trying to alter a natural condition.

APPLYING THE CONTROL CHARTS

The control charts for sample averages and ranges are called "control charts for variables." This is because they provide the firm with a method for controlling the value of a variable characteristic of a product. Once the charts have been constructed, they are used to control the quality of the output in the manner outlined earlier. Periodic samples would be taken, and the average and range of each sample would be plotted on the respective charts. Samples would have to be of uniform size if we want to maintain constant control limits, since the position of the limits is affected by the sample size. The individual sample averages and ranges would be plotted in the order in which the corresponding samples are drawn by using the central line as a time axis. This permits the analyst to approximate the time at which an out-of-control condition arose, and this may be useful in determining the cause of the variation.

REVISING THE CONTROL LIMITS   It should be noted that, if the control limits are based on estimated values of μ and σ', they may be changed when the analyst accumulates more data. With the procedure presented, initial control limits will be calculated from estimates based on, at most, 25 samples, and even fewer if some of these samples yield out-of-control points. However, the larger the number of samples, the greater the reason to believe that the resultant estimates are sound. The reason the analyst does not wait until he takes more samples before he constructs his control charts is that it might take too long to do so. But the analyst can do the following: After the initial control charts are constructed, periodic samples will be taken to determine whether the process continues to remain in control. There is no reason why this additional information cannot be used to revise the estimates if necessary. For example, after he has taken 50 more samples, the analyst can use these data plus the data from his initial samples to reestimate the population mean and standard deviation. If these differ appreciably from the original estimates, the control charts can be revised. New estimates of this type, based on the cumulative samples taken to date, can be made periodically.

RECOGNIZING A POPULATION CHANGE   We know that a lack of control is assumed whenever a point on either of the charts falls outside the control limits. While this is the most obvious evidence of the presence of an assignable cause of variation, there are other signs.

For quality control purposes, it is assumed that the distribution of sample averages, on which the $\overline{X}$ chart is based, and the distribution of sample ranges, on which the R chart is based, are for all practical purposes symmetrical. Therefore, the probability of getting a point above the central line on either of the charts is about equal to the probability of getting a point below the line. This means that if the analyst were to get an extended run of consecutive points or an undue proportion of points on one side of the central line, he would be justified in suspecting that a change had occurred in the population.

Consequently, not only points outside the control limits are interpreted as signifying a change in the population average or dispersion. Consideration is also given to extended runs or an undue proportion of points on one side of the central line. These are determined on the basis of probability computations and assume the form of somewhat arbitrary guides to which a firm can adhere. Typical of these is one which states that a change in the population is to be assumed when 7 or more consecutive points appear on one side of the central line or when 10 out of 11, or 12 out of 14, or 14 out of 17, or 16 out of 20 points appear on one side of the central line.

THE SAMPLE SIZE Mention has been made of the fact that most populations generated by manufacturing processes are such that a minimum sample size of 4 will probably be required to obtain an approximately normal distribution of sample averages. But the firm must make a decision concerning whether the sample size in a given case should be this minimum number or something greater.

We know that the larger the sample size, the less likely it is that an error will be made when passing judgment on the population on the basis of the characteristics of the sample. However, as the sample size is increased, the higher will be the cost of sampling, particularly if destructive testing is involved. Consequently, the one factor encourages the firm to adhere to larger sample sizes and the other to smaller ones. About all that can be said is that, for a particular application of the charts, the analyst must reach a decision by taking into consideration the cost of making an error and the cost of sampling. Because the magnitudes of these costs are often very difficult to estimate, the sample size is usually selected on the basis of judgment. A very common practice is to take samples of size 5, but it would be impossible to ascertain how this practice evolved.

NATURE OF THE SAMPLE Another matter that must be considered is the manner in which samples should be drawn. We know that the samples should be random, but it is also important that all the items included in the sample be drawn from the same population. This is because the sample's characteristics are used as a basis for inferring the characteristics of the population from which it comes. Obviously, if the sample contains items taken from more than one population, it is no longer useful for its intended purpose.

The means for satisfying this requirement become evident when we consider that the probability of population shifts is greater for, say, eight hours of a production activity than for, say, five minutes of the same activity. The reason is that there are more opportunities for something to change in eight hours than in five minutes. It follows that, if the analyst wants his sample items to be drawn from the same population, he can maximize the probability of this occurring by selecting items in such a way that they consist of units produced as close to the same time as possible. This can be accomplished with little difficulty. For example, the analyst can stand at the work station and take, say, five successive parts as they come off the machine. Or he can take a number of parts which are close together in a container in which the output is temporarily stored, on the assumption that the items were placed in the container in the order in which they were produced.

FREQUENCY OF SAMPLING Insofar as the frequency of sampling is concerned, this will be affected by two factors. The cost of sampling will, of course, encourage infrequent sampling. But frequent sampling is encouraged by a desire to discover an out-of-control condition as soon as possible after it occurs. This second factor requires that the risk of such a condition be taken into consideration. Whether this risk is high or low can usually be determined from experience. As a result, it may be that, at the time the control charts are established, the analyst will take a sample every hour if unit processing times permit this. However, if the process remains in control for two or three days, the frequency of sampling may be reduced to one sample every three or four hours. If the process continues in control for a period of a few weeks, the frequency may be reduced still further. On the other hand, if difficulties are encountered in keeping the process in control, more frequent samples are taken. As this suggests, unless reliable cost estimates of the relevant factors can be made, judgment must be relied upon to arrive at the most economical frequency.

AREA OF APPLICATION There is also a question regarding the degree to which $\overline{X}$ and R charts should be used in the plant. In general, any operation is a candidate for these charts if that operation is generating a substantial amount of product that must be reworked or scrapped and if the method of inspection yields a measurement for the variable involved. On the other hand, if little or no difficulty is experienced in meeting the specifications at a particular work station, there will be no good reason for maintaining control charts for this operation. And even in the case of a troublesome operation, it may be found that only an $\overline{X}$ chart is necessary because the difficulty is limited to an unsatisfactory population mean, or that only an R chart is necessary because the difficulty is limited to an unsatisfactory population dispersion.

In brief, no specific rules can be established and adhered to. The cost of controlling the operation must be compared with the potential saving to be realized from a reduction in scrap and rework. And what is currently an operation with which we associate poor quality and a need for control techniques may in time become an operation with which we shall associate good quality and no need for control techniques. Conversely, what is currently an operation with which we associate good quality and no need for control techniques may become an operation with which we shall associate poor quality and a need for control techniques. Further, the required control technique in one case may be both $\overline{X}$ and R charts, while in some other case the $\overline{X}$ or the R chart will suffice.

EVALUATION OF CONTROL CHARTS FOR VARIABLES

The presentation of the areas of application of $\overline{X}$ and R charts concludes our discussion of control charts for variables. The more important limitations of this technique, such as the risk of making an error, have already been mentioned. But in spite of these limitations, the approach has much to be said in its favor.

Of primary importance is the effectiveness of this technique in controlling the quality of future output. Furthermore, it permits the firm to determine an operation's capabilities, which often suggest revisions in specification limits or result in the establishment of realistic quality standards. Finally, the technique may reduce defective output to a level such that the firm might be able to eliminate the need for 100 percent inspection. It may be, however, that, regardless of how low the proportion of defective output is, the nature of the product and the demands of the consumer are such that the output must be screened for unsatisfactory items, if it is possible to do so without destroying the product. But even in such cases, the use of control charts will serve to keep the amount of defective output to a minimum.

QUESTIONS

15-1   What is the difference between quality control and inspection?

15-2   Define the following with reference to the output at a given work station: (*a*) population, (*b*) distribution of a variable, (*c*) population mean, (*d*) population range, and (*e*) population standard deviation.

15-3   What are the characteristics of a normal distribution?

15-4   How can one obtain a normal distribution from a population which is not normally distributed? How does this distribution reflect the population mean?

15-5   What are the characteristics of a distribution of sample ranges? Why is it said that this distribution reflects the population standard deviation?

15-6   What two alternatives does a firm theoretically have for determining whether a change has taken place in a population characteristic? Evaluate each of these methods.

15-7   What is the difference between a chance and an assignable cause of variation between a sample characteristic and a desired population characteristic?

15-8   What two types of error are possible when judgment is passed on a population on the basis of a sample from that population? What are the consequences of each of these errors? How can their size be controlled?

15-9   Why do most firms adhere to 3-sigma limits in the quality control activity?

15-10   What do the central line and control limits represent in the control chart for averages? In the control chart for ranges?

15-11   Describe the procedure for estimating the values of the population mean and standard deviation for use in constructing the control charts for variables. For selecting aimed-at values.

15-12   While applying the control charts, when will the firm assume that a change has taken place in the population?

15-13   What approach can be employed to determine whether a process is in control at a satisfactory level?

15-14   In quality control, what action follows a conclusion that an assignable cause of variation is present? A chance cause?

15-15   What factors does the firm take into consideration when determining (a) the sample size, (b) the manner in which items should be selected for inclusion in the sample, (c) the frequency of sampling, and (d) the operations to be controlled by control charts for variables?

15-16   Evaluate control charts for variables.

PROBLEMS

15-1   Four parts of the following lengths, in inches, have been produced:

6.612   5.907   5.901   6.136

What are the mean, range, and standard deviation of these lengths?

15-2   A large department store has 142 salespeople. Steps have been taken to determine how many customers were served by each salesperson during a specific period. The results can be summarized as follows:

Customers served	*Number of salespeople*
8	15
9	22
10	50
11	34
12	21
Total	142

As an example, this distribution reveals that 22 salespeople served 9 customers each. What is the mean, range, and standard deviation of the distribution? (Ans. 10.2; 4; 1.17)

15-3   One of the characteristics of a population of parts has an average dimension of 2.653 inches, with a standard deviation of 0.012 inch. Given that the individual items are normally distributed, find the percentage of parts whose dimension is:

a Greater than 2.671 inches.

b Less than 2.623 inches. (Ans. 0.62)

c Between 2.623 and 2.671 inches.

d Less than 2.684 inches.

e More than 2.618 inches. (Ans. 99.82)

f Between 2.655 and 2.659 inches.

g Between 2.628 and 2.642 inches. (Ans. 16.0)

15-4   Large quantities of light bulbs are used in an office building for replacement purposes. These bulbs have an average life of 1,350 hours, with a standard deviation of 140 hours. If repeated samples of 25 bulbs are taken from such a population of bulbs and their average life ascertained, what will be the average and the standard error of the mean of the resultant distribution of sample means? What would these be if the sample size were increased to 100 bulbs? (Ans. 1,350; 28; 1,350; 14)

15-5   The light fixtures in one of the offices in the building referred to in the preceding problem contain 49 bulbs. What is the probability that the average life of these 49 bulbs will be:

a More than 1,385 hours? (Ans. 4.01%)

b Less than 1,309 hours?

c Between 1,309 and 1,385 hours?

d Between 1,350 and 1,385 hours?

e Between 1,309 and 1,350 hours?

f Less than 1,385 hours?

g More than 1,309 hours?

15-6   A population of parts is being generated which has a mean of 0.750 inch and a standard deviation of 0.006 inch. The firm wants to maintain this average and will attempt to do so by taking samples of size 9, plotting the sample averages on an $\overline{X}$ chart, and evaluating the results. All computations will be carried out to three decimal places.

   a What will be the values of the central line and control limits on the chart if 2.33-sigma limits are adhered to? If 1.96-sigma limits are adhered to? (Ans. 0.755, 0.750, 0.745; 0.754, 0.750, 0.746)

   b What will be the probability of a type 1 error with the 2.33-sigma limits? With the 1.96-sigma limits?

   c If the population average increases to 0.752 inch but the standard deviation remains the same, what is the probability of making a type 2 error with the 2.33-sigma limits? With the 1.96-sigma limits? (Ans. 0.9332, 0.8399)

   d What would have been the probability of making a type 2 error with 2.33-sigma limits, if samples of size 36 were being taken and the population mean increased to 0.752 inch? If the population mean decreased to 0.746 inch under the same conditions?

15-7 The nature of the material being checked by a proofreader is such that the required time for this activity varies from page to page. Specifically, the distribution of the required time per page has a standard deviation of 1.4 minutes. Assume that samples of 20 pages each are taken, the proofreading time for each page recorded, and the range of these values computed for each sample. In the long run, what will be the mean and the standard error of the resultant distribution of sample ranges? What will these values be if the sample size is reduced to 10 pages? (Ans. 5.229, 1.021)

15-8 Suppose that, in the situation described in the preceding problem, an attempt will be made to maintain the standard deviation at 1.4 minutes with the use of an R chart. The sample size will be 10 pages, and 2.5-sigma control limits will be adopted. Compute the appropriate values for the central line and the control limits. (Ans. 7.099, 4.309, 1.519)

15-9 Parts of a certain length are being produced. The firm wants to control the length of these parts so that the distribution of lengths will have an average of 5.750 inches and a standard deviation of 0.003 inch. It will do this by setting up appropriate control charts and taking periodic samples of size 6. What will be the values of the central line and the control limits for the $\overline{X}$ and R charts if the company has decided to adhere to 3-sigma limits?

15-10 The blueprint specifies that a dimension should be 4.640 ± 0.006 inches. The company would like to construct $\overline{X}$ and R charts for this variable on the basis of aimed-at values of μ and σ'. What should these values be if the firm stipulates that good parts are to account for 95 percent of the output? With the use of these values and a sample size of 9, what control limits will be obtained for the control charts if the probability of a type 1 error is to be 0.10? (Ans. 4.640, 0.0031; 4.6417, 4.6383; 0.0133, 0.0051)

15-11 A delivery service operates within a single metropolitan area. The owner believes that the average time per delivery should be 0.75 hour, but he is willing to accept any time within 0.25 hour of this average as being satisfactory. To control the time taken by his employees to make deliveries, he decides to establish control charts for variables on the basis of aimed-at values of the population mean and standard deviation. He considers a satisfactory population to be one such that 90 percent of the deliveries will require a time between the 0.50 and 1.00 hour suggested earlier.

What should be the aimed-at values of μ and σ'? If the charts will be applied with the use of samples of 25 deliveries each and a stipulated risk of a type 1 error of 0.02, what will be their control limits?

15-12 A company adheres to 2-sigma control limits on its control charts for variables. These charts are established and maintained for a part whose critical dimension is its thickness. The analyst begins by taking 30 samples of size 8 which he will use to estimate the population mean and standard deviation. He finds that the sum of the sample averages is 6.318 inches and that the sum of the sample ranges is 0.891 inch.

a If the process is in control, what should be the values of the central line and control limits for the $\overline{X}$ and R charts?

b If the estimates prove to be accurate, the underlying population is normally distributed, the process remains in control, and the specification is 0.215 ± 0.020 inch, what percent of the output will be undersized? Oversized? Defective? (Ans. 6.68, 0.94, 7.62)

15-13 Control charts for $\overline{X}$ and R are to be established at a work station at which a hole of a certain diameter is being drilled in a part. The analyst begins by estimating the values of μ and $\overline{R}$. He does this by taking 20 samples of size 4, measuring the diameter of the holes contained in each sample, and calculating the sample averages and ranges. These averages and ranges are given in the following table:

Sample number	Sample average, in.	Sample range, in.
1	1.0052	0.007
2	1.0001	0.001
3	0.9964	0.009
4	1.0047	0.011
5	0.9999	0.003
6	0.9985	0.027
7	1.0027	0.005
8	1.0036	0.006
9	1.0044	0.010
10	1.0059	0.008
11	1.0040	0.012

Sample number	Sample average, in.	Sample range, in.
12	0.9978	0.012
13	0.9986	0.010
14	0.9998	0.002
15	1.0031	0.004
16	1.0006	0.006
17	0.9970	0.001
18	1.0092	0.013
19	0.9990	0.011
20	1.0062	0.003

a Determine the values of the central line and the 3-sigma limits for the control charts. (Ans. 1.0065, 1.0014, 0.9963; 0.016, 0.007, 0)

b The specification for the dimension under consideration is 1.000 ± 0.007 inches. If the individual items are normally distributed, what percentage defective output can the firm expect if the process remains in control at the present level?

c What will be the percentage of defective output if the tolerances are increased to ± 0.008 inch?

15-14 The estimation procedure suggested in the preceding problem was followed in another case in which the variable involved was the breaking strength of an item. Twenty-five samples of size 5 were taken, and the average and range of the breaking strength of the units in each sample were ascertained. The sum of the sample averages was found to be 255 pounds and of the sample ranges to be 50 pounds.

Three-sigma trial control limits are calculated for the $\overline{X}$ and R charts, and it is found that two sample averages and three sample ranges exceed these limits. The sample averages are 12.8 and 8.2 pounds, and the sample ranges are 6, 5, and 7 pounds.

After the control limits have been revised, it is found that no sample ranges but one sample average exceeds these limits. The value of the average is 9.2 pounds. Consequently, a third set of trial control limits is computed. Their values are such that all the remaining points fall within these limits.

a What are the values of the trial and the final control limits?

b If the specifications call for a minimum breaking strength of 8.0 pounds and it is assumed that the population is normally distributed, what proportion of defective output can be expected if the indicated population continues to be produced?

SIXTEEN

CONTROL CHARTS FOR ATTRIBUTES

Control charts for variables require that the quality of an individual item be determined by first measuring the magnitude of a given characteristic of that item and then comparing this dimension with that called for by the specification. Although this is often done, on occasion a somewhat different approach is employed. It may be that the inspection procedure followed does not yield the exact dimension of the part but simply reveals whether the part is defective or not. For example, when inspecting shaft diameters, instead of using a micrometer, the inspector may use a *go-no go* gauge. As a result, the inspector can ascertain whether the shaft is within specification limits but cannot ascertain the exact diameter of the shaft. Consequently, $\overline{X}$ and R charts could not be used as a means for controlling quality in this case.

In another case, a manufacturer of bulbs may inspect his output by inserting each of the bulbs into a socket. If the bulb lights up, it is satisfactory and accepted. If not, it is unsatisfactory and rejected. Once again, the characteristic being inspected is not measured and expressed in numbers, and this precludes the use of control charts for variables.

Finally, there are instances in which each characteristic of the product being inspected is measured and recorded in numerical terms, and yet $\overline{X}$ and R charts will not be appropriate for use. For example, a firm may be producing a part involving six different dimensions. At final inspection, each of the dimensions is measured and compared with the corresponding specification limits. If any one of these six dimensions does not meet specifications, the part is rejected. Although $\overline{X}$ and R charts could be maintained for each of the six dimensions, it might be uneconomical to do so. Therefore, the manufacturer might prefer to pass judgment on the processes involved in the production of this part by analyzing the final inspection reports which would simply state the numbers of good and defective units produced.

In all such cases, where each part is simply classified as having been accepted or rejected, the quality of future output must be controlled by some method other than control charts for variables. This other method also involves the use of control charts, but they are of a different type. The charts that can be employed are called "control charts for defectives."

THE BINOMIAL DISTRIBUTION

The theory underlying control charts for defectives differs in certain respects from that on which control charts for variables are based. Therefore, we must begin with a consideration of the specific statistical concepts that are involved.

DISTRIBUTIONS OF NUMBER AND PROPORTION OF OCCURRENCES

To illustrate the new concepts with which we shall be working, let us return to the work station at which shaft diameters were being produced. We saw earlier that the established combination of factors of production would generate a population of shafts. This population was described in terms of the diameter to be associated with each of the manufactured shafts. However, it is also possible to describe each shaft in this population in terms of whether or not its diameter is within specification limits, that is, in terms of whether the shaft is good or defective. This means that a given combination of factors of production can be said to generate a population of shafts, some of which will be good and some of which will be defective.

The simplest way in which to describe such a population is to state the proportion of defectives it contains. For example, it may be that, over an extended period of time, a total of 100,000 shaft diameters is produced. Of these, 80,000, or 0.80, might be within specification limits and, hence, good. Consequently, 20,000, or 0.20, would be outside specification limits and, hence, defective. In brief, it could be said that a population of shafts was produced of which 20 percent were defective.

Let us now assume that random samples of, say, size 10 are taken from this population, that the items in each sample are inspected and classified as being good or defective, and that the number of defective items in each sample is recorded. If sampling is with replacement, which it should be when the population is of finite size, it would be theoretically possible to take an infinite number of such samples. In spite of the fact that the population proportion of defectives is 0.20, we should find that, as a result of chance causes, not every sample would contain a proportion of defectives equal to 0.20; this is to say that not every sample of 10 items would contain exactly 2 defectives. Instead, the following different numbers and corresponding proportions of defectives per sample would be obtained:

Number of defectives per sample	Proportion of defectives per sample	Number of defectives per sample	Proportion of defectives per sample
0	0		
1	0.1	6	0.6
2	0.2	7	0.7
3	0.3	8	0.8
4	0.4	9	0.9
5	0.5	10	1.0

However, not all of these outcomes would appear with the same relative frequency. For example, given that the population proportion of defectives is 0.20, the most likely sample proportion would be 0.20. Other sample proportions would appear with a lower relative frequency. In fact, if we were to plot the different values of either the number or proportion of defectives per sample against their expected frequencies of occurrence, we should obtain the distribution shown in Figure 16-1.

The distribution depicted in Figure 16-1 is called the "binomial distribution." In general terms, the variable consists of either the number or proportion of occurrences per sample; an occurrence is represented by a defective in our illustration. The relative frequency, that is, the probability of occurrence to be associated with a particular value of the variable, can be found by substitution in a formula that has been developed for this purpose; however, we shall have no need for computing these prob-

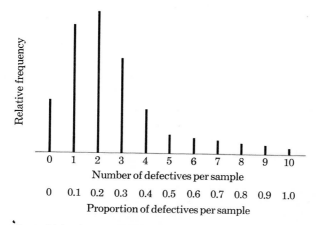

Figure 16-1 A binomial distribution

abilities, so we shall not consider the formula. Finally, the distribution is generated by sampling with replacement from a finite population or by sampling with or without replacement from an infinite population.

MEAN AND DISPERSION OF THE BINOMIAL DISTRIBUTION We saw, in the preceding chapter, that a combination of factors of production can yield, for example, a population of shaft diameters. This population, in turn, can generate a distribution of individual shaft diameters, a distribution of sample averages, and a distribution of sample ranges. We now see that this population can also generate a distribution of proportion of defectives per sample or a distribution of number of defectives per sample, that is, a binomial distribution.

The binomial distribution has a mean and a dispersion as does any distribution. If we concentrate, for the moment, on the distribution of sample proportions, we can say that the arithmetic mean μ_p of this distribution would simply be the average of these proportions. However, it has been found that as the number of samples approaches infinity, the average of the sample proportions is equal to the population proportion of defectives. This means that

$$\mu_p = p' \tag{16-1}$$

The dispersion of the distribution of sample proportions can be described in terms of its standard deviation σ_p, which is called the "standard error of the proportion." The value of this measure is calculated in the same way as is any standard deviation, that is, in the way indicated by Eq. (15-3). However, it has been found that, when the number of samples approaches infinity, the expression for the standard error will assume the following simplified form:

$$\sigma_p = \sqrt{\frac{p'(1 - p')}{n}} \tag{16-2}$$

An examination of Eq. (16-2) reveals that, as the sample size increases, the dispersion of the resultant distribution of sample proportions decreases. This was to be expected, because the larger the sample size, the more likely it is that the sample proportion p will be equal to the population proportion p'. Hence, the individual sample proportions would not be as widely dispersed as they otherwise would be.

Turning to the distribution of number of defectives per sample, we know that this distribution will also have a mean and a dispersion. If p represents the proportion of defectives in a given sample, the number of defectives in that sample will be equal to np. Therefore, the mean μ_{np} of this distribution could be found by computing the average value of the number of defectives in each sample. But it has been found that, if the number of samples approaches infinity, this mean is equal to

$$\mu_{np} = np'$$

(16-3)

Insofar as the standard deviation σ_{np} of this distribution is concerned, it too could be calculated with the use of Eq. (15-3), the basic formula for the standard deviation. But again, if the number of samples approaches infinity, this basic expression will assume the following special form:

$$\sigma_{np} = \sqrt{np'(1 - p')}$$

(16-4)

This standard deviation of the distribution of the number of occurrences per sample is called the "standard error of the occurrences."

To illustrate the application of the foregoing equations, let us return to our example in which we assumed that samples of size 10 would be taken from a population of shafts which was 20 percent defective. If repeated samples were taken, we should find, from Eq. (16-1), that the resultant distribution of sample proportions would have a mean of

$$\mu_p = 0.20$$

With the use of Eq. (16-2), we should calculate the standard error of this distribution to be

$$\sigma_p = \sqrt{\frac{0.20\,(0.80)}{10}} = 0.13$$

On the other hand, Eq. (16-3) tells us that the resultant distribution of number of defectives per sample would have a mean equal to

$$\mu_{np} = 10\,(0.20) = 2$$

The standard error of this distribution, as calculated from Eq. (16-4), would be

$$\sigma_{np} = \sqrt{10\,(0.20)\,(1 - 0.20)} = 1.3$$

It is interesting to note that the mean of 2 and the standard error of 1.3 for this latter distribution are equal to the mean and standard error of the distribution of sample proportions multiplied by the sample size of 10. This is not surprising, because the number of defectives per sample is equal to the proportion of defectives multiplied by the sample size.

THE BINOMIAL DISTRIBUTION IN SUMMARY The characteristics of the binomial distribution can now be summarized as follows: Beginning with the distribution of sample proportions, we can say that this distribution is not continuous but discrete, because the possible values of the variable increase in steps of size $1/n$. The minimum possible value of the sample proportion is 0, and the maximum is 1. The highest relative frequency of occurrence is to be associated with the sample proportion which is equal to the population proportion; consequently, the distribution will be skewed to the right if the population proportion is less than 0.5, skewed to the left if the population proportion is more than 0.5, and symmetrical if the population proportion is equal to 0.5.

The distribution of the number of occurrences per sample is also discrete, because the possible values of the variable increase in steps of size 1. The minimum value of this variable is 0, and the maximum is n. Furthermore, whether the distribution is skewed right, skewed left, or symmetrical depends on the value of the population proportion.

It is obvious from all this that the binomial differs from the normal distribution. Nevertheless, it has been found that, if the sample size is large, the normal distribution can be used as an approximation of the binomial without introducing any serious error into the results. This means, for example, that it can be assumed that 68.3 percent of the samples will have a proportion or number of defectives within 1 standard error of the population average, 95.5 percent within 2 standard errors, and 99.7 percent within 3 standard errors. The actual percentages could be calculated, but because of the computational difficulties involved, a common practice in the area of statistical quality control is to make use of the normal curve approximation. Having noted this, we can go on to relate the binomial distribution and its approximation to a method for controlling quality when a product is described simply as being good or defective.

CONTROL CHARTS FOR FRACTION DEFECTIVE

As has been suggested, when the result of an inspection procedure is that the firm knows only whether a given item is good or defective, it becomes necessary to think of the population involved as consisting of parts of which a certain percentage is defective. A satisfactory population would be defined as one which contains an acceptable proportion of defective parts. Therefore, the firm will attempt to establish a combination of equipment, materials, and manpower that will yield a population that is satisfactory in this sense of the term. After such a combination has been established, the next step is to maintain conditions such that the plant continues to produce this population.

To ascertain whether these conditions are being maintained, it is necessary to provide some means for detecting a change in the population proportion of defectives. This could be done by inspecting and classifying every item in the population of parts produced at a work station. But this approach, as explained when discussing control charts for variables, may be uneconomical, especially when destructive testing is involved; will not reveal any periodic variations in the population proportion; and, at best, will provide the required information too late. The alternative, as before, is sampling. This alternative will now be discussed.

DETECTING A CHANGE IN THE POPULATION PROPORTION   In this presentation, we shall continue to work with our shaft illustration. Let us suppose that the production department has established a combination of factors of production such that 10 percent of the shafts will have diameters outside the specification limits. For one reason or another, this is considered to be satisfactory, and, therefore, an attempt will be made to maintain conditions as they are so that no change will take place in this population proportion.

We know that if periodic samples of, say, size 100 were drawn from this population of shafts, in any one sample the analyst could theoretically find 0 defectives, 1 defective, 2 defectives, 3 defectives, or any number of defectives up to and including 100. This means that the sample proportions could assume any one of the following values: 0.00, 0.01, 0.02, . . . , 0.98, 0.99, 1.00. But while each of these values is possible and will, in time, occur, we should not expect each of them to occur with the same relative frequency. For example, since 10 percent of the population is defective, that is, 10 shafts out of every 100 are defective, we should expect 10 defectives to appear in our respective samples more frequently than any other number of defectives. On the other hand, a sample with 85 defectives would be rare, with 90 defectives still less probable, and so on. Actually, after an infinite or an extremely large number of samples, we should expect the frequency distribution of our sample proportions to appear somewhat as shown in Figure 16-2.

With a finite population, this distribution will result only if the sampling

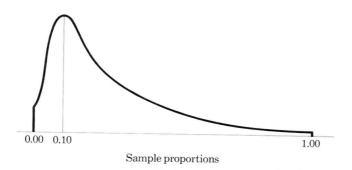

Figure 16-2   Distribution of sample proportions of defectives

is with replacement. However, with a large population, such as is ordinarily associated with a production process, failure to replace makes little difference. In any event, the average of this binomial distribution will be equal to the population proportion p' which in this case is 0.10. Its dispersion, expressed in terms of the standard error of the proportion σ_p, will be equal to

$$\sigma_p = \sqrt{\frac{(0.10)(0.90)}{100}} = 0.03$$

We can now say that, given a sample size of 100, maintaining the population proportion at 0.10 is equivalent to maintaining a population which will generate a distribution of sample proportions whose average will be 0.10 and whose standard error of the proportion will be 0.03. In this case, it is only necessary to control the average of the distribution, because the standard error of the proportion is a function of the population proportion p' and the sample size n. Therefore, with a given sample size, if the population proportion is satisfactory, the standard error of the proportion must also be at the desired level.

To go on, if we assume that the binomial can be approximated with the normal distribution, we can say that, in our illustration, 68.3 percent of the samples will have a proportion of defectives between $0.10 \pm 1(0.03)$; 95.5 percent, a proportion between $0.10 \pm 2(0.03)$; and 99.7 percent, a proportion between $0.10 \pm 3(0.03)$. Therefore, the distribution can be partially described as shown in Figure 16-3.

In effect, then, the firm will want to maintain a population which will generate the distribution shown in Figure 16-3. If a change takes place in the population proportion and, consequently, in this distribution, the firm

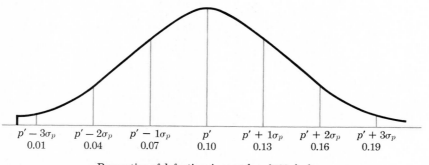

| $p' - 3\sigma_p$ | $p' - 2\sigma_p$ | $p' - 1\sigma_p$ | p' | $p' + 1\sigma_p$ | $p' + 2\sigma_p$ | $p' + 3\sigma_p$ |
| 0.01 | 0.04 | 0.07 | 0.10 | 0.13 | 0.16 | 0.19 |

Proportion of defectives in samples of 100 shafts

Figure 16-3   Partial description of a specific binomial distribution being approximated by the normal

will want to learn of this as soon as possible so that corrective action can be inaugurated. The method by which a shift in the population proportion can be detected is as follows: The analyst will go to the work station, take a random sample of 100 items, inspect and classify each item as being either defective or nondefective, and calculate the proportion of defectives in the sample. This value of the sample proportion will then be evaluated to determine whether it is likely that it was drawn from a population of sample proportions with an average equal to 0.10. Naturally, if the sample proportion is equal to 0.10, the analyst will have no reason to believe that a change has taken place in the population proportion. But even if the sample proportion differs to some degree from the desired population proportion, the analyst will not necessarily assume a change, because he does expect some variation in the sample proportions. However, if the difference between the sample proportion and the desired population proportion is sufficiently great, a shift in the population proportion will be assumed. "Sufficiently great" is usually defined in the same manner as it was with control charts for variables; namely, if the sample proportion differs from the population proportion by more than 3 standard errors of the proportion, the presence of an assignable cause of variation will be assumed. Again, industry adheres to the 3-sigma criterion as a compromise between the costs of type 1 and type 2 errors.

METHOD OF APPLICATION   As in the case of control charts for variables, the analyst will construct a chart which will aid him in the evaluation of the sample proportion he obtains. This chart will have a central line which will represent the satisfactory population proportion p', an upper control limit which will be equal to $p' + 3\sigma_p$, and a lower control limit which will be equal to $p' - 3\sigma_p$. It will appear as shown in Figure 16-4.

This chart is called a "control chart for fraction defective" and is commonly referred to as the "p chart." Once it is constructed, the analyst will

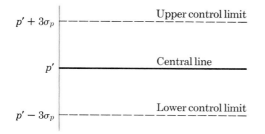

Figure 16-4   **General form of the control chart for fraction defective**

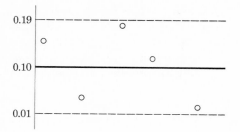
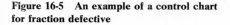

**Figure 16-5   An example of a control chart
for fraction defective**

take periodic random samples of a given size. Varying sample sizes can be drawn, but this necessitates revising the control limits because the magnitude of the standard error of the proportion is affected by the sample size. In any event, the proportion or fraction defective in each sample is computed and plotted on the control chart in the order in which the samples are taken. Therefore, the control chart for our illustration of shafts, for which the control limits can be found from Figure 16-3, might appear, after some time, as shown in Figure 16-5.

Any point outside either of the control limits would be interpreted as signifying a change in the population proportion. However, the same interpretation would be placed on extended runs of points on either side of the central line, for the same reason that extended runs on either side of the central lines of $\overline{X}$ and R charts were assumed to signify population shifts. Extended runs for the control chart for fraction defective are defined just as they were for control charts for variables.

An indicated shift in the population average would be followed by an investigation of the equipment, materials, and operator to determine the assignable cause of variation. This is true even when there is an apparent reduction in the proportion of defectives in the population, which might be indicated by a point falling below the lower control limit. The reasons for this are the same as those given for not ignoring a point that may fall below the lower control limit on the R chart.

THE PROBLEM OF ESTIMATION

By means of an illustration, we have shown how the control chart for fraction defective is constructed. In these computations, it was assumed that the sample size and the population proportion of defectives were known. Consequently, we were able to substitute in the following expressions to obtain the central line and control limits for the p chart:

$$\text{Upper control limit} = p' + 3\sigma_p = p' + 3\sqrt{\frac{p'(1 - p')}{n}} \qquad (16\text{-}5)$$

$$\text{Central line} = p' \qquad (16\text{-}6)$$

$$\text{Lower control limit} = p' - 3\sigma_p = p' - 3\sqrt{\frac{p'(1 - p')}{n}} \qquad (16\text{-}7)$$

As an examination of these expressions reveals, the necessary values cannot be calculated until the sample size n and the population proportion p' are ascertained. We shall now consider how this is done.

THE SAMPLE SIZE   The sample size is decided upon by the analyst. In doing so, he will take cognizance of the fact that the larger the sample, the more likely it is that the sample proportion will approach the population proportion, and, hence, the smaller will be the risk of making an error. On the other hand, the larger the sample, the greater will be the cost of sampling. Therefore, an attempt must be made to select a sample size which will minimize the total of these two costs.

However, the sample size must be fairly large, so that the normal distribution will approximate the binomial distribution to a sufficient degree. What this size is cannot be readily determined. We can only say that the closer the population proportion is to 0.50, the smaller will be the sample size required to make our assumption of normality fairly realistic when applied to the binomial distribution; this is because, with a p' of 0.50, the resultant distribution is symmetrical.

One of the more sophisticated rules of thumb followed by some firms is that the sample size should be such that both np' and $n(1 - p')$ are 5 or more; therefore, if the population proportion is 0.02, a minimum sample size of 250 would be required. A somewhat simpler rule, and it is the one we shall adhere to for illustration purposes, is that the sample size should be no less than 100. But in either case, the resultant sample size is significantly greater than that involved in the application of $\bar{X}$ and R charts.

Because of the large sample size requirement, one might be inclined to conclude that the inspection costs to be associated with control charts for defectives are appreciably greater than those to be associated with control charts for variables. This is not always true. To begin with, the inspection procedure for classifying an item as defective or nondefective is ordinarily less costly than the procedure for getting a precise measurement. For example, 10 shafts might be inspected with a *go-no go* gauge in the time required to measure a single shaft diameter with a micrometer. Also, control charts for defectives are often used on operations from which the output must be subjected to 100 percent inspection because of the nature of the product and the quality demands of the consumer. In those cases, no additional cost is incurred in obtaining the information required to determine whether the process is in control.

ESTIMATING THE POPULATION PROPORTION   Since the decision regarding the sample size is made by the analyst, the sample size is not an unknown in the strict sense of the term. This is not true, however, for the population proportion p'. Here we have an unknown whose value must be ascertained before the control chart can be constructed. As in the case of the control charts for variables, the analyst has two alternatives. With the first, a desired value of p' is selected, the control chart constructed, and an attempt made to keep the process in control at this level.

The second and more common approach is to set up the operation in the best possible manner and then to estimate the proportion defective p' of the resultant stream of product. Again, there is a variety of estimation procedures that can be employed. A typical one requires that the analyst take about 25 random samples, calculate the fraction defective in each, find the average of these sample proportions, and assume that this average is equal to the population proportion of defectives. Let us illustrate this approach with a numerical example.

Suppose that the analyst is interested in constructing a p chart at the work station at which our shafts are being produced. He will begin by taking 25 samples of, say, size 100. The shafts in each sample would be inspected and classified as being either defective or nondefective. Then the proportion defective in the respective samples would be calculated and recorded. It may be that the results of the analysis of 25 samples are found to be as shown in Table 16-1.

The analyst estimates the value of the population proportion of defectives by calculating the average of these sample proportions. This can be done by substituting in the following expression:

$$p' = \frac{\sum\limits_{j=1}^{k} r_j}{\sum\limits_{j=1}^{k} n_j} \qquad (16\text{-}8)$$

where r_j = number of defectives in the jth sample
n_j = size of the jth sample
k = number of samples

In effect. Eq. (16-8) calls for finding the ratio of the total number of defectives found to the total number of items inspected. When the sample size is constant, as it is in our case, Eq. (16-8) can be expressed in the following form:

Table 16-1 Data for Estimating the Population Proportion of Defectives

Sample number (j)	Sample size (n_j)	Number of defectives (r_j)	Sample proportion $(p_j = r_j/n_j)$
1	100	2	0.02
2	100	0	0.00
3	100	12	0.12
4	100	6	0.06
5	100	4	0.04
6	100	7	0.07
7	100	0	0.00
8	100	1	0.01
9	100	6	0.06
10	100	3	0.03
11	100	2	0.02
12	100	5	0.05
13	100	0	0.00
14	100	5	0.05
15	100	3	0.03
16	100	7	0.07
17	100	4	0.04
18	100	6	0.06
19	100	3	0.03
20	100	0	0.00
21	100	10	0.10
22	100	5	0.05
23	100	1	0.01
24	100	6	0.06
25	100	2	0.02
Total	2,500	100	1.00

$$p' \doteq \frac{1}{k}\Sigma p_j \tag{16-9}$$

where $p_j =$ the proportion defective in the jth sample

Therefore, the estimated population proportion, in our example, in which the sum of the sample proportions is 1.00, will be

$$p' \doteq 100/2,500 = 1.00/25 = 0.04$$

With this estimate of the population proportion, the analyst can now determine the locations of the central line and control limits for his p chart with the use of Eqs. (16-5) to (16-7). These will yield the following:

$$\text{Upper control limit} = 0.040 + 3\sqrt{\frac{(0.04)(0.96)}{100}} = 0.099$$

$$\text{Central line} = 0.040$$

$$\text{Lower control limit} = 0.040 - 3\sqrt{\frac{(0.04)(0.96)}{100}} = 0$$

If we carried out the indicated computation for the lower control limit, we should find that a negative value would be obtained. In cases such as this, since it is never possible to obtain a negative proportion of defectives, the value of zero is used as the lower control limit.

TRIAL CONTROL LIMITS   These computed control limits are referred to as "trial" control limits because the analyst has no assurance that all his samples were drawn from the same population. Whether a stable population was being maintained during the sampling period is ascertained in the same manner as it was when control limits were being determined for the $\overline{X}$ and R charts.

In our illustration, a comparison of the sample proportions listed in Table 16-1 with the computed trial control limits reveals that samples 3 and 21 have proportions which exceed the upper control limit. Discarding these two samples leaves the analyst with 23 samples with proportions whose sum is 0.78. Therefore, the revised estimate of the population proportion will be

$$p' \doteq 0.78/23 = 0.034$$

The resultant new set of control limits and central line for the p chart will be as follows:

$$\text{Upper control limit} = 0.034 + 3\sqrt{\frac{(0.034)(0.966)}{100}} = 0.088$$

$$\text{Central line} = 0.034$$

$$\text{Lower control limit} = 0.034 - 3\sqrt{\frac{(0.034)(0.966)}{100}} = 0$$

A comparison of these revised trial control limits with the 23 remaining sample proportions reveals that each of the sample values falls within the limits, and, therefore, the designation "trial" is dropped. These now become the control limits which will be adhered to.

Again, as with the $\overline{X}$ and R charts, these limits may be changed as the analyst accumulates more data. Further, it may be that, after some time, the control chart indicates that a permanent change has taken place in the fraction defective; in that case, the population proportion would be reestimated from 25 or more samples drawn from the new population and new control limits established.

EVALUATING AND MAINTAINING THE LEVEL OF CONTROL

Control limits established in the manner which has just been described will be adhered to if the indicated level of control is considered to be satisfactory, that is, if the firm concludes that the involved population proportion of defectives is acceptable. What an acceptable proportion is will vary from case to case. At best, we can only say that the firm must find that level of quality which will provide an economical balance between the cost of defective work and the cost of maintaining the process at that quality level. This can be determined by means of judgment or cost comparisons.

In the event that it is concluded that the level of control is unsatisfactory, steps must be taken to bring about an improvement. One alternative is to investigate the equipment, materials, and operator's work methods with a view to finding conditions which can be altered so as to reduce the population proportion of defectives. If this fails, or succeeds only partially, consideration can be given to modifying the specification limits. If either or both courses of action are taken and result in some improvement, new control limits will have to be developed. But after all the changes that are economically and technologically feasible are made and a certain proportion of defectives remains, management must accept the fact that this proportion is inherent in the process and evaluate the results of the production activity accordingly.

NATURE OF THE SAMPLE AND FREQUENCY OF SAMPLING

The samples taken in the course of applying control charts for defectives should be taken in such a way that they contain items produced as close to the same time as possible. The reasons for this and the methods for obtaining this kind of sample were presented in our discussion of control charts for variables.

With regard to the frequency of sampling, judgment must be used. If the time span between samples is great, a shift in the population proportion will go undetected for some time, and the cost of this must be considered. On the other hand, frequent samples will increase the cost of sampling and maintaining the control chart; of course, if 100 percent inspection is being performed anyway, inspection costs will remain constant and only the cost of maintaining the chart must be considered. In any event, the costs of infrequent sampling must be compared with the costs of frequent sampling, and an attempt made to minimize these costs.

In general, if control problems are being encountered at a particular work station, the analyst will take more frequent samples than he will at a trouble-free location. At the other extreme, there may be work stations at which uninterrupted control has been maintained for so long that, after some time, the analyst may decide that there is no real need for the continued use of a p chart.

AREA OF APPLICATION

Any activity which yields a product that can be classified as either a defective or nondefective is a candidate for a p chart. This, of course, includes just about every operation in the plant. And, consequently, we must generalize by stating that the control chart for defectives should be used wherever it is profitable to do so. This same statement was made with regard to $\overline{X}$ and R charts, but because of the lower inspection and maintenance costs of p charts, they usually have a greater area of economical application than do control charts for variables.

Frequently, first consideration will be given to the use of $\overline{X}$ and R charts if inspection is by measurement and quality problems are being experienced. The reason for this lies in the greater amount of information made available by these charts. For example, the $\overline{X}$ chart will tell the analyst whether the parts are undersized or oversized, whereas the p chart will only reveal that parts are defective, which means that they can be either undersized or oversized. Also, an $\overline{X}$ chart will be maintained for a single characteristic of the part, whereas a p chart can be maintained for a number of characteristics. To illustrate, the firm may be producing shafts which must be of a specified diameter and length. If it wants to control each of these two characteristics, two sets of $\overline{X}$ and R charts must be maintained. However, a single p chart could be established in which a defective would be any part whose length or diameter, or both, were unsatisfactory. As a result, this chart would not tell the analyst whether the diameter or the length was the source of an undue proportion of defectives, whereas the $\overline{X}$ and R charts would. But in spite of the additional information provided by control charts for variables, their use, in many instances, cannot be economically justified. In those cases, consideration would be given to the use of control charts for defectives.

Very often, the procedure just outlined is reversed. If quality problems are being experienced with a given operation, a p chart is initially introduced. Then, after some time, if there is reason to believe that the information made available by the p chart is inadequate and that the potential benefits are substantial, $\overline{X}$ and R charts are resorted to if inspection is by measurement. But regardless of the order of introduction, the use of any control chart is dependent on the savings it is expected to yield.

EVALUATION OF CONTROL CHARTS FOR DEFECTIVES

This brings us to the end of the discussion of control charts for defectives. In spite of the fact that their use involves approximations, estimation, and risks of error, they do provide a means of controlling the quality of future output which is economical and sufficiently effective in many cases. The method often reduces inspection costs if it eliminates the need for 100 percent inspection, tells us whether an operation is in control, and provides us with information which permits the determination of the expected proportion of defectives. For these reasons, the use of control charts for defectives is an alternative which often can make an important contribution to the attainment and maintenance of high-quality standards.

CONTROL CHARTS FOR DEFECTS

There is another control chart that is based on statistical concepts similar to those which underlie the control chart for fraction defective. This other control chart is used when the quality of a product is evaluated in terms of the number of *defects* the individual items possess. For example, a manufacturer of furniture may be producing, among other things, dining-room tables. It might be that the quality of each table is determined on the basis of the number of surface imperfections it has. A surface imperfection would be a scratch or nick, and each such imperfection would be considered to be a defect. Therefore, an attempt would be made to keep the number of surface imperfections, or defects, to a minimum. In another case, a producer of plate glass may pass judgment on the quality of his output of sheets of glass on the basis of the number of air pockets contained in each sheet. Every air pocket would be considered to be a defect, and control of quality would be synonymous with the control of the number of air pockets, or defects, to be found in each sheet.

It is important that defects not be confused with *defectives*. A defective is an article which fails to meet specification requirements. Every defective, however, may contain one or more defects. To return to our manufacturer of dining-room tables, it may be that a certain grade of table is being produced such that a single scratch, or one defect, results in the table being classified as defective. As opposed to this, a cheaper grade of table may be produced in which 10 surface imperfections must be found before the table is classified as a defective. In this case, every defective would contain 10 or more defects.

The point is that there are instances in which a firm will attempt to keep defectives to a minimum by controlling the number of defects to be found in its product. In these instances, the product will not be inspected by measuring and recording a particular dimension, and, hence, control charts for variables will not be applicable. Nor will the product be inspected and simply classified as defective or nondefective; hence, control charts for defectives will not be applicable. Instead, the product will be inspected by counting the number of defects it contains, and an attempt will be made to keep this number of defects at a satisfactory level. This will be done with the aid of a chart called the "control chart for defects."

THE POISSON DISTRIBUTION

The statistical concepts underlying control charts for defects are closely related to those presented in the discussion of the binomial distribution of the number of occurrences per sample. We know that if samples of a certain size are taken from a population which contains a given proportion of occurrences, a distribution of number of occurrences per sample will result. But let us now assume that: (1) the population from which the samples are being taken has a very small proportion of occurrences, or more specifically, that this proportion approaches zero, and (2) the sample is extremely large, or more specifically, that the sample size approaches infinity.

The effect of the first event on the shape of the resultant binomial distribution is that its peak will now be far to the left. The effect of the second event is that, with a sample size of infinity, it is now theoretically possible to draw a sample which will contain an infinite number of occurrences. Therefore, under these two conditions, the binomial distribution of the number of occurrences per sample would take the form shown in Figure 16-6.

This special case of the binomial distribution is called the "Poisson distribution." It represents the expected relative frequencies with which samples containing various numbers of occurrences will appear when samples of infinite size are drawn from a population in which the proportion of occurrences is nearly zero. A further condition is that np', the product of the sample size and population proportion of occurrences, be constant. The probability of obtaining some number of occurrences per sample under these conditions can be ascertained by a method we shall consider when we discuss acceptance sampling.

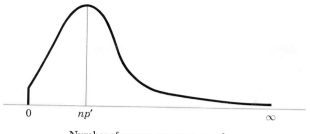

Number of occurrences per sample

Figure 16-6 **The Poisson distribution**

Because of the relationship between the Poisson distribution and the binomial distribution of the number of occurrences per sample, both distributions have the same expression for their respective averages. This means that the average of the Poisson distribution is as follows:

$$\mu_{np} = np' \tag{16-10}$$

To designate the fact that it is the Poisson, and not the binomial, distribution that is being considered, the symbol μ_c is substituted for μ_{np} and c' for np', with the result that the more common expression for the average of the Poisson distribution is as follows:

$$\mu_c = c' \tag{16-11}$$

The expression for the measure of dispersion of the Poisson distribution differs somewhat from the one for the binomial distribution. We know that the standard error of the occurrences is

$$\sigma_{np} = \sqrt{np'(1 - p')} \tag{16-12}$$

However, it was stated that, in the Poisson distribution, np' is constant and that p' approaches zero. Because of the latter, the term $(1 - p')$ in Eq. (16-12) approaches the value of 1. Consequently, if we substitute 1 for $(1 - p')$ in Eq. (16-12), we obtain

$$\sigma_{np} = \sqrt{np'} \tag{16-13}$$

This, then, is the measure of dispersion for the Poisson distribution. Once again, to designate the fact that it is the Poisson distribution which is being considered, we substitute the symbol σ_c for σ_{np} and c' for np' in Eq. (16-13) and obtain the following:

$$\sigma_c = \sqrt{c'} \tag{16-14}$$

In brief, the Poisson is a special case of the binomial distribution of the number of occurrences per sample. As such, it differs from the normal

distribution. Nevertheless, it has been found that no serious error is introduced if we treat it as a normal distribution to determine the probability
of obtaining some number of occurrences per sample, rather than compute such probabilities by an exact method. Consequently, we shall assume, for example, that in the Poisson distribution, 68.3 percent of the
samples will have a number of occurrences within 1 standard error of the
population average, 95.5 percent within 2 standard errors, and 99.7 percent
within 3 standard errors. Let us now see how all this can be employed to
control the quality of a product which is evaluated in terms of the number
of defects it contains.

DISTRIBUTION OF DEFECTS PER SAMPLE   To return to our illustration involving dining-room tables, we can say that the manufacturer will
establish a combination of equipment, materials, and manpower which will
generate a stream of tables. It may be that the appearance of the surfaces
of these tables is the characteristic in which he is interested, in the sense
that he wants these surfaces to be as free of imperfections as possible. For
purposes of analysis, we can consider the surface of each table to be
comprised of infinitesimally small areas. If we do, the population to be
associated with a particular combination of factors of production can be
defined, in this case, as consisting of the sum of the infinitesimally small
areas in terms of which the stream of tables can be described.

But regardless of the care taken in setting up and maintaining the production process, some of these areas will contain a scratch or a nick, that is,
a defect. As a result, a certain proportion of the population of the infinites-
imal areas will contain defects, while the remainder will not. It is likely
that the nature of the manufacturing process is such that the proportion
of areas with defects in the population of areas is so small that we can say
that it approaches zero.

Thus far, we appear to have a set of circumstances which suggests the
applicability of the Poisson distribution. We have a population of occurrences and nonoccurrences. The population is the collection of infinitesimally small table areas; the occurrences are those areas with defects; and
the nonoccurrences are those areas without defects. In addition, an extremely small proportion of the population of areas contains defects. All
we require at this point is some means for drawing repeated samples of
infinite size. This is not difficult to accomplish. In fact, in our illustration,
a sample of a single table will satisfy the requirement of an infinite sample
size, because the surface of a single table is composed of an infinite number
of minute areas. Each of these areas can, theoretically, contain a defect,
and, consequently, a single table can have an infinite number of defects.
Therefore, one table provides us with a sample consisting of an infinite

number of areas from a population of areas. Any one table may have a minimum of zero defects or a maximum of an infinite number of defects. The latter is true, because regardless of the number of defects a table contains, there is always room for one more. In brief, if a sample provides an opportunity for an infinite number of defects to occur, this sample must be of infinite size.

Therefore, if the manufacturer of these tables were to take random samples of one table each from the stream of tables being produced, he would find that some of the tables, that is, samples, would contain 0 defects, some 1 defect, some 2 defects, some 3 defects, and so on, the maximum possible number of defects being infinity. Further, each of these different numbers of defects per sample would appear with some relative frequency. For example, if the population proportion of defects was such that the average number of defects per sample c' is 10, we should expect 10 scratches per table to appear more often than any other number of scratches per table, 15 scratches per table more often than 20, 20 more often than 25, and so on. The general shape of the resultant distribution would be as shown in Figure 16-7.

In summary, what is exemplified in Figure 16-7 is a distribution based on samples of infinite size drawn from a population composed of defects and nondefects. The possible number of defects in a given sample is any value from zero to infinity. Also, the proportion of defects in the population is likely to be close to zero. Consequently, what we have is a Poisson distribution.

CONSTRUCTING THE CONTROL CHART

If the manufacturer wants to control the number of surface imperfections or defects per table, he will establish a combination of equipment, materials, and manpower which he expects will provide him with tables with

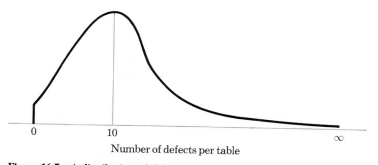

Number of defects per table

Figure 16-7   A distribution of defects per sample

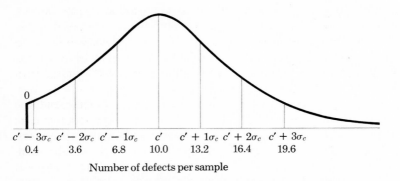

0

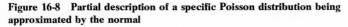

$c' - 3\sigma_c$ $c' - 2\sigma_c$ $c' - 1\sigma_c$ c' $c' + 1\sigma_c$ $c' + 2\sigma_c$ $c' + 3\sigma_c$
0.4   3.6   6.8   10.0 13.2   16.4   19.6

Number of defects per sample

Figure 16-8   Partial description of a specific Poisson distribution being approximated by the normal

a satisfactory finish. A satisfactory population of such tables would be defined as one with a satisfactory average number of defects per table.

Let us assume that the firm in our illustration has established a combination of factors of production which is generating a stream of tables with an average number of defects per table equal to 10 and that this is considered to be satisfactory. Therefore, the manufacturer will want to control conditions so that no undesirable change takes place in this average number of defects per table.

We know that samples of one table each drawn from such a population will vary in the number of defects they contain because of chance causes. Consequently, a distribution of the number of defects per sample will result. Because this is a Poisson distribution, its mean c' will be equal to 10, and its dispersion σ_c, the standard error of the defects, will be equal to $\sqrt{10}$, or 3.2.

If we treat this distribution as if it were normal, we can say that 68.3 percent of the tables will have a number of defects between $10 \pm 1(3.2)$; 95.5 percent, a number between $10 \pm 2(3.2)$; and 99.7 percent, a number between $10 \pm 3(3.2)$. This is to say that the manufacturing process will generate a population of surface areas which will yield a distribution of number of defects per sample which can be partially depicted as shown in Figure 16-8.

Consequently, to say that we want to maintain a population which will yield an average of 10 defects per table is synonymous with saying that we want to maintain a population which will generate the distribution shown in Figure 16-8. As in the case of the binomial distribution, this requires controlling only the distribution average c', because the standard error of the defects is a function of the distribution average. This means that, if we maintain the average at the desired level, the dispersion will also be satisfactory.

One way to ascertain whether the average is satisfactory would be to inspect the entire population of tables. But this is an unsatisfactory approach, for reasons given when we considered the other types of control charts. The alternative is to pass judgment on the population being produced on the basis of a sample drawn from that population. This would be done in the following manner: The analyst would take a random sample of infinite size, which in our example would be one table, and count the defects contained in the sample. He would then compare this number with the desired population average. If an insignificant difference exists, it would be assumed that the variation is attributable to chance causes. But if a significant difference exists, the presence of an assignable cause would be suspected, and an assumption would be made that a change has taken place in the population. A significant difference is usually defined in the same manner as it was in the case of the other control charts. If the number of defects in the sample is more than 3 standard errors away from the desired average, it is assumed that a change has taken place in the underlying population. As before, this 3-sigma criterion represents a compromise between the costs of type 1 and type 2 errors.

METHOD OF APPLICATION   The analyst makes the comparison between the number of defects in the sample and the desired average with the aid of a chart, which is called the "control chart for defects," or more commonly, the "c chart." This chart will have a central line which will represent the desired average number of defects per sample c', an upper control limit which will be equal to $c' + 3\sigma_c$, and a lower control limit which will be equal to $c' - 3\sigma_c$. The general appearance of this chart will be as shown in Figure 16-9.

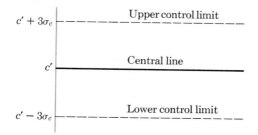

Figure 16-9   **General form of the control chart for defects**

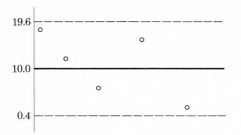

Figure 16-10   An example of a control chart for defects

After having constructed the control chart, the analyst will take periodic random samples, count the number of defects a given sample contains, and plot this number on the control chart. As a result, the control chart, applicable to the case being considered in our illustration and for which the locations of the central line and control limits can be found from Figure 16-8, might appear, after some time, as shown in Figure 16-10.

Out-of-control conditions are recognized in the same manner as they were with control charts for variables and defectives. In the case of a suspected increase in the distribution average, the factors of production would be examined with a view to finding and eliminating the assignable cause of variation. In the event of a suspected decrease, an investigation would be made for reasons mentioned when control charts for ranges and defectives were discussed; if the result is a permanent reduction in the population average, the control chart would have to be revised accordingly.

THE PROBLEM OF ESTIMATION

The assumption was made in the preceding illustration that the average of the distribution of defects per sample c' was known. In practice, this is not true. Yet, the control chart cannot be constructed in the absence of this knowledge. This is apparent from an examination of the following expressions for the central line and control limits for the control chart for defects:

$$\text{Upper control limit} = c' + 3\sigma_c = c' + 3\sqrt{c'} \qquad (16\text{-}15)$$

$$\text{Central line} = c' \qquad (16\text{-}16)$$

$$\text{Lower control limit} = c' - 3\sigma_c = c' - 3\sqrt{c'} \qquad (16\text{-}17)$$

ESTIMATING THE AVERAGE NUMBER OF DEFECTS PER SAMPLE

Some firms solve the problem by selecting a desired value of c' and then making an attempt to keep the process in control at this level. Ordinarily, however, an alternative approach is employed. The firm will establish what it considers to be the best combination of factors of production. An attempt is then made to estimate the average of the distribution of defects per sample being generated by this combination of equipment, materials, and manpower. This is usually done in the following manner: About 25 random samples are drawn from the stream of product being produced, the number of defects in each sample is counted, the average number of defects per sample is calculated, and this average is assumed to be the average of the distribution of defects per sample. Let us now demonstrate this approach.

Returning to our illustration, suppose the analyst goes to the location at which the last operation is being performed on the tables and takes 25 random samples of one table each. He inspects each of these tables and records the number of surface imperfections each contains. The results may be as shown in Table 16-2.

The average of the distribution of defects per sample can be estimated by substituting in the following expression:

$$c' \doteq \frac{1}{k} \Sigma c_j \qquad (16\text{-}18)$$

where $c_j =$ the number of defects in the jth sample
$k =$ the number of samples

In our example, in which the total number of defects in the 25 samples is 125, substitution in Eq. (16-18) yields the following:

$$c' \doteq \frac{1}{25}(125) = 5.0$$

This estimate of c' is now substituted in Eqs. (16-15) to (16-17) to obtain the following values for the central line and control limits:

Upper control limit $= 5.0 + 3\sqrt{5.0} = 11.7$
Central line $= 5.0$
Lower control limit $= 5.0 - 3\sqrt{5.0} = 0$

If the computation for the lower limit were carried out, a negative value would be obtained. But since a negative number of defects is not possible, 0 is used as the lower limit.

TRIAL CONTROL LIMITS These control limits are referred to as "trial" control limits because the analyst has no assurance that his samples were

Table 16-2   Data for Estimating the Average Number of Defects per Sample

Sample number (j)	Number of defects per sample (c_j)
1	5
2	3
3	7
4	4
5	8
6	14
7	5
8	0
9	6
10	5
11	5
12	3
13	6
14	7
15	1
16	4
17	2
18	8
19	2
20	8
21	7
22	3
23	6
24	5
25	1
Total	125

drawn from a stable population. The same approach discussed with reference to other control charts is used to determine whether this requirement has been satisfied.

A comparison of the data in Table 16-2 with the trial control limits reveals that sample 6, which contained 14 defects, exceeds the upper control limit. Discarding this sample leaves 24 samples, with a total number of defects equal to 111. The average number of defects per sample now becomes

$$c' \doteq \frac{1}{24}(111) = 4.6$$

If we substitute this value in our expressions for the central line and control limits, we obtain the following points for our revised c chart:

Upper control limit $= 4.6 + 3\sqrt{4.6} = 11.0$

Central line $= 4.6$

Lower control limit $= 4.6 - 3\sqrt{4.6} = 0$

A comparison of these limits with the remaining data in Table 16-2 shows that each of the 24 samples falls within the control limits, and these limits are now adhered to. But as with the other control charts, the control limits might be changed periodically as more data are accumulated for the reasons and in the manner described in our discussion of those charts.

EVALUATING THE LEVEL OF CONTROL

It is imperative, of course, that the process be in control at a satisfactory level. For example, in the preceding illustration, management must decide whether an average of 4.6 defects per table is acceptable. This can be done solely on the basis of judgment or by approximating, with the normal curve, the percentage of defective tables that will be manufactured if this average is maintained. This approximation would be made in the following manner:

Suppose that the specification states that any table which contains more than 8 surface imperfections is to be classified as a defective. Using the normal distribution as an approximation, we can estimate the percentage of the tables that will contain more than 8 defects by finding the area under the curve that would lie to the right of 8. We begin by substituting in the following modified form of Eq. (15-4):

$$Z = \frac{c - \mu_c}{\sigma_c} = \frac{c - c'}{\sqrt{c'}} \tag{16-19}$$

From this equation, we find that 8 defects is the following number of standard errors away from the mean:

$$Z = \frac{8 - 4.6}{\sqrt{4.6}} = +1.6$$

From Table C-5, we learn that 5.48 percent of the area lies to the right of $c' + 1.6\sigma_c$, and, therefore, we estimate that this will be the percent of defective output if an average of 4.6 defects per table is maintained.

After having calculated such a percentage, the firm can decide whether it is acceptable. A reduction in this percentage, that is, in the average number of defects per sample, will have certain advantages but may bring about an increase in manufacturing costs. But if the decision calls for a reduction in the average number of defects per sample, changes must be made in the production process or the specification to bring about this reduction. Once all the possible changes have been made, an appropriate control chart would be established, and the resultant average number of defects would now be considered to be normal.

At this point, it might also be mentioned that, if the firm decides to construct the control chart on the basis of an aimed-at value of c', the value selected would be one that will yield an acceptable percentage of defective output. Whether a suggested aimed-at value does so can be ascertained by the same procedure that was employed to evaluate a c' value that is actually being realized.

CLASSIFICATION OF DEFECTS

We should note that not all defects are equally serious. For example, the longer and deeper a scratch, the more objectionable it is when it appears on a table surface. Consequently, the firm may establish classes of defects, such as very serious, serious, moderately serious, and not serious.

Although we have not considered this refinement in our example, the existence of such classes calls for weighting the involved defects accordingly. To illustrate, point values might be assigned to the various classes as follows:

Class of defect	Point value
Very serious	3.0
Serious	2.0
Moderately serious	1.0
Not serious	0.5

If an item contains two moderately serious defects, these two defects would be multiplied by the point value of 1 assigned to each to arrive at a total of 2. If another item contains one very serious and one moderately serious defect, a total point value of 4 would be obtained, which indicates that these two defects are equivalent to four moderately serious defects. As all this suggests, because a value of 1 is assigned to a moderately serious defect, the actual number of defects found is expressed in terms of the number of moderately serious defects to which it is equivalent.

This process of classification and weighting would be adhered to when inspecting samples taken for purposes of estimating the distribution average, when constructing the control chart, and in the subsequent application of the resultant chart. The specification for the product would be expressed in terms of a maximum acceptable number of points per unit of output.

THE FREQUENCY OF SAMPLING

After a satisfactory level of control has been attained, whether this level is being maintained will be determined by means of continued sampling. The frequency of this sampling will vary with conditions. At one extreme, every single unit of output may be inspected and the number of defects it contains plotted on the control chart. This would be the case when management feels that the nature of the product and the demands of the consumer make 100 percent inspection mandatory. In such cases, the control chart for defects will not reduce inspection costs but will contribute toward keeping the number of defects and the cost of eliminating these defects, subsequent to inspection, to a minimum by providing the means for recognizing unfavorable changes in the manufacturing process at the time they take place or soon after.

As opposed to this, there are products whose nature is such that 100 percent inspection is unnecessary, in the sense that the consumer will accept a certain number of defects per unit or does not object to finding a small proportion of unsatisfactory items in the product he receives. The use of the control chart for defects will, in these instances, reduce inspection costs and will also serve to keep the process in control at a satisfactory level. However, the question of frequency of sampling now arises. Nothing can be said here that has not already been said with reference to control charts for variables and defectives. More frequent samples will increase inspection costs but will probably permit detecting changes in the population sooner after they occur than will less frequent samples. In general, if control problems are being encountered, sampling will be more frequent than it will be if out-of-control conditions are few and far between. If no problems of control have been experienced over an extended period of time, the use of the control chart may be discontinued completely.

AREA OF APPLICATION

A final matter that must be considered is the selection of those operations to be controlled by means of control charts for defects. As a rule, the conditions required for the correct application of c charts are such that relatively few operations satisfy these requirements. To begin with, the quality of most products is not described in terms of the defects they contain. Further, even if it is, the nature of the operation must be such that the proportion of defects in the population it generates is extremely small. Also, the drawing of a sample whose size approaches infinity must be possible. In most firms, these processes are not too common. This does not mean, however, that the control chart for defects is never used unless all the theoretical requirements regarding the population proportion and sample size are completely satisfied. Sometimes, conditions which approximate those required suffice.

THE SAMPLE SIZE REQUIREMENT To illustrate the approximate satisfaction of the sample size requirement, let us consider a firm which is producing a product which contains 500 rivets. A defective rivet would be considered to be a defect in the product. The population in this case would be all the rivets contained in the items produced. Obviously, a sample of one unit of output would not provide an opportunity for the occurrence of an infinite number of defects. However, it may be believed that the maximum 500 possible defects per sample is sufficiently large, in the sense that the Poisson distribution will adequately approximate the actual distribution. Another alternative is to take a sample, in cases such as this, of more than 1 unit. For example, in this illustration, a sample of 4 units would provide an opportunity for 2,000 defects to occur, and this is still closer to infinity, with the result that the Poisson distribution would be a still better approximation.

But whether the sample is of infinite size or simply very large, it is important that it remain constant, unless the firm is willing to recalculate control limits to reflect variations in the sample size. If the sample is of finite size and the Poisson distribution has been adopted as an approximation, uniform sample sizes will be samples that contain the same number of items. But with samples of infinite size, it is necessary to think in terms of constant "areas of opportunity" rather than the same number of items. For example, a sample of one sheet of plate glass with an area of 20 square feet is not the same as a sample of a single sheet with an area of 10 square feet, in spite of the fact that they are both of infinite size and contain one item each.

An additional point is that, if a sample consists of more than one article, the items included in each sample should be those produced as close to the same time as possible so as to maximize the probability that all the items come from the same population.

POPULATION PROPORTION REQUIREMENT Thus far, we have considered the need for defining quality in terms of defects and the requirement of an infinite sample size as limiting factors in the application of c charts. Another requirement is that the population proportion of defects p' should be extremely small. Unfortunately, what is sufficiently small cannot be precisely defined.

The problem is further complicated by the fact that, when sample sizes are infinite, no estimate of p' is possible. For example, in our table illustration, we could not total the minute areas in our samples and divide this infinite number into the total defects to get an estimate of the population proportion of defects. It was for this reason that the population characteristic estimated was np', the average number of defects per sample, and not p', the population proportion. Consequently, when the population proportion cannot be ascertained, the analyst must base his decision about whether the population proportion is extremely small on judgment. This combination of unknown population proportions and the absence of a quantitative definition of an extremely small population proportion sometimes makes it difficult to determine whether an operation satisfies the requirement of a small proportion of defects in the population it generates.

In the event that all the required conditions are approximately satisfied, whether a c chart should be used must be decided on the basis of the same factors considered when investigating the economic applicability of the other control charts discussed. If no quality problems are being encountered, there would be no reason for introducing a c chart at that work station. If quality problems are being encountered, management must compare the cost of maintaining the chart with the potential savings to be realized from doing so.

In conclusion, it should be noted that a c chart is used to control a population in which every item is described as either having or not having a certain characteristic, that is, attribute. For example, each infinitesimally small area in our population of table areas was classified as either containing or not containing a defect. Similarly, the p chart is used to control a population of the same type. In that case, every item is classified as either being or not being a defective. For this reason, both charts are referred to as "control charts for attributes."

QUESTIONS

16-1   Under what conditions are control charts for defectives employed? Why cannot control charts for variables be used in these cases?

16-2   What are the characteristics of a binomial distribution? What are the replacement requirements when samples are being taken to generate this distribution?

16-3   When can the normal distribution be used as a good approximation of the binomial distribution?

16-4   What do the central line and control limits represent on the control chart for fraction defective?

16-5   Describe the procedure for estimating the value of the population mean for use in constructing a control chart for fraction defective.

16-6   While applying control charts for defectives, when will the firm assume that a change has occurred in the population?

16-7 How does the firm decide whether the process is in control at a satisfactory level when the control chart for defectives is being applied?

16-8 Is a point that falls below the lower control limit on a control chart for defectives of any significance? Explain.

16-9 What factors does the firm take into consideration when determining (*a*) the sample size, (*b*) the manner in which items should be selected for inclusion in the sample, (*c*) the frequency of sampling, and (*d*) the operations to be controlled by control charts for defectives?

16-10 What is the difference between a defect and a defective?

16-11 Under what conditions is the control chart for defects employed?

16-12 What are the characteristics of the Poisson distribution?

16-13 What do the central line and control limits represent on the control chart for defects?

16-14 Describe the procedure for estimating the value of the population mean for use in constructing a control chart for defects.

16-15 When will the firm assume that a change has taken place in the average number of defects per sample?

16-16 How does the firm decide whether a process is in control at a satisfactory level when the control chart for defects is being applied?

16-17 Is a point that falls below the lower control limit on a chart for defects of any significance? Explain.

16-18 What is meant by the classification of defects?

16-19 What factors affect (*a*) the frequency of sampling and (*b*) the choice of operations to be controlled by control charts for defects?

16-20 Does the use of any kind of control chart eliminate the need for 100 percent inspection? Explain.

PROBLEMS

16-1 A university finds that 27 percent of the applications for admission it receives are defective in the sense that they have not been completed properly. Suppose that samples of 50 applications each are taken from the university's files. Sampling is with replacement. In the long run, what will be:

    a The mean and standard error of the resultant distribution of number of defective applications per sample? (Ans. 13.5, 3.14)

    b The mean and standard error of the resultant distribution of proportion of defective applications per sample? (Ans. 0.27, 0.0628)

16-2 In the preceding problem, how would the respective means and standard errors be affected if the sample size were doubled?

16-3 A public utility makes use of punched cards in its data processing system. The firm wants to control the proportion of defective cards, that is, the proportion of cards that contain errors after being keypunched. A control chart for fraction defective will be set up for this purpose. Its central line and control limits will be based on the aimed-at value of 0.02 for the population proportion of defectives and on a decision to assume a risk of making a type 1 error equal to 0.0028.

    a Determine the values of the central line and control limits for a sample size of 250 cards.

    b If at a subsequent point the sample size is increased to 500 cards, what effect will this have on the control chart?

16-4 An analyst takes 20 samples of size 200 each from the output of a final assembly line. The items in each sample are inspected, and the number of defectives in each sample recorded. The results are as follows:

Sample number	Number of defectives	Sample number	Number of defectives
1	9	11	26
2	7	12	18
3	14	13	11
4	15	14	8
5	8	15	10
6	7	16	10
7	9	17	15
8	11	18	13
9	16	19	9
10	12	20	12

    a Basing your estimate of the population mean on these results, compute the values of the central line and 2-sigma control limits for a chart for fraction defective which the analyst wants to maintain at the last station of this assembly line. Assume that the sample size will remain at 200. (Ans. 0.086, 0.054, 0.022)

    b Suppose that some time after the chart has been established, a sample of 300 items is taken and found to contain 25 defectives. Does this result suggest that a satisfactory population mean is or is not being maintained?

16-5 Merchandise distributed by a chain of office supply stores located in a given city is first delivered to a warehouse from which it is shipped to the various stores as the need to do so arises. One of the items stocked is a ball-point pen for which the demand is extremely large. Management wants some assurance that the proportion of defective pens of this type being received from its supplier is maintained at an acceptable level. Consequently, it is going to estimate this proportion and, if it is satisfactory, a p chart will be established and periodic samples taken from future deliveries to determine whether the satisfactory proportion is being maintained.

Twenty-five samples of size 300 are taken to estimate the population proportion of defective pens. The sum of the sample proportions is found to be 0.75. When 2.5-sigma trial control limits are determined, it is noted that a sample proportion of 0.003 falls outside these limits. When the limits are revised, it is found that all the remaining sample proportions fall within the new limits.

a What are the values of the trial and the final control limits for the p chart?

b Some time after the p chart based on these values is introduced, a sample of 100 pens is taken and found to contain seven defectives. What is the significance of this?

16-6 Twenty samples of size 250 and thirty samples of size 500 are taken to estimate the population proportion of defectives. The average proportion of defectives in the 20 samples is 0.013 and in the 30 samples is 0.017. Assume that the process was in control during the entire sampling period.

a How many defectives did the 20 samples contain?

b How many defectives did the 30 samples contain?

c What should the estimate of the population proportion of defectives be?

16-7 A control chart for fraction defective is to be established on the basis of an aimed-at value of p'. Some variation is expected in the size of the samples that will be taken in the course of applying the chart. Specifically, it is estimated that one-half of the samples will contain 2,000 items each, one-third will contain 2,100 items, and one-sixth will contain 2,400 items. Because these fluctuations are relatively small, it is decided to work with a single set of control limits based on the average sample size. What is this average value? (Ans. 2,100)

16-8 An airline company receives an average of 147 phone calls an hour from people requesting information. In the long run, what will be the mean and the standard error of the distribution of number of calls per hour?

16-9 A retail rug dealer receives rugs of a certain size from one of his suppliers. He inspects each such rug he receives by examining it for defects. To control the quality of this item, he decides to maintain a control chart for defects with which he is willing to assume a risk of 0.08 of making a type 1 error.

a What should be the values of the central line and control limits for this chart, if the dealer believes that an average of four defects per rug is acceptable? (Ans. 7.5, 4.0, 0.5)

b If every rug of this type that contains more than seven defects is classified as a defective and returned to the manufacturer for rework, what percentage of the rugs will fall into this category even though the desired distribution of defects per rug is being realized? Determine this with the normal approximation. (Ans. 6.7)

16-10 A lumber company sells, among other things, wooden wall panels of a fixed size. The firm wants to establish a c chart to determine whether the panels it is receiving from its supplier contain an acceptable average number of imperfections per panel. It begins by estimating this average for the panels currently being received. Specifically, 50 samples of one panel each are taken and found to contain a total of 104 defects. The mean is estimated, 2-sigma trial control limits computed, and all 50 points found to fall within these limits.

The estimated average is considered to be satisfactory, so the firm decides to apply this chart in the future by taking periodic samples from incoming shipments of wall panels, inspecting them, and determining whether they suggest that a satisfactory population is being maintained. What are the values of the central line and the control limits for the chart that has been constructed?

16-11 A control chart for defects is to be constructed at a work station in the plant. The analyst estimates the value of the average of the distribution of defects per sample by taking and inspecting 30 samples. The results of this inspection are as follows:

Sample number	Defects per sample	Sample number	Defects per sample
1	5	16	13
2	26	17	14
3	27	18	25
4	15	19	5
5	8	20	27
6	20	21	23
7	9	22	5
8	6	23	6
9	27	24	12
10	22	25	18
11	11	26	26
12	17	27	9
13	7	28	10
14	19	29	26
15	18	30	24

a What will be the values of the central line and 3-sigma limits on the resultant chart?

b Suppose that every item is subjected to final inspection and that any unit that contains more than 23 defects is classified as a defective. What proportion of the output will be defective if the estimated distribution mean is maintained? Use the normal approximation.

16-12 A company manufactures a product which contains 1,000 rivets. Each defective rivet represents a defect in the product. The average number of such defects per unit of output is estimated to be 15, and this is considered to be satisfactory. For quality control purposes, the firm will treat the actual distribution of defects per sample as if it were a Poisson distribution.

a If each sample contains 2 units of output, what will be the mean and standard error of the assumed distribution? (Ans. 30, 5.48)

b If each sample contains 4 units of the product, what will be the mean and the standard error of the assumed distribution? In this case, what would be the appropriate values for the central line and 3-sigma control limits of a c chart?

16-13 The specifications for a product stipulate that any unit that contains more than three defects is unacceptable. Management wants the production process to be controlled at a level such that only 2.28 percent of the output will be defective. What should the aimed-at value of the average number of defects per unit be? Use the normal approximation. (Ans. 1)

SEVENTEEN
ACCEPTANCE SAMPLING

Quality control has been defined as an activity in which measures are taken to control the quality of future output. There are cases, however, in which management is interested solely in the quality of past output. For example, the firm may be procuring raw materials or component parts from an outside source and wants to know whether the quality of a delivered lot is satisfactory. It may, therefore, engage in receiving inspection. If the quality is satisfactory, the lot will be accepted; if it is not, the lot will be rejected. As another example, the firm may want to determine, prior to shipment, whether a particular lot of its own finished goods is of satisfactory quality. It may be that the product under consideration consists of a number of component parts and that, in the course of production, the quality of each of these parts and the assembly was controlled by means of control charts. This, however, provides no assurance that each finished assembly will be satisfactory because the use of control charts does not guarantee that no defective parts will be produced. Therefore, the firm may feel that there is a need for ascertaining the quality of the finished product prior to shipment by means of final inspection.

Whether it is receiving inspection or final inspection, the sole interest of the firm is in the determination of the quality of the product which it or someone else has already produced. One way of accomplishing this is by inspecting each of the items in the lot. However, this approach has its limitations. First, its cost may be high. Second, where large lots are involved, the inspectors are apt to overlook defective items; this is attributable to the fact that the task of inspecting large numbers of articles is monotonous and tedious with the result that errors will occur. Finally, the testing may be destructive, and, hence, 100 percent inspection is not possible.

Because of these limitations of 100 percent inspection, an alternative approach has been developed. This approach is called "acceptance sampling." In brief, the quality of a lot, consisting of a single product or material, is ascertained by taking a random sample from this lot. The items in this sample are then inspected. On the basis of the quality of the items contained in the sample, judgment is passed on the quality of the entire lot which is considered to be the population from which the sample has been drawn.

The advantage of this approach, relative to 100 percent inspection, is that it reduces inspection costs and is the only real alternative when the required testing is destructive. But whenever judgment is passed on a population on the basis of a sample, there is always some probability of making an error. However, the risk is often no greater, and sometimes less, than the risk of error with 100 percent inspection. The reason for this is that, in the inspection of a sample, greater care will be taken, and the results may be more accurate than with 100 percent inspection where monotony, tedium, and boredom may be causes of error.

In the selection of an acceptance sampling plan, the company has a number of alternatives. There are plans in which a single sample is taken, plans in which two samples may be taken, and plans in which an indefinite number of samples may be taken from a single lot. Also, there are plans in which the items in the sample are inspected by precise measurement of the characteristics under consideration, as with control charts for variables, and plans in which the items are inspected in a way which simply identifies each item as being defective or nondefective, as with control charts for fraction defective. In this presentation, we shall concentrate on one type of plan, namely, a plan in which a single sample is drawn from a lot and in which the items in the sample will be classified as being defective or nondefective. This is called "single-sample acceptance sampling by attributes."

THE OPERATING CHARACTERISTIC CURVE

Once management decides that a given product lot will be accepted or rejected on the basis of a sample taken from the lot, a specific sampling plan must be designed. This calls for the determination of the sample size and of the quality of the items in the sample that will lead to the acceptance or rejection of the lot.

In the design of the plan, the firm is governed by two considerations: (1) It wants the plan to be such that satisfactory lots will be accepted and not rejected, and (2) it wants the plan to be such that unsatisfactory lots will be rejected and not accepted. But this statement creates a need for defining "satisfactory lots" and "unsatisfactory lots." In this definition, it will be necessary to refer to the producer of the items contained in the lot and to the consumer of these items. The producer will be that company or department from which the lot has been received. In the case of purchased goods, the producer will be the outside vendor, while in the case of manufactured goods, the producer will be the firm's own production department. The consumer, of course, will be the firm itself.

Naturally, the consumer would like the lot to be completely free of defectives. As a rule, this is not feasible because it is inevitable that lots will contain some defectives due to conditions which cannot be economically controlled. Therefore, the consumer and producer usually get together and agree on what maximum proportion of defectives in the lot constitutes satisfactory quality. For example, they may agree that, if the lot contains 2 percent defectives or less, the lot is acceptable, but if the lot contains more than 2 percent defectives, it is unacceptable and should be rejected. Rejection of the lot may mean returning the lot to the producer, who might screen it for defectives and then send it back, or it may mean screening by the consumer, with the producer, in one way or another, bearing the cost of this screening.

The only way in which it can definitely be determined whether the lot meets the established quality standard is by 100 percent inspection. This procedure, if we ignore the possibility of inspection errors, will reveal the exact proportion of defectives in the lot. This proportion can then be compared with the maximum acceptable proportion, and if it exceeds the maximum acceptable proportion, the lot will be rejected. Obviously, the advantage of an acceptance plan based on 100 percent inspection is that there is no probability of the consumer's accepting a lot which has a proportion of defectives which exceeds the maximum acceptable proportion, and there is no probability of the consumer's rejecting a lot which has a proportion of defectives which does not exceed the maximum acceptable proportion.

The first probability, that of accepting an unsatisfactory lot, is called the "consumer's risk"; the second probability, that of rejecting a satisfactory lot, is called the "producer's risk." Therefore, with 100 percent inspection, the probability of accepting a satisfactory lot is 1.0, and the probability of accepting an unsatisfactory lot is 0.0. This characteristic of an acceptance plan calling for 100 percent inspection can be depicted graphically. If we use the symbol P_a to represent the probability of accepting a lot, the symbol p_s to represent the maximum acceptable proportion of defectives in the lot, and the symbol p' to represent the actual proportion of defectives in the lot, we can say that P_a is 1.0 when p' is less than or equal to p_s and that P_a is 0.0 when p' is greater than p_s. Graphically, this would appear as shown in Figure 17-1.

A curve such as the one shown in Figure 17-1, which serves to describe an acceptance plan in terms of the probability of accepting lots of various quality levels with the plan, is called an "operating characteristic" (OC) curve. The OC curve of a 100 percent inspection plan is said to be an ideal

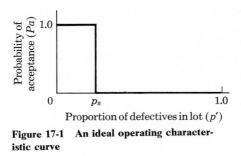

Figure 17-1   **An ideal operating characteristic curve**

curve because the plan it represents has associated with it a producer's risk equal to zero and a consumer's risk equal to zero.

But in spite of the fact that there is no theoretical risk of error to be associated with such a plan, it is often rejected because of the disadvantages mentioned earlier. Due to these disadvantages, sampling may be a more attractive alternative. However, the advantages of sampling inspection entail a price, namely, the risk of making a mistake. We shall now consider the nature and magnitude of this risk.

CALCULATING PROBABILITIES OF ACCEPTANCE   Let us begin by considering a specific single-sample acceptance plan. A sampling plan can be described in terms of three values: (1) N, the lot size, (2) n, the sample size, and (3) c, the acceptance number. The acceptance number c is the maximum allowable number of defectives in the sample. This means that if the sample contains c or fewer defectives, the lot will be accepted, but if it contains more than c defectives, the lot will be rejected. Therefore, a specific single-sample acceptance plan might be as follows:

$N = 100$
$n = 10$
$c = 1$

This tells us that if the lot size is 100, a random sample of size 10 should be taken. If the sample contains 0 or 1 defective, the lot will be accepted; if it contains 2 or more defectives, the lot will be rejected.

To determine the risk of making an error with this particular plan, we must construct its operating characteristic curve. This calls for ascertaining the respective probabilities of acceptance to be associated with lots of various quality levels. To do so, we begin by noting that a specific lot of 100 items will be accepted if a sample of 10 items taken from that lot contains 0 or 1 defective. Consequently, the probability of accepting a lot which is, say, 4 percent defective would be equal to the probability of obtaining a sample which contains either 0 or 1 defective from such a lot. This probability will be equal to the probability of obtaining 0 defectives plus the probability of obtaining 1 defective in the sample. This is so because when individual events are mutually exclusive, which is to say that more than one of them cannot occur at the same time, the probability of one of a number of such events occurring is the sum of the probabilities to be associated with the individual events. Therefore, in our example, we can say that

$$P(0 \text{ or } 1 \text{ defective}) = P(0 \text{ defectives}) + P(1 \text{ defective})$$

or, in general, that the probability of accepting a lot with a plan, in which the acceptance number is c, is equal to

$$P_a = P(0) + P(1) + \cdots + P(c-1) + P(c)$$

To calculate the respective probabilities of the individual events' occurring, we must take into consideration the method of sampling. In industrial practice, samples for acceptance sampling purposes are customarily taken from a finite lot, without replacement, and with no regard to the order in which the items are drawn. Under these conditions, the probability $P(r)$ of obtaining a sample which contains exactly r defectives is equal to

$$P(r) = \frac{C_r{}^D C_g{}^G}{C_n{}^N} \tag{17-1}$$

In this formula, the symbol $C_r{}^D$, for example, is read "the number of combinations of D things taken r at a time" and represents the following expression:

$$C_r{}^D = \frac{D!}{r!(D-r)!}$$

Similarly,

$$C_g{}^G = \frac{G!}{g!(G-g)!}$$

and

$$C_n{}^N = \frac{N!}{n!(N-n)!}$$

Furthermore,

$D =$ number of defectives in the lot
$r =$ number of defectives in the sample
$G =$ number of good items in the lot
$g =$ number of good items in the sample

$N =$ lot size

$n =$ sample size

Another symbol that appears in the foregoing expressions is the factorial symbol, which assumes the form of an exclamation mark. The factorial of any number X is equal to

$$X! = (X)(X - 1)(X - 2) \cdots (2)(1)$$

For example, we should find that

$$5! = (5)(4)(3)(2)(1) = 120$$

Furthermore, by definition, 0! is equal to 1, and the factorial of a negative number does not exist. It should also be noted that the determination of the factorial of a large number can be a difficult task; this task can be simplified with the use of tables of logarithms of factorials which are contained in many mathematical and statistical handbooks.

To illustrate the use of Eq. (17-1), let us return to the sampling plan in our illustration and compute the probability of taking a sample of 10 items, from a lot of 100 items which is 4 percent defective, and finding that the sample contains 0 defectives. Such a lot will contain 0.04 times 100, or 4, defectives and, therefore, 96 good items. Also, a sample of 10 items which contains 0 defectives will contain 10 good items. Consequently, with the use of Eq. (17-1), we find the probability to be

$$P(0) = \frac{C_0{}^4 C_{10}{}^{96}}{C_{10}{}^{100}} = \frac{\dfrac{4!}{0!(4-0)!} \dfrac{96!}{10!(96-10)!}}{\dfrac{100!}{10!(100-10)!}} = 0.65164$$

In a similar manner, the probability of obtaining 1 defective in the sample would be found to be

$$P(1) = \frac{C_1{}^4 C_9{}^{96}}{C_{10}{}^{100}} = 0.29961$$

Therefore, the probability of obtaining a sample which contains 0 or 1 defective will be equal to

$$P(0 \text{ or } 1) = 0.65164 + 0.29961 = 0.95125$$

Given that the lot will be accepted if the sample contains 0 or 1 defective, this result tells us that, with the acceptance plan under consideration, the probability of accepting an incoming lot which is 4 percent defective is approximately 0.95.

The calculations up to this point have yielded one point on the OC curve for the assumed acceptance plan. The other points would be determined in a similar manner. With a lot size of 100, a lot could theoretically con-

Table 17-1 Expressions for Determining Points on an Operating Characteristic Curve

Lot proportion of defectives (p')	Number of defectives in the lot $(D = 100p')$	Probability of finding 0 defectives $[P(0)]$	Probability of finding 1 defective $[P(1)]$
0.00	0	$C_0^0 \cdot C_{10}^{100} \div C_{10}^{100}$	$C_1^0 \cdot C_9^{100} \div C_{10}^{100}$
0.01	1	$C_0^1 \cdot C_{10}^{99} \div C_{10}^{100}$	$C_1^1 \cdot C_9^{99} \div C_{10}^{100}$
0.04	4	$C_0^4 \cdot C_{10}^{96} \div C_{10}^{100}$	$C_1^4 \cdot C_9^{96} \div C_{10}^{100}$
0.08	8	$C_0^8 \cdot C_{10}^{92} \div C_{10}^{100}$	$C_1^8 \cdot C_9^{92} \div C_{10}^{100}$
0.15	15	$C_0^{15} \cdot C_{10}^{85} \div C_{10}^{100}$	$C_1^{15} \cdot C_9^{85} \div C_{10}^{100}$
0.25	25	$C_0^{25} \cdot C_{10}^{75} \div C_{10}^{100}$	$C_1^{25} \cdot C_9^{75} \div C_{10}^{100}$
0.40	40	$C_0^{40} \cdot C_{10}^{60} \div C_{10}^{100}$	$C_1^{40} \cdot C_9^{60} \div C_{10}^{100}$
0.70	70	$C_0^{70} \cdot C_{10}^{30} \div C_{10}^{100}$	$C_1^{70} \cdot C_9^{30} \div C_{10}^{100}$
1.00	100	$C_0^{100} \cdot C_{10}^0 \div C_{10}^{100}$	$C_1^{100} \cdot C_9^0 \div C_{10}^{100}$

tain any one of the following proportions of defectives: 0.00, 0.01, 0.02, . . . , 0.99, 1.00. However, rather than compute the probabilities of acceptance to be associated with each of these possible quality levels, we shall do so only for a selected few. These will be the following: 0.00, 0.01, 0.04, 0.08, 0.15, 0.25, 0.40, 0.70, and 1.00. This will provide us with a sufficient number of points to permit determination of the general shape of the curve. Going on to make the necessary computations for these lots, we obtain the expressions shown in Table 17-1, which yield the results shown in Table 17-2.

With this information, we can construct the operating characteristic

Table 17-2 Probabilities of Accepting Lots with a Given Acceptance Sampling Plan

Lot fraction defective (p')	Probability of finding 0 defectives in sample $[P(0)]$	Probability of finding 1 defective in sample $[P(1)]$	Probability of accepting the lot (P_a)
0.00	1.00000	0.00000	1.00000
0.01	0.90000	0.10000	1.00000
0.04	0.65164	0.29961	0.95125
0.08	0.41655	0.40150	0.81805
0.15	0.18077	0.35678	0.53755
0.25	0.04789	0.18140	0.22929
0.40	0.00436	0.03416	0.03852
0.70	0.00017	0.00006	0.00023
1.00	0.00000	0.00000	0.00000

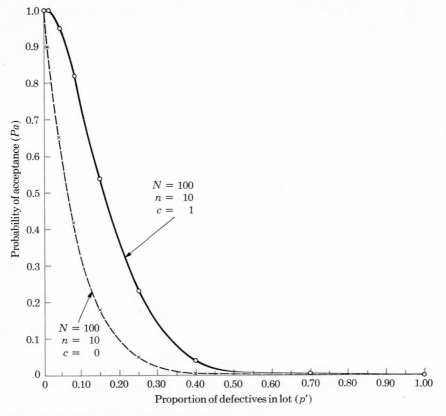

Figure 17-2   Typical operating characteristic curves

curve for the plan under consideration. The OC curve depicts, for a particular plan, the probabilities of accepting lots containing various proportions of defective items. Therefore, if we plot the values in the first column
versus the values in the last column of Table 17-2, that is, p' versus P_a, we
obtain the curve shown as a solid line in Figure 17-2.

It will be noted that Figure 17-2 also contains a broken line. This line
represents the OC curve of a sampling plan which involves a lot size of 100,
a sample size of 10, and an acceptance number of 0. The line was drawn in
for two reasons: First, the data required for locating it were readily available. It will be recalled that we had calculated the probability of finding 0
defectives in single samples drawn from various lots. These probabilities
$P(0)$ appear in the second column of Table 17-2. If the acceptance number
had been 0, these probabilities would also have been the probabilities of
acceptance.

The second reason for showing the line is to bring out the fact that each acceptance plan has a unique OC curve. In general, if the lot and sample sizes are held constant, decreasing the acceptance number shifts the curve to the left. This can be seen from Figure 17-2. Further, if the lot size and acceptance number are held constant, increasing the sample size results in an OC curve with a steeper slope. The extreme case is reached when the sample size equals the lot size, which is true only in 100 percent inspection. In that case, the OC curve is rectangular in shape with as steep a slope as is possible. This was shown in Figure 17-1.

Let us now return to Figure 17-2 and to the OC curve for the plan with an acceptance number of 1 and a sample size of 10. The purpose of our development of this OC curve was to show that there is always some risk of error whenever the acceptance plan involves less than 100 percent inspection. The nature and size of this error become apparent from a study of a typical operating characteristic curve, such as the one shown in Figure 17-2.

It was mentioned that the consumer and producer will agree on some acceptable proportion of defectives in the lot. This may be, for example, 4 percent. Let us assume for the moment that it is. With the acceptance plan under consideration, we found that lots of size 100 containing 4 percent defectives would be accepted approximately 95 percent of the time. This means that 5 percent of the lots containing 4 percent defectives, which is the maximum acceptable proportion of defectives, would be rejected. This 5 percent is referred to as the "producer's risk" because the producer would have some of his satisfactory lots rejected. On the other hand, the consumer also incurs a risk. There is a probability that, even if a lot contains more than 4 percent defectives, it will be accepted. This risk of accepting unsatisfactory lots is referred to as the "consumer's risk." For example, the OC curve tells us that, if a lot containing 8 percent defectives is received, there is a probability of 0.82 that this lot will be accepted.

Of course, the producer and consumer know that there is some risk to be associated with acceptance plans based on something less than 100 percent inspection. However, an attempt would be made to control the degree of risk involved, and, as we shall see at a later point, this is done by designing a plan which involves risks that are not considered to be excessive.

AVERAGE OUTGOING QUALITY LIMIT

We have seen that a given acceptance sampling plan can be described in terms of the operating characteristic curve it will generate. Under certain conditions, a plan can also be described in terms of the resultant "average outgoing quality" (AOQ) of the product being inspected by means of the plan. These conditions are that (1) rejected lots be screened and all the defectives they contain be replaced by good articles and (2) lot sizes of the product be constant.

To demonstrate what is meant by the average outgoing quality, let us return to the lot size and sampling plan we have been considering for purposes of illustration. It was found, for example, that incoming lots which are 4 percent defective will be accepted 95 percent of the time and rejected 5 percent of the time. This means that, in the long run, 95 out of 100 such lots will be accepted and 5 out of 100 rejected. The accepted lots will, of course, be 4 percent defective. But if the rejected lots are screened and all their defectives replaced by good articles, the end result will be lots that are 0 percent defective. In summary, of the incoming lots that are 4 percent defective, 0.95 will be 4 percent defective at the time of their acceptance, and 0.05 will be 0 percent defective at the time of their acceptance following the screening process. The average quality of the outgoing lots of this type will therefore be as follows if the lot sizes are equal:

AOQ = 0.95(4%) + 0.05(0%) = 0.038

In more general terms, we can say that the AOQ of incoming lots that contain a proportion of defectives equal to p' is as follows:

$$\text{AOQ} = P_a(p') + (1 - P_a)(0.0) = P_a(p') \tag{17-2}$$

By making appropriate substitutions in Eq. (17-2), we can find the AOQ for each of the other types of lots considered in our illustration. The results would be as shown in Table 17-3 and in Figure 17-3.

An examination of the calculated AOQ values reveals that a maximum

Table 17-3   Average Outgoing Quality with a Given Acceptance Sampling Plan

Proportion of defectives in incoming lots (p')	Probability of acceptance (P_a)	Average proportion of defectives in outgoing lots (AOQ $= P_a \cdot p'$)
0.00	1.00000	0.00000
0.01	1.00000	0.01000
0.04	0.95125	0.03805
0.08	0.81805	0.06544
0.15	0.53755	0.08063
0.25	0.22929	0.05732
0.40	0.03852	0.01541
0.70	0.00023	0.00016
1.00	0.00000	0.00000

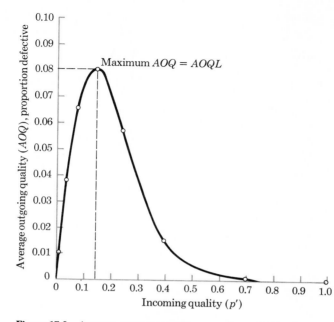

Figure 17-3 **Average outgoing quality curve for a given acceptance sampling plan**

value of 0.08063 is reached for incoming lots with a proportion of defectives equal to 0.15. Consequently, we can say that, with the sampling plan involved, accepted outgoing lots will be, at worst, approximately 8 percent defective. In stating this, we are ignoring, for purposes of simplicity, that a very incomplete set of p' values is being considered and, hence, that the actual maximum value of the AOQ may occur when the p' value is somewhat higher or lower than 0.15.

In any case, this maximum value of the AOQ is called the "average outgoing quality limit" (AOQL), and each acceptance sampling plan can be described in terms of the AOQL it will generate. As this suggests, this characteristic provides a firm with another criterion on the basis of which an acceptance sampling plan can be designed.

To summarize, management can place the emphasis on the risk of making an error with a given plan and, as a consequence, design a plan which will yield a satisfactory OC curve. On the other hand, management can place the emphasis on the average outgoing quality of incoming lots when a given plan is employed and, as a consequence, design a plan which will yield a satisfactory AOQ curve. Finally, consideration can be given to the design of a plan which will be satisfactory both from the standpoint of the risk it involves and the AOQL it will generate. We shall next consider selected approaches to the design of acceptance plans in which cognizance is taken of these alternative criteria.

PLANS WITH STATED RISKS

It has been mentioned that single-sample acceptance plans can be designed so that the resultant consumer's and producer's risks will prove to be satisfactory to all concerned parties. There are various ways of governing the degree to which these risks of error will exist, but we shall consider only one in detail. However, the one to be described is representative and suggestive of the others. This method calls for designing a plan whose OC curve will pass through two stipulated points agreed upon by the consumer and producer. The approach employed is as follows:

Instead of agreeing simply on a single proportion of defectives to represent the acceptable proportion of defectives in the lot, the consumer and producer will agree on two proportions. The first of these is called the "acceptable quality level" (AQL), and it represents the maximum proportion of defectives which the consumer finds definitely acceptable. For example, the consumer may state that he wants to accept all lots which have a fraction defective of 0.01 or less. However, this does not mean that the consumer is unwilling to accept any lots with a fraction defective in excess of this stipulated proportion. But there will be some proportion, and this will be the second stipulated proportion, which represents the minimum proportion of defectives which the consumer finds definitely unacceptable. For example, the consumer may state that he wants to reject all lots which have a fraction defective of 0.25 or more. This second proportion is called the "lot tolerance percent defective" (LTPD). In this illustration, therefore, the AQL is equal to 0.01, and the LTPD to 0.25. Insofar as lots with a fraction defective between 0.01 and 0.25 are concerned, the consumer is said to be "indifferent" to them.

But to take advantage of the economies made available by acceptance sampling, the consumer must be willing to assume a risk of accepting some lots which he finds definitely unacceptable, that is, whose proportion of defectives equals or exceeds the LTPD. Also, the producer must be willing to assume some risk of having some of the definitely acceptable lots rejected, that is, some of the lots whose proportion of defectives equals or is less than the AQL. What is usually done is that the maximum consumer's and producer's risks are agreed upon and explicitly stated in quantitative terms. For example, the producer may agree to accept the risk that 10 percent of the lots with a fraction defective of 0.01 will be rejected, and the consumer may agree to accept the risk that 5 percent of the lots with a fraction defective of 0.25 will be accepted.

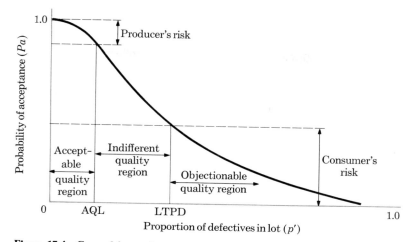

Figure 17-4   General form of an operating characteristic curve that passes through two specified points

The problem that now presents itself is the need for designing an acceptance plan which will meet these requirements. Whether a particular plan does or does not can be ascertained from its operating characteristic curve. But we must now think of the OC curve in the terms shown in Figure 17-4.

In our example, the consumer defined the AQL as being 0.01 and the LTPD as being 0.25. The producer was willing to accept a 10 percent risk that lots with a proportion of defectives of 0.01 would be rejected, and the consumer was willing to accept a 5 percent risk that lots with a proportion of defectives of 0.25 would be accepted. These conditions and the symbols commonly used to represent them are:

$p_1 = AQL = 0.01$
$p_2 = LTPD = 0.25$
$\alpha = $ maximum producer's risk $= 0.10$
$\beta = $ maximum consumer's risk $= 0.05$

When we say that the producer's risk is to be 0.10, this means that the probability of accepting a lot which contains 1 percent defectives should be 1 minus 0.10, or 0.90. Also, a consumer's risk of 0.05 means that there should be a probability of 0.05 of accepting a lot which contains 25 percent defectives. The OC curve for this set of conditions would have the form shown in Figure 17-5.

In effect, what the consumer and producer agree upon is a set of two points for the OC curve; these points are $(p_1, 1 - \alpha)$ and (p_2, β). To phrase this differently, they agree that any acceptance plan whose OC curve passes through these preselected points will be satisfactory. It is assumed

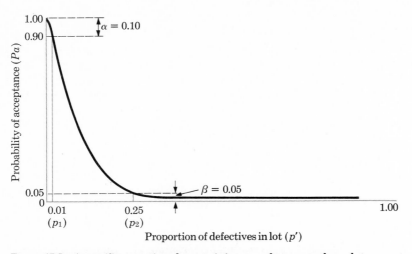

Figure 17-5   A specific operating characteristic curve that passes through two stipulated points

that all the remaining points, which serve to describe the rest of the curve, will be satisfactory. An assumption such as this is almost mandatory, given the difficulty of designing a plan whose OC curve is required to pass through just two points. If the number of stipulated points were to be increased, the task would become an almost impossible one.

THE PROBLEMS OF DESIGN   The problems of acceptance plan design stem from the fact that a trial-and-error approach must be employed in this design. To illustrate this, let us assume that the two stipulated points are those with which we have been working. The question may be: Given a lot size of 100, what should the sample size and acceptance number be? The only way in which this can be determined is by arbitrarily selecting a sample size and an acceptance number, calculating the respective probabilities of acceptance for the acceptable quality level and lot tolerance percent defective, and hoping that they coincide with $(1 - \alpha)$ and β. Chances are that they will not. Another combination of sample size and acceptance number must then be selected, and the procedure repeated. Actually, as an examination of Figure 17-2 will reveal, a sample size of 10 and an acceptance number of 0 will just about satisfy the stipulated requirements. However, the values of p_1, p_2, α, and β used in this illustration were selected so that this would prove to be the case.

The problem of design is further complicated by the fact that, even if p_1, p_2, α, and β remain fixed, a different plan would be required for each lot size because the lot size enters into the probability computations.

Further, one cannot assume that the two points through which the OC curve must pass will remain fixed. They may vary for different products, so that different plans may be required even for lots of equal size.

Although every trial-and-error approach is not inherently tedious and time-consuming, the one involved in acceptance sampling is, because of the nature of the required probability computations. If these could be simplified, the task would be less formidable. Fortunately, if we are willing to make certain assumptions, simplification is possible.

THE POISSON APPROXIMATION   We have adhered to a method for computing the probability of accepting a lot which is known as the "*hypergeometric* method." It takes into account that the sample is taken without replacement from a finite lot. However, other methods for computing probabilities of occurrence are employed under other conditions. For example, when sampling is without replacement and a sample size which approaches infinity is taken from an infinite population whose proportion of defectives approaches zero, these probabilities are calculated by the Poisson method. It is this method that is commonly employed to simplify the task of designing an acceptance sampling plan.

The Poisson method calls for determining probabilities by means of the following expression:

$$P(r) = \frac{(np')^r}{r!} e^{-np'} \tag{17-3}$$

where $e = 2.71828+$, the base of natural logarithms.

If Eq. (17-3) were used to calculate probabilities in acceptance sampling, the results would definitely be approximations. This is so because lot and sample sizes are not of infinite size, and incoming lots may contain a relatively large proportion of defectives.

Nevertheless, it has been found that the Poisson method yields satisfactory approximations when we have (1) fairly large lot sizes, in which case the requirement that the population be of infinite size is somewhat satisfied; (2) fairly large sample sizes, in which case the requirement that the sample size approach infinity is somewhat satisfied; and (3) fairly small lot proportions of defectives, in which case the requirement that the population proportion of defectives approach zero is somewhat satisfied.

However, lot and sample sizes do not have to be very large, and lot proportions do not have to be very small in order that an adequate approximation be obtained. To demonstrate this, let us return to the example with which we have been working. In that example, probabilities of acceptance were computed by the hypergeometric method for a lot size of 100, from which a sample of 10 items would be taken and which would be

accepted if the sample contained 0 or 1 defective. We shall now compute
these probabilities by the Poisson method for the same lot proportions
of defectives considered earlier.

To illustrate the application of the method, we shall assume that a particular lot contains a fraction defective equal to 0.08. The probability of
accepting this lot will be equal to the probability of finding 0 defectives
in a sample of 10 items plus the probability of finding 1 defective. These
individual probabilities can be found by making the required substitutions
in Eq. (17-3). With a lot proportion of 0.08, np' becomes 10 times 0.08,
or 0.8, and the probability of finding 0 defectives in the sample is equal to

$$P(0) = \frac{(0.8)^0}{0!} e^{-0.8} = 0.44933$$

The probability of finding 1 defective in the sample is equal to

$$P(1) = \frac{(0.8)^1}{1!} e^{-0.8} = 0.35964$$

The sum of these probabilities, which is the probability of accepting the lot,
is equal to

$$P_a = 0.44933 + 0.35964 = 0.80897$$

Similar computations would be made for each of the other lot proportions of defectives, and the results would be as shown in Table 17-4.

We can now compare these values of P_a, from which the OC curve for
this acceptance plan would be constructed, with those obtained by the
hypergeometric method of computation. The two sets of points are shown
in the following table:

Lot proportion of defectives	Probability of acceptance	
	Hypergeometric	Poisson
0.00	1.00000	1.00000
0.01	1.00000	0.99532
0.04	0.95125	0.93845
0.08	0.81805	0.80897
0.15	0.53755	0.55775
0.25	0.22929	0.28728
0.40	0.03852	0.09160
0.70	0.00023	0.00728
1.00	0.00000	0.00055

Table 17-4 Poisson Probabilities of Accepting Lots with a Given Acceptance Sampling Plan

Lot proportion of defectives (p')	Probability of finding 0 defectives [$P(0)$]	Probability of finding 1 defective [$P(1)$]	Probability of acceptance [$P_a = P(0) + P(1)$]
0.00	$\dfrac{(0.0)^0}{0!}e^{-0.0}$	$\dfrac{(0.0)^1}{1!}e^{-0.0}$	1.00000
0.01	$\dfrac{(0.1)^0}{0!}e^{-0.1}$	$\dfrac{(0.1)^1}{1!}e^{-0.1}$	0.99532
0.04	$\dfrac{(0.4)^0}{0!}e^{-0.4}$	$\dfrac{(0.4)^1}{1!}e^{-0.4}$	0.93845
0.08	$\dfrac{(0.8)^0}{0!}e^{-0.8}$	$\dfrac{(0.8)^1}{1!}e^{-0.8}$	0.80897
0.15	$\dfrac{(1.5)^0}{0!}e^{-1.5}$	$\dfrac{(1.5)^1}{1!}e^{-1.5}$	0.55775
0.25	$\dfrac{(2.5)^0}{0!}e^{-2.5}$	$\dfrac{(2.5)^1}{1!}e^{-2.5}$	0.28728
0.40	$\dfrac{(4.0)^0}{0!}e^{-4.0}$	$\dfrac{(4.0)^1}{1!}e^{-4.0}$	0.09160
0.70	$\dfrac{(7.0)^0}{0!}e^{-7.0}$	$\dfrac{(7.0)^1}{1!}e^{-7.0}$	0.00728
1.00	$\dfrac{(10.0)^0}{0!}e^{-10.0}$	$\dfrac{(10.0)^1}{1!}e^{-10.0}$	0.00055

An examination of this table reveals that, for the acceptance plan under consideration, the Poisson provides us with an extremely good approximation for population proportions of defectives up to 0.15 and with fairly good approximations for population proportions of defectives up to 0.25. Beyond this last point, the results leave something to be desired. This was to be expected, because the Poisson distribution applies only when the population proportion is extremely small. However, this limitation of the method is of little consequence, because the selected value of the lot tolerance percent defective is rarely anything as high as 0.25. In any case, the important thing is that, if the approximation is quite good for a lot size of 100 and a sample size of 10, it will be even better for larger lot and sample sizes; and in industrial practice, lot and sample sizes are usually significantly larger than those involved in this illustration.

Because the Poisson method yields satisfactory approximations of hypergeometric probabilities, it provides the firm with a simpler approach to the design of a sampling plan whose OC curve is to pass through two preselected points. This is not to say that there is something inherent in the method that eliminates the need for a trial-and-error approach to the design of such a plan; basically, it is still necessary to assume different values for the sample size and the acceptance number until that combination is found which will yield the desired OC curve. The advantage of the Poisson approximation is, first, that it eliminates the need for designing a different plan for every different lot size if the two preselected points on the OC curve are constant and, second, that it provides us with a method for computing probabilities which is decidedly less difficult than the hypergeometric. Also, tables have been constructed and are available from which one can determine Poisson probabilities, such as the ones we have found it necessary to compute, for various values of np'. This means that, if the Poisson approximation is used, it is not necessary to calculate the probabilities of acceptance under different assumed conditions; they can simply be found in a table. Although these tables are not presented here because of their length, the information they contain is depicted in graphical form in Figure 17-6. With the use of this figure, the probabilities computed in Table 17-4 can be obtained to two decimal places.

USE OF AVAILABLE TABLES   For the reasons given, it is customary to employ the Poisson method of computing probabilities when designing an acceptance plan. To develop a plan whose OC curve is required to pass through two preselected points, one can assume different combinations of the sample size n and the acceptance number c and find the probabilities of accepting lots with various proportions of defectives from the Poisson tables. This is continued until the correct combination of sample size and acceptance number is found. Thus, the trial-and-error approach is greatly simplified. In fact, the existence of the Poisson tables, which eliminate the need for making the actual probability computations, has encouraged the development of still other tables which eliminate the need for even this simplified trial-and-error approach. These are tables for developing single-sample acceptance plans. A typical one is shown in Table 17-5.

Let us demonstrate how Table 17-5 is used. Suppose that the acceptable quality level p_1 is 0.02, the lot tolerance percent defective p_2 is 0.08, the producer's risk α is to be 0.05, and the consumer's risk β is to be 0.10. According to the instructions given at the top of the table, we first compute p_2/p_1. This is equal to

$$\frac{p_2}{p_1} = \frac{0.08}{0.02} = 4$$

Next, we find the tabular value in the column for the given α and β which

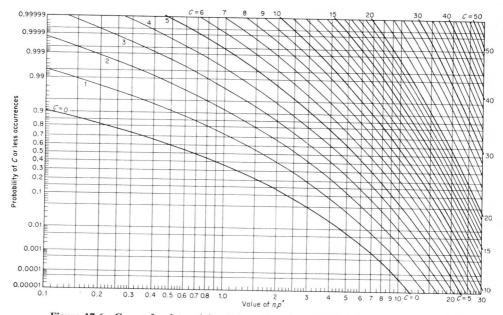

Figure 17-6 Curves for determining Poisson probabilities of obtaining c or less defectives in a sample of size n taken from a population in which the proportion defective is p' (Reprinted by permission from H. F. Dodge and H. G. Romig, *Sampling Inspection Tables—Single and Double Sampling*, 2d ed., John Wiley & Sons, Inc., New York, 1959)

is equal to or just exceeds the ratio p_2/p_1. In this case, the tabular value is 4.057. We then go to the left until we reach the c column, where we find a value of 4. This means that our plan should have an acceptance number c equal to 4. Then we go to the right until we reach the np_1 column, where we find a value of 1.970. To obtain the required sample size n, we divide np_1 by p_1. This is equal to

$$n = \frac{np_1}{p_1} = \frac{1.970}{0.02} = 99$$

Therefore, if our acceptance plan calls for a sample size of 99 and an acceptance number of 4, the resultant OC curve will go through the points (0.02, 0.95) and (0.08, 0.10). This means that the probability of accepting lots which contain 2 percent defectives will be 0.95, and the probability of accepting lots which contain 8 percent defectives will be 0.10.

Table 17-5 Values of np_1 and c for Constructing Single-sampling Plans Whose OC Curve is Required to Pass through the Two Points $(p_1, 1-\alpha)$ and (p_2, β)*

(Here p_1 is the fraction defective for which the risk of rejection is to be α, and p_2 is the fraction defective for which the risk of acceptance is to be β. To construct the plan, find the tabular value of p_2/p_1 in the column for the given α and β which is equal to or just greater than the given value of the ratio. The sample size is found by dividing the np_1 corresponding to the selected ratio by p_1. The acceptance number is the value of c corresponding to the selected value of the ratio.)

| | Values of p_2/p_1 for: | | | | | Values of p_2/p_1 for: | | | |
c	$\alpha = 0.05$ $\beta = 0.10$	$\alpha = 0.05$ $\beta = 0.05$	$\alpha = 0.05$ $\beta = 0.01$	np_1	c	$\alpha = 0.01$ $\beta = 0.10$	$\alpha = 0.01$ $\beta = 0.05$	$\alpha = 0.01$ $\beta = 0.01$	np_1
0	44.890	58.404	89.781	0.052	0	229.105	298.073	458.210	0.010
1	10.946	13.349	18.681	0.355	1	26.184	31.933	44.686	0.149
2	6.509	7.699	10.280	0.818	2	12.206	14.439	19.278	0.436
3	4.890	5.675	7.352	1.366	3	8.115	9.418	12.202	0.823
4	4.057	4.646	5.890	1.970	4	6.249	7.156	9.072	1.279
5	3.549	4.023	5.017	2.613	5	5.195	5.889	7.343	1.785
6	3.206	3.604	4.435	3.286	6	4.520	5.082	6.253	2.330
7	2.957	3.303	4.019	3.981	7	4.050	4.524	5.506	2.906
8	2.768	3.074	3.707	4.695	8	3.705	4.115	4.962	3.507
9	2.618	2.895	3.462	5.426	9	3.440	3.803	4.548	4.130
10	2.497	2.750	3.265	6.169	10	3.229	3.555	4.222	4.771
11	2.397	2.630	3.104	6.924	11	3.058	3.354	3.959	5.428
12	2.312	2.528	2.968	7.690	12	2.915	3.188	3.742	6.099
13	2.240	2.442	2.852	8.464	13	2.795	3.047	3.559	6.782
14	2.177	2.367	2.752	9.246	14	2.692	2.927	3.403	7.477
15	2.122	2.302	2.665	10.035	15	2.603	2.823	3.269	8.181
16	2.073	2.244	2.588	10.831	16	2.524	2.732	3.151	8.895
17	2.029	2.192	2.520	11.633	17	2.455	2.652	3.048	9.616
18	1.990	2.145	2.458	12.442	18	2.393	2.580	2.956	10.346
19	1.954	2.103	2.403	13.254	19	2.337	2.516	2.874	11.082
20	1.922	2.065	2.352	14.072	20	2.287	2.458	2.799	11.825
21	1.892	2.030	2.307	14.894	21	2.241	2.405	2.733	12.574
22	1.865	1.999	2.265	15.719	22	2.200	2.357	2.671	13.329
23	1.840	1.969	2.226	16.548	23	2.162	2.313	2.615	14.088
24	1.817	1.942	2.191	17.382	24	2.126	2.272	2.564	14.853
25	1.795	1.917	2.158	18.218	25	2.094	2.235	2.516	15.623
26	1.775	1.893	2.127	19.058	26	2.064	2.200	2.472	16.397
27	1.757	1.871	2.098	19.900	27	2.035	2.168	2.431	17.175
28	1.739	1.850	2.071	20.746	28	2.009	2.138	2.393	17.957
29	1.723	1.831	2.046	21.594	29	1.985	2.110	2.358	18.742
30	1.707	1.813	2.023	22.444	30	1.962	2.083	2.324	19.532

Table 17-5   Values of np_1 and c for Constructing Single-sampling Plans Whose OC Curve is Required to Pass through the Two Points $(p_1, \ 1-\alpha)$ and (p_2, β)* *(Continued)*

	Values of p_2/p_1 for:					Values of p_2/p_1 for:			
c	$\alpha = 0.05$ $\beta = 0.10$	$\alpha = 0.05$ $\beta = 0.05$	$\alpha = 0.05$ $\beta = 0.01$	np_1	c	$\alpha = 0.01$ $\beta = 0.10$	$\alpha = 0.01$ $\beta = 0.05$	$\alpha = 0.01$ $\beta = 0.01$	np_1
31	1.692	1.796	2.001	23.298	31	1.940	2.059	2.293	20.324
32	1.679	1.780	1.980	24.152	32	1.920	2.035	2.264	21.120
33	1.665	1.764	1.960	25.010	33	1.900	2.013	2.236	21.919
34	1.653	1.750	1.941	25.870	34	1.882	1.992	2.210	22.721
35	1.641	1.736	1.923	26.731	35	1.865	1.973	2.185	23.525
36	1.630	1.723	1.906	27.594	36	1.848	1.954	2.162	24.333
37	1.619	1.710	1.890	28.460	37	1.833	1.936	2.139	25.143
38	1.609	1.698	1.875	29.327	38	1.818	1.920	2.118	25.955
39	1.599	1.687	1.860	30.196	39	1.804	1.903	2.098	26.770
40	1.590	1.676	1.846	31.066	40	1.790	1.887	2.079	27.587
41	1.581	1.666	1.833	31.938	41	1.777	1.873	2.060	28.406
42	1.572	1.656	1.820	32.812	42	1.765	1.859	2.043	29.228
43	1.564	1.646	1.807	33.686	43	1.753	1.845	2.026	30.051
44	1.556	1.637	1.796	34.563	44	1.742	1.832	2.010	30.877
45	1.548	1.628	1.784	35.441	45	1.731	1.820	1.994	31.704
46	1.541	1.619	1.773	36.320	46	1.720	1.808	1.980	32.534
47	1.534	1.611	1.763	37.200	47	1.710	1.796	1.965	33.365
48	1.527	1.603	1.752	38.082	48	1.701	1.785	1.952	34.198
49	1.521	1.596	1.743	38.965	49	1.691	1.775	1.938	35.032

* Reprinted by permission from J. M. Cameron, "Tables for Constructing and for Computing the Operating Characteristics of Single-sampling Plans," *Industrial Quality Control*, July 1952, pp. 37–39.

It will be noticed in Table 17-5 that provision is made for relatively few values of α and β, and anyone wanting to use the table would have a limited selection. This, however, is not serious, because prevalent practice is to use an α of 0.05 and a β of 0.10. Those firms that do not adhere to these values would probably find the selection offered adequate.

This concludes our discussion of the design of a sampling plan which involves certain stated risks. The specific plan considered was one which would generate an OC curve that would pass through two preselected points. However, other requirements can and have been established. To illustrate, some firms want a plan which will yield an OC curve that will pass through a single stipulated point; for example, the plan may be required to provide a 0.50 probability of accepting a lot which is 2 percent defective. Plans such as the latter can be designed by means of trial and error, with the use of tables of Poisson probabilities, or with the use of special tables which have been developed to yield the sample size and acceptance number directly. But the basic concepts underlying the design of any plan, in which the emphasis is on the control of risk, are those that we have considered.

PLANS WITH STATED AVERAGE OUTGOING QUALITY LIMITS

As mentioned earlier, sampling plans can also be designed to satisfy an established average outgoing quality limit. In theory, the development of such a plan calls for (1) selecting a sample size and acceptance number, (2) calculating the resultant probabilities of acceptance for lots of different quality levels, (3) computing the corresponding AOQ values, (4) comparing the maximum AOQ with the established AOQL, and (5) repeating the procedure with a new sample size and acceptance number if the resultant AOQL proves to be unsatisfactory. The procedures for making the calculations involved have been presented and need not be repeated. Suffice it to say that this approach usually proves to be quite time-consuming.

Fortunately, tables have been developed which provide the required sample size and acceptance number for certain AOQL values. Typical of these are those prepared by Dodge and Romig. An example of one such table is shown as Table 17-6.

This specific table would be used when the established AOQL is 2.0 percent. The first step in its application calls for estimating, on the basis of past experience, the most likely proportion of defectives in the lot, that is, the process average; if this cannot be done, the highest process average, which appears in the last column of the table, is used. Next, the value of the lot size involved is located in the first column. Finally, the required sample size and acceptance number are found by moving to the right until the appropriate process average column is reached.

To illustrate all this, suppose that an incoming lot contains 1,500 items. In the past, lots of this particular product have been approximately 1.5 percent defective. From Table 17-6, we find that an n of 95 and a c of 3 will yield the desired AOQL of 2 percent.

It will be noted that a third value p_t is shown under each process average heading; in our example, this value is equal to 7.0 percent. This number represents the lot proportion of defectives for which the probability of acceptance will be 0.10. Consequently, in our example, an n of 95 and a c of 3 will result in a probability of acceptance of 0.10 for incoming lots that are 7.0 percent defective.

Dodge-Romig tables of this kind are available for thirteen different AOQL values, beginning with 0.1 percent and ending with 10.0. In each

Table 17-6   Example of a Dodge-Romig AOQL Table for an AOQL of 2.0 Percent*

Process average %	0–.04			.05–.40			.41–.80			.81–1.20			1.21–1.60			1.61–2.00		
Lot size	n	c	pt %	n	c	pt %	n	c	pt %	n	c	pt %	n	c	pt %	n	c	pt %
1–15	All	0	....	All	0	....	All	0	....	All	0	....	All	0	....	All	0	....
16–50	14	0	13.6	14	0	13.6	14	0	13.6	14	0	13.6	14	0	13.6	14	0	13.6
51–100	16	0	12.4	16	0	12.4	16	0	12.4	16	0	12.4	16	0	12.4	16	0	12.4
101–200	17	0	12.2	17	0	12.2	17	0	12.2	17	0	12.2	35	1	10.5	35	1	10.5
201–300	17	0	12.3	17	0	12.3	17	0	12.3	37	1	10.2	37	1	10.2	37	1	10.2
301–400	18	0	11.8	18	0	11.8	38	1	10.0	38	1	10.0	38	1	10.0	60	2	8.5
401–500	18	0	11.9	18	0	11.9	39	1	9.8	39	1	9.8	60	2	8.6	60	2	8.6
501–600	18	0	11.9	18	0	11.9	39	1	9.8	39	1	9.8	60	2	8.6	60	2	8.6
601–800	18	0	11.9	40	1	9.6	40	1	9.6	65	2	8.0	65	2	8.0	85	3	7.5
801–1000	18	0	12.0	40	1	9.6	40	1	9.6	65	2	8.1	65	2	8.1	90	3	7.4
1001–2000	18	0	12.0	41	1	9.4	65	2	8.2	65	2	8.2	95	3	7.0	120	4	6.5
2001–3000	18	0	12.0	41	1	9.4	65	2	8.2	95	3	7.0	120	4	6.5	180	6	5.8
3001–4000	18	0	12.0	42	1	9.3	65	2	8.2	95	3	7.0	155	5	6.0	210	7	5.5
4001–5000	18	0	12.0	42	1	9.3	70	2	7.5	125	4	6.4	155	5	6.0	245	8	5.3
5001–7000	18	0	12.0	42	1	9.3	95	3	7.0	125	4	6.4	185	6	5.6	280	9	5.1
7001–10,000	42	1	9.3	70	2	7.5	95	3	7.0	155	5	6.0	220	7	5.4	350	11	4.8
10,001–20,000	42	1	9.3	70	2	7.6	95	3	7.0	190	6	5.6	290	9	4.9	460	14	4.4
20,001–50,000	42	1	9.3	70	2	7.6	125	4	6.4	220	7	5.4	395	12	4.5	720	21	3.9
50,001–100,000	42	1	9.3	95	3	7.0	160	5	5.9	290	9	4.9	505	15	4.2	955	27	3.7

* H. F. Dodge and H. G. Romig, *Sampling Inspection Tables—Single and Double Sampling*, 2d ed., John Wiley & Sons, Inc., New York, 1959.

case, the described plan will yield the required AOQL value and a probability of 0.10 of accepting lots whose proportion of defectives is equal to p_t. Also, if rejected lots are subject to 100 percent inspection, the sampling plan will be such that the total number of items inspected will be less than it would be with some other plan that would yield the same AOQL; this total number consists of the items inspected in each sample and the remaining items inspected in the rejected lots which are assumed to be subject to 100 percent inspection.

LOT TOLERANCE TABLES   The emphasis in the aforementioned tables is placed on the AOQL. Nevertheless, they provide information with regard to a single point through which the resultant OC curve will pass. Another set of Dodge-Romig tables is available for use by those firms who want a plan whose OC curve will pass through a stipulated point but who also want to know the value of the resultant AOQL. The point involved is described in terms of the lot tolerance percent defective and the corresponding probability of acceptance. This probability of acceptance, which is the maximum consumer's risk, is 0.10 for all the seven LTPD values for which tables have been prepared. These values begin with 0.5 percent and end with 10.0. A typical table, which is applicable when the established LTPD is 5.0 percent, is shown as Table 17-7.

To illustrate the use of this table, suppose that a firm establishes an LTPD of 5.0 percent and is willing to accept a maximum consumer's risk of 0.10. Each incoming lot of a given product contains about 700 items. However, the firm is unable to estimate the value of the process average; consequently, it will work with the highest process average represented

Table 17-7 Example of a Dodge-Romig LTPD Table for an LTPD of 5.0 Percent*

Process average %	0–.05			.06–.50			.51–1.00			1.01–1.50			1.51–2.00			2.01–2.50		
Lot size	n	c	AOQL %	n	c	AOQL %	n	c	AOQL %	n	c	AOQL %	n	c	AOQL %	n	c	AOQL %
1–30	All	0	0	All	0	0	All	0	0	All	0	0	All	0	0	All	0	0
31–50	30	0	.49	30	0	.49	30	0	.49	30	0	.49	30	0	.49	30	0	.49
51–100	37	0	.63	37	0	.63	37	0	.63	37	0	.63	37	0	.63	37	0	.63
101–200	40	0	.74	40	0	.74	40	0	.74	40	0	.74	40	0	.74	40	0	.74
201–300	43	0	.74	43	0	.74	70	1	.92	70	1	.92	95	2	.99	95	2	.99
301–400	44	0	.74	44	0	.74	70	1	.99	100	2	1.0	120	3	1.1	145	4	1.1
401–500	45	0	.75	75	1	.95	100	2	1.1	100	2	1.1	125	3	1.2	150	4	1.2
501–600	45	0	.76	75	1	.98	100	2	1.1	125	3	1.2	150	4	1.3	175	5	1.3
601–800	45	0	.77	75	1	1.0	100	2	1.2	130	3	1.2	175	5	1.4	200	6	1.4
801–1000	45	0	.78	75	1	1.0	105	2	1.2	155	4	1.4	180	5	1.4	225	7	1.5
1001–2000	45	0	.80	75	1	1.0	130	3	1.4	180	5	1.6	230	7	1.7	280	9	1.8
2001–3000	75	1	1.1	105	2	1.3	135	3	1.4	210	6	1.7	280	9	1.9	370	13	2.1
3001–4000	75	1	1.1	105	2	1.3	160	4	1.5	210	6	1.7	305	10	2.0	420	15	2.2
4001–5000	75	1	1.1	105	2	1.3	160	4	1.5	235	7	1.8	330	11	2.0	440	16	2.2
5001–7000	75	1	1.1	105	2	1.3	185	5	1.7	260	8	1.9	350	12	2.2	490	18	2.4
7001–10,000	75	1	1.1	105	2	1.3	185	5	1.7	260	8	1.9	380	13	2.2	535	20	2.5
10,001–20,000	75	1	1.1	135	3	1.4	210	6	1.8	285	9	2.0	425	15	2.3	610	23	2.6
20,001–50,000	75	1	1.1	135	3	1.4	235	7	1.9	305	10	2.1	470	17	2.4	700	27	2.7
50,001–100,000	75	1	1.1	160	4	1.6	235	7	1.9	355	12	2.2	515	19	2.5	770	30	2.8

* H. F. Dodge and H. G. Romig, *Sampling Inspection Tables—Single and Double Sampling*, 2d ed., John Wiley & Sons, Inc., New York, 1959.

in the table. Doing so, it will find that the sample size should be 200, and the acceptance number 6. Furthermore, this plan will yield an AOQL of 1.4 percent.

It should also be mentioned that, as in the case of the Dodge-Romig AOQL tables, the LTPD tables will provide the firm with a plan which will require the inspection of fewer items, if rejected lots are screened, than would any other plan whose OC curve passes through the same stipulated point.

DOUBLE AND MULTIPLE SAMPLING PLANS

Although we have concentrated on typical single-sample acceptance plans, it should be repeated that other plans do exist. One of these calls for double sampling. With such a plan, it may be necessary to take two samples before reaching a decision concerning whether a lot should be accepted or rejected. For example, a specific plan of this type might be described as follows:

$$n_1 = 35 \qquad n_2 = 60$$
$$c_1 = 0 \qquad c_2 = 2$$

where $n_1 =$ size of first sample

$n_2 =$ size of second sample

$c_1 =$ maximum number of defectives in the first sample that will permit acceptance of the lot

$c_2 =$ maximum number of defectives in the *combined* samples that will permit acceptance of the lot

This means that, in our example, an initial sample of 35 items would be taken. If the sample contained 0 defectives, the lot would be accepted, and if the sample contained 3 or more defectives, the lot would be rejected. However, if the sample contained 1 or 2 defectives, a second sample of 60 items would be taken. If the combined sample of 95 items contained more than 2 defectives, the lot would be rejected; otherwise, it would be accepted.

SEQUENTIAL SAMPLING   Multiple sampling plans are those in which three or more samples might be taken before a decision is reached regarding the acceptability of a lot. An extreme case is sequential sampling in which sampling might continue until the lot is exhausted. A plan such as this is partially described in Figure 17-7.

In general, sequential sampling calls for inspection on an item-by-item basis and making a decision after each item is inspected concerning whether the lot should be accepted or rejected or sampling continued. Let us illustrate this with reference to Figure 17-7. Suppose 5 items had been inspected. If 0 defectives had been found, the resultant point on the graph would fall in the area "accept lot," and the lot would be accepted. If 4

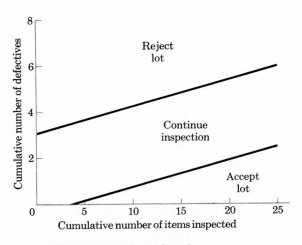

Figure 17-7   A sequential sampling plan

defectives had been found, the lot would be rejected. But if 3 defectives had been found, inspection would continue; specifically, one more item would be selected and inspected, and the resultant point located on the graph. This would continue until the lot was accepted or rejected. Actually, graphs are rarely employed. Instead, a table is prepared in which acceptance and rejection numbers are shown for the different values of the cumulative number of items inspected.

Double and multiple sampling plans can be designed to satisfy such requirements as those considered in our discussion of single-sample plans. As a rule, these plans require less total inspection for a given level of quality protection than do single-sample plans. However, the latter can be more easily interpreted and, hence, are less likely to be applied incorrectly by inspectors.

NATURE OF THE SAMPLE

This concludes our discussion of acceptance sampling. Its advantages and disadvantages, as compared with 100 percent inspection, have been presented and will not be repeated here. However, it is worth emphasizing that all sampling has associated with it some risk of error.

Also, it is important to note that the theory we have employed is based on the assumption that the sample taken is a random one. This means that the items should be drawn in such a way that every article in the population has the same chance of being selected. Often this is difficult to accomplish, but at least an effort can be made to avoid any obvious type of bias.

For example, it would be incorrect to establish a practice of always selecting the items to be included in the sample from the top of the containers in which the lot might have been delivered, because with this approach, the other items have no chance of being included in the sample.

Furthermore, there is no need to choose items that were produced at about the same time, as was the case in sampling for control chart purposes. In acceptance sampling, an incoming lot is, by definition, a single population, and, as a result, there is no risk of items from more than one population appearing in the sample.

PROCESSING DATA

Having completed the last topic we shall consider in the area of quality control, we might note that this is another area in which a need arises for the handling of numerical data and, hence, provides an opportunity for the application of automatic data processing equipment. When control charts are being employed, the equipment can be used to process the information that has been obtained for the purpose of estimating population means and dispersions and calculating trial control limits. In the case of control charts for variables and for defects, determination of the level at which the involved process is in control can be followed by the calculation of the percent defective work that can be expected at that level.

Insofar as acceptance sampling is concerned, we know that special tables have been prepared for use in the design of an appropriate plan. However, a given firm may want a plan with characteristics such that existing tables prove to be unsuitable, and, consequently, a trial-and-error approach must be employed. When this is the case, data processing equipment can be utilized to make the computations necessary to ascertain such things as probabilities of acceptance and average outgoing quality limits to be associated with alternative plans.

OTHER APPLICATIONS

We have seen how control charts and acceptance sampling plans can be used to maintain or determine product quality. Although our examples were chosen from the manufacturing area, the techniques of statistical quality control can be applied, as well, to the results of other types of activities. To illustrate, let us consider the output of office activities, such as filling out forms, typing letters, maintaining records, processing data, and the like. In these instances, satisfactory output would consist of forms, letters, records, and reports that would contain no, or some acceptable number of, errors. For quality control purposes, each error could be defined as a defect, or each unit of output that contains an error could be defined as a defective. It follows that a control chart for attributes could be constructed and maintained, and with its use, the average number of errors per sample or the population proportion of defectives could be controlled at an acceptable level.

As another illustration, let us consider the need, in both manufacturing and nonmanufacturing organizations, to determine whether records of such things as inventories, accounts receivable, accounts payable, and the like are accurate. The complete record of any one of these things represents a population. For example, a bank can be said to have a population of savings accounts. Periodically, a need arises to audit records to determine whether they are accurate. There is no reason why an approach based on the principles of acceptance sampling cannot be applied. To continue with the savings account example, a sample of accounts could be taken and verified. If the sample proves to be satisfactory, the entire population of accounts would be accepted as being satisfactory. Otherwise, every account in the population would be verified; that is, the population would be subjected to 100 percent inspection.

Mention should also be made of the fact that the techniques of statistical quality control have applications other than that of maintaining or determining the quality of an organization's output. For example, in either a manufacturing or nonmanufacturing enterprise, it may be important that a certain average time to perform a repetitive task be maintained so that a target completion date can be met or so that labor costs do not become excessive. In this case, control charts for variables can be established in which the variable is the elapsed time. Samples of elapsed times for the task could be taken and evaluated to determine whether a satisfactory population of times is being realized.

As another example of this type of application, we can consider the need to keep at an acceptable level the proportion of time spent on nonessential activities by an organization's personnel. The individuals involved might be teachers, salesmen, doctors, administrators, service personnel, machine operators, and the like. The desired control could be maintained with the use of a p chart in which p' would represent the acceptable proportion of total time spent on nonessential tasks. Work sampling studies could be made, by means to be discussed in a subsequent chapter, to determine sample proportions of nonessential-activity time, and these sample proportions could be located on the control chart to ascertain whether the desired population proportion is being maintained.

In brief, the statistical approaches we have considered have product and nonproduct applications. Furthermore, the opportunities for these applications exist in every type of organization.

QUESTIONS

17-1 What is acceptance sampling? Why is it often a better approach than 100 percent inspection?

17-2 Define single-sample acceptance sampling by attributes.

17-3 What must be determined when a sampling plan is being designed?

17-4 Define consumer's risk. Producer's risk.

17-5 What is an operating characteristic curve?

17-6 How does an *ideal* OC curve differ from others?

17-7 What does the acceptance number represent?

17-8 What is the usual method of sampling in industry?

17-9 How is the shape of the OC curve affected by an increase in the sample size? By an increase in the acceptance number?

17-10 What is meant by the average outgoing quality of incoming lots?

17-11 What is the average outgoing quality limit?

17-12 An operating characteristic curve that is required to pass through two stipulated points can be described in terms of the following: (*a*) acceptable quality level, (*b*) acceptable quality region, (*c*) lot tolerance percent defective, (*d*) indifferent quality region, (*e*) objectionable quality region, (*f*) producer's risk, and (*g*) consumer's risk. Define each of these terms.

17-13 Under what conditions are Poisson probabilities good approximations of hypergeometric probabilities?

17-14 In the absence of available tables, what approach must be employed in the design of an acceptance plan that will yield a desired OC curve?

17-15 In the absence of available tables, what approach must be employed in the design of an acceptance plan that will yield a stipulated AOQL?

17-16 What are double sampling plans? Sequential sampling plans?

17-17 The sample taken from an incoming lot should be a random sample. What is a random sample?

17-18 How can data processing equipment be used in the area of quality control?

17-19 What are some examples of activities, other than manufacturing, to which the techniques of statistical quality control can be applied?

17-20 Can the methods of statistical quality control be used to control things other than the quality of an organization's output? Explain.

PROBLEMS

17-1 An auditing firm periodically examines a bank's savings accounts. The bank operates in a small town and has only 200 such accounts. In any case, the procedure calls for taking a random sample of 20 accounts and determining whether or not they contain errors. If none do, it is assumed that all the bank's accounts are in order. But if one or more of the accounts prove to be inaccurate, that is, defective, the entire population of 200 accounts is checked. In brief, the auditors adhere to a single-sample acceptance plan with an acceptance number of 0 and a sample size of 20 for a lot of size 200.

Construct the operating characteristic curve which serves to describe this plan. Do this by calculating the respective probabilities of accepting populations of accounts which are 0, 1, 3, 6, 10, 15, 20, 30, and 100 percent defective and then plotting the results. When computing probabilities, do so by the hypergeometric method, that is, with the use of Eq. (17-1). (Ans. 1.000, 0.810, 0.527, 0.272, 0.108, 0.032, 0.009, 0.001, 0)

17-2 Assume that the sampling plan described in the preceding problem is revised so that the acceptance number is now 1. If the other data remain unchanged, what will be the new probabilities of acceptance? Construct the resultant OC curve on the same graph that contains the original curve.

17-3 With the data given and the results obtained in problem 17-1, compute the average outgoing quality for each of the given population proportions and identify the average outgoing quality limit. Ignore the fact that an incomplete set of population proportions of inaccurate accounts has been considered. Construct the resultant AOQ curve and note the location of the AOQL. (Ans. 0, 0.0081, 0.0158, 0.0163, 0.0108, 0.0048, 0.0018, 0.0003, 0)

17-4 Do all the things called for in the preceding problem with the data given and the results obtained in problem 17-2.

17-5 Compute the probabilities of acceptance in problem 17-1 by the Poisson method. Do this by, first, making the appropriate substitutions in Eq. (17-3) and, then, solving the resultant expressions with the use of Figure 17-6. Compare the results with those obtained by the hypergeometric method in problem 17-1. (Ans. 1.000, 0.819, 0.549, 0.301, 0.135, 0.050, 0.018, 0.002, 0)

17-6 Compute the probabilities of acceptance in problem 17-2 by the Poisson method and compare the results with those obtained in problem 17-2. In your determination of the probabilities, make the necessary substitutions in Eq. (17-3) and solve the resultant expressions with the use of Figure 17-6.

17-7 With the use of Table 17-5, design a single-sample acceptance plan for each of the following conditions:

  a Acceptable quality level is 0.02; lot tolerance percent defective is 0.07; producer's risk is to be 0.05; and consumer's risk is to be 0.01. (Ans. 235, 8)

  b Acceptable quality level is 0.03; lot tolerance percent defective is 0.08; consumer's risk is to be 0.10; and producer's risk is to be 0.01.

  c Lot tolerance percent defective is 0.12; acceptable quality level is 0.01; producer's risk is to be 0.05; and consumer's risk is to be 0.05.

17-8 A city purchasing department wants to design a single-sample acceptance plan for use in passing judgment on the quality of shipments from the firms with which it places orders. The only requirement is that the plan be such that the probability be 0.50 that incoming lots that are 2.5 percent defective will be accepted. With the use of Figure 17-6, determine three such plans.

17-9   A company wants to adopt a single-sample acceptance plan which will yield
an average outgoing quality limit of 2.0 percent. With the use of Table 17-6,
design such a plan for each of the following conditions and determine what
lot proportion of defectives will have a probability of acceptance of 0.10
with this plan:

   a Lot size is 4,200, and the process average is 1.0 percent. (Ans. 125, 4,
   6.4%)

   b Lot size is 10,000, and the process average is unknown.

   c Lot size is 15, and the process average is 0.3 percent.

17-10   A firm has established a lot tolerance percent defective of 5.0 and a maximum consumer's risk of 0.10 and wants a single-sample acceptance plan
whose OC curve will pass through the point these values represent. With
the use of Table 17-7, design such a plan for each of the following conditions and determine the resultant average outgoing quality limit:

   a Lot size is 17,500, and the process average is unknown. (Ans. 610, 23,
   2.6%)

   b Lot size is 25, and the process average is 2.0 percent.

   c Lot size is 475, and the process average is 1.4 percent.

17-11   The following double sampling plan has been adopted for use by a company:

$$n_1 = 100 \qquad n_2 = 200$$
$$c_1 = 1 \qquad c_2 = 3$$

What maximum *proportion* of defectives can the second sample contain if
the lot is to be accepted after the first sample has been found to contain:

   a No defectives?

   b Two defectives?

   c Four defectives?

   d Three defectives?

   e One defective?

17-12   Assume that the sequential sampling plan described in Figure 17-7 is in
effect and is being applied in the evaluation of a lot which has just been
received. What action would be taken at each of the following possible
points in the sampling procedure?

   a Six items are found to contain no defectives.

   b Twenty-two items are found to contain eight defectives.

   c Two items are found to contain no defectives.

   d Nineteen items are found to contain one defective.

   e Twelve items are found to contain three defectives.

   f Nine items are found to contain six defectives.

PART EIGHT
WORK METHODS

EIGHTEEN
METHODS ANALYSIS

Thus far, we have considered measures that can be employed by a firm in its attempt to manufacture a satisfactory product, in the required quantities, and in time to meet established delivery dates. At various points in this discussion, reference was made to the need for efficient work methods. However, specific approaches to the development of such methods have not been presented. These approaches will now be considered.

METHODS IMPROVEMENT OPPORTUNITIES

The firm that is concerned with efficient work methods realizes that the planning for these methods must begin with the design and process engineers. Therefore, the design engineer will take care to develop a design which will minimize production costs without affecting the function and consumer acceptability of the product adversely. This means that he will recognize that some materials are more costly than others, that extremely close tolerances will increase operating times and the amount of defective output, that smoother finishes may make additional operations necessary, and that a more complicated design will increase the required number of operations and possibly necessitate the use of more costly equipment and manpower.

Similarly, the process engineer will take care to select production methods which will involve the most economical sequence of operations and the use of the most efficient equipment and accessories available and will specify how the production facilities are to be operated so as to minimize processing times. It will be recalled that all this information is presented in the form of an operation, or routing, sheet such as the one shown earlier in Figure 3-1.

However, the instructions provided by the process engineer are fairly general in nature. To illustrate, he may state that an operation is to be performed on a punch press, but he will not describe the work methods which should be employed at that work station; yet one layout or pattern of activity at this work station may be more efficient than some other. In brief, there are factors that will influence the effectiveness of work methods but with which the process engineer does not concern himself. For this reason, the firm will have methods analysts study these other factors.

Thus far, we have concentrated on those activities whose nature will be directly affected by the decisions reached by the design and process engineers. However, there are numerous activities in every plant for which nothing comparable to an operation sheet is prepared. These would include work performed by members of the shipping and receiving department, by personnel in stockrooms, by members of machine-repair crews, by members of the inspection department, and the like. If the best methods of performing these functions are to be employed, someone must ascertain what these methods are. This will be the responsibility of the firm's methods analysts, and the firm which is interested in the use of efficient work methods will provide for the study of these activities at the time they are to be inaugurated.

In summary, the company which is concerned with the development of efficient original work methods will realize that the proper development of these methods calls for the cooperative efforts of the design engineer, process engineer, and methods analyst. However, even a firm such as this will find that opportunities for methods improvements present themselves. The reason for this is that the best available methods at one point in time will not necessarily be the best available methods at some later point. Subsequent investigations may reveal that more economical materials are available; more efficient machines, tools, jigs, and fixtures have been designed; better inspection methods have evolved; more satisfactory materials handling equipment can now be procured; the existing plant layout is obsolete because of a change in the product mix; and so on. This suggests that there is a continuing need for analyzing existing methods even in the case in which special efforts are expended to develop efficient original work methods.

As all this suggests, the methods analysis activity is one in which an attempt is made to develop efficient methods for tasks which are to be performed for the first time and to improve existing work methods. Nevertheless, in our presentation of the various techniques of methods analysis, we shall concentrate on the approach to be followed in the improvement of existing methods rather than that to be followed in the selection of original work methods. The reason for this is that, in most cases, methods for performing tasks already exist, which is to say that new activities account for a relatively small proportion of a firm's total activities; therefore, the usual problem confronting a methods analyst is one of methods improvement. Furthermore, the same principles and guides that enable the firm to improve upon an existing method will serve as a basis for the development of efficient original methods. This is true because any proposed method can be considered to be an existing method and evaluated accordingly.

THE PROCESS CHART APPROACH

All the techniques for making an analysis of existing work methods have one common characteristic: They call for ascertaining and describing the method that is currently being employed. This can be done in a number of different ways, but a particularly effective one is the process chart approach.

In general, a process chart is a unique manner of describing an existing method. It is unique in the sense that there is reason to believe that, if the description assumes this form, the analyst is more likely to get ideas for possible improvements than he otherwise would.

A number of different kinds of process charts are available for use. The specific chart to be constructed in a given case will depend on the nature of the activity being studied and the amount of detail the analyst would like to include in his description. We shall consider only the basic process charts, the conditions under which they are employed, and the manner in which they are used to make a methods improvement. The first of these is the *flow process chart.*

THE MATERIAL FLOW PROCESS CHART

A flow process chart is defined by the American Society of Mechanical Engineers in the following manner:

A graphic presentation of the sequence of all operations, transportations, inspections, delays, and storages occurring during a process or procedure, and includes information considered desirable for analysis such as time required and distance moved. [1]

There are two types of flow process charts. The first is the *material type,* in which the analyst records what happens to the materials involved in the production process he is studying. The points at which these materials enter the process are shown, and then the operations, transportations, inspections, delays, and storages to which the materials are subjected are described in the order in which they occur. This raises the question of what an operation is, what a transportation is, and so on. Definitions of these respective activities are also included in the ASME standards.

OPERATIONS   The definition of an "operation" is as follows:

An operation occurs when an object is intentionally changed in any of its physical or chemical characteristics, is assembled or disassembled from another object, or

---

[1] *ASME Standard Operation and Flow Process Charts,* American Society of Mechanical Engineers, New York, 1962.

is arranged or prepared for another operation, transportation, inspection, or storage. An operation also occurs when information is given or received or when planning or calculating takes place.

The definition states that an operation occurs when an object is changed in any of its physical characteristics. An example of this would be an activity in which a hole is drilled in a block of metal. The physical characteristics of the drilled block differ from those of the solid block, and, hence, the material has been subjected to an operation. Insofar as a change in chemical characteristics is concerned, some processes call for, say, the mixing of liquids. The resultant mixture may have all the physical characteristics, such as color, of the component liquids, and yet its chemical characteristics are unlike those of the component liquids. As a result, an operation has taken place.

We are also told that an assembly or a disassembly is an operation. It may be that at some point it is necessary to assemble or disassemble component parts. Although the physical and chemical characteristics of each of the parts remain unchanged, the analyst would classify the activity as an operation.

Next, the definition states that arranging or preparing material for some subsequent activity is an operation. For example, the operator may be placing the material in a machine prior to drilling a hole in it, and, hence, the material is being arranged or prepared for an operation. Consequently, this arrangement or preparation would be called an operation. In another case, the operator may be placing objects in a container in which they will be transported to another location. Again, this is an arrangement or a preparation for a transportation and, hence, would be classified as an operation. As another illustration, parts may have been delivered to an inspector who unloads and positions them at his work station prior to inspecting them. This is an arrangement or a preparation for an inspection and would be considered to be an operation. Finally, the inspected parts may be delivered to the stockroom, where they are placed in bins. Placing them in the bins is synonymous with arranging them for storage and, hence, would be classified as an operation.

The definition ends with a reference to an exchange of information and to a planning or calculating activity. Information is given, for example, when a foreman tells the operator what job he should perform next. Information is received, for example, when an operator is told how a machine should be set up. Planning and calculating may take place when an operator studies a blueprint to determine how the part is to be processed and to determine how he should operate his machine. All such activities would be called operations.

TRANSPORTATIONS The next term in the description of a material flow process chart is "transportation." This activity is defined as follows:

A transportation occurs when an object is moved from one place to another, except when such movements are a part of the operation or are caused by the operator at the work station during an operation or an inspection.

This definition can be best understood by concentrating on the exceptions. We are told that movements which are a part of the operation are not considered to be transportations. For example, in a planing operation, the material moves back and forth against a stationary cutting tool. Although the material is moving from one place to another, this movement is an integral part of the operation itself and, hence, would not be considered to be a transportation. It is also stated that movements of the material caused by the operator at the work station are not transportations. As an example, it will be necessary for the operator to move materials when placing them in the machine or removing them from the machine. However, this movement is necessary to prepare or arrange the material for an operation or a transportation, and, therefore, it is considered to be an operation and not a transportation.

In general, a transportation occurs only when materials are moved from one work station to another. This may be from one production center to another production center, from the raw-material stockroom to a production center, from a production center to the finished-goods stockroom, from the finished-goods stockroom to the shipping department, and so on.

From this definition of a transportation and the earlier definition of an operation, we can conclude that the material flow process chart would be used when the process being studied is one in which materials move from one work station to another rather than one in which materials remain at a single work station.

INSPECTIONS The third activity which might appear in a material flow process chart is called an "inspection." It is defined in the following manner:

An inspection occurs when an object is examined for identification or is verified for quality or quantity in any of its characteristics.

An example of an examination for identification would be the case of the individual in the stockroom who receives parts which are to be placed in appropriate bins. It will be necessary for him to identify the parts before he can decide where they should be stored. This identification would be an inspection.

Insofar as verification for quality is concerned, the individual who determines whether a particular part meets established specifications is performing an inspection.

Finally, we have verifications for quantity. An example of this would be what occurs at the receiving dock when a shipment of materials is received. The invoice may state that the shipment contains 50 cases of a certain item. Before signing the invoice, the receiving clerk will probably count the cases to see whether the stipulated quantity is correct. This verification for quantity is an inspection.

STORAGES AND DELAYS   Another term that appears in the definition of the material flow process chart is "storage." The storage activity is defined as follows:

A storage occurs when an object is kept and protected against unauthorized removal.

There is little one can add to this. If raw materials are received and placed in a stockroom from which they are removed as they are needed, the materials are being stored. If finished parts are sent to a finished-goods stockroom from which they are shipped as orders are received, the finished goods are being stored. Unfortunately, confusion concerning whether a storage is taking place under certain conditions is sometimes created by the presence of a fifth activity, which is included in the description of the material flow process chart. This is "delay." Delay is defined in the following manner:

A delay occurs to an object when conditions, except those which intentionally change the physical or chemical characteristics of the object, do not permit or require immediate performance of the next planned step.

This definition may raise the question of the difference between a storage and a delay. To illustrate, to take advantage of quantity discounts, the company may buy its raw materials in such large lots that they must be stored for about three weeks before they are actually used. But if the company decides that it is economical to do so, it will buy the large lots, and the storage becomes a planned and required step which prevents the subsequent step from being performed. Because it is planned and required, the activity will be a storage and not a delay. But let us now turn to a different type of storage. In many plants, when work in process is delivered to a work station, the operator is unable to begin the required operation immediately on all the material that has been delivered to him. Instead, there will be a time lag. Everyone knows and accepts this, although no formal decision had been made to store these materials at the various work stations. Informally, however, it had been decided that it would be uneconomical to make other arrangements. In effect, the resultant storage was not planned; on the contrary, it just evolved over a period of time. As a result, the analyst often wonders whether the activity should be called a delay or a storage.

Fortunately, the question is of no consequence in practice. If something is not an operation, inspection, or a transportation, all of which are easily identified, then it must be a storage or delay. Whether the analyst calls it a storage or a delay is of little importance in the subsequent analysis so long as what is occurring is clearly described.

OTHER PROCESS CHART CHARACTERISTICS The description of the material flow process chart also states that the chart is a graphic presentation. This means that the information it contains is recorded in the form of a diagram in which the analyst makes use of both verbal descriptions and symbols to depict the various activities involved in the process being studied. The symbols for the five activities we have discussed are as follows:

Activity	Symbol
Operation	○
Transportation	→
Inspection	□
Storage	▽
Delay	D

Finally, the definition of the chart contains a clause to the effect that any other information considered desirable for analysis can be recorded. Time required and distances moved are mentioned specifically. Other items of information occasionally included are such things as the locations at which the various activities take place, machine names and numbers, and so forth.

AN ILLUSTRATION Let us supplement the preceding explanation with an illustration of what a completed material flow process chart looks like.

Suppose that a company is interested in improving upon the method employed in the production of a sliding panel door used in a certain type of cabinet it manufactures. The analyst examines one of the completed doors and finds that it consists of three different component parts. One of these is an 8- by 10- by ¼-inch flat aluminum plate which contains two holes; the second is an aluminum handle which has a rivet hole in each end; and the third is a pair of standard ⅜-inch diameter rivets by means of which the handle is fastened to the plate.

The analyst begins by describing the existing method for manufacturing the door. His description takes the form of the material flow process chart shown in Figure 18-1.

At this point, what the analyst has is a record of the method being em-

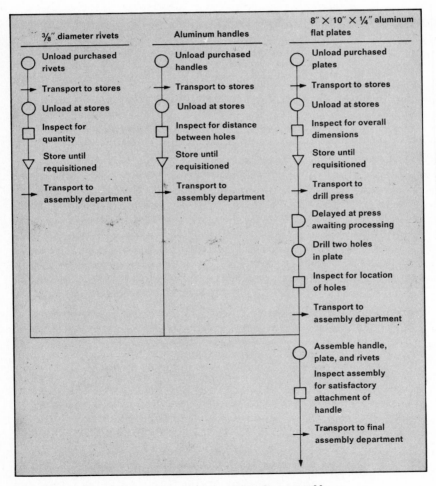

Figure 18-1 Material flow process chart for sliding-door assembly

ployed at the present time. This is extremely important because a knowledge of what is taking place must precede any attempt to improve upon the method. However, the construction of the process chart is not an end in itself. The analyst is now confronted by the task of improving upon the method. But there is nothing about the completed chart which will generate a stream of ideas. These must come from the analyst, and unfortunately, there is no procedure which, if followed, will reveal with certainty what the most efficient method is.

However, it has been found that there is an approach which, more often than not, will prove to be effective. This approach is as follows: The analyst examines the activities described in the material flow process chart and directs the following questions toward each of these activities: Why, What, How, Where, Who, and When? There is reason to believe that the answers to these questions will, as a rule, provide the analyst with ideas for possible improvements. Let us see what happens when we apply the approach to a few of the activities included in the production of the sliding panel door assembly.

The analyst has found that the purchased materials are first unloaded. He may ask himself: How are they unloaded? and find that a man unloads them from a truck manually by carrying out one case at a time. A possible improvement might be to use a forklift truck to unload the materials. Turning to another activity, the analyst may ask himself: Who unloads the materials at the storeroom prior to inspection? and find that this work is done by the inspectors, who fall into the category of skilled labor and are paid accordingly. A possible improvement might be to have this work done by lower-priced unskilled labor. Insofar as the inspection activities are concerned, the analyst may ask: How is the part or material inspected? and find that every unit of a specific part is subjected to inspection and that a certain kind of gauge is used. A possible improvement may be to engage in sampling inspection, or possibly, a special gauge can be designed which will reduce the inspection time. With regard to the storage activities, he can ask: Why are the materials kept in stores for an average of so-many days? An investigation may reveal that it would be more economical to procure the materials in smaller lot sizes and thereby increase the inventory turnover. Keeping in mind the delay experienced with the flat plates at the drill press, the analyst may ask: When are the materials delivered to this work station? and find that they are delivered at the beginning of each shift, with the result that valuable floor space in the plant is being utilized for storage. An improvement may be to schedule periodic deliveries of the material to the drill press throughout the day. With regard to the assembly activity, the analyst may ask: Where are the component parts assembled? and find that the location of this production center is such that the component parts must be transported relatively large distances to reach the assembly area and, further, that the completed assemblies must be transported relatively large distances to reach the final assembly department, where they will be installed in cabinets. Relocating this production center may be an alternative which would represent an improvement. As a final illustration, the analyst may ask: What is the nature of the materials from which the component parts are produced? In this case they happen to be aluminum. However, it may be that savings could be realized from the substitution of some cheaper metal alloy which would be just as satisfactory.

These few examples suffice to demonstrate the manner in which the general approach is applied. They also suffice to demonstrate a number of other things. One is that the approach is effective only if the analyst has

---

I. WITH REGARD TO OPERATIONS:

1. Can the operation be eliminated by:
   a. The use of different material?
   b. A change in the design of the part?
2. Can the operation be combined with some other activity in a way which will reduce the unit production cost?
3. Will a change in the sequence of the operations be of value?
4. Can the operation be performed more economically through the use of different:
   a. Equipment?
   b. Tools, jigs, and fixtures?
5. Can the layout of the work station at which the operation is performed be improved upon?
6. Would it be economical to subcontract the work?
7. Will subdividing the operation help?
8. Is the operation performed by personnel who will minimize the labor cost per unit?
9. Should the operation be performed at some other location in the plant so as to minimize handling costs?
10. Are working conditions, such as heat, light, and ventilation, satisfactory?
11. Is the equipment being operated properly?
12. Are the most economical materials being used?
13. Can anything be done to reduce scrap and defective output?
14. Is the work scheduled in economic lot sizes?

II. WITH REGARD TO INSPECTIONS:

1. Is the inspection necessary?
2. Are the best-suited gauges being used?
3. Can sampling inspection be substituted for 100 per cent inspection?
4. Can the finish, tolerance, and allowance requirements be relaxed?
5. Can the inspection be more economically performed by the machine operator than by an inspector?
6. Is anything to be gained by using statistical quality control techniques in the manufacturing departments?
7. Can the layout of the station at which the inspection is performed be improved upon?
8. Will it help to have parts delivered to a central location for inspection, or is it better to have inspections performed at various production centers?

Figure 18-2   A typical flow process chart checklist

some knowledge of alternative methods. The few questions that were presented in our illustration suggested that it would be desirable that the analyst know something about inspection procedures, statistical quality control, materials handling equipment, plant layout, and available raw materials. But just as important, it is necessary that the analyst be able to formulate correct specific questions and that he be able to use the answers as a basis for getting ideas. To aid him in doing so, checklists have been developed. These consist of questions whose nature is such that they often succeed in providing the analyst with ideas for possible improvements when applied to the activities recorded in a material flow process chart. Many guides of this kind have been developed. A typical one is shown in Figure 18-2.

9. Does the inspector have the required skill; that is, is the company paying for more skill than is necessary or, conversely, utilizing personnel who possess less skill than is necessary?
10. Can a number of inspections be combined to reduce handling time?

III. WITH REGARD TO TRANSPORTATIONS:

1. Can the distances traveled be reduced by a change in the plant layout?
2. Can quantities transported at one time be increased to reduce unit handling costs?
3. Will it be economical to replace manual methods by mechanical methods or mechanical methods by manual methods?
4. Are materials loaded and unloaded at the correct locations?
5. Can the means for dispatching equipment be improved upon?
6. Is the most efficient kind of mechanized equipment being used?
7. Is the equipment being operated at the correct speed?
8. Can handling be made easier by the use of containers, racks, and trays of appropriate design?
9. Can an operation, such as painting, be performed while the material is being transported?
10. Can cheaper labor be used to handle and transport material?

IV. WITH REGARD TO STORAGES AND DELAYS:

1. Can the delivery of materials be scheduled to eliminate or reduce storage time?
2. Are storages caused by order quantities which are too large?
3. Are materials stored at the most convenient locations?
4. Are materials stored in such a way as to minimize breakage, deterioration, and theft?
5. Is the layout of the storeroom such that materials being delivered or received can be loaded and unloaded with little difficulty?
6. Can the number or length of storages and delays be minimized by:
   a. Establishing better production schedules?
   b. Providing wider aisles or more aisles?
   c. Increasing the output capacity of the plant?
   d. Combining certain activities?
   e. Performing more than one activity at a given location?
7. Is time lost because of frequent job transfers?
8. Do the employees experience delays because instructions are not made available on time or because production facilities, such as men, machines, and materials, are not available when needed?

It will be noted that the questions listed in Figure 18-2 are fairly general so that they would prove to be relevant in a large number of situations. However, a given company can compile more specific check questions, related to its activities, which would prove to be of greater value to its methods analysts than the check questions of a more general nature. In any case, even the best checklists are only aids, and there is nothing inherent in them which will ensure the development of the most economical method.

THE MAN FLOW PROCESS CHART

The second kind of flow process chart is the *man type*. The general definition of this chart is the same as the one given for the material flow process chart. However, there are differences between the two. Whereas the material flow process chart describes the activities to which materials are subjected, the man type depicts the operations and inspections performed by a man, the transportations in which he engages, and the delays he experiences. But the storage activity is not considered, because it cannot be performed by a man.

Another difference between the two types of process charts lies in their area of application. While the material flow process chart is used when the analyst is interested in learning of the activities to which materials are subjected, the man flow process chart is used when the analyst is interested in learning of the activities which a man is performing. The man who would be studied by means of a chart such as this would be a man whose activities require that he move from one work station to another. Examples of such tasks would be the work of a messenger, a watchman, a materials handler, a maintenance man, and the like. But this is similar to the condition under which a material flow process chart would be employed. It will be recalled that the process described by means of a material flow process chart was one in which materials moved from one work station to another rather than one in which materials remained at a single work station.

AN ILLUSTRATION   Let us now illustrate the application, construction, and analysis of a man flow process chart. In doing so, we shall return to the production of the sliding panel door referred to earlier. One of the materials used in the production of this assembly was an aluminum flat plate. If we refer back to our material flow process chart, we find that, after being stored, these plates are taken from the storeroom and delivered to the drill press. Following the drilling operation, they are taken to an area where they are assembled with rivets and handles. Finally, the assembled door is delivered to the assembly area, where it is installed in a cabinet.

Suppose that there is one man whose responsibility it is to perform these materials handling functions and that the analyst is interested in improving upon the methods employed by this man. He begins by constructing a man flow process chart in which the present method is described. This description is shown in Figure 18-3.

With this information at his disposal, the analyst uses the same method of analysis described in the discussion of the material flow process chart. This approach calls for his directing the following questions toward each of the activities described in this process chart: What is done? Who does this? When is this done? Where is this done? How is this done? Why? Let us now apply this method of analysis to our illustration and see what the results are.

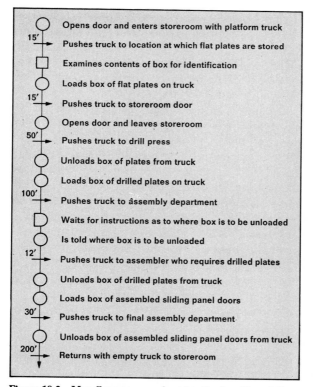

Figure 18-3 Man flow process chart for the handling of flat plates and assembled sliding panel doors

First, the analyst may concern himself with where the flat plates are kept in the storeroom. As can be seen from the chart, it is at some location which requires the materials handler to walk 15 feet to obtain the plates after he enters the room. It may be that the storage area can be relocated in the room so as to reduce this distance. Next, the analyst might ask why the man loads only one box of plates in the storeroom, one box of drilled plates at the drill press, and one box of sliding panel doors at the assembly station. It might be possible to have him transport more than one box at a time. Also, the analyst might question the efficiency of the plant layout, which creates a need for the handler to travel relatively large distances from one work station to another. It might be that one or more of these stations can be effectively relocated with respect to the others. Further, the analyst might ask why it is necessary for the man to wait for instructions concerning where the drilled plates are to be unloaded in the assembly department. A more satisfactory alternative may be to provide him with a single and fixed set of instructions indicating the order in which the assemblers are to receive the plates. Finally, the analyst might ask how the materials are transported and why these means are employed. For example, it may be that the use of a forklift truck would be a more economical method for transporting the plates, or it might be expedient to install a belt conveyor for the purpose of carrying the assembled doors to the final assembly department.

These are but a few of the aspects of the overall activity that might be questioned and only some of the ideas for possible improvements that these questions may suggest. But again, we can never be sure that a particular analyst will be capable of raising the appropriate questions or that the answers to these questions will generate ideas for a more effective method. For this reason, analysts are usually furnished with more specific aids. As in the case of the material flow process chart analysis, these aids take the form of checklists which are designed to guide the analyst in his investigation. However, a single checklist is usually prepared for both types of flow process charts. Consequently, the checklist presented in the discussion of the material flow process chart serves to suggest the kind of list which might be prepared to help the analyst in his study of a man whose activities call for his moving from one work station to another.

WORK-STATION FLOW PROCESS CHARTS

In the course of analyzing processes in which either materials or men move from one work station to another, the analyst will examine the methods being employed at the various work stations. A work station was defined earlier as the area occupied by the operator and the equipment with which he works. This suggests that the work station may consist of a number of *locations* at which the operator carries out his activities. For example, he may go to one location to obtain the part to be placed in the machine. The actual machining would then be performed at a second location. Finally, the machined part may be placed in a container situated at a third location.

However, such activities at a work station would be reported on the flow process chart as a single operation. In his analysis, the analyst would probably study this operation by first spending some time at the work station and making mental or written notes of what is being done and how it is being done. Following this, he would question each of the detailed work-station activities in the hope of making some salutary changes. But on occasion, the analyst will find that the work station under consideration contains such a number of different locations, at which so many different activities take place, that he has difficulty obtaining and retaining a complete picture of what is taking place if he does not employ a systematic approach to the acquisition of the required information. This systematic approach can take the form of another process chart.

There is no single chart that has been developed for use in a situation such as this. It is not unusual, however, to employ what amounts to a man flow process chart.

In this application, the man flow process chart and the activities which it comprises are defined just as they were before. The only difference is that every *location* at the work station is treated as if it were a *work station.* This means that a raw-material storage area is considered to be a work station; a machine, a second work station; the workbench, a third work station; a finished-part storage area, a fourth work station; and so on. The analyst then proceeds to construct a man flow process chart in which the man is considered to be moving from one work station to another as he moves from one location to another.

To illustrate this, let us consider one of the activities which appeared in the material flow process chart for the sliding-door assembly. It will be recalled that the flat plates, after having been unloaded, were inspected. In Figure 18-1, this activity was noted in the following manner:

☐ Inspect for overall dimensions

But in analyzing this activity at the work station, the analyst may find it expedient to describe the activity in greater detail by means of the work-station man flow process chart shown in Figure 18-4. With this information at his disposal, he would then go on to analyze the method by means of the same general approach described earlier. This is to say that each activity that now appears in the work-station flow process chart would be

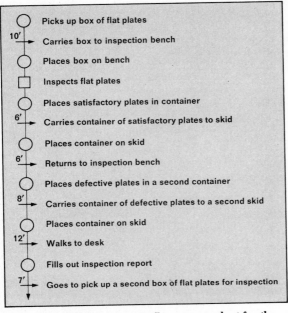

Places box on bench

Inspects flat plates

Places satisfactory plates in container

Carries container of satisfactory plates to skid

Places container on skid

Returns to inspection bench

Places defective plates in a second container

Carries container of defective plates to a second skid

Places container on skid

Walks to desk

Fills out inspection report

Goes to pick up a second box of flat plates for inspection

Figure 18-4   Work-station man flow process chart for the inspection of flat plates

subjected to the questions of Why, What, How, Where, Who, and When? Furthermore, each activity would be examined in light of an appropriate checklist. The result may be that sampling inspection will be substituted for 100 percent inspection, more efficient gauges will be adopted for use, the layout of the work station will be improved, the inspection will be performed by less skilled personnel, or the inspection may be completely eliminated on the grounds that it is unnecessary.

Of course, if a clearer presentation can be made by describing what happens to the material at the work station rather than what the man does, a work-station material flow process chart can be substituted for the man flow process chart.

THE MAN AND MACHINE CHART

We have seen that, on some occasions, no chart may be needed to analyze the activities at a work station. On other occasions, a flow process chart can be adapted to an analysis of the activities at a particular work station if the analyst feels that there is a need to do so. But there are cases in which the nature of the activity taking place at a work station and the reason for the analyst's making the study are such that unique process charts must be constructed. One of these is a chart which would be used to study an activity which involves a man working with a machine when the analyst has reason to believe that there is excessive idle time on the part of either the man or the machine or both. This chart is called a "man and machine chart." Its nature is such that it provides the analyst with information which will enable him to take steps to eliminate or reduce the amount of idle time.

SOME DEFINITIONS   The man and machine chart is defined as follows:

A graphic presentation of the coordinated activities of a man and a machine described in terms of independent work, combined work, and waiting. The duration of the various activities is represented by bars which are drawn to length against a time scale.

Let us consider this definition by beginning with the activities in terms of which the work is described. These are (1) independent work, (2) combined work, and (3) waiting. Insofar as independent work is concerned, this classification may be applied to either the man or the machine. The man is said to be engaged in independent work when he is working independently of the machine. This means that the nature of his activity is such that it could be performed even if the machine were not present at that work station. For example, at some point in the work cycle, the man may have to study a blueprint, inspect a part, obtain raw materials, place a finished part in a container, or receive instructions from the foreman. Any of these tasks could be performed even if the machine were not there.

The machine is said to be engaged in independent work when the nature of one of its activities is such that it could be performed even if the operator were not present at the work station during that portion of the work cycle. An example of this would be the case in which the machine is designed to operate and stop automatically after it has been set up and started by the operator. Care must be taken, however, not to assume that the machine is working independently whenever the operator is not engaged in any physical activity involving the machine. To illustrate, a drill press may be equipped with power feed. This suggests that the man is free to do some other work during the drilling portion of the cycle. But it may be that, if something goes wrong while the machine is operating automatically, the consequences will be serious. For example, if the cutting tool breaks, the damage done to the part or machine may be quite costly. For this reason, the operator may have to monitor the machine while it is operating automatically. In the event of a mishap, he would be able to stop the ma-

chine immediately and thereby minimize the adverse effects of the breakdown. Where this is true, the man is not free to perform some other work,
and, hence, the machine is not operating independently of the man.

The second activity which may appear in a man and machine chart is
combined work. Again, this classification can be applied to either the
man or the machine. The man is said to be engaged in combined work
when he is working with the machine. Similarly, the machine is said to be
engaged in combined work when it is performing a function which also
requires the services of the operator. In other words, combined work is
work which can be performed by the man only when the machine is present
at the work station and also work which can be performed by the machine
only when the man is present at the work station. Examples of this activity
would be setting up, loading, unloading, cleaning, maintaining, or monitoring the machine. Each of these tasks can be performed by the operator
only if the machine is there to be set up, loaded, unloaded, cleaned, maintained, or monitored. Another example would be that portion of the work
cycle in which the machine is being operated by hand feed, because the
machine is capable of processing the material only for so long as the man
is there to operate the machine.

The third and last activity is waiting. Waiting is idleness on the part
of either the man or the machine. If waiting is to occur on the part of the
man, it can occur only while the machine is working independently. For
example, when a machine which does not require monitoring is operating
automatically, it may be that the man is idle or waiting in the sense that he
is not engaged in or making preparations for productive work. Also, if waiting is to occur on the part of the machine, it can occur only while the man
is working independently. For example, when a man is at his workbench
inspecting a part he has just produced, it may be that the machine is standing idle or is waiting in the sense that it is not engaged in or being prepared
for any productive work.

The definition of the man and machine chart also tells us that the chart
is a graphic presentation. This means that the descriptions of the various
activities are accompanied by symbols and are presented in the form of a
diagram. The symbols for the respective activities are as follows:

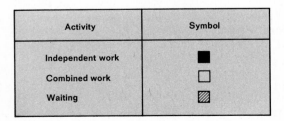

Activity	Symbol
Independent work	■
Combined work	□
Waiting	▨

The definition goes on to state that the length of these bars will vary with the duration of the activity each represents. The manner in which this is done can best be seen from an actual chart, which we shall construct in just a moment. A time scale is also referred to in the definition. The purpose of the time scale is to enable the analyst to show the duration of the various activities and also to show how the activities of the man and the machine are coordinated. The latter means that the activities are recorded in a way which permits one to study the chart and determine what both the man and the machine are doing at a given moment in time. But just how this is done can also be best seen from an examination of a completed chart.

AN ILLUSTRATION Suppose that the analyst had constructed a material flow process chart for the sliding-door assembly. After having done so, he studied each of the activities. One of these involved drilling the two holes in the flat plate. He found that the drill-press operator was performing the operation in the following manner: He would take a single plate, mark the locations at which the holes were to be drilled with the use of a pattern, drill the two holes using hand feed, and set the plate aside. The analyst improved upon this activity by first designing a jig which was capable of holding four plates simultaneously. The nature of the jig was such that it contained two holes which served to guide the cutting tool, and this eliminated the need for the operator to mark the locations at which the holes were to be drilled. Also, a fixture was developed which served to hold the jig and the four stacked plates in the correct position in the drill press. The operator was then instructed to use automatic feed and to operate the machine at a faster speed. As a result, the method of operation was now as follows: The operator would stack four plates in the jig, position the jig in the machine, drill two holes in the four plates using power feed, remove the jig, remove the four drilled plates, and set the plates aside. In addition to all this, the analyst made some changes in the layout of the workplace. This brought the points at which raw materials and finished parts were stored at the work station closer to the machine, placed the operator's workbench in a more convenient location, and made it easier for the materials handler to deliver raw materials and to remove the drilled plates.

After having completed all this, the analyst noticed that the nature of the resultant work cycle was such that the operator and machine were intermittently idle. As a result, he decided to construct a man and machine chart which might suggest changes that would bring about a more effective utilization of both the man and the machine. Therefore, he observed the operation for a few cycles and recorded the respective activities of the man and the machine and the amount of time required to perform each of these activities. On the basis of this information, he constructed the man and machine chart shown in Figure 18-5.

A study of this chart reveals that the total cycle time is 3.9 minutes. During these 3.9 minutes, the operator and the machine are each idle 1.4 minutes, or approximately 36 percent of the time. The task now confronting the analyst is to develop some means of reducing these percentages. In general, the analyst has the following alternatives:

1 Change the work method in a way which will minimize the idle time on the part of the man or the machine or both.

2 Assign additional manpower to the machine so as to minimize the idle time on the part of the machine.

OPERATOR		TIME		DRILL PRESS
1. Obtains 4 plates from box and places plates in jig		0.5 min		1. Idle
2. Positions jig under drill, turns on power, and throws in automatic feed		0.4 min		2. Being loaded and started for drilling of first hole
3. Idle		0.7 min		3. Drills hole
4. Raises drill, shuts off power, and positions drill for second hole		0.4 min		4. Being stopped and prepared for drilling of second hole
5. Idle		0.7 min		5. Drills hole
6. Raises drill, shuts off power, and removes jig		0.3 min		6. Being stopped and unloaded
7. Sets jig aside, removes plates from jig, places plates in container, and cleans chips out of jig		0.9 min		7. Idle

Figure 18-5   Man and machine chart for the drilling of holes in flat plates

3 Assign some other task to the operator, such as inspection, assembly, or tending another machine, which he can perform during his idle time.

Let us apply these guides to the operation under consideration. Insofar as the work method is concerned, it will be noticed that the machine is idle on two occasions. One is when the operator is making preparations to load the machine, and the second is after the operator has unloaded the machine. Now, it may be possible to supply the man with additional jigs which would permit the following change: During his waiting times, the operator could be placing undrilled plates in empty jigs and removing drilled plates from filled jigs. As soon as the drilling operation is completed, the machine could be loaded with a prefilled jig. Consequently, not only the man's waiting time would be reduced, but so would the machine's.

With regard to assigning additional manpower to a machine, there are cases in which it is extremely important to keep the machine running as close to 100 percent capacity as possible. This may be necessary in order to meet production schedules or to keep the investment in relatively expensive equipment to a minimum. Where this is true, the analyst may find it economical to have two men assigned to one machine, three men to two machines, or some other such combination which will permit the other man to operate the machine while the first man is engaged in independent work. In our illustration, this would call for a second man to load, operate, and unload the machine while the first man was busy removing the four drilled plates from the jig, setting the plates aside, and cleaning and reloading the jig.

The third alternative, assigning other work to the operator, would be given serious consideration in those cases where waiting time on the part of the man is the more important problem. When this is true, one man may be instructed to tend two machines, two men to tend three machines, or some other such combination which will enable the man to load, operate, or unload the other machine while the first machine is engaged in independent work. Other possibilities might be to have the man tend only one machine but to have him perform an inspection or an assembly operation during what would otherwise be his waiting time.

From a casual observation, it is difficult to tell which one or combination of these alternatives would be the most desirable in the case under consideration. A specific decision could be made only after the analyst had described each alternative in greater detail and made a cost comparison. This has not been done for this illustration because we are interested only in the general approach that would be employed.

This concludes our description of the man and machine chart. The man and machine chart is only one of a number of charts which are referred to as "multiple-activity charts." Similar charts, involving the same activities, symbols, and method of construction, can be prepared to record the co-ordinated activities of two or more men, or of any combination of men and machines. These will not be discussed here because in principle they do not differ from the chart presented.

QUESTIONS

18-1   What does the methods analysis activity encompass?

18-2   Give a general definition of a process chart.

18-3   Describe a material flow process chart in terms of the information it contains.

18-4   Under what conditions would a material flow process chart be used to make a methods analysis?

18-5   How is the material flow process chart analyzed to improve upon the method it describes?

18-6   Describe a man flow process chart in terms of the information it contains.

18-7   Under what conditions would a man flow process chart be used to make a methods analysis?

18-8   How is the man flow process chart analyzed to improve upon the method it describes?

18-9   Define the following activities that might appear in a flow process chart: (*a*) operation, (*b*) inspection, (*c*) transportation, (*d*) storage, and (*e*) delay.

18-10   What symbols are used to represent the activities that might appear in a flow process chart?

18-11   Describe a work-station flow process chart in terms of the information it contains.

18-12   Under what conditions would a work-station flow process chart be used to make a methods analysis?

18-13   How is the work-station flow process chart analyzed to improve upon the method it describes?

18-14   Describe a man and machine chart in terms of the information it contains.

18-15   Define the following activities that might appear in a man and machine chart: (*a*) machine working independently, (*b*) man working independently, (*c*) combined work, and (*d*) waiting or idleness.

18-16   What symbols are used to represent the activities that might appear in a man and machine chart?

18-17   Under what conditions would a man and machine chart be used to make a methods analysis?

18-18   How is the man and machine chart analyzed to improve upon the method it describes?

PROBLEMS

18-1 Select an activity whose nature is such that it requires the movement of materials or work in process from one work station to another. The activity considered in this and subsequent problems in this chapter can take place in a manufacturing firm, service organization, or home. Then go on to do the following:

    a Describe the present method for carrying out the activity by means of a material flow process chart.

    b Analyze the chart with a view toward improving the method.

    c Prepare a brief description of each of the changes you recommend.

    d Describe the proposed method by means of a material flow process chart.

18-2 Select an activity whose nature is such that it requires the movement of a person from one work station to another. Then proceed to do everything called for in problem 18-1, with the difference that the present and proposed methods are to be described by means of a man flow process chart.

18-3 Select an activity whose nature is such that it requires the movement of material or work in process from one location to another at a single work station. Then proceed to do everything called for in problem 18-1, with the difference that the present and proposed methods are to be described by means of a work-station material flow process chart.

18-4 Select an activity whose nature is such that it entails the movement of a person from one location to another at a single work station. Then proceed to do everything called for in problem 18-1, with the difference that the present and proposed methods are to be described by means of a work-station man flow process chart.

18-5 Select an activity which involves a person working at a work station with a machine or some other type of equipment. Then proceed to do everything called for in problem 18-1, with the difference that the present and proposed methods are to be described by means of a man and machine chart.

18-6 It was stated that a man and machine chart is only one of a number of charts which are referred to as multiple-activity charts. Suppose you wanted to prepare a chart of this type to record the coordinated activities of two people. In that case, how would independent work, combined work, and waiting be defined? Supplement your definitions of these three activities with an example of each.

NINETEEN
MOTION STUDY

In addition to work-station flow process charts and multiple-activity charts, there is a third class of process charts which can be used to analyze the activities taking place at a single work station. These charts are employed when the analyst wants to study and improve upon the motions an operator employs in the course of performing his task. Therefore, an examination of these techniques will take us into the realm of motion study.

The process charts employed in the course of conducting a motion study are applicable only when the activities involved are performed at a single *location* in a work station. It is unlikely that the analyst would be interested in a man's motions as the man moves from one location to another in a given work station; it is only after he has arrived at a particular location where he will perform some task that there would be anything to be gained from a study of his motions.

THE OPERATOR PROCESS CHART

The purpose of the process charts involved in a study of an operator's motions is to provide the analyst with a description of the motions being employed by the operator at the present time. One of the most commonly used charts is the *operator process chart*. This chart is defined as follows:

A graphic presentation of the coordinated activities of an operator's right and left hands. These activities are described in terms of operations, transportations, holds, and delays.

In this definition, we are told that the chart is a graphic presentation. This means that the analyst records the information in diagram form, in which verbal descriptions are accompanied by symbols used to depict the various activities the analyst may observe. For each of the activities mentioned in the definition, the respective symbols are as shown on the following page.

Next, the definition states that the coordinated activities are presented. This is similar to what was done in the man and machine chart. In this case, the activities of the left hand are shown in one column and the activities

Activity	Symbol
Operation	◯
Transportation	→
Hold	▽
Delay	D

of the right hand in another. These activities are recorded in the respective columns in the order in which they occur and are positioned so as to permit one to examine the chart and determine what both the right and left hands were doing at a particular moment in time.

THE ACTIVITIES DEFINED Let us now turn to the activities themselves. Although practically the same activities are involved as those which appeared in the flow process charts, these activities are defined differently. The new definition for an operation is as follows:

An operation occurs whenever the hand picks up, drops, lays down, positions, uses, or assembles something.

This definition appears to cover everything that a hand can possibly do. However, there are a few motions which do not involve picking up, dropping, laying down, positioning, using, or assembling something. What these motions are can best be seen from the definitions of the remaining activities. If we can recognize a transportation, a hold, and a delay, we can assume that any motion which does not fall into any one of these three classifications is an operation. Therefore, let us go on to the transportation activity. A transportation is defined as follows:

A transportation occurs whenever the hand moves from one position to another at the workplace.

This becomes clear if we define the term "position." A simple illustration will be the best means for doing so. Suppose that an operator is engaged in the assembly of two parts. The parts to be assembled are stored at a certain point at the workplace, the actual assembly takes place at another point, and the assembled parts are stored at a third point. Each of these points would be considered to be a position. Let us now concentrate on the activities of only the right hand. The operator begins by reaching for a part. This would be considered to be a transportation, because the hand is moving from one position to another. When the hand reaches the position at which the part is located, the part is picked up. Now, it is true that some movement is involved in picking up the part. However, the movement takes place at the position at which the part is stored, and, hence, it would be classified as an operation rather than a transportation. Next, the hand carries the part to the position at which it will be assembled with the other part. Because of the change in position, a transportation is taking place. At this point, the actual assembly activity takes place. In the course of assembling the part, some movement again occurs. But since this movement takes place at the position at which the assembly activity is performed, the hand would be engaged in an operation and not in a transportation. This is followed by the finished assembly's being carried by the hand to the position at which the assemblies are stored. Because the hand is moving from one position to another, it would be engaged in a transportation. When the hand reaches the storage area, the assembly is dropped or laid down. Again, in the course of dropping or laying down the assembly, some movement of the hand is involved. But since the movement is taking place at the position at which the assembly is stored, the dropping or laying down of the part would be classified as an operation rather than a transportation. Finally, the empty hand moves back to its starting position, and this would be a transportation.

At this point, we can make the following generalization with regard to the operation and transportation activities: In both, the hand is engaged in some type of motion. The basic difference between the two is that, in an operation, the motion takes place as the hand performs some function at a single position at the workplace, while in a transportation, the motion takes place as the hand moves from one position to another.

The remaining activities, hold and delay, are distinguished by the fact that they occur when the hand is not in motion. That this is true for hold can be seen from its definition, which is as follows:

A hold occurs whenever the hand holds an object so that the other hand may do something to that object.

We can illustrate this by returning to the assembly example. It was mentioned that two parts were to be fitted together. The actual assembly activity may consist of the left hand holding the one part in a relatively fixed position while the right hand is fitting the other part onto it. If this is true, the analyst would say that the left hand is engaged in a hold while the right hand is engaged in an operation.

The last activity which appears in the definition of an operator process chart is delay. This activity is defined as follows:

A delay occurs when the hand is idle, in the sense that it is not performing an operation, a transportation, or a hold.

There is little that can be added to this. If during a given portion of the work cycle the analyst finds that one of the hands is doing nothing which contributes to the successful completion of the task, he concludes that the hand is idle or experiencing a delay. For example, in our assembly illustration, it may be that the finished assembly is transported to the finished assembly area at the workplace by just the right hand. While this is going on, the left hand may be hanging at the operator's side or resting on the table. If so, the hand is not doing anything essential to the completion of the overall task, and, hence, it would be said to be experiencing a delay during this portion of the work cycle.

In conclusion, it might be noted that the inspection activity does not appear in the operator process chart. This is because of the way in which an operation is now defined. In this definition, no distinction is made between, for example, the hand's positioning and using an object in order to change the physical characteristics of something and the hand's positioning and using an object in order to verify something for quality. This suggests that, if a hand picks up and positions a part for an inspection, the picking up and positioning is identified as an operation and not as an inspection. Also, if the hand positions and uses a gauge to inspect a part, the positioning and use of the gauge is identified as an operation and not an inspection. This means that, even if the overall task is an inspection, this inspection would be described in an operator process chart in terms of operations, transportations, holds, and delays.

AN ILLUSTRATION   Let us now construct an operator process chart. In doing so, we shall return to our sliding-door assembly.

One of the last activities shown on the material flow process chart was the assembly of the drilled plates, the handles, and the rivets into finished sliding doors. Suppose that the analyst decides that something is to be gained from an analysis of the motions which the operator employs in the course of assembling the four component parts of the sliding door. He begins by describing the motion pattern being adhered to by the operator at the time. The description will take the form of an operator process chart.

The analyst finds that the general method followed by the operator is as follows: The operator obtains the drilled flat plate, the handle, and a single rivet from containers located at the workplace. He positions the handle, which has a hole in each end, over the two holes in the plate and then inserts the rivet in the one set of matching holes. Following this, the plate, handle, and rivet are placed and held on an anvil as shown in Figure 19-1.

Then the operator picks up a hammer and flattens out the end of the rivet. Next, the operator removes the partially assembled door from the anvil, obtains a second rivet, inserts it in the second set of matching holes, positions the partially assembled door on the anvil, and flattens out the end of the second rivet. Finally, the assembled door is placed in a container provided for that purpose at the workplace. All these activities are de-

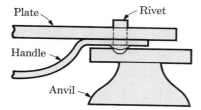

Figure 19-1 Position of component parts of sliding-door assembly on anvil

scribed in detail in the operator process chart shown in Figure 19-2.

As can be seen in Figure 19-2, the chart also contains a sketch of the layout of the workplace. This is customary because such a sketch is often of value in the subsequent analysis. Another thing that might be mentioned is that the chart does not contain a time scale. This does not mean that one cannot be included; however, it usually is not because of the cost of obtaining this information.

PRINCIPLES OF MOTION ECONOMY Once the analyst has made an operator process chart in which the current method is described, he is in a position to begin his analysis.

The approach he employs is as follows: He studies every activity performed by the operator's left and right hands with a view to eliminating or simplifying the motions involved. There is no fixed way of accomplishing this, but the analyst does have fairly detailed guides provided for his use. The basic principles on which these guides are based were developed by Frank and Lillian Gilbreth, who did much of the pioneering work in the field of motion study. Since that time, others have added to and elaborated upon these principles. Among these individuals, Ralph M. Barnes has probably made the most notable contribution. These principles are known as the principles, or laws, of motion economy, and they have been presented by Barnes as shown in Figure 19-3.

These principles of motion economy serve as guides to the analyst. As guides, they are used as follows: The analyst studies every activity which appears in his chart to determine whether any of the activities violate the laws of motion economy. Those activities that do are scrutinized, and every attempt is made to alter them so as to have them performed in accordance with the appropriate principle. This is done because the research on which these principles are based revealed that adherence to them will minimize idle time, reduce fatigue, and decrease the amount of time required to perform certain activities. In brief, adherence to these principles will increase labor productivity.

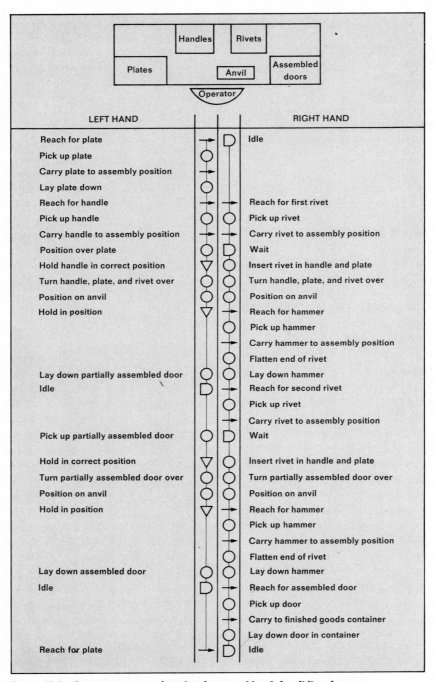

Figure 19-2   Operator process chart for the assembly of the sliding door

APPLYING THE PRINCIPLES OF MOTION ECONOMY Of course, to know and understand the principles of motion economy is one thing, and to apply them is another. A person may accept the fact that symmetrical motions are desirable, but this does not solve the problem of determining how the activity can be performed by means of symmetrical motions. Also, there will always be those situations in which a specific principle cannot be put into effect and also situations in which a specific principle does not apply.

Nevertheless, given that there may be some difficulty in applying the principles of motion economy and that there is no certainty that a particular individual will be capable of developing a more effective work method, a knowledge of the principles will certainly aid the analyst in his attempt to improve upon the existing method of operation. To demonstrate this, let us return to our illustration in which the sliding-door assembly was being considered and see whether any of the rules of motion economy are capable of suggesting changes of a beneficial nature.

If we reexamine Figure 19-2, we will notice two things that call for corrective action: (1) For a relatively large proportion of the work cycle, the operator's left hand is holding the handle, plate, and rivet while the right hand is getting the hammer and flattening the end of the rivet, and (2) an appreciable amount of time is spent by the left and right hands in idleness.

With regard to the holding activity, the rules of motion economy suggest the use of a fixture of some type. In this case, the analyst may find that a fixture of the kind shown in Figure 19-4 would be of help. It consists of a heavy iron block with a depressed center section. Each of the raised sections has a hole which is of the same size and shape as the rivet head. At the base of each of these holes is a magnet capable of holding the rivet which would be positioned head downward in the hole. With the use of this fixture, the operator could take two rivets, position them in the respective holes, take the handle, position it over the rivets, take the drilled plate, and position it over the handles and the rivets. All this is shown in Figure 19-4. Following this, the operator could take the hammer and flatten the ends of the rivets. However, a slight change in the design of the rivet head would probably be necessary. It will be recalled that the original rivet had an oval head. In order to enhance the holding qualities of the magnet, it would be necessary that a flat-headed rivet be used.

Once a tentative decision is made to use a fixture of this design, another change involving a principle of motion economy suggests itself. If only one fixture were to be employed, the operator would obtain only one handle at a time, and this means that one of the hands would be idle during this part of the work cycle. The solution to this lies in supplying the operator with

I. USE OF THE HUMAN BODY:

1. The two hands should begin as well as complete their motions at the same time.
2. The two hands should not be idle at the same time except during rest periods.
3. Motions of the arms should be–made in opposite and symmetrical directions and should be made simultaneously.
4. Hand motions should be confined to the lowest classification with which it is possible to perform the work satisfactorily. General classifications of hand motions are as follows:
   a. Finger motions.
   b. Motions involving fingers and wrist.
   c. Motions involving fingers, wrist, and forearm.
   d. Motions involving fingers, wrist, forearm, and upper arm.
   e. Motions involving fingers, wrist, forearm, upper arm, and shoulder.
5. Momentum should be employed to assist the worker wherever possible, and it should be reduced to a minimum if it must be overcome by muscular effort.
6. Smooth continuous motions of the hands are preferable to zigzag motions or straight-line motions involving sudden and sharp changes in direction.
7. Ballistic movements are faster, easier, and more accurate than restricted or controlled movements.
8. Rhythm is essential to the smooth and automatic performance of an operation, and the work should be arranged to permit easy and natural rhythm wherever possible.

II. ARRANGEMENT OF THE WORK PLACE:

9. There should be a definite and fixed place for all tools and materials.
10. Tools, materials, and controls should be located close in and directly in front of the operator.

*R. M. Barnes, Motion and Time Study, 6th ed., John Wiley & Sons, Inc., New York, 1968.

Figure 19-3   Principles of motion economy

two fixtures. Doing so would permit the operator's hands to reach for and position the first pair of rivets simultaneously. The next step would call for doing the same thing with a second pair of rivets. Then the hands could obtain a pair of handles simultaneously and position them on the respective fixtures. Following this, because of the size of the plates and the greater difficulty in positioning them, both hands would obtain one plate and locate it on the first fixture, and next, both hands would obtain a second plate and locate it on the second fixture. The rest of the task would be performed as shown in Figure 19-5.

It can be seen in Figure 19-5 that a need remains for holding the plate while the ends of the rivets are being flattened, but the amount of time required for this activity will probably be less than in the original method because the operator has to reach for, pick up, and lay down the hammer once, rather than twice as before, in the course of flattening four rivets. The idle time, on the other hand, has been completely eliminated. With regard to the hammer itself, the operator process chart for the revised method also indicates that, as suggested by another principle of motion

11. Gravity feed bins and containers should be used to deliver material close to the point of use.
12. Drop deliveries should be used wherever possible.
13. Materials and tools should be located to permit the best sequence of motions.
14. Provisions should be made for adequate conditions for seeing. Good illumination is the first requirement for satisfactory visual perception.
15. The height of the work place and the chair should preferably be arranged so that alternate sitting and standing at work are easily possible.
16. A chair of the type and height to permit good posture should be provided for every worker.

III. DESIGN OF TOOLS AND EQUIPMENT:

17. The hands should be relieved of all work that can be done more advantageously by a jig, a fixture, or a foot-operated device.
18. Two or more tools should be combined wherever possible.
19. Tools and materials should be pre-positioned wherever possible.
20. Where each finger performs some specific movement, such as typewriting, the load should be distributed in accordance with the inherent capacities of the fingers.
21. Handles such as those used on cranks and large screwdrivers should be designed to permit as much of the surface of the hand to come in contact with the handle as possible. This is particularly true when considerable force is exerted in using the handle. For light assembly work the screwdriver handle should be so shaped that it is smaller at the bottom than at the top.
22. Levers, crossbars, and hand wheels should be located in such positions that the operator can manipulate them with the least change in body position and with the greatest mechanical advantage.

economy, the hammer is kept in a holder which serves to preposition the tool. This eliminates the need for the operator's spending time in getting the hammer in the correct position for the flattening operation. Further, the holder could be kept in a fixed position, which would eliminate searching for the hammer every time it is needed.

From the sketch of the revised layout of the workplace, it can be seen that other improvements can be and have been made on the basis of still

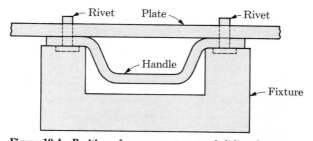

Figure 19-4 Position of component parts of sliding-door assembly in fixture

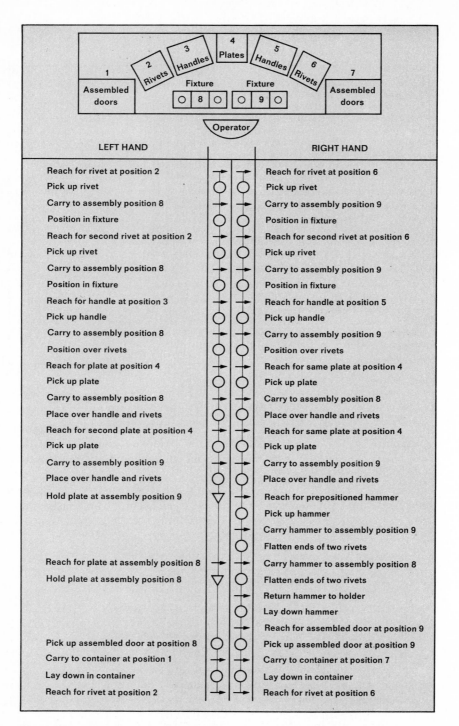

Figure 19-5 Operator process chart for the assembly of the sliding door by an improved method

other principles of motion economy. One of these is that materials are arranged so that they are closer to the operator and so that most of the motions of the arms can now be made in opposite and symmetrical directions. Also, the assembled doors are stored close to the position of the rivets, and this improves the sequence of motions, in the sense that the last activity is completed near the point at which the first activity begins. Finally, the containers in which the assembled doors are placed rest on two sections of the workbench which are at a lower level than the remainder of the surface. This provision permits the operator to reach down when setting the completed work aside, probably a less fatiguing and time-consuming motion than carrying the doors straight ahead at shoulder level and then positioning them in a container.

Other changes related to the principles of motion economy which could be made but which cannot be seen from the operator process chart are (1) to have the rivets and handles stored in gravity feed containers and (2) to have the drilled plates stacked in a box with the open end facing the operator. Doing so would eliminate the need for reaching down into containers and groping for the required parts. Finally, the analyst could check on such things as illumination, height of the workbench, and the height and type of chair.

In brief, it is fairly evident that the suggested changes would bring about a method which is less fatiguing and time-consuming than the original method. Further, there is reason to believe that the probability of a given analyst's originating these changes is increased if he has a record of the existing method in the form of an operator process chart. In the absence of such a record, many of the deficiencies of the method may not be apparent. Also, the availability of the principles of motion economy undoubtedly is an aid to the analyst in his attempt to eliminate or minimize these deficiencies.

THE SIMULTANEOUS MOTION CYCLE CHART

There is a second chart that is sometimes used when making a motion study. This is the simultaneous motion cycle chart, usually referred to as the "simo chart." The simo chart is employed under conditions similar to those under which an operator process chart is employed. The basic difference between the two charts lies in the fact that the simo chart yields a more detailed description of the observed motion pattern and, hence, is often more capable of revealing deficiencies in the motion pattern than is an operator process chart. Because of this, the analyst may be able to make improvements which would not be suggested by an analysis of an operator process chart. That this is true will become evident after we have defined, described, and illustrated the simo chart. Let us begin with the definition which is as follows:

A graphic presentation of the coordinated activities of an operator's body members. These activities are described in terms of basic or fundamental motions known as therbligs. The time required for the performance of these motions is also shown.

In this definition, reference is made to the operator's body members. Although the chart can be employed to record the activities of any of the operator's body members, the members usually studied are the right and left hands. But on occasion, the analyst may find it worthwhile to study the motions of such things as the fingers or feet. We shall limit our discussion to a right- and left-hand analysis, because this is the most prevalent application.

The definition also states that the activities are described in terms of basic or fundamental motions. At the time Frank Gilbreth was doing his work in the field of motion study, he concluded that any manual activity could be described in terms of 17 fundamental motions. This is comparable to our being able to describe every word in the English language in terms of some of the 26 letters of the alphabet. Each of these fundamental motions is called a "therblig." The operator's activities, when recorded by means of a simo chart, are described in terms of these therbligs, which in their present form vary only slightly from those developed by Gilbreth. As opposed to this, the operator process chart is based on only four activities. This means that the simo chart provides a more minute description of the method being followed. It is for this reason that a study involving the use of a simo chart is often called a "micromotion study," that is, a study of small motions. What these motions are will be discussed in just a moment.

We are also told that the chart is a graphic presentation. This suggests that the description of the motion pattern will be presented in the form of a diagram. In this diagram, use is made of verbal descriptions of the activities and of symbols. In some cases, the analyst will also show a letter abbreviation for each of the 17 different activities he may encounter. The names of these activities, their symbols, and their letter abbreviations are as shown in Figure 19-6.

In addition to the symbols and abbreviations listed, bars of different shading or color are often used to describe the therbligs symbolically. These would be similar to the devices used in the construction of a man and machine chart. However, we shall not consider this notation, because it will add nothing to our understanding of the simo chart.

Let us now turn to the definitions of each of the therbligs. Although these definitions are fairly well standardized, those presented in some references are somewhat more clearly self-explanatory than those pre-

NAME OF THERBLIG	SYMBOL	LETTER ABBREVIATION
Search	⊂⊃	Sh
Select	→	St
Grasp	∩	G
Transport empty	⌣	TE
Transport loaded	⌣	TL
Hold	⌓	H
Release load	⌢	RL
Position	9	P
Pre-position	△	PP
Inspect	0	I
Assemble	#	A
Disassemble	‡	DA
Use	U	U
Unavoidable delay	⌒	UD
Avoidable delay	⌐	AD
Plan	₿	Pn
Rest for overcoming fatigue	ℓ	R

Figure 19-6   Therbligs

sented in others. One of these expository sets of definitions is the one developed by Ralph M. Barnes, who defines the fundamental motions as shown in Figure 19-7.

MECHANICS OF CONSTRUCTING A SIMO CHART   The analyst constructs an operator process chart by observing the operator and recording what is taking place. The approach to the construction of a simo chart is somewhat different. The reason for this is that the duration of the various therbligs is often so short that it would be extremely difficult for even a highly skilled analyst to record the sequence and synchronization of these therbligs by direct observation. Also, the completed chart contains information with regard to the amount of time spent by the operator on each of the therbligs. It is not unusual for some of these times to be as short as two- or three-thousandths of a minute. Obviously no analyst would be capable of obtaining these times by direct observation. And yet, it is believed that this information is essential to a complete analysis of this type

Search is that part of the cycle during which the eyes or the hands are hunting or groping for the object. Search begins when the eyes or hands begin to hunt for the object and ends when the object has been found.

Select is the choice of one object from among several. In many cases it is difficult, if not impossible, to determine where the boundaries lie between search and select. For this reason, it is often the practice to combine them, referring to both as the one therblig, select. Using this broader definition, select then refers to the hunting and locating of one object from among several. Select begins when the eyes or hands begin to hunt for the object and ends when the desired object has been located.

Grasp is taking hold of an object, closing the fingers around it preparatory to picking it up, holding it, or manipulating it. Grasp begins when the hand or fingers first make contact with the object and ends when the hand has obtained control of it.

Transport empty is moving the empty hand in reaching for an object. It is assumed that the hand moves without resistance toward or away from the object. Transport empty begins when the hand begins to move without load or resistance and ends when the hand stops moving.

Transport loaded is moving an object from one place to another. The object may be carried in the hands or fingers, or it may be moved from one place to another by sliding, dragging, or pushing it along. Transport loaded also refers to moving the empty hand against resistance. Transport loaded begins when the hand begins to move an object or encounter resistance and ends when the hand stops moving.

Hold is the retention of an object after it has been grasped, no movement of the object taking place. Hold begins when the movement of the object stops and ends with the start of the next therblig.

Release load is letting go of the object. Release load begins when the object starts to leave the hand and ends when the object has been completely separated from the hand or fingers.

Position is turning or locating an object in such a way that it will be properly oriented to fit into the location for which it is intended. It is possible to position an object during the motion transport loaded. Position begins when the hand begins to turn or locate the object and ends when the object has been placed in the desired position or location.

Preposition is locating an object in a predetermined place or locating it in the correct position for some subsequent motion. Preposition is the same as position except that the object is located in the approximate position that will be needed later. Usually a holder, bracket, or special container of some kind is used for holding the object in a way that permits it to be grasped easily in the

*Adapted from R. M. Barnes, Motion and Time Study, 6th ed., John Wiley & Sons, Inc., New York, 1968.

Figure 19-7   Therblig definitions

because elapsed times often suggest areas which present the greatest opportunities for improvement.

For these reasons, the approach employed in the construction of the chart calls for making a motion picture of the operator performing the task. The film is then projected frame by frame, and the analyst analyzes each of these frames and determines what therblig is being performed by the body member under consideration at a given moment. The film also enables the analyst to ascertain the elapsed time for each therblig. To illustrate, the analyst may know that the camera he is using operates at a speed of 1,000 frames per minute. This means that each frame represents one-thousandth of a minute. If the projector is equipped with a frame position in which it will be used. Preposition is the abbreviated term used for "preposition for the next operation."

Inspect is examining an object to determine whether or not it complies with standard size, shape, color, or other qualities previously determined. The inspection may employ sight, hearing, touch, odor, or taste. Inspect is predominantly a mental reaction and may occur simultaneously with other therbligs. Inspect begins when the eyes or other parts of the body begin to examine the object and ends when the examination has been completed.

Assemble is placing one object into or on another object, with which it becomes an integral part. Assemble begins as the hand starts to move the part into its place in the assembly and ends when the hand has completed the assembly.

Disassemble is separating one object from another object of which it is an integral part. Disassemble begins when the hand starts to remove one part from the assembly and ends when the hand has separated the part completely from the remainder of the assembly.

Use is manipulating a tool, device, or piece of apparatus for the purpose for which it was intended. Use may refer to an almost infinite number of particular cases. It represents the motion for which the preceding motions have been more or less preparatory and for which the ones that follow are supplementary. Use begins when the hand starts to manipulate the tool or device and ends when the hand ceases the application.

Unavoidable delay is a delay beyond the control of the operator. Unavoidable delay may result from either of the following causes: (1) a failure or interruption in the process; (2) a delay caused by an arrangement of the operation that prevents one part of the body from working while other body members are busy. Unavoidable delay begins when the hand stops its activity and ends when activity is resumed.

Avoidable delay is any delay of the operator for which he is responsible and over which he has control. It refers to delays which the operator may avoid if he wishes. Avoidable delay begins when the prescribed sequence of motions is interrupted and ends when the standard work method is resumed.

Plan is a mental reaction which precedes the physical movement, that is, deciding how to proceed with the job. Plan begins at the point where the operator begins to work out the next step of the operation and ends when the procedure to be followed has been determined.

Rest for overcoming fatigue is a fatigue or delay factor or allowance provided to permit the worker to recover from the fatigue incurred by his work. Rest begins when the operator stops working and ends when the work is resumed.

counter, the analyst, when projecting the film frame by frame, can record the frame number which marks the beginning of a particular therblig and the frame number which marks the end of that therblig. If, for example, a total of six frames covers the performance of a specific motion, the analyst knows that the activity required six-thousandths of a minute. In this way, he can construct his simo chart.

THE SIMO CHART ILLUSTRATED   Let us now illustrate the construction of such a chart. Suppose that the analyst is interested in making a more detailed analysis of the motions employed by the operator who is assembling the component parts of the sliding door. This is the same task we

LEFT HAND				TIME, $\frac{1}{1000}$ min			RIGHT HAND
Reach for plate	TE	⌣	15				
Select plate	St	→	2				
Grasp plate	G	∩	5	51	↷	UD	Waiting
Carry plate to assembly position	TL	⌣	20				
Lay plate down	RL	⌢	9				
Reach for handle	TE	⌣	12	12	⌣	TE	Reach for rivet
Select handle	St	→	2	2	→	St	Select rivet
Grasp handle	G	∩	3	3	∩	G	Grasp rivet
Carry handle to assembly position	TL	⌣	13	13	⌣	TL	Carry rivet to assembly position
Position handle over plate	P	9	15	15	↷	UD	Wait
Hold handle in correct position	H	⌂	29	9	9	P	Position rivet over handle
				20	#	A	Insert rivet through handle and plate
Grasp handle, plate and rivet	G	∩	4	4	∩	G	Grasp handle, plate and rivet
Turn over	TL	⌣	14	14	⌣	TL	Turn over
Position on anvil	P	9	11	11	9	P	Position on anvil
Hold in position	H	⌂	86	12	⌣	TE	Reach for hammer
				7	∩	G	Grasp hammer
				16	⌣	TL	Carry hammer to assembly position
				51	U	U	Flatten end of rivet
Lay down partially assembled door	RL	⌢	10	10	⌢	RL	Lay down hammer

Figure 19-8. Simo chart for a portion of the assembly of the sliding door.

described earlier by means of the operator process chart. But now a film is made and analyzed. The resultant description of the present motion pattern takes the form of the chart shown in Figure 19-8.

Figure 19-8 depicts only about the first half of the entire task. The complete description would be quite lengthy and would not provide us with either a clearer picture of the form of a simo chart or a better basis for an explanation of the approach employed in its analysis. Therefore we shall limit our discussion to just the portion of the task that has been described.

As with all the other process charts, the analyst must now study this description with a view to making some improvements. One of the guides available to him for this purpose will continue to be the principles of motion economy. However, in addition to these principles, guides of a somewhat more detailed nature have been developed. These take the form of check questions to be applied to the various therbligs. The questions are designed to provide the analyst with a more specific means for determining whether one or more of the rules of motion economy are applicable to a given activity and, if so, how they can be implemented. This can best be seen from an examination of a typical set of such questions which has been suggested for use. This is the one developed by Ralph M. Barnes and shown in Figure 19-9.

The analyst would direct each of these questions to the activity to which it applies. By doing so, he might get ideas for improvements which otherwise would not be forthcoming. To illustrate this, we shall apply some of the questions to that portion of the task described in our simo chart. But before we do so, let us assume that, with the simo chart, the analyst will think of the improvements already described in our presentation of the operator process chart. If the simo chart is to be of any greater value than the operator process chart, it should be capable of suggesting additional improvements.

To begin with, a review of the questions related to the therblig "grasp" would compel the analyst to consider the possibility of having the operator grasp more than one object at a time. As a result, the operator may be instructed to reach for, grasp, and transport two rivets with each hand rather than just one rivet. After the four rivets have been transported to the two fixtures, the operator could position the first two rivets in the fixture and then the second two rivets. While it is true that the rivets may be a little more difficult to manipulate when held two at a time, this may be more than offset by the fact that the need for reaching for, grasping, and transporting a second pair of rivets is eliminated.

Turning to the checklist for transport empty and transport loaded, the analyst will be confronted by the question of whether the distance traveled

WITH REGARD TO SELECT:

1. Is the layout such as to eliminate searching for articles?
2. Can tools and materials be standardized?
3. Are parts and materials properly labeled?
4. Can better arrangements be made to facilitate or eliminate select—such as a bin with a long lip, a tray that pre-positions parts, and a transparent container?
5. Are common parts interchangeable?
6. Are parts and materials mixed?
7. Is the lighting satisfactory?
8. Can parts be pre-positioned during preceding operation?
9. Can color be used to facilitate selecting parts?

WITH REGARD TO GRASP:

1. Is it possible to grasp more than one object at a time?
2. Can objects be slid instead of carried?
3. Will a lip on front of the bin simplify grasp of small parts?
4. Can tools or parts be pre-positioned for easy grasp?
5. Can a special screwdriver, socket wrench, or combination tool be used?
6. Can a vacuum, magnet, rubber finger tip, or other device be used to advantage?
7. Is the article transferred from one hand to another?
8. Does the design of the jig or fixture permit an easy grasp in removing the part?

WITH REGARD TO TRANSPORT EMPTY AND TRANSPORT LOADED:

1. Can either of these motions be eliminated entirely?
2. Is the distance traveled the best one?
3. Are the proper means used—hand, tweezers, conveyors, etc.?
4. Are the correct members (and muscles) of the body used—fingers, forearm, shoulder, etc.?
5. Can a chute or conveyor be used?
6. Can "transports" be effected more satisfactorily in larger units?
7. Can transport be performed with foot-operated devices?
8. Is transport slowed up because of a delicate position following it?
9. Can transports be eliminated by providing additional small tools and locating them near the point of use?
10. Are parts that are used more frequently located near the point of use?
11. Are proper trays or bins used and is the operation laid out correctly?
12. Are the preceding and following operations properly related to this one?
13. Is it possible to eliminate abrupt changes in direction? Can barriers be eliminated?
14. For the weight of material moved, is the fastest member of the body used?
15. Are there any body movements that can be eliminated?
16. Can arm movements be made simultaneously, symmetrically, and in opposite directions?
17. Can the object be slid instead of carried?
18. Are the eye movements properly coordinated with the hand motions?

WITH REGARD TO HOLD:

1. Can a vise, clamp, clip, vacuum, hook, rack, fixture, or other mechanical device be used?
2. Can an adhesive or friction be used?
3. Can a stop be used to eliminate hold?
4. When hold cannot be eliminated, can arm rests be provided?

WITH REGARD TO RELEASE LOAD:

1. Can this motion be eliminated?

*R. M. Barnes, Motion and Time Study, 6th ed., John Wiley & Sons, Inc., New York, 1968.

Figure 19-9   A therblig checklist

2. Can a drop delivery be used?

3. Can the release be made in transit?

4. Is a careful release load necessary? Can this be avoided?

5. Can an ejector (mechanical, air, gravity) be used?

6. Are the material bins of proper design?

7. At the end of the release load, is the hand or the transportation means in the most advantageous position for the next motion?

8. Can a conveyor be used?

WITH REGARD TO POSITION:

1. Is positioning necessary?

2. Can tolerances be increased?

3. Can square edges be eliminated?

4. Can a guide, funnel, bushing, gauge, stop, swinging bracket, locating pin, spring, drift, recess, key, pilot on screw, or chamfer be used?

5. Can arm rests be used to steady the hands and reduce the positioning time?

6. Has the object been grasped for easiest positioning?

7. Can a foot-operated collet be used?

WITH REGARD TO PRE-POSITION:

1. Can the object be pre-positioned in transit?

2. Can tool be balanced so as to keep handle in upright position?

3. Can holding device be made to keep tool handle in proper position?

4. Can tools be suspended?

5. Can tools be stored in proper location to work?

6. Can a guide be used?

7. Can design of article be made so that all sides are alike?

8. Can a magazine feed be used?

9. Can a stacking device be used?

10. Can a rotating fixture be used?

WITH REGARD TO INSPECT:

1. Can inspect be eliminated or overlapped with another operation?

2. Can multiple gauges or tests be used?

3. Can a pressure, vibration, hardness, or flash test be used?

4. Can the intensity of illumination be increased or the light sources rearranged to reduce the inspection time?

5. Can a machine inspection be used to replace a visual inspection?

6. Can the operator use spectacles to advantage?

WITH REGARD TO ASSEMBLE, DISASSEMBLE, AND USE:

1. Can a jig or fixture be used?

2. Can an automatic device or machine be used?

3. Can the assembly be made in multiple? Or can the processing be done in multiple?

4. Can a more efficient tool be used?

5. Can stops be used?

6. Can other work be done while machine is making cut?

7. Should a power tool be used?

8. Can a cam or air-operated fixture be used?

is the best one. As a result, he may notice that, in transporting the component parts to the two fixtures, the operator finds it necessary to carry
the parts in an upward direction because of the height of the fixtures. An
improvement may be to have the section of the assembly bench on which
the fixtures are positioned depressed a few inches so that the surface of the
fixtures will now be at a lower level, with the result that the materials can
be carried in a horizontal plane. This might serve to reduce both the travel
time and operator fatigue.

Next, with regard to the holding activity, the checklist suggests that,
when hold cannot be eliminated, an armrest might be provided. The improved method, based on the operator process chart analysis, did not
completely eliminate the need for holding the assembly during the operation in which the rivets were flattened. However, a more detailed study
of this therblig now suggests that providing an armrest for the operator
may enable him to hold the part more effectively and with less fatigue.

The checklist for position raises the possibility of increasing tolerances.
As a consequence, in the process of designing the fixture, the analyst may
take care not to have the diameter of the holes of such a size that an extremely snug fit of the rivet head would result. A slightly larger hole would
permit the operator to position the rivets with less difficulty and in less
time.

Finally, among the questions related to the assemble, disassemble, and
use activities, the question of whether a more efficient tool can be used
is asked. The only tool involved in the assembly of the sliding door is a
hammer. However, it is conceivable that the design of the hammer is not
the best one for the flattening of the rivets and that a hammer with a head
of a particular size and shape will enable the operator to perform this operation in a shorter period of time.

These few examples are representative of the ideas that the analyst may
get by reviewing each of the therbligs recorded on his simo chart in light
of the detailed checklists based on the principles of motion economy. And
of course, the rules of motion economy and their supplementary checklists
would have also suggested all the modifications made earlier as a result
of the operator process chart analysis.

One could maintain that these additional improvements could have been
made on the basis of an operator process chart and that there was no real
need for constructing a simo chart. This may be true. In fact, there may be
analysts who could observe the assembly activity without making any kind
of chart and who would have thought of even more changes than we
proposed. At the other extreme, there may be analysts who would have
thought of few, if any, changes even after analyzing a simo chart. However,
there is reason to believe that, for a given analyst, a more detailed de-

scription of the task will increase the probability of his recognizing opportunities for improvements. It is on the basis of this assumption that we conclude that an analysis of a simo chart is more likely to yield a greater number of salutary changes than will an analysis of an operator process chart.

SELECTING THE MOTION STUDY APPROACH   The reason that a simo chart is not always preferred to an operator process chart for use in a motion study is the higher cost of conducting a micromotion study. To begin with, extra costs are incurred because the firm must make an investment in such things as a camera, photo flood lamps, an exposure meter, tripods, a projector, screen, and cabinets for storing film and equipment. Second, production is more likely to be disrupted when a movie is being taken than when the analyst simply stands at the work station and observes what is going on, because time is required to set up the equipment, the work station may have to be rearranged to make room for the equipment, the operator has to be given special instructions, and it takes time for everybody to return to the normal routine after the movie has been taken. Third, there is the cost of developing the film and the cost of studying it frame by frame during the course of constructing the simo chart itself.

All this is worthwhile if it can be shown that the extra cost of making a simo chart analysis as compared with an operator process chart analysis is more than offset by the extra savings to be realized from the methods improvements made possible by such an analysis. However, it is impossible to make an evaluation of this type prior to inaugurating the study. While it may be feasible to make fairly accurate estimates of the costs of conducting the respective studies, there is no way to predict what potential methods improvements can be associated with the respective approaches. This will depend on the inherent characteristics of the operation being analyzed in the sense that some operations have a higher potential for being improved upon than others, and it will also depend on the inherent ability of the analyst in the sense that some analysts are more capable of making improvements than others. Consequently, the analyst is compelled to rely upon his judgment when deciding on how detailed an analysis should be made. However, his judgment will be better if he keeps in mind certain factors.

The operator process chart is usually capable of providing a basis for making the more important improvements in a motion pattern. Therefore, the additional improvements made possible by a micromotion study probably will not amount to much in terms of a time saving per unit of output. If the total additional time saving is to be of any significance, it will be necessary that the volume of output to be associated with the activity under consideration be quite high. This volume would have to be defined in terms of both the output per time period and the number of time periods during which the operation will be performed. Admittedly, it is impossible to say what volume of output falls into the "quite high" classification, but this can often be decided upon on an intuitive basis.

But just as the total additional time saving would be affected by the anticipated future volume of output, the total additional dollar saving would be affected by still another factor. This is the operator's hourly wage rate. For a given total additional time saving attributable to a micro-motion study, the dollar saving will be at one level if the operator is paid $3 per hour and at another if the operator is paid $5 per hour. Therefore, high wage rates encourage the more costly simo chart analysis, while low wage rates do not. Again, it is impossible to say what a high wage rate is, but as before, the analyst can probably decide upon this on an intuitive basis. And, of course, he will never consider this factor independently of the factor of volume of output, because it is the two of them in com-bination that will influence the magnitude of the total additional saving.

THE NEED FOR PROCESS CHARTS

The simo chart is the last process chart we shall consider. Although all the charts we have discussed can be an effective means for making methods improvements, it would be incorrect to state that a process chart of some kind should always be used when making an analysis. In many cases, the caliber of the methods analyst and the nature of the process involved are such that a visual observation of what is taking place suffices to suggest all the possible improvements.

On other occasions, the process involved may be fairly complex, with the result that the analyst will find it helpful to prepare some type of written description of what is taking place. In these cases, it is not mandatory that the written description of the existing method take the form of a process chart. There is no reason why, in a particular case, a description in essay form might not be just as satisfactory. But in general, most firms lean to-ward the use of process charts when a complicated task is involved which makes a written description necessary. There are a number of reasons for this. First, the form in which the chart is constructed and the activities in terms of which the process it depicts is described practically ensure that the analyst will not overlook any of the steps in the process. Second, the process chart, being a graphic presentation, provides a description which is extremely easy to follow. And third, the use of symbols often proves to be of great value to the analyst. Let us see why this last point is true.

To begin with, the nature of many activities is such that they very often provide the greatest opportunities for improvements. These are such things as delays, storages, holds, and idleness. Now, it is much easier to recognize the presence of these activities by examining symbols than to go through what may be a lengthy verbal description. A similar observation can be made with regard to transportations. The number of transportations and the kinds of transportations which are necessary are usually a reflection of the plant, work station, and workplace layouts and of the existing materials handling system. Therefore, a study of transportations is usually a study of the layout and handling methods. Since the layout and the materials handling system are often studied as a whole, the analyst will most likely prefer to analyze not an individual transportation, but all the transportations collectively. He can do this with greater ease if he is able to separate the transportation activities from the others. Again, he is better able to do this if he has some simple means for recognizing the occurrence of a transportation. The transportation symbol provides him with this means. Next, the operation and inspection activities that appear in a flow process chart are the ones that may call for further analysis in the form of a man and machine chart, a motion study, or a work-station flow process chart. As before, the symbols serve to point out these activities better than verbal descriptions can. On the basis of all this, we conclude that symbols are not absolutely necessary, but they do serve to simplify the task of the analyst.

These, then, are the reasons for preferring process charts as a means of describing the process being studied when a written description is necessary. It could be that these advantages might be completely offset if the construction of a process chart were more difficult and time-consuming than the preparation of some other description. But this is not the case. Regardless of the form of the description, the same information would have to be obtained. The process chart is unique only in the manner in which this information is presented.

EVALUATION OF PROPOSED METHODS

The end result of most methods analyses is that the firm will be confronted by at least two alternatives. One is represented by the old method and the other by the proposed method. In some cases, alternative new methods will be developed in the course of the study.

On occasion, the new method will generate savings at no additional cost and is, obviously, more economical than the old. But as a rule, there will be some expense to be associated with the adoption of the new method, and consideration must be given to whether this cost offsets the expected savings. As this suggests, the result of most methods analyses is a proposed method which must then be evaluated by comparing its cost with that of the existing method. This can be done by means of the uniform annual cost method.

Before closing, we might note that, in our presentation of the process chart approach to the development of more efficient work methods, the illustrations were related in the sense that they all involved tasks that were being performed in the course of manufacturing a sliding-door assembly. Specifically, we began with a study of the entire process by constructing a comprehensive material flow process chart. Following this, selected portions of the process were studied in greater detail with the use of other charts. However, it would be incorrect to conclude from this that every methods analysis begins with the construction of a comprehensive flow process chart for an entire product and that it continues with the construction of a series of work-station flow process charts, man and machine charts, operator process charts, and simo charts for the various activities that appear in the comprehensive flow process chart. In any number of cases, the study will begin and end with the construction and analysis of a comprehensive flow process chart. And in still other cases, the study will begin and end with the construction and analysis of, say, a man and machine chart for an operation being performed at a single work station. As all this suggests, the scope of the methods analysis activity will vary from one situation to another. The jobs to be studied and the extent to which they should be studied will depend, of course, on the opportunities they seem to provide for making improvements and on the cost of making various types of process chart analyses.

The illustrations employed in this presentation were also characterized by the fact that they were based on manufacturing activities. But it should be apparent that the approaches described lend themselves for use in the analysis of any type of activity. Process charts can be, and are being, used to describe and improve office procedures, building construction methods, registration procedures in educational institutions, troubleshooting techniques, ways of serving customers, motion patterns adhered to in surgery, and so on.

QUESTIONS

19-1   Describe an operator process chart in terms of the information it contains.

19-2   Define the following activities that might appear in an operator process chart: (*a*) operation, (*b*) hold, (*c*) transportation, and (*d*) delay.

19-3   What symbols are used to represent the activities that might appear in an operator process chart?

19-4 Under what conditions would an operator process chart be used to make a methods analysis?

19-5 How is the operator process chart analyzed to improve upon the method it describes?

19-6 Describe a simo chart in terms of the information it contains.

19-7 What are therbligs?

19-8 Describe the procedure for constructing a simo chart.

19-9 How is the simo chart analyzed to improve upon the method it describes?

19-10 Under what conditions would a simo chart, rather than an operator process chart, be used to make a methods analysis? Explain.

19-11 Should the process chart approach always be employed when making a methods analysis? Explain.

19-12 Of what value are the symbols that appear in a completed process chart?

19-13 The end result of a methods analysis is usually a proposed new method. What is the procedure for evaluating such proposals?

19-14 What are some examples of nonmanufacturing activities that might be subjected to a methods analysis?

PROBLEMS

19-1 Select a manual activity which is being carried out by a person working at a single location at a work station. The activity considered in this and the following problem can take place in a manufacturing firm, service organization, or home. Then go on to do the following:

  a By means of an operator process chart, describe the present motion pattern being adhered to in the course of performing the task.

  b Analyze the chart with a view toward improving the work method.

  c Prepare a brief description of each of the changes you recommend.

  d Describe the proposed method by means of an operator process chart.

19-2 Select an activity of the same general nature considered in problem 19-1. Then proceed to do everything called for in that problem, with the difference that the present and proposed methods are to be described by means of a simo chart. In these descriptions, do not concern yourself with the elapsed times for the therbligs involved if their short duration precludes your obtaining these times.

PART NINE

WORK MEASUREMENT AND INCENTIVES

TWENTY
STOPWATCH
TIME STUDY

We have seen that, at various points in the production management activity, it is necessary to know the amount of time required to perform a task by an operator following a prescribed method. Thus far, we have assumed, at each of these points, that these times were known, and no consideration was given to the techniques for obtaining this information. These techniques will now be considered.

Determination of time requirements is commonly referred to as "work measurement." In this activity, the firm may ascertain one or more of three different kinds of time. These are: (1) actual time, (2) normal time, and (3) standard time. For the moment, we shall limit ourselves to general definitions of these terms. *Actual time* is the time that will elapse when a task is performed. As opposed to this, the *normal time* is the amount of time required to perform a task by an operator who is working at 100 percent efficiency and experiences no avoidable or unavoidable delays. Finally, the *standard time* is the amount of time required to perform a task by an operator who is working at 100 percent efficiency and experiences no avoidable delays but does experience unavoidable delays.

As a rule, the firm will be interested in either the actual time or standard time, although the latter can be obtained only after the normal time is known. For example, the relevant time in the preparation of an operation schedule or the determination of equipment requirements will be the actual time. However, in the course of developing performance standards with a view toward controlling labor costs, the firm will be interested in the standard time.

Of the two, actual time is the more easily ascertained. In general, this information can be obtained either by timing the operator or from an analysis of past production records. Standard time, however, involves the somewhat elusive concept of 100 percent efficiency and, consequently, is much more difficult to determine. For this reason we shall assume in this presentation of work measurement techniques that the firm is interested in the determination of standard times. The first technique to be considered is the stopwatch time study approach.

THE GENERAL APPROACH

The stopwatch time study, or, more simply, the time study procedure can be summarized as follows: The analyst goes to the work station at which a task is being performed and times the operator with the use of a stopwatch. This is done in a way which will yield the time spent on the elements of work that are *essential* to the successful completion of the task; as this suggests, this elapsed time will not include the time spent on avoidable and unavoidable delays. In the course of timing the operator, the analyst will also pass judgment on the operator's efficiency. These two items of information, the elapsed time and the operator's efficiency, are then used to compute the normal time for the task; this is done by multiplying the elapsed time by the efficiency.

To illustrate this, suppose that the analyst finds that the operator requires an average of 10 minutes per unit of output to perform the essential elements of a task. Furthermore, the analyst concludes that the operator was working at 120 percent efficiency while being timed. To obtain the normal time, that is, the time that would have been required had the operator been working at 100 percent efficiency, the analyst would multiply the elapsed time by the efficiency and find that

Normal time = elapsed time × efficiency

$$= 10 \text{ min/unit} \times 1.20 = 12 \text{ min/unit}$$

After this portion of the procedure has been completed, the analyst makes a separate study to determine the degree to which unavoidable delays occur. For the task under consideration, this study may reveal that the normal time should be increased by, say, 30 percent to allow for the occurrence of these delays. This would be done by multiplying the normal time by 130 percent, which is called the "allowance factor." By doing so, the analyst obtains the standard time which, in our example, would be

Standard time = normal time × allowance factor

$$= 12 \text{ min/unit} \times 1.30 = 15.6 \text{ min/unit}$$

As all this reveals, neither the normal nor the standard time takes into account the time spent on avoidable delays. This is so because, being avoidable, these activities are unnecessary, and, hence, no time will be allowed for them.

In summary, the analyst goes to the work station to obtain three items of information. These are (1) the time spent by the operator on the essential elements of the job, (2) the operator's efficiency, and (3) the frequency with which unavoidable delays occur. With these data, he is able to compute the standard time. Let us now consider the specific steps of the procedure for obtaining these three items of information.

SELECTING THE METHOD

The first step in the time study procedure is to select the method to be followed by the operator. It is not unusual for the operator to employ a less efficient method while being observed than he otherwise does. If the analyst accepts this less efficient method, the result will be an excessive allowed time for the job.

But even in the absence of a situation such as this, the best method is desirable because of the contribution it makes to reduced operating costs. Also, if an improvement is not introduced until after a time standard based on the old method is established, the entire time study procedure must be repeated to obtain a new standard time.

SOME PRELIMINARY STEPS

Having selected the method to be followed, the analyst instructs the operator accordingly. He then goes on to note certain facts on an observation sheet of the type shown in Figure 20-1. As a rule, the name of the operator, a description of the operation, and the department in which the operation is taking place are among the items of information recorded. In addition, the analyst makes a sketch of the layout of the workplace and lists the equipment, tools, jigs, fixtures, and materials being used. These additional data are important because they provide a general description of the method being employed; hence, they will aid the firm, at some later date, to determine whether a methods change has taken place which may justify a revision in the time standard.

DETERMINING JOB ELEMENTS

Following this, the analyst breaks the job down into its elements. The elements of a job are the distinct steps an operator must go through in the process of performing the task. For example, a typical breakdown of a packaging operation might be as follows:

1 Obtain supply of cartons and wrapping paper.
2 Position wrapping paper.
3 Position part on wrapping paper.
4 Wrap.
5 Place in carton.
6 Cover carton.
7 Stamp identification number on carton.
8 Set aside.

For any given job, a number of different elemental breakdowns are possible. Certain restrictions exist, however, and these limit the number of available alternatives. Some of these restrictions become apparent when

OBSERVATION SHEET

SHEET 1 OF 1 SHEETS

ELEMENTS	SPEED	FEED		1	2	3	4	5	6	7	8	9	10	11	12	13	14	15	MIN. TIME	AV. TIME	SELECT. TIME	OCC. PER CYCLE	RATING	NORMAL TIME
1. Fill core box with 3 handfuls of sand. Press sand down each time.			UPPER	.09	.09	.09	.09	.08	.08	.10	.07	.08	.08	.09	.07	.08	.09	.06	.06	.081	.081	1	115	.093
			LOWER	.09	.41	.71	1.07	.38	.67	.98	.28	.57	.87	.18	.46	.76	4.05	.32						
2. Press sand down with one trowel stroke. Strike off with one trowel stroke.			UPPER	.06	.05	.08	.06	.05	.05	.06	.05	.05	.06	.06	.05	.05	.06	.06	.05	.059	.059	1	125	.074
			LOWER	15	.46	.79	.13	.43	.72	2.04	.33	.62	.93	.24	.51	.81	.11	.38						
3. Get and place plate on core box, turn over, rap, and remove box.			UPPER	.13	.13	.15	.14	.13	.13	.14	.13	.14	.13	.12	.14	.12	.13	.13	.10	.126	.126	1	135	.170
			LOWER	.28	.59	.94	.27	.56	.85	.18	.46	.76	3.06	.36	.65	.93	.24	.51						
4. Carry plate with core 4 feet. Dispose on oven truck.			UPPER	.04	.03	.04	.03	.03	.03	.03	.03	.03	.03	.03	.03	.03	.02	.03	.02	.032	.032	1	125	.040
			LOWER	.32	.62	.98	.30	.59	.88	.21	.49	.79	.09	.39	.68	.96	.26	.54						
(1)			UPPER	.07	.10	.08	.08	.07	.08	.07	.08	.08	.08	.07	.07	.08	.09	.09						
			LOWER	.61	.95	.25	.53	.83	.12	.41	.71	7.01	.28	.55	.84	.16	.48	.77						
(2)			UPPER	.05	.05	.05	.05	.06	.06	.06	.06	.05	.06	.06	.07	.06	.05	.05						
			LOWER	.66	5.00	.30	.58	.89	.18	.47	.77	.06	.34	.61	.91	.22	.53	.82						
(3)			UPPER	.14	.13	.12	.13	.12	.13	.13	.12	.11	.12	.13	.13	.14	.13	.13						
			LOWER	.80	.13	.42	.71	6.01	.31	.60	.89	.17	.46	.74	8.04	.36	.66	.95						
(4)			UPPER	.05	.04	.03	.04	.03	.03	.03	.03	.02	.02	.03	.04	.03	.02	.03						
			LOWER	.85	.17	.45	.75	.04	.34	.63	.93	.20	.48	.77	.08	.39	.68	.98						
(1)			UPPER	.07	.07	.08	.08	.08	.08	.07	.08	.09	.08	.09	.08	.08	.08	.09						
			LOWER	9.05	.34	.64	.93	.21	.50	.78	11.07	.39	.69	.99	.29	.59	.89	.19						
(2)			UPPER	.05	.06	.05	.06	.06	.07	.06	.07	.08	.07	.06	.06	.07	.06	.08						
			LOWER	.10	.40	.69	.99	.27	.57	.84	.14	.47	.76	12.05	.35	.66	.95	.27						
(3)			UPPER	.14	.13	.13	.11	.12	.11	.11	.12	.10	.12	.12	.13	.12	.12	.11						
			LOWER	.24	.53	.82	10.10	.39	.68	.95	.26	.57	.88	.17	.48	.78	13.07	.38						
(4)			UPPER	.03	.03	.03	.04	.03	.03	.04	.04	.04	.03	.03	.03	.03	.03	.03						
			LOWER	.27	.56	.85	.14	.42	.71	.99	.30	.61	.91	.20	.51	.81	.10	.41						

FOREIGN ELEMENTS:

Tally-by elements

No. 1	No. 2	No. 3	No. 4
.06-╵	.05-▦▦▦╵	.10-╵	.02-▦
.07-▦▦	.06-▦▦▦╵	.11-▦	.03-▦▦▦
.08-▦▦	.07-▦	.12-▦	.04-▦▦
.09-▦╵	.08-▦	.13-▦▦▦╵	.05-╵
.10-╨		.14-▦▦	
		.15-╵	

TOOLS, JIGS, GAUGES, PATTERNS, ETC.
Core box No. C-1D-7253, Size 1⅞" x 3½"x8½", Wt. 1 lb.; 5"Molder's trowel
Plates 4" x 9"; weight with core 3½ lb. Core sand No. A16

OVERALL RATING	BEGIN	END	ELAPSED	UNITS FINISHED	ACTUAL TIME PER PIECE
125	9:18	9:32	14:00	45	0.31 Min.

| OPERATION: | Make core for crank frame No. 7253 | | | | OP. NO.: | C-10-A |

SUMMARY

NO.	ELEMENTS	NORMAL TIME	FAT'G & PER'L ALLOW.	OTHER ALLOW.	TOTAL ALLOW.	STD TIME
1.	Fill core box with 3 handfuls of sand. Press sand down each time.	.093	12	—	12	.106
2.	Press sand down with one trowel stroke. Strike off with one trowel stroke.	.074	15	—	15	.087
3.	Get and place plate on core box, turn over, rap, and remove box.	.170	15	—	15	.200
4.	Carry plate with core 4 feet. Dispose on oven truck.	.040	12	—	12	.046
						.439

TOTAL STD. TIME PER CYCLE: .439

NO. PIECES PER CYCLE: 1   STD. TIME PER PIECE: Use .44

DRAWING OF PART:

Core:

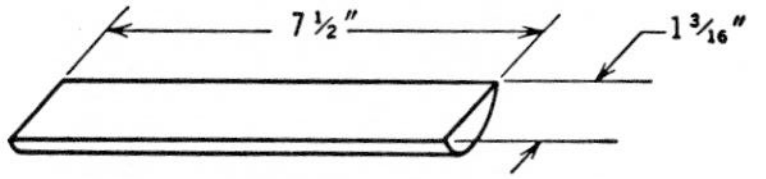

One half of cylinder 1 3/16" x 7 1/2"

Wt. of core before baking = 1/4 lb.

7 1/2"   1 3/16"

PART NAME: Core for crank frame No. 7253		PART NO.: —
MACH. NAME: Bench No. 62		MACH. NO.: —
OPERATOR'S NAME & NO.: S.R. Martin		MALE ☑ FEMALE ☐
EXPERIENCE ON JOB: Six months		FOREMAN: M.L. Ray
NO. MACHINES OPER'D: — MACH. SPEED —		DEPT. NO.: 17

MATERIAL: Dry core sand—specification No. A16

SKETCH OF WORK PLACE   SCALE: One square = 4 inches

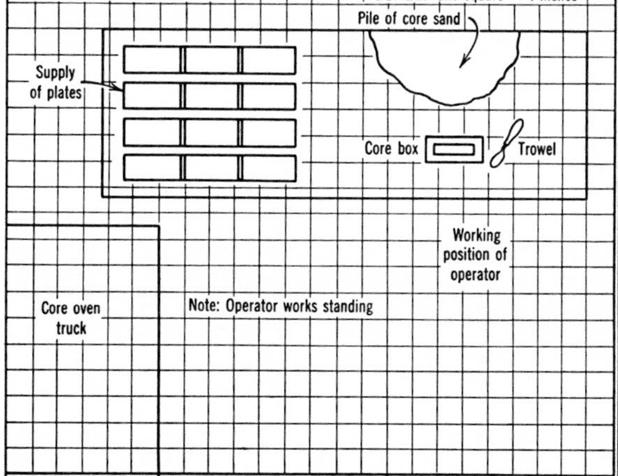

Pile of core sand

Core box

Trowel

Working position of operator

Supply of plates

Note: Operator works standing

Core oven truck

| DATE OF STUDY | OBSERVER C.A. Clark | APPROVED J.S.R. |

Figure 20-1 A stopwatch time study observation sheet (R. M. Barnes, *Motion and Time Study*, 6th ed., John Wiley & Sons, Inc., New York, 1968)

consideration is given to a few of the reasons for timing the elements of a job rather than the entire job as a single unit.

First, studying a job in terms of its elements permits separating man-controlled from machine-controlled activities. *Man-controlled elements* are those over which the operator has control from the standpoint of the amount of time he takes to perform them. For example, the amount of time required to position a part in a machine is affected by the pace at which the operator works and the skill he possesses. *Machine-controlled elements* are those over which the operator does not have control from the standpoint of the amount of time he takes to perform them. For example, given a specified speed, feed, and depth of cut, the amount of time required to complete a machining step is beyond the control of the operator. As a result, the analyst, who will estimate the operator's efficiency for each element at a subsequent point in the study, rates the performance of the operator only on those elements over which he has control; machine-controlled elements are assumed to have been performed at 100 percent efficiency. Separating these elements permits the analyst to do this. For this reason, a breakdown, in which a man-controlled activity is combined with a machine-controlled activity in a single element, would be unsatisfactory.

Second, breaking a job down into its elements permits separating repetitive from intermittent activities. Repetitive elements are those which appear in every cycle of the work, while intermittent elements are those which appear less frequently. For example, the operator positions a part in a machine every time he gets ready to machine a part, and, hence, positioning the part is a repetitive element. However, the machine must be set up only at the beginning of the first cycle; the operator can then machine the entire lot of parts without making another setup, and, hence, setup is an intermittent element. Since the time standard ordinarily is expressed in terms of minutes or hours per unit, it is necessary that intermittent elements be evaluated. This means that the time per intermittent element must be averaged over the number of parts which can be produced following the completion of the intermittent activity. To illustrate, if 30 minutes are required per setup and 15 parts are to be produced with each setup, the setup time would appear in the standard as 2 minutes per unit of output. But such a calculation can be made only if the time required for the intermittent activity is known, and the analyst can determine this time if he separates the intermittent elements from the others when timing the job. Therefore, any elemental breakdown in which an intermittent element is combined with a repetitive one is unsatisfactory.

Third, describing and timing a task in terms of its elements permits separating necessary from unnecessary activities. The latter are represented by delays. Since the normal time is the time that should be required to perform the essential elements of a job, it would not include time spent on delays. Consequently, the analyst would ignore delay times when developing the normal time. He can do this if the unnecessary elements are separated from the others. It follows, therefore, that any elemental breakdown in which an unnecessary element is combined with a necessary one is unsatisfactory.

These, then, are three reasons for timing the elements of an operation, which also serve to reduce the number of possible elemental breakdowns. Additional restrictions exist. One of these is that the elements must be long enough to be timed. What this length is varies with the skill of the analyst, but 0.04 minute is close to the minimum. Further, the elements should have definite and recognizable starting and ending points. This eliminates the need for the analyst's using judgment in the determination of when a given step begins and ends.

Additional reasons also exist for timing a job in terms of its elements. One of these is that an elemental breakdown of a job serves as an excellent detailed job description against which future methods can be compared to determine whether any change has taken place. A final reason is that this practice permits the company to develop "standard data" which can be used to establish time standards for other tasks. Since standard data will be discussed later, it will suffice to say, at this point, that if a firm accumulates elemental times for a variety of elements, a new operation can possibly be described in terms of these elements and a time standard developed without taking additional stopwatch studies.

In any event, after ascertaining the elements and recording them on his observation sheet, the analyst is ready to go on with the actual timing of the activity.

TIMING THE ELEMENTS OF A TASK

Timing is usually done with a decimal stopwatch of the type shown in Figure 20-2. The mechanics of its operation are as follows: The analyst will begin his observations with the large hand in the zero position. Timing is begun by moving the side slide, which is identified in the figure by the letter A, forward. As soon as this is done, the large arm will begin rotating and will continue to do so until the side slide is moved backward. One complete revolution of the large hand represents 1 minute, and, since the dial is divided into 100 parts, readings to within 0.01 minute can be obtained. Every time the large hand makes one complete revolution, the small hand will register 1 minute and is able to register up to 30 minutes.

If the analyst stops the watch at any point by moving the side slide backward, he can return both hands to zero by pressing down on the crown, which is mounted on the winding stem. The crown is identified in the figure by the letter B. So long as the side slide remains in the backward position, the hands will not begin rotating again.

Figure 20-2 Decimal stop-
watch for time study

If the side slide is in the forward position, which means that the hands are rotating, depressing the crown will also return the hands back to zero. However, as soon as the crown is released, the hands will begin rotating again. This is because the watch had not been stopped by moving the side slide backward.

Keeping this in mind, we can now discuss the two different methods of timing which can be employed. One of these is the continuous method; the other is the snapback.

METHODS OF TIMING   In the *continuous method,* the watch is started from the zero position at the beginning of the study by moving the side slide forward and is not touched again throughout the entire study. This means that at no point in the study is the watch ever stopped or are the hands brought back to zero. The watch runs continuously, and the analyst simply records the stopwatch reading at the end of each element. The elapsed times are obtained at the end of the study by taking the difference between successive readings. For example, the results of a continuous study of one cycle of a job consisting of five elements might be as follows:

Element number	Stopwatch reading, min	Calculated elemental time, min
1	0.17	0.17
2	0.49	0.32
3	1.02	0.53
4	1.23	0.21
5	2.18	0.95

In the *snapback method,* the watch is also started from the zero position at the beginning of the study by moving the side slide forward. But from this point on, although the side slide is not touched again, the crown is very much in use. At the end of each element, the analyst simultaneously notes the stopwatch reading and depresses the crown. As soon as the hands reach zero, the crown is released and the hands begin rotating again. Since the hands are snapped back to zero at the beginning of each element, the recorded stopwatch readings represent elapsed times. The results of a snapback study of one cycle of a job consisting of six elements might be as follows:

Element number	Stopwatch reading and elemental time, min
1	0.06
2	1.14
3	0.17
4	0.10
5	0.79
6	0.23

ADVANTAGES OF THE CONTINUOUS METHOD Each of the timing methods has its advantages. One of the advantages of the continuous method is that no time is lost in snapping the watch back to zero, and, hence, more accurate elemental times are obtained. In the snapback method, some time is lost while the hand is traveling back to zero and in the interval between the points at which the hand reaches zero and the analyst releases the crown. The seriousness of this loss varies with the length of the element. To illustrate, a loss of 0.01 minute is significant with elemental times of 0.05 minute but negligible with elemental times of 2.00 minutes, if we consider the error in terms of a percentage of the elemental time.

A second advantage of the continuous method is that it compels the analyst to account for all the time which elapsed during the study. Since the method requires that the watch run continuously throughout the study, the analyst is forced to record everything that takes place and to record the stopwatch readings he observes. Failure to do so would result in incorrect elemental times, because these times are obtained by taking the differences between successive readings. To illustrate why a complete record is an advantage, let us suppose that the analyst obtains the readings shown in the table on the following page when timing a representative cycle of a task by the continuous method.

When establishing the time standard, the analyst may decide that adjusting the machine was unnecessary. The resultant standard, therefore, will include no time for this activity. But subsequently, the operator may

Element	Stopwatch reading, min	Elemental time, min
1. Obtain material and position in machine	0.10	0.10
2. Adjust machine	3.50	3.40
3. Machine	4.52	1.02
4. Remove part and set aside	4.60	0.08

complain that the standard is tight. A review of the time study will reveal that although the operator had been adjusting the machine, this activity was considered to be an avoidable delay. What is important, however, is that this decision is now a matter of record, and the analyst can be called upon to defend his action.

But if the snapback method had been used, the hands could have been snapped back to zero at the beginning and end of the "adjusting the machine" element without making any record of the activity. Doing so would not affect the recorded elemental time for the following element, and no record would exist of the decision involved.

ADVANTAGES OF THE SNAPBACK METHOD An advantage of the snapback method is that, with its use, elemental times are obtained directly. This eliminates the need for making a series of subtractions and, hence, reduces clerical costs.

Another advantage is that it permits the analyst to see what the elapsed times are at the time he is making his study. This can be important on occasion. To illustrate, it may be that the following readings are obtained for an element which involves obtaining a part: 0.05, 0.07, 0.09, 0.15, 0.06, 0.08, 0.12, 0.18, 0.07. The analyst cannot help but wonder why the values vary from a minimum of 0.05 minute to a maximum of 0.18 minute. If he notes the variation while making the study, which he will if he is using the snapback method, he can immediately investigate and find an explanation. It may be that the parts are positioned at the workplace in such a manner that the operator has to travel varying distances when obtaining the individual items. But if the continuous method had been used, the analyst might not have noted the wide variation until after he had returned to the office and made his subtractions. A return to the workplace may not be feasible, because it is possible that the work has already been completed and may not reappear in the production schedule for some time. The analyst must then consider a number of likely explanations. First, it may be that he made an error in reading the stopwatch, and this would explain the extreme values; if this is the case, he would want to discard these times. Or possibly the operator's pace varied considerably, and this would explain the extreme values; if this is the case, the analyst may want to ignore these values on the grounds that his rating of the operator's efficiency was based on the operator's prevalent, and not average, pace. In other words, the analyst is uncertain about whether these values should be retained and must rely on judgment.

In most cases, the decision concerning which timing method should be used is not made by the analyst. Ordinarily, management will stipulate the method to be employed. At the present time, the continuous method is used more widely than the snapback. The consensus is that its advantages more than offset its disadvantages.

DETERMINING THE REQUIRED NUMBER OF OBSERVATIONS

At some point in his study, the analyst must decide whether he has made an adequate number of observations. Of course, this number must be large enough to provide the analyst with an opportunity to observe the work elements that occur intermittently. On the other hand, it cannot exceed the number made possible by the lot size with which the operator may be working. But the question regarding a specific value remains. This value has been defined in two different ways, and each suggests a different approach to its determination.

METHOD BASED ON JUDGMENT In the first approach, cognizance is taken of the fact that the goal of the analyst is the determination of the normal time, that is, the time required to complete an element by an operator working at 100 percent efficiency. Consequently, an adequate number of observations is considered to be that number which will permit the analyst to determine, or rate, the efficiency of the operator. As this suggests, there is no single number which will satisfy this requirement in all cases. Instead, the number will vary from analyst to analyst.

To illustrate this, let us assume that it is known, which it never is, that the normal time for a particular element is 3.60 minutes. An analyst could make a single observation of this activity and find that the elapsed time is 4.00 minutes. If he estimates the operator's efficiency to be 90 percent, he will calculate a normal time of 4.00 minutes times 90 percent, or 3.60 minutes, which happens to be correct. Another analyst, however, may feel more confident in his rating if he observes the operator for five cycles. After having done so, he may find the average elapsed time to be 3.60 minutes. If he estimates the efficiency to be 100 percent, he will also obtain the correct normal time of 3.60 minutes. However, there may be an analyst who studies the operator for 100 cycles and obtains an average elapsed time of 3.00 minutes. But if he estimates that the operator worked at an efficiency of 110 percent, he will calculate a normal time which will be incorrect in spite of the fact that he has made 100 observations. All this proves is that one observation may be adequate for one analyst and 100 observations inadequate for some other analyst. Consequently, it can be maintained that no one can say quantitatively what an adequate number of observations is. Only a generalization is possible, namely, that every analyst must make that number of observations which will enable him to rate accurately the performance of the operator he is observing.

THE STATISTICAL APPROACH   The second approach to the determination of an adequate number of observations is statistical in nature.[1] The reasoning which underlies this method is as follows: Any operator performing an element of work at a fairly constant pace will not always complete the element in exactly the same length of time. The reason for what is assumed to be a random variation in performance times is that there will be chance variations in the operator's movements and pace and also in the position of parts and tools with which he works. As a result, if the analyst were to observe the operator for an extended period, he would find that the elapsed times for a given element would have a distribution with a mean μ and a standard deviation σ'. This distribution may or may not be normal. But even though the population of individual time values for the element may not be normally distributed, if the analyst were to take a large number of samples of size n, the distribution of the resultant average elapsed times would approach normality. Therefore, with a given operator, we can associate a normal distribution of average elapsed times for a given element of work, and this distribution will have a mean μ and a standard error $\sigma_{\bar{x}}$. This mean will be equal to the mean of the distribution of individual elapsed times, but the standard error will be equal to σ' divided by $\sqrt{n}$.

The advocates of the statistical approach to the determination of an adequate number of observations maintain that the object of this phase of the time study is to determine the mean of the distribution of elapsed times to be associated with the operator being studied. Therefore, they define an adequate number of observations to be that number which will permit the analyst to determine this mean for each element with a satisfactory degree of accuracy. This differs from the earlier definition, in which it was maintained that an adequate number is that number which will permit the analyst to pass sound judgment on the efficiency of the operator.

---

[1] The statistical concepts underlying this approach were explained in pp. 347–354 and are only being applied here.

To go on, the time study is looked upon as a way of taking a single sample of the operator's performance times. The number of observations represents the sample size. The question now becomes: What must the sample size be to enable the analyst to determine the mean of the population of elapsed times which the operator will eventually generate for a given element of work? The efficiency rating problem is considered to be independent of this one.

An obvious answer is that the analyst should begin timing the operator on the first day the latter begins this work and continue timing him until he is retired from this work. The analyst would then have a sample size equal to the population size and could calculate the true population mean. This, however, is not practical. Observing the operator for what may be an extended period of time would involve a prohibitive cost. Also, the time standard is required to satisfy fairly immediate needs, and the information, if obtained too late, would be of no value. Consequently, a smaller sample must be taken.

The actual size of the sample will be affected by the degree of accuracy the analyst demands and the risk of making an error that he is willing to assume. For example, he may decide that he wants chances to be 95.5 out of 100 that his sample average will be within 5 percent of the population average. To ascertain the required sample size, he will utilize the following approach:

If the sample average $\overline{X}$ is to be within 5 percent of the population average μ, the maximum acceptable value of the sample average is $1.05\,\mu$ and the acceptable minimum is $0.95\,\mu$. Furthermore, if the chances are to be 95.5 out of 100 that a sample average between these two values will be obtained, it becomes necessary that the maximum value coincide with $\mu + 2\sigma_{\overline{x}}$ and the minimum value with $\mu - 2\sigma_{\overline{x}}$; this is so because 95.5 out of 100 sample averages in a normal distribution of sample averages will have values between $\mu \pm 2\sigma_{\overline{x}}$. In brief, the desired distribution of sample means is as shown in Figure 20-3. As an examination of this figure reveals, the following requirement must be satisfied:

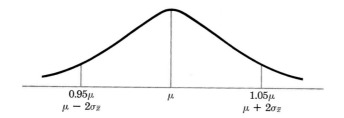

| 0.95μ | μ | 1.05μ |
| $\mu - 2\sigma_{\overline{x}}$ | | $\mu + 2\sigma_{\overline{x}}$ |

Figure 20-3 Example of a desired distribution of sample averages

$$0.05\mu = 2\sigma_{\bar{x}} \qquad\qquad (20\text{-}1)$$

However, because of the relationship that exists between the standard deviation of the distribution of individual values and the standard error of the distribution of sample averages, we can say that

$$0.05\mu = 2\frac{\sigma'}{\sqrt{n}}$$

which yields

$$n = \left(\frac{2\sigma'}{0.05\mu}\right)^2 \qquad\qquad (20\text{-}2)$$

The nature of this expression is such that the sample size can be found only if the population average and standard deviation are known. However, the population average is what the analyst wants to find. Consequently, Eq. (20-2) can be applied only after the values of μ and σ' are estimated. This is done as follows:

The analyst goes to the work station and takes some arbitrary number of observations for a given element. Let us call this number n'. He then calculates the average of these n' readings and uses this average as an estimate of the population average. In effect, the population average is now represented by the following expression:

$$\mu \doteq \frac{\sum\limits_{i=1}^{n'} X_i}{n'} \qquad\qquad (20\text{-}3)$$

where X_i signifies the observed times and $\doteq$ denotes an approximation. The same n' readings are used to estimate the population standard deviation. This is done with the use of the following expression:

$$\sigma' \doteq \sqrt{\frac{\sum\limits_{i=1}^{n'} (X_i - \mu)^2}{n'}} \qquad\qquad (20\text{-}4)$$

Substituting the estimate of μ in this expression, we obtain the following as an estimate of σ':[2]

$$\sigma' \doteq \sqrt{\frac{\sum (X_i - \sum X_i/n')^2}{n'}} \qquad\qquad (20\text{-}5)$$

---

[2] When we estimate the standard deviation from a sample, a better estimate is obtained if we use $(n'-1)$ in the denominator of Eq. (20-5). However, this is a refinement we can ignore in this application without introducing any appreciable error, especially if n' is fairly large.

If Eq. (20-5) is subjected to a few algebraic operations, it will assume the following form:

$$\sigma' \doteq \frac{1}{n'}\sqrt{n'\Sigma X_i{}^2 - (\Sigma X_i)^2} \tag{20-6}$$

Let us now substitute the approximations for the population average and standard deviation in Eq. (20-2). When we substitute Eq. (20-3) for μ and Eq. (20-6) for σ' and simplify, we obtain

$$n = \left[\frac{40\sqrt{n'\Sigma X_i{}^2 - (\Sigma X_i)^2}}{\Sigma X_i}\right]^2 \tag{20-7}$$

For other combinations of probabilities and acceptable percentages of error, we should obtain different formulas. To illustrate, if a probability of 0.997 were established of getting a sample average within 10 percent of the population average, we should want 0.10μ to equal $3\sigma_{\bar{x}}$. With the described procedure, the following expression would be derived:

$$n = \left[\frac{30\sqrt{n'\Sigma X_i{}^2 - (\Sigma X_i)^2}}{\Sigma X_i}\right]^2 \tag{20-8}$$

Each such formula is to be interpreted as follows: If the population average and standard deviation are what they have been estimated to be on the basis of n' readings, the calculated n represents the required sample size.

Let us now illustrate the application of this approach with the use of Eq. (20-7). For purposes of simplicity, we shall assume that the task under consideration consists of only one element. The first step requires that the analyst take some unspecified number of readings. Suppose he takes 5 and finds the elapsed times X_i in hundredths of a minute and their squares to be as follows:

X_i	$X_i{}^2$
5	25
6	36
5	25
5	25
6	36
$\Sigma X_i = 27$	$\Sigma X_i{}^2 = 147$

Making the necessary substitutions in Eq. (20-7), he obtains the following:

$$n = \left[\frac{40\sqrt{5(147) - (27)^2}}{27} \right]^2 = 13.2 \text{ or } 14$$

Because the actual sample size n' of 5 is less than the calculated required sample size n of 14, the sample size must be increased. However, we cannot say that exactly 9 more observations will be required. When additional elapsed times are obtained, the cumulative total number of observations will be used to reestimate μ and σ', and these revised estimates may yield a required sample size which is smaller, equal to, or greater than 14. For example, the analyst in our illustration may go on to take only 5 more observations so that n' is now 10. The 10 elapsed times and their squares may be as follows:

X_i	X_i^2
5	25
6	36
5	25
5	25
6	36
5	25
5	25
5	25
5	25
5	25
$\Sigma X_i = 52$	$\Sigma X_i^2 = 272$

The necessary substitutions in Eq. (20-7) will now yield the following:

$$n = \left[\frac{40\sqrt{10(272) - (52)^2}}{52} \right]^2 = 9.5 \text{ or } 10$$

The actual sample size of 10 is now equal to the calculated value, so it can be concluded that no additional observations are necessary. The same would be true if n' exceeded n. However, if n' were less than n, additional elapsed times would have to be obtained and a new required sample size computed. This would continue until n' equaled or exceeded n.

This, then, is the statistical approach to the determination of the number of stopwatch observations to be made on a particular operator for a given element. The outlined procedure would have to be followed for every element of the job being studied.

EVALUATION OF THE STATISTICAL APPROACH   The statistical approach has a number of limitations. One of these stems from the assumption that the variation in readings is due to chance. Very often this is not true. Time study analysts have found that an important cause of variation is an intentional change in pace by the operator at various times during the study in order to mislead or confuse the analyst. When this occurs, the requirement of randomness is not being satisfied, and the theory is no longer applicable.

Also, the mechanics of the approach are troublesome. As an examination of the formulas indicates, the sample size will vary with the population average. This means that a different sample size may be required for every element of the study if no two elements appear to have the same average. As a result, if the continuous method of timing is being used, the number of complete cycles to be observed will be governed by that element which calls for the largest sample size. In some instances, it may be a fairly large number. This increases the cost of the study. Further, lot sizes may be such that it is impossible to obtain the necessary number of readings at the time they are required. Finally, there is a chance that the obtained sample average differs significantly from the population average because the sample average came from one of the tails of the distribution.

All this does not mean that there is general agreement that the approach would be any more valuable if these limitations did not exist. The question arises concerning the value of knowing the operator's true average performance time. The purpose of the study is not to ascertain this but to determine the average of an operator working at 100 percent efficiency. And as was shown earlier, the correct normal time can be found without knowing the operator's true average time. But knowing the operator's true average time provides no assurance that the correct normal time will be found. This brings us to the subject of performance rating.

RATING THE OPERATOR'S PERFORMANCE

Either while making his observations or after completing them, the analyst must rate the operator's performance. We know that the goal of the analyst is the determination of the elemental times that would be required by an operator working at 100 percent efficiency. This kind of operator is called a "normal operator."

A normal operator has been described as one who possesses an average amount of skill and expends an average amount of effort. Further, the normal time is the time that will be required by such an operator following a given method and working under average conditions. This raises the question of how average skill, effort, and working conditions are to be defined. Those who attempt to answer this question invariably conclude that average skill and effort are the skill and effort to be associated with a normal operator, and average working conditions are those under which a normal operator can complete a task in normal time. This, of course, completes the vicious circle.

In any case, the problem of performance rating can be broken down into two parts. First, the analyst must know what a normal operator is. Second, he must be able to evaluate any operator on the basis of this abstract concept of normality. But in the time study activity, the analyst usually finds himself in the position of not having a precise measure of what normal performance is and of then being compelled to pass judgment on an operator in terms of this intangible normal operator. For this reason, performance rating is one of the most controversial aspects of the stopwatch time study procedure.

In our discussion of performance rating, we shall assume that the analyst will rate the operator's efficiency on each element of the job. If he does, the end result of a time study may be as follows:

Element	Average elapsed time, min	Rating factor	Normal time, min
1	2.00	0.65	1.30
2	0.50	1.00	0.50
3	1.50	1.20	1.80
Total	4.00		3.60

An alternative to elemental performance rating is to rate the operator's average efficiency on the entire job. With reference to our example, this means that, instead of estimating three elemental rating factors and calculating three elemental normal times to obtain the total normal time, the analyst would simply estimate the operator's average efficiency and apply this to the total average elapsed time to obtain the total normal time. If we assume that the three given elemental ratings are correct, the overall rating factor would have to be 0.90 which, when applied to the total average time of 4.00 minutes, would yield the correct total normal time of 3.60 minutes. It should be noted that this overall rating factor must be a weighted average of the elemental ratings, because each element does not account for the same proportion of total elapsed time.

Proponents of overall rating maintain that, at best, the analyst can obtain an overall impression of the operator's efficiency. But there are a number of reasons why rating elements is preferred to rating the entire job. First, if normal elemental times are available, the company can develop standard data which may enable it to describe a new job in terms of elements for which normal times are known; this would eliminate the need for making stopwatch studies of these new jobs. And second, there is reason to believe that more accurate ratings can be made of the parts of a job than of the entire job because of the weighting which is innate in the overall rating factor; in brief, there is a danger that the analyst may be unduly influenced in his selection of an overall rating factor by the operator's performance on job elements which account for a small proportion of the total time.

But whether elemental or overall rating is employed, a very common practice is to have the analyst rate the operator strictly on the basis of judgment. However, a number of different performance rating methods have been developed which, although they do not eliminate the need for judgment, provide guides for making better judgments. No attempt will be made to present each of these methods. Instead, we shall limit our discussion to a few which are representative of those suggested for use.

THE WESTINGHOUSE SYSTEM   The first of these methods is the Westinghouse system. Although it was designed to be used when the analyst wants to rate the entire job, there is no reason why the system cannot be applied to each work element to obtain elemental ratings. With this method, the operator's performance on either the entire job or a given element of the job is evaluated in terms of four factors. These are skill, effort, consistency, and conditions. In brief, skill is defined as the proficiency at following a given method; effort, as the will to work; consistency, as the degree of variation in performance times; and conditions, as the characteristics of the physical environment which affect the operator, such as heat, light, humidity, and noise. The analyst is required to decide upon the level of skill the operator possesses, the amount of effort he is expending, the degree of consistency in his performance times, and the nature of the working conditions. Categories have been established for each of these factors, and the analyst must select that category into which the operator falls. A complete listing of these categories is shown in Table 20-1.

It will be noted that a positive or negative point value is assigned to each category. These values are handled as follows: If the analyst rates the operator's skill as B1, his effort as D, his consistency as C, and conditions as E, the operator will be rated in quantitative terms by totaling the point values assigned to each of these categories. In this case, the total will be

$$0.11 + 0.00 + 0.01 - 0.03 = 0.09$$

This total is then added to 1.00 to yield 1.09, or 109 percent, which is now assumed to represent the operator's efficiency. The average elapsed time is multiplied by 1.09 to obtain the normal time.

When one turns to the details of the system, it becomes apparent that the analyst must use judgment when deciding what level of skill the operator possesses, the amount of effort he is expending, his degree of consistency, and the nature of the conditions.

Insofar as the factors themselves are concerned, effort must be evaluated

Table 20-1   Factors and Point Values in the Westinghouse System of Performance Rating*

Skill			Effort		
+0.15	A1	Superskill	+0.13	A1	Excessive
+0.13	A2		+0.12	A2	
+0.11	B1	Excellent	+0.10	B1	Excellent
+0.08	B2		+0.08	B2	
+0.06	C1	Good	+0.05	C1	Good
+0.03	C2		+0.02	C2	
0.00	D	Average	0.00	D	Average
−0.05	E1	Fair	−0.04	E1	Fair
−0.10	E2		−0.08	E2	
−0.16	F1	Poor	−0.12	F1	Poor
−0.22	F2		−0.17	F2	

Conditions			Consistency		
+0.06	A	Ideal	+0.04	A	Perfect
+0.04	B	Excellent	+0.03	B	Excellent
+0.02	C	Good	+0.01	C	Good
0.00	D	Average	0.00	D	Average
−0.03	E	Fair	−0.02	E	Fair
−0.07	F	Poor	−0.04	F	Poor

*S. M. Lowry et al., *Time and Motion Study and Formulas for Wage Incentives*, 3d ed., McGraw-Hill Book Company, New York, 1940.

separately from skill, but the difficulty of doing so can be appreciated by anyone who has watched an exceptionally skilled individual give an "effortless" performance, that is, an individual whose skill permitted him to perform a task without any apparent effort.

The factor of consistency also poses a problem. It may be that the nature of the work is such that inconsistency is the natural result of a constant pace; parts may be positioned in different locations, materials may vary, and so on. Or an inconsistent operator may generate a lower average elapsed time than a consistent one. Yet, in each of these cases, the operator would be penalized for inconsistency. Because of the questionable relevance of this factor, it has become fairly common practice to designate consistency as being average when using this method of performance rating.

The factor of conditions presents another difficulty. The reasoning behind this factor is as follows: The normal time is the time that should be required under average conditions. If conditions at the time of the study are "ideal," less time will supposedly be taken by the operator than would have been taken if the conditions had been average, and, therefore, the elapsed time will be increased by 6 percent to obtain the normal time. If conditions are "poor," more time will be taken by the operator, and, therefore, the elapsed time will be reduced by 7 percent to obtain the normal time. However, a difficulty arises from the fact that in evaluating effort, there is a natural tendency to take into consideration the conditions under which the operator is working; in effect, the two factors are not independent.

A final observation in regard to the system is that there is no way of demonstrating that the point values involved are correct.

Because of these limitations of the system, one is forced to conclude that it leaves, as it must, many of the problems of performance rating unsolved.

OBJECTIVE RATING   The second method we shall consider is objective rating, which was developed by Mundel.[3] With this method, each element of the task is rated by taking into consideration two factors. One of these is *observed pace;* the other is *job difficulty.*

Observed pace is used synonymously with speed of movement, and, therefore, its consideration takes into account the fact that operating efficiency will be reflected in the pace, or speed, at which the operator works while following a prescribed method. However, it is recognized that job difficulty will affect the pace at which an operator can be expected to work.

Job difficulty is described in terms of six categories of job characteris-

[3] M. E. Mundel, *Motion and Time Study,* 2d ed., Prentice-Hall, Inc., Englewood Cliffs, N.J., 1955.

Table 20-2   Secondary Adjustments in the Objective Rating System*

Category no.	Description	Reference letter	Condition	Percent adjustment
1	Amount of body used	A	Fingers used loosely	0
		B	Wrist and fingers	1
		C	Elbow, wrist, and fingers	2
		D	Arms, etc.	5
		E	Trunk, etc.	8
		E2	Lift with legs from floor	10
2	Foot pedals	F	No pedals or one pedal with fulcrum under foot	0
		G	Pedal or pedals with fulcrum outside of foot	5
3	Bimanualness	H	Hands help each other or alternate	0
		H2	Hands work simultaneously doing the same work on duplicate parts	18
4	Eye-hand coordination	I	Rough work, mainly feel	0
		J	Moderate vision	2
		K	Constant, but not close	4
		L	Watchful, fairly close	7
		M	Within $\frac{1}{64}$ inch	10
5	Handling requirements	N	Can be handled roughly	0
		O	Only gross control	1
		P	Must be controlled, but may be squeezed	2
		Q	Handle carefully	3
		R	Fragile	5
6	Weight		Identify by the letter W, followed by actual weight or resistance	Use table below

Weight, lb	Percent adjustment arm lift	Percent adjustment leg lift	Weight, lb	Percent adjustment arm lift	Percent adjustment leg lift	Weight, lb	Percent adjustment arm lift	Percent adjustment leg lift
1	2	1	18	34	14	35	55	32
2	5	1	19	35	15	36	56	34
3	6	1	20	37	16	37	58	35
4	10	2	21	38	17	38	59	36
5	13	3	22	39	18	39	61	38
6	15	3	23	39	19	40	63	39
7	17	4	24	40	20	41	65	40
8	19	5	25	41	21	42	67	42
9	20	6	26	42	22	43	68	43
10	22	7	27	43	23	44	71	44
11	24	8	28	45	24	45	73	
12	25	9	29	46	25	46	74	
13	27	10	30	47	26	47	76	
14	28	10	31	48	28	48	78	
15	30	11	32	50	29	49	80	
16	31	12	33	52	30	50	82	
17	32	13	34	53	31			

* M. E. Mundel, *Motion and Time Study*, 2d ed., Prentice-Hall, Inc., Englewood Cliffs, N.J., 1955.

tics. Each of these categories is broken down into classes or "conditions," and each condition has associated with it a stipulated percent adjustment which is used to arrive at a performance rating factor. These categories, conditions, and percent adjustments are shown in Table 20-2.

The system is applied as follows: The firm must first select a simple job and choose a pace which it considers to be normal for that job. A simple job would be one which can be described in terms of Table 20-2 by the reference letters A, F, H, I, and N and involves negligible weight; in brief, it is a task which is not difficult in any respect. Having selected such a job, the firm can arrange to have an operator perform the task at various speeds. The actual performances or films of these performances can be viewed by responsible individuals and a decision reached regarding which pace is to be considered normal. Normal pace for a given firm will, of course, depend on the caliber of its personnel, and this will be affected by the wage rates, fringe benefits, working conditions, and opportunities for advancement with which the firm provides its employees. In any case, the time study analyst is then exposed to demonstrations or films of this simple job being performed at various tempos until he has acquired the ability to identify the speed he is observing in terms of a percent of normal speed.

When actually timing a job, the analyst rates the operator's pace for each element. While doing so, he ignores the difference between the actual work situation and the one used to define normal pace. In other words, the pace rating is not adjusted to reflect job differences. For example, if moving a 50-pound casting was done at one-half the speed of, let us say, the simple job of moving a sheet of paper at normal speed, the pace rating would be recorded as 50 percent.

Next, the factor of job difficulty is considered. It is this factor which compensates for differences between work situations and is used to make a secondary adjustment in the average elapsed elemental time. To illustrate how this is done, let us return to our element of moving a 50-pound casting to which a pace rating of 50 percent was assigned. The analyst must now describe the difficulty of this element in terms of the categories and conditions contained in Table 20-2 and, in this manner, obtain the called-for percent adjustment values. For moving the casting, let us assume these to be as shown in the following table:

Category	Condition	Adjustment, %
1	Arms, elbows, wrists, and fingers used	5
2	No pedals	0
3	Hands help each other	0
4	Moderate vision	2
5	Only gross control	1
6	50-lb arm lift	82
Total		90

The secondary adjustment factor is obtained by adding the total percent adjustment to 100 percent, which in this case results in a secondary adjustment factor of 190 percent. The normal time for the element would be the average elapsed time multiplied by the pace rating times the secondary adjustment factor; as this suggests, the performance rating factor is equal to the product of the pace rating and the secondary adjustment factor. In our example, if the average time had been 1.00 minute, a pace rating of 50 percent and a secondary adjustment factor of 190 percent would result in a normal time of

$$1.00 \text{ min} \times 0.50 \times 1.90 = 0.95 \text{ min}$$

The foregoing procedure would be followed by the analyst to arrive at a pace rating and secondary adjustment factor for each work element.

The contribution of the objective rating system is that it attempts to quantify differences between jobs. However, one cannot say with certainty that it has done so in a satisfactory manner. An immediate question is whether all differences between jobs can be described in terms of the six categories considered; for example, maybe consideration should also be given to the conditions under which a job is performed. Next, there is no way of proving that the percent adjustment assigned to each condition is correct.

In addition, the system has a number of subjective elements. Someone must decide what normal pace is. Also, the analyst must use judgment in determining the pace rating. And finally, the nature of some of the categories is such that no one condition is obviously the correct one; one analyst may decide, for example, that "moderate" vision is required, while another may feel just as strongly that it must be "constant but not close."

TEMPO RATING   The last system to be considered will be called "tempo rating." In this method, which can be applied to obtain either elemental ratings or an overall rating, the time study analysts in a given firm are acquainted with management's concept of normal tempo in the following manner: First, all the jobs in the plant are reviewed and placed in various classes. Each class consists of jobs which are similar, in the sense that similar equipment is employed; working conditions are not appreciably different; little variation exists in the size, shape, and weight of the materials involved; and the work elements have much in common. In brief, jobs are classified in accordance with their difficulty.

Next, one job is selected from each of these classes of work which is considered to be typical of that class. Then, films are made of each of these typical jobs being performed at various tempos. Now it becomes the responsibility of management, which may be represented by the plant manager and his superintendents, to view these films and select that tempo which it considers to be normal for a specific class of work. This normal tempo will, of course, vary from one class of work to another.

Then, the time study analysts are trained to recognize normal tempo for each class of work and to describe some other tempo as a percent of this normal tempo. The training procedure is as follows: A movie of a given typical job, being performed at a normal tempo for that type of job, is shown to the analysts and identified as representing 100 percent efficiency. Other films are shown of the same job being performed at other levels of efficiency, and each of these efficiencies is made known at the time the corresponding film is being shown. After the analysts are exposed to a number of films for which the corresponding efficiencies are made known, they are then shown films from which they must estimate the efficiencies of the performing operators. The correct ratings are then made known to them for purposes of comparison. This procedure is repeated for every typical job until the analysts acquire sufficient skill to arrive at fairly accurate ratings.

When the analyst is making the time study, he will rate a given element or the entire job by comparing the tempo he observes with what he was trained to recognize as normal tempo in one of the films in which an activity of comparable difficulty appeared. For example, if a 50-pound casting is being moved, the analyst may decide that the rating factor should be 110 percent, because the observed tempo appears to be 10 percent faster than the tempo he was trained to recognize as being normal for an activity of comparable difficulty.

The tempo rating system, like the others, has its limitations. Judgment must be used when defining normal tempo. Also, difficulties may be encountered in selecting typical jobs, and judgment must play a role in their selection. Next, the cost of making the required films is fairly high; films can be rented or purchased, but this is an alternative only when the kinds of films required are available from other sources.[4] Further, the required initial and continuing training of the firm's analysts may prove to be costly and time-consuming. Finally, the analysts must still exercise judgment when rating operators.

Offsetting all this to some degree is the fact that there is reason to believe that the resultant performance ratings, if not accurate, will at least be consistent. It is not unusual for employees to pass judgment on a time standard by comparing it with other standards which have been established. Any apparent inconsistency is quickly detected, and dissatisfaction is a natural consequence.

This concludes the discussion of performance rating methods. Not all firms, of course, adhere to some such systematic method. Often the ana-

---

[4] One source of such films is the Society for the Advancement of Management.

lyst simply uses his own judgment and intuition. In any event, one is compelled to conclude that performance rating is inherently subjective. This does not mean that the application of the stopwatch time study procedure cannot be justified because of the subjective nature of some of its steps. The fact remains that management requires time standards, and if methods for obtaining them are somewhat subjective, these methods must nevertheless be employed because of the lack of a better alternative.

DETERMINING THE TOTAL NORMAL TIME

Having recorded the performance rating factors, the analyst has all the information he is capable of obtaining at the work station. He is now in a position to determine the total normal time required for the task. In presenting the details of this procedure, we shall assume that the continuous method of timing was employed, each element was rated, and more than one operator was studied on the job to provide a check on the consistency of the analyst's performance ratings.

The analyst begins by making the necessary subtractions to obtain elapsed times. Next, he reviews the elements to determine whether any of them were unnecessary. These would be considered to be delays and would be ignored in the computation of the total normal time. Unfortunately, it is not always clear whether an element is necessary or unnecessary. If a machine operator periodically stops to obtain instructions from the foreman or to study a blueprint, there may be some uncertainty about the need for these activities. In doubtful cases such as this, the analyst must base his decision on judgment.

Once this is done, the analyst will usually review the individual elemental times for abnormal times. These are times which, for a given element, are inconsistent with the other times for that element. For example, the elapsed times for the element of positioning materials may be as follows:

0.12   0.14   0.10   0.10   0.25   0.13   0.11   0.05

The values 0.25 and 0.05 would probably be considered to be abnormal, and an attempt would be made to find an explanation for their occurrence. In some cases, the answer may be obvious. For example, the 0.25 value may have resulted from the operator's dropping the material while positioning it. If the analyst had made a note of this while making the study, he will now have his explanation, and since the element was not performed correctly, this particular time will be ignored when computing the average elemental time. In other cases, the answer may not be as obvious. For example, the 0.05 value might be the result of an error in the stopwatch reading; instead of recording, say, 12.57, the analyst might have recorded 12.47. However, this would mean that the time for the succeeding element in this cycle would be overstated by 0.10 minute. If the succeeding element is relatively short, this overstatement will be readily apparent. When the analyst has reason to believe that this is the explanation, he will ignore the two elemental times. Finally, there are cases in which the analyst, by recalling what took place during the study, may discover something innate in the operation which will explain the extreme time values. In that event, there would be no justification for not including these values in his computations.

However, if the analyst finds that none of the above explanations is valid, he must arrive at only one conclusion, namely, that the abnormal times were caused by a radical change in pace by the operator. What he does in this case varies from company to company. In some firms, the analyst is instructed not to discard time values for this cause, because it is assumed that the elemental rating represents the average pace maintained and, hence, reflects these major variations in pace. Other companies believe that these values should be ignored, because the performance rating probably reflects the prevalent pace maintained, and no analyst can be expected to incorporate the effects of unusual pace variations in his final rating.

After the analyst has decided which, if any, time values should be discarded, he proceeds to compute his average elemental times. For repetitive elements, this is usually done by calculating the arithmetic mean of the retained times. Intermittent elements, however, present a special problem. In order to obtain average elemental times, each of which will be expressed in terms of minutes per unit of output, it is necessary to take into consideration the frequency with which intermittent elements must be performed.

Once average elemental elapsed times, all expressed in minutes per unit of output, have been computed, the analyst applies his rating factors to obtain elemental normal times. If only one study has been taken, the sum of these elemental normal times will yield the total normal time for the task.

When more than one study has been made of the job, the procedure for calculating the elemental normal times is followed for each study. Then, to determine the total normal time for the task, the analyst computes the average normal time for each element and then totals these averages to obtain the total normal time. If performance ratings have been fairly consistent, no appreciable difference should exist between the elemental normal times found from each study. Where appreciable differences do exist, the analyst may simply discard inconsistent normal times or may make additional studies if an insufficient amount of data remains.

THE ALLOWANCE FACTOR

At this point, the analyst has the total normal time for an operation. This time must now be adjusted to provide for the occurrence of unavoidable delays.

One example of a delay of this type is the time the operator loses because of machine breakdowns. Other unavoidable delays of the same nature may be experienced because of a lack of materials, faulty materials, or a delay on the part of the foreman in assigning a task to the operator. Also, the operator will always experience a need for personal time to visit the washroom, take authorized rest periods, and so on.

A second category of unavoidable delays includes those activities which are not delays in the strict sense of the term but have not been included in the total normal time. Typical of these would be making minor machine adjustments, cleaning and oiling the machine, replacing cutting tools, obtaining jigs and fixtures, and maintaining the work area. The reason for not providing for these activities in the total normal time is that their nature may be such that the analyst believes it impossible to estimate their time requirements or frequency of occurrence or both.

In brief, there will always be occurrences and activities which have a time requirement and yet have not been included in the total normal time. To compensate for this, the analyst must establish a standard time for the task which exceeds the normal time. As we know, he does this by multiplying the normal time by an allowance factor. The problem at this point is the determination of the allowance factor. Firms that wish to employ other than a rule-of-thumb approach to the determination of allowance factors have recourse to two methods for doing so. One is the *continuous production study;* the other is the *ratio-delay study.* In general, each of these methods calls for determining the frequency with which unavoidable delays occur. It might be maintained that the analyst could determine this during the time study, but as a rule, the amount of time spent on such a study is not sufficiently long for this purpose.

THE CONTINUOUS PRODUCTION STUDY In the continuous production study, the analyst observes the operation for which an allowance factor is to be determined for some continuous period of time. This period may be anything from 8 to 40 hours. During this observation period, he records what activities are taking place and the amount of time spent on each. There is no fixed manner in which the task must be broken down into the various activities it encompasses. However, since the analyst's goal is the determination of an allowance factor for unavoidable delays, he will want to learn what proportion of the total time is spent on these delays.

Therefore, unavoidable delays must be separated from the other activities. Also, since no allowance will be granted for avoidable delays, the analyst will want to ignore the time spent on these delays. Therefore, avoidable delays must be separated from the other activities. Delays having been considered, only one class of activities remains, that is, those activities covered by the total normal time. We shall call these "normal activities." Consequently, the analyst cannot have a coarser breakdown than the following: (1) normal activities, (2) avoidable delays, and (3) unavoidable delays.

Let us assume, for the moment, that the analyst decides on this breakdown and makes a 40-hour study of some task. It could be that he finds these hours to be distributed among the three activities in the following manner:

Activity	Observed hours	Percent of total time
Normal activities	25	62.5
Avoidable delays	10	25.0
Unavoidable delays	5	12.5
Total	40	100.0

These data are now used to calculate the allowance factor. However, in doing so, one must be careful not to make a fairly common error. This error is to say that, since 12.5 percent of the total time is attributable to unavoidable delays, the allowance factor should be 112.5 percent. The correct approach is to express the amount of time spent on unavoidable delays as a percentage of the time spent on normal activities. Doing so in this case yields the following:

Activity	Observed hours	Percent of total time	Percent of normal-activities time
Normal activities	25	62.5	100.0
Avoidable delays	10	25.0	40.0
Unavoidable delays	5	12.5	20.0
Total	40	100.0	

The percentages shown in the last column can be found in either of two ways. For example, unavoidable-delay time, expressed as a percentage of normal-activities time, can be found by taking the ratio of the hours spent on unavoidable delays to the hours spent on normal activities; this is 5 hours divided by 25 hours, or 20 percent. The same result can be obtained by taking the ratio of the percentage of total time spent on unavoidable delays to the percentage of total time spent on normal activities; this is 12.5 percent divided by 62.5 percent, or 20 percent.

In any case, since unavoidable-delay time is equal to 20 percent of the normal-activity time, the allowance factor should be 120 percent. That this approach is correct can be demonstrated by means of a somewhat simpler illustration. Let us assume that the results of a 40-hour study are as follows:

Activity	Observed hours	Percent of total time	Percent of normal–activities time
Normal activities	20	50	100
Unavoidable delays	20	50	100
Total	40	100	

These results indicate that the operator will spend as much time on unavoidable delays as he will on normal activities. Therefore, the standard time for the job should be twice the normal time, which is to say that the allowance factor should be 200 percent. If the results in our illustration are used in the suggested manner, this value of the factor will be obtained.

The validity of this approach is not changed by the fact that avoidable delays may be present. The reason for this is that the logical assumption is made that, if the operator had attempted to do productive work during the avoidable-delay time, the same distribution of normal activities and unavoidable delays would have taken place during this period as took place during the hours not spent on avoidable delays.

EVALUATION OF THE PRODUCTION STUDY APPROACH   The continuous production study method has a number of limitations. The first of these is that, while making his study, the analyst must often rely on judgment to decide whether a delay is avoidable or unavoidable. To illustrate, if the operator stops to adjust the machine, the analyst must decide whether this is necessary. Or if the machine breaks down, the analyst must decide whether it was the operator's fault. Because this type of judgment is required, many companies insist that the analyst break down the task he is observing more finely than shown in the preceding illustration. Instead of having a single activity called "unavoidable delays," the analyst may be required to list every different activity he considers to be an unavoidable delay and record the time spent on each. The same would be done for avoidable delays. Normal activities, however, would be shown as a single activity, because the elements included in the total normal time provide an adequate description. The result is that, instead of having only three activities recorded on his observation sheet, the analyst may have many more.

With a detailed record of this type, a review can be made of the individual activities for which an allowance was granted if there is some complaint that the allowance is unsatisfactory. In effect, the analyst's decision about which of these activities were avoidable or unavoidable is now known and can be discussed and evaluated.

A second reason for a more detailed description is that the allowance eventually incorporated in the time standard will not necessarily be equal to that called for by an initial study of this type. For example, it may be found that the time spent on unavoidable delays is equal to 80 percent of the time spent on normal activities. This may be considered to be excessive. If a detailed listing of these delay times is available, reviewing them may reveal that most of the 80 percent is attributable to machine breakdowns. Corrective action can then be inaugurated to reduce this specific occurrence to a reasonable level, and a new allowance factor can be determined. In the absence of this detailed information, management would have no basis on which to act.

In addition to the fact that the continuous production method is subjective to some degree, it has the further limitation of being costly because of the relatively long observation periods.

Further, the constant presence of the analyst may alter the nature of the activities taking place. At one extreme, an operator, because he is being observed, may not take time to perform such necessary tasks as oiling and cleaning the machine, getting an occasional drink of water, and maintaining the work area in a satisfactory condition. At the other extreme, another operator, because he is being observed, may spend an excessive amount of time adjusting and repairing the machine, consulting with the foreman, filling out production reports, reading blueprints, and so on.

A final criticism becomes apparent when consideration is given to the fact that the goal of the analyst is the determination, for a particular operation, of the true ratio of unavoidable-delay time to normal-activity time which will prevail in the future. Actually, the only way in which this can be ascertained with complete reliability is to have an analyst make a continuous production study beginning at the present time and ending when the operation is no longer being performed. This, of course, is not an acceptable alternative. It would be too expensive, and the information would be obtained too late for use. As a result, a study is made for a limited time period; in effect, a sample of the future is taken. This, naturally, raises the question: What is an appropriate sample size? The answer is that, with this method, there is no way of knowing. As a result, most firms select a study period on the basis of judgment.

Another important point is that, even if the study period is adequate in the sense that it does yield the correct allowance factor, the factor remains correct only while operating conditions remain unchanged. And there is no assurance that conditions prevailing at the present time will prevail in the future. To illustrate, the physical condition of the machine used to perform an operation may be such that, on the average, it is down one hour out of every eight. The length of the continuous production study may be sufficient to bring this out, and, hence, the allowance for machine breakdown will be correct. However, a year from now, the physical condition of the machine may be such that it is down two hours out of every eight, and, consequently, the allowance factor will no longer be adequate. This suggests a need for a periodic review of allowances incorporated in standards to determine whether they continue to reflect actual conditions.

Although there is no approach to the determination of allowance factors which will eliminate all these limitations of the continuous production study method, there is one approach which will eliminate some of them and minimize others. This is the ratio-delay method.

THE RATIO-DELAY METHOD The ratio-delay method, or work sampling, as it is often called, is similar in many respects to the continuous production study. The analyst begins by determining the activities in terms of which the job to be observed will be described. These activities can be either very broad or limited in scope. But for reasons presented, the coarsest breakdown possible is (1) normal activities, (2) avoidable delays, and (3) unavoidable delays. Then, with the use of an observation sheet, such as the one suggested by Figure 20-4, the analyst begins his study.

The study consists of a series of random intermittent visits to the work station at which the task is being performed. Every time the analyst arrives at the work station, he notes which one of the various activities is taking place by making a tally on his observation sheet next to that activity. He then leaves the work station, returns at some later time, notes the activity taking place at that time, and leaves again. This is continued until a sufficient number of observations has been made.

After having made his last observation, the analyst will have a series of tallies for each activity. These tallies are totaled, and the respective totals shown on the observation sheet. A completed observation sheet might, therefore, appear as shown in Figure 20-4.

With these results, the allowance factor would be determined as follows: First, it is assumed that the distribution of the total tallies among the var-

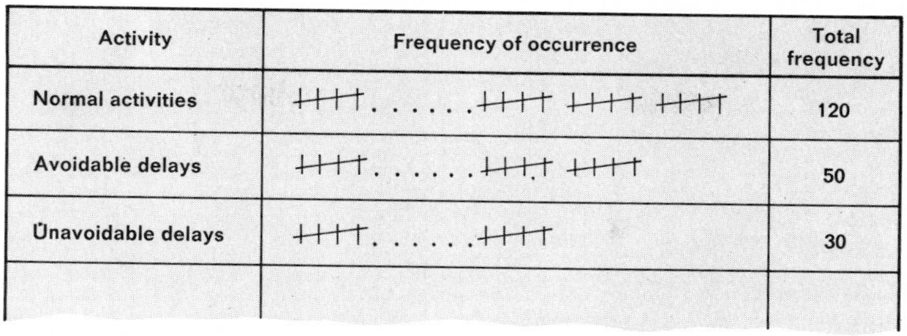

Activity	Frequency of occurrence	Total frequency
Normal activities	⊬⊬⊬ . . . . . . ⊬⊬⊬ ⊬⊬⊬ ⊬⊬⊬	120
Avoidable delays	⊬⊬⊬ . . . . . . ⊬⊬⊬ ⊬⊬⊬	50
Unavoidable delays	⊬⊬⊬ . . . . . . ⊬⊬⊬	30

Figure 20-4   A completed ratio-delay study

ious activities coincides with the distribution of the total time among these activities. This means that the data in our illustration can be expressed in the following form:

Activities	Number of observations	Percent of total observations or total time	Percent of "normal-activities" observations or "normal-activities" time
Normal activities	120	60	100
Avoidable delays	50	25	42
Unavoidable delays	30	15	25
Total	200	100	

The respective percentages are computed in the same manner as they were in the continuous production study. In this case, therefore, the indicated allowance factor would be 125 percent. If this does not appear to be excessive, this factor would be applied to the normal time to obtain the standard time. Otherwise, the analyst may be required to investigate the various unavoidable delays with a view toward reducing their frequency of occurrence. This is more easily done if a finer breakdown than that used in our illustration is available. In any event, if corrective action is taken, a new allowance factor would then have to be developed.

Although this entire procedure is extremely simple, one problem was ignored in its presentation. This deals with the determination of an adequate number of observations. One approach to this determination is as follows: In general, the method calls for the analyst to continue making observations until each of the respective proportions for the various activities no longer fluctuates to any significant degree. For example, it may be that the analyst makes 500 observations, in increments of 100, and finds the results to be as follows:

Cumulative number of observations	Proportion of cumulative observations		
	Normal activities	Avoidable delays	Unavoidable delays
100	0.60	0.10	0.30
200	0.70	0.15	0.15
300	0.65	0.12	0.23
400	0.66	0.13	0.21
500	0.65	0.13	0.22

As an examination of these results reveals, after 300 observations had been made, each of the respective proportions remained fairly stable. Consequently, with a total sample size of 500, the analyst would probably decide that any additional observations would not alter his results significantly, and he would therefore determine his allowance factor on the basis of the proportions obtained from his sample of 500.

A STATISTICAL APPROACH   A second approach to the determination of an adequate number of observations in a ratio-delay study calls for determining the sample size by statistical methods.[5]

When we speak of the activities taking place at a work station, we can think in terms of what is occurring at various moments in time. Insofar as the allowance factor is concerned, the relevant moments in time are the future moments. If we know the percent of these moments that will consist of normal activities, the percent of unavoidable delays, and the percent of avoidable delays, we can divide the unavoidable-delays percent by the normal-activities percent and add the result to 1.00 to obtain the allowance factor. These three percentages can be ascertained with certainty by observing every future moment in time, that is, every item in the population of moments. However, this would be an expensive procedure and would yield the desired information too late. The alternative is to estimate these percentages from a sample.

For the time being, let us assume that the analyst is interested in determining only the proportion of moments which consists of normal activities. If so, he can think of the population in terms of occurrences and nonoccurrences, with the occurrences being represented by normal activities. The task is to determine the population proportion of occurrences p'.

[5] The statistical concepts underlying this approach were explained in pp. 386–390 and are only being applied here.

We know that if samples of a given size n are taken from this population, a distribution of sample proportions will be obtained. This distribution will have a mean p' and a standard error of the proportion σ_p. If the analyst wants to estimate this mean on the basis of a sample, he must begin by stipulating his requirements. For example, he might state that he wants chances to be 95.5 out of 100 that the sample proportion will be within 6 percent of the population proportion.

If we assume that we can approximate the binomial distribution by treating it as if it were normal, we can say that the requirements of the analyst in our example will be satisfied if $p' \pm 2\sigma_p$ coincides with $p' \pm 0.06\,p'$, because 95.5 percent of the sample proportions will fall between $p' \pm 2\sigma_p$. Therefore, as can be seen in Figure 20-5, the requirement is that

$$0.06p' = 2\sigma_p \tag{20-9}$$

When we substitute the expression for σ_p in Eq. (20-9), we obtain

$$0.06p' = 2\sqrt{\frac{p'(1 - p')}{n}}$$

Solving this expression for the sample size n, we find that

$$n = \left(\frac{2}{0.06p'}\right)^2 \left[p'(1 - p')\right] \tag{20-10}$$

An examination of Eq. (20-10) reveals that its use requires that the population proportion be known before the required sample size can be computed. But if this proportion were known, there would be no need for taking a sample. Therefore, as in similar situations we have considered, it is necessary to begin with an estimate of the value of this unknown. To illustrate the procedure involved, let us continue with our example in which the analyst wants the probability to be 0.955 that the sample proportion of normal activities will be within 6 percent of the population proportion.

The analyst begins the study by making some arbitrary number of observations, say, 500. He then calculates what percentage of these observations consists of normal activities; in the case being considered, it may be that 300, or 60 percent, of the 500 observations fall into this category. Next, this percentage is used as an estimate of the population proportion of normal activities and substituted in Eq. (20-10). Doing so yields a required sample size of 741. This means that, if p' is 0.60, the actual sample size of 500 is inadequate and must be increased. However, there is no way of determining exactly how many more observations must be made, because p' will be reestimated on the basis of the cumulative number of observations made, since a larger number is likely to provide a better estimate. In

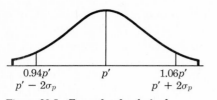

$$
\begin{array}{ccc}
0.94p' & p' & 1.06p' \\
p' - 2\sigma_p & & p' + 2\sigma_p
\end{array}
$$

Figure 20-5   Example of a desired distribution of sample proportions

any case, the analyst may go on to make only 150 more observations and find that 416, or 64 percent, of the cumulative total of 650 represent normal activities. Substituting 0.64 for p' in Eq. (20-10), he would find the required sample size to be 625. Since this is less than 650, it would be concluded that the actual sample size of 650 is adequate, and the population proportion of normal activities would be assumed to be 0.64. As this suggests, observations continue to be made until the actual sample size equals or exceeds the required size.

This outlined procedure would be followed for each of the activities being considered in the study. This is not to say that a different sample must be taken for each activity. Instead, a single sample is taken, and the respective proportions or percentages estimated from this sample. For example, after having taken one sample of appropriate size, the analyst can examine this sample and determine what proportion of the observations consists of normal activities; the balance would be attributable to other activities. Then, this same sample can be analyzed to determine what proportion of the observations consists of unavoidable delays; now the balance would be attributable to activities other than unavoidable delays. Finally, this same sample can be analyzed to determine what proportion of the observations consists of avoidable delays; in this instance, the balance would be attributable to activities other than avoidable delays. The only requirement is that the sample be large enough to satisfy the obligation imposed upon it by the most demanding activity. This would be the activity which requires the largest sample size. In the case of a uniform probability and accuracy requirement, an examination of the sample-size formula will reveal that this would be the activity which has the smallest population proportion associated with it. If the sample satisfies the demands of this activity, it will more than satisfy the demands of the others.

Of course, the probability and accuracy requirements can vary. For example, the analyst may want chances to be 68.3 out of 100 that the sample proportion will be within 2 percent of the population proportion. This suggests that a variation of $1\sigma_p$ from the mean should coincide with a variation of $0.02p'$ or that

$$0.02\,p' = 1\sigma_p \tag{20-11}$$

Beginning with this expression and following the outlined procedure, we should obtain the following:

$$n = \left(\frac{1}{0.02p'}\right)^2 \left[p'(1 - p')\right] \tag{20-12}$$

In any event, once the respective proportions are determined from the sample, the allowance factor is computed in the manner described earlier.

EVALUATION OF THE RATIO-DELAY APPROACH It was mentioned that the ratio-delay method would eliminate some but not all of the difficulties inherent in the continuous production study approach. The analyst must continue to use judgment when classifying many of the activities he observes, because it may not be obvious whether something is an avoidable or unavoidable delay. Further, even if the sample does provide an accurate allowance factor, this factor is based on the assumption that conditions existing at the present time are the same as those which will exist in the future, which is not necessarily true. Finally, there is some probability that the sample proportions will be poor estimates of the population proportions.

Offsetting these limitations are a number of advantages. The first of these is that the analyst is able to determine the required sample size in a rational manner by means of a statistical approach. Second, even though there is a probability of error, the magnitude of this probability can be calculated. Third, there is reason to believe that comparable results can be obtained more economically by means of the ratio-delay method than by the continuous production study; the savings stem from the relatively smaller amount of time the analyst must devote to the observation of the job activities. Finally, operators and shop supervisors find occasional visits by the analyst to be less disruptive than his constant presence during a continuous production study, and intermittent visits are less likely to alter the nature of the activities taking place.

It should be mentioned, however, that the statistical theory underlying the ratio-delay method is based on the assumption that the visits are made in such a way that the result is a random sample. To increase the probability of the sample's being random, various means have been developed for establishing a schedule of visits. In some firms, the analyst may write out the various times of day, to the closest minute, on individual slips of paper. These are then placed in a container, and slips of paper are drawn at random. For example, if the analyst plans to make 100 visits during an eight-hour shift, 100 slips are selected, and the times noted on them make up the schedule to which he will adhere. A more sophisticated approach calls for the use of tables of random numbers, which can be employed to establish a schedule. Finally, some analysts make a visit whenever they are able to. It may be that one analyst is assigned to making observations on 20 different operations. His day will consist of making the rounds of these work stations. His arrival time at a particular location will be determined by the time it took him to visit the other 19 locations. Since this time will usually vary because of chance, his visits to any one location will probably be random.

Schedules developed by some such means have certain advantages. For all practical purposes, they result in the analyst's making his observations at nonuniform intervals, which prevents the operator's anticipating the next visit and arranging his activities accordingly. Also, they prevent the analyst from deciding not to make a visit at a particular time because "the operator is probably having a rest period" or because "the machine is probably still being repaired."

But regardless of how the allowance factor is determined, the resultant percentage, even if correct, is still an average. For any one day, the allowance may be too large, too small, or just right. At best, it will be correct over the long run.

It might also be noted that the allowance factor, as we have determined it, provides only for the occurrence of unavoidable delays, which were defined to include personal time required by the operator. But some firms also include an allowance for "fatigue." For example, the normal time may be increased by, say, 20 percent to provide for unavoidable delays and by, say, another 15 percent to provide for fatigue brought on by the difficulty of the job; in this case, the total allowance factor would be 135 percent. A fatigue allowance was not considered in our illustrations, because it was assumed that job difficulty would be reflected in the performance rating factors and, therefore, in the normal time for the task.

Having shown how the allowance factor is determined and applied to the normal time to obtain the standard time, we have considered the last step in the time study procedure. We shall now go on to discuss another method for the development of standard times.

QUESTIONS

20-1   Define actual time, normal time, and standard time.

20-2   Express the relationship among normal time, elapsed time, and efficiency.

20-3   Express the relationship among standard time, normal time, and the allowance factor.

20-4   Why is it advisable to select the best method of operation prior to making a time study of a task?

20-5 What general information should the analyst record after he has selected the work method? Why?

20-6 Why is it desirable to obtain elemental elapsed times instead of the total elapsed time for the job?

20-7 To what guides can the analyst adhere when breaking a job down into its elements?

20-8 Define each of the following types of elements: (*a*) man-controlled, (*b*) machine-controlled, (*c*) repetitive, and (*d*) intermittent.

20-9 What is the continuous method of timing? What are its advantages and disadvantages?

20-10 What is the snapback method of timing? What are its advantages and disadvantages?

20-11 Describe the rationale underlying the proposed use of judgment in the determination of the required number of time study observations. Evaluate this approach.

20-12 Describe the rationale underlying the statistical method for determining the required number of time study observations. Evaluate this approach.

20-13 Describe and evaluate each of the following performance rating methods: (*a*) Westinghouse system, (*b*) objective rating, and (*c*) tempo rating.

20-14 After the operators have been timed and their performances rated, in what way does the analyst determine the total normal time for the job?

20-15 Give some examples of things for which time will be allowed in the time standard by means of the allowance factor.

20-16 Describe and evaluate the continuous production study approach to the determination of allowance factors.

20-17 Describe and evaluate the ratio-delay, or work sampling, method for determining the value of the allowance factor.

20-18 What are the two methods for ascertaining whether a sample of adequate size has been taken in a ratio-delay study?

PROBLEMS

20-1 The following elements were selected from a collection of stopwatch time studies. Comment on each from the standpoint of whether it represents a correct elemental breakdown. Explain your decisions.

a Wind wristwatch and obtain supply of punched cards.

b Reach for order form.

c Study blueprint and then place part in machine.

d Type address on envelope.

e Transport six cases and unload first one.

f Iron shirt.

g Clean up work area.

h Machine part, remove, and set aside.

20-2   A necessary work element is involved in each of the cases that follow. For
the element under consideration in a given case, determine:

a The normal time when the elapsed time is 0.120 hour and the efficiency
is 110 percent.

b The standard time when the normal time is 3.56 minutes and the allowance factor is 125 percent.

c The standard time when the elapsed time is 11.48 minutes, the efficiency
is 90 percent, and the allowance factor is 1.40. (Ans. 14.465)

d The elapsed time when the normal time is 0.631 hour and the efficiency
is 120 percent.

e The normal time when the standard time is 7.35 minutes and the allowance factor is 1.30.

f The efficiency when the normal time is 0.233 hour and the elapsed time
is 0.233 hour.

g The allowance factor when the standard time is 25.20 minutes and the
normal time is 16.80 minutes.

h The elapsed time when the standard time is 2.70 minutes, the allowance
factor is 135 percent, and the efficiency is 80 percent. (Ans. 2.50)

20-3   An analyst wants to determine by statistical means the number of observations he should make of an element which appears in a repetitive office
operation he is timing. For each of the following requirements, derive the
formula for the necessary sample size:

a The probability is to be 0.98 that the sample average will be within 10
percent of the population average.

b The probability is to be 0.90 that the sample average will be within 2
percent of the population average.

c The probability is to be 0.95 that the sample average will be within 6
percent of the population average

20-4   A time study is being made of a task being performed in a laundry. For one
of the job elements under observation, the following elapsed times, in
minutes, are obtained:

0.20   0.21   0.20   0.22   0.23   0.21   0.20   0.23

If the probability is to be 0.997 that the sample average will be within 10
percent of the population average, have a sufficient number of observations
been made? Explain.

20-5   A typist is being timed while addressing envelopes. After six cycles, the
elapsed times, in minutes, for one of the elements of the task are found to be
as follows:

0.07   0.08   0.07   0.09   0.09   0.07

The analyst wants chances to be 95 out of 100 that the average time he obtains for this element will be within 6 percent of the population average. Does he have a sufficient number of observations? If not, how many more must he make?

20-6 Suppose that the analyst in the preceding problem goes on to time the typist for five more cycles. For the element under consideration, the elapsed time is 0.08 minute in three of these cycles and 0.07 in the remaining two. Does the analyst now have a sufficient sample size?

20-7 A market research firm has received a large number of completed question-naires which it had sent out at an earlier date. Four elements of work are performed in the course of extracting the relevant data from each question-naire. A time study of the activity has yielded the following average elapsed elemental times and the indicated corresponding estimated efficiencies:

Element	Time, min	Rating factor, %
1	0.64	90
2	0.25	105
3	1.39	110
4	4.70	75

What is the unweighted average of the elemental rating factors? How does this compare with the actual average efficiency at which the individual studied was working? (Ans. 95%, 84.4%)

20-8 A handyman completes a routine maintenance job in 0.475 hour. His per-formance is rated by means of the Westinghouse system, and it is concluded that his skill is fair (E1), effort is good (C2), consistency is excellent, and that conditions are average. What will be the calculated normal time for the activity?

20-9 A stockroom attendant completes an element of work in an average of 0.51 minute. His performance is rated by means of the objective rating sys-tem. The analyst rates the attendant's pace as 80 percent. Job difficulty is described in terms of the following reference letters: D, F, H, K, and P. The weight involved is 5 pounds, and arm lift is required. What is the at-tendant's efficiency considered to be? What will be the calculated normal time for the element?

20-10 An investment advisory service occasionally mails out large amounts of promotional materials. Among other things, this activity calls for folding descriptive brochures and inserting them in a supply of preaddressed en-velopes. A time study is made of one of the employees engaged in this opera-tion. The employee is observed for 12 cycles of the work and her efficiency is estimated by the tempo rating system. The following results were ob-tained with the continuous method of timing:

| | Cycle | | | | Efficiency |
Element	1	2	3	4	
1. Position & fold brochure	0.12	0.31	0.53	0.73	120
2. Insert & put aside	0.20	0.40	0.61	0.80	95
1.	0.94	1.16	1.36	1.55	
2.	1.03	1.24	1.45	1.62	
1.	1.73	1.94	2.16	2.35	
2.	1.81	2.02	2.25	2.42	

a What value will be obtained for the normal time in terms of minutes per unit of output?

b Suppose that, on the basis of judgment, it is decided that an allowance is required only for personal time and that one hour out of an eight-hour day will suffice to take care of personal needs. What standard time will the resultant allowance factor yield?

20-11 A printer packs books prior to shipment. For purposes of establishing a time standard, two packers were timed by two different analysts on the same job. The first analyst used the continuous method of timing and obtained the following results:

| | Cycle | | | | | | Performance rating |
Element	1	2	3	4	5	6	
1. Obtain two cases	1.05	....	4.99	....	8.74	.....	105
2. Place six books in case	1.56	2.89	5.47	6.95*	9.23	10.60	95
3. Set case aside	2.36	3.65	6.25	7.76	10.08	11.34	100
4. Light cigarette	....	3.87					

*Dropped book.

The second analyst used the snapback method when timing the other packer and obtained the following results:

| | Cycle | | | | | Performance rating |
Element	1	2	3	4	5	
1. Obtain two cases	0.82	....	0.80	....	0.85	125
2. Place six books in case	0.44	0.42	0.46	0.40	0.41	110
3. Set case aside	0.71	0.67	0.69	0.71	0.68	115

Using the data contained in both studies, calculate the total normal time for the job in terms of hours per 100 cases. (Ans. 3.002)

20-12 An eight-hour continuous production study is made of the job considered in the preceding problem. A summary of the results is as follows:

Activity	Observed hours
Normal activities	5.50
Unavoidable delays	1.65
Avoidable delays	0.85

a Calculate the percentage of total time attributable to each activity.

b Compute the allowance factor, first, by working with the observed hours and, second, by working with the percentage of total time spent on the respective activities.

c Determine the standard time for the job in terms of hours per 100 cases. (Ans. 3.903)

20-13 Five time studies are made of an assembly activity. The elemental normal times are found to be as follows:

Element	Normal time, min/pc				
	Study 1	Study 2	Study 3	Study 4	Study 5
1	0.126	0.130	0.124	0.127	0.129
2	4.235	4.401	3.192	4.313	4.250
3	0.864	0.888	0.875	1.267	0.892
4	1.498	1.503	1.526	1.511	1.492
5	0.737	0.417	0.419	0.424	0.421
6	0.064	0.059	0.060	0.062	0.066

On the basis of these data, determine the total normal time for the job in terms of minutes per piece.

20-14 After the five time studies referred to in the preceding problem have been completed, a ratio-delay study is made of the assembly activity. A summary of the results is as follows:

Activity	Frequency of occurrence
Normal activities	1,512
Unavoidable delays	227
Avoidable delays	261

a Calculate the percent of total observations attributable to each activity.

b Compute the allowance factor, first, by working with the frequencies of occurrence and, second, by working with the percentage of total observations attributable to the respective activities. Assume that the sample size is adequate.

c Determine the standard time for the job in terms of minutes per piece. (Ans. 8.389)

20-15 An analyst wants to determine by statistical means the number of observations to be made in a work sampling study. For each of the following requirements, derive the formula for the necessary sample size:

a Chances are to be 99.7 out of 100 that the sample proportion will be within 5 percent of the population proportion.

b Chances are to be 95.5 out of 100 that the sample proportion will be within 10 percent of the population proportion.

c Chances are to be 68.3 out of 100 that the sample proportion will be within 12 percent of the population proportion.

20-16 A ratio-delay study of a machining operation is being conducted. The 1,200 observations made thus far are distributed among the various activities in the following manner:

Normal activities	852
Unavoidable delays	228
Avoidable delays	120

The accuracy requirement established for the normal-activity proportion is as described in part *a* of problem 20-15, for the unavoidable-delay proportion as described in part *b*, and for the avoidable-delay proportion as described in part *c*. Has a sufficient number of observations been made?

20-17 Suppose that the study in the preceding problem is continued and that 300 more observations are made. The cumulative total of 1,500 observations is now found to be distributed as follows:

Normal activities	1,062
Unavoidable delays	316
Avoidable delays	122

What sample size requirement is generated by these new frequencies of occurrence? Are additional observations necessary? (Ans. 1,499)

20-18 The chairman of a department in a university wants to know what proportion of the time he spends in his office is devoted to activities related to administration, what proportion to activities related to teaching, and what proportion to activities related to research. He asks a graduate assistant to make this determination by means of a work sampling study, and the assistant begins to do so. But at the end of every 200 observations, he stops to compute the percentage of the cumulative observations attributable to each class of activity. Up to this point, he has obtained the following results:

Cumulative observations	Percent of cumulative observations		
	Administration	Teaching	Research
200	47	43	10
400	41	48	11
600	37	51	12
800	40	49	11
1,000	48	41	11

On the basis of judgment, would you conclude that the current sample size of 1,000 is sufficiently large? Explain.

TWENTY-ONE

THE STANDARD DATA METHOD

After taking a number of stopwatch time studies, the analyst will have normal times for a variety of elements. Eventually, a point will be reached at which many of the elements appearing in new jobs are the same as elements for which normal times have already been determined. In some cases, every single element of a new job is an element which appeared in some earlier task and for which the normal time had been determined. Where this is true, there is no need for making a time study of the new job. Instead, the analyst can simply list the elements of the task and refer to his files to learn what the normal times are for these elements. In this manner, he can ascertain the total normal time for the task. If he applies an appropriate allowance factor to this total, he can obtain the standard time.

This procedure for determining the time standard is the standard data method. We say that the analyst compiles "standard data" for a variety of elements by means of stopwatch time studies and then makes use of these standard data to develop time standards for other tasks.

Standard data are not usually developed by the analyst's haphazardly making a large number of stopwatch time studies with the hope that he will eventually be in a position to describe new jobs in terms of elements which appeared in jobs he has already studied. Instead, a planned approach is employed which enables the analyst to obtain the required information more economically and in a shorter period of time. We shall now consider the steps in such a planned approach.

ESTABLISHING CLASSES OF WORK

The analyst begins by reviewing the operations being performed in the plant with a view toward establishing classes of work. A given class of work would contain those jobs that involve similar elements and are performed by the same method. For example, it may be that, at a number of locations in the plant, cases of finished products are coming off packaging lines. At the end of every line is a man whose job it is to remove each case from the conveyor, seal it, identify its contents, and set it aside. Although there are a number of such lines on which a variety of products are being packaged, the men stationed at the end of these lines perform the same elements by the same method. To illustrate, it may be that each of these jobs can be described in terms of the following elements:

1 Remove the case from conveyor and position on table.
2 Apply glue with 4-inch brush to two of the four case flaps.
3 Press the other two flaps against the glued surfaces.
4 Stamp product number on the case.
5 Remove case from table and place on skid.

However, because jobs are similar does not mean that they will not differ. In the packaging operation we are using for purposes of illustration, one would expect the cases handled to vary in size and weight. Consequently, it may be that the same amount of time will not be required to perform each of these similar tasks. For example, it may take more time to position a heavier case than a lighter one. In fact, it is conceivable that, if 50 cases which differ from each other are being considered, 50 different time standards may be called for.

SELECTING AND STUDYING TYPICAL OPERATIONS

After he has identified a number of similar jobs as belonging to a particular class of work, the analyst will select those jobs which he considers to be representative of this activity. For example, in our final packaging operation, the analyst might want to select cases which range from the lightest to the heaviest in weight and from the smallest to the largest in size. If 50 different cases are involved, he may decide that five of them will suffice to satisfy this requirement. Let us assume that these five cases can be described as follows:

Case type	Volume, cu ft	Weight when filled, lb	Area of glued flaps, sq ft
1	1	10	1
2	4	15	4
3	6	35	2
4	9	50	6
5	15	20	9

The analyst will now make stopwatch time studies of these typical jobs to determine their respective elemental normal times; in these studies, the jobs would be broken down into the same elements, and the operators would be rated on the basis of a uniform concept of normal performance. If the analyst were to do this for the five cases in our illustration, he might find the normal times to be as follows:

Element	Normal time, min per case				
	Case 1	Case 2	Case 3	Case 4	Case 5
1. Remove case from conveyor and position on table	0.11	0.12	0.15	0.1?	0.13
2. Apply glue with 4-in. brush to two of the four case flaps	0.20	0.50	0.28	0.73	0.97
3. Press the other two flaps against the glued surfaces	0.07	0.08	0.08	0.09	0.07
4. Stamp product number on the case	0.04	0.05	0.04	0.05	0.05
5. Remove case from table and place on skid	0.12	0.14	0.18	0.21	0.15
Total	0.54	0.89	0.73	1.25	1.37

ASCERTAINING CAUSES OF VARIATION

It will be noted that the total normal times shown in the preceding table are not uniform, and this fact dictates the nature of the next step. The analyst must determine the cause of the variation. A logical way to begin is to examine each of the elements to see which are constant and which are variable insofar as their normal times are concerned.

An examination of the preceding table reveals that, for all practical purposes, the third and fourth elements are constant. What little variation exists can probably be attributed to inconsistent performance ratings. The same is not true for the remaining elements. Here the analyst must seek some inherent characteristic of the work which caused the variation. It is in this phase of the standard data approach that the analyst's judgment and experience will play an important role, for he must analyze each of the tasks to find the characteristic or combination of characteristics which will provide the required explanation. For example, in regard to the second element, which involves applying glue to the case flaps, the analyst may suspect that the time required is affected by the size of the area to which the glue must be applied. To confirm this suspicion, he can plot the respective normal times for this element against the corresponding areas which were given in the description of the five typical cases. When he constructs his graph, he will find the resultant relationship between the normal time

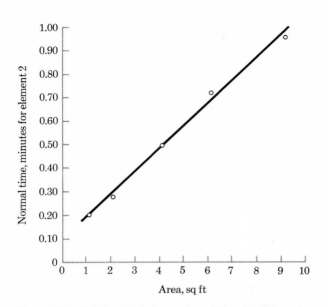

**Figure 21-1   Relationship between normal time for element 2
and area of case flaps**

and surface area to be as shown in Figure 21-1. This figure reveals that the
analyst was correct in his assumption that the variation in area is the cause
of the variation in the normal time for this element. The specific relationship between the two variables is a linear one.

   The analyst would now make the same analysis for the remaining two
variable elements. Both the first and fifth elements involve moving the
case from one location to another. It might be assumed, to begin with, that
the time required to complete each of these elements is dependent on the
volume of the case handled. The analyst could then plot the normal times
against the corresponding case volumes for each of these elements. If he
did, he would find an apparent absence of a cause-and-effect relationship.
As a result, the analyst must turn to some other characteristic. If he now
assumes that the case handling time is affected by the weight of the case,
he can check this by plotting the normal times against case weights. Doing
so for the first element, which involves removing the case from the conveyor, will yield the results shown in Figure 21-2.

   Again it appears that a linear relationship exists between the two variables. The same thing would be found if the analyst were to plot the normal
times for the fifth element, which involves removing the case from the
table, against the corresponding case weights. This is shown in Figure 21-3.

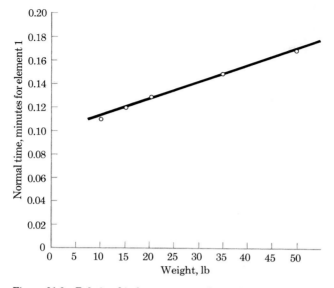

Figure 21-2   Relationship between normal time for element 1 and weight of case

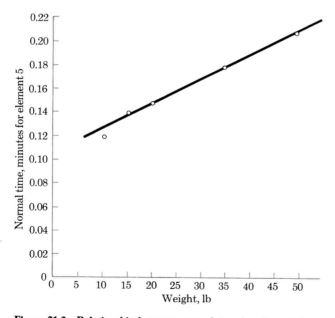

Figure 21-3   Relationship between normal time for element 5 and weight of case

It will be noted that, in our example, a linear relationship was found to exist between the normal times for each of the variable elements and some job characteristic. Obviously, the analyst will find, on occasion, that existing relationships are curvilinear. However, for purposes of simplicity, we shall consider only linear ones. It might also be mentioned that, in our example, the strength of the respective linear relationships could probably be ascertained by a visual examination of the constructed graphs. However, if a quantitative measure is desired, coefficients of correlation could be computed with the use of Eq. (2-8). In the application of this equation, the job characteristic would be treated as the independent variable and the normal time as the dependent variable.

But to continue, having identified the constant and variable elements and determined what characteristics of the work affect the normal times for the variable elements, the analyst is in a position to develop the standard data for the class of work under consideration.

FORMS OF STANDARD DATA

The standard data for the constant elements are found by calculating the arithmetic mean of the available normal times for each of these elements. To illustrate, for the third element in our example, pressing the two flaps against the glued surfaces, this average would be

$$\frac{0.07 + 0.08 + 0.08 + 0.09 + 0.07}{5} = 0.078 \text{ min}$$

For the fourth element, stamping the product number on the case, it would be

$$\frac{0.04 + 0.05 + 0.04 + 0.05 + 0.05}{5} = 0.046 \text{ min}$$

The standard data for a variable element can be left in the form of the chart in which the relationship between the normal time for the element and some characteristic of the work is shown. It is not unusual, however, to express the standard data for variable elements in the form of equations. This calls for finding the algebraic expression for the line that describes the relationship between the normal time for a given element and some job characteristic. If this relationship is linear, this can be done by the method of least squares in which the Y-intercept and slope of the line are found with the use of Eqs. (2-4) and (2-5).

Another alternative is to express the standard data for variable elements in table form. A table for a particular element can be constructed by first listing the different values that might be assumed by the work characteristic that determines the normal time for the element. Then one can go to the graph for that element, read off the corresponding normal times for each of these work characteristic values, and list these times in a second column of the table. Another way of constructing such a table would be to calculate a series of normal times for the variable element by substituting different values of the work characteristic in the equation of the least-squares line for that particular element.

In spite of the availability of these alternative methods of presenting standard data for variable elements, we shall assume that the analyst chooses to express these data in the form of graphs. This means that the standard data for our final packaging operation will appear as follows:

Element	Normal time per case, min
1. Remove case from conveyor and position on table	(Fig. 21-2)
2. Apply glue with 4-in. brush to two of the four case flaps	(Fig. 21-1)
3. Press the other two flaps against the glued surfaces	0.078
4. Stamp product number on case	0.046
5. Remove case from table and place on skid	(Fig. 21-3)

APPLYING THE DATA

Once the standard data are available, the analyst can find the total normal time for any job in this class of work without making a time study. For example, suppose that the analyst wants to find the total normal time required to obtain, glue, seal, stamp, and set aside a case which weighs 25 pounds and has an area of 7 square feet to be glued. It is mandatory that each case be described in these terms because these characteristics will determine the values of the variable elemental times. We know that the time for the first element, removing the case from the conveyor, is to be found from Figure 21-2. If we go to 25 pounds on the X axis, project this point up to the curve, and then read the corresponding time value on the Y axis, we shall find it to be 0.135 minute. The time for the second element, applying glue, would be found in the same manner from Figure 21-1; an area of 7 square feet yields a time of 0.790 minute. The time for the third element, pressing the flaps against the glued surfaces, is a constant 0.078 minute regardless of the nature of the case handled. The same is true for the fourth element, stamping the case, for which we obtained a value of 0.046 minute. Finally the time for the fifth element, removing the case from the table, would be found from Figure 21-3; a weight of 25 pounds yields 0.158 minute. The total normal time would be the sum of these elemental times, which is 1.207 minutes. All this can be summarized as follows:

Element	Normal time per case, min
1. Remove case from conveyor and position on table	0.135
2. Apply glue with 4-in. brush to two of the four case flaps	0.790
3. Press the other two flaps against the glued surfaces	0.078
4. Stamp product number on the case	0.046
5. Remove case from table and place on skid	0.158
Total	1.207

To obtain the standard time for the task under consideration, the analyst must now apply an allowance factor to the calculated normal time. Allowance factors would be determined by one of the methods discussed earlier. This does not mean, however, that either a ratio-delay or continuous production study must be made of every job in a class of work to obtain a unique allowance factor for that job. Very often, it will be found that unavoidable delays occur with approximately the same frequency in every job in a given class of work. In such cases, the representative jobs can be studied to obtain the appropriate allowance factor. This factor becomes the standard allowance factor for the entire class of work and is applied to the total normal time for every job in that class; as we have seen, this normal time can be obtained by either the stopwatch time study or standard data method.

If a firm decides that the same allowance factor is applicable to every job in a class of work, it will sometimes express its standard data in terms of the standard time per element rather than the normal time as we did in our illustration. This would be done by applying the selected allowance factor to each of the elemental normal times obtained from the stopwatch time studies of typical jobs. These elemental standard times are then used to develop the standard data. When standard data are expressed in terms of elemental standard times, applying these data will yield the total standard time directly. This approach, however, restricts, to some degree, the use of these data. If a particular job calls for an allowance factor which differs from the one incorporated in the standard data, these data would not be applicable to that job.

A word of caution on the use of standard data is in order at this point. Although it is true that these data are derived to permit the determination of time standards for all jobs in a given class of work, it is usually not advisable to apply them to jobs whose characteristics fall outside the range of characteristics covered by the time studies from which the standard data were developed. For example, in our packaging illustration, the typical cases studied ranged from 10 to 50 pounds in weight and from 1 to 9 square feet in area to be glued. While we know that, within this range of values, certain elemental times are constant and others vary in a predictable manner, we have no way of knowing what will take place beyond this range. It may be that, if we had studied a much larger or much smaller case, the element of pressing down the two flaps might not have been found to be a constant 0.078 minute. The same holds true for the variable elements. It may be that, if we had studied cases whose weights exceeded 50 pounds, we would have found that the line representing the relationship between weight and handling time would turn up sharply as we went beyond the 50-pound point. In brief, there is some danger in projecting lines beyond the points for which we have time study data. Consequently, one would use the standard data in our illustration with some misgivings to determine a time standard for a case which has, for example, a weight of 60 pounds and an area to be glued of 11 square feet.

EVALUATION OF THE STANDARD DATA METHOD

The described procedure for developing standard data must be followed for every class of work which exists in the plant if extensive coverage is desired. However, the use of standard data will never eliminate completely the need for establishing some time standards by means of other techniques. Even if these data are developed for every class of work in the plant, there will be occasions when the nature of a new job is such that its characteristics exceed the range of characteristics considered when developing the data. Further, it is likely that a number of operations, both present and future, will be unique in the sense that they do not fall into any particular class of work. Time standards for all such tasks would have to be determined by other means.

This is not to suggest that an operation must be exactly like other operations in a given class of work in order that the analyst be able to apply standard data to it. For example, to return to our packaging illustration, it may be that there are some cases being sealed in the plant which do not require that the product number be stamped on them. In those instances, the analyst would use the standard data he developed, but with the difference that no time would be included in the time standard for stamping the case. Or, going to an extreme situation, there may be a task in the plant whose nature is such that it does not fall into any of the classes of work for which the analyst has developed standard data. Yet, a study of the job may reveal that, although in its entirety it is dissimilar from any other job in the plant, it is composed of elements each of which appears in some class of work for which standard data are available. There would be no reason why these data could not be used to determine the time standard. However, it should be mentioned that studies have been made which indicate that the amount of time required to complete an element is affected by the nature of the preceding and succeeding elements. This suggests that a correct application of the standard data can be made only if the job to which the data are applied contains the same elements, performed in the same sequence, as the jobs studied to develop the data. While this is undoubtedly true, the percentage of error introduced is probably negligible when the elements are of fairly long duration, as they are when standard data are compiled from stopwatch time studies.

Those firms that have developed standard data with care have found that the results are worth the effort. Once the data have been derived, time standards can be determined more economically and in a shorter period of time than by means of stopwatch time studies. Also, the resultant time standards will possess a degree of consistency not attainable by any other means. In addition, there is reason to believe that time standards determined from standard data are more reliable than those determined from stopwatch time studies. This is attributable to the fact that, as a rule, standard data are based on more information than is accumulated when setting a time standard for a single task by some other method. Finally, standard data permit establishing a time standard prior to the inception of production. For example, a need may arise for performing a new operation which can be described in terms of elements for which standard data exist. This would permit establishing a time standard before the activity actually takes place. This is extremely desirable for purposes of production scheduling, determining manpower and equipment requirements, and controlling labor costs.

This is not to say, however, that standard data yield perfect time standards. These data are determined on the basis of stopwatch time studies, and, hence, the resultant time standards have many of the limitations of standards established by the stopwatch time study technique, if for no other reason than that judgment must still be used in performance rating when timing typical jobs and in the determination of whether certain activities are necessary.

EXTERNAL SOURCES OF STANDARD DATA

In this discussion of the standard data approach, it has been assumed that the firm will develop its own standard data. This will not always be the case. A growing number of firms are applying data which have been developed by individuals or groups outside their own organizations.

One external source of standard data is the so-called predetermined elemental time systems which have been developed by consultants, educators, and independent research workers. Some of these are the work-factor system, methods-time measurement, basic motion-time study, and motion-time analysis. In essence, each of these systems provides time requirements for elements which can be used to describe many manual activities. Their distinguishing characteristic is that the elements considered are much more basic and of much shorter duration than those considered in stopwatch time studies. In fact, they are on the order of therbligs. Because of the more fundamental nature of the elements, they can be used to describe a greater variety of jobs than can be described with the usual stopwatch time study type of element.

One of the better known of these systems is methods-time measurement (MTM).[1] In this approach, use is made of time data compiled for the following basic activities: reach, move, turn and apply pressure, grasp, position, disengage, release, eye travel time and eye focus, and body, leg, and foot motions. These data are shown in Table 21-1.

[1] A detailed description of this system can be found in H. B. Maynard et al., *Methods-Time Measurement,* McGraw-Hill Book Company, New York, 1948.

Table 21-1   MTM Time Data (Courtesy of MTM Association for Standards and Research)

TABLE I—REACH—R

Distance moved, in.	Time TMU				Hand in motion		Case and description
	A	B	C or D	E	A	B	
¾ or less	2.0	2.0	2.0	2.0	1.6	1.6	A Reach to object in fixed location, or to object in other hand or on which other hand rests.
1	2.5	2.5	3.6	2.4	2.3	2.3	
2	4.0	4.0	5.9	3.8	3.5	2.7	
3	5.3	5.3	7.3	5.3	4.5	3.6	B Reach to single object in location which may vary slightly from cycle to cycle.
4	6.1	6.4	8.4	6.8	4.9	4.3	
5	6.5	7.8	9.4	7.4	5.3	5.0	
6	7.0	8.6	10.1	8.0	5.7	5.7	
7	7.4	9.3	10.8	8.7	6.1	6.5	
8	7.9	10.1	11.5	9.3	6.5	7.2	C Reach to object jumbled with other objects in a group so that search and select occur.
9	8.3	10.8	12.2	9.9	6.9	7.9	
10	8.7	11.5	12.9	10.5	7.3	8.6	
12	9.6	12.9	14.2	11.8	8.1	10.1	
14	10.5	14.4	15.6	13.0	8.9	11.5	D Reach to a very small object or where accurate grasp is required.
16	11.4	15.8	17.0	14.2	9.7	12.9	
18	12.3	17.2	18.4	15.5	10.5	14.4	
20	13.1	18.6	19.8	16.7	11.3	15.8	
22	14.0	20.1	21.2	18.0	12.1	17.3	E Reach to indefinite location to get hand in position for body balance or next motion or out of way.
24	14.9	21.5	22.5	19.2	12.9	18.8	
26	15.8	22.9	23.9	20.4	13.7	20.2	
28	16.7	24.4	25.3	21.7	14.5	21.7	
30	17.5	25.8	26.7	22.9	15.3	23.2	

Table 21-1   MTM Time Data (*Continued*)

TABLE II—MOVE—M

Distance moved, in.	Time TMU				Wt allowance			Case and description
	A	B	C	Hand in motion B	Wt lb Up to	Fac-tor	Con-stant TMU	
¾ or less	2.0	2.0	2.0	1.7	2.5	1.00	0	A Move object to other hand or against stop.
1	2.5	2.9	3.4	2.3				
2	3.6	4.6	5.2	2.9				
3	4.9	5.7	6.7	3.6	7.5	1.06	2.2	
4	6.1	6.9	8.0	4.3				
5	7.3	8.0	9.2	5.0	12.5	1.11	3.9	
6	8.1	8.9	10.3	5.7				
7	8.9	9.7	11.1	6.5	17.5	1.17	5.6	
8	9.7	10.6	11.8	7.2				
9	10.5	11.5	12.7	7.9	22.5	1.22	7.4	B Move object to approximate or indefinite location.
10	11.3	12.2	13.5	8.6				
12	12.9	13.4	15.2	10.0	27.5	1.28	9.1	
14	14.4	14.6	16.9	11.4				
16	16.0	15.8	18.7	12.8	32.5	1.33	10.8	
18	17.6	17.0	20.4	14.2				
20	19.2	18.2	22.1	15.6	37.5	1.39	12.5	
22	20.8	19.4	23.8	17.0				
24	22.4	20.6	25.5	18.4	42.5	1.44	14.3	
26	24.0	21.8	27.3	19.8				
28	25.5	23.1	29.0	21.2				C Move object to exact location.
30	27.1	24.3	30.7	22.7	47.5	1.50	16.0	

TABLE III—TURN AND APPLY PRESSURE—T AND AP

Weight	Time TMU for degrees turned										
	30°	45°	60°	75°	90°	105°	120°	135°	150°	165°	180°
Small—0 to 2 lb	2.8	3.5	4.1	4.8	5.4	6.1	6.8	7.4	8.1	8.7	9.4
Medium—2.1 to 10 lb	4.4	5.5	6.5	7.5	8.5	9.6	10.6	11.6	12.7	13.7	14.8
Large—10.1 to 35 lb	8.4	10.5	12.3	14.4	16.2	18.3	20.4	22.2	24.3	26.1	28.2

APPLY PRESSURE CASE 1—16.2 TMU
APPLY PRESSURE CASE 2—10.6 TMU

Table 21-1 MTM Time Data (*Continued*)

TABLE IV—GRASP—G

Case	Time TMU	Description
1A	2.0	*Pick up grasp*—Small, medium or large object by itself, easily grasped.
1B	3.5	Very small object or object lying close against a flat surface.
1C1	7.3	Interference with grasp on bottom and one side of nearly cylindrical object. Diameter larger than ½″.
1C2	8.7	Interference with grasp on bottom and one side of nearly cylindrical object. Diameter ¼″ to ½″.
1C3	10.8	Interference with grasp on bottom and one side of nearly cylindrical object. Diameter less than ¼″.
2	5.6	*Regrasp.*
3	5.6	*Transfer grasp.*
4A	7.3	Object jumbled with other objects so search and select occur. Larger than 1″ × 1″ × 1″.
4B	9.1	Object jumbled with other objects so search and select occur. ¼″ × ¼″ × ⅛″ to 1″ × 1″ × 1″.
4C	12.9	Object jumbled with other objects so search and select occur. Smaller than ¼″ × ¼″ × ⅛″.
5	0	Contact, sliding or hook grasp.

TABLE V—POSITION*—P

	Class of fit	Symmetry	Easy to handle	Difficult to handle
1—Loose	No pressure required	S	5.6	11.2
		SS	9.1	14.7
		NS	10.4	16.0
2—Close	Light pressure required	S	16.2	21.8
		SS	19.7	25.3
		NS	21.0	26.6
3—Exact	Heavy pressure required	S	43.0	48.6
		SS	46.5	52.1
		NS	47.8	53.4

* Distance moved to engage—1″ or less.

TABLE VI—RELEASE—RL

Case	Time TMU	Description
1	2.0	Normal release performed by opening fingers as independent motion.
2	0	Contact Release.

TABLE VII—DISENGAGE—D

Class of fit	Easy to handle	Difficult to handle
1—*Loose*—Very slight effort, blends with subsequent move.	4.0	5.7
2—*Close*—Normal effort, slight recoil.	7.5	11.8
3—*Tight*—Considerable effort, hand recoils markedly.	22.9	34.7

Table 21-1   MTM Time Data (*Continued*)

TABLE VIII—EYE TRAVEL TIME AND EYE FOCUS—ET AND EF

Eye travel time $= 15.2 \times \dfrac{T}{D}$ TMU, with a maximum value of 20 TMU.

where T = the distance between points from and to which the eye travels.

D = the perpendicular distance from the eye to the line of travel T.

Eye focus time = 7.3 TMU.

TABLE IX—BODY, LEG, AND FOOT MOTIONS

Description	Symbol	Distance	Time TMU
Foot Motion—Hinged at Ankle.	FM	Up to 4″	8.5
With heavy pressure.	FMP		19.1
Leg or Foreleg Motion.	LM	Up to 6″	7.1
		Each add'l. in.	1.2
Sidestep—Case 1—Complete when leading leg contacts floor.	SS-C1	Less than 12″	Use REACH or MOVE time
		12″	17.0
		Each add'l. in.	.6
Case 2—Lagging leg must contact floor before next motion can be made.	SS-C2	12″	34.1
		Each add'l. in.	1.1
Bend, Stoop, or Kneel on One Knee.	B,S,KOK		29.0
Arise.	AB,AS,AKOK		31.9
Kneel on Floor—Both Knees.	KBK		69.4
Arise.	AKBK		76.7
Sit.	SIT		34.7
Stand from Sitting Position.	STD		43.4
Turn Body 45 to 90 degrees—			
Case 1—Complete when leading leg contacts floor.	TBC1		18.6
Case 2—Lagging leg must contact floor before next motion can be made.	TBC2		37.2
Walk.	W-FT	Per Foot	5.3
Walk.	W-P	Per Pace	15.0

If we consider the move activity for purposes of illustration, it will be noted that the allowed time is a function of the type of move, the distance involved, and the weight of the object. The time itself is given in TMUs, where one TMU is equal to 0.00001 hour and represents the normal time for the activity.

The analyst applies these data by, first, describing the task in terms of the basic activities. Established normal times are then obtained from the available tables. The total of these times yields the total normal time for the job. However, the firm must now determine the appropriate allowance factor by some method such as those we have considered and apply this factor to the normal time to obtain the standard time.

The adoption of such a system eliminates the need for performance rating by the firm using the system. However, it is important to recognize the fact that all such predetermined times are derived by means similar to those with which a firm develops its own standard data. This is to say that someone must exercise judgment when determining how much time is required to complete an element of work by an operator working at 100 percent efficiency. If the company does not do this for itself, it can choose to have someone else do it. But the underlying approach is the same in either case.

The standard data method is the last approach to time requirement determination we shall consider. Although we have treated this and the stopwatch time study approach in some detail, it should be stressed that, on many occasions, a firm may ascertain these requirements on the basis of estimates and past production records. However, these methods are likely to be less satisfactory than those we have considered.

DETERMINATION OF OPERATING EFFICIENCY

Once the standard time has been established, an operator's efficiency can be determined with little difficulty. To illustrate, suppose that the standard time for a given job has been found to be 1 hour per unit and that, during an 8-hour period, an operator has produced 10 units. We should say that the hours produced H_p by this operator are as follows:

H_p = standard time/unit $\times$ units produced

= 1 hr/unit $\times$ 10 units

= 10 hr

From time records, we know that the hours worked H_w are 8. Therefore, the operator produced 2 more hours of work than was required. This is 2 divided by 8, or 25 percent more work than was required, and, therefore, we conclude that the operator's efficiency was 125 percent. More directly, we can state that the efficiency E is equal to

$$E = \frac{H_p}{H_w} \qquad\qquad (21\text{-}1)$$

or, in our example, that

$$E = 10/8 = 125\%$$

It is also worth noting that

$$H_w = \text{actual time/unit} \times \text{units produced}$$

Substituting this general expression for H_w and the general expression for H_p in Eq. (21-1), we obtain

$$E = \frac{\text{standard time/unit} \times \text{units produced}}{\text{actual time/unit} \times \text{units produced}}$$

$$= \frac{\text{standard time/unit}}{\text{actual time/unit}}$$

With the use of this expression, the actual time per unit can be ascertained for production management purposes if the standard time and labor efficiency are known. For example, let us assume that the firm is in the process of forecasting actual manpower needs for a given operation. If the standard time for the job is 1 hour per unit and past operating efficiencies of, say, 80 percent are expected to continue in the future, the actual time per unit would be calculated to be

$$0.80 = \frac{1 \text{ hr/unit}}{\text{actual time/unit}}$$

or

$$\text{Actual time/unit} = \frac{1 \text{ hr/unit}}{0.80} = 1.25 \text{ hr/unit}$$

It will be recalled that such calculated actual time requirements were used in production planning and control to determine manpower requirements. This was done by multiplying the units to be produced by the hours required per unit and then dividing the result by the number of hours one man would be available during the period under consideration. But there are cases in which manpower requirements cannot be ascertained in this straightforward manner. Let us consider one such case.

WAITING LINES

Situations arise in which manpower requirements are affected not only by the time required to complete an activity but also by the pattern of demand for the man's services. To illustrate this, let us consider the case of a toolcrib attendant. Machine operators will arrive at the crib to obtain the machine accessories they require. In the simplest case, the time required to serve an operator and the times at which operators arrive will be constant. Under these circumstances, the determination of manpower requirements for the toolcrib presents no difficulty. For example, if the service time is 10 minutes per machine operator and one machine operator arrives every 10 minutes, it is obvious that one attendant should be assigned to the crib. If this is done, the events during a typical one-hour period can be described as follows:

Operator arrival time	Time service begins	Time service ends	Attendant's idle time, min	Operators' waiting time, min	Operators waiting to be served
1:00	1:00	1:10	0	0	0
1:10	1:10	1:20	0	0	0
1:20	1:20	1:30	0	0	0
1:30	1:30	1:40	0	0	0
1:40	1:40	1:50	0	0	0
1:50	1:50	2:00	0	0	0

As can be seen, neither the attendant nor the operators lose any time, and no *waiting line* or *queue* forms. Consequently, there would be no question but that only one attendant should be assigned to the crib. However, the actual situation is usually more complex. To illustrate, it would be more likely that only the *average* service time is 10 minutes and that an operator will arrive every 10 minutes on the *average*. As this suggests, a single service time and a single interval between arrival times may be more or less than 10 minutes. In a case such as this, service delays may occur, and a waiting line may form. To demonstrate this, let us consider another hypothetical time period during which average service and arrival times are 10 minutes but the individual values vary. Specifically, we shall assume that the arrival and service times are as shown in the first two columns of the table that follows. Given these data and assuming that one attendant will be present, we can construct the pattern of events which is described in the balance of the table.

Operator arrival time	Required service time, min	Time service begins	Time service ends	Atten- dant's idle time, min	Operators' waiting time, min	Operators waiting to be served
1:00	12	1:00	1:12	0	0	0
1:08	8	1:12	1:20	0	4	1
1:18	10	1:20	1:30	0	2	1
1:30	6	1:30	1:36	0	0	0
1:45	14	1:45	1:59	9	0	0
1:50	10	1:59	2:09	0	9	1

An examination of the results reveals that, during the 69-minute study period, the attendant was idle 9 minutes and operators were waiting 15 minutes in spite of the fact that the average service time was 10 minutes and that an average of one operator arrived every 10 minutes. Furthermore, because of the waiting time experienced by the operators, a queue formed. If we assume for purposes of discussion that the study period was sufficiently long to reflect the conditions that will generally prevail, the cost to be associated with the idle and waiting times can be calculated. For example, the firm may conclude that the cost of the attendant's idle time is $8 per hour and of the operators' waiting time $12; these costs would include such items as the wage rate, fringe benefits, and equipment downtime. Therefore, the cost for the 69-minute period would be

$$\text{Cost} = 9\ (\$8/60) + 15\ (\$12/60) = \$4.20$$

If the working day contains 480 minutes, the average daily cost would be

$$\text{Cost per day} = \$4.20\ (480/69) = \$29.22$$

Consideration must now be given to whether this represents the minimum possible cost. To reduce the length of the queue and, thereby, the operators' waiting time, the firm could assign one more attendant to the crib. However, this reduction would be offset to some degree by an increase in the attendants' idle time. Nevertheless, it may be that the resultant total cost would be lower than that experienced with one attendant. Whether this is the case could be ascertained by taking the arrival and required service times indicated in the preceding table, determining the idle and waiting times that would be experienced with two attendants serving the operators, and computing the resultant cost. This would be repeated for alternatives calling for three or more attendants until the alternative yielding the minimum cost was found.

METHODS OF ANALYSIS The foregoing illustration serves to indicate the nature of so-called waiting-line, or queuing, problems. In general, the firm finds that, by increasing the available service capacity and, therefore, the service cost, it can reduce the length of the waiting line, and, therefore, the waiting cost. For some combination of service capacity and corresponding waiting line, the cost will be a minimum, and the task is to determine this combination.

The task is a difficult one, because very often service and arrival times will vary. Therefore, it becomes necessary to ascertain the different values these times can assume in a given problem and to estimate the probability of occurrence to be associated with each. Quantitative approaches to the solution of waiting-line problems have been developed in which some assumption is made with regard to the nature of the distribution of service and arrival times. For example, a common assumption is that the Poisson distribution is applicable. But the theory underlying these methods is quite complex, and there is reason to believe that the assumed distributions very often differ from the actual ones. For these reasons, we shall not consider these analytical methods.

Another approach is Monte Carlo simulation. This method calls for estimating, on the basis of past experience if possible, the probabilities of occurrence to be associated with the various possible service and arrival times. Then, in the manner described in our earlier discussion of simulation, a series of arrival times and corresponding service times can be generated. The resultant idle and waiting times and their cost can be calculated for alternative service capacities and the most economical capacity selected. At all times, however, care must be taken to generate a fairly long series so as to obtain an accurate indication of the long-term effects of a given policy.

As all this reveals, the determination of manpower requirements sometimes calls for taking into consideration more than just the time required to perform a job and the number of times a job must be performed. This has been demonstrated by means of an example involving a toolcrib attendant. Similar examples could be given involving machine repairmen, materials handlers, setup men, cashiers, sales personnel, nurses, telephone operators, and the like. In all these cases, the pattern of service demands must be described and a waiting-line analysis performed. It should also be noted that the emphasis in our discussion of this approach has been placed upon the determination of manpower requirements. However, service requirements generate a demand not only for labor but also for other factors of production. Consequently, just as the basic work measurement methods enable the firm to determine both manpower and equipment requirements, so does a waiting-line analysis.

OTHER APPLICATIONS

It has been mentioned that waiting-line analyses can be made of activities that occur in areas other than manufacturing. A similar observation can be made with regard to work measurement. Time standards have been, and are being, determined for such activities as typing, mail sorting, keypunching, order filling, check writing, filing, floor sweeping, window washing, bricklaying, typesetting, auto repairing, and so on. This is not intended to suggest that a standard time can be ascertained for every activity. A prerequisite is that the task be such that it is possible to develop a specific series of steps by means of which the task can be completed successfully, and that the nature of these steps be such that their execution does not involve a significant amount of judgment and intuition. Consequently, one does not encounter time standards for activities such as product design, preparation of advertising copy, computer programming, report writing, diagnostics, and policy determination. But even when we exclude such work, abundant opportunities for determining standard times exist in every type of enterprise.

In closing, we might note that data processing equipment may prove to be useful at various points in the work measurement procedure. The stopwatch time study approach involves arithmetical steps in which a determination is made of elapsed times, normal times, and standard times. At each of these points, data processing equipment could be used to make the necessary computations.

Furthermore, the firm may adhere to the statistical method for determining what number of observations must be made in the course of timing an operator or making a ratio-delay study. It will be recalled that this method calls for estimating the average of the population under consideration, computing the required sample size, and concluding whether the actual sample size is adequate. The procedure can be simplified to some degree by preparing tables, in advance, of required sample sizes for different population averages and for a variety of accuracy requirements and levels of risk. To illustrate, a table could be constructed for use in ratio-delay studies when the analyst wants chances to be 90 out of 100 that his sample proportion will be within 5 percent of the population proportion. The table might contain required sample sizes for population proportions beginning with, say, 0.01 and increasing in steps of one-hundredth until a proportion of 1.00 is reached. After estimating the population proportion to the closest one-hundredth, the analyst need not take the time to calculate the required sample size but could simply turn to the table to determine whether additional observations are necessary. Although the preparation of an adequate set of such tables by manual methods would be very time-consuming, the task becomes relatively simple when data processing equipment is available for this purpose.

The equipment can also be used when standard data are being developed and applied. Coefficients of correlation can be computed to determine the strength of the relationship between the normal time for a variable element and some work characteristic which is suspected of causing the variation. When the cause is determined, the equation of the least-squares line which describes the relationship between the two variables can then be determined. In addition, the equipment could be utilized to compute the normal time for a variable element from the equation of this line as the need to do so arises, or to prepare a table of normal times for different values of the variable for a given element. And of course, any other steps of an arithmetic nature that must be taken to obtain the standard time by means of the standard data method could be performed automatically.

Finally, if a waiting-line analysis is to be performed by means of simulation, a computer can be employed in the manner described when we considered an earlier application of this approach. However, the queuing analysis is sometimes made with the use of quantitative techniques which are based on some assumed theoretical distribution of service and arrival times. The mechanics of these methods are such that significant reductions can be realized in processing times through the utilization of computers.

QUESTIONS

21-1 For purposes of developing standard data by means of stopwatch time studies, what jobs would be considered to be representative of a single class of work?

21-2 On what basis are operations to be time-studied selected from a given class of work?

21-3 What is the difference between a constant and a variable element?

21-4 How are standard data for constant elements determined?

21-5 How are standard data for variable elements determined and expressed?

21-6 If standard data consist of elemental normal times, what is the procedure for developing a time standard with their use?

21-7 Under what condition would the firm be inclined to maintain standard data in the form of elemental standard times? How are these data used to develop a time standard?

21-8 Evaluate the standard data method for determining time standards.

21-9 Describe the methods-time measurement (MTM) system for establishing time standards.

21-10 What is the relationship among the operator's efficiency, the units he produces per time period, the length of the time period, and the standard time per unit of output?

21-11 In waiting-line, or queuing, problems, what do service times and arrival times represent?

21-12 What is the nature of the relationship between the service capacity and the length of the resultant waiting line? Between service capacity and service cost? Between service capacity and waiting cost?

21-13 In general terms, describe the method for determining the most economical service capacity when arrival and service times are known.

21-14 Under what conditions can Monte Carlo simulation be employed in the analysis of waiting-line, or queuing, problems? Describe this approach in general terms.

21-15 What are some examples of activities, other than manufacturing, for which time standards can be established? Which lend themselves to waiting-line analyses?

21-16 How can data processing equipment be used in the area of work measurement? In a waiting-line analysis?

PROBLEMS

21-1 The results of time studies taken to develop standard data were summarized in the table on page 551. Elements 1, 2, and 5 were found to be variable elements, and the standard data for these elements were expressed in the form of graphs. For each of these elements, do the following:

a With the use of Eqs. (2-4) and (2-5), determine the equation of the least-squares line which describes the relationship between the normal time and the independent variable.

b With the use of Eq. (2-8), calculate the value of the coefficient of correlation.

21-2 It is decided to develop standard data for the job of washing windows in a condominium apartment building. These data will be expressed in terms of standard times, because the allowance factor will be constant for all such jobs.

In any case, four stopwatch time studies are made of an individual washing windows of various sizes. The activity involves a number of elements, one of which is "Dry window using a 12-inch squeegee." The analyst correctly assumes that the time required for this element will depend on the size of the window. He begins the determination of the relationship between these two variables by listing the calculated standard times and the corresponding window sizes. The results are as follows:

Standard time, min	Window area, sq ft
0.61	16
0.35	8
0.82	24
0.39	12

a What is the value of the coefficient of correlation for the two variables as determined with the use of Eq. (2-8)? (Ans. 0.98)

b What is the equation of the least-squares line, as determined with the use of Eqs. (2-4) and (2-5), which serves to describe the relationship between the variables? (Ans. $Y' = 0.0745 + 0.0312X$)

c Construct a graph which describes the relationship between the two variables.

d Prepare a table which describes the relationship between the two variables. Do this by beginning with a window area of 8 square feet and increasing the value of the area in steps of 1 square foot until a maximum of 24 square feet is reached.

21-3 Suppose that, in the preceding problem, an allowance factor of 120 percent was used to obtain the standard times on the basis of which the standard data for the element were developed. A need has now arisen for calculating the standard time for drying windows whose areas are 18 square feet each. However, for unexpected reasons, it has become necessary to apply an allowance factor of 135 percent to this new job. What will be the calculated standard time for the element under consideration?

21-4 A metalworking firm makes use of formulas in the determination of normal times for various machining elements. These formulas were not developed on the basis of time studies but derived by taking into consideration such things as the distance the cutting tool must travel and the speeds and feeds at which the equipment is to be operated. As an example, it has been found that the required cutting time for drills is as follows:

Cutting time = distance drill must move ÷ feed

Suppose that a drill must move 2.25 inches in the course of cutting a hole and that the feed is to be 3.82 inches per minute. Determine the normal time for this element of work.

21-5 Containers of various sizes are filled with a powdery material of a certain kind. The task requires that the operator obtain and position the empty container on a roller conveyor, open a spout, wait while the container is being filled, close the spout, and push the container aside. For purposes of developing standard data, time studies have been taken of this job with three different-sized containers. The distances the operator had to walk to obtain and position the containers and the dimensions of the containers are as follows:

Distances and dimensions	Container		
	1	2	3
Distance, ft	10.0	30.0	20.0
Width, ft	1.0	2.0	1.0
Length, ft	1.0	3.0	2.0
Height, ft	1.0	2.0	1.5

The results of the time studies have been summarized as follows:

Element	Normal time, min/case		
	Case 1	Case 2	Case 3
Obtain and position container	0.139	0.243	0.191
Open spout	0.052	0.049	0.055
Fill container	0.170	1.990	0.520
Close spout	0.044	0.048	0.046
Push container aside	0.080	0.084	0.079

a Develop standard data for each of the constant elements.

b Develop standard data for each of the variable elements in the form of an equation of the least-squares line. Then locate these lines on a graph.

c For each of the variable elements, measure the strength of the relationship between the normal time and the assumed cause of variation by means of the coefficient of correlation.

21-6 With the use of the data developed in the preceding problem, determine the total normal time for filling a container whose dimensions are 1.5 by 2.25 by 2 feet and which necessitates the operator's walking 25 feet in the course of obtaining and positioning it. If the company uses an allowance factor of 1.30 for each job in this class of work, what will be the standard time for filling this container? (Ans. 1.524, 1.981)

21-7 The MTM system is to be used to establish a time standard for a task which requires that an operator simply move a large quantity of objects from one location to another. Specifically, the job can be described in terms of the following activities:

a *Reach* 18 inches with the right hand for a very small object which requires an accurate grasp.

b With the right hand, *grasp* the object which is lying close against a flat surface.

    c *Move* the object 24 inches to the other hand.

    d Place the object in the left hand with a *transfer grasp*.

    e *Move* the object 12 inches with the left hand to an approximate location.

    f *Position* the object. The class of fit is loose; the object is easy to handle; and the symmetry class is *S*.

    g *Release* the object normally.

    With the use of Table 21-1, determine the normal time for moving 1,000 units of the object from the one location to the other. If the allowance factor is 118 percent, what will be the standard time? (Ans. 0.709, 0.837)

21-8 Time standards have been established for various operations in a meat processing firm. Calculate the operator's efficiency in each of the following cases:

    a The time standard is 0.125 hour per unit. A total of 76 units is produced in 10 hours. (Ans. 95%)

    b The time standard is 0.240 hour per unit. A total of 22 units is produced in 4 hours.

    c The time standard is 1.500 hours per 100 units. A total of 3,000 units is produced in 45 hours.

21-9 A mail-order house has established time standards for some of its operations. For each of the following cases selected from the firm's records, calculate the actual time per unit of output:

    a The time standard is 0.980 hour per unit, and the efficiency was 142 percent. (Ans. 0.690)

    b The time standard is 2.024 hours per unit, and the efficiency was 100 percent.

    c The time standard is 4.123 hours per 100 units, and the efficiency was 73 percent.

21-10 In the example of a waiting-line analysis presented on pp. 565–566, the average daily cost with one attendant was found to be $29.22. What would have been the cost with two attendants?

21-11 Trucks arrive at a dock where they are unloaded by a method such that only a single man can be assigned to unloading a given truck. By means of Monte Carlo simulation, the firm involved finds that, for a typical eight-hour day, the schedule of arrival and service times is as follows:

Truck arrival time	Required unloading time, hr
0:00	2.0
1:30	2.5
4:00	1.5
5:00	0.5
7:00	1.0

The cost of idle time on the part of unloaders is $10 per hour, and the cost of waiting time on the part of trucks is $75 per hour. For a typical day, determine the total of these costs under each of the following conditions:

a One man is available to unload trucks. (Ans. $155)

b Two men are available to unload trucks. (Ans. $85)

21-12 Suppose that a typical one-hour period in a stockroom can be described as follows: A man arrives at the beginning of the hour and requests service. He is followed by a second man 10 minutes after the hour begins, by a third man 20 minutes after the hour begins, and finally, by a fourth man 30 minutes after the hour begins. The service time is 15 minutes in each case. Because one attendant can service four men per hour and four men will arrive per hour, it is recommended that one attendant be assigned to the stockroom. An alternate proposal is that two attendants be assigned so as to reduce waiting time. If the cost of waiting time is $13 per hour and the cost of an attendant's idle time is $6.50 per hour, which of these two proposals should be adopted?

TWENTY-TWO
WAGE INCENTIVES

The establishment of work standards permits the firm to determine the efficiency of employees assigned to the tasks involved. However, the existence of such standards is not always sufficient in itself to provide the work force with the necessary incentive to maximize its efficiency. Consequently, a firm may decide to pay the more productive employee a bonus whose magnitude will vary in some proportion with the employee's output. In brief, the firm offers a financial incentive which is called a "wage incentive."

A number of different wage incentive plans are available for use. All have certain characteristics in common. One is that every plan is based on some established standard of performance. This means that every plan calls, first, for a decision on the part of management concerning what output it has a right to expect from a normal operator; this level of output represents 100 percent efficiency. With regard to the need for such time standards, it might be noted that, if machine-controlled elements account for a large proportion of the work cycle, the time standard may differ from the one that would have been established in the absence of a wage incentive plan. It will be recalled that machine-controlled elements were rated at 100 percent to obtain normal times because the operator has no control over the time they require. Therefore, if machine time is a significant part of the total time, the operator is limited in his ability to increase his efficiency beyond 100 percent. To provide him with an incentive to keep the equipment operating properly, the firm may increase the time standard by rating machine-controlled elements, say, 130 percent or by including a so-called incentive factor of, for example, 20 percent in the allowance factor.

A second characteristic of every incentive plan is that it involves a decision on the part of management concerning what level of efficiency will mark the point at which the incentive payment will start. For example, one firm may pay incentive earnings to all employees whose efficiency exceeds 100 percent and another to all employees whose efficiency exceeds 80 percent.

Finally, every plan stipulates the manner in which the incentive payment will be determined. To illustrate, one plan may provide that, for every 1 percent increase in efficiency beyond 100 percent, the employee's earnings will increase by 1 percent, while another plan may provide that, for every 1 percent increase in efficiency, the employee's earnings will increase by ½ percent.

Having brought this out, we are now in a position to go on to a study of the basic types of incentive plans. We shall begin with a wage payment plan, which is not an incentive plan in the strict sense of the term. However, a knowledge of its characteristics contributes to an understanding of incentive plans as such. The plan to be considered is called the "day rate plan."

DAY RATE PLAN

In a day rate plan, the operator is paid his base rate regardless of what his level of output happens to be. Therefore, as labor efficiency increases, the labor cost per unit of output decreases. This will be demonstrated by means of an illustration in which we shall consider five different levels of efficiency.

Suppose that the standard time for an operation is 2 hours per unit. To determine the actual time that corresponds to some level of efficiency, we make use of the following expression which was developed earlier:

$$\text{Actual time/unit} = \frac{\text{standard time/unit}}{\text{efficiency}}$$

By substituting in this expression, we shall find that, for the efficiencies shown in the first column of the following table, the actual times per unit will be as shown in the second column.

Efficiency (E), %	Hours worked per unit (H_w)	Operator's earnings per hour (R_a)	Labor cost per unit ($H_w \times R_a$)
50	4.00	$4.00	$16.00
80	2.50	4.00	10.00
100	2.00	4.00	8.00
125	1.60	4.00	6.40
160	1.25	4.00	5.00

Let us now assume that the operator assigned to this job is paid a base rate of $4 per hour. Under a day rate plan, as shown in the third column of the table, his earnings per hour will be this $4, regardless of the efficiency at which he works.

Finally, we can obtain the labor cost per unit for a given level of efficiency by multiplying the labor cost per hour by the hours required to produce one unit. This has been done in the last column of the table.

An examination of the results confirms what was stated earlier. With a day rate plan, in which the operator's actual earnings per hour R_a are always equal to his base rate per hour R_b, direct labor costs per unit decrease as efficiency increases.

AN EVALUATION   It was mentioned that the day rate plan is not an incentive plan in the strict sense of the term. The reason is that there is nothing in the plan which provides a direct financial reward for extra output. This is not to say that, where this method of wage payment is in effect, the employee can work at, say, 20 percent efficiency for an extended period of time without repercussion. The firm would undoubtedly have some formal or informal standard of performance which the employee would be required to meet if he is to qualify for the base rate. However, the base rate is not ordinarily thought of as an incentive.

Also, because an employee is not rewarded directly for a higher level of output, it does not follow that the operator will produce just the required minimum. It may be that greater efficiency will result in a promotion to a better-paying position. But where this incentive for greater efficiency does prevail, it does not exist because of any inherent characteristic of a day rate plan, and hence the plan, as such, does not provide the incentive.

In spite of this lack of an incentive feature, the day rate plan is probably the most widely used method of wage payment. This is true for a number of reasons. First, although we assumed the presence of a time standard for purposes of illustration, there are many tasks whose nature is such that it is impossible to determine what the standard times for their performance should be. For example, a machine repairman may be responsible for diagnosing the trouble and correcting it when a machine breaks down. It would be the rare time study analyst who would try to ascertain the normal time for an activity such as this. Consequently, the absence of a time standard precludes computing the man's operating efficiency and necessitates paying him a fixed hourly rate.

In another case, it may be possible to establish a time standard, but an accurate production count may not be economically feasible. For example, a forklift-truck operator's duties may call for his handling and transporting materials which vary in size, quantity, and location. While a time standard could be established for each different activity, the design of an economical procedure for determining exactly what he had done during a particular day may not be possible. Again, this would prevent anyone from determining his efficiency, and he too would have to be paid on an hourly basis.

Also, there may be tasks for which a time standard can be established and a production count obtained, and yet, the firm may believe that the presence of an incentive to increase the quantity of output may affect the quality of output adversely. For example, a given inspection may be extremely important. In the absence of an incentive plan, the inspector may exercise the required care, but the presence of an opportunity to increase earnings may encourage him to hurry at the expense of the quality of his work. If this cannot be prevented, the firm may prefer simply to pay the inspector his base rate.

In addition, there are some companies which prefer a day rate plan because they find the cost of installing and maintaining an incentive plan prohibitive. An incentive plan may require additional personnel for establishing accurate time standards, making production counts, computing efficiencies, calculating incentive earnings, and maintaining records. On occasion, the cost of all this exceeds the benefits to be realized from the plan.

Also, there are cases in which the presence of an incentive plan creates labor problems which management wants to avoid. The plant's labor force may oppose incentives in principle, or may be constantly inaugurating grievances which stem from the manner in which the incentive plan has been designed or is being maintained. Where this is true, the firm may find it expedient to adhere or revert to the day rate method of wage payment.

Finally, the nature of some firms' operations is such that they want the operating efficiency to be neither above nor below a stipulated level. This would be difficult to accomplish in the presence of a wage incentive plan. For example, there may be three subassembly lines feeding into a final assembly line. These respective lines may have been constructed so that they are balanced if each is operated at the same level of efficiency. If the desired level is 100 percent, one of the lines operating at 120 percent efficiency, which might occur if an incentive plan is in effect, would create as many problems as would a line operating at 80 percent efficiency. Therefore, management would prefer a wage payment plan which will encourage uniform operating efficiencies. One alternative would be a day rate plan, coupled with an understanding that the employees must operate at the desired level of efficiency.

Sometimes, a variation of the day rate plan is used to increase the probability of the desired efficiency being maintained. This variation consists of adding an incentive feature to the day rate plan. For example, if efficiency is to be maintained at 100 percent, management will pay the employees only the base rate if they work at any efficiency less than 100 percent. However, if they work at an efficiency of 100 percent or more, the base rate will be increased by some factor such as 1.20. This has the effect of increasing the base rate by 20 percent for an employee who attains 100 percent efficiency. But there is no incentive for the employee to exceed 100 percent efficiency. This variation of the day rate plan is called the "differential time plan," and, of course, it can involve the use of some factor other than 1.20.

These, then, are the reasons why a company may adhere to a day rate plan or some variation of it. In the absence of such circumstances, it will probably adopt one of many available incentive plans.

FULL PARTICIPATION PLAN BEGINNING AT 100 PERCENT EFFICIENCY

One of the simplest and most widely used incentive plans is the full participation plan, in which an employee becomes eligible for incentive payments when his efficiency reaches 100 percent. With this plan, for every 1 percent increase in output beyond 100 percent, the operator receives a 1 percent increase in earnings. For this reason, the plan is often referred to as a "1-for-1" plan.

To illustrate the mechanics of computing the earnings per hour under this plan, let us assume that, as before, the standard time per unit of output is 2 hours and that the base rate is $4 per hour. Unless stated otherwise, this is the assumption we shall make in all our computations from this point on. But to continue, if an employee's efficiency is, say, 125 percent, his earnings would exceed his base rate by 25 percent.

This 25 percent can be obtained by taking the *difference* between the actual efficiency of 125 percent and the 100 percent efficiency at which incentive payments begin. While this yields the correct answer, it is an incorrect method. The correct method is as follows: Since incentive payments begin at 100 percent efficiency, 100 percent efficiency is, in effect, the required output. An operator working at 125 percent efficiency is therefore producing 125 percent *divided* by 100 percent, or 1.25, times as much work as is demanded of him. Because the 1.25 means that he is producing 25 percent *more* work than he is required to, we say that he will be paid 25 percent more.

Admittedly, the incorrect method yields the same answer, but this is true only when incentive payments begin at 100 percent efficiency. If they were to begin at 80 percent, as they will in another plan we shall discuss, the method would yield an incorrect answer. To illustrate, under such a plan, an operator working at 125 percent efficiency would actually be producing 125 percent *divided* by 80 percent, or 1.5625, times as much work as is demanded of him and, if it is a 1-for-1 plan, would have his earnings increased by 56.25 percent. The *difference* between 125 percent and 80 percent would suggest an increase in earnings of only 45 percent, which is not correct.

Keeping this in mind, let us return to the case of the 125 percent operator working under a full participation plan in which incentive payments begin at 100 percent efficiency. As we saw, his earnings per hour would increase by 25 percent. This would yield earnings per hour equal to

$$R_a = \$4 \times 1.25 = \$5$$

The same approach would be employed in calculating earnings per hour at any level of efficiency from 100 percent on. For efficiencies less than 100 percent, the approach differs because it is customary to guarantee the employee his base rate. This was not always the prevalent practice. At one time, if the employee operated at 80 percent efficiency, his earnings per hour were 80 percent of his base rate; if he operated at 50 percent efficiency, his earnings per hour were 50 percent of his base rate; and so on. The motive underlying the change to a guaranteed base rate was a desire on the part of management to make the incentive plan more acceptable to labor by eliminating the insecurity and uncertainty which prevail in the absence of such a guarantee. Therefore, a provision of a full participation plan is that, so long as the employee is assigned to a task, he is assured of receiving at least his base rate per hour.

In any case, for the same efficiencies considered in the discussion of the day rate plan, the indicated approach would yield the earnings per hour shown in the third column of the table that follows. The actual times per unit would, of course, be those determined earlier, and the labor costs per unit would again be found by multiplying these times by the corresponding earnings per hour. These costs are also shown in the table.

Efficiency (E), %	Hours worked per unit (H_w)	Operator's earnings per hour (R_a)	Labor cost per unit ($H_w \times R_a$)
50	4.00	$4.00	$16.00
80	2.50	4.00	10.00
100	2.00	4.00	8.00
125	1.60	5.00	8.00
160	1.25	6.40	8.00

A study of the results permits us to make a number of generalizations. First, up to 100 percent efficiency, the full participation plan, in which incentive payments begin at 100 percent efficiency and the base rate is guaranteed, does not differ from the day rate plan. Earnings per hour remain constant, and labor costs per unit decrease as efficiencies increase. Second, from 100 percent efficiency on, earnings per hour increase in direct proportion to the increase in efficiency, and labor costs per unit remain constant. The latter was to be expected. Once 100 percent efficiency is reached, the plan provides for passing on to the employee all the labor savings to be realized from a reduction in labor time per unit of output. Hence, management realizes none of these benefits, with the result that unit labor costs remain fixed.

The full participation plan beginning at 100 percent efficiency can be applied to any activity for which a time standard can be developed and an accurate production count obtained. This assumes, of course, that information about the amount of time spent on the task can be made available, which, as a rule, is a correct assumption. The pay formula is relatively simple, and because it impresses most employees as being equitable and is easily understood, the plan is probably more widely used than any other incentive plan. However, on occasion, there are special circumstances which encourage the use of some other plan. One of these is the less than 1-for-1 incentive plan beginning at 100 percent efficiency.

LESS THAN FULL PARTICIPATION BEGINNING AT 100 PERCENT EFFICIENCY

There are a number of plans which can be described as being less than full participation plans beginning at 100 percent efficiency. All are alike in the sense that each pays incentive earnings to the employee whose efficiency exceeds 100 percent. Also, at the present time, each plan usually provides a guaranteed base rate for those employees who operate at less than 100 percent efficiency. But unlike the full participation plan, each of these plans is characterized by the fact that, for every 1 percent increase in output beyond 100 percent, the employee receives a less than 1 percent increase in earnings. The plans differ in the degree to which the operator is compensated for his additional output. For example, some firms have adopted a "50-50" plan, in which the employee's earnings increase by $\frac{1}{2}$ percent for every 1 percent increase in output beyond 100 percent. Others have a "70-30" plan, in which the employee's earnings increase by $\frac{7}{10}$ percent for every 1 percent increase in output beyond 100 percent. Still others adhere to a "60-40" plan, in which the employee's earnings increase by $\frac{6}{10}$ percent for every 1 percent increase in output beyond 100 percent. In the discussion to follow, we shall consider the so-called 50-50 plan for purposes of illustration.

At efficiencies below 100 percent, the operator is paid his base rate, which we shall continue to assume to be $4 per hour, for as long as he is retained on the job. But if he works at an efficiency of, say, 160 percent on the job for which we assumed a standard time of 2 hours per unit, he is eligible for an incentive payment. The magnitude of this payment is computed as follows: At 160 percent efficiency, the employee is producing 60 percent more work than is demanded of him. With a 50-50 plan, he will receive an increase in earnings of one-half of this 60 percent, or 30 percent. As a result, his earnings per hour would be equal to

$$R_a = \$4 \times 1.30 = \$5.20$$

The product of this labor cost per hour and the elapsed hours per unit is the labor cost per unit, which is equal to

1.25 hr/unit $\times$ \$5.20/hr = \$6.50

In the same manner, we can find the earnings per hour and the labor cost per unit at the various other levels of efficiency considered when discussing the preceding two methods of wage payment. The results would be as follows:

Efficiency (E), %	Hours worked per unit (H_w)	Operator's earnings per hour (R_a)	Labor cost per unit ($H_w \times R_a$)
50	4.00	$4.00	$16.00
80	2.50	4.00	10.00
100	2.00	4.00	8.00
125	1.60	4.50	7.20
160	1.25	5.20	6.50

As can be seen, because of the guaranteed base rate, the plan is exactly like the day rate plan for efficiencies up to 100 percent. The employee's earnings per hour remain fixed at the base rate, and increased efficiency is reflected in a reduced labor cost per unit. Once 100 percent efficiency is reached, the operator's earnings per hour begin to increase. But they do not increase at as great a rate as they do with the full participation plan; this is because the employee does not realize the entire labor saving to be associated with a reduction in the labor time per unit of output. For the same reason, labor costs per unit continue to decrease as efficiencies increase beyond 100 percent. However, they decrease at a slower rate than they do with the day rate plan, because now management does not realize the entire labor saving to be associated with a reduction in the labor time per unit of output.

AN EVALUATION   As a rule, an incentive plan of this type is adopted when a firm has reason to believe that its time standards are liberal, that is, loose. This usually is the case when standards are developed by taking average actual times from past production records and adopting them as standard times. Consequently, it is likely that the standard in effect with a less than 1-for-1 plan will be more liberal than the standard in effect with a 1-for-1 plan. For this reason, it would not be correct to compare the results of our computations and conclude that labor costs per unit will be less with a 50-50 plan than with a 1-for-1 plan at some particular level of efficiency.

In any event, the sharing feature of the plan is designed to offset the overstatement of an operator's efficiency attributable to liberal standards. But given that the degree of overstatement is not known, there is no way of ascertaining whether this adjustment is correct.

Also, labor usually resents sharing the benefits of its greater efficiency with management in spite of the fact that the time standards are more liberal than they would otherwise be. Some of the employees just refuse to believe this is so, and others feel that the degree of liberality is more than offset by the sharing feature of the plan.

Furthermore, many managements are troubled by the relatively high labor efficiencies which usually are attained because of the liberal time standards. Pointing out that labor costs per unit decrease as efficiencies increase sometimes helps, but many managements suspect that the costs might be even lower with some other plan based on more accurate standards. In maintaining this position, they may be right.

For these reasons, more and more firms are discarding such plans and taking it upon themselves to establish more accurate time standards by means of stopwatch time studies or through the use of standard data. These standards are then used as a basis for some incentive plan such as a full participation plan.

FULL PARTICIPATION PLAN BEGINNING AT LESS THAN 100 PERCENT EFFICIENCY

We have discussed a full participation plan in which the employee's earnings increased by 1 percent for every 1 percent increase in output beyond a certain point. This point was 100 percent efficiency. We shall now consider a full participation plan in which incentive earnings begin at some point below 100 percent efficiency. For example, a firm may have a 1-for-1 plan in which the operator becomes eligible for an incentive payment as soon as his efficiency reaches 80 percent; another may begin incentive payments at $66\frac{2}{3}$ percent efficiency. It is customary with such plans, as it was with the others, to guarantee the employee his base rate per hour.

With a plan of this type, computations of earnings per hour and labor costs per unit are made just as they were in a full participation plan beginning at 100 percent efficiency. The only thing that must be kept in mind is that the required output is now represented by some efficiency less than 100 percent. How this is handled was suggested earlier, but we shall illustrate the approach by computing the earnings per hour at the various levels of efficiency we considered when discussing the wage payment plans presented earlier. In these computations, we shall assume, as before, that the time standard for the task under consideration is 2 hours per unit and that the operator's base rate is $4 per hour. Further, let us suppose that the specific plan involved is a full participation plan beginning at 80 percent efficiency.

If the employee is, for example, working at 100 percent efficiency, we begin the determination of his earnings by taking this efficiency of 100 percent and dividing it by the required efficiency of 80 percent. This yields 1.25, which means that the employee is producing 25 percent more work than is demanded of him. Consequently, because of the full participation feature of the plan, his earnings per hour would be increased by 25 percent, which is to say that they will be 125 percent of his base rate. This is equal to

$$R_a = 1.25 \times \$4 = \$5$$

We found that the operator is producing 125 percent as much work as is required of him by computing the ratio of the actual efficiency to the required efficiency. This ratio, which we shall call the "adjusted efficiency," can always be found from the following expression:

$$\text{Adjusted efficiency} = \frac{\text{actual efficiency}}{\text{required efficiency}}$$

The adjusted efficiency, expressed as a decimal, will yield a factor which, when applied to the base rate, will give us the earnings per hour, unless the factor is less than 1. In that case, because of the guaranteed base rate, the earnings per hour will be equal to the base rate.

Having shown how earnings per hour are calculated, we can now summarize what these earnings and the resultant unit labor costs would be, under the full participation plan beginning at 80 percent efficiency, for the selected levels of performance we considered with the other wage payment plans. This summary is presented in the following table:

Efficiency (E), %		Hours worked per unit (H_w)	Operator's earnings per hour (R_a)	Labor cost per unit ($H_w \times R_a$)
Actual	Adjusted			
50	62.50	4.00	$4.00	$16.00
80	100.00	2.50	4.00	10.00
100	125.00	2.00	5.00	10.00
125	156.25	1.60	6.25	10.00
160	200.00	1.25	8.00	10.00

AN EVALUATION   As can be seen, for efficiencies up to the point at which the employee becomes eligible for incentive payments, the plan is just like the day rate plan because of the guaranteed base rate. This means that, as efficiencies increase, earnings per hour remain constant and labor costs per unit decrease. But once the point is reached at which incentive payments begin, increasing efficiencies result in increasing earnings per hour and constant labor costs per unit. This is true because of the full participation feature of the plan. However, it should be noted that the labor costs per unit remain constant at a higher level than they do with a full participation plan in which incentive payments begin at 100 percent efficiency. In fact, with our plan in which the incentive payments begin at 80 percent, the minimum labor cost per unit is $10, which is 25 percent higher than the $8 minimum labor cost per unit we obtained with the full participation plan beginning at 100 percent efficiency.

A firm would consider adopting a full participation plan beginning at less than 100 percent when the preincentive efficiency is quite low. For example, it may be 50 percent. If the firm were to establish a requirement of 100 percent efficiency, the employees might react in one of two undesirable ways. First, many might feel that it is not worth the effort required to become just eligible for incentive earnings. In this case, the required effort would be that necessary to double their output, for which there would be no reward. On the other hand, if incentive payments began at 80 percent efficiency, doubling the present output would mean an increase in earnings of 25 percent, and this, of course, would provide a greater incentive. The second undesirable reaction might be psychological in nature. Because the established requirement of 100 percent is so much higher than the efficiency at which they have been working, the employees might believe that it is impossible to produce that much more work. And with this attitude, they might find this to be true.

Of course, if relatively few employees fail to perform satisfactorily, management can inaugurate disciplinary action. But if most of the employees fall into this category, there is not much the firm can do. For this reason, if there is a strong likelihood that the results will be unsatisfactory if the required level of performance is 100 percent, management may decide to begin incentive payments at some lower percent. It may be argued, however, that, as a result, labor costs per unit will be higher than they would be if incentive payments began at 100 percent efficiency. There is no reason to believe that this is true. If incentive payments begin at, say, 80 percent, the employees may do their best, and their efficiency may eventually reach 100 percent. Using our earlier figures for purposes of illustration, we can say that labor costs per unit would then be $10. But if incentive payments begin at 100 percent, the employees may react adversely, with the result that their efficiency may remain at 50 percent and labor costs per unit would then be $16. It is on the basis of an assumption such as this that some firms begin incentive payments at some point below 100 percent efficiency when the preincentive efficiency is relatively low.

In spite of the fact that there are situations which encourage the adoption of such a plan, there is some tendency on the part of many firms to avoid its use. It has been found that the computations are a little complicated and are often subject to misunderstanding by the employees. Further, most managements feel that they have a right to demand 100 percent efficiency, regardless of how low the preincentive efficiency happens to be, without paying an incentive to obtain it. And of course, if this demand can be enforced, a full participation plan beginning at 100 percent efficiency will yield lower unit labor costs.

THE STEP PLAN

The next plan we shall discuss is the step plan. It can best be described in terms of the pay formulas from which earnings per hour with a plan of this type can be computed. In the most elementary step plan, incentive payments begin at 100 percent efficiency. For efficiencies below 100 percent, the base rate R_b is guaranteed. Therefore, the expression for earnings per hour R_a at efficiencies up to 100 percent would be

$$R_a = R_b \tag{22-1}$$

At efficiencies equal to or greater than 100 percent, earnings per hour would be larger. The amount of these earnings would depend on the specific nature of the plan, but in one of the more common ones, it would be found from the following expression:

$$R_a = 1.25E \cdot R_b \tag{22-2}$$

where $E =$ the operator's efficiency.

To illustrate the use of these formulas, let us suppose that an operator's efficiency is 50 percent on the job for which the time standard was 2 hours per unit and the base rate $4 per hour. Since the efficiency is less than 100 percent, the operator's earnings per hour will be equal to his base rate of $4.

As another example, let us assume that the operator's efficiency is 100 percent. To find his earnings per hour, we should make the appropriate substitutions in Eq. (22-2), which is the pay formula at operating efficiencies equal to or greater than 100 percent. From Eq. (22-2), we should find that

$$R_a = 1.25 \times 100\% \times \$4 = \$5$$

If we were to make similar computations for the various efficiencies we considered when discussing the other incentive plans and, also, for an additional efficiency of 99.5 percent, we should find the resultant earnings and unit labor costs to be as summarized in the following table:

Efficiency (E), %	Hours worked per unit (H_w)	Operator's earnings per hour (R_a)	Labor cost per unit ($H_w \times R_a$)
50.0	4.00	$4.00	$16.00
80.0	2.50	4.00	10.00
99.5	2.01	4.00	8.02
100.0	2.00	5.00	10.00
125.0	1.60	6.25	10.00
160.0	1.25	8.00	10.00

An examination of this table reveals that, as efficiencies increase up to 100 percent, the step plan, like the day rate plan, yields constant earnings per hour and, therefore, decreasing labor costs per unit. But because of the additional efficiency level of 99.5 percent we included, it is clear that there is an upward "step" in the labor cost per unit as soon as the operating efficiency reaches 100 percent. The reason for this upward step is that the operator realizes an increase in earnings of 25 percent as soon as his efficiency reaches 100 percent.

From 100 percent on, labor costs per unit remain constant, and the operator's earnings per hour increase as his efficiency increases. However, these labor costs are constant at a higher level than they would be in a 1-for-1 plan beginning at 100 percent efficiency. In fact, they are higher by 25 percent because of the 1.25 factor in our pay formula.

AREA OF APPLICATION   Let us now consider the conditions under which a plan of this type is ordinarily adopted. In some cases, preincentive efficiencies may be quite low, and the firm may want to provide an added incentive for the employees to reach 100 percent efficiency. A step plan would be used to accomplish this instead of a full participation plan beginning at less than 100 percent efficiency when the company believes that the step plan will be just as effective. In such cases, the step plan would be more economical than a full participation plan beginning at less than 100 percent efficiency because the labor cost per unit would continue to decrease until 100 percent efficiency is reached.

In other cases, the step plan would be used instead of the full participation plan beginning at 100 percent efficiency if the nature of the firm's production costs was such that appreciable savings were to be realized in areas other than labor cost from an increase in output per man-hour. For example, at higher labor efficiencies, the output to be realized from equipment will be greater than it will be at lower efficiencies. Consequently, for some required volume of total output, the amount of equipment needed, and hence the capital investment in equipment, will decrease as the labor efficiency increases. It follows, therefore, that higher efficiencies will be accompanied by lower equipment costs per unit of output. In a situation such as this, the firm would want its employees to reach their maximum efficiency. Naturally, the employees would have a greater incentive to reach this efficiency under a step plan, such as the one we have described, than they would under a full participation plan beginning at 100 percent efficiency. This can be shown by means of the figures with which we have been working. With the step plan, earnings per hour at 160 percent efficiency would be $8 as compared with $6.40 with the full participation plan beginning at 100 percent efficiency. As a result, the employees may feel that $8 justifies the extra effort required to reach 160 percent, whereas $6.40 does not.

Of course, labor costs at any efficiency beyond 100 percent will be higher with the step plan than with a full participation plan beginning at 100 percent efficiency. But there are situations in which management can economically justify the increase in labor costs. These situations would be those in which the additional incentive provided by the step plan would serve to raise efficiencies sufficiently to bring about reductions in other costs which would more than offset the increase in labor costs. These potential savings in other operating costs would serve to determine the value of the "step" which management would provide for in the plan. We have considered a plan in which a factor of 1.25 was involved. But plans have been used where factors other than 1.25 were believed to be more adequate.

In fact, there are plans which contain two or three steps. To illustrate, one firm adheres to the following pay formulas:

For efficiencies up to 100 percent: $R_a = R_b$

For efficiencies equal to or greater than 100 percent but less than 125 percent:
$R_a = 1.10E \cdot R_b$

For efficiencies equal to or greater than 125 percent but less than 140 percent:
$R_a = 1.15E \cdot R_b$

For efficiencies equal to or greater than 140 percent: $R_a = 1.25E \cdot R_b$

A plan such as this would be used when there is reason to believe that the additional steps will provide a greater motivation and, thereby, minimize total unit production costs.

The step plan is the last incentive plan we shall consider. Those discussed are the basic types, and all kinds of variations and combinations are possible.

GROUP VERSUS INDIVIDUAL PLANS

In each of the incentive plans considered, we spoke of earnings per hour for an individual employee who was working at a specific efficiency. In doing so, we assumed that the incentive plan was an individual plan. Under a plan such as this, the hours produced and the hours worked are determined for a given employee, and his efficiency is computed. This efficiency is then used to calculate his earnings.

As opposed to this, there are so-called group plans. A group consists of a number of employees who are looked upon as a single production unit. The calculated efficiency is the average efficiency of all the members of the group. Because this average must be weighted to reflect the hours worked at each efficiency, it is best determined by finding the sum of the hours produced by the members of the group and then dividing this total by the sum of the hours worked by the members of the group. Every employee in the group is then treated as if he worked at this efficiency, and his earnings are computed accordingly. Let us illustrate this by means of an example in which we shall assume that a full participation plan beginning at 100 percent is in effect.

Suppose we have a group consisting of three operators. At the end of the incentive period, it may be that the hours worked and the hours produced for each of these individuals are as follows:

Operator	Hours worked	Hours produced	Efficiency, %
A	40	22	55
B	40	42	105
C	40	62	155
Total	120	126	105

An examination of the table reveals that the average efficiency of the group is 126 divided by 120, or 105 percent. As a result, each of the three operators would experience an increase in earnings of 5 percent. This would not have been the case had the plan been an individual rather than a group plan. With an individual plan, operator A would have received his base rate if this had been guaranteed; operator B, an incentive payment equal to 5 percent of his base earnings; and operator C, an incentive payment of 55 percent of his base earnings. As a result, because of the group feature, operator A is overpaid, operator C is underpaid, and only operator B is being compensated correctly. Furthermore, the total incentive payment would be lower than with an individual plan, because while A earns 5 percent more than he would under an individual plan, C's earnings are increased by only 5 rather than 55 percent.

As a rule, group plans are less effective than individual plans. To begin with, the inefficient employee's unsatisfactory performance is not always recognized by management because output and efficiency are ascertained only for the group rather than for each individual; consequently, such an employee is more secure and, therefore, less highly motivated than he would otherwise be. Also, efficient employees, who will be compelled to share the benefits of their efficiency with the less productive members of the group, tend to lose some, if not all, of their motivation.

Admittedly, administrative costs will be lower with a group plan than with an individual plan. Individual incentive payments would still have to be ascertained, because the payment would vary with the hours worked; if base rates are equal and the group efficiency was, say, 110 percent, the person who spent 40 hours in the group would get twice as large an incentive payment for this activity as would a person who spent only 20 hours. However, there is no need to measure and record individual outputs, calculate individual hours produced, and compute individual efficiencies. Instead, this is done for the group as a whole.

In addition to this saving in administrative costs, as has been shown, the total incentive payment may be less with the group plan for a given average efficiency than with an individual plan.

Nevertheless, there is reason to believe that, more often than not, these advantages are more than offset by the fact that individual efficiencies will be lower with the group plan. Therefore, it is ordinarily recommended that individual incentives be adopted.

Of course, there are cases in which the firm has no choice but to use a group plan. For example, five or six people may be assigned to a progressive assembly line on which an individual is unable to work at a pace which is independent of the others'; instead, the speed of the entire line is governed by the pace of the bottleneck operator. Or a machine may be run by an operator and a helper; with this arrangement, it would be impossible to ascertain what fraction of the output is attributable to either one of these individuals. But even in such cases, much is to be gained by keeping the group as stable, homogeneous, and small as possible, for it has been found that the smaller, the more stable, and the more homogeneous the group, the greater is the resultant cooperation among members of the group.

Further, with some group activities, care must be taken when establishing the time standard. For example, in a three-station progressive assembly line, the required time for the first operation may be 1.0 minute per unit; for the second, 1.2 minutes; and for the third, 1.1 minutes. If the work cannot be redistributed more equitably, the time for the most demanding operation, which in this case is 1.2 minutes, should be allowed for each of the other two operations. As a result, the standard time for the three operations would be 3 times 1.2 minutes, or 3.6 minutes, and not 1.0 plus 1.2 plus 1.1, or 3.3, minutes. The reason for this is that if the bottleneck operator works at the required 100 percent efficiency, each operation will require 1.2 minutes.

INCENTIVE PERIODS

In all our computations of earnings per hour, we assumed that the operator would work at some uniform level of efficiency. In practice, however, the assumption is not usually valid. For example, in an eight-hour day, the operator may spend two hours on each of four different jobs. His efficiencies on each of these tasks may be 110, 90, 120, and 80 percent, respectively. For purposes of computing his earnings for the day, it becomes necessary to decide how these varying efficiencies are to be handled. If the plan is a full participation plan beginning at 100 percent efficiency, one alternative would be to pay the operator 10 percent more than his base rate for the first task, his guaranteed base rate for the second, 20 percent more than his base rate for the third, and his guaranteed base rate for the fourth. If his base rate is $4 per hour, this method will involve the computations and yield the results shown in the following table:

Job number (1)	Hours worked (2)	Hours produced (3)	Efficiency, % (4 = 3 ÷ 2)	Earnings per hour (5)	Earnings per job (6 = 5 × 2)
1	2	2.20	110	$4.40	$8.80
2	2	1.80	90	4.00	8.00
3	2	2.40	120	4.80	9.60
4	2	1.60	80	4.00	8.00
Total	8	8.00			$34.40

As shown in the table, his earnings for the day would be $34.40. However, the approach which yields these earnings is undesirable to the firm in several respects. First, it necessitates extremely accurate timekeeping, and this may be costly; if it were incorrectly shown that only 1.5 hours were spent on job 1, the earnings would be affected. Second, efficiencies and earnings have to be computed for every job, and this raises the cost of administering the plan. Third, allowance factors included in time standards are not expected to be correct for a limited time period spent on a single job; this method of computation favors the operator because he is protected by a guaranteed base rate if the allowance factor is inadequate but he reaps all the benefits if the allowance is too liberal for any one job assignment. Fourth, the operator is able to work at an exceptionally fatiguing pace on the first job, rest on the second, speed up again on the third, rest on the fourth, and so on; this method of computation would serve to overstate his average efficiency, since it would treat the "rest" periods as periods of 100 percent efficiency.

For one or more of these reasons, companies prefer to base their computations on the operator's average efficiency over a longer period of time. For example, some companies adhere to a one-day incentive period. This means that the operator's average efficiency for the day is calculated, and this average, which is weighted to reflect the hours worked at each efficiency, is then used to compute his earnings for the day. To illustrate, in the case we have been considering, the operator produced 8 hours while working 8 hours. This yields an average efficiency of 8 divided by 8, or 100 percent. Therefore, his earnings for the day would be only his base rate per hour, $4, times the hours worked, 8, or $32. With this method, only the total hours worked and the total hours produced during the day must be recorded; only one efficiency computation is required; only one earnings calculation is necessary; and a more realistic picture of actual efficiency is presented.

The most commonly used incentive period is probably one week. Where this is the case, the average efficiency for the week is calculated and used to determine the earnings for the week. A few firms even adhere to a one-month incentive period, but this is usually considered to be unsatisfactory by the employees. As opposed to management's preference, the employees favor a short incentive period. They want to take advantage of allowance factors which work in their favor, and they do not want to be penalized for occasional job efficiencies of less than 100 percent. In any event a one-week period has usually proven to be an acceptable compromise.

A relatively short incentive period also allows the firm to make fairly frequent incentive payments. If the incentive period is one month, the company usually pays its employees their incentive earnings once a month. This is not a particularly satisfactory arrangement to the employees because they ordinarily feel that they have a right to receive incentive payments they earned earlier in the month without experiencing this type of delay. Also, it has been found that employees are more highly motivated when they receive more frequent incentive payments. When the operator receives an incentive payment every week, this frequent reminder of the benefits to be realized from higher efficiencies encourages him to work at higher efficiencies. While there is a greater administrative cost to be associated with more frequent payments of incentive earnings, most firms have found that the disadvantage is more than offset by the advantage of increased motivation.

GUARANTEED INCENTIVE EARNINGS

Ordinarily, an employee is eligible for incentive earnings only when working on a job covered by an incentive plan. For time spent on an activity for which no time standard has been established, he would simply be paid his base rate. For example, suppose that, during a particular day, an employee spends 6 hours on a standard job, that is, one covered by the incentive plan, and 2 hours on a nonstandard job. Further, he produces 7.5 hours of work while on the standard job, which represents an efficiency of 125 percent. If his base rate is $4 per hour and the plan is a full participation plan beginning at 100 percent efficiency, his earnings per hour for the standard job would be equal to

$$R_a = 1.25 \times \$4 = \$5$$

But for the time he spends on the nonstandard job, which is often called "daywork," he would be paid his base rate of $4 per hour. Therefore, his earnings for the day, which we shall assume is the length of the incentive period, would be

Earnings/day = ($5/hr)(6 hr) + ($4/hr)(2 hr) = $38

All this appears to be straightforward and just, but it can and does create problems. Although some employees are inclined to oppose incentive plans in principle, once the plan is installed, they often want to take full advantage of the opportunity to increase earnings the plan presents. But the employee in our illustration does not have this opportunity. If he had been able to work on a standard job for the 2 hours he was assigned to the nonstandard job, it is possible that he could have performed at 125 percent efficiency during this 2-hour period just as he did during the 6-hour period. As a result, his earnings per hour for the full 8-hour period would have been $5, and, consequently, his earnings for the day would have been

Earnings/day = $5/hr $\times$ 8 hr = $40

This, of course, is more than $38, and the employee reacts unfavorably because he has lost $2. This reaction often results in a demand by the employees that they be paid their average incentive earnings while assigned to daywork. Under this arrangement, it would be assumed, in our illustration, that the operator worked at 125 percent efficiency on the nonstandard job just as he did on the standard job, and he would be paid accordingly.

Most firms oppose a demand of this type. They argue that only extra effort warrants extra payment and that there is reason to believe that the employee does not expend extra effort on a nonstandard job. Labor, on the other hand, will maintain that, if the firm expects the employees to support the plan, it must not penalize them by assigning them to nonstandard work and, thereby, reducing their earnings. This implied threat of a lack of support often succeeds in forcing management to agree to pay the employee his average incentive earnings for the time he spends on nonstandard work. When this decision is reached, it is usually because the company has decided that the advantages to be associated with a plan which has the support of the employees more than offset the cost of this undesirable provision. Other companies, however, have successfully resisted this pressure and refused to yield to labor's demands on this issue.

INCENTIVE PLAN BENEFITS AND COSTS

Thus far, we have demonstrated that earnings and, therefore, unit labor costs are affected by the choice of incentive plan, by whether individual or group incentives are adhered to, by the length of the incentive period, and by whether incentive earnings are guaranteed. When choosing the specific provisions that will characterize its incentive plan, a firm will be governed by its desire to have a successful plan, that is, a plan that will minimize unit production costs. That an incentive plan is capable of doing so has already been shown with reference to unit labor costs. It will be recalled that, in every incentive plan discussed, labor costs per unit decreased as operating efficiencies increased, until the point was reached at which incentive payments began. As a result, if the preincentive efficiency is lower than the efficiency at which incentive payments begin and the plan succeeds in raising operating efficiencies up to this point, the plan has contributed to a reduction in labor costs per unit.

As efficiencies increase beyond the point at which incentive payments begin, whether there is a continued reduction in labor costs per unit depends on the nature of the plan. For example, if the plan is a less than full participation plan beginning at 100 percent efficiency, labor costs per unit will continue to decrease as efficiencies increase beyond 100 percent. The same cannot be said for some of the other plans. For example, if the plan is a full participation plan beginning at 100 percent efficiency, labor costs per unit reach their minimum at 100 percent efficiency and remain at that level as efficiencies increase beyond 100 percent. Therefore, if the plan succeeds in raising efficiencies to some level beyond 100 percent, there is no additional advantage to the company, from the standpoint of labor costs per unit, to be associated with this occurrence. Because of this, the question arises concerning why the company would want efficiencies to exceed 100 percent. The answer to this question is that there are unit production costs, other than those of labor, that will decrease not only as efficiencies increase up to 100 percent, but also as efficiencies increase beyond 100 percent. Let us now consider some examples of these other costs.

We know that labor efficiency reflects the output per man-hour. Therefore, the number of employees required to attain a given level of output eventually decreases as labor efficiency increases. Admittedly, with certain incentive plans, less manpower will not bring about a reduction in total wage payments when efficiencies increase beyond a certain point. However, in addition to wages, every employee receives fringe benefits, such as paid vacations and holidays, life and health insurance, and the firm's contribution to pension plans. These costs are relatively fixed per employee, and, consequently, the total fringe benefit expense continues to decrease as increasing labor efficiency continues to reduce the required number of employees.

Furthermore, as efficiency increases, less equipment and machinery is required to attain a given level of output. In the long run, this will bring about a decrease in depreciation charges, cost of invested capital, maintenance and repair costs, utility expenses, floor space requirements, and cost of supervision. And the higher the efficiency, the greater will be the reduction in such costs.

In brief, maximum labor efficiency is to the firm's advantage, because total unit costs continue to decrease even though unit labor costs may remain constant after a certain efficiency has been reached. Hence, a successful wage incentive installation is one that maximizes operating efficiencies.

Of course, a successful installation is possible only because of the benefits an incentive plan also makes available to the firm's employees. Insofar as they are concerned, the advantage of an incentive plan is that it presents them with an opportunity to increase their earnings. This assumes that people are interested in earning more money and, consequently, will be motivated by plans of this kind to increase their output.

This is not to say that wages is the only job factor with which employees are concerned. They are also interested in such things as security, opportunities for advancement, the work involved, plant location, working conditions, fringe benefits, and the type of supervision and coworkers. The nature of these other factors will also affect the employees' attitude toward the firm and the degree to which employees are motivated. Nevertheless, the factor of wages continues to be an important one.

However, it is necessary to recognize that, from the standpoint of the employees, the introduction of a wage incentive plan will very often be accompanied not only by an opportunity to increase earnings but also by an unfavorable change in certain job factors. To begin with, the required output may now be higher than it was during the preincentive period, and therefore, at a given base rate, more is demanded of the employee. Next, individual operating efficiencies will now be determined and recorded, and this may affect an employee's security and opportunity for advancement. Also, the presence of an incentive plan often changes employees' relationships with each other; there may now be a struggle for jobs with more liberal standards, or one worker may accuse another of working too hard and thereby placing the rest of the labor force in an unfavorable light. In addition, the relationship between the supervisors and their employees may be affected adversely. There is no denying that changes in these other job factors can be so serious that, not only will the introduction of the incentive plan fail to motivate the employees, but its introduction may be followed by serious personnel problems.

It should also be noted that the firm invariably finds itself in a position analogous to that of the employees, in the sense that it also must pay a price to realize the benefits of an incentive installation. This is the expense of installing and administering the plan. Time and money will have to be spent on designing the plan, establishing standards, computing efficiencies, maintaining records, calculating incentive earnings, and issuing incentive payments. In the absence of an incentive plan, some of these costs might be incurred anyway. For example, the company may establish time standards even if a day rate plan is adhered to. Similarly, employees may experience certain undesirable changes in job factors even if an incentive plan is not in effect. For example, the company may insist on a 100 percent operating efficiency even if a day rate plan is adhered to. But just as some of the changes in job factors are directly attributable to the wage incentive plan, so some of the aforementioned costs to the company are directly attributable to the wage incentive plan. And there have been cases in which the magnitude of these costs more than offset the benefits to be associated with the incentive plan, with the result that some companies have rejected incentives as a method of wage payment. These cases correspond to those in which employees in some firms have found that the unfavorable changes in other job factors have more than offset the opportunity to increase earnings, with the result that they have reacted adversely to incentives as a method of wage payment.

RECOMMENDATIONS FOR A SUCCESSFUL INSTALLATION

It has been shown that both management and labor will find that incentive plans have certain advantages and disadvantages. In some cases, the advantages more than offset the disadvantages, and the result is a successful wage incentive installation. In other cases, the disadvantages more than offset the advantages, and the result is an unsuccessful wage incentive installation.

No one knows what the exact formula is for a successful wage incentive installation. However, a sufficient number of successes and failures have occurred and been analyzed with the result that certain recommendations have evolved for the design, installation, and maintenance of an incentive plan. Some of these have already been mentioned. Specifically, it was pointed out earlier that (1) base rates should be guaranteed so long as the employee is employed by the firm, (2) an individual rather than a group incentive plan should be adopted whenever feasible, (3) incentive periods should be relatively short, (4) incentive payments should be made fairly frequently, and (5) incentive earnings should be guaranteed if conditions warrant.

Other recommendations call for things whose desirability is fairly obvious. Among these are that the firm should (1) establish and maintain correct work standards, (2) enforce production standards, (3) train workers in the work methods on which time standards are based, and (4) explain the incentive plan to the employees and their supervisors.

With reference to the last point, the suggested explanation is advocated because, as is to be expected, the individual employee is interested in knowing and understanding how his incentive earnings are computed. Because of this, it is also recommended that the company adhere to a simple plan. In fact, the specific recommendation is that, if at all possible, the firm should adopt a full participation plan beginning at 100 percent efficiency. The belief is that, if anything more complicated is in effect, the work force may have difficulty understanding it. In the absence of this understanding, the employees may assume that the plan works against their interests. As a result, they will be less highly motivated to increase their operating efficiencies. Of course, if conditions suggest the use of a slightly more complicated plan, it would also be wrong for the company to go to the other extreme and assume that anything which is somewhat more difficult will be beyond the employees' comprehension. Plans such as step plans or plans beginning at less than 100 percent efficiency do have their areas of application. But in all cases, it is mandatory that the firm take it upon itself to acquaint the work force with the reasons for adopting a particular plan and with the manner in which incentive earnings are computed. If it does, potential difficulties will be minimized.

It is also recommended that the firm strive for high incentive coverage, that is, strive to have as many activities as possible covered by the incentive plan. When this has been accomplished, a larger number of the firm's employees are motivated to maximize their efficiency than would otherwise be the case. Furthermore, there is then a smaller chance that a given employee will have to spend a part of his time on daywork, that is, on work not covered by the incentive plan; this reduces the likelihood of the firm's having to guarantee incentive earnings for this kind of work or, if nothing else, minimizes the amount of incentive payments of this type. And finally, high incentive coverage reduces the risk of awkward differentials in earnings that might otherwise occur among the firm's employees.

A point related to incentive coverage is that there is no reason why personnel other than those engaged in manufacturing activities cannot be provided with an opportunity to realize incentive earnings. In the earlier discussion of work standards, it was pointed out that time standards can be determined for such activities as typing, mail sorting, keypunching, order filling, check writing, filing, floor sweeping, window washing, bricklaying, typesetting, and auto repairing. Having established such standards, the firm can go on to include the individuals involved in the incentive plan. This also suggests that an incentive plan can be developed for individuals performing tasks of this type in organizations of a nonmanufacturing nature.

The last recommendation for an incentive installation we shall consider is that the plan should contain some provision for the maintenance of quality. If it does not, employees are often inclined to neglect quality so as to increase the quantity of their output. The result may be that the cost of defective work attributable to the incentive plan exceeds the savings in other costs.

By far the most prevalent practice is to credit the employee only for the good parts he produces. This means that the time standard is expressed in terms of hours or minutes per good part. To obtain the hours produced, the allowed time per part is multiplied by the number of good parts produced. More often than not, this discourages the operator from adhering to work methods which will have a detrimental effect on quality since he receives no credit for the defective output. When this approach proves to be ineffective, the firm may find it necessary to establish quality standards expressed in terms of the maximum permissible percent of defective output. Any operator who consistently exceeds this limit is subject to some kind of disciplinary action. But the fact remains that an incentive plan usually intensifies the problem of quality. And situations arise in which the cost of maintaining quality in the presence of a wage incentive plan more than offsets the other benefits to be realized from the plan. It is for this reason that, in every plant, there are a number of activities to which the incentive plan is not applied.

This brings us to the close of our discussion of the factors that management should take into consideration when designing, installing, and maintaining an incentive plan. It is being taken for granted that cognizance will be taken of the fact that the presence of a wage incentive plan calls for such things as (1) maintaining records of output and hours worked, (2) calculating hours produced and efficiencies, and (3) computing incentive earnings. Also, a need may be created for various special reports; one such report may list operating efficiencies for individual employees, another may identify the employees whose efficiencies are below a satisfactory level, still another may describe incentive earnings by employee for a given incentive period, and so on. If data processing equipment is available, it can be used to process whatever data and information serve as the basis for these calculations and reports. An example of a report prepared with the use of such equipment is shown in Figure 22-1.

A FINAL OBSERVATION

The topic of wage incentives is the last we shall consider in this presentation of the principles of production and operations management. In one respect, it is appropriate that the selected order of presentation resulted in our ending with a subject which drew our attention to the need for motivating operating personnel. This is because it is the operating personnel

EMPLOYEE EFFICIENCY REPORT		DEPT. NO. 60			EMPLOYEE NUMBER 197030			SHOP DATE 615

SHOP ORDER		OPER. NO.	QUAN. COMP.	ST'D. RATE	STD. HRS.	ACT. HOURS	EFFIC. %	REMARKS
PART NO.	LOT NO.							
0358117	040—0	1200	50	140	70	68	1029	
2103526	060—0	70	10	20	2	2	1000	
38264	100—0	50	50	22	11	10	1100	

Figure 22-1   An efficiency report (Courtesy of International Business Machines Corporation)

who produce the real goods and services, and the purpose of all the analytical techniques upon which we focused our attention is simply to enable these individuals to perform their function in the most efficient manner.

QUESTIONS

22-1   Answer the following with reference to the day rate method of wage payment:

    a What happens to earnings per hour as efficiency increases?

    b What happens to unit labor costs as efficiency increases?

    c Under what conditions is a firm likely to adopt this wage payment plan?

22-2   Why do some firms adhere to a differential time plan?

22-3   Answer question 22-1 with reference to the following wage incentive plans in which the base rate is guaranteed:

    a Full participation beginning at 100 percent efficiency.

    b Less than full participation beginning at 100 percent efficiency.

    c Full participation beginning at less than 100 percent efficiency.

    d Step plan.

22-4   What are the limitations of a less than full participation plan beginning at 100 percent efficiency?

22-5   Define each of the following:

    a Guaranteed base rate

    b Individual incentive plan
    c Group incentive plan
    d Incentive period
    e Incentive coverage
    f Guaranteed incentive earnings

22-6 What benefits can a firm realize from the installation of a wage incentive plan?

22-7 What benefits can employees derive from methods of wage payment based on incentive plans?

22-8 What are the disadvantages of an incentive plan from the standpoint of the employee? From the standpoint of the firm?

22-9 Under what conditions does it become necessary to adhere to a group rather than to an individual incentive plan?

22-10 What provisions can the firm make for the maintenance of quality in the presence of a wage incentive plan?

22-11 With regard to the design, introduction, and maintenance of a wage incentive plan, why is it recommended that:
    a Work standards be correct?
    b The plan be simple?
    c The base rate be guaranteed?
    d Production standards be enforced?
    e Individual rather than group plans be adopted?
    f Provision be made for the maintenance of quality?
    g Workers be trained in correct methods?
    h Incentive periods be short?
    i Incentive payments be frequent?
    j Incentive coverage be high?
    k The plan be explained to employees?

22-12 Can wage incentives be applied to nonmanufacturing activities? Explain.

22-13 How can data processing equipment be employed in the implementation of a wage incentive plan?

PROBLEMS

22-1 A firm adheres to a day rate plan. The time standard for a given task is 1.200 hours per unit, and the base rate is \$4.40 per hour. Compute the operator's earnings per hour and the labor cost per unit at efficiencies of 70, 100, and 140 percent. (Ans. \$4.40 and \$3.77 at 140 percent)

22-2 A firm adheres to a differential time plan which provides for an increase of 10 percent in the base rate when the employee's efficiency reaches 100 percent and an increase of 15 percent when the efficiency reaches 120 percent. Three employees have been assigned to a job for which the time standard is 0.500 hour per unit. The first employee requires an average of 0.8 hour per unit of output; the second, 0.5 hour; and the third, 0.4 hour. If the base rate is $6 per hour, what are the earnings per hour and the labor cost per unit to be associated with each of these employees? (Ans. $6.60 and $3.30 for second employee)

22-3   A firm adheres to a full participation incentive plan beginning at 100 percent efficiency. The time standard for a given activity is 4.000 hours per 100 units of output, and the guaranteed base rate is $4.80 per hour. Compute the operator's earnings for an eight-hour day and the unit labor cost when the operator produces 160 units, 200 units, and 230 units per day. (Ans. $38.40 and $0.24 at 160 units)

22-4   A firm adheres to a 60–40 incentive plan beginning at 100 percent efficiency. The time standard for a certain operation is 0.265 hour per unit, and the guaranteed base rate is $5.70 per hour. Calculate the employee's earnings per hour and the labor cost per unit at efficiencies of 100, 130, and 200 percent. (Ans. $9.12 and $1.21 at 200 percent)

22-5   A firm adheres to a 1-for-1 plan beginning at 75 percent efficiency. The time standard for a given task is such that, at 100 percent efficiency, an operator would be expected to produce 600 units in a 40-hour workweek. In a specific week, one employee produces 675 units, and another 420 units. If the guaranteed base rate is $7.20 per hour, what will be their respective earnings for that week? Also, what will be the average labor cost per unit of their combined output for that week? (Ans. $0.658 per unit)

22-6   A firm adheres to a 70–30 incentive plan beginning at 66⅔ percent efficiency. The time standard for a given job is 1.050 hours per unit, and the guaranteed base rate is $5.20 per hour. Compute the employee's earnings per hour and the labor cost per unit at efficiencies of 76 and 104 percent. (Ans. $7.24 and $7.31 at 104 percent)

22-7   A firm adheres to a step plan which can be described in terms of the following pay formulas:

Up to 100 percent efficiency: $R_a = R_b$

From 100 to 130 percent efficiency: $R_a = 1.10E \cdot R_b$

From 130 percent efficiency on: $R_a = 1.20E \cdot R_b$

The time standard for a job is 8.250 hours per 100 units, and the guaranteed base rate is $3.60 per hour. Calculate the operator's earnings per hour and the labor cost per unit at 80, 105, and 140 percent efficiency. (Ans. $4.158 and $0.327 at 105 percent)

22-8   During a one-week period, three employees have been assigned to an activity covered by a time standard. The hours they worked and produced while performing the operation are as follows:

Operator	Hours worked	Hours produced
X	40	28.4
Y	40	56.2
Z	40	42.8

If the operators' guaranteed base rate is $3.97 per hour and a full participation plan beginning at 80 percent efficiency is in effect, what would be their respective total earnings for the 40-hour week under each of the following arrangements?

a Incentive payments are to be determined on an individual basis. (Ans. $158.80, $278.89, $212.40)

b Incentive payments are to be determined on a group basis with the three employees being considered as making up a single group. (Ans. $210.81)

22-9   During a given month, four employees have worked on a job covered by a time standard. The hours they worked on the job and their efficiencies while doing so are as follows:

Operator	Hours worked	Efficiency, %
1	84	123
2	120	95
3	170	137
4	60	89

The guaranteed base rate is $6.16 per hour; the length of the incentive period is one month; and a full participation plan beginning at 100 percent efficiency is in effect. What incentive payment will the respective employees have earned on the job if the following plans are in effect?

a An individual incentive plan.

b A group plan with these four employees being considered as making up the group.

22-10   With reference to the computations carried out in the table on page 592, it was stated that the earnings would be affected if it were incorrectly reported that only 1.5 hours were spent on job 1 and that 2.5 hours were spent on, say, job 2. What would be the earnings if this occurred?

22-11 An employee has spent the entire 40-hour week on tasks covered by time standards and an incentive plan. His performance on each of these days is summarized in the following table:

Day	Hours worked	Efficiency, %
1	8	126.2
2	8	75.0
3	8	137.5
4	8	100.0
5	8	84.3

If his guaranteed base rate is $7.03 per hour and a 55–45 plan beginning at 100 percent efficiency is in effect, what will be his incentive earnings for the week if the firm adheres to:

a A one-day incentive period? (Ans $19.70)

b A one-week incentive period? (Ans. $7.11)

22-12 An operator has worked 40 hours per week for four weeks at a guaranteed base rate of $5.28 per hour. During each of these weeks, he spent some time on tasks covered by a full participation plan beginning at 100 percent efficiency. The hours he worked and produced on these jobs are as follows:

Week	Hours worked	Hours produced
1	24	34.8
2	38	36.1
3	14	16.8
4	30	27.3

What will his total earnings be for the four-week period if the length of the incentive period is one week? Four weeks?

22-13 Incentive coverage in a company is quite high, but employees are occasionally assigned to daywork, that is, to jobs not covered by time standards. For example, during a 40-hour week, one employee spent 35 hours on incentive work and the balance on other jobs. The time standard for the incentive task is 2.988 hours per 100 good units. In the week under consideration, the operator produced 1,525 units of which 4 percent were found to be defective.

The operator's guaranteed base rate is $4.37 per hour. The firm adheres to a full participation plan, beginning at 100 percent efficiency, and a one-week incentive period.

a What will be the operator's total earnings for the week if he is paid the base rate for daywork? (Ans. $213.04)

b What will these earnings be if there is an agreement that, for incentive payment determination, it will be assumed that the operator worked at the same efficiency on nonstandard work as he did on the 35 hours of work covered by time standards? (Ans. $218.50)

22-14 In the preceding problem, suppose that the firm adheres to a 70–30 plan beginning at 90 percent efficiency. Furthermore, incentive earnings are guaranteed. However, for the employee under consideration, total earnings for the week will be computed in the following manner: For the 35 hours spent on incentive work, the earnings will be determined by taking into account the efficiency at which the employee worked during those hours; this will have been found to be 125 percent. But for the 5 hours spent on daywork, the earnings will be determined by applying the average efficiency at which the employee worked during the preceding incentive period; assume that this was 111 percent. What will be the employee's total earnings for the week under this arrangement?

22-15 A company is currently producing an item in one of its plants at a rate of 200,000 units per year. The average efficiency of the direct labor force involved is 80 percent. Any increase in this efficiency is accompanied by a proportional increase in output.

A number of different costs are incurred in the course of manufacturing the product. Among these are a supervisory expense of $130,000 per year, an equipment depreciation expense of $90,000 per year, and fringe benefit expenses of $80,000 per year. Any increase in output attributable to an increase in direct labor efficiency generates no increase in these expenses, because no additional supervisors, equipment, or employees are required.

a At an efficiency of 80 percent, what is the total of these expenses in terms of an amount per unit of output?

b If the efficiency increases to 100 percent and the firm has a need for the resultant additional output, what will be the total of these expenses in terms of an amount per unit of output? (Ans. $1.20)

c If the efficiency increases to 120 percent and the firm has a need for the resultant additional output, what will be the total of these expenses in terms of an amount per unit of output?

22-16 It will have been found in the preceding problem that, when efficiency increased from 80 to 100 percent, output increased from 200,000 to 250,000 units per year. Let us now suppose that the firm has no need for any of this additional output. Consequently, over a period of time, it reduces its direct labor work force, the number of supervisors, and the amount of equipment on hand. The result is that the annual expense of fringe benefits, supervision, and depreciation drops from $300,000 to $260,000. What will these expenses now be in terms of an amount per unit of output?

Next, suppose that the efficiency goes on to increase to 120 percent. But again, the firm wants to maintain the level of output at 200,000 units, and it does so by making further reductions in the work force, supervisory staff, and available equipment with the result that the corresponding expenses decrease from $260,000 to $230,000. What will these expenses now be in terms of an amount per unit of output?

APPENDIXES

A

METALWORKING MANUFACTURING PROCESSES

There are six basic metalworking operations. These are as follows: (1) drilling and boring, (2) turning, (3) milling, (4) planing and shaping, (5) grinding, and (6) metal forming. For our purposes, a brief description of each of these processes will suffice.

DRILLING AND BORING

In the drilling operation, a round hole is cut by means of a rotating drill. On occasion, after this has been done, the hole is finished by means of a rotating, offset, single-point tool; this is called "boring." Figure A-1 serves to illustrate both operations.

Two other activities can be placed under this classification; these are reaming and tapping. Reaming involves finishing a drilled hole to very close tolerances. In tapping, a thread is cut inside a hole so that a cap screw can be used in it.

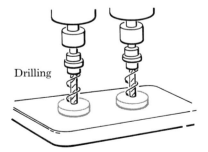
Drilling

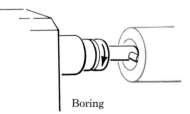
Boring

Figure A-1   Drilling and boring

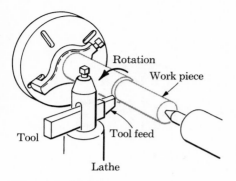

Rotation

Work piece

Tool

Tool feed

Lathe

Figure A-2   Turning

TURNING

The turning operation is performed with the use of a lathe. As can be seen in Figure A-2, the material to be machined is rotated and the cutting tool pressed against it. The result is an external cylindrical or conical surface.

It might also be noted that the feed is the rate of axial advance of the cutting tool along the workpiece. Speed is represented by the relative surface speed between the tool and the work. Depth of cut is the depth to which the tool's cutting edge engages the work.

MILLING

Milling consists of machining a piece of metal by bringing it into contact with a rotating cutting tool which has multiple cutting edges.

As indicated in Figure A-3, different types of cutters can be employed. A narrow milling cutter resembles a circular saw. Other cutters have spiral edges which give the tool the appearance of a huge screw. The shapes most commonly produced by milling machines are slots and flat surfaces.

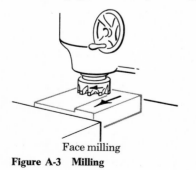

Face milling

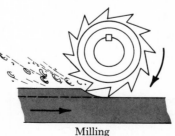

Milling

Figure A-3   Milling

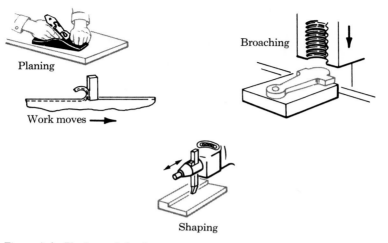

Figure A-4   Planing and shaping

PLANING AND SHAPING

Planing metal with a machine tool is similar to planing wood with a carpenter's hand plane. Of course, the machine tool is of much larger size than the hand plane and is not portable. Another difference is that, as shown in Figure A-4, the cutting part of the tool remains stationary while the part to be planed is moved back and forth beneath it.

A similar operation is performed by a shaper. However, in shaping, the workpiece is held stationary while the cutting tool travels back and forth. When this operation is done vertically, it is called "slotting."

Broaches can also be classified as planing machines. A broach has a series of cutting teeth, with each cutting edge a little higher than the one before it, graduated to the exact finished size required.

GRINDING

In grinding, a piece of work is shaped by bringing it into contact with a rotating abrasive wheel. As can be seen in Figure A-5, the grinding operation can be performed on external cylindrical surfaces, in holes, and on flat surfaces.

Lapping and honing are also placed in the grinding classification. Lapping entails the use of abrasive pastes or compounds to remove very small amounts of material. Honing machines make use of rotating heads that carry abrasive inserts to finish holes with extreme accuracy.

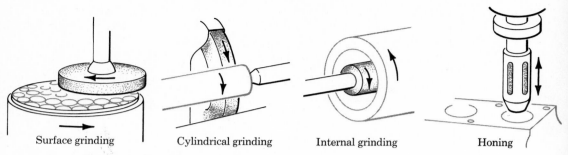

| Surface grinding | Cylindrical grinding | Internal grinding | Honing |

Figure A-5   Grinding

METAL FORMING

The major processes included in metal forming are shearing, pressing, and forging. A shear is used to cut metal into shape. Various types of presses are available to bend strips or sheets, to punch holes in metal sheets, and to blank out the desired shape from a sheet and squeeze it into its final shape in a die. Forging machines are used to squeeze a piece of white-hot metal in a die so that it flows into every part of the die and assumes the desired shape. Some of these processes are illustrated in Figure A-6.

NUMERICAL CONTROL

A great deal of progress has been made toward controlling metalworking processes with the use of a computer. To illustrate, a technique known as "numerical control" has been developed which permits a machine tool to produce parts repetitively in an automatic manner. Programs have been prepared which enable the computer to store and select procedures needed

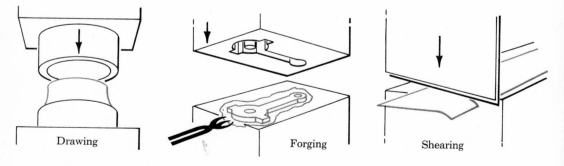

| Drawing | Forging | Shearing |

Figure A-6   Metal forming

to perform a specific operation and to govern such things as cutting sequences, operating speeds and feeds, and tool selection. All this can be done without the aid of an operator.

In any case, it is well to remember that, regardless of the simplicity or complexity of any machine tool, it performs one or more of the six basic operations we have considered.

QUESTIONS

A-1 Describe the following manufacturing processes:

a Drilling	**g** Planing	
b Boring	**h** Shaping	
c Reaming	**i** Grinding	
d Tapping	**j** Shearing	
e Turning	**k** Pressing	
f Milling	**l** Forging	

A-2 What is numerical control?

PROBLEMS

A-1 Describe and prepare a sketch of a finished part whose production will involve drilling and boring.

A-2 Describe and prepare a sketch of a finished part whose production will involve milling, drilling, and tapping.

A-3 Describe and prepare a sketch of a finished part whose production will involve turning and shaping.

A-4 Describe and prepare a sketch of a finished part whose production will involve forging and grinding.

A-5 Describe and prepare a sketch of a finished part whose production will involve planing.

A-6 Describe and prepare a sketch of a finished part whose production will involve shearing and pressing.

B

AUTOMATIC DATA PROCESSING

Every method of data processing, whether it be manual or automatic, calls for putting data into the processing system. To illustrate, if the company wants to determine what component parts must be on hand to satisfy the demand for one of its products which happens to be an assembly, it must have access to the following information: (1) the number of assemblies to be produced, (2) a listing of the different component parts required for each assembly, and (3) the number of each of these parts needed for one assembly. Once these data are obtained and introduced into the system, the determination can begin. This portion of the system is called the "input" phase.

After the required information has been fed into the system, the data are processed, which is to say that the "processing" phase occurs. In our example, this would be represented by the multiplication of the number of component parts required per unit by the number of units to be assembled.

Finally, the results of the processing activity must be presented in a form which will enable concerned individuals to make use of these data. This means that information must be taken out of the system, and, hence, every system must have an "output" phase. To return to our illustration, the end result of the output phase might be a printed summary sheet in which the component parts and the quantities required would be listed.

If relatively few computations of the type suggested by our example are required, a manual data processing system would undoubtedly prove to be adequate. Otherwise, the firm would probably be inclined to introduce the use of automatic equipment. This equipment may be punched card machines or a computer. Let us now consider each of these possible installations, beginning with punched card machines.

PUNCHED CARD EQUIPMENT

A punched card installation is characterized by the fact that data are fed into and processed in the system by means of cards such as the one shown

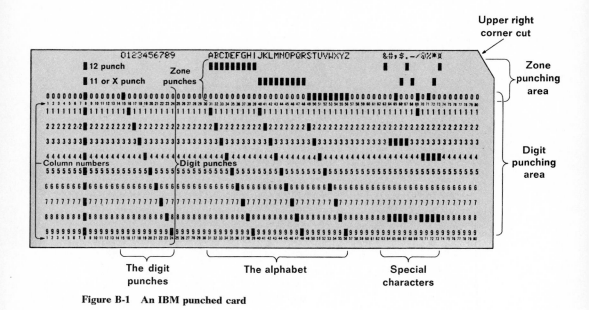

Figure B-1   An IBM punched card

in Figure B-1.[1] As an examination of this figure reveals, data are recorded on the card by means of holes. In our example of component-part determination, one such card could be prepared for each different part required for the assembly. A given card might identify the component part, the assembly in which it is used, the quantity required per assembly, and the source of the part. In brief, a set of such cards could be the form assumed by the bill of materials; that is, it serves as the parts list for the product involved.

The specific equipment that serves to make up a punched card installation in a given firm varies with the demands imposed upon the system. However, the general types are recording units, classifying units, calculating units, and printing units. We shall now describe the more important machines included in each of these classifications.

RECORDING UNITS   Punched card data processing begins with the recording of information on cards by punching holes in appropriate locations. The "key punch" is the device used for this purpose. The punching is accomplished by depressing keys on a keyboard which is similar to that found on a typewriter.

[1] All the illustrations in this appendix have been supplied by and printed with the permission of the International Business Machines Corporation.

Because a card containing only holes is somewhat difficult to interpret, the recorded data are sometimes also printed on the card. This is done with an "interpreter."

After the punching has been completed, a "verifier" can be used to determine whether this has been done accurately. If the data have been printed on the card in addition to being punched, visual rather than machine verification is sometimes employed.

In summary, the key punch, interpreter, and verifier are involved in the recording of source information on a card. When this has been completed, there is sometimes a need for reproducing a portion or all of this recorded information on another card. The equipment used for this purpose is a "reproducer." In some cases, a reproducer will be used to punch a duplicate set of cards from the original deck; however, the order in which the data are recorded on the new cards can be changed, or only some of the original data reproduced, if this is desired. Reproducers can also be used for gang punching. This is a process in which an item of information punched in the first card in a deck is punched in all the cards that follow this lead card; for example, the number of an assembled product might be gang punched in all the cards which will serve as the bill of materials for that product.

CLASSIFYING UNITS Once data have been recorded on cards, they are in the form required for processing. What specific processing is done depends on the desired end result. But in general, processing calls for passing cards through an appropriate machine. The machine converts the data, as represented by punched holes, into electrical impulses. These impulses then cause the machine to generate the desired output.

In some cases, the nature of the desired output is such that the information contained in the cards must be classified. Most classification of data is done with the use of a "sorter." A sorter is capable of sequencing, grouping, and selecting data. Sequencing involves arranging data in alphabetical or numerical order; this might be done, for example, when preparing a report of individual operating efficiencies in which the employees' names are to be listed alphabetically. Grouping consists of arranging data so that like items will be brought together; to illustrate, prior to an equipment replacement analysis, all the cards describing repair costs during a given period for the equipment might be grouped together. Selecting data is the extraction of specific items from a larger body of information; for example, past sales of a single product might be extracted for sales forecasting purposes from more comprehensive sales records being maintained on punched cards. All these operations are illustrated in Figures B-2, B-3, and B-4.

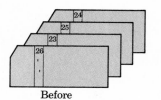
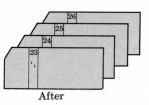

Before   After

Figure B-2 An example of sequencing

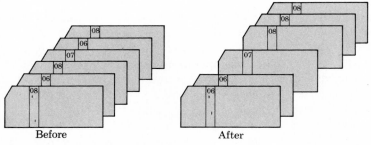

Before   After

Figure B-3 An example of grouping

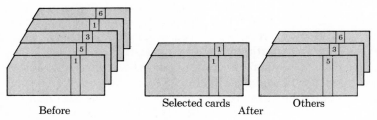

Before   Selected cards Others
After

Figure B-4 An example of selecting

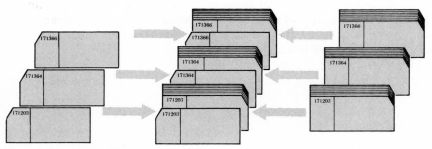

Figure B-5 An example of merging

Another type of classifying unit is the "collator." One of the main functions of this machine is that of merging two sets of cards as illustrated in Figure B-5. This might be necessary, for example, in the course of determining the amount of stock on hand for various items. The set of cards representing the beginning-of-period balance by item could be merged with the set which describes the number of units of each item withdrawn during the period. The collator can also be employed to match cards that are identical with respect to a given element of information and to check whether cards are arranged in sequence.

CALCULATING UNITS If the processing function calls for the addition, subtraction, multiplication, or division of data, the necessary steps can be performed with a "calculator." As indicated in Figure B-6, the factors to be subjected to one or more of these operations are punched into a single card, the card is fed into the machine which reads the information and makes the required computations, and the result is automatically punched into the same card. An example of such an application would be the determination of machine-hours of a certain type required to process a given order; data with regard to units to be produced, standard time per unit, expected scrap, and probable operating efficiency could be fed into the calculator and the required hours obtained.

PRINTING UNITS The end result of a punched card data processing application is a printed report in which the outcome of the processing phase is described. This report may contain operators' names and their operating efficiencies, part numbers and the quantities in stock, product numbers and the quantities sold during the past month, and so on.

Such reports, which represent the output of the system, are printed with the use of a unit called either a "tabulator" or an "accounting machine." The tabulator is also capable of summarizing data by means of addition or subtraction. To illustrate, the tabulator might be used to prepare a machine load report. In doing so, it would list the order numbers already scheduled on a specific type of production equipment and the

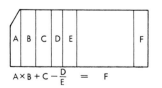

$$A \times B + C - \frac{D}{E} \;=\; F$$

Figure B-6   An example of calculating

hours required for each order. At the same time, it is able to add these hours and print the total hours of work scheduled on the equipment.

EVALUATION OF THE SYSTEM   A description of the units which may make up a punched card data processing installation and the examples of their applications bring out the fact that the system lends itself for use when there is a need for routine, continuous, and repetitive processing of large amounts of data. However, in every firm, situations will arise in which certain data must be handled in an irregular manner and by means of procedures which call for the use of judgment. If these are the exception rather than the rule, a punched card installation may still prove to be profitable in spite of the fact that these special cases must be handled manually.

ELECTRONIC DATA PROCESSING

The speed with which data can be processed in a punched card system is governed by the rate at which the machines can handle the cards mechanically. Although this speed exceeds that which is possible with manual methods, it is appreciably slower than that possible with an electronic system in which data move through the system in the form of electrical pulses. For this reason, the firm that has a need for extremely rapid data processing will give serious consideration to the procurement of a computer.

The computer most commonly used in business firms is the digital computer which works solely with information that has been expressed in the form of numbers. Every such installation contains the following functional units: (1) input devices, (2) storage devices, (3) central processing unit, and (4) output devices.

INPUT DEVICES   Data to be processed by a computer can be recorded in a number of ways. The first of these is recording by means of punched

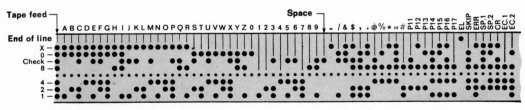

Figure B-7   Paper tape

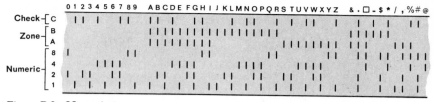

Figure B-8   Magnetic tape

cards of the type already discussed with reference to punched card data processing.

A second medium is paper tape. As opposed to punched cards, tape is not of any fixed length and, hence, can be used to record information of any length. The actual recording of information is done by punching holes in the tape with manually operated tape-punching devices. The special arrangements of holes used to depict various characters are shown in Figure B-7.

Another method calls for the use of magnetic tape. In this case, information is recorded on tape by means of a special arrangement of magnetized spots or bits; the specific patterns used to represent various characters are shown in Figure B-8.

Data can also be recorded in the form of magnetic ink characters of the type shown in Figure B-9. These are printed on paper with the use of a machine called an "inscriber." The result has the advantage of lending itself to easy visual interpretation.

Finally, data can be expressed on paper in the form of optically readable characters, which include all the letters of the alphabet, the digits 0 through 9, and special characters. An example of this type of input is shown in Figure B-10.

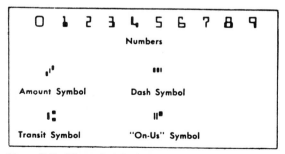

Figure B-9   Magnetic ink characters

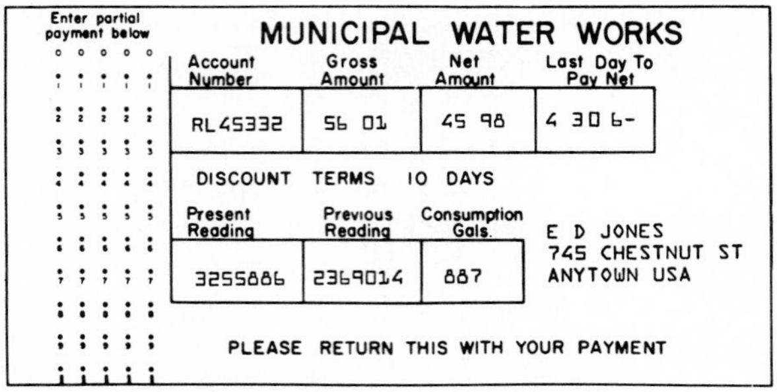
Enter partial payment below

MUNICIPAL WATER WORKS

Account Number	Gross Amount	Net Amount	Last Day To Pay Net
RL45332	56 01	45 98	4 30 6-

DISCOUNT TERMS 10 DAYS

Present Reading	Previous Reading	Consumption Gals.
3255886	2369014	887

E D JONES
745 CHESTNUT ST
ANYTOWN USA

PLEASE RETURN THIS WITH YOUR PAYMENT

Figure B-10 An optically readable document

After data have been recorded by one of the aforementioned methods, they are read or sensed by an input device. This device is simply a machine which converts the holes, magnetic characters, magnetized spots, or optically readable characters into electronic impulses. From this point on, it is these impulses that are used as data by the computer system.

STORAGE DEVICES Data from the input unit are transmitted directly to a storage device or, as it is often called, a "memory unit." The information is held there until it is needed for processing. The memory unit is also used to store reference data such as tables or constant factors, the instructions to the computer about what operations are to be performed on the input data, the intermediate results obtained in the course of processing, and the end result of the processing procedure.

There are various types of storage devices. One of these involves the use of magnetic cores. The core is a small ring made of ferromagnetic material. Data are stored by a process which entails sending electrical current through the cores and magnetizing them. Whether the resultant magnetic polarity is positive or negative depends on the direction in which the current flows through the core. Consequently, a unit of data can be stored by means of a combination of cores magnetized, from the standpoint of polarity, in a unique order.

Data can also be stored with the use of magnetic drums. The drum is a steel cylinder enclosed by a copper sleeve which is coated with magnetic material. Data are recorded by magnetizing spots on the drum surface. A given item of data will be represented by some special combination of magnetized and nonmagnetized spots.

Another storage medium is the magnetic disk. The disk is made of thin metal which is coated on each side with a magnetic recording material. A number of such disks are mounted on a vertical shaft with each disk being separated from the adjoining ones by a small distance. Data are recorded on both sides of the disks by means of magnetic spots.

Still another storage device is the data cell. The data cell contains several hundred oxide-coated plastic strips on which the data are recorded in the form of magnetic spots.

Memory units also differ in the storage capacity they possess. What capacity is needed depends, of course, on the demands imposed upon the system by a given firm. It should also be mentioned that every storage device is divided into locations and that each of these locations is assigned an address. Data are inserted in the memory unit in specific locations, and the addresses of these locations are recorded. This is necessary, because when the actual computing begins, the equipment must be told the location number or address of the data to be processed.

CENTRAL PROCESSING UNIT Required calculations are performed by the central processing unit of the system. It is this unit that is known as the computer, and it consists of two sections. The one performs arithmetic and logical operations on the data; the other engages in the control function.

The arithmetic portion of the arithmetic-logical section contains the circuitry which enables the computer to add, subtract, multiply, and divide numbers; to ascertain whether a number is positive, negative, or zero; and to compare two values to determine whether they are equal.

At some point in the processing procedure, the computer may be required to select one of alternative sets of processing instructions. It is the logical portion of the arithmetic-logical section that carries out this decision-making operation.

The control section of the central processing unit directs and coordinates all the activities in the system. To illustrate, it tells (1) the input device what information is to be placed in storage and when this is to be done, (2) the memory unit the locations at which the information should be stored, (3) the arithmetic-logical section of the computer how the data are to be processed and where the results are to be stored, and (4) the output device what is to be punched or printed. As a result of the control activity, the entire installation operates as a single automatic machine. However, the control section is capable of accomplishing all this only if it is furnished with proper instructions.

The instructions to a computer are known as a "program," and this program must be prepared by individuals trained to do so. The program will consist of the steps in the required procedure, in the sequence in which they must be performed. Each step will contain a description of the operation to be carried out and an identification of the information and the mechanism required for this purpose.

Preparation of a computer program ordinarily begins with the construction of a program flow chart or block diagram. In general, the flow chart is a graphical presentation of the procedure for processing the data within the system. Or more specifically, it is a detailed outline of the steps to be performed by the computer if the desired output is to be obtained. For example, if assembly requirements are to be translated into the demand they generate for component parts, the program flow chart may appear as shown in Figure B-11.

Construction of the program flow chart is followed by preparation of the program; this is sometimes referred to as "coding." The program can be written directly in machine language, that is, in a form recognizable to the circuitry of the computer. But because this is somewhat difficult, problem-oriented languages, such as COBOL and FORTRAN, have been developed. These languages permit the programmer to use words and mathematical notations that are similar to those ordinarily used to describe and solve problems.

The program is then read into the memory unit of the system. If a problem-oriented language has been used, a special program, called a "compiler," will have been prepared to enable the computer to translate the problem-oriented language into machine language. In any case, the computer is now ready to begin data processing.

Processing can be either "on-line" or "sequential." With on-line processing, records are updated whenever a transaction occurs; for example, if some quantity of an item is withdrawn from stock, this datum is entered into the system, and the inventory record is updated immediately. As opposed to this, with sequential processing, a number of such transactions would be accumulated, or batched, and fed into the system at intervals to update the affected record or file.

OUTPUT DEVICES   We saw that various input media are available, and the same holds true for output media. The output of the computer can assume the form of punched cards, paper tape, magnetic tape, printed information, or graphic displays. If punched cards, paper tape, or magnetic tape are acceptable, the same unit used for input purposes with each of these media can be employed as the output device. However, if a printed report is required for use by individuals in the organization, a machine called a "printer" is used. And if a graphic display is desired, a display unit similar to a television set is employed, and the output appears on the cathode-ray tube screen.

EVALUATION OF THE SYSTEM   As in the case of a punched card data processing system, a firm would give consideration to the procurement of a computer when large amounts of data must be subjected to routine, continuous, and repetitive tasks. However, an electronic system has the advantage of greater speed and accuracy. The lower degree of accuracy

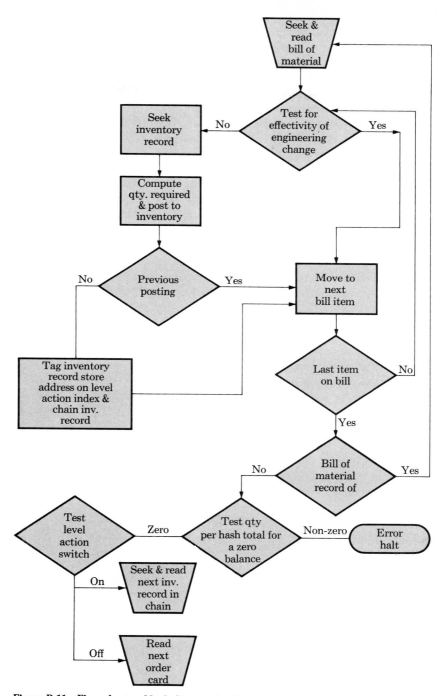

Figure B-11   Flow chart or block diagram for determination of component-part requirements

with a punched card system is attributable to the mechanical aspects of the equipment involved. Whether these advantages of electronic data processing offset the disadvantage of higher equipment costs can only be determined on the basis of a study of the alternatives.

We know that the three general alternatives in any analysis of data processing methods are manual, punched card, and electronic processing. However, there are a variety of manual approaches, different types of punched card equipment, and many kinds of computers. Consequently, the more specific alternatives must be ascertained, described, and compared from the standpoint of cost. Relevant factors to be considered would be either the rental charges or the required investment, equipment lives and salvage values, and such things as installation expenses, maintenance costs, operating expenses, programming costs, the value of an improved information system, and the like. After as many of these factors as possible have been expressed in quantitative terms, the average annual cost of each alternative can be calculated. By taking these costs and existing irreducible factors into consideration, management would be able to select what is likely to be the most economical alternative.

APPLICATIONS IN OPERATIONS MANAGEMENT

We have discussed automatic data processing systems in a fairly general manner. But this will suffice to enable us to recognize and explain the ways in which such equipment can be used, as we consider the various areas of production and operations management. The applications to be presented are intended only to suggest the role data processing equipment and procedures can assume in this area of business decision making. Other applications exist, and, undoubtedly, still others will be developed.

But in spite of the fact that so many opportunities exist for the utilization of automatic data processing methods, many companies continue to find that the nature of their requirements is such that the procurement of the necessary equipment would prove to be uneconomical. Consequently, a significant number of organizations continue to adhere to manual methods; some of these firms, however, have found it worthwhile to have certain of their processing tasks performed by computer service bureaus which sell computer time and computer related services.

Furthermore, even those firms that conclude that an automatic data processing installation is justified will reach different decisions concerning which type of equipment is most suitable. In one case, the kind and amount of data processing to be performed are such that a punched card installation is found to be adequate. In another, a computer installation may be found to be mandatory. And of course, the specific components of either of these installations will differ from firm to firm depending upon the needs of the organization.

We should also recognize that, even though a company may already possess automatic data processing equipment, not every task that can be theoretically performed by the equipment will be done so. For a given application, programming and operating costs may be excessive in the sense that manual methods will prove to be more economical.

Finally, it might be noted that care must be taken not to exaggerate the contribution that automatic data processing equipment can make to sound decision making in production management. Where a specific course of action must be selected primarily on the basis of judgment, intuition, and experience, the firm must continue to rely on qualified individuals in the organization to make the required selection. But admittedly, many decisions can be reached by means of specific procedures for the accumulation, interpretation, and processing of information. In these situations, the computer is at least as capable of applying these procedures as is a human being. However, it is first necessary that these procedures be developed and then that the computer be instructed in their application; these functions can, in the final analysis, be performed only by the firm's personnel. If these individuals are to be able to perform these functions in the area of production management, they must be acquainted with the nature of the production activity, with the problems encountered in this activity, with the quantitative and qualitative approaches to the solution of these problems, and with automatic data processing methods. It is the purpose of this book to provide concerned individuals with this acquaintance.

QUESTIONS

B-1 What are the advantages and disadvantages of manual as compared with automatic data processing methods?

B-2 What are the advantages and disadvantages of punched card equipment as compared with computers?

B-3 Under what conditions do manual methods of data processing usually prove to be adequate? Automatic methods?

B-4 Describe the following phases of any data processing system: (a) input, (b) processing, and (c) output.

B-5 What functions are performed by the following equipment which is often a part of a punched card system: (a) key punch, (b) interpreter (c) verifier, (d) reproducer, (e) sorter, (f) collator, (g) calculator, and (h) tabulator or accounting machine?

B-6 State the purpose of each of the following functional units in a computer installation: (a) input device, (b) memory unit, (c) central processing unit, and (d) output device.

B-7   By means of what media can data be recorded for input purposes in electronic data processing?

B-8   Describe the various types of available storage devices which represent the computer's memory unit.

B-9   What functions are performed by the arithmetic portion of the arithmetic-logical section of the central processing unit? By the logical portion?

B-10   What does the control section of the central processing unit do?

B-11   What is the purpose of a computer program?

B-12   What is a program flow chart or block diagram?

B-13   What is (*a*) coding, (*b*) a machine language, (*c*) a problem-oriented language, (*d*) a compiler, (*d*) on-line processing, and (*f*) sequential or batch processing?

B-14   What forms can the output of a computer assume?

B-15   What approach should be employed in the determination of the most efficient data processing system?

C
TABLES

Table C-1 Single-payment Compound Amount Factor (F/P)

Number of years (n)	*Interest rate per year (i)*							
	4%	5%	6%	7%	8%	10%	12%	15%
1	1.040	1.050	1.060	1.070	1.080	1.100	1.120	1.150
2	1.082	1.103	1.124	1.145	1.166	1.210	1.254	1.322
3	1.125	1.158	1.191	1.225	1.260	1.331	1.405	1.521
4	1.170	1.216	1.262	1.311	1.360	1.464	1.574	1.749
5	1.217	1.276	1.338	1.403	1.469	1.611	1.762	2.011
6	1.265	1.340	1.419	1.501	1.587	1.772	1.974	2.313
7	1.316	1.407	1.504	1.606	1.714	1.949	2.211	2.660
8	1.369	1.477	1.594	1.718	1.851	2.144	2.476	3.059
9	1.423	1.551	1.689	1.838	1.999	2.358	2.773	3.518
10	1.480	1.629	1.791	1.967	2.159	2.594	3.106	4.046
11	1.539	1.710	1.898	2.105	2.332	2.853	3.479	4.652
12	1.601	1.796	2.012	2.252	2.518	3.138	3.896	5.350
13	1.665	1.886	2.133	2.410	2.720	3.452	4.363	6.153
14	1.732	1.980	2.261	2.579	2.937	3.797	4.887	7.076
15	1.801	2.079	2.397	2.759	3.172	4.177	5.474	8.137
16	1.873	2.183	2.540	2.952	3.426	4.595	6.130	9.358
17	1.948	2.292	2.693	3.159	3.700	5.054	6.866	10.761
18	2.026	2.407	2.854	3.380	3.996	5.560	7.690	12.375
19	2.107	2.527	3.026	3.617	4.316	6.116	8.613	14.232
20	2.191	2.653	3.207	3.870	4.661	6.727	9.646	16.367
21	2.279	2.786	3.400	4.141	5.034	7.400	10.804	18.821
22	2.370	2.925	3.604	4.430	5.437	8.140	12.100	21.645
23	2.465	3.072	3.820	4.741	5.871	8.954	13.552	24.891
24	2.563	3.225	4.049	5.072	6.341	9.850	15.179	28.625
25	2.666	3.386	4.292	5.427	6.848	10.835	17.000	32.919
30	3.243	4.322	5.743	7.612	10.063	17.449	29.960	66.212
35	3.946	5.516	7.686	10.677	14.785	28.102	52.799	133.175
40	4.801	7.040	10.286	14.974	21.725	45.259	93.051	267.862
45	5.841	8.985	13.765	21.002	31.920	72.890	163.987	538.767
50	7.107	11.467	18.420	29.457	46.902	117.391	289.001	1083.652

Table C-2   Single-payment Present Worth Factor (P/F)

Number of years (n)	Interest rate per year (i)							
	4%	5%	6%	7%	8%	10%	12%	15%
1	0.9615	0.9524	0.9434	0.9346	0.9259	0.9091	0.8929	0.8696
2	0.9246	0.9070	0.8900	0.8734	0.8573	0.8264	0.7972	0.7561
3	0.8890	0.8638	0.8396	0.8163	0.7938	0.7513	0.7118	0.6575
4	0.8548	0.8227	0.7921	0.7629	0.7350	0.6830	0.6355	0.5718
5	0.8219	0.7835	0.7473	0.7130	0.6806	0.6209	0.5674	0.4972
6	0.7903	0.7462	0.7050	0.6663	0.6302	0.5645	0.5066	0.4323
7	0.7599	0.7107	0.6651	0.6227	0.5835	0.5132	0.4523	0.3759
8	0.7307	0.6768	0.6274	0.5820	0.5403	0.4665	0.4039	0.3269
9	0.7026	0.6446	0.5919	0.5439	0.5002	0.4241	0.3606	0.2843
10	0.6756	0.6139	0.5584	0.5083	0.4632	0.3855	0.3220	0.2472
11	0.6496	0.5847	0.5268	0.4751	0.4289	0.3505	0.2875	0.2149
12	0.6246	0.5568	0.4970	0.4440	0.3971	0.3186	0.2567	0.1869
13	0.6006	0.5303	0.4688	0.4150	0.3677	0.2897	0.2292	0.1625
14	0.5775	0.5051	0.4423	0.3878	0.3405	0.2633	0.2046	0.1413
15	0.5553	0.4810	0.4173	0.3624	0.3152	0.2394	0.1827	0.1229
16	0.5339	0.4581	0.3936	0.3387	0.2919	0.2176	0.1631	0.1060
17	0.5134	0.4363	0.3714	0.3166	0.2703	0.1978	0.1456	0.0929
18	0.4936	0.4155	0.3503	0.2959	0.2502	0.1799	0.1300	0.0808
19	0.4746	0.3957	0.3305	0.2765	0.2317	0.1635	0.1161	0.0703
20	0.4564	0.3769	0.3118	0.2584	0.2145	0.1486	0.1037	0.0611
21	0.4388	0.3589	0.2942	0.2415	0.1987	0.1351	0.0926	0.0531
22	0.4220	0.3418	0.2775	0.2257	0.1839	0.1228	0.0826	0.0462
23	0.4057	0.3256	0.2618	0.2109	0.1703	0.1117	0.0738	0.0402
24	0.3901	0.3101	0.2470	0.1971	0.1577	0.1015	0.0659	0.0349
25	0.3751	0.2953	0.2330	0.1842	0.1460	0.0923	0.0588	0.0304
30	0.3083	0.2314	0.1741	0.1314	0.0994	0.0573	0.0334	0.0151
35	0.2534	0.1813	0.1301	0.0937	0.0676	0.0356	0.0189	0.0075
40	0.2083	0.1420	0.0972	0.0668	0.0460	0.0221	0.0107	0.0037
45	0.1712	0.1113	0.0727	0.0476	0.0313	0.0137	0.0061	0.0019
50	0.1407	0.0872	0.0543	0.0339	0.0213	0.0085	0.0035	0.0009

Table C-3 Capital Recovery Factor (A/P)

Number of years (n)	Interest rate per year (i)							
	4%	5%	6%	7%	8%	10%	12%	15%
1	1.04000	1.05000	1.06000	1.07000	1.08000	1.10000	1.12000	1.15000
2	0.53020	0.53780	0.54544	0.55309	0.56077	0.57619	0.59170	0.61512
3	0.36035	0.36721	0.37411	0.38105	0.38803	0.40211	0.41635	0.43798
4	0.27549	0.28201	0.28859	0.29523	0.30192	0.31547	0.32923	0.35027
5	0.22463	0.23097	0.23740	0.24389	0.25046	0.26380	0.27741	0.29832
6	0.19076	0.19702	0.20336	0.20980	0.21632	0.22961	0.24323	0.26424
7	0.16661	0.17282	0.17914	0.18555	0.19207	0.20541	0.21912	0.24036
8	0.14853	0.15472	0.16104	0.16747	0.17401	0.18744	0.20130	0.22285
9	0.13449	0.14069	0.14702	0.15349	0.16008	0.17364	0.18768	0.20957
10	0.12329	0.12950	0.13587	0.14238	0.14903	0.16275	0.17698	0.19925
11	0.11415	0.12039	0.12679	0.13336	0.14008	0.15396	0.16842	0.19107
12	0.10655	0.11283	0.11928	0.12590	0.13270	0.14676	0.16144	0.18448
13	0.10014	0.10646	0.11296	0.11965	0.12652	0.14078	0.15568	0.17911
14	0.09467	0.10102	0.10758	0.11434	0.12130	0.13575	0.15087	0.17469
15	0.08994	0.09634	0.10296	0.10979	0.11683	0.13147	0.14682	0.17102
16	0.08582	0.09227	0.09895	0.10586	0.11298	0.12782	0.14339	0.16795
17	0.08220	0.08870	0.09544	0.10243	0.10963	0.12466	0.14046	.16537
18	0.07899	0.08555	0.09236	0.09941	0.10670	0.12193	0.13794	0.16319
19	0.07614	0.08275	0.08962	0.09675	0.10413	0.11955	0.13576	0.16134
20	0.07358	0.08024	0.08718	0.09439	0.10185	0.11746	0.13388	0.15976
21	0.07128	0.07800	0.08500	0.09229	0.09983	0.11562	0.13224	0.15842
22	0.06920	0.07597	0.08305	0.09041	0.09803	0.11401	0.13081	0.15727
23	0.06731	0.07414	0.08128	0.08871	0.09642	0.11257	0.12956	0.15628
24	0.06559	0.07247	0.07968	0.08719	0.09498	0.11130	0.12846	0.15543
25	0.06401	0.07095	0.07823	0.08581	0.09368	0.11017	0.12750	0.15470
30	0.05783	0.06505	0.07265	0.08059	0.08883	0.10608	0.12414	0.15230
35	0.05358	0.06107	0.06897	0.07723	0.08580	0.10369	0.12232	0.15113
40	0.05052	0.05828	0.06646	0.07501	0.08386	0.10226	0.12130	0.15056
45	0.04826	0.05626	0.06470	0.07350	0.08259	0.10139	0.12074	0.15028
50	0.04655	0.05478	0.06344	0.07246	0.08174	0.10086	0.12042	0.15014

Table C-4 Series Present Worth Factor (P/A)

Number of years (n)	Interest rate per year (i)							
	4%	5%	6%	7%	8%	10%	12%	15%
1	0.962	0.952	0.943	0.935	0.926	0.909	0.893	0.870
2	1.886	1.859	1.833	1.808	1.783	1.736	1.690	1.626
3	2.775	2.723	2.673	2.624	2.577	2.487	2.402	2.283
4	3.630	3.546	3.465	3.387	3.312	3.170	3.037	2.855
5	4.452	4.329	4.212	4.100	3.993	3.791	3.605	3.352
6	5.242	5.076	4.917	4.767	4.623	4.355	4.111	3.784
7	6.002	5.786	5.582	5.389	5.206	4.868	4.564	4.160
8	6.733	6.463	6.210	5.971	5.747	5.335	4.968	4.487
9	7.435	7.108	6.802	6.515	6.247	5.759	5.328	4.772
10	8.111	7.722	7.360	7.024	6.710	6.144	5.650	5.019
11	8.760	8.306	7.887	7.499	7.139	6.495	5.938	5.234
12	9.385	8.863	8.384	7.943	7.536	6.814	6.194	5.421
13	9.986	9.394	8.853	8.358	7.904	7.103	6.424	5.583
14	10.563	9.899	9.295	8.745	8.244	7.367	6.628	5.724
15	11.118	10.380	9.712	9.108	8.559	7.606	6.811	5.847
16	11.652	10.838	10.106	9.447	8.851	7.824	6.974	5.954
17	12.166	11.274	10.477	9.763	9.122	8.022	7.120	6.047
18	12.659	11.690	10.828	10.059	9.372	8.201	7.250	6.128
19	13.134	12.085	11.158	10.336	9.604	8.365	7.366	6.198
20	13.590	12.462	11.470	10.594	9.818	8.514	7.469	6.259
21	14.029	12.821	11.764	10.836	10.017	8.649	7.562	6.312
22	14.451	13.163	12.042	11.061	10.201	8.772	7.645	6.359
23	14.857	13.489	12.303	11.272	10.371	8.883	7.718	6.399
24	15.247	13.799	12.550	11.469	10.529	8.985	7.784	6.434
25	15.622	14.094	12.783	11.654	10.675	9.077	7.843	6.464
30	17.292	15.372	13.765	12.409	11.258	9.247	8.055	6.566
35	18.665	16.374	14.498	12.948	11.655	9.644	8.176	6.617
40	19.793	17.159	15.046	13.332	11.925	9.779	8.244	6.642
45	20.720	17.774	15.456	13.606	12.108	9.863	8.283	6.654
50	21.482	18.256	15.762	13.801	12.233	9.915	8.305	6.661

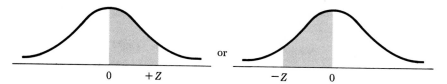

Table C-5 Areas of the Normal Curve

Z	.00	.01	.02	.03	.04	.05	.06	.07	.08	.09
0.0	.0000	.0040	.0080	.0120	.0160	.0199	.0239	.0279	.0319	.0359
0.1	.0398	.0438	.0478	.0517	.0557	.0596	.0636	.0675	.0714	.0753
0.2	.0793	.0832	.0871	.0910	.0948	.0987	.1026	.1064	.1103	.1141
0.3	.1179	.1217	.1255	.1293	.1331	.1368	.1406	.1443	.1480	.1517
0.4	.1554	.1591	.1628	.1664	.1700	.1736	.1772	.1808	.1844	.1879
0.5	.1915	.1950	.1985	.2019	.2054	.2088	.2123	.2157	.2190	.2224
0.6	.2257	.2291	.2324	.2357	.2389	.2422	.2454	.2486	.2517	.2549
0.7	.2580	.2611	.2642	.2673	.2704	.2734	.2764	.2794	.2823	.2852
0.8	.2881	.2910	.2939	.2967	.2995	.3023	.3051	.3078	.3106	.3233
0.9	.3159	.3186	.3212	.3238	.3264	.3289	.3315	.3340	.3365	.3389
1.0	.3413	.3438	.3461	.3485	.3508	.3531	.3554	.3577	.3599	.3621
1.1	.3643	.3665	.3686	.3708	.3729	.3749	.3770	.3790	.3810	.3830
1.2	.3849	.3869	.3888	.3907	.3925	.3944	.3962	.3980	.3997	.4015
1.3	.4032	.4049	.4066	.4082	.4099	.4115	.4131	.4147	.4162	.4177
1.4	.4192	.4207	.4222	.4236	.4251	.4265	.4279	.4292	.4306	.4319
1.5	.4332	.4345	.4357	.4370	.4382	.4394	.4406	.4418	.4429	.4441
1.6	.4452	.4463	.4474	.4484	.4495	.4505	.4515	.4525	.4535	.4545
1.7	.4554	.4564	.4573	.4582	.4591	.4599	.4608	.4616	.4625	.4633
1.8	.4641	.4649	.4656	.4664	.4671	.4678	.4686	.4693	.4699	.4706
1.9	.4713	.4719	.4726	.4732	.4738	.4744	.4750	.4758	.4761	.4767
2.0	.4772	.4778	.4783	.4788	.4793	.4798	.4803	.4808	.4812	.4817
2.1	.4821	.4826	.4830	.4834	.4838	.4842	.4846	.4850	.4854	.4857
2.2	.4861	.4864	.4868	.4871	.4875	.4878	.4881	.4884	.4887	.4890
2.3	.4893	.4896	.4898	.4901	.4904	.4906	.4909	.4911	.4913	.4916
2.4	.4918	.4920	.4922	.4925	.4927	.4929	.4931	.4932	.4934	.4936
2.5	.4938	.4940	.4941	.4943	.4945	.4946	.4948	.4949	.4951	.4952
2.6	.4953	.4955	.4956	.4957	.4959	.4960	.4961	.4962	.4963	.4964
2.7	.4965	.4966	.4967	.4968	.4969	.4970	.4971	.4972	.4973	.4974
2.8	.4974	.4975	.4976	.4977	.4977	.4978	.4979	.4979	.4980	.4981
2.9	.4981	.4982	.4982	.4983	.4984	.4984	.4985	.4985	.4986	.4986
3.0	.4986	.4987	.4987	.4988	.4988	.4988	.4989	.4989	.4989	.4990

Table C-6 Values of d_2 and d_3 Factors for the R Chart*

Sample size	d_2	d_3
2	1.128	0.853
3	1.693	0.888
4	2.059	0.880
5	2.326	0.864
6	2.534	0.848
7	2.704	0.833
8	2.847	0.820
9	2.970	0.808
10	3.078	0.797
11	3.173	0.787
12	3.258	0.778
13	3.336	0.770
14	3.407	0.762
15	3.472	0.755
16	3.532	0.749
17	3.588	0.743
18	3.640	0.738
19	3.689	0.733
20	3.735	0.729
21	3.778	0.724
22	3.819	0.720
23	3.858	0.716
24	3.895	0.712
25	3.931	0.709

**ASTM Manual on Quality Control of Materials*, American Society for Testing Materials, Philadelphia, 1951.

BIBLIOGRAPHY

Abramowitz, Irving: *Production Management: Concepts and Analysis for Operation and Control,* The Ronald Press Company, New York, 1967.

Ammer, Dean S.: *Manufacturing Management and Control,* Appleton-Century-Crofts, Inc., New York, 1968.

Amrine, Harold T., et al.: *Manufacturing Organization and Management,* 2d ed., Prentice-Hall, Inc., Englewood Cliffs, N.J., 1966.

Apple, James M.: *Plant Layout and Materials Handling,* 2d ed., The Ronald Press Company, New York, 1963.

Archibald, R., and R. Villoria: *Network-based Management Systems (PERT/CPM),* John Wiley & Sons, Inc., New York, 1967.

Barish, Norman N.: *Economic Analysis for Engineering and Managerial Decision Making,* McGraw-Hill Book Company, New York, 1972.

Barnes, Ralph M.: *Motion and Time Study,* 6th ed., John Wiley & Sons, Inc., New York, 1968.

Barrett, D. A.: *Automatic Inventory Control Techniques,* International Publishers, New York, 1969.

Berry, W. L., and D. C. Whybark: *Computer Augmented Cases in Operations and Logistics Management,* South-Western Publishing Co., Cincinnati, 1972.

Biegel, John E.: *Production Control: A Quantitative Approach,* 2d ed., Prentice-Hall, Inc., Englewood Cliffs, N.J., 1971.

Bierman, Harold, Jr., Charles P. Bonini, and Warren H. Hausman: *Quantitative Analysis for Business Decisions,* 4th ed., Richard D. Irwin, Inc., Homewood, Ill., 1973.

———and Seymour Smidt: *The Capital Budgeting Decision,* 2d ed., The Macmillan Company, New York, 1966.

Bolz, H. A., and G. E. Hagemann: *Materials Handling Handbook,* The Ronald Press Company, New York, 1958.

Bowman, Edward H., and Robert B. Fetter: *Analysis for Production and Operations Management,* 3d ed., Richard D. Irwin, Inc., Homewood, Ill., 1967.

Broom, H. N.: *Production Management,* rev. ed., Richard D. Irwin, Inc., Homewood, Ill., 1967.

Brown, Robert G.: *Decision Rules for Inventory Management,* Holt, Rinehart and Winston, Inc., New York, 1967.

Buffa, Elwood S.: *Basic Production Management,* John Wiley & Sons, Inc., New York, 1971.

————: *Modern Production Management,* 3d ed., John Wiley & Sons, Inc., New York, 1969.

————: *Operations Management: Problems and Models,* 3d ed., John Wiley & Sons, Inc., New York, 1972.

————: *Readings in Production and Operations Management,* John Wiley & Sons, Inc., New York, 1966.

————and William H. Taubert: *Production-Inventory Systems: Planning and Control,* rev. ed., Richard D. Irwin, Inc., Homewood, Ill., 1972.

Burack, Elmer H.: *Manpower Planning and Programming,* Allyn & Bacon, Inc., Boston, 1972.

Burgess, Leonard R.: *Wage and Salary Administration in a Dynamic Economy,* Harcourt, Brace & World, Inc., New York, 1968.

Burnstein, Herman: *Attribute Sampling,* McGraw-Hill Book Company, New York, 1971.

Canada, John R.: *Intermediate Economic Analysis for Management & Engineering,* Prentice-Hall, Inc., Englewood Cliffs, N.J., 1971.

Caplen, R. H.: *A Practical Approach to Quality Control,* Brandon Systems Press, Inc., Princeton, N.J., 1969.

Chase, Richard B., and Nicholas J. Aquilano: *Production and Operations Management,* Richard D. Irwin, Inc., Homewood, Ill., 1973.

Communications Oriented Production Information and Control System, International Business Machines Corporation, White Plains, N.Y., 1972.

Conway, R. W., W. L. Maxwell, and L. W. Miller: *Theory of Scheduling,* Addison-Wesley Publishing Company, Inc., Reading, Mass., 1967.

De Garmo, E. Paul: *Engineering Economy,* 4th ed., The Macmillan Company, New York, 1967.

Di Roccaferrera, Giuseppe M. Ferrero: *Introduction to Linear Programming Processes,* South-Western Publishing Co., Cincinnati, 1967.

Dodge, H. F., and H. G. Romig: *Sampling Inspection Tables,* 2d ed., John Wiley & Sons, Inc., New York, 1959.

Dooley, Arch R., et al.: *Casebooks in Production Management,* John Wiley & Sons, Inc., New York, 1964.

Driebeck, Norman J.: *Applied Linear Programming,* Addison-Wesley Publishing Company, Inc., Reading, Mass., 1969.

Duncan, Acheson J.: *Quality Control and Industrial Statistics,* 3d ed., Richard D. Irwin, Inc., Homewood, Ill., 1965.

Dunn, J. D., and Frank M. Rachel: *Wage and Salary Administration,* McGraw-Hill Book Company, New York, 1970.

Elmaghraby, Salah E.: *The Design of Production Systems,* Reinhold Publishing Corporation, New York, 1966.

Enrick, N. L.: *Quality Control and Reliability,* 5th ed., Industrial Press, Inc., New York, 1966.

Fabrycky, W. J., P. M. Ghare, and P. E. Torgersen: *Industrial Operations Research,* Prentice-Hall, Inc., Englewood Cliffs, N.J., 1972.

———and Paul E. Torgersen: *Operations Economy: Economic Applications of Operations Research,* Prentice-Hall, Inc., Engelwood Cliffs, N.J., 1966.

Fetter, Robert B.: *The Quality Control System,* Richard D. Irwin, Inc., Homewood, Ill., 1967.

———and Winston C. Dalleck: *Decision Models for Inventory Management,* Richard D. Irwin, Inc., Homewood, Ill., 1961.

Garrett, Leonard J., and Milton Silver: *Production Management Analysis,* 2d ed., Harcourt Brace Jovanovich, Inc., New York, 1973.

Gass, S. I.: *Linear Programming,* 3d ed., McGraw-Hill Book Company, New York, 1969.

Gavett, J. William: *Production and Operations Management,* Harcourt Brace Jovanovich, Inc., New York, 1968.

Gedye, Rupert: *A Manager's Guide to Quality and Reliability,* John Wiley & Sons, Inc., New York, 1969.

Giffin, W. C.: *Introduction to Operations Engineering,* Richard D. Irwin, Inc., Homewood, Ill., 1971.

Gordon, G.: *System Simulation,* Prentice-Hall, Inc., Englewood Cliffs, N.J., 1969.

Goslin, Lewis N.: *The Product-planning System,* Richard D. Irwin, Inc., Homewood, Ill., 1967.

Grant, Eugene L., and W. Grant Ireson: *Principles of Engineering Economy,* 5th ed., The Ronald Press Company, New York, 1970.

———and Richard S. Leavenworth: *Statistical Quality Control,* 4th ed., McGraw-Hill Book Company, New York, 1972.

Greene, James H.: *Operations Planning and Control,* Richard D. Irwin, Inc., Homewood, Ill., 1967.

———: *Production and Inventory Control Handbook,* McGraw-Hill Book Company, New York, 1970.

———: *Production Control: Systems and Decisions,* Richard D. Irwin, Inc., Homewood, Ill., 1965.

Groff, Gene K., and John F. Muth: *Operations Management: Analysis for Decisions,* Richard D. Irwin, Inc., Homewood, Ill., 1972.

———: *Operations Management: Selected Readings,* Richard D. Irwin, Inc., Homewood, Ill., 1969.

Hackamack, Lawrence C.: *Making Equipment-replacement Decisions,* American Management Association, New York, 1969.

Harris, Douglas H., and F. B. Chaney: *Human Factors in Quality Assurance,* John Wiley & Sons, Inc., New York, 1969.

Harris, Roy D., and Michael J. Maggard: *Computer Models in Operations Management: A Computer-augmented System,* Harper & Row, Publishers, New York, 1972.

Hoffman, Thomas R.: *Production: Management and Manufacturing Systems,* Wadsworth Publishing Company, Inc., Belmont, Calif., 1967.

Hopeman, Richard J.: *Production: Concepts, Analysis, Control,* 2d ed., Charles E. Merrill Books, Inc., Columbus, Ohio, 1970.

———: *Systems Analysis and Operations Management,* Charles E. Merrill Books, Inc., Columbus, Ohio, 1969.

Horowitz, Joseph: *Critical Path Scheduling: Management Control Through CPM and PERT,* The Ronald Press Company, New York, 1967.

Hottenstein, Michael P.: *Models and Analysis for Production Management,* International Textbook Co., Scranton, Pa., 1968.

Iannone, A. L.: *Management Program Planning and Control with PERT, MOST and LOB,* Prentice-Hall, Inc., Englewood Cliffs, N.J., 1967.

Ireson, W. Grant, and Eugene L. Grant: *Handbook of Industrial Engineering and Management,* 2d ed., Prentice-Hall, Inc., Englewood Cliffs, N.J., 1971.

Juran, Joseph M.: *Quality Control Handbook,* 2d ed., McGraw-Hill Book Company, New York, 1967.

——— and F. M. Gryna, Jr.: *Quality Planning and Analysis,* McGraw-Hill Book Company, New York, 1970.

Karaska, Gerald J., and D. F. Bramhall: *Locational Analysis for Manufacturing,* M.I.T. Press, Cambridge, Mass., 1969.

Kaufmann, A., and G. Desbazeille: *The Critical Path Method,* Gordon and Breach, Science Publishers, Inc., New York, 1969.

Killeen, Louis M.: *Techniques of Inventory Management,* American Management Association, New York, 1970.

Kirkpatrick, Elwood G.: *Quality Control for Managers and Engineers,* John Wiley & Sons, Inc., New York, 1970.

Lanford, H. W.: *Technological Forecasting Methodologies,* American Management Association, New York, 1972.

Levin, Richard I., et al.: *Production/Operations Management: Contemporary Policy for Managing Operating Systems,* McGraw-Hill Book Company, New York, 1972.

——— and Charles A. Kirkpatrick: *Planning and Control with PERT/CPM,* McGraw-Hill Book Company, New York, 1966.

——— and Rudolph P. Lamone: *Linear Programming for Management Decisions,* Richard D. Irwin, Inc., Homewood, Ill., 1969.

Lewis, Bernard R.: *Developing Maintenance Time Standards,* Industrial Education Institute, Boston, 1968.

Lipman, Burton, E.: *How to Control and Reduce Inventory,* Prentice-Hall, Inc., Englewood Cliffs, N.J., 1972.

Lockyer, K. G.: *An Introduction to Critical Path Analysis,* 2d ed., Pitman Publishing Corporation, New York, 1967.

Magee, John F., and David M. Boodman: *Production Planning and Inventory Control,* 2d ed., McGraw-Hill Book Company, New York, 1967.

Martino, R. L.: *Critical Path Networks,* McGraw-Hill Book Company, New York, 1970.

Mayer, Raymond R.: *Financial Analysis of Investment Alternatives,* Allyn & Bacon, Inc., Boston, 1966.

Maynard, Harold B.: *Handbook of Modern Manufacturing Management,* McGraw-Hill Book Company, New York, 1970.

McKenney, J. L., and R. S. Rosenbloom: *Cases in Operations Management,* John Wiley & Sons, Inc., New York, 1969.

Meier, R. C., W. T. Newell, and H. L. Pazer: *Simulation in Business and Economics,* Prentice-Hall, Inc., Englewood Cliffs, N.J., 1969.

Miller, Ernest C.: *Objectives and Standards of Performance in Production Management,* American Management Association, New York, 1967.

Mize, Joe H., et al.: *Production System Simulator (Prosim V) A User's Manual,* Prentice-Hall, Inc., Englewood Cliffs, N.J., 1971.

———, Charles R. White, and George H. Brook: *Operations Planning and Control,* Prentice-Hall, Inc., Englewood Cliffs, N.J., 1971.

Moore, Franklin G.: *Production Management,* 6th ed., Richard D. Irwin, Inc., Homewood, Ill., 1973.

——— and R. Jablonski: *Production Control,* 3d ed., McGraw-Hill Book Company, New York, 1969.

Moore, James M.: *Plant Layout and Design,* The Macmillan Company, New York, 1962.

Morris, William T.: *Analysis for Materials Handling Management,* Richard D. Irwin, Inc., Homewood, Ill., 1962.

———: *The Capacity Decision System,* Richard D. Irwin, Inc., Homewood, Ill., 1967.

Morrow, L. C.: *Maintenance Engineering Handbook,* 2d ed., McGraw-Hill Book Company, New York, 1966.

Mundel, Marvin E.: *Motion and Time Study: Principles and Practice,* 4th ed., Prentice-Hall, Inc., Englewood Cliffs, N.J., 1970.

Murdick, Robert C., and Donald D. Deming: *The Management of Capital Expenditures,* McGraw-Hill Book Company, New York, 1968.

Muther, Richard, and Knut Haganas: *Systematic Handling Analysis,* Cahners Books, Boston, 1969.

Naddor, Eliezer: *Inventory Systems,* John Wiley & Sons, Inc., New York, 1966.

Nadler, Gerald: *Work Design: A Systems Concept,* rev. ed., Richard D. Irwin, Inc., Homewood, Ill., 1970.

———: *Work Systems Design: The Ideals Concept,* Richard D. Irwin, Inc., Homewood, Ill., 1967.

Nance, Harold W., and Robert W. Nolan: *Office Work Measurement,* McGraw-Hill Book Company, New York, 1971.

Naylor, T. H., E. T. Byrne, and J. R. Vernon: *Introduction to Linear Programming: Methods and Cases,* Wadsworth Publishing Company, Inc., Belmont, Calif., 1971.

Niebel, Benjamin W.: *Motion and Time Study,* 5th ed., Richard D. Irwin, Inc., Homewood, Ill., 1972.

Niland, Powell: *Production Planning, Scheduling, and Inventory Control: A Text and Cases,* The Macmillan Company, New York, 1970.

O'Brien, J. J.: *Scheduling Handbook,* McGraw-Hill Book Company, New York, 1969.

Panico, J. A.: *Queuing Theory: A Study of Waiting Lines for Business, Economics and Science,* Prentice-Hall, Inc., Englewood Cliffs, N.J., 1969.

Plossl, G. W., and O. W. Wright: *Production and Inventory Control: Principles and Techniques,* Prentice-Hall, Inc., Englewood Cliffs, N.J., 1967.

Prabhu, N. U.: *Queues and Inventories,* John Wiley & Sons, Inc., New York, 1965.

Prichard, James W., and Robert H. Eagle: *Modern Inventory Management,* John Wiley & Sons, Inc., New York, 1965.

Quirin, G. David: *The Capital Expenditure Decision,* Richard D. Irwin, Inc., Homewood, Ill., 1967.

Ramlow, Donald E., and Eugene H. Wall: *Production Planning and Control,* Prentice-Hall, Inc., Englewood Cliffs, N.J., 1967.

Reed, Ruddell, Jr.: *Plant Location, Layout, and Maintenance,* Richard D. Irwin, Inc., Homewood, Ill., 1967.

Riggs, James L.: *Production Systems: Planning, Analysis, and Control,* John Wiley & Sons, Inc., New York, 1970.

Roscoe, Edwin Scott, and Dorman G. Freark: *Organization for Production,* 5th ed., Richard D. Irwin, Inc., Homewood, Ill., 1971.

Schmidt, J. W., and R. E. Taylor: *Simulation and Analysis of Industrial Systems,* Richard D. Irwin, Inc., Homewood, Ill., 1970.

Shaffer, Louis R., et al.: *Critical Path Method,* McGraw-Hill Book Company, New York, 1965.

Shore, Barry: *Operations Management,* McGraw-Hill Book Company, New York, 1973.

Smith, C. S.: *Quality and Reliability: An Integrated Approach,* Pitman Publishing Corporation, New York, 1969.

Smith, Gerald W.: *Engineering Economy: Analysis of Capital Expenditures,* The Iowa State University Press, Ames, 1968.

Smythe, William R., Jr., and Lynwood A. Johnson: *Introduction to Linear Programming, with Applications,* Prentice-Hall, Inc., Englewood Cliffs, N.J., 1966.

Starr, Martin K.: *Production Management: Systems and Synthesis,* 2d ed., Prentice-Hall, Inc., Englewood Cliffs, N.J., 1972.

———: *Systems Management of Operations,* Prentice-Hall, Inc., Englewood Cliffs, N.J., 1971.

Stockton, R. Stansbury: *Introduction to Linear Programming,* Richard D. Irwin, Inc., Homewood, Ill., 1971.

Thomas, A. B.: *Inventory Control in Production and Manufacturing,* Cahners Books, Boston, 1969.

Thompson, Gerald E.: *Linear Programming,* The Macmillan Company, New York, 1971.

Throsby, C. D.: *Elementary Linear Programming,* Random House, Inc., New York, 1970.

Thuesen, H. G., W. J. Fabrycky, and G. J. Thuesen: *Engineering Economy,* 4th ed., Prentice-Hall, Inc., Englewood Cliffs, N.J., 1971.

Timms, Howard L.: *Introduction to Operations Management,* Richard D. Irwin, Inc., Homewood, Ill., 1967.

—— and M. F. Pohlen: *The Production Function in Business,* 3d ed., Richard D. Irwin, Inc., Homewood, Ill., 1970.

Von Kaas, H. K.: *Making Wage Incentives Work,* American Management Association, New York, 1971.

Voris, William: *Production Control,* 3d ed., Richard D. Irwin, Inc., Homewood, Ill., 1966.

Wetherill, G. B.: *Sampling, Inspection and Quality Control,* Barnes & Noble, Inc., New York, 1969.

Wiest, J. D., and F. K. Levy: *A Management Guide to PERT/CPM,* Prentice-Hall, Inc., Englewood Cliffs, N.J., 1969.

Zeyher, Lewis R.: *Production Manager's Desk Book,* Prentice-Hall, Inc., Englewood Cliffs, N.J., 1969.

——: *Production Manager's Handbook of Formulas and Tables,* Prentice-Hall, Inc., Englewood Cliffs, N.J., 1972.

Zimmerman, H. J., and M. G. Sovereign: *Quantitative Models for Production Management,* Prentice-Hall, Inc., Englewood Cliffs, N.J., 1974.

Zollitsch, Herbert G., and Adolph Langsner: *Wage and Salary Administration,* 2d ed., South-Western Publishing Co., Cincinnati, 1970.

INDEX

INDEX

PRODUCTION AND OPERATIONS MANAGEMENT

McGRAW-HILL SERIES IN MANAGEMENT
Keith Davis, Consulting Editor